PAGE 29
ON THE ROAD

YOUR COMPLETE DESTINATION GUIDE
In-depth reviews, detailed listings
and insider tips

TOP EXPERIENCES MAP NEXT PAGE

Lviv & Western Ukraine p86

Central Ukraine p70

Kyiv p30

The Carpathians p114

D028B104

Eastern Ukraine p205

Odesa & Southern Ukraine p139

Crimea p159

PAGE 265
SURVIVAL GUIDE

YOUR AT-A-GLANCE REFERENCE
How to get around, get a room,
stay safe, say hello

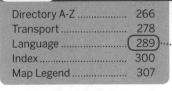

THIS EDITION WRITTEN AND RESEARCHED BY

Marc Di Duca
Leonid Ragozin

Ukraine

Andriyivsky Uzviz
Explore Kyiv's most
captivating street (p35)

Pyrohovo Museum
Ukraine's best open-air museum
of folk architecture (p48)

Ploshcha Rynok
Join the crowds on the city's
central piazza (p89)

Carpathian Landscapes
Bike and hike Ukraine's
relaxing uplands (p119)

Kamyanets-Podilsky
Wander this town atop a
rock island (p79)

Kolomyya
An engaging base for
Carpathian exploration (p124)

Odesa's Nightlife
Beach parties by the
Black Sea (p150)

**Danube Delta
Biosphere Reserve**
Bird spotting and watery
vistas (p156)

Top Experiences ›

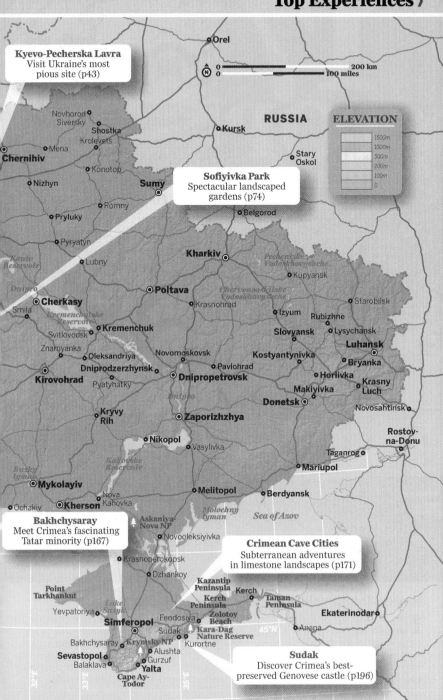

Kyevo-Pecherska Lavra
Visit Ukraine's most
pious site (p43)

Sofiyivka Park
Spectacular landscaped
gardens (p74)

RUSSIA

ELEVATION

1500m
1000m
500m
200m
100m
0

0   200 km
0   100 miles

Orel

Novhorod
Siversky
Shostka
Krolevets
Mena
Chernihiv
Konotop
Nizhyn
Pryluky
Pyryatyn
Kaniv
Reservoir
Lubny
Dnipro
Cherkasy
Smila
Kremenchutske
Reservoir
Svitlovodsk
Znamyanka
Kremenchuk
Oleksandriya
Dniprodzerzhynsk
Kirovohrad
Pyatykhatky
Kryvy
Rih
Nikopol
Kakhovske
Reservoir
Vasylivka
Buzky
lyman
Mykolayiv
Nova
Kahovka
Ochakiv
Kherson
Molochny
lyman

Kursk
Stary
Oskol
Belgorod
Kharkiv
Pechenitske
Vodoskhovyshche
Kupyansk
Poltava
Chervonooskilske
Vodoskhovyshche
Krasnohrad
Izyum
Starobilsk
Rubizhne
Slovyansk
Lysychansk
Novomoskovsk
Kostyantynivka
Luhansk
Pavlohrad
Bryanka
Dnipropetrovsk
Horlivka
Krasny
Luch
Dnipro
Makiyivka
Zaporizhzhya
Donetsk
Novosahtinsk
Rostov-
na-Donu
Taganrog
Mariupol
Melitopol
Berdyansk
Sea of Azov
Sumy
Romny

Bakhchysaray
Meet Crimea's fascinating
Tatar minority (p167)

Askaniya-
Nova NP
Novooleksiyivka
Krasnoperokopsk
Dzhankoy
Point
Tarkhankut
Yevpatoriya
Lake
Sivash
Simferopol
Bakhchysaray
Krymsky NP
Sevastopol
Alushta
Balaklava
Gurzuf
Yalta
Cape Ay-
Todor

Crimean Cave Cities
Subterranean adventures
in limestone landscapes (p171)

Kazantip
Peninsula
Kerch
Kerch
Peninsula
Taman
Peninsula
Zolotoy
Beach
Feodosiya
Sudak
Kara-Dag
Nature Reserve
Kurortne
45°N
Anapa
Ekaterinodar

Sudak
Discover Crimea's best-
preserved Genovese castle (p196)

32°E   33°E   35°E

17 TOP EXPERIENCES

Kyevo-Pecherska Lavra, Kyiv

1 Discover mysteries of Eastern Orthodoxy and descend into catacombs to see mummies of much-revered saints on an excursion to the holy of holies for all eastern Slavs. Founded as a cave monastery in 1051, the *lavra* (p43) is filled with golden-domed churches, baroque buildings and orchards. Religious ceremonies take place in lavishly decorated, icon-filled interiors, accompanied by beautiful choir singing and attended by crowds of pilgrims and monks. There are great collections of Scythian gold, micro-miniatures and more in museums located on the premises. Dormition Cathedral (p45)

2 By and large Ukraine is as flat as a topographically challenged *blin* (pancake), which makes its bumpy bits all the more special. Ukraine's slice of the Carpathian arc barely reaches over 2000m, but its soothing wooded slopes, rough stony trails, flower-filled upland pastures and wide, snaking valleys make this prime hiking, biking and skiing territory. Needless to say, the Carpathians (p119) are home to Ukraine's highest peak, Mt Hoverla, a fairly easy trek from nearby villages, as well as several ski resorts. Carpathian countryside, near Uzhhorod

Lviv's Ploshcha Rynok

3 Lviv is the pulsating heart of Ukraine, and the main square, pl Rynok (p89), is the bustling heart of Lviv. Plonked in the middle is the huge *ratusha* (town hall), around which mill clutches of camera-toting tourists and quick-footed locals. The aroma of freshly milled coffee beans wafts across the square from the city's legendary cafes, and summer tables tumble out across the Habsburg-era cobbles as old Soviet-era trams rumble past. Take a seat, order a coffee and watch it all roll by.

MARTIN MOOS

Andriyivsky Uzviz, Kyiv

4 The apostle Andrew is said to have climbed this steep ascent to erect a cross and prophesise the rise of Kyiv. Today it's the haunt of artists, who install their canvases on this cobbled Montmartre-like street, which – in true decadent style – Kyivites call Andrew's Descent (p35). Packed with souvenir stands selling all sorts of junk, the uzviz has heaps of Bohemian charm and is great for people-watching. Here Russian writer Mikhail Bulgakov wrote *The White Guard*, perhaps the best novel about Kyiv and its people; his house is now a museum.

JOHN WARBURTON-LEE PHOTOGRAPHY/ALAMY

Kamyanets-Podilsky

5 Ringed by the dramatic gorge of the Smotrych River, there are few more eye-pleasing spots in Ukraine than this Podillyan town (p79). A stroll from the new bridge takes you through the cobbled quarters of this once divided community, past beautifully renovated churches, crumbling palaces and forgotten pieces of the once beefy defences, to the town's impossibly picturesque fortress, surely one of the highlights of any visit to Ukraine. And the best thing? Outside high season you may have the place entirely to yourself.

MARTIN MOOS

Pyrohovo Museum of Folk Architecture, Kyiv

6 You can safely claim you've seen all of Ukraine after a visit to Pyrohovo (p48) – a large chunk of countryside just outside Kyiv filled with traditional wooden architecture representing all parts of the country. Whole churches, windmills, shops and houses were brought here from their original villages, providing a wonderful backdrop for folk festivals, which frequently take place on the grounds. Here Transcarpathia is walking distance from the Poltava region, although it might be a strenuous walk, as the area is huge indeed. Country-house interior, Pyrohovo

ALLOVER PHOTOGRAPHY/ALAMY

Odesa's Nightlife

7 By day Odesa's museums, parks, beaches and, of course, the celebrated Potemkin Steps provide ample distraction, but it's at night that the city really comes alive. With its imaginatively styled dance temples and chill-out zones just steps from the Black Sea, Arkadia Beach is the place to strut and pose until the wee summer hours. But Odesa (p150) also has a stomping alternative scene, with several hip venues serving up cool ales to the sound of guitar-happy indie bands and local DJs.

Bakhchysaray's Crimean Tatar Culture

8 Back from a 50-year exile, Crimean Tatars are busy turning their capital Bakhchysaray (p167) into what its name means – garden city. Their family-run guesthouses provide some of the best (and cheapest) accommodation in Crimea, while their Asian-influenced food is now served across the peninsula. Ancient crafts, such as embroidery and filigree, are being revived by small co-operatives. Tatars are wonderful hosts, on a mission to spread the word about their unique culture. Prepare to consume large amounts of mouth-watering sweets while listening to their stories.

ULANA SWITUCHA/ALAMY

Kolomyya

9 With its traveller-friendly places to stay, two fascinating museums and effortless access to the surrounding forested hills, Kolomyya (p124) is one of the best bases from which to scale the heights of the Carpathian Mountains. The town's central Pysanky Museum, housed in a giant Easter egg, is the obvious highlight, but aimless wandering also bears fruit in the shape of some twirling art nouveau architecture from the town's Austro-Hungarian days.

Sheshory (ArtPole) Festival

10 Think Woodstock meets Burning Man and you have Sheshory (p20), an annual three-day gathering in mid-July of musicians and artists from all over Eastern Europe. For the first few years the event was held in the Carpathian village of Sheshory, but has since gone walkabout, and now the action takes place in rural Podillya. If your experience of Ukraine has been mostly scowling receptionists and shop assistants with dyed hair, the hippy spirit of the Sheshory festival comes as a very pleasant surprise.

Sofiyivka Park, Uman

11 Forget boxes of chocolates, bouquets of roses or even diamond rings – how about wowing your loved one with a gift measuring 150 hectares, complete with grottoes, water features and an entire town's worth of architectural follies? That was the grandiose way one 18th-century Polish magnate chose to express adoration for his wife, Sofia, and the legacy of his devotion is this amazing landscaped park (p74) intended to resemble the countryside of Sofia's native land. Her response – an affair with his son.

GREG BLOOM

Sudak's Crumbling Castle

DFWALLS/ALAMY

12 Once the far corner of the Roman Empire, Crimea was rediscovered by medieval Genovese traders, who came here to link up with caravans bringing silk and spices from the Orient. Their trade outposts were protected by mighty fortresses, most of which were razed by Mongol hordes. But at least one remains intact. Imagine yourself surrounded by knights, doges and silk merchants when you climb the Consul's Tower and look down the vertiginous cliff from the wall of Sudak fortress (p196), waiting for white sails to appear on the horizon.

Danube Delta Biosphere Reserve

13 The Danube Delta Biosphere Reserve (p156) is Europe's largest wetland, located in a huge delta in Ukraine's far southwest where the Danube dumps its cargo of water and silt into the Black Sea. Few make the effort to reach this far-flung chunk of fertile Ukrainian territory (few Ukrainians have been here), but those who do are rewarded with some astoundingly beautiful scenery, colourful birdlife, memorable days out on the water and serene evenings in drowsy Vylkovo, nicknamed the 'Ukrainian Venice' thanks to its network of canals.

EYE UBIQUITOUS/PHOTOLIBRARY

Crimean Cave Cities

14 It was not breathtaking views but the need to hide and protect themselves from blood-thirsty nomads that prompted ancient Crimeans to carve dwellings out of limestone atop high plateaus. Goths, Alans, Feodorites – these long-forgotten peoples come to life when you hear the story of Mangup-Kale (p171), preferably after you've hiked to the top of the plateau. Another cave city, Chufut-Kale, the Jewish fortress, remains the Zion of Karaites – a small Turkic group that has managed to preserve its unique culture and religion, rooted in Judaism, for centuries. Chufut-Kale (p168)

ITAR-TASS PHOTO AGENCY/ALAMY

Watching Football

15 Preparing to host European Cup football in 2012, Ukraine has been sprucing up its stadiums or rebuilding them from scratch. Even if you are not here for the cup, it's worth joining the crowds of fans to watch leading Ukrainian teams, such as Shakhtar Donetsk or Dynamo Kyiv. The pride of Ukraine is the brand new Donbass Arena in Donetsk. At the time of writing, reconstruction of the Olympic arena in Kyiv, the scheduled venue of Euro 2012, was in full swing. Stadiums in Kharkiv and Lviv were also bracing for the challenge. Donbass Arena (p219)

Train Journey on Ukrainian Railways

16 A quintessential experience anywhere in the former USSR is an overnight journey on the rails. Most trains have sleeper carriages with either four-bed compartments or open dorms, meaning you soon get to know your fellow travellers. Food is shared, stories told, drinks passed round, and the foreigner (you) at this impromptu party is the centre of attention (prepare for some odd questions). Finally beds are rolled out and you are left to drop off to the clickety-clack of wheel on track as the carriage sways through the darkness. Train station, Khmelnytsky

MARTIN MOOS

Colourful Markets

17 In the market for a 5L jar of gherkins, a Lada gearbox, a kilo of pig fat or a bottle of fake-brand perfume? You'll probably find them all, plus almost everything else under the sun, at Ukraine's amazing bazaars. They're the best spots to source seasonal fruit and veg, and if you're looking to pack a picnic, these are the places to get supplies. Towns large and small have sprawling markets, but the biggest and best can be found in Odesa, Kharkiv, Kyiv and Chernivtsi. Bessarabsky Rynok (p59), Kyiv

welcome to Ukraine

Big, diverse and largely undiscovered, Ukraine is one of Europe's last genuine travel frontiers, a poor nation rich in colour-splashed tradition, warm-hearted people and off-the-map travel experiences

Land on the Edge

The word 'Ukraine' means 'land on the edge', an apt title for this vast slab of Eurasia in more ways than one. This is the Slavic hinterland on Europe's periphery, European Russia's underbelly on the doorstep of Central Asia and the fringe of the Black Sea, but it's also a country creeping slowly towards the edge of change and modernity. The 2004 Orange Revolution lit a bitterly disappointing false dawn, the world economic slowdown walloped this country hard and recent political changes have been labelled Ukraine's great leap backwards, but things are, nonetheless, shifting forward little by little in Europe's biggest country. One look at the renovated city centres, well-dressed townsfolk, resurfaced roads and all the glistening infrastructure bolted in place for the 2012 European Soccer Championships (the world's third-largest sporting event) is enough to see that after two decades of independence, Ukraine is edging long-term toward where it aspires to be, despite its squabbling politicians and meddlesome neighbours.

Ukraine – Yes You Can!

A trip to what is, for many, an unfamiliar destination can seem slightly daunting, but fear not – Ukraine is currently taking a soccer-inspired crash course in how to look after travellers. Long gone are the days when, visa in hand, you were group-herded around approved sights by the state travel agency, though some Ukrainians, particularly the elderly, are still shocked to learn Westerners dare travel independently or solo. Visas have (hopefully) gone forever, getting around the country has never been easier, frayed Soviet hotels are renovating, imaginative restaurants are being created in big cities and even (drum roll) bona fide tourist information centres are springing up, at least in the country's west. Whether you come for lazy beach holidays in Crimea, hire a mountain bike in the Carpathians, stay in European-style luxury in Kyiv or camp out at an ethno rock festival, you'll be doing something that was barely possible a decade and a half ago.

Warts & All Experience

Travel may be simpler and more entertaining than it once was, but the whiff of Soviet 'hospitality' does remain. Ukraine still specialises in blind waiters, dumbstruck receptionists, nail-filing ticket sellers and devious policemen. Very few people outside Kyiv and Lviv speak English and facilities are often shoddy, antiquated or just not up to the job. But embrace the post-Soviet disarray, select your itinerary carefully and engage with Ukraine's wonderfully kind and generous people, and we guarantee your time in Ukraine will be well spent.

need to know

Currency
» Hryvnya (UAH; *hriv*-nya)

Language
» Ukrainian and Russian

When to Go

Warm to hot summers, cold winters

Lviv
GO May–Sep

Kyiv
GO May-Jun, Sep

Kharkiv
GO May-Jun, Sep

Donetsk
GO May-Jun, Sep

Odesa
GO May–Sep

Yalta
GO May-Jun, Sep

High Season
(Jul–Aug)

» Expect stifling heat and heavy thunderstorms

» Accommodation rates rise in Crimea but fall in the Carpathians

» Cities empty as people head for the coast and their country cottages

Shoulder (May–Jun & Sep–Oct)

» Travel now to dodge the extreme temperatures of summer or winter

» Spring can be chilly, but it's a pleasant time to be in blossoming Kyiv

» Visit Crimea in autumn and avoid the summer crowds

Low Season
(Nov–Apr)

» Expect temperatures well below zero, heavy snowfalls and hard frosts

» The Carpathians skiing season runs November to March

» Book ahead for New Year and early January

Your Daily Budget

Budget less than
250uah

» Travel on overnight sleeper trains and cut accommodation costs

» Cafeteria-style meal: from 30uah

» Dorm beds: 100-150uah

Midrange
250-1000uah

» Double room with breakfast in a good hotel: 400-800uah

» Lunch and dinner in restaurants with waiters

» English guides and tours where available

Top end over
1000uah

» Double room in a comfortable, European standard hotel: from 800uah

» Taxis between cities: 2-3uah per kilometre

» English speaking guide and driver per day: 400-600uah

Money

» ATMs widespread, even in small towns. Credit cards accepted at most hotels but only upmarket restaurants.

Visas

» Generally not needed for stays of up to 90 days.

Mobile Phones

» Local SIM cards can be used in European and Australian phones. US and other phones aren't compatible; consider a cheap Ukrainian mobile.

Transport

» Trains for longer distances; buses for local and inter-regional travel.

Websites

» **Lonely Planet** (www.lonelyplanet. com/ukraine) Info, hotel bookings, traveller forum and more.

» **Brama** (www. brama.com) Most useful gateway site.

» **Infoukes** (www. infoukes.com) Ukrainian-Canadian pages with online maps and tips on where to visit.

» **Ukraine.com** (www. ukraine.com) Gateway site with news and lots of background info.

» **Ukraine Encyclopaedia** (www. encyclopediaofukraine. com) One of the largest sources of info on Ukraine.

Exchange Rates

Australia	A$1	7.50uah
Canada	C$1	7.60uah
EU	€1	10.50uah
Japan	¥100	9uah
New Zealand	NZ$1	6uah
Poland	1zł	2.70uah
Russia	R10	2.50uah
UK	UK£1	12.50uah
US	US$1	8uah

For current exchange rates see www.xe.com.

Important Numbers

When calling within a city, leave off the city code. When calling abroad from landlines, dial 0 then wait for another tone before pressing 0 again.

Country code	+38
International access code	0-0
General emergency number	112

Arriving in Ukraine

» **Kyiv Borispil Airport**

Buses – regular round-the-clock departures from outside the terminal

Taxis – 200-300uah; around 40 minutes to the city centre

Train – new express train planned for Euro 2012

» **Lviv Airport**

Buses – trolleybus 9 or *marshrutka* (fixed-price minibus) 95 to the city centre

Taxis – around 50uah; 15 minutes to the city centre

New connections may appear for Euro 2012

Packing for Ukraine

What you choose to stuff into your bags depends very much on when you are heading to Ukraine and what you plan to do there. We'll leave you to decide if those Ugg boots are the best footwear for a Carpathian trek, but the following is gear we've found essential over the years.

When the power fails (and it does) a torch means you won't be left fumbling. Insect repellent is absolutely essential everywhere from June to October and a basic first-aid kit (painkillers, diarrhoea tablets and plasters) is useful in rural areas. A sewing kit is handy as buttons regularly pop off in the metro crush. Pack sunglasses summer and winter, as well as a pair of flip-flops, good for beaches and long train journeys. A universal sink plug is helpful on trains and in no-frills hotels.

if you like...

Folk Culture

Traditional folk culture has boomed in recent years with new festivals and events added to an ever-growing calendar. The mountain-dwelling Hutsuls are the embodiment of Ukrainian folk culture and Carpathian souvenirs of fleece and carved wood are touted across the land.

Hutsuls Festivals, weddings and red-letter days are the best times to see the culture of the Carpathians' Hutsul people in all its woolly glory (p127)

Sheshory (ArtPole) Festival One of many festivals held around the country celebrating all things folkloric (p9)

Pyrohovo Museum of Folk Architecture This is the best open-air museum in the country highlighting local crafts and customs (p48)

Crimean Tatars Bakhchysaray is the best place to track down traditional Crimean Tatar culture and some delicious ethnic food (p167)

Kosiv craft market Ukraine's biggest traditional craft market is the place to pick up genuine hand-made souvenirs (p127)

Castles

In the west of the country many a hilltop castle and chateau gazes out across the landscape. The Polish nobility transformed the region's draughty medieval fortresses into Renaissance and baroque palaces, but decades of communism saw many left to crumble.

Kamyanets-Podilsky A photogenic creation in stone and a highlight for any Ukraine-bound castle-chaser (p80)

Khotyn A dramatic sight rising high above the River Dnister (p134)

Sudak A 14th-century Genoese fortress draped over a limestone peak (p196)

Palanok Castle Perched above the town of Mukacheve and the surrounding plains, this commanding fortress remembers turbulent and blood-stained days (p137)

Czerwonogrod Our expert in off-the-beaten-track Ukrainian castles rates this as the country's best (p83)

Churches

Stalin did his levelling best to destroy Ukraine's stock of magnificent church buildings, but somehow many survived. Musty church interiors, perfumed with beeswax candles and decorated with gilt icons, colourful frescoes and intricately carved iconostases, are an unmissable element of any visit to Ukraine.

Pecherska Lavra This gathering of golden domes is Ukraine's holiest site (p43)

St Sophia's Cathedral Kyiv's most atmospheric place of worship (p34)

St Andrew's Church Many a 19th-century aristocratic wedding took place in this magnificent chunk of baroque architecture (p35)

Chernihiv The town's collection of exquisite church buildings has earned it Unesco recognition (p207)

Carpathian wooden churches Miniature timber churches and chapels can be found the length of the Carpathian arc from Romania to the Czech Republic (p91)

Pochayiv This golden-domed huddle of churches and monastery buildings can be seen for miles around (p108)

>> Khotyn Fortress (p134), the site of an epic confrontation between Poles, Cossacks and Turks, overlooks the Dnister River

MARTIN MOOS

PLAN YOUR TRIP IF YOU LIKE

Soviet Architecture

Taxi-hailing Lenin statues, brutish war memorials, plinthed tanks, Karl Marx busts and the odd Stalin monument may one day be carted off to a nostalgia museum, but some things would need copious amounts of dynamite to demolish. We list some of them here.

Rodina Mat This 62m-tall titanium goddess wields sword and shield high above the River Dnipro (p47)

Derzhprom This megalomaniac's dream in concrete even manages to dominate the world's second largest square (p180)

Kyiv metro Some of Kyiv's metro stations are proof that the Soviets did sometimes create things of ornate beauty (p67)

Friendship of Nations Monument A huge Soviet realist monument under a tin rainbow that radiates different colours at night (p51)

Jewish Sites

Jewish cemeteries, former synagogues and tombs can be found across western and central Ukraine. *Shtetls* were established in Central Ukraine in the 19th-century Pale of Settlement. The holocaust and recent emigration have left few to tend to memorials at WWII mass burial sites.

Uman The tomb of Rabbi Nachman draws thousands of pilgrims at Jewish New Year (p75)

Berdychiv The highlight here is the tomb of Levi Yitzhak set amid toppling, Hebrew-inscribed graves (p73)

Bratslav Rabbi Nachman wrote most of his works in this small town 50km southeast of Vinnytsya (p78)

Sharhorod One of the region's best preserved *shtetls* (p78)

Babyn Yar A sobering site in Kyiv's western suburbs where most of the city's Jews were shot in September 1941 (p48)

Museums

Most of Ukraine's museums are threadbare affairs, tended by an army of eagle-eyed *babushkas,* who follow visitors round switching lights on and off and making sure they don't err from the prescribed tour route. However, there are some fantastically quirky exceptions out there.

Museum of One Street Relates the story of Kyiv's Andriyivsky uzviz in a delightful jumble of knickknacks (p35)

Korolyov Cosmonaut Museum A blast off from the Soviet space program past (p72)

Nuclear Missile Museum See how close the world was to mass destruction at this remote former nuclear missile launch site (p78)

Chornobyl Museum Tells the horrific story of the world's worst nuclear disaster (p42)

Pysanky Museum The yoke's on you if you miss this folksy museum housed in a huge painted egg (p125)

If you like...caves, Crimea has whole subterranean cities of them, buried deep below the peninsula's limestone plateau (p168)

Beaches

An increasing number of travellers are coming to Ukraine to spend at least part of their trip frolicking on the beach. Naturally most head straight for the Black Sea but Ukrainians will make use of any body of water.

Hydropark Didn't think you'd need your Speedos in Kyiv? Think again. (p59)

Arkadia Not so much about the beach as the all-night clubbing and hedonistic hoo-ha that goes on beside it (p146)

Yashmovy Beach The 800 steps down to this stunningly beautiful stretch of Crimean sand put many off, meaning a less crowded experience (p181)

Lisya Bay This Crimean nudist beach attracts naturists from across the ex-USSR (p199)

Mountain Sports

Ukraine's vast plains and steppe are typically as flat as prehistoric seabeds come, but things do get crumply in the far west of the country (the Carpathian Mountains) and in southern Crimea. Increasingly these two locations are becoming mountain sports playgrounds.

Bukovel Ukraine's premier ski resort with facilities and prices to match (p123)

Bikeland This network of cycling trails in the Carpathian Mountains is one of the most promising developments in the region (p122)

Hoverla An ascent of Ukraine's highest peak is not as difficult as it sounds (p120)

Hiking Both the Carpathians and Crimea are superb places to lace up your walking boots for a trek (p120)

Wildlife

In a land of nuclear disasters, environmental neglect and post-Soviet disarray, you'd be excused for thinking there would be little wildlife left – but you'd be wrong. Ukraine boasts several well-stocked nature reserves and protected areas.

Askaniya Nova Reserve Zebras, camels and wild horses roaming the Eastern European steppe? You better believe it. (p155)

Danube Delta Biosphere Reserve A watery haven for all kinds of birdlife (p156)

Kara-Dag Nature Reserve Hike through a weird and wonderful landscape of volcanic rock formations to spot eagles and storks (p199)

Carpathian Biosphere Reserve Several stretches of Carpathian virgin forest provide habitats for all kinds of fauna and flora (p129)

Shatsky National Nature Park Ukraine's under-visited 'lake district' is a superbly soggy region of marshes, ponds and wetlands in the far northwest of the country (p112)

month by month

Top Events

19

1 **Carnival Humorina**, April

2 **Sheshory (ArtPole) Festival**, June

3 **Ivan Kupala**, July

4 **Koktebel International Jazz Festival**, September

5 **New Year's Eve**, December

January

Winter bites cold in January and you'll have to wrap up pretty snugly to do any sightseeing. However, this is a great time to snap on skis or snowboard in the Carpathian Mountains.

Orthodox Christmas

Only revived in recent years, Ukrainians celebrate Orthodox Christmas according to the old Julian Calendar on 7 January. On Christmas Eve families gather for the 12-course meal of *Svyata Vecherya* (Holy Supper), while children might go carolling (*kolyadky*).

Old New Year's Eve

Not only do Ukrainians get to celebrate two Christmases (Catholic and Orthodox), they also get two stabs at New Year – according to the Julian Calendar Orthodox New Year falls on 13 January. No day off work for the hungover, though.

Epiphany

Across Ukraine during 18–19 January, mad individuals can be seen leaping into icy rivers to celebrate the arrival of Christianity in Kyivan Rus. Kyiv sees the biggest event with scores of men braving the numbing waters of the Dnipro.

March

There's usually little sign of spring in March, with temperatures hovering around zero and occasional snow falls. The Carpathian skiing season begins to wind up mid-month and hikers and bikers reclaim the peaks.

International Women's Day

Nowadays this relic from the days of the USSR is just a good excuse for the menfolk to get out of their gourd. The day starts with much hand kissing, flower giving and toasts to 'our ladies', before deteriorating into *horilka* (vodka) fuelled abandon.

April

Things begin to warm up along the southern coast, but inland you'll still need those chunky Hutsul woollen socks. A pleasant time to visit Kyiv is the end of the month when thousands of chestnut trees are just beginning to bloom across the city.

Carnival Humorina

Odesa's biggest fiesta of the year takes the shape of a one-day street parade on 1 April. Floats, music, dancing and lots of food flood the streets to celebrate the city's status as Ukrainian capital of humour.

Orthodox Easter

Falling two weeks after Catholic Easter, colourful Orthodox *paskha* arrives in April two years out of three. This is more of a religious festival than in the West, with churchgoers taking baskets of *pysanky* (painted eggs) and specially baked loaves to be blessed by priests.

May

Ukraine is most definitely a shoulder season destination and May is the first of those shoulders. Colour returns

to the snow-bleached land, the last river ice fades and the first seedlings nudge through Ukraine's black soil.

Kamyanets-Podilsky Days

Mid-May sees street parties, concerts, choirs, parades, exhibitions, sporting events and a picturesque hot-air balloon festival take over the rock-island town of Kamyanets-Podilsky for almost a week. It's one of the few times of the year when things come to life here.

Kyiv Day

A colourful spring celebration and festival in honour of the capital city held on the last weekend of May. The day of fun events comes to an end around 10pm with a huge firework display over the Dnipro.

June

Comfortable temperatures continue across the steppe but things begin to heat up in Crimea. Along with September, this is one of the most pleasant months to travel, before the worst of the heat arrives.

Sheshory (ArtPole) Festival

The most talked-about ethnic music festival (www. artpolefest.org) in the country has taken on a more experimental character in recent years. The roving festival was held in rural Podillya in 2010; check the website for this year's destination and program.

July

Alas, most visitors arrive in the hottest months of the year when travel becomes a sweaty ordeal. Give Crimea a wide berth at this time of year and head instead for the cooler Carpathians.

Ivan Kupala

An exhilarating pagan celebration of midsummer involving fire jumping, maypole dancing, fortune-telling, wreath floating and strong overtones of sex. Celebrated July 7, head for the countryside for the real heathen deal.

Kazantip

The huge, seaside Kazantip rave festival (www.kazantip.com) kicks off in late July and runs for five weeks, into August. It's held in Popivka north of Yevpatoriya and attracts over 100,000 party people.

Kraina Mriy Festival

This free three-day festival of ethnic music (www. krainamriy.com) attracts traditional musicians from across the country. Performances take place on several stages erected in the park next to Kyiv's Pecherska Lavra, and there's also a book fair and kids' events.

Taras Bulba Festival

Held in the small Rivne region town of Dubno, this hard-rock festival (www. tarasbulba-fest.kiev.ua) is in honour of Gogol's legendary Cossack character. Most of the guitar thrashing happens within the walls of the town's castle.

Festival 'Under the Rock'

Held in the tiny village of Pidkamin (meaning 'under the rock'), this popular ethnic music, jazzy–type festival is held around a huge hilltop rock formation. It's one of the most popular festivals in the west with a tent city and loads of side events.

August

Crowded and superheated, Crimea is still the place to avoid during August. Colossal sunflower fields are a gobsmacking sight across Ukraine's agricultural heartlands this month, and by the end the harvest is in full swing.

Independence Day

On the 24th, cities across the land lay on festivals and parades with performances and special events. But the place to be is Kyiv's maydan Nezalezhnosti (Independence Square), which bops to an evening pop concert followed by a mega firework show.

September

Temperatures mellow out, people return to the cities and everyday life resumes in the hazy light of the Ukrainian autumn. By far the best time to travel and to gorge on Ukraine's legendary fruit and veg.

★ Koktebel International Jazz Festival

In mid-September international jazz stars join locals at this cool festival (http://jazz.koktebel.info) after Crimea's summertime crush has passed. Over 20,000 fans swamp tiny Koktebel to tap feet in rhythm with almost 200 musicians, making this one of Ukraine's largest music festivals.

★ Gogolfest

The biggest festival of the autumn in Kyiv, Gogolfest (www.gogolfest.org.ua) takes place at the new Mystetsky Arsenal venue opposite the Lavra. The highlight of the two weeks of art, theatre and music is the Moloko Music Fest.

★ Lviv Coffee Festival

Disciples of the bean should go west to Ukraine's caffeine capital for the country's only coffee festival (www.coffeefest.lviv.ua). Highlights of the three-day event include the presentation of an award for 'Lviv coffeehouse of the year', various concerts and coffee-themed tours.

October

The comfortable temperatures give way to chilly days, falling leaves and the first frosts. Ukrainians head out to their country cottages and gardens to wind up the season and lock up for the long winter.

★ Terra Heroika Festival

This riotous festival pitches Polish hussars against moustachioed Turks and ponytailed Cossacks in slightly over-authentic battle re-enactments. Ever seen a guy with a 2m-long broadsword in a nightclub? You might during this festival – but hey, this is Ukraine.

★ Kyiv International Film Festival Molodist

Late October sees Kyiv host this superb film festival (www.molodist.com), a great opportunity to check out new cinematic talent from Ukraine and other countries. Forty years old in 2010, it's recognised as one of Eastern Europe's top film events.

December

End-of-year commercialism is yet to take off in a big way here, so if you're looking to flee the Christmas shopping blues, decidedly unfestive Ukraine could be the antidote. Bring your woollies as temperatures head south.

★ Catholic Christmas

On 25 December Catholic Ukrainians celebrate the first of two Christmases the country marks every year. However, for most people, especially in the predominantly Orthodox and Russian-speaking areas, this is just an ordinary working day.

★ New Year's Eve

This is by far the biggest bash of the year and if you think you've seen it all on New Year's Eve, you haven't been to Kyiv. Needless to say, gallons of *horilka* and cheap bubbly are involved.

itineraries

Whether you've got six days or 60, these itineraries provide a starting point for the trip of a lifetime. Want more inspiration? Head online to lonelyplanet. com/thorntree to chat with other travellers

Two Weeks
Essential Ukraine

> The quintessential Ukrainian experience kicks off in **Kyiv**, the cradle of Slavic civilisation. Three days are just enough to absorb the mix of gold-domed Orthodox churches, monumental Stalinist architecture, leafy parks and raucous nightlife.

From Kyiv catch an overnight train to the former Habsburg city of **Lviv**. With its Italianate buildings and Austrian-style cafes, it's a cosy contrast to the colossal capital.

From there, it's a simple ride south to **Kolomyya**, a great base from which to explore the Carpathian Mountains and perhaps climb **Mt Hoverla**, Ukraine's highest peak. A short ride from here brings you to stunning **Kamyanets-Podilsky**, where the medieval Old Town perches atop a tall rock in the middle of a river loop.

Next stop, **Odesa**, famous for the Potemkin Steps and weekend clubbing at Arkadia Beach. Then take an overnight train to **Simferopol**, before heading to the Crimean Tatar capital of **Bakhchysaray**, with its captivating Khans' Palace and cave city of Chufut Kale.

Then head south to kitschy **Yalta**, a handy base for exploring Crimea's southern coast.

Two Weeks
Best of the West

> Launch your loop around Ukraine's far west in **Lviv**, an eastern outpost of central Europe with a strong cafe culture and some gobsmacking architecture that make it one of Ukraine's top stops for any visitor. Outside the city centre the Lychakivske Cemetery is a must-see. The city also has some of the country's wackiest restaurants, with the Masonic Restaurant and Dim Lehend topping a zany list.

If you can tear yourself away from Lviv's European charms, hop on board a slow train south to low-key **Mukacheve**, where one of Ukraine's most dramatic hilltop castles awaits. From here it's into soothingly forested mountain country, the **Carpathians** to be exact. Ukraine's section of the Carpathian arc is etched with long broad valleys, and a great place to start your exploration is **Rakhiv**. Here you can have your first brush with Hutsul culture and head off into the hills for some exhilarating hiking and biking, before picking your way north along the A265 road linking resort villages, ski centres and hiking bases en route. Call a halt at quaint **Kolomyya**, a superb launch pad for more hikes. The town also has two intriguing museums including the famous Pysanky Museum housed in a giant Easter egg. It also boasts one of the best places to stay in all Ukraine in the shape of the On the Corner B&B.

Consider short stops at energetic **Chernivtsi**, to visit the psychedelic university building, and the spectacular **Khotyn** fortress on the banks of the wide River Dnister, before you next unpack your bags in the show-stopping island town of **Kamyanets-Podilsky**. One of Ukraine's must-see attractions, the town is as historically fascinating as it is dramatically situated in a loop of the river Smotrych.

A long haul by bus across giant fields of sunflowers and sugar beet via off-the-beaten-track Ternopil delivers you to picturesque **Kremenets**, another town boasting a superb fortress as well as an eerie Cossack cemetery. From here it's a short *marshrutka* (fixed-price minibus) hop to the polished golden domes of **Pochayiv**, Ukraine's second most important monastery after Kyiv's Pecherska Lavra. Lviv is a four-hour bus ride away.

Ten Days
Best of the East

> This venture into the less frequented east begins with a quick jump north from Kyiv to atmospheric **Chernihiv**, with its amazing Unesco-listed collection of monasteries and cathedrals. Most make this a day-trip from the capital but staying the night gives more time to appreciate the wonderful collection of ancient church buildings.

Unless you're up for some slow and complicated train journeys, backtrack to the capital and jump aboard an express train heading east – first stop the spa town of **Myrhorod**. Gogol was born nearby, and the town and surrounding area feature in many of his tales. Get off the beaten track in these parts by spending a couple of days on the Gogol Circuit, which visits many sites associated with the author. Local guesthouses can put you up for a few hryvnya.

Reboard the express for the short trip to **Poltava**, a pleasant, park-dotted place and the scene of a key battle in Ukrainian history. Designed as a kind of mini–St Petersburg, this grand city contrasts with the surrounding bucolic scenery and is well worth half a day's exploration. The final stop of the express is **Kharkiv**, a huge student city of 1.5 million. Essential viewing here is the world's second-largest city square, which is dominated by the mammoth, Stalinist-era Derzhprom building.

From Kharkiv it's a smooth roll south to another of Ukraine's eastern megacities – **Dnipropetrovsk** – still a major centre for Ukraine's rocket and aviation industries (so be careful what you aim your camera at!). Take a stroll by the Dnipro River before continuing south to **Zaporizhzhya**, an ugly industrial city but also the location of Khortytsya Island, where the Ukrainian Cossacks once gathered at the *sich* (fort). This is the best place in the country to learn about the Cossacks, their way of life and their influence on the country's history. From the banks of the Dnipro, catch a bus or train to **Donetsk**, the powerbase of the east. The main industry is still coalmining, but among the slag heaps you'll also glimpse Eastern Europe's most cutting-edge football stadium, a Euro 2012 venue. Donetsk is an overnight bus or train journey back to Kyiv.

Regions at a Glance

Kyiv

History ✓✓✓
Architecture ✓✓
Walks ✓✓

Kyivan Rus
One of those places 'where it all started', Kyiv is the cradle of all things Russian, Ukrainian and Belarusian. While visiting St Sophia cathedral or Kyevo-Pecherska Lavra, you'll step on the stones that remember the Viking princes and Greek bishops who shaped East Slavic civilization. Walking down Andrew's Descent towards the Dnipro, you'll follow the same route as Kyivites did when Prince Volodymyr ordered that they plunge into the river in a mass baptism ceremony that heralded the adoption of Christianity by Kyivan Rus.

Eclectic Cityscape
Early medieval monasteries, Polish-influenced baroque, Russian art nouveau, Soviet constructivism and post-Soviet kitsch – Kyiv's architecture is a charming disorderly cocktail of epochs and styles. Check out landmark buildings designed by Wladislaw Horodecki, particularly his famous House of Chimeras.

Riverside Promenade
You might feel as if you are flying above the mind-bogglingly wide Dnipro when you observe it from the hilly right bank. Here, a chain of parks forms a long green belt separating Kyiv's centre from the river. It's a great place for walks and bicycle or Segway rides, as well as for watching Kyivites in their element, while being curiously inspected by them.

Central Ukraine

Jewish Heritage ✓✓✓
Architecture ✓✓
Museums ✓✓✓

Jewish Sites
The Nazis and post-Soviet emigration emptied Central Ukraine's cities of Jews, but many a crooked, Hebrew-inscribed gravestone and synagogue remain. The region is also the birthplace of Hasidism, its founders' tombs attracting a stream of pilgrims every year.

Architectural Landscape
Central Ukraine boasts one of the country's most spectacular castles at Kamyanets-Podilsky, but there are many other fortresses and mansions. Zhytomyr flaunts a stern Soviet style while Uman wows with its romantically landscaped Sofiyivka Park.

Quirky Museums
What do an embalmed doctor, a real nuclear missile launch site and assorted junk from the space race have in common? Well, Central Ukraine has a museum dedicated to them all – surely the most fascinating collection in the country.

Lviv & Western Ukraine

Architecture ✓✓✓
Coffee ✓✓
Castles ✓✓✓

Architectural Style

From the handsome austerity of Gothic churches to box-ugly Soviet apartment blocks, Lviv is a textbook of European architectural styles from the last seven centuries. Echoes of the past can be found in towns and villages across the region.

Cafe Culture

Lviv has a distinct central European coffeehouse tradition that sets it firmly apart from the rest of Ukraine. One of the city's delights is ducking in and out of its many intimate, bean-perfumed coffeehouses, sampling the best doses of Arabica in the land.

Castles & Fortresses

No other region of Ukraine possesses such a large number of castles, fortresses, chateaux and mansions. When the Polish nobility ruled the roost, the Polish nobility converted many crumbling medieval castles into noble baroque residences. In a strange way their current shabby state just adds to the magic.

p86

The Carpathians

Outdoor Fun ✓✓✓
Landscapes ✓✓✓
Food ✓✓

Boot & Bike

The mountains are becoming a mecca for more adventurous outdoorsy types with routes for both knobbly tyre and treaded boot crisscrossing the forested ranges. Volunteers from the superb Bikeland project have marked out many new cycling trails but the going is still quite rough.

Alpine Eye Candy

Only Crimea can rival the Carpathians for mountain vistas and peak-top views. Carpeted in thick forest, the Carpathians are generally more soothing than dramatic, but some of the views out across the valleys are spectacular.

Carpathian Menu

The mountain-dwelling Hutsuls have a traditional diet dominated by the ingredients they fish and pluck from the Carpathians' rivers and forests. But star of the food show in these parts is the delicious local cheese, made in special huts high up in the mountains.

p114

Odesa & Southern Ukraine

Nightlife ✓✓✓
Beaches ✓
Wildlife ✓✓✓

Seaside Clubbing

Odesa's nightlife comes a close second to the capital's, with bars, clubs and music venues to suit every taste and hairstyle. The blingy beachside megaclubs attract the glitterati for nights of see-and-be-seen clubbing, but the city centre hides more low-key spots for an alternative crowd.

Black Sea Fun

The Black Sea's sand-fringed shores attract once-a-year holidaymakers from across the former USSR, who tan until crisp before wallowing in the tepid waters. Not the cleanest beaches in the world, but the further you go, the better they get.

Ukrainian Safari

Southern Ukraine is a magnet for wildlife spotters with two unique areas teeming with winged and hooved critters. Go on safari around the Askaniya Nova Reserve, where zebra, camels and Przewalski horses roam free, or venture into the Danube.

p139

Crimea

Mountains ✓✓✓
Palaces ✓✓
Battlefields ✓

Stunning Landscapes

A chain of plateaus with vertiginous near-vertical slopes loom above the dark-blue sea. Looking like cream topping on a cake, their limestone hats hide ancient cave cities and bizarrely eroded forms. In spring, they turn into flower-filled Oriental tapestries.

Royal Retreats

Russian aristocrats and moguls squandered fortunes on whimsical creations of fin de siècle architects. These monuments of imperial decadence dot the Crimean coast, surrounded by lush parks and filled with memories of the last Romanovs.

Crimean War

The Crimean War was fought on some of the world's most picturesque battlefields. While observing terrain that remembers Florence Nightingale and the Charge of the Light Brigade, you may plunge into a turquoise sea or discover that Balaklava is more about seafood than ski hats.

p159

Eastern Ukraine

Cossacks ✓✓✓
Quirky Donbass ✓✓
Village Life ✓✓

Cossack Stronghold

Wondering about the Cossacks? Spend a day on the island of Khortitsa in Zaporizhzhya, the site of their main stronghold known as the Sich. History aside, the place is beautiful with its rocky cliffs and rapids, and Dniproges dam looming in the distance.

Caves & Mines

There are some gems lurking behind those heaps of coal dust – a particularly cute Orthodox cave monastery and a mindboggling salt mine. Besides, the escapist culture of Britain-obsessed Donetsk has produced some great places to eat and have fun.

Northern Countryside

It's Ukrainian to the core, complete with sunflowers, pumpkins and villagers that seem to have walked out of Nikolai Gogol's books. Tourist infrastructure is embryonic here, so be the first to discover it!

p205

Look out for these icons:

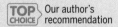 Our author's recommendation

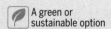 A green or sustainable option

 No payment required

On the Road

Kyïv Київ

🎵 044 / POP 5.6 MILLION

Best Places to Eat

» Spotykach (p57)
» Vernisazh (p57)
» Garbuzyk (p57)
» Concord (p56)
» Kyivska Perepichka (p56)

Best Places to Stay

» Rented Apartment (p53)
» Hotel Opera (p54)
» Sunflower B&B Hotel (p52)
» Hyatt Regency (p53)
» Central Station Hostel (p54)

Why Go?

Ancients were spoilt for choice when they needed a pretty spot to settle down. One can't help thinking this in Kyiv, the birthplace of Eastern Slavic civilization, which spread from here as far as the Pacific coast of Eurasia. Its lovely forested hills overlook the Dnipro – a river so wide that birds fall down before reaching its middle, as writer Nikolai Gogol jokingly remarked.

Those hills, numbered seven as in Rome, cradle a wonderfully eclectic city that has preserved the legacy of its former possessors, from Viking chieftains to Soviet dictators. History buffs can indulge in unrestrained epoch-hopping, but it's rewarding enough just to stroll along the streets lined by trademark chestnut trees, stopping by an open-air cafe or diving into a basement bar. That's where one meets Kyivites – a merry, tongue-in-cheek and perfectly bilingual lot, whose distinct urban identity outweighs their ethnic allegiance. They are the city's main asset.

When to Go?

Kyiv

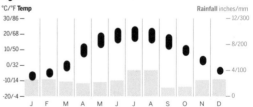

January Party on New Year's night, then repent at an Orthodox Christmas service a week later.

May Frolic in Kyiv's two Botanical Gardens, where just about every tree is blossoming.

July Witness ancient pagan ceremonies and enjoy great world music at the Kraina Mriy festival.

History

Legend has it that three Slavic brothers and their sister founded Kyiv. The eldest, Kyi, gave the city its name. The names of brothers Shchek, Khoriv and sister Lybid now appear in its topography. An iconic statue of the four siblings – the Foundation of Kyiv Monument (Пам'ятник засновникам; Map p32) – stands on the banks of the Dnipro River.

Four hundred years later the city really started to prosper, after Vikings from Novgorod took control. Circa 864 two Novgorod warlords Askold and Dir settled down in Kyiv after a failed raid on Constantinople. Novgorod's new prince Oleh journeyed to Kyiv in 882, dispatched the two Vikings and declared himself ruler. This was the beginning of Kyivan Rus ('Rus' being the Slavic name for the red-haired Scandinavians). The city thrived on river trade, sending furs, honey and slaves to pay for luxury goods from Constantinople. Within 100 years its empire stretched from the Volga to the Danube and to Novgorod.

In 989 Kyivan prince Volodymyr decided to forge a closer alliance with Constantinople, marrying the emperor's daughter and adopting Orthodox Christianity. Kyiv's pagan idols were destroyed and its people driven into the Dnipro for a mass baptism.

Under Volodymyr's son, Yaroslav the Wise (1017–54), Kyiv became a cultural and political centre in the Byzantine mould. St Sophia's Cathedral was built to proclaim the glory of both God and city. However, by the 12th century, Kyiv's economic prowess had begun to wane, with power shifting to northeast principalities (near today's Moscow).

In 1240 Mongol raiders sacked Kyiv. Citizens fled or took refuge wherever they could, including the roof of the Desyatynna Church, which collapsed under the weight.

The city shrank to the riverside district of Podil, which remained its centre for centuries. Only when Ukraine formally passed into Russian hands at the end of the 18th century did Kyiv again grow in importance. The city went through an enormous boom at the turn of the 20th century when it was essentially the third imperial capital after St Petersburg and Moscow. Many new mansions were erected at this time, including the remarkable House of Chimeras.

During the chaos following the Bolshevik Revolution, Kyiv was the site of frequent battles between Red and White Russian forces, Ukrainian nationalists, and German and Polish armies. Author Mikhail Bulgakov captured the era's uncertainty in his first novel, *The White Guard*. The home in which he wrote this book is now a museum (see p35).

In August 1941, German troops captured Kyiv and more than half a million Soviet soldiers were caught or killed. The entire city suffered terribly. Germans massacred about 100,000 at Babyn Yar and 80% of the city's inhabitants were homeless by the time the Red Army retook Kyiv on 6 November 1943.

The postwar years saw rapid industrialisation and the construction of unsightly suburbs. During the late 1980s nationalistic and democratic movements from western Ukraine began to catch on in the capital. Throughout the presidency of Leonid Kuchma, Kyiv and its young population increasingly became a base of opposition politics. During the Orange Revolution of 2004, activists from around Ukraine poured into the capital to demonstrate on maydan Nezalezhnosti (Independence Sq) and outside the parliament building. In the 2010 presidential elections, two-thirds of voters in Kyiv supported Orange Revolution leader Yulia Tymoshenko, although she still lost to Viktor Yanukovych.

◉ Sights

Some of Kyiv's main attractions are half-day adventures and not always terribly central. So, rather than plunging right in, it's highly recommended you warm up with an initial stroll. The Walking Tour (p50) provides a quick introduction to the city.

CENTRE

Maydan Nezalezhnosti CENTRAL SQUARE
(майдан Незалежності; Independence Square; Map p36; MMaydan Nezalezhnosti) Fountain-filled maydan Nezalezhnosti is the city's most popular meeting place. This was made plain on worldwide TV at the end of 2004 when the square became ground zero for Ukraine's Orange Revolution and a makeshift tent city.

The square has held protests since the Orange Revolution and will probably see many more. Some **graffiti** left from those events is preserved under plexiglass on one of the post office columns near the corner of Khreshchatyk. Since 2001, the square has been dominated by kitschy post-Soviet

Kyiv Highlights

1 Stroll up and down **Kreshchatyk** (p31) munching on a hotdog from **Kyivska Perepichka** (p56)

2 Admire the beauty of Orthodox ritual and meet the mummies at **Kyevo-Pecherska Lavra** (p43)

3 Explore the nuclear ghostland of **Chornobyl** (p68) on a guided tour

4 Share a few beers and *horilka* (vodka) shots with local bohemians in a smoke-filled dive, such as **Palata No.6** (p60)

5 Step on the rugged cobblestones of **Andriyivsky uzviz** (p35), inhale its Parisian air and sample some quality French food in one of its cafes

2 km
1 miles

To **3** Chornobyl
(105km)

Velyka Kiltseva doroha

pr Pravdy

Dniprovsky Park

vul Onore de Balzaka

pr Henerala Vatutina

Dnipro River

bul Perova

Dolobetsky Island

Trukhaniv Island

M Heroyiv Dnipra

M Minska

M Obolon

M Petrivka

vul Bohatyrska

pr Moskovsky

vul Vyshgorodska

vul Frunze

Babyn Yar

M Dorohozhychi

vul Stetsenka

Lukyanivska

vul Dekhtyarivska

M Shulyavska

vul Hihorovicha

vul Artema

Shulyavska

M Beresteyska

pr Peremohy

See Podil Map (p42)

PODIL

Kontraktova pl

M Andriyivsky **5** uzviz

Poshtova pl **M**

vul Velyka Zhytomyrska

Maydan

M

M

M

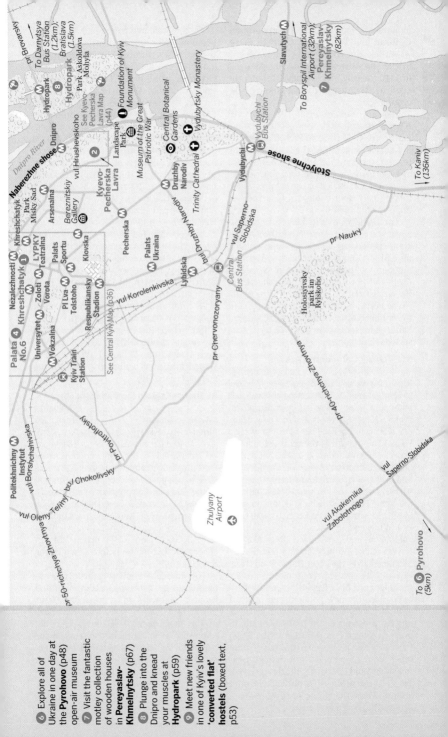

To Darnytsya
Bus Station
(1.2km);
Bratislava
(1.5km)

pr Brovarsky

To Boryspil International
Airport (32km);
Pereyaslav-
Khmelnytsky
(82km)

Hydropark 8
Park Askoldova
Mohyla

Hydropark

Foundation of Kyiv
Monument 1

See Kyevo-
Pecherska
Lavra Map
(p44)

Central Botanical
Gardens

Dnipro

Dnipro River

Naberezhne shose

Vydubytsky Monastery

vul Hrushevskoho

Landscape
Park 2

Museum of the Great
Patriotic War

Kyevo-
Pecherska
Lavra

Trinity Cathedral

Vydubychi

Park
Misky Sad

Druzhby
Narodiv

Vydubychi
Bus Station

Arsenalna

Bereznitsky
Gallery

Vydubychi

Stolychne shose

Pecherska

To Kaniv
(136km)

Palats
Sportu

bul Druzhby Narodiv

vul Saperno-
Slobidska

Palats
Ukraina

pr Nauky

Lybidska

Slavutych

LYPKY
Khreshchatyk 1

Teatralna

Zoloti
Vorota

Klovska

Nezalezhnosti
Khreshchatyk

Respublikansky
Stadion

Central
Bus Station

Holosiyivsky
park im
Rylskoho

Pl Lva
Tolstoho

See Central Kyiv Map (p36)

vul Korolenkivska

Universytet

Vokzalna

pr Chervonozoryany

Palata 4
No.6

Kyiv Train
Station

vul Oleny Teliny

pr 50-richchya Zhovtnya

bul Chokolivsky

vul Borshchahivska

pr Pontoflotsky

Politekhnichny
Instytut

Zhulyany
Airport

pr 40-richchya Zhovtnya

pr Nauky

vul
Saperno-Slobidska

vul Akademika
Zabolotnogo

To 6 Pyrohovo
(5km)

6 Explore all of
Ukraine in one day at
the **Pyrohovo** (p48)
open-air museum

7 Visit the fantastic
motley collection
of wooden houses
in **Pereyaslav-
Khmelnytsky** (p67)

8 Plunge into the
Dnipro and knead
your muscles at
Hydropark (p59)

9 Meet new friends
in one of Kyiv's lovely
'converted flat'
hostels (boxed text,
p53)

monuments, including the **Independence Column** and the rebuilt **Lyadski Gate**, which had turned out to be the weak link in the city's defence against the Mongols in 1240. Nearby, you can peer through the glass at the excavated foundation of the original gate.

Maydan Nezalezhnosti lies on **vul Khreshchatyk**, Kyiv's broad, 1.5km-long main street. During WWII the retreating Soviet army mined the buildings here, turning them into deadly booby traps for any German soldiers setting foot inside. Most places exploded or caught fire, which is why the rebuilt boulevard is in such an imposing Stalinist style.

Khreshchatyk is at its best on weekends, when it's closed to traffic and becomes a giant pedestrian zone. Getting gussied up and strolling Khreshchatyk is Kyivans' number-one pastime. Maydan Nezalezhnosti and both ends of Khreshchatyk (pl Bessarabska to the south and pl Evropeyska to the north) host frequent free concerts in the summer, often involving big Ukrainian bands and sometimes big Western acts, such as Elton John.

St Sophia's Cathedral & Around

MEDIEVAL CATHEDRAL

(Софійський собор; Sofiysky Sobor; Map p36; pl Sofiyska; grounds 3uah, cathedral 40uah, bell tower 8uah, weekly full access ticket regular/student 50/22uah; ☉grounds 9am-7pm daily, cathedral 10am-6pm Thu-Tue, 10am-5pm Wed; Ⓜ Zoloti Vorota) The interior is the most astounding aspect of Kyiv's oldest standing church, St Sophia's Cathedral. Many of the mosaics and frescoes are original, dating back to 1017–31, when the cathedral was built to celebrate Prince Yaroslav's victory in protecting Kyiv from the Pechenegs (tribal raiders). While equally attractive, the building's gold domes and 76m-tall wedding-cake bell tower are 18th-century baroque additions.

Named after the great Hagia Sofia (Holy Wisdom) Temple (currently mosque) in Istanbul, St Sophia's Byzantine architecture announced the new religious and political authority of Kyiv. It was a centre of learning and culture, housing the first school and library in Kyivan Rus. Adjacent to the Royal Palace, it was also where coronations and other royal ceremonies were staged, treaties signed and foreign dignitaries received. Prince Yaroslav himself is buried here, or at least everyone thought so until a few years ago (see the boxed text, p40).

Each mosaic and fresco had its allotted position according to Byzantine decorative schemes, turning the church into a giant three-dimensional symbol of the Orthodox world order. There are explanations in English of individual mosaics, but the one that immediately strikes you is the 6m-high **Virgin Orans** dominating the central apse. The Virgin Orans is a peculiarly Orthodox concept of the Virgin as a symbol of the earthly church interceding for the salvation of humanity. Having survived this long, this particular Orans is now thought indestructible by Orthodox believers. (Unesco was slightly less certain, adding the cathedral to its protective World Heritage List in 1990.)

Less obvious, but worth seeking out, are fragments in the central nave and the north stairwell of two group portraits of Yaroslav and family. The prince's tomb is found on the ground floor, in the far left corner from the main entrance.

In front of the cathedral complex on pl Sofiyska is a **statue** of Cossack hero Bohdan Khmelnytsky. Just before the bell tower lies the ornate **tomb** of Kyiv Patriarch Volodymyr Romanyuk. Religious disputes prevented him from being buried within the complex (see p249).

St Michael's Gold-Domed Monastery

MONASTERY

(Михайлівський Золотоверхий Монастир; Mykhaylivsky Zolotoverkhy Monastyr; Map p42; admission free; ☉8am-8pm; Ⓜ Poshtova pl) Looking from St Sophia's past the Bohdan Khmelnytsky statue, it's impossible to ignore the gold-domed blue church at the other end of proyizd Volodymyrsky. This is St Michael's Gold-Domed Monastery, named after Kyiv's patron saint. As the impossibly shiny cupolas imply, this is a fresh (2001) copy of the original St Michael's (1108), which was torn down by the Soviets in 1937.

The church's fascinating history is explained in great detail (in Ukrainian and English placards) in a **museum** (9uah; ☉10am-6pm Tue-Sun, ticket office 10am-5pm) in the monastery's bell tower. The museum also explains the sad history of the neighbouring Tryokhsvyatytelska Church, destroyed by the Soviets in 1934. They then added insult to injury by building the gargantuan **Ministry of Foreign Affairs** (Міністерство закордонних справ; pl Mykhaylivska 1; Ⓜ Poshtova pl) on the site.

Two Days

Stroll down the main boulevard, vul Khreshchatyk, from **Bessarabsky Rynok** market (p59) to **maydan Nezalezhnosti** (p31). Head up to **Zoloti Vorota** (p39) for a drink on the terrace before moving on to **St Sophia's Cathedral** (p34) and **St Michael's Monastery** (p34). Catch the funicular down to **Podil** (p41), visit the **Chornobyl Museum** (p42) and then walk up **Andriyivsky uzviz** (p35). Choose a good **Ukrainian restaurant** (p55) for dinner.

Arrive early on the second day at the **Lavra** (p43), before visiting **Rodina Mat** (p47) and the **Museum of the Great Patriotic War** (p47). Return to the centre on Kyiv's astonishingly deep **metro** (p67). Wander around Shevchenko Park and sample authentic Ukrainian *blyny* (pancakes) from the **O'Panas blyny stand** (p57). Check out the **Bohdan and Varvara Khanenko Museum of Arts** (p40), then rest up before hitting a few **bars** (p60) and **clubs** (p61).

Four Days

Follow the two-day itinerary and on the third day visit the **Pyrohovo Museum of Folk Architecture** (p48). Visit **Babyn Yar** (p48) and a few more museums. For some local flavour in summer, head to **Hydropark** (p59).

Heading around the left of the church to the rear, you'll find the quaint **funicular** (1.5uah; ☺6.30am-11pm; ⓂPoshtova pl) that runs down a steep hillside to the river terminal in the mercantile district of Podil. Although in the summer trees partially obscure your view, this is still the most fun public-transport ride in town.

Andriyivsky uzviz   HISTORICAL STREET
(Andrew's Descent; Map p42; ⓂKontraktova pl) It says a lot for Andriyivsky uzviz (or Andreyevsky Spusk, as the Russian-speaking majority calls it) that it has retained its charm despite the souvenir stalls overflowing on its cobblestones. Historically this curving incline linked the high ground of the administrative centre, or Upper Town, to Podil. Nowadays it's frequented by purveyors of Ukrainian crafts, Soviet memorabilia, Osama bin Laden *matryoshky* (stacking dolls), Yuri Gagarin T-shirts and the occasional stunning photo of Kyiv. Yet the quaint houses and crooked pavements still give the place plenty of atmosphere.

The street is named after Apostle Andrew, who is believed to have climbed the hill here, affixed a cross to its summit and prophesied that this would be the site of a great Christian city. That blue, beautiful piece of baroque dominating the view as you walk up the *uzviz* is **St Andrew's Church** (Андріївська церка; ☺10am-6.30pm Thu-Tue; ⓂKontraktova pl). Built in 1754 by Italian architect Bartolomeo Rastrelli,

who also designed the Winter Palace in St Petersburg, this is a magnificent interpretation of the traditional Ukrainian five-domed, cross-shaped church. The rich interior has English placards explaining the history of the church.

There are diversions galore along Andriyivsky uzviz, including a few wonderful cafes, restaurants, galleries, craft shops and museums. At the foot of the *uzviz*, the individual histories of the Descent's buildings are laid out in the **Museum of One Street** (Музей одної вулиці; Andriyivsky uzviz 2B; admission 20uah; ☺noon-6pm Tue-Sun; ⓂKontraktova pl). The sheer jumble-sale eclecticism of the collection – showcasing the lives of dressmakers, soldiers, a rabbi, a Syrian-born orientalist and more – exudes bags of charm.

A little way up on the left, the early home of the much-loved author of *The Master and Margarita* has become the strange and memorable **Bulgakov Museum** (Музей Булгакова; Andriyivsky uzviz 13; tours in Russian/English 20/70uah; ☺10am-4pm Thu-Tue; ⓂKontraktova pl), designed as an alternative universe populated by the author's memories and characters. Mikhail Bulgakov lived here long before writing the novel, between 1906 and 1919, but this building was the model for the Turbin family home in *The White Guard,* his first full-length novel. A restaurant just down the street has a bolder reference to *The Master and Margarita,*

KYIV

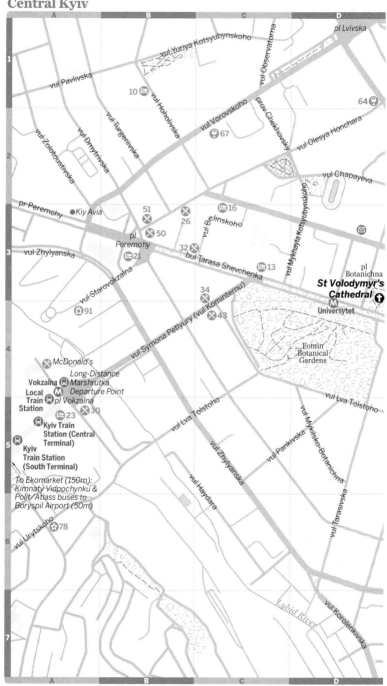

Central Kyiv

pl Lvivska

vul Yuriya Kotsyubynskoho

vul Observatorna

vul Pavlivska

vul Hoholivska

10

64

vul Vorovskoho

prov Chekhovsky

67

vul Olesya Honchara

vul Turgenivska

vul Dmytrivska

vul Zolotoustivska

vul Chapayeva

Pr Peremohy   ●Kiy Avia

51

26

16

vul Belinskoho

pl
Peremohy

50

vul Mykhayla Kotsyubynskoho

vul Zhylyanska

21

32

bul Tarasa Shevchenka

13

pl
Botanichna

vul Starovokzalna

34

**St Volodymyr's
Cathedral**

91

43

Universytet

vul Symona Petlyury (vul Kominternu)

Fomin
Botanical
Gardens

McDonald's

Long-Distance
Vokzalna Marshrutka
Local   Departure Point
Train   pl Vokzalna
Station

30

vul Lva Tolstoho

vul Lva Tolstoho

23

vul Mykilsko-Botanichna

Kyiv Train
Station (Central
Terminal)

Kyiv
Train
Station
(South Terminal)

vul Zhylyanska

vul Pankivska

vul Tarasivska

To Ekomarket (150m);
Kimnaty Vidpochynku &
Polit/Atlass buses to
Boryspil Airport (50m)

vul Haydara

vul Urytskoho

78

Lubid River

vul Korolenkivska

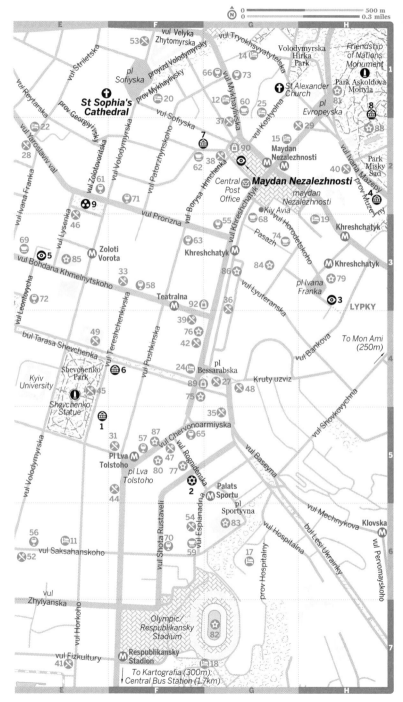

KYIV SIGHTS

vul Velyka Zhytomyrska

vul Tryokhsvyatytelska

53

pl Sofiyska

prov Mykhaylivsky

proyizd Volodymyrsky

vul Striletska

vul Reytarska

prov Georgiyivsky

St Sophia's Cathedral

vul Volodymyrska

vul Yaroslaviv val

vul Ivana Franka

22

28

61

vul Zolotovoritska

71

vul Lysenka

9

46

vul Patorzhynskoho

vul Borysa Hrinchenka

vul Prorizna

Zoloti Vorota

69

5

85

vul Bohdana Khmelnytskoho

33

58

vul Leontovycha

72

Teatralna

49

bul Tarasa Shevchenka

vul Tereshchenkivska

Kyiv University

Shevchenko Park

6

Shevchenko Statue

1

45

31

57

87

Pl Lva Tolstoho

pl Lva Tolstoho

80

47

77

44

vul Volodymyrska

56

11

52

vul Saksahanskoho

vul Zhylyanska

vul Horkoho

vul Fizkultury

41

Volodymyrska Hirka Park

14

66

73

12

vul Mykhaylivska

60

25

37

7

62

38

90

St Alexander Church

pl Evropeyska

Friendship of Nations Monument

Park Askoldova Mohyla

8

88

15

Maydan Nezalezhnosti

Maydan Nezalezhnosti

maydan Nezalezhnosti

Kiy Avia

68

vul Horodetskoho

55

Central Post Office

63

Khreshchatyk

vul Pushkinska

vul Sofiyska

vul Kostyolna

29

40

Park Misky Sad

4

19

Khreshchatyk

Pasazh

74

84

86

pl Ivana Franka

79

3

Khreshchatyk

LYPKY

92

36

vul Lyuteranska

39

76

42

24

pl Bessarabska

89

27

75

48

Kruty uzviz

35

vul Chervonoarmiyska

65

vul Rognidenska

vul Bankova

To Mon Ami (250m)

vul Shovkovychna

vul Baseyna

vul Esplanadna

2

Palats Sportu

pl Sportyvna

83

vul Mechnykova

Klovska

54

70

59

17

vul Shota Rustaveli

vul Hospitalna

prov Hospitalny

bul Lesi Ukrainky

vul Pervomayskoho

Olympic/ Respublikansky Stadium

82

Respublikansky Stadion

18

To Kartografia (300m); Central Bus Station (1.7km)

Central Kyiv

with the figure of a smug, fat black cat – the devil's mischievous sidekick, Behemoth – adorning its facade.

Continuing up Andriyivsky uzviz past St Andrew's Church, look for a dense cluster of vendors selling Dynamo Kyiv and other sports paraphernalia on the right. The fenced-off archaeological site behind them covers the foundations of the **Desyatynna Church ruins** (Десятинна церка). Prince Volodymyr ordered the church built in 989 and devoted 10% of his income to it, hence the name (*desyatyna* means 'one-tenth'). The church collapsed under the weight of the people who took refuge on its roof during the Mongol sacking of Kyiv in 1240. Today the Moscow and Kyiv patriarchates of the Ukrainian Orthodox Church are fighting over the fate of the site – the latter wants to rebuild the church.

The huge Stalinist building behind that is the **National Museum of Ukrainian History** (Національний музей історії

України; vul Volodymyrska 2; admission 18uah; ☉10am-5pm Thu-Tue; ⓂKontraktova pl). It has exhibits of archaeological and recent historical interest, including books and coins. To the left of the museum begins **Peyzazhna Alley**, an uncrowded promenade with excellent views of Podil. It skirts the ravine and abuts vul Velyka Zhytomyrska.

St Volodymyr's Cathedral CATHEDRAL
(Володимирський собор; Map p36; bul Tarasa Shevchenka 20; ⓂUniversytet) Although not one of Kyiv's most important churches, St Volodymyr's Cathedral arguably has the prettiest interior. Built in the late 19th century to mark 900 years of Orthodox Christianity in the city, its yellow exterior and seven blue domes conform to standard Byzantine style. However, inside it breaks new ground by displaying art nouveau influences.

Huge murals, flecked with golden accents, include a painting of Volodymyr the Great's baptism into Orthodox Christianity in Chersoneses (now Khersones; see p30) and of Kyiv's citizens being herded into the Dnipro River for a mass baptism soon afterwards.

Across the boulevard and behind the Universytet metro station lie the landscaped **Fomin Botanical Gardens**, best visited in spring when just about everything there is blooming. A short walk to the left from the entrance, you'll find a leaning apronclad bronze figure wielding something that looks like a bow. This strange-looking monument is dedicated to the professors and students who died defending Kyiv in WWII. Students cynically call it 'monument to the deceased botanist' – 'botanist' being the Russian slang word for nerd.

Zoloti Vorota   CITY GATE

(Золоті Ворота; Golden Gate; Map p36; vul Volodymyrska; Ⓜ Zoloti Vorota) Part of Kyiv's fortifications during the rule of Yaroslav the Wise, the famous Zoloti Vorota sounds much better than it looks, but the sum-

mer patio around the fountain out front is a great place to have a drink. Erected in 1037 and modelled on Constantinople's Golden Gate, this was the main entrance into the ancient city, with ramparts stretching out from both sides. However, the gate was largely destroyed in the 1240 Mongol sacking of Kyiv, and what you see today is a 1982 reconstruction that encloses whatever remains of the original. You can get inside for 10uah. The statue to the side is of Yaroslav, although people call it 'monument to the Kyiv cake' – you'll understand why when you see it.

House of Chimeras   MANSION HOUSE

(Будинок з химерами; Map p36; vul Bankova 10; Ⓜ Khreshchatyk) With its demonic-looking animals and gargoyles, the House of Chimeras is Kyiv's weirdest building. Built at the start of the 20th century by architect Wladislaw Horodecki (p41), it's been more recently used for government receptions. There are plenty of other interesting old

MY BONES LIE OVER THE OCEAN

Moscow-based reporter Nikita Maximov had no modern mysteries to solve when he came to Kyiv in September 2009. Instead, he wanted to trace the Viking roots of Yaroslav the Wise, one of the greatest Kyivan princes, with the help of DNA analysis. He was preparing to deliver a sample of the royal tissue to a lab in Moscow. Scientists at St Sophia's would open the tomb that enclosed the remains of the prince and his wife Ingegerda, and take it for him.

But all at once his hopes were dashed. The grave appeared to contain only one skeleton, and it belonged to a female. Beside it lay a Pravda newspaper dated 1964.

Maximov embarked on the search for truth in this murky story. One thing was clear: the remains had been extracted from the tomb by Soviet scientists who took them to Leningrad in 1936 and meticulously described every bone. Documents prove that in 1940 they returned the skeletons to Kyiv. After that, they supposedly remained in storage until being placed back into the tomb in 1964. At least, that's what St Sophia's guides had been telling tourists for decades. But having uncovered the disappearance, scientists looked at the 1964 handover documents. To everyone's amazement, papers only mentioned one skeleton. So what happened to the other?

The leading version at the time of writing was that the bones could have been taken by Ukrainian collaborators who left the city with the Nazis in 1943. Several sources claimed they ended up in New Jersey and spent over 50 years lying under the bed of a Ukrainian priest who handed them to a Brooklyn-based bishop before passing away. The bishop was alleged to have admitted this fact in the spring of 2010 in a conversation with a Ukrainian scientist, but speaking to *Newsweek* in August the same year he flatly denied it.

Maximov's investigation was not anywhere near the end at the time of writing. But something was brewing – the Ukrainian foreign ministry got involved, raising hopes that some secret transatlantic talks could be in progress.

mansions in this district, known as **Lypky** – see the Walking Tour, p50.

Bohdan & Varvara Khanenko Museum of Arts
EUROPEAN ART

(Музей художнього мистецтва Богдана та Варвари Ханенко; Map p36; vul Tereshchenkivska 15/17; regular/student 25/12uah; free last Wed of month; ⊙10.30am-5.30pm Wed-Sun, 10.30am-2pm last Wed of month; ⓂPl Lva Tolstoho). Kyiv's most impressive collection of European art boasts Bosch, Velázquez and Rubens among the many masters represented, but they are only part of the attraction. The house, with its frescoed ceilings and intricately carved woodwork, alone is worth the price of admission. All the better that it's packed with priceless antique furniture, ancient Greek sculptures, porcelain ceramics and dazzling paintings, such as a version of Hieronymus Bosch's *Temptation of St Anthony*. The museum's climax is on the top floor: four rare religious icons from the 6th and 7th centuries. Even if icons aren't your thing, it's hard not to be moved by these primitive Byzantine treasures. And we've only described the 'Western' wing.

The 'Eastern' wing has Buddhist, Chinese and Islamic art.

PinchukArtCentre
MODERN ART

(Map p36; http://pinchukartcentre.org; Arena City complex, vul Baseyna 2A; admission free; ⊙noon-9pm Tue-Sun; ⓂPl Lva Tolstoho/Teatralna) The rotating exhibits at this world-class gallery feature elite names in the world of European contemporary art and design, all financed by billionaire mogul Viktor Pinchuk. Works by British giants Antony Gormley and Damian Hirst have recently been exhibited. If you don't feel like coming inside, you can download the whole exhibition on your mobile phone, if you position yourself near the entrance and switch on Bluetooth.

Russian Art Museum
RUSSIAN ART

(Музей російського мистецтва; Map p36; vul Tereshchenkivska 9; regular/student 25/10uah; ⊙10am-6pm Tue, Fri & Sun, 11am-6pm Mon, noon-8pm Sat, closed last Mon of month; ⓂTeatralna/Pl Lva Tolstoho) With 2000 paintings, it is the largest collection of Russian artwork outside Moscow and St Petersburg.

National Art Museum
UKRAINIAN ART

(Національний художній музей; Map p36; vul Hrushevskoho 6; regular/student 20/5uah; ☺10am-6pm Tue-Sun, closed last Fri of month; Ⓜ Maydan Nezalezhnosti) Displays early Ukrainian icons, and paintings from the 14th to the 19th centuries, including some by polymath national poet Taras Shevchenko.

Taras Shevchenko Memorial House Museum
POET'S HOUSE

(Літературно-Меморіальний Будинок-музей Тараса Шевченка; Map p36; prov Tarasa Shevchenka 8A; admission 5uah; ☺10am-6pm Wed-Sun, noon-8pm Tue; Ⓜ Maydan Nezalezhnosti) A beautifully restored, 19th-century wooden house where the great man (see p261) once lived.

Water Museum
MUSEUM

(Музей води; Map p36; vul Grushevskoho 1v; tour 20uah; ☺10am-5pm; Ⓜ Maydan Nezalezhnosti) Inside a historical water pump, this Danish-funded museum is a fun place, especially for children. On the obligatory tour, you're taken on a walk through a rainwater collector, allowed to sit on a giant loo or stand inside a bubble, and introduced to a yellow fish called Vasily.

PODIL

The funicular and Andriyivsky uzviz both lead down to this riverside mercantile quarter. An appealing grid of streets lined with quaint lanterns and eclectic turn-of-the-20th-century buildings, it's the antidote to all those Soviet facades that dominate vul Khreshchatyk. Dating back to the earliest settlements, the area grew quickly around the port. Podil was last rebuilt in 1811 after a devastating fire and emerged largely unscathed from WWII. Today it's a buzzing restaurant district.

St Nicholas Naberezhny
CHURCH

(Перка Святого Миколая Набережного; Nicholas by the River; Map p42; vul Pochaynynska 4; Ⓜ Kontraktova pl) Church lovers will find several attractive and historic specimens in Podil, including this church right on the river, which is dedicated to sailors and others journeying along the river to do business.

Florivsky Monastery
CONVENT

(Флорівський жіночий монастир; Map p42; vul Prytytsko Mykilska; Ⓜ Kontraktova pl) This is a 15th-century women's convent that remained open during the communist era. Pass through the bell tower to the grounds,

---

GAME OF ARCHITECTURE

Beautifying Kyiv's skyline was obviously his vocation, but Wladislaw Horodecki had very little time for it. There were so many exciting things to do in Kyiv at the start of the 20th century, like riding first motorcars or taking to the skies in flimsy biplanes built by aspiring aviation engineers. One of them was Igor Sikorsky, a fellow Kyivite, destined to become the father of the US helicopter industry. But Horodecki's main passion was big-game hunting, which took him to Siberia, Central Asia, Afghanistan and Africa. He even authored a book about his exploits in the savannah.

That is why his contribution to Kyiv's cityscape appears relatively modest. But discounting all the storehouses and public toilets the architect designed to fund his adventures, it is fair to say that all his creations became Kyiv's architectural icons. Those include the classical-styled National Museum (p38), the neo-Gothic St Nicholas Catholic Cathedral (p63), the Karaite prayer house (see p51) on vul Yaroslaviv val and – most famously – House of Chimeras. The latter he built for himself, placing it on a high cliff so it appears as a six-storey structure on one side and three-storey on the other.

Looking at it, you might notice that the whimsical chimeras look nothing like Gothic gargoyles, but instead largely resemble Horodecki's exotic hunting trophies. He kept real stuffed animals inside the house. It is a mystery whether any of them are still there, as unfortunately only visiting presidents can admire the opulent interior, which includes a giant octopus made of concrete, as are the chimeras. An official promise that the house would be open to the general public on certain days has failed to materialise.

These days, Wladislaw Horodecki (or at least his bronze statue) seems to be in no hurry and is always available for a coffee and a chat in the Pasazh. There is a vacant seat by his (also bronze) table, which you are free to take, without worrying that he will dash off to walk his pet monkey on Khreshchatyk, as he did a century ago.

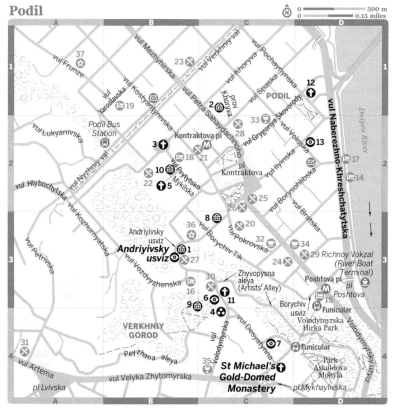

which contain several attractive churches; there are great views from here of St Andrew's Church. Dress appropriately to enter the grounds.

Pharmacy Museum MUSEUM
(Музей-аптека; Map p42; vul Prytitsko-Mykilska 7; regular/student 10/7uah; ⊗9am-4pm; MKontraktova pl) Right by the monastery, you will find this excellent museum, set in the premises of an early-19th-century German pharmacy. There are separate rooms dedicated to alchemy and witchcraft.

Church of Mykola Prytysk CHURCH
(Церква Миколи Притиска; Map p42; vul Prytytsko Mykilska; MKontraktova pl) The nearby Church of Mykola Prytysk survived the 1811 fire that destroyed much of Podil. This 1631 church is the oldest structure in the district and is surrounded by several pastel-coloured brick buildings exhibiting the eclectic style in vogue in Kyiv at the end of the 19th century.

Chornobyl Museum MEMORIAL MUSEUM
(Музей Чорнобиль; Map p42; prov Khoryva 1; admission 10uah; ⊗10am-6pm Mon-Sat, closed last Mon of month; MKontraktova pl) It's hard to convey the full horror of the world's worst nuclear accident, but the Chornobyl Museum makes a valiant attempt. It is not so much a museum as a shrine to all the firemen, soldiers, engineers, peasants and whole villages that perished in the aftermath of the explosion of Chornobyl power plant reactor No 4, on 26 April 1986. The location in a former fire-squad garage evokes strong associations with 9/11. Chornobyl is indeed Ukraine's Ground Zero.

The exhibits are predominantly in Russian and Ukrainian, but there is plenty here of interest for English speakers, including several videos, distressing photos of the sorts of deformities – in animals and humans – the accident caused, and a few jarred specimens of mutant animals such as an eight-legged baby pig. Front pages of the *New York Times* and *Philadelphia Inquirer* from the days immediately following the accident are on display, and the largest hall contains poignant anti-nuclear posters sent in by artists from around the world on the 20th anniversary of the accident.

The signs above the stairs as you enter represent the 'ghost' cities evacuated from the Chornobyl area in the wake of the disaster. If you wish to see for yourself, it's possible to take a tour to the Chornobyl exclusion zone (see p68).

English-language audioguides are available, but they are in short supply.

LAVRA AREA & BEYOND

Any day and in any weather Arsenalna metro station discharges a steady flow of tourists and pilgrims moving along vul Ivana Mazepy (Sichnevoho Povstannya) towards pl Slavy. Their main magnet is the Lavra – the holiest of holy sites in Ukraine and beyond, but there are a few other things to see in its vicinity.

The Lavra is a pleasant 15-minute walk from the metro. On the way back, you may take trolleybus 38 or *marshrutka* (fixed-route minibus) 520 or 406, which will bring you to the metro station.

Holodomor Memorial   MEMORIAL
(off Map p42; admission free; ⓂArsenalna) At the far end of Vichnoy Slavy, centred around a Soviet-era war memorial, you will find a monument from an entirely different epoch. President Viktor Yushchenko's pet project, it is dedicated to almost four million victims of the famine, artificially induced by Stalin's policy of collectivisation in 1932–33. Inside the round-shaped structure, village household objects are contrasted against bloodthirsty quotes from Bolshevik leaders, such as Lenin's: 'We should resolve the Cossack issue by the means of their full extermination; all assets and property to be confiscated'.

Kyevo-Pecherska Lavra   MONASTERY
(києво-печерська лавра; Map p44; Caves Monastery; www.lavra.ua; vul Sichnevoho Povstannya 21; admission upper lavra 20uah,

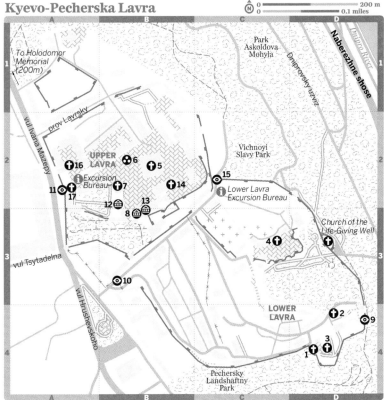

lower lavra free; ⊘upper lavra 9am-7pm Apr-Sep, 9.30am-6pm Oct-Mar, lower lavra sunrise-sunset, caves 8.30am-4.30pm) Tourists and Orthodox pilgrims alike flock to the Lavra. It's easy to see why the tourists come. Set on 28 hectares of grassy hills above the Dnipro River, the monastery's tight cluster of gold-domed churches is a feast for the eyes, the hoard of Scythian gold rivals that of the Hermitage in St Petersburg, and the underground labyrinths lined with mummified monks are exotic and intriguing.

For pilgrims the rationale is much simpler. To them, this is the holiest ground in all three East Slavic countries – Ukraine, Russia and Belarus.

A *lavra* is a senior monastery, while *pecherska* means 'of the caves'. The Greek St Antoniy founded this *lavra* in 1051, after Orthodoxy was adopted as Kyivan Rus' official religion. He and his follower Feodosiy progressively dug out a series of catacombs,

where they and other reclusive monks worshipped, studied and lived. When they died their bodies were naturally preserved, without embalming, by the caves' cool temperature and dry atmosphere. The mummies survive even today, confirmation for believers that these were true holy men.

The monastery prospered above ground as well. The Dormition Cathedral was built from 1073 to 1089 as Kyiv's second great Byzantine-inspired church, and the monastery became Kyivan Rus' intellectual centre, producing chronicles and icons and training builders and artists.

Wrecked by the Tatars in 1240, the Lavra went through a series of revivals and disastrous fires before being mostly rebuilt, with its prevailing baroque influences, in the 18th century. It was made a museum in 1926, but partly returned to the Ukrainian Orthodox Church (Moscow Patriarch) in 1988.

KYIV SIGHTS

The complex is divided into the upper *lavra* (owned by the government and Kyiv Patriarchy and the lower *lavra* (which belongs to Moscow Patriarchy and contains the caves).

Visiting the Lavra

As this is the city's single most fascinating and extensive tourist site, you will need at least half a day to get a decent introduction. Try to avoid the Lavra on weekends, when it gets extremely busy. If you must go, then visit early and head for the caves first.

Entrance to the upper *lavra* is free from 6am to 9am, and for a couple of hours after closing (until sunset). Admission to the upper *lavra* allows access to the churches, but several museums on-site levy additional fees.

The **excursion bureau** (Екскурсійне бюро; www.kplavra.kiev.ua, in Ukrainian), just to the left past the main entrance to the upper *lavra,* sells two-hour guided tours in various languages (375uah per group of up to 10 people). Book in advance during peak periods. The excursion bureau also runs regularly scheduled group tours in Russian and/or Ukrainian every 30 minutes (16uah per person).

Entrance to the lower *lavra* and the caves is free of charge for pilgrims. Foreign tourists are likely to be asked to join one of the Russian-language tours that depart from the **lower lavra excursion bureau** (Екскурсійне бюро нижньої лаври; tours per person 25uah), located near the exit from the upper *lavra.*

To enter the caves, women must wear a headscarf and either a skirt that extends below their knees or, at a pinch, trousers.

(Trousers are officially forbidden but nowadays a blind eye is frequently turned.) Men are obliged to remove their hats, and wearing shorts and T-shirts is forbidden. Men and women will also feel more comfortable donning scarves and doffing hats in the monastery's churches.

Upper Lavra

The main entrance to the upper *lavra* is through the striking **Trinity Gate Church** (Троїцька надбрамна церква; Troitska Nadbramna Tserkva), a well-preserved piece of early-12th-century Rus architecture. Rebuilt in the 18th century, it once doubled as a watchtower and as part of the monastery fortifications. It's well worth going inside to observe its rich frescoes and lavish gilded altar. To access the church, turn left immediately after entering through the main gate. Also in this northwest section of the grounds is the small, late-17th-century **St Nicholas' Church** (Церква Св Миколая), its unique blue dome adorned with golden stars. It's now an administrative building.

Back out on the main path, you can't miss the seven gleaming gold domes of the **Dormition Cathedral** (Успенський собор; Uspensky Sobor), a year-2000 replica of the famous and sacred original. It was blown up during WWII – most probably by Soviet partisans, although pro-Russian historians still blame it on the Nazis. You can enter the church only during services, typically held Saturday afternoons at 5pm and Sunday mornings at 7am. The big rock in the square between the cathedral and the bell tower is a **fragment** of the original cathedral.

Towering over the cathedral is the 96.5m-tall **Great Bell Tower** (Дзвіниця). Climbing the 174 steps to the top is an essential experience; however, the tower was shut down for renovations in 2005 and is unlikely to reopen before 2012.

Beneath the bell tower on the south side, the **Museum of Microminiature** (Музей мікромініатюр; admission 20uah; ☉10am-5pm Wed-Mon) provides something even for atheists within this holiest of holies – and, boy, is it popular! Possibly the most orderly queues in unruly Kyiv form in front of Russian artist Nikolai Siadristy's tiny creations. The world's smallest book (with some verses of Shevchenko), a balalaika with strings one-fortieth the width of a human hair and a flea fitted with golden horseshoes are just some of his works of whimsy. Each is so small that microscopes are needed to view them, but you can occupy yourself with the brief English explanations while you wait.

The cluster of buildings just south of the Assumption Cathedral includes the mildly interesting **Museum of Ukrainian Folk and Decorative Arts** (Музей українського фольклору та прикладного мистецтва; admission 20uah; ☉10am-6pm Mon, Wed & Thu, 10am-8pm Fri & Sat) and also the **Refectory Church of St Antoniy & St Feodosiy** (Трапезна церква Св Антонія та Феодосія), sporting the monastery's most famous gold-striped dome (1885–1905). The main domed space is slightly reminiscent of Istanbul's Hagia Sophia, with its ring of small narrow windows along the base of the drum. The interior is beautifully painted with biblical scenes, saints and art nouveau patterns. The generously frescoed **refectory** (Трапезна палата) attached to the church is a sight in itself.

The **Historical Treasures Museum** (Музей історичних коштовностей України; admission 12uah; ☉10am-4.45pm Tue-Sun), behind the Dormition Cathedral, has an astounding collection of precious stones and metal found or made in Ukraine. The highlight is the fabulous hoard of gold jewellery worked for the Scythians by Greek Black Sea colonists. Much of the treasures come from two 4th-century BC burial mounds: the Tolstaya grave in the Dnipropetrovsk region and the Gaimana grave in the Zaporizhzhya region.

To get to the lower *lavra* from the upper *lavra,* find the path behind the Refectory Church of St Antoniy & St Feodosiy and head downhill under the flying buttress.

Lower Lavra

The entrance to the **Nearer Caves** (Вхід у Ближні печери; ☉8.30am-4.30pm) is inside the **Church of the Raising of the Cross** (Хрестовоздвиженська церква; 1700). Before the stairs head downwards, there's a table selling candles (3uah) to light your way through the dark passages. The use of cameras is forbidden in the caves.

Underground, the mummified monks' bodies, preserved in glass cases, are clothed and you only see the occasional protruding toe or finger. The coffins are arranged in niches in the tunnels, underground dining hall and three **subterranean churches**. Antoniy, the monastery's founder, and Nestor the Chronicler are just two of the 123 bodies down here. Students consider the latter their patron saint and leave candles near his mummy to have luck at exams. Another notable monk lying here is Ioann the Long-Sufferer, who fought the sin of womanising by half-burying himself in the ground every year for the duration of Lent. As a result, his sinning lower half completely decayed, while his saintly upper half remained intact. Would it be accurate to call him a half-saint, we wonder?

Tourists are only allowed into the first section of the caves, as many areas are cordoned off for Orthodox pilgrims and clergy. Monks frequently guard the entrance to restricted tunnels and are expert at spotting foreigners and nonbelievers.

Visiting the caves when they're not crowded can be a very moving experience. However, their low, narrow passageways are not for the seriously claustrophobic. If you visit on a busy day, it's total chaos down there. The monks' bodies are believed to have healing powers and pilgrims will bow to kiss the feet of one, before quickly diving to the other side of the tunnel to kiss the hand of another. Lost in religious ecstasy or sheer novelty, people wave their lit candles dangerously close to your back and face, particularly if you're a woman wearing a flammable headscarf – you will, frankly, feel more vulnerable than in the mosh pit of a punk-rock concert. It's an experience you will never forget, but if you like to take things calmly, choose a weekday visit.

The **Farther Caves** (admission free; ☉8.30am-4.30pm) were the original caves built by Antoniy and Feodosiy. Their en-

During WWII, when Kyiv was occupied by Nazi Germany, the members of the talented Dynamo football team were challenged to a public match with a team of German soldiers. The Ukrainians formed a team called Start, and despite physical weakness brought on by the occupation, they were soon ahead in their first match. At half-time, German officers came into the dressing room and commanded them to let up. Nevertheless, Start continued to play hard, and before the game finished the referee blew the whistle and called it off (with a score of four to one).

The Germans reshuffled their players, and Start was offered another chance to lose. Instead they won. Next, Start was pitted against a Hungarian team – and won again. Finally, the enraged Germans challenged Start to a match against their finest, undefeated team, Flakelf. When the *Übermensch* of Flakelf lost, the Nazis gave up – and proceeded to arrest most of the Start players, several of whom were executed at Babyn Yar (p48). A monument to them still stands in Dynamo Stadium (p63). Their story inspired the movie *Victory,* starring Sylvester Stallone and soccer legend Pele. Andy Dougan's *Defending the Honour of Kyiv* (2001) is a readable, well-researched account of the incident.

trance (Вхід у Дальні печери) is in the **Church of the Conception of St Ann** (Аннозачатіївська церква; 1679), reached from the Nearer Caves by a viaduct. This cave system is also lined with ornamented mummified monks and contains three underground churches. Uphill from the Church of the Conception of St Ann is the seven-domed **Church of the Nativity of the Virgin** (Різдва Богородиці церква; 1696). Rising to the right is the unusual high-baroque **Bell Tower of Farther Caves** (Дзвіниця на Дальніх печерах; 1761).

From the Farther Caves it's a long walk back up the hill to the **main entrance** (Вхід до Нижньої лаври) on vul Sichnevoho Povstannya, or you can exit (or enter) at the nearby **lower entrance** (Нижній вхід до Нижньої Лаври). There may be taxis waiting at the lower entrance, or you can walk 15 minutes north along busy Naberezhne shose to the Dnipro metro station.

Rodina Mat
MEMORIAL

(Родина Мать; Map p32; Ⓜ Arsenalna) There's not much to say about Rodina Mat (literally 'Nation's Mother', but formally called the Defence of the Motherland Monument). However, from certain parts of Kyiv it's highly visible and so requires a high-profile explanation. Especially when you're approaching from the left (or east) bank, this 62m-tall statue of a female warrior is liable to loom on the horizon and make you wonder, 'What the hell is that?'

In fact, it's the icing on top of the **Museum of the Great Patriotic War** (Музей Великої Вітчизняної; Map p32; www.warmuseum.kiev.ua; vul Sichnevoho Povstannya 44; regular/student 10/3uah; ⊙10am-5pm Tue-Sun). The statue has been nicknamed 'the Iron Lady' and 'Tin Tits'. Even if you don't like such Soviet pomposity, don't say too much; you'd be taking on a titanium woman carrying 12 tonnes of shield and sword. You can get right into her head – literally, via an elevator in the museum (200uah).

While the museum was built belatedly in 1981 to honour Kyiv's defenders during WWII, it seems to be straight out of the 1950s, with gloomy lighting and huge display halls covered in creaky parquet flooring. This is a sombre and sometimes even macabre exhibition, such as in Hall No 6, where you find yourself looking at a pair of gloves made from human skin. The overall effect is as moving as it is shocking. Westerners often don't appreciate how much Ukraine suffered as Nazi troops moved eastwards towards Moscow. Here you get a better idea.

The grounds around Rodina Mat are popular for strolling and contain a number of intriguing relics of the communist era, including an eternal flame in memory of WWII victims; various old tanks, helicopters and anti-aircraft guns; and a veritable garden of Soviet realist sculpture in and around the underpass leading towards the Lavra.

OUT OF THE CENTRE
Central Botanical Gardens
PARK

(Центральний Ботанічний Сад; Map p32; vul Tymiriazivska 1; adult/student 15/10uah) The long, steep hill running along the Dnipro River from Dynamo Stadium and Mariyinsky Palace (see p50) to Rodina Mat continues south for several kilometres, eventually becoming the Central Botanical Gardens. The gardens' fastidiously manicured grounds are criss-crossed by a network of paths leading to hidden viewpoints and churches frozen in time.

The botanical gardens are tricky to reach by public transport. Take a taxi or pick up bus 14 anywhere along bul Lesi Ukrainky.

Vydubytsky Monastery   CHURCH
(Видубицький Монастир; Map p32; vul Vydubytska 40; M Druzhby Narodiv) Few churches appear more frozen in time than those of the Vydubytsky Monastery, nestled into the hill's dense foliage beneath the botanical gardens. If you found the crowds at the Lavra a little too much to bear – or if you're just into intense serenity – you should not hesitate to come here. The monastery, which is thought to be at least as old as Kyiv, is looking in fine fettle today after centuries of catastrophes followed by years of Soviet neglect. The monastery is home to a small community of monks, who, quite frankly, have chosen a much more monk-friendly place to practise their faith than the increasingly touristy Lavra.

The bucolic church looking down on the monastery from the crest of the hill is the recently restored **Trinity Cathedral** (Троїцький собор).

Pyrohovo Museum of Folk Architecture
OPEN-AIR MUSEUM
(off Map p32; vul Chervonopraporna; regular/student 15/7uah, English-language excursion from 45uah; ☺museum 10am-5pm, grounds sunrise-sunset) Ukraine is dotted with 'open-air' museums like this, full of life-size models of different rustic buildings. However, the Pyrohovo Museum of Folk Architecture, 12km south of Kyiv, is one of the most fun and best maintained.

Two things make it stand out. Firstly, the quaint 17th- to 20th-century wooden churches, cottages, farmsteads and windmills are divided into seven 'villages' representing regional areas of Ukraine. So in just one long afternoon you can journey from the architecture of eastern to western to southern Ukraine.

Secondly, in summer, workers enact different village roles, carving wood, making pottery, doing embroidery and driving horses and carts. There are restaurants,

pubs and stalls selling barbecued *shashlyk* (shish kebab). The place is perfect for kids.

Throughout the year Pyrohovo hosts various festivals – the biggest is during the countrywide Ivan Kupala festival (see p248). Ukrainian musicians play at weekends.

The museum is near Pyrohovo village. From Lybidska metro station take *marshrutka* 172, which stops right by the entrance. *Marshrutky* 3 and 156, as well as trolleybus 11, stop at the turn to the museum. A taxi will cost about 80uah one way.

Babyn Yar   MEMORIAL
On 29 September 1941, Nazi troops rounded up Kyiv's 34,000-strong Jewish population, marched them to the Babyn Yar ravine (Бабин Яр; Map p32), and massacred them all in the following 48 hours. Victims were shot and buried in the ravine. Over the next two years, many thousands more lost their lives at Babyn Yar when it was turned into a concentration camp, called Syrets after the Kyivan suburb it was in. Romany people, partisans and even footballers (see the boxed text, p47) would be among those killed.

The place's dreadful history only came to light after the war, and three monuments have been erected over time. The first was a colossal Soviet effort dating from 1976, which is found in the southern sector of the park. Typical of Soviet Holocaust memorials, it makes no mention of Jews. It's also in the wrong spot; the massacre took place north from here.

Follow the path from vul Melnykova 44, past a TV station, to the secluded spot where you'll find the 1991 Jewish memorial, a menorah, which better marks the spot. From here several paths lead to points overlooking the ravine itself. Another monument was erected in 2001 beside metro Dorohozhychi to commemorate the Jewish children who perished at Babyn Yar. Babyn Yar is easily reached from metro Dorohozhychi.

Central Synagogue   SYNAGOGUE
(Центральна синагога; Map p36; www. greatsynagogue.kiev.ua; vul Shota Rustaveli 13; M Palats Sportu) Despite the Holocaust, today's Kyiv has an active Jewish community numbering about 60,000. The largest synagogue is the Central Synagogue.

🏃 Activities
Contact details for organisers of regular football, cricket and Ultimate Frisbee

Bereznitskiy Gallery
GALLERY
(Галерея Березницького; Map p32; vul Rybalska 22; ⊙11am-7pm Tue-Sun; ⓂKlovska) Doesn't settle for anything less than the best Ukrainian artists.

Da Vinci Gallery
GALLERY
(Галерея Да Вінчі; Map p36; Arena City complex, vul Chervonoarmiyska 5; ⊙10am-8pm; ⓂPl Lva Tolstoho/Teatralna) Kyiv's best sculpture gallery.

Gallery-36
GALLERY
(Галерея-36; Map p42; www.gallery36.org.ua; Andriyivsky uzviz 36; ⊙11am-6pm Tue-Sun; ⓂKontraktova pl) Arguably Kyiv's most beloved gallery, on Kyiv's most beloved street.

Ra Gallery
GALLERY
(Укртелеком; Map p36; www.ragallery.net; vul Bohdana Khmelnytskoho 32; ⊙11am-7pm; ⓂZoloti Vorota) Long-running favourite; also runs a prestigious art school.

Tsekh
GALLERY
(Цех; Map p42; vul Ilyinska 16; ⊙1-7pm Tue-Sun; ⓂKontraktova pl) Refuge for underground artists; can be either spectacular or substandard.

---

games are in the *Kyiv Post* community listings. For lists of bowling alleys, fitness centres, swimming pools, tennis courts and golf ranges, consult *In Your Pocket* or the *Kyiv Business Directory*.

Thanks to a dam a few kilometres downstream, the Dnipro around Kyiv is full of islands and beaches, which are packed with sunbathers in summer. Water sports like wake-boarding and sailing are popular summer pursuits, while in the winter ice fishers descend on the frozen river en masse and intrepid 'walrus' swimmers take to the frigid bouillabaisse. It's better to merely sunbathe than to spend much time in the river, which isn't the cleanest – although that doesn't deter thousands of locals from diving right in.

Richnoy Vokzal
RIVER CRUISES
(river port; Map p42; cruise 200uah; ⓂPoshtova pl) In summer you can get the whole picture (and choose a beach for yourself) by taking a river cruise from the river port (1½ hours).

Hydropark
BEACHES
(Map p32; ⓂHydropark) The most central beaches are found on Trukhaniv Island or in the two-island recreation zone of Hydropark, where you'll find gay, straight, clothed and nude beaches. This is also the best place to observe the Kyevo-Pecherska Lavra, which looms majestically just across the river.

Other popular activities in Hydropark include beach volleyball, beach football, basketball, bungee jumping from a giant crane near the footbridge and – most popular –

drinking vodka. In the winter you can hire cross-country skis.

Hydropark has its own metro stop, so getting there's a snap. To get to Trukhaniv Island take the footbridge directly below the rainbow arch (see p51).

Outdoor Gym
GYMNASIUM
(Map p32; Hydropark; admission free; ⓂHydropark) Kyiv's quirkiest sight might just be Hydropark's giant, makeshift gym. The machines here are cobbled together from used truck parts and salvaged scrap metal. It's a testosterone-fuelled affair, although you'll usually see one or two women amid the muscle. On weekends and summer evenings the gym is packed. Beware: the sight of hundreds of sweaty dudes in Speedos pumping primitive iron could be a little offputting. To get here, cross the footbridge and bear right. Next to the outdoor gym is a gymnastics zone that sees surprisingly competent amateurs swinging from horizontal bars.

Sun City
WATER SPORTS
(Map p32; Hydropark; admission 60-70uah; ⓂHydropark) Entertainment complex Sun City is a private beach at Hydropark with a swimming pool that rents out jet-skis. When the sun goes down it turns into a fashionable nightclub.

✯✯ Festivals & Events

Epiphany
RELIGIOUS HOLIDAY
In January scores of the faithful leap into the Dnipro River in Hydropark and elsewhere to celebrate the baptism of Christ.

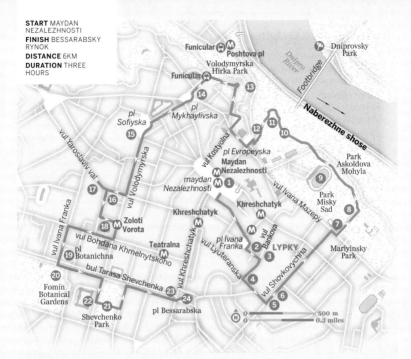

START MAYDAN
NEZALEZHNOSTI
FINISH BESSARABSKY
RYNOK
DISTANCE 6KM
DURATION THREE
HOURS

Funicular 🚇M
Poshtova pl
Dniprovsky
Park
Volodymyrska
Hirka Park
Funicular 🚇M
14
13
pl
Sofiyska
pl
Mykhaylivska
15
12 11 10
vul Kostyolna
pl Evropeyska
Maydan
Nezalezhnosti
Park
Askoldova
Mohyla
maydan
Nezalezhnosti
M
M 1
9
vul Ivana Mazepy
Park
Misky
Sad
Khreshchatyk
M
8
Khreshchatyk
7
pl Ivana
Franka
vul Bankova
M 2
3
LYPKY
Mariyinsky
Park
Teatralna
M
vul Lyuteranska
Zoloti
Vorota
pl
Botanichna
4
vul Bohdana Khmelnytskoho
19
bul Tarasa Shevchenka
5
6
vul Shovkovychna
Fomin
Botanical
Gardens
22 21
23 24
pl Bessarabska
Shevchenko
Park
0   500 m
0   0.3 miles

Walking Tour
Eras & Chimeras

❯ Set out from ❶ **maydan Nezalezhnosti** (p31), walking south along cobbled
vul Horodetskoho, named after the city's
best-known architect, to pl Ivana Franka.
Set your sights on Wladislaw Horodecki's
(p41) bizarre ❷ **House of Chimeras**
(p39) on the hill behind the square. Ascend
this hill via a path to the right of the House
of Chimeras. At the top you'll be face-
to-face with the huge ❸ **Presidential
Administration building** on vul Bankova.
Take a right, proceed to the corner of vul
Lyuteranska, named so after German
Lutherans who resided here, and turn left
again, pausing to glance at the art nouveau
façade of the ❹ **Weeping Widow House**
at vul Lyuteranska 23. It is best seen when
it rains and water is dripping down the
cheeks of the sad female face on the façade. Sometimes the square by the Presidential Administration is closed for official
receptions, in which case retreat from pl
Ivana Franka to vul Zankovetskoyi and walk
left to vul Lyuteranska.

Continue straight and take a left at the
next corner onto vul Shovkovychna – Mul-
berry Street. Many of Kyiv's aristocrats
built mansions in this area, known as Lypky,
at the turn of the 20th century. Examples
include the neo-Gothic ❺ **mansion** at vul
Shovkovychna 19 and the brown-coloured
❻ **Chocolate House** next door. Follow vul
Shovkovychna until it terminates at the
❼ **Verkhovna Rada** (Parliament Building).
You might now bump into a colourful crowd
of demonstrators. If blue flags prevail, they
must be supporters of the current president
Viktor Yanukovych. Orange colours suggest
the protesters' allegiance to the pro-
Western ideals of the Orange revolution.

Cross the street and walk through Park
Misky Sad to the right of the Verkhovna
Rada. The blue baroque building on your
left is ❽ **Mariyinsky Palace**, based on a
design by Italian architect Bartelomeo Rastrelli, who built St Andrew's Church (p35)
and much of St Petersburg. A former Kyiv
residence of the Russian royals, it is now

used for official ceremonies attended by the Ukrainian president.

Behind the palace, follow a path leading northwest through the park. Eventually you'll spy **9** **Dynamo Stadium** (p63), just before crossing the high **10** **Devil's Bridge** adorned with hundreds of locks left by newly wed couples who defiantly ignore the bridge's infernal name. Continue straight until you come to a giant, dull, metal parabola. This is the inappropriately named Rainbow Arch, part of the **11** **Friendship of Nations Monument** celebrating the 1654 'unification' of Russia and Ukraine. Beneath the arch stand two 'brothers' - Russia and Ukraine - with fists raised in textbook Soviet-realist style. There are stunning views here of the Dnipro and Trukhaniv Island, which you can cross to at this point via a pedestrian bridge.

Descend the hill via a path leading by the **12** **National Philharmonic** (p62), and cross pl Evropeyska. On the other side, follow vul Tryokhsvyatytelska uphill, turning right into Volodymyrska Hirka Park beyond the intersection of vul Kostyolna. All trails in here lead to the viewpoint looking down on the **13** **statue of Volodymyr the Great** – who brought Christianity to the eastern Slavs in 989 – and out across the Dnipro and the monolithic suburbs beyond. Russian writer Mikhail Bulgakov, who grew up in the vicinity, simply called this spot 'the best place in the world'.

Continue round the elevated riverbank, past a children's playground to the blue and gold **14** **St Michael's Monastery** (p34). From pl Mykhaylivska you can see the tall bell tower and gold domes of **15** **St Sophia's Cathedral** (p34), which you should now head towards. Turn left into vul Volodymyrska, and two long blocks along, on your right, you'll see **16** **Zoloti Vorota** (p39). From here, turn right to vul Yaroslaviv wall and make a quick detour to **17** **Karaite Ke-**

nasa (p166) built by Wladislaw Horodecki (p41). Karaites are a small Crimean ethnic group who have preserved a peculiar religion mixing Judaism and Turkic paganism. Having lost a massive cupola in the Soviet period, the temple now houses a theatre.

Back on vul Volodymirska walk towards **18** **Taras Shevchenko National Opera Theatre** (p62) before turning right into vul Bohdana Khmelnytskoho and, two blocks later, left into vul Ivana Franka. At the end of this road, on the left, stands **19** **St Volodymyr's Cathedral** (p38). Across the road, you'll see the beginning of the landscaped **20** **Fomin Botanical Gardens**, named after 1920s botanist Alexander Fomin. In spring definitely venture inside to sit on a bench under blossoming fruit trees and observe the beautiful scenery.

Turning left, you're on bul Tarasa Shevchenka, named after the Ukrainian national poet, Taras Shevchenko (see p261). On the right is his **21** **statue** in Shevchenko Park. A quick detour will give you a look at **22** **Kyiv University**. According to a Communist-period urban legend, Tsar Nicholas I ordered this building to be painted blood red in response to student protests against army conscription. When the building was reconstructed after WWII, it was kept the same shade of red.

At the end of the street stands Kyiv's last remaining **23** **Lenin statue**, a fairly modest affair. An army-styled tent was set nearby by local Communists guarding their leader against vandals and the authorities who were threatening to remove the monument. Lenin is looking straight at the last stop on your tour, the wonderfully atmospheric **24** **Bessarabsky Rynok** (p59) on the other side of pl Bessarabska. Even a small piece of *salo* – cured pig fat, a quintessential Ukrainian foodstuff sold at the market – will instantly compensate for all calories lost during the walk.

Kraina Mriy Festival   MUSIC FESTIVAL
(www.krainamriy.com) VV frontman Oleh Skrypka (see p260) organises a three-day festival of ethnic music from Ukraine and elsewhere in July during the countrywide Ivan Kupala festival (see p248). Over the last three years the same festival has also taken place in January around Orthodox Christmas.

Kyiv Days   CITY HOLIDAY
This celebration of spring brings musicians and street performers to Andriyivsky uzviz, maydan Nezalezhnosti and other streets of the capital on the last weekend of May.

Baptism of Rus   RELIGIOUS HOLIDAY
Kyivans plunge into the Dnipro again on 12 August, just as they did in 988 AD on the orders of Prince Volodymyr, who decided that his land should join the Christian world.

Gogolfest   ART FESTIVAL
A lively festival of modern theatre, music, cinema, architecture and all imaginable kinds of art dedicated to writer Nikolai Gogol takes place in early September. It's new and not necessarily annual.

Kyiv International Film Festival Molodist   CINEMA FESTIVAL
(www.molodist.com) An annual event that takes place during the last week of October.

🛏 Sleeping

Kyiv's typical hotel is an unappealing Soviet high-rise with an array of rooms to suit different budgets, from unrenovated economy-class (think old, funny-coloured wallpaper, creaky furniture and not-so-clean bathrooms) to perfectly acceptable if faceless modern standards, usually equipped with air-con and internet access.

Conveniently for tourists, many hotels offer considerable discounts during weekends and long holiday periods (22 December to 12 January, 24 April to 11 May, and 30 June to 30 August) when business travellers stay home. Yet generally prices in midrange hotels are at least double those in other Ukrainian cities.

You can significantly reduce your expenses without compromising on comfort by renting an apartment. This cannot be overemphasised and applies even for short stays. Apartments are available in all budget categories and offer substantial savings (up to 40%) on the same level of hotel accommodation.

Kyiv has a lovely hostel scene, a typical hostel being a large converted apartment sleeping about 20 people. Owners and staff are often fellow travellers who you will find cooking in the kitchen and sleeping on a mat in the common room. For more Kyiv hostels check www.hihostels.com.ua and international hostel sites.

MAYDAN, KHRESHCHATYK & OLYMPIC STADIUM AREA

Sunflower B&B Hotel   GUESTHOUSE $$$
(Map p36; ☏279 3846; www.sunflowerhotel. kiev.ua; vul Kostyolna 9/41; r from 950uah; ❄ @; Ⓜ Maydan Nezalezhnosti) The name is an oxymoron – it's more B&B than hotel – but we're not complaining. The highlight is the continental breakfast (with a warm pastry) delivered to your room, on request, by English-speaking staff. It's centrally located but nearly impossible to find – calling for a pick-up is not a bad idea.

Chillout Hostel   HOSTEL $
(Map p36; ☏093 332 4306; chillouthostel@ gmail.com; vul Saksahanskoho 30v; dm 120uah, r with shared bathroom 350uah; ☎; Ⓜ Pl Lva Tolstoho) This Polish-run place has the bonus of balconies with Thai-styled mats for chilling out. Enter through the arch at Gorkoho 22, cross the courtyard diagonally bearing left towards a yellow building. The hostel is on the 2nd floor. The owners' Ukrainian friend, Mykola, takes people on free guided tours once in a while.

Gintama Hotel   NEW LUXURY $$$
(Готель Джинтама; Map p36; ☏278 5092; www.gintama.com.ua; vul Tryokhsvyatytelska 9; s/d 1300/1500uah; ❄ ❄ ❄; Ⓜ Maydan Nezalezhnosti) This friendly family-run hotel has an understated style, with smallish, individually decorated rooms tending towards the traditional, but with cleaner lines and fewer florals than usual. The hotel is in a quiet spot just a three-minute walk from maydan Nezalezhnosti.

St Petersburg Hotel   HISTORIC HOTEL $$
(Готель Санкт-Петербург; Map p36; ☏279 7472; www.s-peter.com.ua; bul Tarasa Shevchenka 4; s/d with shared bathroom 280/440uah, with private bathroom from 500/680uah; ☎; Ⓜ Pl Lva Tolstoho) If you're pinching pennies, this once-grand old classic is a fine option. The cheapest rooms are worn and simple, but shared showers and toilets are clean, which

turns the place into a bargain, considering the central location.

Hotel Ukraine
SOVIET HIGH-RISE **$$**

(Готель Україна; Map p36; ☑279 0347; www.ukraine-hotel.kiev.ua; vul Instytutska 4; s/d from 660/740uah; @; MMaydan Nezalezhnosti) This Stalin-era giant presiding over maydan Nezalezhnosti offers the best view of future revolutions, orange or otherwise. All rooms have air-con to protect you from natural and political heat.

Hotel Rus
SOVIET HIGH-RISE **$$$**

(Готель Русь; Map p36; ☑256 4000; www.hotel rus.kiev.ua; vul Hospitalna 4; r from 850uah; ❄ @; MPalats Sportu) The Hotel Rus is not a bad deal – hallways are well lit, rooms are only slightly tacky, and the views can be great. It's perched above Olympic Stadium, so it's a bit of an uphill grind to walk here. But it's perfect if you're in town for a football match.

Hotel Sport
SOVIET HIGH-RISE **$$**

(Готель Спорт; Map p36; ☑289 0252; www.hotelsport.com.ua; vul Chervonoarmiyska 55A;

s/d from 480/510uah; MRespublikansky Stadion) Musty monstrosity next to Olympic Stadium. Breakfast extra.

Hotel Khreschatik
HOTEL **$$$**

(Готель Хрещатик; Map p36; ☑279 7339; www.khreschatik.kiev.ua; vul Khreshchatyk 14; s/d from 800/960uah; ❄; MMaydan Nezalezhnosti) Popular with journalists who tend to book it because of the location and then grumble about conditions and service.

UPPER CITY

Hyatt Regency Kyiv
INTERNATIONAL CHAIN **$$$**

(Map p36; ☑581 1234; http://kiev.regency.hyatt.com; vul Tarasova 5; r from 3300uah; ☻ ❄ @ ☎; MMaydan Nezalezhnosti) Other Ukrainian hotels can only dream of having the Hyatt's view of duelling 11th-century churches. Inside, everything is just as perfect, from the fabulous gym to the spacious and eminently comfortable rooms, to its popular panorama bar and Grill Asia restaurant. Western leaders tend to stay here and we've never heard them complain.

APARTMENTS

Kyiv has dozens of apartment agencies and sorting through them all can be a chore. Most reputable agencies have websites where you can browse their apartments. Booking is best done online or via phone or text message; only a few firms have offices. Most agencies require that you pay the first night's accommodation in advance in order to book.

See p267 for more tips on apartment rental. All of the following have English-speaking representatives and accept credit cards.

Absolut
APARTMENTS **$$**

(☑541 1740, 099 214 6480; www.hotelservice.kiev.ua) Reasonable, if not great, service.

Best Kiev Apartment
APARTMENTS **$$$**

(☑067 506 1875, 067 442 2533; www.bestkievapartment.com; apt from $65) Smartly renovated apartments.

Grata Apartments
APARTMENTS **$$**

(Грата; Map p36; ☑468 0757, 238 2603; www.accommodation.kiev.ua; vul Mykhaylivska 9A; apt from $55; MMaydan Nezalezhnosti) Service-oriented firm has nice range of apartments.

Rentguru
APARTMENTS **$$**

(☑044 228 7509, 050 381 8586; www.rentguru.com.ua/en) Canadian-educated doctor Valentyn offer some of the cheapest, though not very central apartments.

Teren Plus
APARTMENTS **$$**

(☑289 3949; www.teren.kiev.ua; apt from $60) Tried and true.

UARent
APARTMENTS **$$**

(☑278 8363, 067 403 6030; www.uarent.com) Tends towards more expensive apartments with superb locations.

UKR Apartments
APARTMENTS **$$**

(☑234 5637, 050 311 0309; www.ukr-apartments.kiev.ua) Has a wide selection of inexpensive apartments.

Radisson Blu INTERNATIONAL CHAIN **$$$**
(Map p36; ☑492 2200; www.radissonsas.com; vul Yaroslaviv val 22; r from 2700uah; ☺✳@; Ⓜ Zoloti Vorota) The city's first international hotel had been well established as the city's best until the 2007 Hyatt opening jeopardised that title. The sumptuous rooms have fluffy beds that invite entry via flying leap, and the Asian spa is a nice touch.

International Youth Hostel Kiev HOSTEL **$**
(Map p36; ☑hostel 481 3838, bookings 331 0260; www.hihostels.com.ua; per person 150uah; Ⓜ Lukyanivska) Ignore the lack of common room, kitchen and services, and concentrate on what this hostel does have: basic doubles and quadruples that you don't have to share with 10 people. Every two rooms share a bathroom/shower. It occupies the 4th and 5th floors of an apartment building off Artema, two trolleybus stops south of Lukyanivska metro station.

ANDRIYIVSKY UZVIZ & PODIL

Bohdan Khmelnitsky Boatel BOAT **$**
(Боатель Богдан Хмельницький; Map p42; ☑578 0190; www.vipteplohid.kiev.ua; vul Naberezhno-Khreshchatytska, moorage 5; r from 250uah; ☺Oct-Apr; Ⓜ Kontraktova pl) Shame it's only a seasonal affair! Built in Budapest in 1954, this paddle boat is still fully operational. The dark-wood panelling in its corridors and rooms looks immaculate after a 2004 facelift. Moored in Podil for most of the year, it works as a regular pleasure boat May to September.

Hotel Vozdvyzhensky BOUTIQUE HOTEL **$$$**
(Готель Воздвиженський; Map p42; ☑531 9900; www.vozdvyzhensky.com; vul Vozdvyzhenska 60; standard s/d 1000/1300uah, superior r from 1400uah; ☺✳@; Ⓜ Kontraktova pl) Tucked away in a nook just off Andriyivsky uzviz, the Vozdvyzhensky is one of Kyiv's few true boutique hotels. The 29 rooms are all individually designed and boast fine art. The hotel highlight is the rooftop summer terrace, which has views overlooking Podil. Our main gripes are the small standard rooms and the difficulty pronouncing 'Vozdvyzhensky'.

Yaroslav Youth Hostel HOSTEL **$**
(Map p42; ☑hostel 417 3189, bookings 331 0260; www.hihostels.com.ua; vul Yaroslavska 10; dm 120uah, shared d per person 140uah; Ⓜ Kontraktova pl) Another no-frills hostel, it has the same pricing scheme as its sister, International Youth Hostel Kiev. The difference is

it's much smaller and cosier – just three rooms in a converted apartment.

Top-end boutique hotels are popping up all over Kyiv's Podil district. The latest and greatest are the intimate **Podol Plaza Hotel** (Готель Поділ Плаза; ☑503 9292; www.podolplazahotel.com.ua; vul Kostyantynivska 7A; s/d from 1650/2000uah; ☺✳@; Ⓜ Kontraktova pl) and the attractive but overpriced **Hotel Riviera** (Готель Рів'єра; ☑581 2828; www.rivierahotel.com.ua; vul Sahaydachnoho 15; r from $340; ☺✳@; Ⓜ Poshtova pl).

TRAIN STATION AREA

Central Station Hostel HOSTEL **$**
(Map p36; ☑098 669 4783; vul Hoholivska 25; apt 15, dm 120-140uah, r with shared bathroom 350uah; Ⓜ Vokzalna) We should thank Ukrainian bureaucracy for leaving the Brazilian owner stranded in Ukraine with an expired visa. Now fully legalised, Aricio runs one of Kyiv's most atmospheric hostels set in a converted flat with bunk beds in two rooms. In the evening, Ukrainian and expat friends drop in for a beer, which inevitably results in everyone setting out on a pub crawl. On the top floor of a heritage house in a leafy upmarket neighbourhood, the place is, however, not as close to the train station as its name might you lead you to believe.

Hotel Opera HOTEL **$$$**
(Готель Опера; Map p36; ☑581 7070; www.opera-hotel.com; vul Bohdana Khmelnytskoho 53; s & d from 2360uah; ✳@; Ⓜ Universytet) Tired of Hyatts and Radissons? Here is Donbass oligarchs' take on the dolce vita. A sister of the legendary Donbass Palace in Donetsk, the Opera offers many of the same luxuries, plus a wonderful setting in an old tranquil neighbourhood. The metro is a little far away, but most clients can easily live without it.

Lybid Hotel HOTEL **$$$**
(Готель Либідь; Map p36; ☑236 0063; www.hotellybid.com.ua; pl Peremohy 1; s/d from 830/950uah; ☺✳@; Ⓜ Universytet) Lybid hails from the same Soviet architectural incubator as many other hotels in Kyiv, but it stands out from its siblings thanks to friendly service and convenient location – a five-minute walk from the train station and metro. All rooms are renovated; they're about 200uah cheaper in July and August and during public holidays.

Hotel Express HOTEL **$$**
(Готель Експрес; Map p36; ☑503 3045; www.expresskiev.com; bul Tarasa Shevchenka 38/40;

s/d without bathroom 420/510uah, with bath-room from 600/780uah; ✳ @; Ⓜ Universytet) The Soviet-style Express has a mix of renovated and unrefurbished rooms. The cheapest have tiny beds and lack showers. Prices increase proportionally as ameni-ties and coats of paint are added. Air-con rooms don't cost extra, but you must re-quest them.

Kimnaty Vidpochynku STATION ROOMS $
(Resting Rooms; off Map p36; ☎239 8962; Kyiv Train Station; dm 150uah, d 380uah; ✳) The 3rd floor of the station's new Southern Terminal has two resting rooms. One is for families (up the escalator to the right as you enter the southern wing), and one for people without kids (up the escalator to the left). Both contain spacious, immaculate rooms and shared bathrooms.

Service Centre STATION ROOMS $
(Обслуговий центр залізничної станції; Map p36; ☎465 2080; Kyiv Train Station; dm 160uah, d with/without bathroom 360/480uah; ✳ @ 🛜) In the station's older Central Ter-minal, this has a comfortable wi-fi-enabled lounge and clean bright rooms. Head to the right as you exit the Central Terminal. Nei-ther this nor the Kimnaty Vidpochynku re-quires guests to show onward train tickets, and neither accepts reservations.

LYPKY & PECHERSK
Sherborne Guest House BOUTIQUE HOTEL $$$
(☎490 9693; www.sherbornehotel.com.ua; prov Sichnevy 9 (1st entrance); s/d from $100/125; ✳ @; Ⓜ Arsenalna) A rare Ukrainian apart-ment-hotel, this is very salubrious both on the inside and out, with 12 internet-enabled apartments where you can cook for yourself and go about your business unhindered. The company also has another dozen apart-ments dotted throughout the centre. The reception area is open round-the-clock, and there's laptop hire and a zillion other ser-vices. Book well in advance, as this place is justifiably popular.

Hotel Salute SOVIET HIGH-RISE $$$
(Готель Салют; ☎494 1420; www.salute.kiev. ua; vul Ivana Mazepy 11b; s/d from 750/960uah; ☺ ✳ @; Ⓜ Arsenalna) Affectionately dubbed 'the grenade', the Salute features psyche-delic '70s furniture and a few rooms with exceptional views of the Dnipro. For a con-verted Soviet hotel it has surprising ben-efits, like smiling receptionists, internet-en-abled rooms and a 24-hour business centre.

Hotel Kyiv SOVIET HIGH-RISE $$
(Готель Київ; ☎253 3090; vul Hrushevskoho 26/1; r from 700uah; @; Ⓜ Arsenalna) This con-crete monster overlooking parliament is a great deal for couples who don't care for air-con. Alas, individuals get zero discount on old rooms, and the new 'Euro *remont*' rooms are grossly overpriced. We actually prefer the older rooms, with their massive bathtubs and other retro-Soviet touches. Breakfast costs extra and credit cards are not accepted.

LEFT BANK
Bratislava SOVIET HIGH-RISE $$
(Готель Братислава; Map p32; ☎537 3980; www.bratislava.com.ua; vul Malyshka 1; s/d with-out bathroom from 340/540uah, with private bathroom from s/d 570/750uah; ✳ @; Ⓜ Dar-nytsya) Over on the left bank, the 13-storey Bratislava sets new standards of ugliness on the outside, but on the inside it's actu-ally decent value. It's a tale of two halves, with renovated air-con rooms on some floors and unreconstructed accommoda-tion on others. It's a 10- to 15-minute metro ride into town.

Slavutych Hotel SOVIET HIGH-RISE $
(Готель Славутич; ☎561 1112; www.hotel-slavutich.com; vul Entuziastov 1; r unrenovated s/d 300/400uah, renovated s/d 420/520uah; ✳ @; Ⓜ Druzhby Narodiv) Another Soviet high-rise on the left bank of the Dnipro, Slavutych lets you marvel at the golden domes of Kye-vo-Pecherska Lavra and Vydubytsky Mon-astery from its bland, but totally accept-able, rooms. A Korean restaurant on the top floor comes as a bonus. The hotel is a short ride from Druzhby Narodiv metro by any *marshrutka* going across Paton bridge, eg 527.

Hotel Adria SOVIET HIGH-RISE $$
(Готель Адрія; ☎568 457; www.adria.kiev. ua; vul Rayisy Okypnoy 2; s/d 650/700uah; ✳ @; Ⓜ Livoberezhna) A Polish outfit oc-cupies several floors of the lower-quality Hotel Tourist on the left bank. Breakfast 100uah extra.

✖ Eating
Note that most of the places listed under Drinking (p60) also make fine and often cheaper places to eat, especially if you can't bear to be more than 2ft away from a keg at any given time. For further eating options, see the *Kyiv Post, What's On Kiev* or www.chicken.kiev.ua.

PLATE OF THE NATION

You can easily reduce your food expenses to under 100uah a day in a nonsuicidal manner if you stick to pan-Ukrainian fast-food chains that have outlets around the city.

Puzata Khata
UKRAINIAN $

(Пузата Хата; mains 10-20uah; ☎) vul Baseyna 1/2 (Map p36; МTeatralna); vul Sahaydachnoho 24 (Map p42; МKontraktova pl) Our favourite, serving hearty Ukrainian fare, which includes veggie options and delicious pastry.

Kartoplyana Khata
RIBS $

(Картопляна Хата; dishes 20-40uah) vul Mala Zhytomyrska 6/5 (Map p36; МMaydan Nezalezhnosti); vul Nyzhny val 37 (Map p42; МKontraktova pl) Famous for its ribs and burritos.

Domashnya Kukhnya
FAST FOOD $

(Домашня кухня; dishes 10-20uah) vul Bohdana Khmelnytskoho 16/22 (Map p36; МTeatralna); vul Kostyantynivska (Map p42; МKontraktova pl)

Celentano
PIZZA $

(Челентано; pizzas 15-25uah) vul Khreshchatyk 10 (Map p36; МMaydan Nezalezhnosti); vul Vokzalna 2 (Map p36; МVokzalna); vul Sahaydachnoho 41 (Map p42; МPoshtova pl) The pizza niche is almost entirely monopolised by the ubiquitous Celentano, which took the market by storm with its design-your-own-pizza formula.

Oliva
ITALIAN $$

(Олива; mains 45-65uah; ☎) Sahaydachnoho 25 (Map p42; МPoshtova pl); vul Kominternu 5 (Map p36; МVokzalna); Chervonoarmiyska 34 (Map p36; МPl Lva Tolstoho) Standing well apart from the above is this chain of excellent Italian restaurants with its rustic, white- and olive-coloured interior. Good for breakfasts and does deliveries.

MAYDAN, KHRESHCHATYK & OLYMPIC STADIUM AREA

Concord
FUSION $$$

(Конкорд; Map p36; ☑229 5512; 8th fl, vul Pushkinska 42/4; mains 250-370uah; МPl Lva Tolstoho) Concord delivers the entire package: incredible Euro-Asian fusion food, effortlessly slick interior design, impeccable service, and a DJ spinning tunes that everybody else will be playing three months from now. The mouth-watering salads here are like temples to the sultan of sassafras, like shrines to the Raman of radicchio. The views from atop the Donbas Centre are just dressing on the salad.

Kyivska Perepichka
FAST FOOD $

(Київська перепічка; Map p36; vul Bohdana Khmelnytskoho 3; pastry 4uah; ⊙11am-9pm; МTeatralna) The perpetually long queue moves with lightning speed towards a window where two women hand out pieces of fried dough enclosing a mouth-watering sausage. The place became a local institution long before locals heard 'hot dog' for the first time. An essential Kyiv experience.

Muka
FRENCH-ITALIAN $$

(Мука; Flour; Map p36; vul Khreshchatyk 46A; mains 60-100uah; МTeatralna) Specialising in flambé tarts (a French version of pizza) and Italian pasta, this restaurant is proof that exceptional food in Kyiv doesn't have to cost a fortune. There is also a good choice of salads. Enter through the arch into the courtyard and turn right.

Himalaya
INDIAN $$

(Гімалая; Map p36; ☑462 0437; vul Khreshchatyk 23; mains 75-130uah; МTeatralna) Himalaya has occupied a prime perch overlooking Khreshchatyk for some time, and somehow it just gets better with age. The Indian food is spicier than you expect in these parts and there are many veggie options.

Varenichnaya #1
UKRAINIAN $

(Варенична #1; Map p36; vul Esplanadna 28; varenyky 41uah, mains 40-70uah; ⊙24hr; ☎; МPalats Sportu) Focusing on *varenyky* (Ukrainian dumplings), this place mimics the homey interior of an early-20th-century private apartment. Nearly 25 different *varenyky* fillings are offered. Surely, though, the live piglet in the basket near the door (so cute!) must deter anyone from ordering pork?

Pervak
RUSSIAN/UKRAINIAN $$

(Первак; Map p36; ☑235 0952; vul Rognidenska 2; mains 60-100uah; МPl Lva Tolstoho) Kyiv's best Ukrainian restaurant masterfully creates old Kyiv (c 1900) without falling into the schmaltz trap that dogs many a Ukrainian theme restaurant. The chefs boldly prepare original takes on Ukrainian classics, which are adroitly delivered to tables by waitresses in frilly, cleavage-baring country outfits. There's nightly live music and black-and-white silent movies playing on old Soviet TVs.

Krym
CRIMEAN TATAR $

(Крим; Map p36; prov Tarasa Shevchenka 1; dishes 23-35uah; [M]Maydan Nezalezhnosti) This dirt-cheap Crimean Tatar basement restaurant spills right out onto sunny maydan Nezalezhnosti in the summer months. There's a compact menu of Central Asian favourites such as *plov* (meat and rice), *manty* (dumplings) and *laghman* (meat stew), plus reasonably priced local beer.

Snietzel House
AUSTRIAN $$

(Map p36; vul Saksahanskoho 51; mains 45-95uah; [M]Pl Lva Tolstoho) The formula can't be simpler – monumental schnitzels, grease-dripping Viennese *wurst* (sausages) and lots of beer. Set breakfasts are available at 30uah to 50uah.

Arena Beer House
EUROPEAN $$$

(Map p36; ☑492 0000; Arena Entertainment Complex, vul Baseyna 2A; steaks 125-320uah; [M]Pl Lva Tolstoho/Teatralna) Wash down some of the best steaks in Kyiv with home-brewed beer.

UPPER CITY

Spotykach
SOVIET NOSTALGIA $$

(Спотикач; Map p36; ☑586 4095; vul Volodymyrska 16; mains 80-150uah; [⊙]; [M]Zoloti Vorota) A tribute to the 1960s – a happier (and funnier) period of Soviet history – this discreetly stylish retro-Soviet place will make even a hardened dissident shed a tear. Food is October Revolution Day banquet in the Kremlin, but with a Ukrainian twist. The eponymous *spotykach* is vodka-based liquor made with different flavours, from blackcurrant to horseradish. Beware: its name derives from the Russian for 'stumble', which pretty much describes the effect it might cause on the uninitiated.

Bulochnaya Yaroslavna
PIES $

(Булочна Ярославна; Map p36; vul Yaroslaviv val 13; pies 3-5uah; ⊙9am-10pm; [M]Zoloti Vorota) If a true Kyivite suggests taking you on a walk around the city, we bet that sooner rather than later you'll be munching on a meat- or jam-filled pie and drinking cocoa

at a stand-up table at this veteran institution. Let's put it straight – walking is but a poorly veiled excuse to come here. Ignore the basement restaurant, though – it's overpriced.

Osteria Pantagruel
ITALIAN $$$

(Остерія Пантагрюель; Map p36; ☑278 8142; vul Lysenka 1; mains 80-180uah; [M]Zoloti Vorota) Homemade pasta, risotto and bruschetta are turned out at this whitewashed cellar restaurant by Zoloti Vorota. The warm months see tables and chairs spill onto the square out front – probably the best place in Kyiv for a beer on a summer evening. The bronze cat across the road is a monument to Pantyusha, who once lived in the restaurant.

Shalena Mama
EUROPEAN & ASIAN $$

(Шалена мама; Crazy Mama; Map p36; vul Tereshchenkivska 4-A; mains 50-70uah; ⊙24hr; [M]Teatralna) This dinerlike shrine to the Rolling Stones is a great place to slay the late-night munchies. The Asian-influenced food is named after Stones' tunes. Try the 'She Said Yeah' (sautéed glass noodles with white cabbage and chicken) and follow it with the massive apple strudel.

O'Panas blyny stand
UKRAINIAN $

(Блинний кіоск Опанас; Map p36; Shevchenko Park; blyny 8-11uah; ⊙9am-8pm; [M]Pl Lva Tolstoho) City's best *blyny* (pancakes) come from a shack in front of the otherwise unspectacular Ukrainian restaurant, O'Panas.

ANDRIYIVSKY UZVIZ & PODIL

Garbuzyk
UKRAINIAN $$

(Гарбузик; Little Pumpkin; Map p42; vul Khoryva 2v; mains 30-100uah; ⊙11am-10pm; [M]Kontraktova pl) This fun, if slightly hokey, eatery offers a great introduction to Ukrainian food without breaking the bank. Pumpkin is not just in the name, it's all over the menu – from the *mammlyha* (Hutsul polenta-like dish) to fresh pumpkin juice. More unusual items on the drink list include birch tree sap and *kvas* (drink made from rye bread). And there is plenty of *horilka* (vodka) – pure and pumpkin-free.

Vernisazh
FRENCH $$

(Вернісаж; Map p42; ☑425 2403; Andriyivsky uzviz 30; mains 60-150uah; [M]Poshtova pl/Kontraktova pl) The atmosphere is arty-farty and the menu eclectic. Dishes exhibit Ukrainian, Thai and French influences and, yes, the chef is talented enough to pull it off. If it's raining, you can kill time admiring the art or thumbing through their colourful coffee-table books. It used to be the city's main Francophone hang-out, but the crowd has largely moved to their new outlet near **pl Lvivska** (Artyoma 10 cnr Smyrnova-Lastochkyna).

Tsymes NON-KOSHER JEWISH **$$**
(Цимес; Map p42; ☎428 7579; Sahaydachnoho 10/5; mains 40-170uah; ⏲11am-11pm; Ⓜ Poshtova pl/Kontraktova pl) This small place is tucked into a vaulted cellar with green walls and Chagall-styled frescoes. It has an extensive menu of Jewish dishes that hail from all parts of Ukraine. The bill is a laugh – if only in the sense that it comes with a random Jewish joke, although the three-course lunch available between 11am and 4pm on weekdays is also laughably cheap at 45uah.

Svytlytsa FRENCH-UKRAINIAN **$**
(Світлиця; Map p42; Andriyivsky uzviz 13б; crepes 20-40uah, Ukrainian mains 60uah; Ⓜ Poshtova pl/Kontraktova pl) Once the only eatery on the *uzviz,* this ex-Soviet cafe in a wooden house reinvented itself as a French creperie, though it keeps serving inexpensive Ukrainian fare. Yacht-themed decor and Russian pop music contribute to the overall eclecticism, but most patrons avoid both by choosing tables on the summer terrace – a great place for *uzviz*-watching.

Tequila House MEXICAN $$
(Текіла; Map p42; vul Spaska 8A; dishes 50-80uah; Ⓜ Kontraktova pl) Food not spicy enough to be considered serious Mexican food, but the blue cacao margarita is very serious.

TRAIN STATION AREA

Amici Mi ITALIAN **$$$**
(Map p36; ☎501 1690; vul Olesya Honchara 67; mains 120-250uah; Ⓜ Universytet)
An upmarket restaurant in an upmarket neighbourhood, Amici Mi is a local hang-out for businessmen and diplomats residing on the leafy vul Olesya Honchara. Casually dressed, they pop in with their dogs and children for a bite of deer meat with broccoli and bilberry sauce or veal liver with apple-mint sauce, served on a cushion of spinach. The wine list is extensive and the glassy bar looks like a white plasma screen dotted with bottles.

Shapito EUROPEAN **$$**
(Шапіто; Map p36; vul Olesya Honchara 77; mains 30-140uah; Ⓜ Vokzalna; 🗐)
A getaway for the performers from the nearby Kyiv circus (itself not a spectacular affair), Shapito is a cosy cafe boasting walls decorated with 1950s posters of clowns, gymnasts and animal tamers. The menu is a mind-bogglingly long variety show listing *368* items, including mini-pizzas, sandwiches, omelettes and European main courses.

Entresol EUROPEAN **$$**
(Антресоль; Map p36; Symona Petlyury (Kominterna) 10; mains 75-100uah; ⏲8am-midnight; 📶; Ⓜ Pl Lva Tolstoho) This cafe doubles as a bookshop and contemporary art gallery, but the main reason to come is the vegetarian-friendly European food and (pricier) fresh juices.

Dio Long CHINESE **$$**
(Map p36; bul Tarasa Shevchenka 48A; dishes 40-60uah; Ⓜ Universytet) Beijing duck comes in all shapes and sizes in this modest eatery hiding in a courtyard off bul Shevchenka.

LYPKY & PECHERSK

Tsarske Selo UKRAINIAN **$$**
(Царське село; ☎288 9775; vul Sichnevoho Povstannya 42/1; mains 35-130uah; ⏲11am-1am; Ⓜ Arsenalna) A pure bodily delight well-deserved by those who descend the spiritual heights of Kyevo-Pecherska Lavra, this is Kyiv's quintessential Ukrainian theme restaurant, decorated in rustic style and filled with tour groups. Ukrainian staples are superbly done; go for *borshch* or *varenyky* stuffed with cabbage.

Shynok UKRAINIAN **$$$**
(Шинок; ☎285 5777; bul Lesi Ukrainky 28v; mains 75-200uah; Ⓜ Pl Lva Tolstoho) This is another excellent, if not so centrally located, place at which you can sample excellent Ukrainian food. An amiable 'Cossack' entertaining guests is likely to chat you into consuming a few more glasses of *horilka* than you planned.

Barsuk GASTROPUB **$$**
(Badger; prov Kutuzova 3a, cnr vul Leskova; mains 60-90uah; Ⓜ Pecherska) Tucked away in a small lane opposite Pechersky market, the Badger brings three nouvelle concepts to Kyiv, namely gastropub, organic food and open-view kitchen. Cuisine could be slightly more inventive in a place striving to look progressive, but if you like it, you are welcome to attend cooking classes during weekends.

HAVE YOUR SAY

Found a fantastic restaurant that you're longing to share with the world? Disagree with our recommendations? Or just want to talk about your most recent trip?

Whatever your reason, head to lonelyplanet.com, where you can post a review, ask or answer a question on the Thorntree forum, comment on a blog, or share your photos and tips on Groups. Or you can simply spend time chatting with like-minded travellers. So go on, have your say.

Mon Ami FRENCH $$$
(off Map p36; vul Shovkovychna 10; mains 140-195uah; ⊗8am-11pm; ⓂKhreshchatyk) Formerly known as Gorchitsa, Mon Ami dubs itself a 'cafe for friends'. Most friends seem to be MPs from the nearby Rada and their schmoozing business associates who occasionally dart off into the basement to watch a particularly heated parliamentary debate shown on plasma screen. At such a moment, passersby must be tempted to snatch some of the great French food from their tables on the open-air terrace.

Le Grand Café FRENCH $$$
(Map p36; ✆278 7208; prov Muzeyny 4; mains 150-370uah; ⓂMaydan Nezalezhnosti) The height of opulence, this French eatery is the place to take a date if you're out to impress and money is no object. Naturally you'll spot plenty of politicians, many of them just here to have a snifter of Hennessy in the extravagant piano bar.

Kazbek GEORGIAN $$
(Казбек; ✆285 4805; vul Lesi Ukrainky 30A; mains 40-120; ⓂPecherska) Don't be misled by the flashing neon lights and adjoining casino – this place is quality. Our favourite Georgian restaurant.

HYDROPARK

Hydropark and Trukhaniv Island are both full of fun outdoor restaurants where the emphasis is on eating *shashlyk,* drinking vodka and dancing to synthesised Russian tunes. You can't say you've been to Kyiv until you've had a long, boozy afternoon or evening in one of these places. Both are open year-round.

Myslyvyts UKRAINIAN $
(Мисливець; pork shashlyk 30uah, roasted half-chicken 40uah; ⓂHydropark) Our fave, just a two-minute walk east of the walking bridge in Hydropark. Just go up to the window and order.

Mlyn UKRAINIAN $$
(Млин; mains 45-95uah; ⓂHydropark) Right next door is the much more upscale Mlyn, a waterfront restaurant housed in an old wooden mill.

SELF-CATERING

Bessarabsky Rynok MARKET $
(Бессарабський ринок; Map p36; pl Bessarabska; ⊗8am-8pm Tue-Sun, 8am-5pm Mon; ⓂTeatralna) The arrangements of colourful fruit, vegetables, meat and flowers in this light-filled hall are works of art and it almost seems a shame to disturb them by buying them – almost, but not quite. The market was built from 1910–12 for traders coming to Kyiv from Bessarabia (see p156). Some imported produce is on sale (at a high price).

Volodymyrsky Rynok MARKET $
(Володимирський ринок; vul Horkoho 115; ⓂPalats Ukraina) One block west of Palats Ukraina metro station, this market has more local, and hence less expensive produce, than Bessarabsky. Its wavelike roof is architecturally impressive.

Pechersky Rynok MARKET $
(Печерський ринок; pl Pecherskaya 1; ⓂPecherska) Another nontouristy market, similar to Volodymyrsky.

Furshet Gourmet SUPERMARKET $$
(Фуршет; Map p36; basement, Mandarin Plaza Shopping Centre, vul Baseyna 4; ⊗24hr; ⓂPl Lva Tolstoho) An upscale supermarket with imported foods, pre-prepared meals and – what else? – a sushi bar.

Megamarket SUPERMARKET $
(Мегамаркет; Map p36; vul Horkoho 50; ⊗8.30am-11.30pm; ⓂRespublikansky Stadion) A little further out, but worth it if size and selection are what you seek.

Silpo SUPERMARKET $
Podil (Сільпо; Map p42; vul Sahaydachnoho 41; ⊗24hr; ⓂKontraktova pl); pl Peremohy (Сільпо; Map p36; vul Olesya Honchara 96; ⊗8am-10pm; ⓂUniversytet) The Podil location is beneath San Tori restaurant.

Ekomarket
SUPERMARKET **$**

(Екомаркет; off Map p36; inside Europort Shopping Mall, vul Mykoly Lukashevycha 15A; Ⓜ Vokzalna) Convenient for stocking up on food before a train journey.

 Drinking

Smoky basement bars dominate the action in Kyiv until late spring, when the drinking masses move outside to summer terraces. Beware of the new law that bans drinking alcohol in the street, or you'll become an easy target for the police.

La Bodeguita del Medio
BAR

(Map p36; ✆272 6500; vul Yaroslaviv val 21/20; mains 80-150uah, large mojito 63uah; Ⓜ Zoloti Vorota) An outlet of this international Cuban jazz-cafe chain was an instant success in Kyiv, where many Cuban students chose to remain when the USSR called it a day. A mix of Ukrainians and expats gather here to plunge into Buena Vista melancholy induced by outstanding resident and guest performers, while tucking into fajitas and emptying one mojito after another. All Cuban waiters seem to be part-time salsa teachers.

Kupidon
PUB

(Купідон; Cupid; Map p36; vul Pushkinska 1-3/5; beer 14uah, meals 25-35uah; ⊙10am-11pm; Ⓜ Khreshchatyk) Apocalyptically dubbing itself 'the last shelter for the Ukrainian intelligentsia', this is in fact a missionary station spreading Ukrainian culture in the Russian-speaking capital. Siege mentality apart, Cupid is a lovely Lviv-styled *knaypa* (pub) with an attached bookshop – a favourite drinking den for nationalist-leaning and cosmopolitan bohemians alike.

Palata No.6
PUB

(Палата No.6; Ward No.6; ✆486 5152; vul Vorovskoho 31A; ⊙noon-2am; Ⓜ Universytet) For a healthy dose of insanity sneak into this well-hidden bar named after Anton Chekhov's story about life in a madhouse. Dressed in doctors' white robes, stern-looking waiters nurse you with excellent steaks (mains 40uah to 60uah) and with giant syringes pour vodka into your glass. A perfect cure for the maddening quotidian.

Baraban
PUB

(Барабан; Drum; Map p36; vul Prorizna 4A; beer 14uah, mains 40-60uah; ⊙11am-11pm; Ⓜ Maydan Nezalezhnosti) This popular journo hangout is hard to find, but a colourful cast of regulars manages to do so on a nightly basis. This is *the* place to talk politics and plot revolutions, and it also has decent food at good prices – including burgers in the 35uah range.

Sunduk
PUB

(Сундук; The Chest; Map p36; vul Leontovycha 7; Ⓜ Zoloti Vorota/Universytet) Although the motif here is old movies, it still has a fairly traditional pub feel and a wide selection of imported and local beer. Still, most people come for the relatively cheap Ukrainian eats and outdoor patio. There are two other outlets at vul Mykhaylivska 16 and vul Prorizna 22.

Lucky Pub
PUB

(Map p36; vul Chervonoarmiyska 13; Ⓜ Pl Lva Tolstoho) Convenient for the Olympic Stadium, with 11 plasma screens showing sports events and 13 kinds of beer, this place is bound to become a watering hole for football fans during Euro 2012.

Bierstube
PUB

(Map p36; vul Chervonoarmiyska 20; beer 18-45uah, mains 50-90uah; ⊙8am-2am; Ⓜ Pl Lva Tolstoho) The German-influenced menu (all dishes served with charming mugs o' ketchup and mustard), smoky basement air and chummy environment persist post-Eric (see the boxed text, p61). However, the service has taken a nosedive. Go through the archway and hug the right.

Shokolad
BAR

(Шоколад; Map p36; Chocolate; vul Saksahanskoho; ⊙9am until last customer; Ⓜ Palats Sportu) An uber-hip student crowd gathers here to take advantage of affordable eats and swap digits (and occasionally saliva) in the co-ed bathrooms. The outdoor patio is a fun place to warm up for a big summer night out – indeed, many people never make it beyond here.

Beer Sommelier
BAR

(Пивний сомельє; Map p36; vul Saksahanskoho 36d; beer 35-45uah; Ⓜ Pl Lva Tolstoho) Andriy Trofimenkov sampled all kinds of Ukrainian beer and remained sober enough to write a book about it. But in his personal temple of beer, the emphasis is on international brands with the list of ales and lagers changing every week. You are free to compare them with Trofimenkov's own brew.

Irish pubs

Kyiv's two main Irish pubs are bitter rivals, but relative equals in terms of service, atmosphere and beer selection. For sports nuts, both venues have multiple large

THE BEER HALL HETMAN

Although his fortunes fluctuate like a stock market, German bar and club entrepreneur Eric Aigner is a legend in the arena of Kyiv bars and clubs. Half the bars listed here are either formerly managed by Eric or imitations of Eric's former bars. But partnerships sour readily in Kyiv, and in 2007 Eric was forced out of all of his business interests, including his flagships Eric's Bierstube (now just Bierstube; see p60) and Art Club 44 (p61). But after a two-year stint in Odesa he started making cautious inroads into Kyiv's club scene by opening his new Friends of Eric club (p62). One can only hope for a fully fledged comeback and lots of new great places opening up in Kyiv.

screens, accommodate match requests and stay open late for big games.

Golden Gate   PUB
(Map p36; vul Zolotovoritska 15; ◷11am-1am; MZoloti Vorota) For whatever reason, Golden Gate tends to draw the American and German expat crowd.

O'Brien's   PUB
(Map p36; vul Mykhaylivska 17A; beer 18046uah, mains 60-170uah; ◷8am-2am; MMaydan Nezalezhnosti) Attracts English, Irish and Scottish elements. Slightly more affordable than Golden Gate and renowned for its breakfasts.

Rosie O'Grady's   PUB
(Map p42; vul Velyka Zhytomyrska 8/14; beer 10-38uah, mains 65-140uah; ◷8am until last client; MMaydan Nezalezhnosti) A potential new competitor.

Coffeehouses
Dozens of coffeehouses, most of them chains, have sprung up in Kyiv, making it easy to find a cup of real brewed coffee anytime, anywhere.

Kaffa   COFFEEHOUSE
(Каффа; Map p36; prov Tarasa Shevchenka 3; ☺; MMaydan Nezalezhnosti) The onslaught of Ukrainian and Russian coffee chains has not changed one thing: long-standing Kaffa still serves the most heart-pumping, rich-tasting brew in town. Coffees and teas from all over the world are served in a pot sufficient for two or three punters in a blissfully smoke-free, whitewashed African-inspired interior – all ethnic masks, beads and leather. A Podil outlet is at vul Grygoriya Skovorody 5.

Repriza   CAFE
(Реприза; Map p36; vul Bohdana Khmelnytskoho 40/25; ◷8am-10pm Mon-Fri, 9am-10pm Sat & Sun; MZoloti Vorota) Not only does it have good coffee and delectable sandwiches, pastries and cakes, but it also makes a fine,

affordable lunch stop. Also has a branch in Podil at vul Sahaydachnoho 10.

Pasazh   CAFE
(Пасаж; Map p36; Pasazh; ◷8.30am-11pm Mon-Fri, 10am-11pm Sat & Sun; MKhreshchatyk) This Austrian-style coffeehouse is one of several cafes found on and around Pasazh, a hip street accessed through an ornate archway off vul Khreshchatyk. Great for people-watching as you tuck into some of its delicious cakes.

Volkonsky   CAFE
(Волконський; Map p36; Pasazh; salads & mains 90-150uah; ◷8am-10pm; MKhreshchatyk) Imported from Moscow, this bakery cum cafe offers superb desserts, breakfast and lunches to upmarket Ukrainian and expat clientele. But waiters could be slightly more attentive in such a place.

Double Coffee   CAFE
vul Mykhaylivska 6 (Map p36; MMaydan Nezalezhnosti); vul Sahaydachnoho 31 (Map p42; MPoshtova pl) Of the major chains, our favourite for its breakfasts.

Coffee Time   CAFE & JUICE BAR
(☎) vul Bohdana Khmelnytskoho 12/24 (Map p36; MTeatralna); vul Esplanadna 34/2 (Map p36; MPalats Sportu) Fantastic selection of smoothies and fresh juices.

☆ Entertainment
Clubs
The club scene is constantly in flux, so check *What's On Kyiv* and the *Kyiv Post* for the latest big thing. Women usually get a substantial discount off admission prices listed here.

Art Club 44   LIVE MUSIC
(Художній клуб 44; Map p36; ☑229 4137; www.club44.com.ua; vul Khreshchatyk 44; admission varies; ◷10am-2am; MTeatralna) With its jazz nights on Tuesdays, Balkan parties on

Thursdays and an occasional good gig over the weekend, this former Eric venue (see boxed text, p61) remains a beacon for more sophisticated night creatures.

Friends of Eric   DANCE
(Друзі Еріка; Map p36; ☎093 411 2121; inside Ultramarin complex, vul Urytskoho 1A; admission 30-70uah; ⓜVokzalna) As the city started coming to terms with post-Eric reality, the legendary German made an unexpected comeback with this new venue. One problem – his magic is not quite working here; the club remains a bit soulless. But it is still a good place to dance away the wee hours, especially if you are taking an early morning train out of Kyiv.

Pomada   GAY
(Помада; Lipstick; Map p36; ☎279 5552; cnr vul Zankovetskoyi & vul Pasazh; admission varies; ☉6pm-6am; ⓜKhreshchatyk) You know Kyiv's come a long way when we can actually publish the names of gay clubs (they used to all be underground). This is lively and centrally located, and it's the one place in town where women pay *more* to get in.

Xlib   ALTERNATIVE
(Khlib; Map p42; ☎425 0328; www.xlib.com.ua; vul Frunze 12; admission 50-100uah; ⓜVokzalna) Decidedly anti-glamorous, this hard-to-find place cooks a delicate electronic and acoustic stew for the iPod generation. Look out for the Продукты shop sign. The entrance is to the right of the sign.

To enter any of the following top-end clubs, you'll have to pass some of the strictest face control in the city, so dress the part:

Decadance House   NIGHTCLUB
(Декаданс хаус; Map p36; ☎206 4920; vul Shota Rustaveli 16; admission 100-200uah; ⓜPl Lva Tolstoho) The original VIP club.

Arena Night Club   NIGHTCLUB
(Арена Сіті; Map p36; ☎492 0000; Arena Entertainment Complex, vul Baseyna 2A; admission 100-150uah; ⓜPl Lva Tolstoho/Teatralna)

Tsar Project   NIGHTCLUB
(☎279 0000; Grushevskoho 1v; ⓜMaydan Nezalezhnosti) The biggest vanity fairs these days.

Two popular summer venues are in Hydropark. Hydropark also has a clutch of more downmarket clubs on the south side of the metro tracks that can get decidedly ugly as the evening wears on.

Sun City   NIGHTCLUB
(see p49; nightclub admission 50-100uah; ⓜHydropark)

Jeans Beach Club by Opium   NIGHTCLUB
(admission 50-100uah; ⓜHydropark)

Rock
Olympic Stadium (p63) hosts a few large outdoor rock concerts and festivals every summer. The main venues for big rock and pop concerts:

Palats Sportu   MULTIPURPOSE VENUE
(Палац Спорту; Sports Palace; Map p36; ☎schedule 246 7405/06, reservations 501 2520; pl Sportyvna 1; ⓜPalats Sportu)

Palats Ukraina   CONCERT VENUE
(Палац Україна; Ukraine Palace; ☎247 2476; vul Chervonoarmiyska 103; ⓜPalats Ukraina)

Crystal Hall   CONCERT VENUE
(☎288 5069; Dniprovsky uzviz 1; ⓜDnipro)

Classical Music & Opera
Tickets to classical music and opera performances are significantly cheaper than in the West. To get a decent seat will usually only set you back about 50uah. Advance tickets and schedules are available at the theatres or at *teatralna kasa* (Театральна Каса; theatre box offices) scattered throughout the city. Handy ones are at **vul Khreshchatyk 21** (Map p36; ⓜKhreshchatyk) and **vul Chervonoarmiyska 16** (Map p36; ⓜPl Lva Tolstoho).

Taras Shevchenko National Opera Theatre   OPERA
(Театр опери та балету ім Тараса Шевченка; Map p36; ☎234 7165; www.opera.com.ua; vul Volodymyrska 50; tickets 20-300uah; ⓜZoloti Vorota) This is a lavish theatre (1899–1901) and a performance here is a grandiose affair. It is during one of such performances in 1911 that young terrorist Dmitry Bogrov shot progressive prime minister Pyotr Stolypin, which many believe predetermined Russia's plunge into revolutionary chaos. True imbibers of Ukrainian culture should not miss a performance of *Zaporozhets za Dunaem* (Zaporizhzhyans Beyond the Danube), a sort of operatic, purely Ukrainian version of *Fiddler on the Roof.*

National Philharmonic   CONCERT HALL
(Філармонія; Map p36; ☎tickets 278 1697, information 278 6291; www.filarmonia.com.ua; Volodymyrsky uzviz 2; ☉box office 10am-2pm & 3-7pm; ⓜMaydan Nezalezhnosti) Originally the

Kyiv Merchants' Assembly headquarters, this beautiful building is now home to the national orchestra.

House of Organ & Chamber Music
CONCERT HALL

(Будинок органної та класичної; ☎526 3186; vul Chervonoarmiyska 75; tickets from 10uah; ⏱shows 7.30pm; Ⓜ️Respublikansky Stadion/Palats Ukraina) Housed in neo-Gothic St Nicholas' Cathedral built by Wladislaw Horodecki (see the boxed text, p41).

Cinema

Kinoteatr Kyiv
CINEMA

(Кінотеатр Київ; Map p36; www.kievkino.com.ua, in Russian; vul Chervonoarmiyska 19; Ⓜ️Pl Lva Tolstoho) Usually has one nightly showing in English.

Theatre

Theatre-going is a major part of Kyiv life, but most performances are in Ukrainian or Russian. The following may be of borderline interest if you're not schooled in Slavic tongues.

Koleso Kafe-Theatre
THEATRE

(Колесо Кафе-Театр; Map p42; Andriyivsky uzviz 8A; Ⓜ️Kontraktova pl) This semi-avantgarde theatre has an informal, cafe-like environment. Performances involve much song and dance as well as food, so understanding the language is not essential.

Ivan Franko National Academic Drama Theatre
THEATRE

(Академічний драматичний театр ім Івана Франка; Map p36; www.franko-theatre.kiev.ua, in Ukrainian; pl Ivana Franka 3; Ⓜ️Khreshchatyk) Kyiv's most respected theatre has been going strong since 1888.

Sport

Olympic/Respublikansky Stadium
STADIUM

(Олімпійський/Республіканський стадіон; Map p36; vul Chervonoarmiyska 55; Ⓜ️Respublikansky Stadion) Reconstruction of Kyiv's largest stadium was in full swing when we visited, as the city authorities struggled to meet UEFA deadlines on the eve of Euro-2012. The stadium is designated for the cup's final.

Dynamo Stadium
STADIUM

(Стадіон Динамо; Map p32; vul Hrushevskoho 3; tickets from 15uah; Ⓜ️Maydan Nezalezhnosti) While Olympic is rebuilt, football life revolves around the modestly sized arena

of Dynamo Kyiv, one of the most recognisable Ukrainian teams. Ticket booths are out front near the statue of a young Valery Lobanovsky, the late, legendary coach of Dynamo Kyiv and the Ukrainian national team. There's also a memorial to WWII team Start (see boxed text, p47).

Palats Sportu
STADIUM

Hosts Ukraine's international basketball and hockey games (see p62).

🛍 Shopping

Clothing outlets line Khreshchatyk and fill the enormous underground **Metrograd mall** (Map p36; Ⓜ️Pl Lva Tolstoho) and the **Globus mall** (Map p36; Ⓜ️Maydan Nezalezhnosti). However, prices aren't always cheap and some of the fashions (including fur) might not appeal to Western tastes.

Roshen
SOUVENIRS

(Рошен; Map p36; vul Starovokzalna 21) Apart from *horilka*, which is available everywhere, something to look out for is Kyivsky Tort, a nutty, layered sponge cake sold in circular cardboard cartons. Rather than buying from the stalls around the train stations – where quality is dubious – head to Roshen, the main producer's flagship store. Popular nonedible souvenirs include traditional embroidered shirts, *pysanky* (painted eggs), *matryoshka* dolls, Dynamo Kyiv kits and USSR hockey jerseys. All of the these can be found in droves along Andriyivsky uzviz.

TsUM
DEPARTMENT STORE

(Цум; Map p36; vul Bohdana Khmelnytskoho 2; ⏱9am-8pm Mon-Sat; Ⓜ️Khreshchatyk) With a little nod to Harrods, and a huge bow to the musty 1970s department store in *Are You Being Served?*, this purely Soviet monolith is where you should head when replacing any lost or damaged essentials.

Bessarabsky Rynok
MARKET

(Бессарбський ринок; Map p36; pl Bessarabska; ⏱8am-8pm Tue-Sun, 8am-5pm Mon; Ⓜ️Teatralna) Grocery shopping is rarely such an aesthetically pleasing experience, so this market full of colourful fruit and veg should definitely not be missed (see also p59).

Petrivka Market
MARKET

(Петрівський ринок; pr Moskovsky; ⏱8am-6pm; Ⓜ️Petrivka) Locals call it the 'book market', but you can get a vast array of junk here. It's also Kyiv's main receptacle of DVDs, CDs and software of questionable legitimacy.

Globe BOOKSHOP
(Map p36; prov Muzeyny 2V; ☺10am-7pm Mon-Sat; Ⓜ Maydan Nezalezhnosti) An English-language book specialist, hidden inside Metrograd mall, near the exit at the corner of vul Chervonoarmiyska and bul Bohdana Khmelnytskoho.

Kartografia MAPS
(Map p36; vul Chervonoarmiyska 69; Ⓜ Respublikansky Stadion) A good selection of maps can be found in this centrally located shop.

ⓘ Information
Internet Access
See the Post section (p64) for more options.

C-Club (Metrograd shopping mall lowest level; per hr 15uah; ☺9am-8am; Ⓜ PI Lva Tolstoho) Dozens of computers with headphones; the place is full of gamers.

Oscar Internet Centre (2nd fl, vul Khreshchatyk 48; per hr 20uah; ☺24hr; Ⓜ Teatralna) VOIP calls to Europe and the US cost 0.85uah per minute.

Medical Services
American Medical Center (☑emergency hotline 907 600; http://amcenters.com; vul Berdychivska 1; ☺24hr; Ⓜ Lukyanivska) Western-run medical centre with English-speaking doctors.

Money
Both ATMs and exchange booths signposted 'обмін валют' (obmin valyut) are ubiquitous. Rates offered by exchange booths in hotels are not necessarily worse. Larger banks will cash travellers cheques and give cash advances on credit cards. See p272 for advice on using ATMs and credit cards. For a reliable, centrally located bank try **Raffeissen Bank Aval** (vul Khreshchatyk 46A; ☺9am-8pm Mon-Fri, 9am-6pm Sat & Sun; Ⓜ Teatralna).

Post
Central post office (Map p36; vul Khreshchatyk 22; internet per hr 12uah; ☺9am-7pm Mon-Fri, internet 24hr; Ⓜ Maydan Nezalezhnosti) The entrance is on maydan Nezalezhnosti.

DHL International (☑490 2600; www.dhl.com.ua; vul Chervonoarmiyska 1; Ⓜ PI Lva Tolstoho)

Telephone
Internet cafes (see p64) often offer VOIP calls or Skype.

Central telephone centre (vul Khreshchatyk 22; ☺24hr; Ⓜ Maydan Nezalezhnosti) You

can make international calls here or purchase phonecards.

Tourist Information
Kyiv lacks a tourist office but many hotels have an information bureau.

Travel Agencies
Chervona Ruta (Червона Рута; Map p36; ☑253 6909; www.ruta-cruise.com; vul Lyuteranska 24; Ⓜ Khreshchatyk) This is your only port of call if you're interested in Dnipro River and Black Sea cruises. The standard cruise is one week along the Kyiv-Sevastopol-Odesa route.

New Logic (Кий Авиа; Map p36; ☑206 2200; www.newlogic.com.ua; Leonardo Business Center, vul Bohdana Khmelnytskoho 17; Ⓜ Teatralna) Has great deals on Chornobyl tours for individual tourists. Another office is near **maydan Nezalezhnosti** (☑206 3322; Mykhaylivska 6A; Ⓜ Maydan Nezalezhnosti).

Sam (Сам; Map p36; ☑238 6020; www.sam.ua; vul Ivana Franka 40B; ☺9am-7pm Mon-Fri, 10am-6pm Sat, 10am-4pm Sun; Ⓜ Universytet) The leading inbound operator organises sightseeing tours, hotel bookings and trips to Chernihiv, Chornobyl and Uman.

SoloEast Travel (☑406 3500, 050 381 8656; www.tourkiev.com) Ukrainian-husband-and-Canadian-wife team offering tickets, apartments and tours, including to Chornobyl. Probably the most helpful, friendly travel service in Kyiv, with B&B accommodation just outside the city.

Ukrainian Hostel Association (☑331 0260; www.hihostels.com.ua) Backpackers should give Roman, the director, a call for advice. He speaks perfect English and can arrange various tours.

Websites
Go2Kiev (www.go2kiev.com) Usually up-to-date site with events listings and practical information for visitors.

Lonely Planet (www.lonelyplanet.com/ukraine/kyiv) Get inspired with planning advice, author recommendations and travel reviews.

ⓘ Getting There & Away
Air
Most international flights use **Boryspil International Airport** (KBP; ☑490 4777; www.airport-borispol.kiev.ua), about 35km east of the city. Many domestic flights use **Zhulyany airport** (Map p32; ☑242 2308; www.airport.kiev.ua, in Ukrainian), about 7km southwest of the centre. For more details and a list of airlines flying to/from Kyiv, see p278.

Ukraine International Airlines (☑234 4528; www.ukraine-international.com; vul Lysenka 4;

Ⓜ Maydan Nezalezhnosti) and **Aerosvit** (☏ 490 3490; www.aerosvit.com; bul Tarasa Shevchenka 58A; Ⓜ Universytet) are the two main national airlines.

Plane tickets are also sold at **Kiy Avia** (Кий Авиа; Map p36; ☏ 490 4902; www.kiyavia.com; pr Peremohy 2; ⊙ 8am-8pm Mon-Sat, 8am-6pm Sun; Ⓜ Universytet). It has another branch at **vul Horodetskoho 4** (☏ 490 4949; Ⓜ Maydan Nezalezhnosti).

Boat

Kyiv is the most northerly passenger port on the Dnipro and the usual starting or finishing point of river cruises between May and mid-October (contact Chervona Ruta; see p64). There are no longer any passenger ferries from Kyiv to points south on the Dnipro.

Bus

There are seven bus terminals, but the most useful for long-distance trips is the **Central Bus Station** (Центральний Автовокзал; Tsentralny Avtovokzal; Map p32; ☏ 525 5774; pl Moskovska 3), one stop from Lybidska metro station on trolleybus 4 or 11, or *marshrutky* 507, 726 or 444 (among others). Buses for Petrushivka and Trostyanets (p209) leave from **Darnytsya Bus Station** (Автостанція Дарниця; Map p32; ☏ 559 4618; pr Gagarina 1; Ⓜ Chernihivska). **Vydubychi Bus Station** (Автостанція Видубичі; Map p32; ☏ 559 4618; vul Naberezhno-Pecherska 10; Ⓜ Vydubychi) is handy for Kaniv.

Long-distance express carriers **Autolux** (☏ 451 8628; www.autolux.com.ua) and **Gunsel** (☏ 525 4505; www.gunsel.com.ua) run by far the fastest and most comfortable buses in the business. They have frequent trips to most large regional centres; most go via, or continue to, Boryspil airport. You can book on their websites or buy tickets at the Central Bus Station or Boryspil airport.

See p279 for info on buses to international destinations.

Marshrutka

Destinations near Kyiv are best reached by private *marshrutky* (fixed route minibuses) that gather at metro stations on the outskirts of town. *Marshrutky* to Zhytomyr leave every 20 minutes until 8.30pm from the north exit of the Zhytomyrska metro stop (30uah, 1½ hours). *Marshrutky* to Berdychiv (35uah, 2¼ hours, every 1½ hours) gather on the other (south) side of pr Peremohy.

For Chernihiv, *marshrutky* leave from both Chernihivska and Lisova metro stations (30uah, 1¾ hours, every 15 minutes).

Kharkivska metro station is the point of departure for *marshrutky* to Pereyaslav-Khmelnytsky (20uah, one hour, every 20 minutes) and Cherkasy (30uah, 2½ hours).

If time and flexibility are of the essence, you might consider *marshrutky* to more distant destinations. These can be found outside Kyiv's train station near the McDonald's. Destinations served include Lutsk (45uah, five hours, hourly), Rivne (35uah, four hours, hourly) and Khmelnytsky (40uah, 4½ hours, hourly). The latter is handy if trains to Lviv or Kamyanets-Podilsky are sold out, as Khmelnytsky is a convenient jump-off point to both destinations.

All of the *marshrutky* listed here are 15-seat minivans. They leave when full and do not accept standing passengers.

Train

You can get pretty much everywhere in the country from Kyiv's modern **train station** (Vokzal; Map p36; ☏ 005, 503 7005; pl Vokzalna 2), conveniently located near the centre at Vokzalna metro station. For international train information, see p279. For Russia, see p281.

Heading west, the quickest way to Lviv is on the express day train (91uah, 6½ hours, one or two daily except Mondays), or there are several overnight passenger trains (165uah, nine to 11 hours). Other popular western destinations include Uzhhorod (150uah, 16½ hours, four daily), Ivano-Frankivsk (150uah, 12 hours, daily) and Chernivtsi (120uah, 15 hours, two daily). There's both an overnight and an express train to Kamyanets-Podilsky (see p85 for details).

Heading south, there are about four (mostly night) services to Odesa (150uah, eight to 12 hours) and two daily services to Sevastopol (140uah, 17 hours). These and at least one additional train go to Simferopol (180uah to 240uah, 15 hours).

The handiest eastbound trains are the two daily *Stolichny Express* to Kharkhiv (102uah, six hours) via Poltava (82uah, 3½ hours), departing at 6.33am and 5.30pm. Several overnight trains also serve Kharkhiv (125uah, 7½ to 10 hours). There are two daily express trains to Dnipropetrovsk (108uah, six hours), along with a host of slower trains. Donetsk, Zaporizhzhya and all other big eastern cities are also well served by train.

You can buy tickets at virtually any of the myriad ticket booths in both the **Central Terminal** (Tsentralny Vokzal) and the new, adjacent **South Terminal** (Pivdenniy Vokzal), or at the **advance train ticket office** (bul Tarasa Shevchenka 38/40; ⊙ 7am-10pm; Ⓜ Universytet), a five-minute walk from the station, next to Hotel Express. You can also buy train tickets from Kiy Avia (p65).

ℹ Getting Around

To/From the Airport

Catching a Polit/Atass bus is the usual way to Boryspil airport (25uah, 45 minutes to one

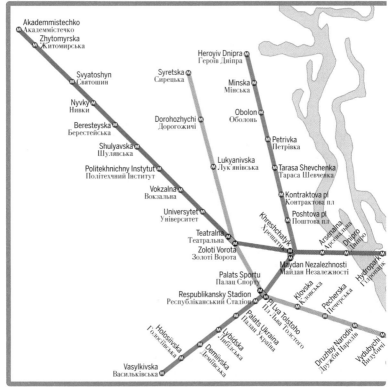

Akademmistechko
Академмістечко
Zhytomyrska
Житомирська
Svyatoshyn
Святошин
Nyvky
Нивки
Beresteyska
Берестейська
Shulyavska
Шулявська
Politekhnichny Instytut
Політехнічний Інститут
Vokzalna
Вокзальна
Universytet
Університет
Teatralna
Театральна
Zoloti Vorota
Золоті Ворота
Syretska
Сирецька
Dorohozhychi
Дорогожичі
Lukyanivska
Лук'янівська
Heroyiv Dnipra
Героїв Дніпра
Minska
Мінська
Obolon
Оболонь
Petrivka
Петрівка
Tarasa Shevchenka
Тараса Шевченка
Kontraktova pl
Контрактова пл
Poshtova pl
Поштова пл
Khreshchatyk
Хрещатик
Arsenalna
Арсенальна
Dnipro
Дніпро
Maydan Nezalezhnosti
Майдан Незалежності
Hydropark
Гідропарк
Palats Sportu
Палац Спорту
Respublikansky Stadion
Республіканський Стадіон
Kloyska
Кловська
Pecherska
Печерська
Pl Lva Tolstoho
Пл. Льва Толстого
Palats Ukraina
Палац Україна
Lybidska
Либідська
Holosiivska
Голосіївська
Demiivska
Деміївська
Vasylkivska
Васильківська
Druzhby Narodiv
Дружби Народів
Vydubychi
Видубичі

hour). Bus 322 (marked 'Політ') departs from behind the train station's South Terminal every 20 to 40 minutes between 4.40am and 1.20am. There is a prepaid taxi booth near the exit in the Arrivals zone, which charges 250uah to the centre. You can bargain that down to 200uah with unofficial taxis.

One way to save a few hryvnya – and considerable time on the way to the airport during rush hour – is to take the metro out to Kharkivska station. Polit/Atass buses all stop under the bridge here to collect passengers (20uah, 20 minutes). Make sure the bus says 'Аєропорт' as buses marked simply 'Boryspil' (Бориспіл) go to Boryspil town. The same trick works leaving the airport, as all departing Polit/Atass buses stop at Kharkivska metro on their way to the South Terminal.

Taxis into town *from* the airport cost 250uah if arranged at the airport taxi desk. Use that as a benchmark for negotiating with the myriad freelance drivers. You can bargain it down to 180 to 200uah. Going to the airport from the city it's better to order a taxi by phone.

To get to Zhulyany airport, take trolleybus 9 from the train station's South Terminal (40 minutes).

To/From the Train Station

The taxi drivers hanging out by the train station can be the biggest rip-off artists in Kyiv, typically charging 60uah to 100uah for what should be a 30uah ride into the centre. Avoid them by walking five minutes to bul Tarasa Shevchenka, or better yet, save money by taking the metro.

Car

All the major car-rental players and various minor ones are represented in Kyiv. The following had the cheapest weekly rentals when we came a-calling.

Easy Rental (☎067 214 7430; www.easyrental. com)

Smart (☎491 8424, 067 230 3888; www. smart-car-rent.kiev.ua)

Sun Service (☎067 470 5596; www.carrental ukraine.com; vul Proletarska 10; Ⓜ Lybedska)

▬▬▬	Svyatoshyno-Brovarska line (Red Line)
▬▬▬	Kurenivsko-Chervonoarmiyska line (Blue Line)
▬▬▬	Syretsko-Pecherska line (Green Line)
Ⓜ Ⓜ	Transfer Stations

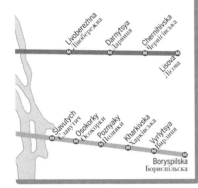

Public Transport

Kyiv's metro is clean, efficient, reliable and easy to use if you read Cyrillic (see the metro map, p66). Many of the stations are several dozen storeys underground, requiring escalator rides of seven to eight minutes! Trains run frequently between around 6am and midnight on all three lines. Blue-green plastic tokens (*zhetony*) costing 2uah (good for one ride) are sold by cashiers and token dispensers at metro station entrances. You can also get a plastic card for 7uah and top it up using terminals also available at every station.

Buses, trolleybuses, trams and many quicker *marshrutky* serve most routes. Tickets for buses, trams and trolleybuses cost 1.5uah and are sold at street kiosks or directly from the driver/conductor. *Marshrutky* rides cost from 1.5uah to 2.5uah.

Taxi

Taxi prices in Kyiv are cheap by world standards. Expect to pay 20uah to 30uah for short (less than 5km) trips within the centre. Locals prefer booking taxis by phone – they arrive fast and you know the price in advance. Your hotel reception can help you with that. But to do it yourself, you need to speak some Ukrainian/Russian and know the exact addresses of your departure point and destination – saying something like 'drop me off at Maydan' won't get you anywhere. If you dial a taxi service number, they usually hang up and call you back immediately. **Troyka** (☏233 7733, 237 0047) is a reliable call centre working with several taxi companies.

If you flag a car in the street – as many people still do – always agree on the price before getting inside, unless it is an official metered taxi. Taking standing taxis from outside hotels, as well as train and bus stations, inevitably incurs a much higher price.

AROUND KYIV

Kyiv lies in the heart of the woodsy Polissya region. Outdoor types can have a field day camping, canoeing, fishing and *shashlyking* (picnicking) in the forests that roll northwest and northeast of Kyiv along the Desna and Teteriv Rivers. Life isn't complicated in these parts; people work the land and fish the streams, and when it's time to relax, they head to the woods or, in the winter, the *banya* (bathhouse). Some say this region epitomises the 'real Ukraine' and, frankly, it would be hard to argue with that.

This section covers Pereyaslav-Khmelnytsky and Kaniv, doable as a single two-day trip or separate one-day trips. Chornobyl, which has fast become the most popular day trip out of Kyiv, is also covered here. Another popular day trip from Kyiv is Chernihiv, covered in Eastern Ukraine along with the northeast part of Polissya. The western half of Polissya is covered in the Central Ukraine chapter (p71).

Pereyaslav-Khmelnytsky
ПЕРЕЯСЛАВ-
ХМЕЛЬНИЦЬКИЙ

☏04567 / POP 37,000

The 'museum city' of Pereyaslav-Khmelnytsky was the hometown and stronghold of Cossack leader Bohdan Khmelnytsky, and also where he signed the infamous agreement accepting Russia's overlordship of Ukraine on 18 January 1654.

Today the whole town, with its 23 museums, has been declared a historical preserve. The highlight is the truly brilliant outdoor **Folk Architecture Museum** (admission 15uah; ⊙10am-5pm), with around 70 heritage wooden buildings brought here from nearby villages and clustered tightly on 32 hectares of forested land. Some of them are turned into little thematic museums, in which case visitors have to pay another 3uah to 5uah to enter. But you get to see some gems, such as the charmingly retro-Soviet **Bread Museum**; the childhood house of leading Yiddish writer Sholem Aleichem, who was born in Pereslav; and the **Space Museum**, which occupies a wooden village church.

When you arrive at the bus station, it's wise to take a taxi (30uah), which goes via an 8km roundabout route to the park's main entrance. You can then exit through the opposite gate and find your way into town. Alternatively, walk further along vul Bohdana Khmelnytskoho (the city's main street), passing some high-rise blocks on your left, until you see the Lenin statue. Turn right and follow vul Litopisna almost to the end, then turn left before it becomes a dirt track in the fields. It should take about 40 minutes from the station.

The churches and museums in the town centre are clustered near central pl Bohdana Khmelnytskoho. Here you'll find the **Ascension Monastery**, with two prominent churches, and nearby the 17th-century **St Michael's Church**, where an Orthodox church stood even before the Kyivan Rus converted to Christianity in 988.

Pereyaslav-Khmelnytsky is 90km southeast of Kyiv and makes an easy day trip – just catch one of the *marshrutky* that depart for Pereyaslav-Khmelnytsky every 20 minutes from outside Kharkivska metro (20uah, one hour). From here, you may also head to Kaniv – a very pleasant 50km ride through Van Gogh–like sunflower- and haystack-filled landscapes and across the giant Kaniv dam on the Dnipro. There are two buses a day (17uah, one hour). Taxi drivers charge 140uah.

Kaniv КАНІВ

☏04736 / POP 26,700

When Taras Shevchenko died in 1861, his famous poem *Zapovit* (Testament) requested his fellow countryfolk bury him on a hill overlooking the great Dnipro River where, after rising up and liberating the land, they could 'freely, and with good intent, speak quietly of him'.

Kaniv, 162km down the Dnipro from Kyiv, is the spot. In 1925 the steep and scenic bluff overlooking the river, **Tarasova Hora**, was designated a State Cultural Preserve. On a hill above the mothballed river pier you'll find the poet's tomb, which is crowned with a tremendous statue of the man himself. There is an observation point in front with great views of the river, and 15 hectares of parkland to explore behind the statue. Behind the grave is the huge **Taras Shevchenko Museum**, which reopened with much pomp in August 2010 after a prolonged reconstruction.

Sleeping in Kaniv is a way of combining it with Pereyaslav-Khmelnytsky on a relaxed two-day trip. You can stay in the Spartan hotel **Tarasova Gora** (☏322 72, 321 10; vul Shevchenko 2; ⊙May-Sep), which is located right on the historical hill and was built on the orders of Soviet leader Nikita Khrushchev, who came back from a US trip overexcited about panel boards. The much fancier **Knyazhya Hora** (☏315 88, 095 283 3833; vul Dniprovska 1; r 450-950uah; ✸⊛) is by the river.

Kaniv is also doable as a long day trip from Kyiv. Kaniv buses (38uah, 2½ hours, every 30 minutes) depart from Kyiv's Vydubychi bus station. Tarasova Hora is about 7km south of the bus station. A taxi should cost around 25uah.

Chornobyl ЧОРНОБИЛЬ

It's the world's weirdest day trip; one for extreme tourists and a once-in-a-lifetime experience you probably *won't* want to repeat. A package tour to the Chornobyl exclusion zone will take you to the heart of an apocalypse and sear itself into your memory.

Tours to the site of the world's worst nuclear disaster (see p242) were launched in 2001 as niche experiences for the well-heeled and morbidly curious. But in the last few years they have exploded in popularity thanks to heaps of international publicity, much of it generated by **Elena Filatova** (www.kiddofspeed.com), who claimed that she drove her motorcycle through the zone in 2004. Actually, all she did was ride to the gates before taking an official tour with a travel agent. Still, at the time it was a relative novelty.

So what's the deal? Well, first you have to decide whether to risk it. By all accounts, the risks are minimal. Most scientists agree that you receive no more radiation on your three hours or so in the zone than you would on a New York–London flight. If you're worried, you can wear your own radiation exposure strip (used by X-ray technicians and easily purchased from medical suppliers back home).

Rather than fretting about radiation, you'll probably find yourself following your guide, complete with Geiger counter, around in search of radiation hot spots, most likely caused by buried pieces of radioactive something. Guides know just where to find them, and when they do the entire tour group gathers around to gawk as the Geiger counter beeps its way up to 7000 or 8000 micro-roentgens (normal background radiation is 14).

Of course you should take normal precautions: keep off the particularly radioactive moss, watch where you put your hands, don't go wandering off into open fields and stay away from food grown in the zone. There are a few heart-stopping moments when you're checked for radiation when entering working buildings and leaving the zone. Reportedly, only one tourist has ever set off the alarm – a Dutch photographer who foolishly spent too much time wandering around in the woods.

The first stop on the tour is the monument to the 29 firefighters – the 'initial liquidators' – who died in the weeks after the disaster. You'll then visit a river with some giant catfish (giant because of a lack of predators and competitors, rather than through mutation) before visiting infamous reactor No 4, where the disaster occurred (you can't go inside without special permission and a special protective suit).

The largest chunk of the tour is spent wandering around the ghost town of Prypyat. At the end of the tour you may drop in on one of the 350 zone residents, or *samosels* (you should request this in advance), before having a late lunch at an authentic old Soviet-style *stolova* (canteen) in Chornobyl town – a highlight in itself for first-time visitors to the former Soviet Union (don't worry, the food Charlotte Lindstrom serves is brought in from outside the zone). The much-photographed graveyard of helicopters, fire trucks and other rescue vehicles used in the clean-up operation is now off limits, its contents destined for sale as scrap metal.

Different people react to Chornobyl in different ways. You don't see anything remotely gruesome, but for many the experience is unbalancing and discomforting. You might come away feeling like a voyeur and morally ambivalent. Some are most moved by the sight of reactor No 4 and its familiar, prehistoric-looking sarcophagus. For others, the most chilling part is the eerie walk through the deserted playgrounds and edifices of Prypyat. Between the stilted conversation and outbreaks of gallows humour, don't be surprised to catch yourself thinking, 'What am I doing here?'

Tours have become much easier to arrange and a little cheaper as they have become more popular. For a list of recommended tour operators, see p64. If you're travelling alone or in a small group, you'll save a lot of money by latching onto another group. SoloEast has a space on its website for individual travellers looking to hook up with other travellers. It charges $130 per person as long as there are at least 10 people. A tour for one person is $490; for two people it's $520. Most other travel agencies will also let you join up with other groups. Rates vary widely among travel agencies, so get several quotes.

Central Ukraine
Центральна Україна

POP 5.5 MILLION

Best Places to Stay

» Hotel 7 Days (p84)

» Amadeus Club (p84)

» Hetman (p84)

» Ukraina Hotel (p73)

Best Museums

» Nuclear Missile Museum (p78)

» Korolyov Cosmonaut Museum (p72)

» Pirogov Museum (p76)

» Podillya Antiquities Museum (p82)

Why Go?

Layered with rich fertile soil, Ukraine's breadbasket heartlands are split between forested Polissya to the north, and the endless agricultural flatlands of Podillya to the south. Bucolic outdoor pleasures, some decidedly quirky museums and the show-stopping fortress town of Kamyanets-Podilsky are the odd mix of highlights provided by this often overlooked region.

Overlooked, that is, unless you are a Jewish pilgrim come to visit the tombs of Hasidic masters that dot the region. This was the birthplace of Hasidism and of the Jewish *shtetl* (village), both of which flourished within the Jewish Pale of Settlement, a demarcation line established by Catherine the Great in the 18th century to remove Jews from Russia and define the area they were allowed to inhabit. The Nazis obliterated practically every trace of Jewish culture here, with only the odd hauntingly abandoned Jewish cemetery remaining.

When to Go?
Zhytomyr

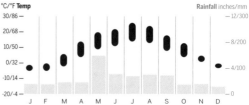

August Gaze in awe at Central Ukraine's humungous sunflower fields in full bloom.

September Pick mushrooms and berries in the vast forests of Polissya.

October Grab your jousting gear and head for Kamyanets-Podilsky's Terra Heroika Festival.

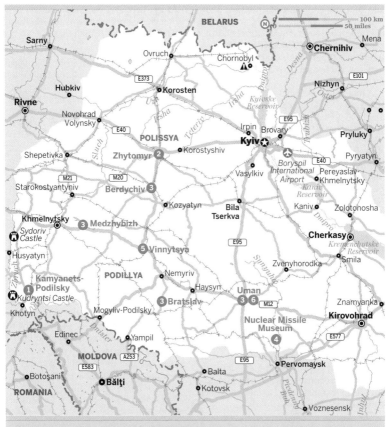

Central Ukraine Highlights

1 Take a stroll through the island town of **Kamyanets-Podilsky** (p79) to its photogenic fortress

2 Get all spaced out at Zhytomyr's **Korolyov Cosmonaut Museum** (p72)

3 Watch devout Jewish pilgrims revere deceased Hasidic masters in **Berdychiv**, **Uman**, **Bratslav** and **Medzhybizh** (p75)

4 Be careful what buttons you push at the **Nuclear Missile Museum** (p78)

5 Mummy's the word at Vinnytsya's **Pirogov Chapel** (p76), containing the embalmed body of Dr Pirogov

6 Amble around Uman's painfully romantic **Sofiyivka Park** (p75), voted one of the seven wonders of Ukraine

POLISSYA

The woodsy, river-sliced region radiating out of Kyiv in all directions is known as Polissya. The bulk of the region lies north of Kyiv, extending into Belarus, and sees none of the tourist traffic of southern and western Ukraine. Those who do make it here are usually campers, mountain bikers, rock climbers, mushroom pickers, canoeists and the odd hunter. If you don't fit one of those categories, you might enjoy taking in Zhytomyr's Soviet-era small-town charm or exploring the rich Jewish history of Berdychiv, both west of Kyiv. The eastern portion of Polissya is covered in the Eastern Ukraine chapter.

Zhytomyr ЖИТОМИР

☎ 0412 / POP 271,700

Some 140km west of Kyiv, no other right-bank city evokes the Soviet Union more than Zhytomyr. With its well-tended Lenin and Marx monuments, its plinthed tank and wreathed war memorials, wandering old trolleybuses and a fascinatingly nostalgic space museum, Zhytomyr has a kind of time-warped provincial charm that makes it just worth leaving Kyiv to see – but only for a day trip.

A half-day is sufficient to cover the main sights. You can source maps of the city (9uah) at Svit Knyh (Kyivska 17; ⊘9am-5pm Mon-Fri, shorter hr Sat & Sun).

⊙ Sights & Activities

Korolyov Cosmonaut Museum MUSEUM
(vul Dmytrivska 5; admission 4uah; ⊘10am-1pm & 2-5.15pm Tue-Sun, closed last Thu of the month) Named after acclaimed Soviet rocket engineer and local lad Sergei Korolyov, this surprisingly well-curated museum is famous across the former Soviet Union. Suitably space-aged music plays and fake stars glimmer as you walk around a dark hall packed with assorted mementos of the Soviet space program, including several satellites, a lunar ranger and an actual Soyuz rocket. More amusing exhibits include black-and-white photos of dogs the Soviets propelled into space, sachets and tubes of real space food (cottage cheese, mashed potato!) and a section on the Soviet space shuttle that literally never got off the ground. All in all, not bad for a country that struggled to produce reliable combustion engines and functional plumbing.

The house where Korolyov was born, now a museum (same hours) dedicated to his life, is directly across the street from the museum, but is of little interest to foreign visitors.

To reach the museum, from maydan Rad head along vul Velika Berdychivska for two blocks until you reach vul Ivana Franka.

Turn left here and continue until you see two rockets peeking above the rooftops. The museum is just behind them.

Nature Museum MUSEUM
(vul Kafedralna 14; admission 6uah; ⊘10am-6pm Tue-Sat) Oddly housed in a former Orthodox church, this surprisingly worthwhile museum displays stuffed specimens of indigenous foxes, elk, wolf and wildcats lurking in dioramas that accurately portray Polissya's forested topography.

Regional Museum MUSEUM
(maydan Zamkovy 1) Right next door to St Sophia's Church, the museum's attractive baroque palace home was receiving much-needed renovation at the time of research. The museum moved out in July 2010, but it's not known when the city's archaeological and cultural exhibits will return.

Gagarin Park PARK
Flanking the Teteriv River about 1.5km south of the centre, this park is a hive of activity in the summer months and serves up great views of the river gorge and the forest beyond, accessible via the Berdychivsky bridge over the gorge. To reach the park, follow bul Stary to its southern terminus.

St Sophia's Church CHURCH
(vul Kafedralna) With its distinctive ochre-and-white exterior, double clock towers and lavish interior, this dinky church dating from 1746 is a must-see for fans of baroque.

Lenin Statue STATUE
(maydan Soborny) The city's main square is dominated by a giant Lenin apparently emerging from a lump of bedrock. Two decades after the collapse of the Soviet Union, it's still as well cared for as ever.

SEVEN WONDERS OF UKRAINE

In 2007 a poll was held across Ukraine to find the 'Seven Wonders of Ukraine'. Over 77,000 people voted for their favourite place from a list of 21 locations. In the end there was no clear winner, but the poll at least raised awareness among Ukrainians about the fascinating places their country possesses.

The results:

» 1/2. Joint winners were Uman's Sofiyivka Park (p75) and Kyiv's Kyevo-Pecherska lavra (p43)

» 3/4. Joint third place went to Kamyanets-Podilsky (p79) and Khortytsya Island (p228)

» 5. Khersones, Crimea (p172)

» 6. St Sophia's Cathedral, Kyiv (p34)

» 7. Khotyn Fortress (p134)

📖 Sleeping & Eating

For more places to eat, head for the attractive pedestrian zone on vul Mykhaylivska where there are several cafes and bars with outdoor summer terraces. There are plenty of supermarkets for snackers, picnickers and self-caterers.

Zhytomyr Hotel　　SEMI-RENOVATED SOVIET **$**
(📞234 43; maydan Peremohy; s/d from 230/260uah) The remaining Soviet-style rooms here are perfectly functional and clean, but not the great deal they once were. Renovated rooms are slightly overpriced for what you get, meaning the classier renovated rooms at the Ukraina Hotel are much better value. A breakfast of sorts is included in the room rate, a rarity at most Soviet slab hotels.

Ukraina Hotel　　RENOVATED SOVIET **$$**
(📞472999; vul Kyivska 3; dm/s/d 116/230/424uah) All rooms here have undergone post-Soviet facelifts and the hotel has a much friendlier feel than the Zhytomyr. The doubles are actually suites, and for those looking for a touch of USSR nostalgia, some balconies have views overlooking the Lenin statue on maydan Soborny. The hotel is also known for its Georgian restaurant, Pirosmani.

Chas Poyisty　　UKRAINIAN CANTEEN **$**
(pl Peremohy 3; meals around 20uah; ⏱9am-11pm Mon-Fri, from 10am Sat & Sun) When it's 'time to eat' (a translation of the name), join the feeding frenzy at this cheap, quick and painless self-service canteen just across from the mounted tank on pl Peremohy. Serves all the usual favourites from across the ex-USSR, plus decent coffees and beers.

Schultz　　BEER HALL **$$**
(vul Peremohy 1; mains 20-90uah; ⏱10.30am-last customer; 🍺) This underground Ukrainian interpretation of a Czech microbrewery restaurant feels more like an American bar abutting a subterranean chemical plant (no romantic copper brewing vats here). But the service is pleasant, the meat-heavy menu tasty and the commendable wheat beer and dark ale, both brewed on the premises, go down a treat on scorching days.

❶ Getting There & Away

BUS The simplest way to make Zhytomyr a day trip from Kyiv is to take a (virtually) nonstop *marshrutka* (fixed-price minibus; 30uah, two hours) from outside the main train station. These arrive at and depart from Zhytomyr's bus station, a 1uah trolleybus ride from the centre. Other *marshrutky* leave from Kyiv's Zhytomyrska metro station (near the western end of the red line) but are harder to track down. Most other public buses (frequent) and trains (sporadic) to and from Kyiv take much longer (three to four hours).

Berdychiv БЕРДИЧІВ

📞0414 / POP 86,200

You'd never guess today that this sleepy town on the southern edge of Polissya was once an important intellectual centre and hotbed of Jewish culture. At the turn of the 19th century, Berdychiv's population was more than 80% Jewish. The Nazis took care of that, executing just about every one of the city's 39,000 Jews and burying them in mass graves on the town's outskirts. These days Berdychiv's Jewish community numbers only several hundred, but the city remains an important pilgrimage site for followers of revered Hasidic master Levi Yitzhak (1740–1810) who is buried in the town's remarkable Jewish cemetery.

The website www.berdichev.org is a good resource for information on the city.

⊙ Sights

Jewish Cemetery　　JEWISH CEMETERY
(Evreysky Kladovyshche; vul Lenina) Levi Yitzhak's mausoleum is in Berdychiv's eerie, overgrown Jewish Cemetery. While the mausoleum itself has been looked after, several-hundred odd boot-shaped tombstones lie hideously askew and virtually hidden by weeds, neglected almost to the point of disbelief. Many tombstones, etched with barely legible Hebrew inscriptions, lie flat on the ground.The graves predate the Nazis by at least several decades, but it was the Nazis who sealed the cemetery's fate by leaving no Jews behind to care for it.

A walk through the cemetery is moving and awe-inspiring. The effect is magnified by the solitude of the place. Despite its sorry state, it has fared better than the many Jewish cemeteries in Ukraine that have been buried and lost forever. It is thus a symbol of defiance and a powerful, important and rare reminder of the country's rich pre-Holocaust Jewish past.

The cemetery is about 15 minutes' walk north of Berdychiv's town centre just beyond where a set of railway lines cross the main road to Zhytomyr. The entrance is across from a petrol station.

BERDYCHIV'S KILLING FIELDS

Those who are interested can try to hunt down the two **mass burial sites** that lie outside the town. The first one is about 3km west of the monastery complex on the Khmelnytsky highway. A memorial on the right side of the highway commemorates the 18,640 'Soviet citizens' killed here in September 1941 – like all Soviet Holocaust monuments it makes no mention of Jews. The actual burial site, marked by a plaque with Hebrew writing, is hidden under a clump of low-lying trees about 150m into the cow pasture behind the Soviet plaque. A second burial site, where another 18,000 Jews died, is another 1km towards Khmelnytsky on the left side of the highway. At both sites the Nazis shot their victims in the back of the head and let their slumped bodies fall into pre-dug pits.

Berdychiv Castle   MONASTERY COMPLEX
(Soborna pl) The impressive brick-walled complex hogging the horizon as you approach Berdychiv from Khmelnytsky is widely known as the castle *(krepost),* but it's actually a 17th-century Carmelite monastery. The fortresslike defensive walls and towers were built in the late 18th century. Sadly, it's not open to the public.

St Barbara Church   CHURCH
(vul Karalipnika) Berdychiv has links to two great 19th-century literary figures: Joseph Conrad was born in Berdychiv (1857), and Honoré de Balzac was married here (1850) in this rose-tinted neoclassical church. Look out for the brass plaque celebrating the event.

⌷ Sleeping

Berdychiv is best visited as a day trip from, or en route to, Vinnytsya or Zhytomyr. If you do want to stay the night there's only one place to bed down, so book ahead.

Hotel Mirabella   HOTEL $
(☑320 190; vul Lenina 20; standard/deluxe r 230/300uah) Well located within walking distance of the Jewish cemetery, Berdychiv's sole lodgings boast unimaginative rooms with satellite TV hook-up and fridge, an erratic hot water supply and occasional power blackouts.

❶ Getting There & Away

BUS Several buses an hour head this way from Zhytomyr (12uah, one hour) terminating at Berdychiv's central bus station. However, the station is a long way from anywhere so ask to be dropped off in the town centre. There are buses or *marshrutky* at least every hour to Vinnytsya (20uah, two hours) and Kyiv (35uah), which is 31 hours away by bus or 21 hours by *marshrutka*.

PODILLYA

Podillya is the borderland within the country whose name means 'borderland'. Podillya is the bridge between the stolid, Russia-leaning east and the pro-European south. A swing district politically, topographically it's more predictable: flat and agricultural. The iconic image of bright blue sky over vast wheat field (possibly the inspiration for the colours of the Ukrainian flag) is practically inescapable here. But Podillya is not all farms and flatlands. Castle hunters will find business to attend to in the region's southern half, particularly in the 'rock island' city of Kamyanets-Podilsky. And there are a handful unusual sites, including a Hitler bunker and a missile museum, scattered about the region for those with time to explore.

Uman УМАНЬ

☑0474 / POP 87,700

All roads in Ukraine seem to pass through this central hub, home of relentlessly romantic Sofiyivka Park and the final resting place of the revered Hasidic Rabbi Nachman of Bratslav. Visiting Uman is a perfect way to break up the journey between Kyiv and Odesa, or in a pinch, the town can be visited as a long day trip from either city. Beyond the park and the tomb, this is one of many places in Ukraine where time seems to have stopped c 1985.

Nash Svit publishes a great city map, filled with information on the park. It's available at **Knyhy** (vul Sadova 1; ⊙9am-5pm Mon-Fri, 9am-2pm Sat) in the town centre.

◉ Sights

Sofiyivka Park   LANDSCAPED PARK
(vul Sadova; admission 12uah, free before 9am, after 6pm & all winter; ⊙6am-10pm summer,

6am-9pm rest of year) Sofia Pototsky was a legendary beauty, and Uman's stunning park is her husband Count Felix' monument to her physical perfection. Having bought Sofia for two million zloty from her former husband (she had been sold into slavery at an early age by her parents), the Polish count set to landscaping this 150-hectare site with grottoes, lakes, waterfalls, fountains, pavilions and 500 species of tree. The result, completed in 1802, was Ukraine's answer to Versailles.

A map at the park entrance describes the history of the park in English and points the way to the various highlights, most bearing sentimental names like **Island of Love** and **Grotto of Venus**. The park is such a superlative piece of landscape architecture that you do not need to be a park lover to appreciate it. In summer, you can hire boats to traverse the park's many ponds. As it turns out, Sofia broke Felix' heart before he died, having an affair with his son.

Tours of the park are available in English (400uah). However, these are tediously detailed, so only commit if you're *really* interested. The park is about a 10-minute walk from the centre of Uman, down vul Sadova.

Rabbi Nachman's Tomb TOMB
(vul Pushkina) To visit the tomb of Rabbi Nachman, head towards Sofiyivka Park, and about halfway down vul Sadova, turn right onto vul Pushkina.

🛏 Sleeping & Eating

During Rosh Hashana most Uman residents rent out their flats to pilgrims or tourists. The rest of the year you're limited to the following.

Hotel Sofiyivka UNRENOVATED SOVIET $
(☑433 527; vul Sadova 53; dm/s/d from 50/100/200uah) This faded number has seen only token renovations since the 1980s, but the location next to the park entrance is a major drawcard. The hilarious price list posted at reception features 'rooms without comfort' (a direct translation of the Russian for 'without bathroom') – perhaps someone should point out this linguistic faux pas (we didn't). The restaurant often heaves with Uman's shaven-headed and short-skirted celebrating weddings to a techno beat.

Uman Hotel UNRENOVATED SOVIET $
(☑452 632; vul Radyanska 7; r with shared/private bathroom per person from 50/92uah) You would expect much, much worse from this centrally located Soviet-style hotel. The rooms, while tatty, are well attended to by Stakhanovite maids, the beds aren't deal-breakers and the communal showers have been spruced up. No breakfast, but still one of Ukraine's true bargains.

Celentano PIZZERIA $
(vul Radyanska 15; pizzas around 20uah) Ukraine's ubiquitous pizza chain is a blessing in restaurant-starved Uman.

Kadubok Shynok UKRAINIAN $
(vul Radyanska 7; mains around 20uah) On the east side of Uman Hotel, this cafe-cum-restaurant serves Ukrainian and Russian classics including tasty *borshch*.

ⓘ Getting There & Away

BUS Uman is located 210km south of Kyiv and 280km north of Odesa. Most Autolux and other buses between the two cities stop at Uman's bus station. To and from Kyiv, these buses are a better option than private *marshrutky* (50uah, three hours) from the main bus station or train station, as the journey time is around the same. Buses take around four hours to reach Odesa. Services for Vinnytsya (three hours) and Khmelnytsky (five hours) are sporadic, but there are a few per day.

PILGRIMS FLOCK TO PODILLYA

Ever since the death of Rabbi Nachman (1772–1810), Jewish pilgrims have flocked to his graveside in Uman every Jewish New Year (Rosh Hashana) to pay homage to this 18th-century sage who founded the Breslov branch of Hasidism.

The rabbi was born in Medzhybizh, made his name in Bratslav (Breslov), near Vinnytsya, and died of tuberculosis in Uman at the young age of 38. On his deathbed, Nachman promised his followers that he would save and protect anyone who came to pray beside his tomb. Today some 20,000 Jews answer his call at Rosh Hashana, and at any time of year you'll find a handful of devout worshippers – male and female – praying at his gravesite.

Pilgrimages also take place to the grave of the Baal Shem Tov (Besht), Rabbi Nachman's grandfather and the founder of Hasidism, in Medzhybizh (p78); to Levi Yitzhak's grave in Berdychiv (p73); and to Bratslav (p78).

Vinnytsya ВІННИЦЯ

☎0432 / POP 370,000

Straddling a kink in the River Pivdenny Buh, Vinnytsya is another perfectly pleasant city that one would never expect to find hidden amid central Ukraine's endless wheat, sunflower and sugar-beet fields. It famously plays host to the embalmed body of a renowned Russian doctor and to one of Hitler's bunkers, but its true appeal lies in its centre, where several churches, a park and a pleasant pedestrian street compete for the attention of travellers. Vinnytsya is also a convenient jumping-off point for some interesting excursions in southern Podillya.

The city has a snazzy website in English, www.vinnytsatourism.com.ua, with loads of practical information, though some sections are slightly out of date.

◉ Sights & Activities

Pirogov Chapel   TOMB

(vul Pyrohova 195; admission 7uah; ◷10am-5.30pm) The second-most famous embalmed corpse in the former Soviet Union (after Lenin in Moscow) rests in the basement of a chapel in the suburb of Pyrohove about 6.5km southwest of Vinnytsya centre. Nikolai Pirogov was a Russian medical pioneer who invented a type of cast as well as a revolutionary anaesthesia technique. His wife had him embalmed when he died in Vinnytsya in 1881 and chose the chapel as his final resting place. The body is said to be much better preserved than Lenin's younger corpse. This is without question one of Ukraine's oddest sites. Take rare bus 13 or *marshrutka* 70 or 48.

SILLY SOUVENIRS

Here are Lonely Planet's five silliest Ukrainian souvenirs, compiled on our travels around the country:

» Pair of woman's breasts fashioned from Carpathian wool fleece

» Replica traffic-police baton with pre-attached $100 dollar bribe

» Made-in-China replica of the Virgin Mary's footprint from Pochayiv

» Caviar on toast fridge magnet

» Osama bin Laden *matryoshka* (Russian doll)

Pirogov Museum   HOUSE MUSEUM

(vul Pyrohova 155; admission 16uah; ◷10am-5.30pm) About 1.5km before you get to the chapel containing Pirogov's body, you can see his house, now a museum. It's actually more interesting than you'd expect, and not just because of the Soviet character of the place (the Soviets claimed Pirogov as a hero many years after his death because his inventions saved countless lives in the world wars). The doctor's anatomical sketches are also quite interesting, and one room remains unchanged from the surgeon's era. Bus 13 or *marshrutka* 70 or 48 pass the entrance on their way to the suburb of Pyrohove.

Wehrwolf   BUNKER RUINS

WWII buffs might fancy a trip out to the remains of Hitler's forward bunker, 8km north of Vinnytsya and 500m to the east of the town of Stryzhavka. Hitler visited this bunker a couple of times (accounts vary) between May 1942 and July 1943. Presumably it was on one of these visits that he ordered the execution of the 15,000 Ukrainian slave labourers who built the complex – he was ostensibly worried that they would spill the beans about the bunker's location. At its peak the Wehrwolf complex consisted of three bunkers and 20 standing structures, complete with swimming pool, movie theatre and casino. The Nazis blew it all up on their retreat in 1944. Today there's not a whole lot to see here besides some large concrete fragments of the bunker in an otherwise empty field – which is arguably more affecting than the typical Soviet monument. To get here take a taxi (for about 60uah return) from Vinnytsya.

Regional Museum   MUSEUM

(vul Soborna 19; admission 5uah; ◷10am-6pm Tue-Sun) This large and diverse museum is well worth an hour or two for its interesting archaeological artefacts, bug-eyed taxidermy and large WWII exhibition with Soviet propaganda posters galore. Other highlights include a 30,000-year-old mammoth skeleton, pieces of Scythian gold ornament and some Scythian-era stone figures.

Orange Revolution Monument   MONUMENT

(maydan Nezalezhnosti) Vinnytsya's epicentre is maydan Nezalezhnosti (Independence Sq), where major demonstrations and meetings were held during the 2004 Orange Revolution. A rather inconspicuous monument on its western side keeps alive the memory of those heady days.

War Veterans Museum   MUSEUM

(admission 3uah; ☺10am-6pm Tue-Sun) The redbrick clock tower at the end of pedestrian vul Kozytskoho houses an interesting museum, where you'll find tributes to the 167 young local men who made the ultimate sacrifice in the Soviet-Afghan War.

Transfiguration Church   CHURCH

(vul Soborna 23) Next door to the Regional Museum, this light-yellow, gold-domed church dating from 1758 is worth checking out for its dim and atmospheric painted interior.

🛏 Sleeping

Podillya   RENOVATED SOVIET $$

(☎592 233; www.vintur.com.ua; vul Pushkina 4; s/d from 300/400uah; ✷) By the time you pitch up in Vinnytsya, the Soviet furnishings and fittings in all the rooms here will be but a faint memory, making this Vinnytsya's top digs, at least for the time being. It also has a handy in-house tourist agency and a swanky restaurant on the premises.

Vinnytsya   RENOVATED SOVIET $

(☎610 332; vul Soborna 69; s/d from 240/300uah) A member of the once prestigious Savoy group (along with the Ukraina across the road), the Vinnytsya is quite a good deal. Even the cheapest rooms are clean and comfortable, and (in places skin-deep) renovation efforts are in evidence throughout. High ceilings and extras such as a minibar and in-room phones make this place feel decidedly un-Soviet. Give the awful and awfully overpriced 42uah breakfast a miss.

Ukraina Hotel   HOTEL

(vul Kozytskoho 36) Occupying an opulent 19th-century building in a prime location at the maydan Nezalezhnosti end of vul Kozytskoho, this grand old dame was undergoing a comprehensive refit at the time of research. It's set to reopen as sorely needed luxury-end lodgings sometime in 2011. When it does, it will be the best place to stay between Kyiv and Lviv.

🍴 Eating

For a city of this size there are surprisingly few places to eat in the centre. The highly visible 'golden arches' just off maydan Nezalezhnosti are a blessing here, even if you ain't lovin' it.

Masay Mara   CAFE $

(vul Hrushevskoho 70; mains 15-50uah) One of a handful of places along Hrushevskoho, this funky coffeehouse has an African theme (think cave drawings and lots of rough-hewn wood), but the menu is firmly Eurasian. The outdoor seating draws a crowd in the evenings, as does the real fire in winter.

Celentano   PIZZERIA $

(vul Soborna 43; pizzas around 20uah; ☺10am-11pm) If you've been in the country a long time, you may have grown weary of Ukrainian flavour pizzas, but the Vinnytsya branch also does a good line in pancakes, salads and soups.

ℹ Getting There & Away

BUS From the **Central Bus Station** (vul Kyivska 8) services fan out to points north, east and south, including frequent buses to Berdychiv (20uah, 1½ hours), Zhytomyr (31uah, 2½ hours) and Bratslav (15uah, 1½ hours). The West Bus Station, about 4km west of the centre on Khmelnytsky shose, services western Ukrainian cities, including Lviv, Khmelnytsky and Sharhorod (16uah, two hours).

TRAIN Vinnytsya is a major stop for many east–west trains, including international services. More than a dozen passenger trains daily connect Vinnytsya with both Kyiv (70uah to 90uah, around three hours) and Lviv (120uah, around seven hours). The quickest way to and from Kyiv is on either the Kyiv–Kamyanets-Podilsky or Kyiv-Khmelnytsky express trains (50uah, 2½ hours). There are also many connections to Odesa (100uah, seven hours).

ℹ Getting Around

The train station is about 3km east of Vinnytsya's centre and is linked to it by trams 1 and 4. If arriving by bus, turn left out of the central bus station and walk around 100m to pl Zhovtneva from where any tram will take you into the city centre.

Around Vinnytsya

There are a couple of interesting side trips from Vinnytsya, especially if you are interested in Jewish heritage sites. The village of Bratslav, 50km southeast of Vinnytsya, is where Rabbi Nachman lived and wrote most of his teachings before moving to Uman. Several of Nachman's disciples are buried in a shrinelike **cemetery** on a lovely hillside overlooking a river. Jewish pilgrims allege that the graves have healing powers.

WORTH A TRIP

NUCLEAR MISSILE MUSEUM

It's not easy to find, but deep in Ukraine's agricultural heartland, 30km north of Pervomaysk, lies arguably Ukraine's coolest museum. The **Museum of Strategic Missile Troops** (☎05161-732 18; admission 20uah), better known as the Nuclear Missile Museum, was formerly a nuclear missile launch facility.

The highlight is the journey taking you 12 storeys underground in a Brezhnev-era elevator to the control room (you may have to pay the guides extra to do this), where you can't help thinking that once upon a time a simple push of a button could have ended civilisation as we know it. You can even sit at the desk of doom, hand hovering over the button, and pretend to take that fateful call on an old Soviet phone.

The facility controlled 10 missiles, each of which lay hidden in subterranean silos near the control room. In the grounds of the museum are four huge decommissioned intercontinental ballistic missiles (ICBM), including a 75ft SS-18 Satan rocket, the Soviets' largest ICBM. There were actually no Satan rockets at this complex and this particular specimen was hauled in from Baikanor, Kazakhstan. Ukraine's facility was for shorter-range missiles targeting Europe.

It's a fascinating museum, but there are no English guides and getting here is a hassle unless you're driving from Kyiv to Odesa. From Kyiv, turn left (towards Holovanivsk) about 50km after Uman and follow the signs to the museum (about 40km). From Uman it's a 270uah, one-hour taxi ride (though finding a taxi driver who's heard of the place is difficult). Another option is to take a *marshrutka* from Mykolayiv in southern Ukraine (see p154) to Pervomaysk (40uah, 2½ hours) and continue by taxi to the museum (90uah one way).

Southwest of Vinnytsya is the *shtetl* of **Sharhorod**. The *shtetl* originated in Ukraine and the one in Sharhorod is said be the best-preserved example in the country. But it may not be that way for long. Sharhorod's *shtetl* is dying; its 16th-century **fortress synagogue** (used as a liquor factory in Soviet times) and many of the houses clustered around it have been abandoned to the elements.

Sharhorod also has a sprawling **Jewish cemetery** with thousands of exquisitely carved tombstones, some dating as far back as the 17th century. To get to it, follow the lane to the right of the post office down the hill, bearing left and crossing the creek. Then follow the trail up the hill bearing left and you will see the black cemetery gate marked with three large Stars of David.

For details on getting to Bratslav and Sharhorod, see p77.

Khmelnytsky & Medzhybizh
ХМЕЛЬНИЦЬКИЙ & МЕДЖИБІЖ

☎0382 / POP 261,600

Khmelnytsky, the gateway to western Ukraine, has little to divert tourists, but it is a convenient transport junction for those looking to get to Lviv from Kamyanets-Podilsky or from other off-the-beaten-track destinations in central Ukraine. It's also a convenient jumping-off point for the village of Medzhybizh, 30km to the east.

Besides being the birthplace of Hasidism, Medzhybizh possesses delightful rural charm, and a mighty 16th-century **fortress** (www.mezhibozh.com; admission 10uah; ⊙10am-6pm Tue-Sun), which stands at the confluence of two rivers.

If you get stuck in Khmelnytsky for a night, try the **train station rest rooms** (s/d 130/170uah) or **Eneida Hotel** (☎718 018; www.eneida.km.ua; vul Teatralna 8; s/d from 160/190uah; ❊), which boasts both tastefully renovated rooms and survivable unrenovated examples of a more Soviet vintage.

❶ Getting There & Away

BUS Private *marshrutky* zip down to Kamyanets-Podilsky every 30 minutes or so from the Maslozavod (Маслозавод; Cooking Oil Factory) stop on Khmelnytsky's southern edge (30uah, 1½ hours). Avoid the slow, packed, public buses and *marshrutky* to Kamyanets-Podilsky that leave from the bus station (300m from the train station). Myriad *marshrutky* connect the train station with the Maslozavod stop.

Any eastbound bus from the bus station gets you to Medzhybizh (8uah, 45 minutes).

TRAIN Over 20 trains pass through Khmel-nytsky on their way to Lviv (80uah, four hours) and Kyiv (95uah, six to eight hours), which is also serviced by two daily express trains (95uah, 4½ hours). One of these continues to Kamyanets-Podilsky. There are also four connections to Odesa (80uah, seven to eight hours), the most convenient of which is overnight train 172 departing at 10.30pm.

Kamyanets-Podilsky
КАМ'ЯНЕЦЬ-ПОДІЛЬСЬКИЙ

☏03849 / POP 102,000

Kamyanets-Podilsky is the sort of place that has writers lunging for their thesauruses in search of superlatives. Even words like 'dramatic', 'stunning' and 'breathtaking' just will not do. Like the Swiss capital of Bern, or Český Krumlov in the Czech Republic, the town is located where a sharp loop in a river has formed a natural moat. However, Kamyanets-Podilsky is much wilder and less commercial than these other places, and attracts a fraction of their visitor numbers.

The wide tree-lined Smotrych River canyon is 40m to 50m deep, leaving the 11th-century old town standing clearly apart on a tall, sheer-walled rock 'island'. According to an oft-told legend, when the Turkish Sultan Osman arrived to attack the town in 1621, he asked one of his generals, 'Who has built such a mighty town?' 'Allah', came the reply, to which the Sultan responded, 'Then let Allah himself conquer it', and bid a hasty retreat.

Schizophrenic KP is really a tale of two cities – the noisy and chaotic Soviet new town, where most of the hotels are located, and the quieter old town where all of the sights are gathered. The latter sometimes gives the impression of having been abandoned by locals c 1950 for the Soviet utopia across the river. Vul Knyaziv Koriatorychiv runs from the bus station in the new town to the New Bridge, which crosses into the old town. There's no tourist office, nor are there any plans to open one.

History

Named after the stone on which it sits, Kamyanets-Podilsky existed as early as the 11th century as a Kyivan Rus settlement. Like much of western Ukraine, the town spent periods under Lithuanian and Polish rule, with the latter dominating from the 15th to 17th centuries. Unlike much of western Ukraine, however, it fell briefly to the Ottoman Turks, who conquered it with a tremendous army in 1672 and ruled for 27 years. After being returned to Polish rule, Kamyanets-Podilsky was conquered in 1793 by the Russians. They used its fortress as a prison for Ukrainian nationalists. In 1919 the town became the temporary capital of the short-lived Ukrainian National Republic. During WWII the Germans used the old town as a Jewish ghetto, where an estimated 85,000 people died. Intensive fighting and air raids destroyed some 70% of the old town.

◉ Sights

Fortress   FORTRESS

(Фортеця; adult/child 12/6uah; ◷9am-7pm, to 6pm Mon) Built of wood in the 10th to 13th centuries, then redesigned and rebuilt in stone by Italian military engineers in the

---

UKRAINE'S WORLD HERITAGE SITES

There are just four Unesco World Heritage sites in Ukraine (http://whc.unesco.org/en/statesparties/ua), although another 15 have been nominated for future consideration, with the town of Kamyanets-Podilsky one of the strongest candidates for inclusion. The four already inscribed on the list include two transnational entries.

The Danube Delta Biosphere Reserve (p156) is also part of Unesco's global network of biosphere reserves.

» **St Sophia's Cathedral** (p34) and **Kyevo-Pecherska lavra** (p43) – a joint entry from Kyiv

» **Lviv** (p89) – Lviv's historic centre made the list in 1998

» **Primeval Beech Forests of the Carpathians** – consisting of 10 separate patches of forest stretching from Rakhiv into Slovakia

» **Struve Geodetic Arc** – a chain of scientific survey markers (1816–55) in a long arc from Norway to the Black Sea

CENTRAL UKRAINE PODILLYA

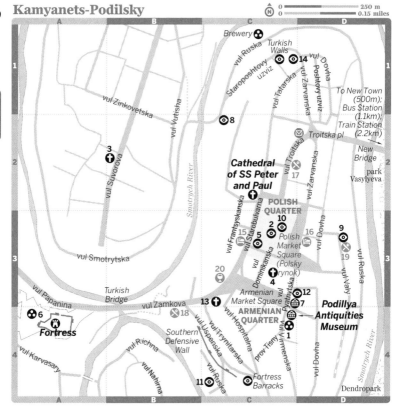

16th century, KP's fortress is a complete mishmash of styles. But the overall impression is breathtaking, and if Ukraine ever gets its act together as a tourist destination, the view from the **Turkish Bridge** leading to the fortress will become one of the country's iconic, front-page vistas. The name of the bridge is slightly misleading, as it's essentially a medieval structure whose arches were filled in and fortified by Turks in the 17th century. It's supposed to be closed to vehicles during the day.

The fortress is in the shape of a polygon, with nine towers of all shapes and sizes linked by a sturdy wall. In the middle of it all is a vast courtyard. The **New East Tower** (1544) is directly to your right as you enter the fortress and contains a well and a huge winch stretching 40m deep through the cliff to bring up water.

Just beyond the New East Tower, an unmarked white building houses a fantastic museum, which romps through the history of KP and Ukraine over the last century in a jumble of nostalgia-inducing exhibits. Two revolutions bookend the collections – the blood-red silken flags of 1917 looking symbolically more potent than the limp orange banners of 2004.

On the right (north) side of the courtyard, stairs lead downwards to the **debtors' hole**, where people behind in loan repayments were kept until their debt was covered. Continue through the debtors' hole and try to spot a cannonball, pink with age, burrowed in the fortress' north wall.

The first tower on your left (south) as you enter the courtyard is the **Papska** (pope's) or **Karmalyuk Tower** (1503–17), which was used as a prison. The wax figure inside is Ustym Karmalyuk, a loveable rogue who, legend has it, was so handsome that women tossed strands of their hair down to him. He eventually accumulated enough hair to make a rope and escape one of his three incarcerations here between 1817 and 1823.

Behind the fortress to the west are the remains of the largely earthen **New Fortress** (Нова фортеця).

POLISH QUARTER

Under the medieval Magdeburg Laws, each of the old town's four major ethnic groups (Poles, Ukrainians, Armenians and Jews) occupied a different quarter. The focus of the old Polish Quarter is the Polish Market Sq (Polsky rynok), the old town's main piazza. In summer this is the site of the **Little Town of Souvenirs** (Сувенірне Містечко; *Suvenirne Mistechko*), basically a mocked-up street of baroque cottages proffering tacky mementos.

Cathedral of SS Peter & Paul   CATHEDRAL
(Кафедральний собор святих Петра та Павла; Polsky rynok) Through a small triumphal gate in the northwest corner of Polish Market Sq lies this fascinating cathedral, KP's busiest place of worship. One feature of the building perfectly illustrates how the Polish and Turkish empires collided in Kamyanets-Podilsky. Built in 1580 by the Catholic Poles, the cathedral was converted into a mosque when the Turks took over in the late 17th century; they even built an adjacent 42m-high minaret. When the town was handed back to the Poles by treaty in 1699, the Turks specifically stipulated that the minaret could not be dismantled. So the Poles topped it with its current 3.5m-tall golden statue of the Virgin Mary instead.

Ratusha   TOWN HALL
(Ратуша; Polsky rynok) Polish Market Sq is lorded over by the tall 14th-century Ratusha (town hall). The renovated peach-hued building now houses three single-room museums that are of limited interest unless you are into coins, medieval justice or the Magdeburg legal system, but there is a decent bar on the ground floor. In front of the Ratusha stands the enclosed **Armenian well** (Вірменська криниця; 1638), which looks more like a baroque chapel than a well.

Dominican Monastery   MONASTERY
(Домініканський монастир; vul Dominikanska) Vul Dominikanska cuts south from Polish Market Sq, linking it with the Armenian Quarter. Here you'll find the Dominican Monastery complex, some parts of which date from the 14th century. The buildings suffered serious damage during WWII but are now under constant restoration. The monastery Church of St Nicholas holds services in Ukrainian and Polish throughout the day.

ARMENIAN QUARTER

The Armenian quarter is centred around the quiet Armenian Market Sq, an elongated cobbled expanse to the south of the Polish Quarter. The Armenians are long gone, but the name remains.

Podillya Antiquities Museum   MUSEUM
(Експозиція старожитностей Поділля; vul Ivano-Predtechynska 2; adult/child 3/2uah; ⊙10am-6pm, to 5pm Mon) This imaginatively

AND THERE'S MORE...

Most visitors content themselves with a stroll from the New Bridge to the fortress and back, stopping off at a restaurant or cafe along the way. But if your legs are up to the job, there's so much more to explore in KP's run-down backstreets and lanes where forgotten chunks of the town's defences lurk.

Looking south from the New Bridge you can spot the **Potters' Tower** (Гончарська башта; 1583), so named because it was looked after by the town's potters. Twelve of these towers once lined the bank of the gorge along the perimeter of the island; seven or eight remain today.

At the northern edge of the old town is the still-functioning 16th-century **Vitryani (Windy) Gate** (Вітряні брама), where Peter the Great's hat blew off in 1711. Connected to the gate is the seven-storey stone **Kushnir (Furriers') Tower**, a defensive structure funded by artisans who lived nearby. From the tower, Staroposhtovy uzviz turns southwest and descends steeply into the ravine down to the **Polish Gate** (Польська брама). This gate was named after the historic Polish section of the city, which was located on the other side of the river, built around the hill dominated by the 19th-century Orthodox **Church of St George** (Церква Св Юрія), with its five cupolas painted in brilliant turquoise.

Both the Polish Gate and the **Ruska Gate** (Російська брама), on the south side of the isthmus in the old Ruthenian (Ukrainian) quarter, were built from the 16th to 17th centuries to guard the two most vulnerable entrances into the old town. Both gates were ingeniously fashioned with dyke mechanisms that could alter the flow of the Smotrych River and flood the entrances – an impressive engineering feat for the time.

presented museum with English explanations takes visitors through the archaeology of Podillya in six easy steps. You begin in a Stone Age cave and end in a courtyard of sculpted Slavic gods, passing through Trypillian, Scythian and early Slav dwellings along the way. Slavophiles will appreciate the exhibit on the Glagolitic script (forerunner to today's Cyrillic alphabet).

Picture Gallery   GALLERY
(Художня галерея; vul Pyatnytska 11; admission 4uah; ☉10am-6pm, to 5pm Mon) The permanent collections here are of wildly varying quality and some works are in downright wretched condition. But temporary exhibitions lift the mood and if the art on the walls doesn't impress, the elaborate parquet floors will.

Armenian Church   CHURCH
(Вірменська церква; vul Virmenska) Huge, decorative wrought-iron gates keep prying tourists out of this set of 15th-century church ruins, its perimeter still weeping masonry onto the cobbles below. The reconstructed defensive bell tower is now a small Ukrainian Orthodox chapel.

Russian Magistrate   MAGISTRATE
(Колишній Руський магістрат; vul Pyatnytska) There are some interesting old buildings on vul Pyatnytska, which branches off Armenian Market Sq. The building with a distinctive metal dragon projecting from its facade is the old Russian Magistrate, now the headquarters of **NIAZ Kamyanets** (НІАЗ Кам'янець; www.niazkamenec.org.ua), the body overseeing KP's conservation area. Check the website for information on occasional tours the organisation offers.

St Jehoshaphat's Church   CHURCH
(Колишній тринітарський; vul Starobulvarna) Heading towards the fortress along the main drag through the old town, you'll pass this baroque 18th-century Greek Catholic Church (formerly St Trinity's), fronted by sculptures of two saints who appear to be boogieing on down.

✖✦ Festivals & Events

Kamyanets-Podilsky has two marvellous festivals.

Kamyanets-Podilsky Days OPEN-AIR FESTIVAL
Held in mid-May; features street parties, concerts, parades and a picturesque hot-air balloon festival.

Terra Heroika Festival RE-ENACTMENT FESTIVAL
In early October; jousting, horsemanship and swordsmanship displays in the fortress and around town.

Sleeping

Hotel 7 Days HOTEL **$$**

(Готель 7 Днів; ☎690 69; www.7dney.com; vul Soborna 4; s/d from 260/440uah; ❄️🛜🏊) This vastly improved place in the new town impresses from the moment you walk into the air-conditioned, design-style lobby. Staff speak English, the service is professional and the room rate includes use of the swimming pool, breakfast *and* dinner, a sure-fire deal-clincher in eatery-poor KP. Our only criticism is the feeble wi-fi coverage, but overall this is a superb place to unzip your pack.

Hetman THEME HOTEL **$$**

(Гетьман; ☎970 27; www.hetman-hotel.com. ua; Polsky rynok 8; r/ste from 385/500uah; ❄️🛜) The mammoth rooms, great location

QUEEN OF THE CASTLE

Iryna Pustynnikova is Ukraine's original castle hunter. She runs the website http://castles.com.ua and doles out castle-hopping itineraries to anybody who asks. We caught up with Iryna in her hometown, Kamyanets-Podilsky, and asked her to pick the top 10 lesser-known castles in Ukraine.

» **Czerwonogrod** (Map p87) 'It's simply...wow! 100 years ago the guidebooks called it the most beautiful manor in Poland. For me it's the most beautiful place in the whole country.' From the 14th to 19th centuries; near Nyrkiv, 50km north of Chernivtsi.

» **Sydoriv Castle** (Map p71) 'It looks like an ocean liner sailing through a sea of maize and other vegetables.' Built in the 17th century; near Husyatyn, 60km northwest of Kamyanets-Podilsky.

» **Kudryntsi Castle** (Map p71) 'The landscapes are unbelievable, the ruins are very scenic and vivid, and tourists are rare birds here.' Early 17th century; 22km west of Kamyanets-Podilsky.

» **Nevytske Castle** (Map p115) 'Legend has it this very picturesque castle served as a shelter for Uzhhorod's girls – *nevesta* is the local word for "girl".' Built in the 16th century; 12km north of Uzhhorod.

» **Hubkiv Castle** (Map p87; Rivne oblast) 'It rises 32m over an area known as "Switzerland on the Sluch River". The views these castle ruins command are simply breathtaking. The fresh air that wafts forth from the surrounding forests inebriates the visitor like a good wine, and heals as well as any medicine.' From the 15th to 16th centuries.

» **Svirzh Castle** (Map p87) 'This picturesque Renaissance castle stands in its own park and is surrounded by water. Watch out for the female ghosts that locals claim wander the grounds.' Built in the 16th century; 55km northeast of Lviv.

» **Starostynsky Castle** (Map p87) 'None other than Batu-Khan (Genghis Khan's grandson, who led the Mongol invasion of Europe) put paid to the first fortress on this hill, overlooking the River Dnister.' Current building from 17th century; 23km north of Ivano-Frankivsk.

» **Olyka Castle** (Map p87) 'In summer, flowers perfume the courtyard of this once noble residence, though today you're more likely to meet white-coated doctors and pale-faced patients rather than the aristocratic Radziwills here, as it's now part of a hospital.' Built between 16th and 18th centuries; halfway between Lutsk and Rivne.

» **Berezhany Castle** (Map p87) 'This mighty, thick-walled Renaissance castle is now the haunt of grazing cows and mums with prams, but is still an impressive sight. The Zolota Lypa River grips the castle on two sides.' Built between 16th and 18th centuries; 50km southwest of Ternopil.

» **Chynadiyeve Castle** (Map p115) 'This striking building was once a hunting castle belonging to the Schönborn family. In the 1890s they gave it a pseudo-Gothic makeover and transformed it into a grand residence.' Ten kilometres northeast of Mukacheve.

in a town house on Polish Market Sq and easy-going staff make this atmospheric, 14-room theme hotel worth the extra hryvna. The walls are lined with paintings of all Ukraine's Hetmans (Cossack heads of state), an 11m-long tapestry bearing the words of the national anthem hangs in the stairwell and the Ukrainian restaurant (mains 20uah to 55uah) serves five types of *borshch*.

Amadeus Club   HOTEL $$$
(Амадеус Клаб; ☎912 10; www.amadeus-club.com; vul Starobulvarna 2; r from 816uah; ❄🛜) KP's plushest place to achieve REM is this spanking-new hotel, occupying a former Polish palace right in the thick of the old town. Not sure what the Polish *szlachta* (nobility) would make of the deep pile carpets, antique-style furniture and the baths in most rooms, but you'll love them. Bigger price just means bigger room here. Staff speak passable English.

TIU Hostel   HOSTEL $
(☎063 982 3048; vul Gagarina 69, apt 4; dm 100uah) The town's only stable backpacker hostel belongs to the TIU group, meaning a good standard of facilities and fun staff – nights out in KP and barbecues at Khotyn are regular activities. Only 10 beds, so book ahead.

Gala Hotel   HOTEL $$
(☎383 70; www.gala-hotel.com; vul Lesi Ukrainky 84; d/ste from 200/580uah) This is a solid midrange choice with a wide range of rooms – from cupboard-size twins to deluxe apartments with their own kitchens. It's about 15 minutes' walk south of the new town.

Filvarky Centre   RESORT HOTEL $
(☎332 31; www.filvarki.km.ua; vul Lesi Ukrainky 99; s/d from 70/95uah) This 30-room place south of the town centre is KP's version of a resort, with deck chairs arranged around a swimming pool outside. Couples will like the large if somewhat worn rooms, which have queen-sized beds, but all the rooms are pretty good value for money. Prices include breakfast.

✘ Eating & Drinking

Kafe Pid Bramoyu   UKRAINIAN $
(Каварня під Брамою; vul Zamkova 1A; mains 20-30uah) Although the service at this *shashlyk* (shish kebab) restaurant-cafe can be spotty, the view overlooking the fortress never takes a day off. The menu covers all the Ukrainian basics, including *deruny* (po-

tato pancakes) and *varenyky* (dumplings), plus fresh fish that you can pick out of their small pond. Portions are on the miserly side.

Hostynny Dvir   RUSSIAN $
(Гостинний двір; vul Troitska 1; mains 15-40uah) If you can forgive the spread-eagled bearskin pinned to the far wall, this refined restaurant has the best food in the old town, although service can be snail slow. The Russian menu is carnivore-friendly.

Stara Fortetsya   UKRAINIAN $
(Стара Фортеця; vul Valy 1; mains 12-30uah) Unfortunately you can only take drinks on the balcony, perched dramatically over a 40m cliff over the gorge. Inside is where the Ukrainian food is served. Located next to the Potters' Tower.

Kava Vid Politsmeystera   BAR
(Кава від Поліцмейстера; vul Zamkova) With cheap Lvivske *pyvo* (beer) on draught and a summer terrace, it's the best place in the old town for a drink.

Celentano   PIZZA $
(Челентано; vul Knyaziv Koriatorychiv 9; pizzas around 20uah) Ukraine's most popular pizza chain is typically mobbed with young locals.

Hunska Krytnytsa   CAFE $
(Ханська криниця; vul Soborna; mains 7-15uah; ⊙8.30am-10pm) No-frills Ukrainian cafe in the new town with summer tables tumbling out onto pedestrianised vul Soborna.

❶ Information

Post, internet & telephone office (Поштамт, Інтернет і Укртелеком; vul Soborna 9; internet per hr 4uah; ⊙post 9am-6pm Mon-Fri, to 4pm Sat, internet 8.30am-9pm Mon-Fri, 10am-10pm Sat & Sun)

Post office (Пошта; vul Troitska 2; ⊙9am-1pm & 2-6pm)

❶ Getting There & Away

BUS Buses to Chernivtsi depart from Kamyanets-Podilsky bus station (Автовокзал; 20uah, 2½ hours, at least every 30 minutes) and go via Khotyn (7uah, 45 minutes). There are two buses per day to Lviv (80uah, 6½ hours), two night buses to Odesa (160uah, 12 hours) and one uncomfortable overnighter to Kyiv (110uah, 10 hours).

TRAIN The express train 177 from Kyiv is the quickest way to reach Kamyanets-Podilsky. It departs Kyiv at 4.43pm (68uah, 6½ hours) and goes via Vinnytsya and Khmelnytsky. The return leg (train 178) departs Kamyanets-Podilsky at

1.55am. There's also an overnight service to and from Kyiv (88uah, 10 hours).

If coming from Lviv, Odesa or eastern Ukraine, your best bet is to take a train to Khmelnytsky and continue by train or *marshrutka* from there. From Lviv and elsewhere in western Ukraine you might also consider taking a train to Chernivtsi, and then a *marshrutka* to Kamyanets-Podilsky. There's one direct train to and from Odesa (104uah, 11½ hours).

 **Getting Around**

The bus station is within walking distance (two blocks east) of the new town centre. The train station is 1km north of the bus station. You can take bus 1 into the new or old town, or catch a taxi, which should cost no more than 20uah.

Marshrutka 19 goes between the new town and the Armenian Market Sq in the old town.

Lviv & Western Ukraine Львів & Західна Україна

POP 5.85 MILLION / AREA: 75,847 SQ KM

Includes »

Best Places to Eat

» Masonic Restaurant (p101)

» Dim Lehend (p101)

» Korona Vitovta (p111)

» Kupol (p101)

Best Places to Stay

» Vintage (p97)

» Leopolis Hotel (p97)

» Hotel Zaleski (p111)

» Kosmonaut Hostel (p97)

Why Go?

More quintessentially Ukrainian than the rest of the country, and distinctly more European, the west is all about its largest city, the Galician capital of Lviv. One of Ukraine's great hopes for tourism, the city is a truly captivating place, rich in historic architecture and with an indulgent coffee-house culture, but only a fraction of the tourist hordes who choke similar city-break destinations such as Krakow and Prague. Early signs of gentrification have yet to smother its shabby authenticity.

The Soviets ruled for only 50 years here, making the west the most foreigner-friendly province with less surly 'no-can-do' bureaucracy than in eastern regions. People here speak Ukrainian (rather than Russian) and show greater pride in Ukrainian traditions than elsewhere.

Away from Lviv, the moody Carpathian Mountains are a short bus ride away, as are historic Lutsk, the olde-worlde spa at Truskavets and the golden domes of Pochayiv Monastery.

When to Go?

Lviv

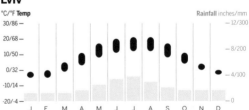

May Stroll through Lviv's centre on Sunday mornings, when church music wafts along the streets.

July Experience a Ukrainian summer of love at Pidkamin's Ethnofestival.

August Crowds of pilgrims gather at Pochayiv Monastery during the Feast of the Assumption.

History

Mongols overrunning Kyivan Rus in 1240 never made it as far west as the powerful province of Galicia-Volynia. They did occasionally knock on its door, but the region was largely left to enjoy self-rule under King Roman Mstyslavych, his son Danylo Halytsky and his descendants.

This idyllic state was shattered in the 1340s when Polish troops invaded, but western Ukraine never lost its taste for independence. Several centuries of Polish domination saw the rise of a unique Ruthenian identity, which is the basis for much contemporary Ukrainian nationalism. Many Galician *boyars* (nobles) – often sent from Poland, Germany or Hungary – adopted the Polish language and Roman Catholicism. However, the peasants, also known as Ruthenians, remained Orthodox. They were

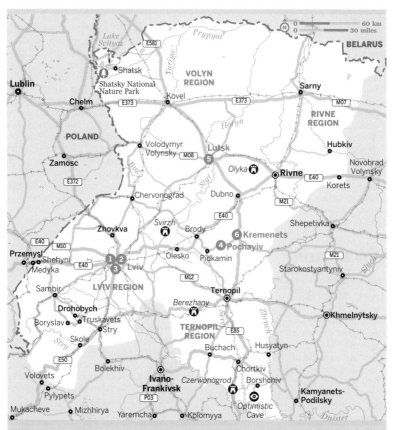

Lviv & Western Ukraine Highlights

1 Do a spot of cobble-surfing in **Lviv's historical centre** (p89), which is packed with churches, museums and eccentric restaurants

2 Make a caffeine-and-cake halt at **Lviv's coffeehouses** (p102), some of the best in the country

3 Pay your respects to Lviv's great and good of yesteryear at the city's amazing **Lychakivske Cemetery** (p89)

4 Join the Orthodox faithful for a pilgrimage to **Pochayiv Monastery** (p108) to find Ukraine's most devout atmosphere

5 Take a turn around **Lutsk's old quarter** (p110) for a blast from Western Ukraine's past

6 Head uphill to **Kremenets Fortress** (p109) for show-stopping views of the town's many churches

only persuaded to join the new Ukrainian Catholic Church, also known as the Uniate Church, in 1596 (thereby acknowledging the pope's spiritual supremacy) because this church agreed to retain Orthodox forms of worship. Other Ruthenians fled southeast to set up Cossack communities.

In 1772, Galicia became part of the Habsburg Austro-Hungarian Empire and to this day western Ukrainians touchingly remember the Austrians as (relatively) liberal, tolerant rulers. In other parts of the empire separatists suffered under the Austrian yoke, but in Ukraine the Habsburgs allowed Ukrainian nationalism to re-emerge and that made them good guys in this country. Western Ukraine even enjoyed a few days' independence as the Habsburg Empire collapsed at the end of WWI, but it soon found itself again under the dreaded Polish thumb.

Following the outbreak of WWII in September 1939, things went from bad to worse in local eyes. The Red Army marched in and asserted Moscow's control over the region for the first time in history. Finally dispatching the Nazis after bloody battles during WWII, the Soviets hung around until 1991, when the USSR imploded.

LVIV REGION

Lviv ЛЬВІВ

POP 735,000

Mysterious, edgy and architecturally lovely, Lviv boasts that it's Ukraine's least Soviet city. It may have a point. The city's Unesco World Heritage–listed centre was built like a rich layer-cake of neoclassical architecture in rococo, baroque, Renaissance and Gothic styles. There's nary a concrete Soviet apartment block in sight (in the centre, at least), and it has a deep-rooted coffee-house culture that is oh-so-central European.

Yet Lviv does retain a whiff of Sovietness that only broadens its appeal. Weathered *babushkas* sell pickled vegetables and honey at the city's Krakivsky Market. There's still the odd *gastronom* (food store), Volga and dodgy neon-lit slot-machine parlour scattered about. Opera tickets and tram rides are still priced for the people and Soviet slab hotels still offer rooms for the price of a five-star breakfast.

Over the past two decades many a travel pundit has predicted a plague of Krakow- or Prague-style stags and hens would descend on Lviv sooner or later. But the crowds have never materialised, possibly as the city 'lacks' budget airline connections to Western Europe. We don't want to emulate those erroneous pundits, but this situation may be about to change. The new airport being thrown up in time for Euro 2012 is very likely to attract an easyJet or Ryanair, so you may want to get here before they do.

The legacy for Lviv of just three football matches in 2012 will be resurfaced roads and straightened tram lines, new hotel rooms, the new-fangled airport and a definite focus on the visitor experience. The city is the only one in Ukraine to have a guide licensing system and one of only two boasting a completely municipally funded tourist office. Some very switched-on guys at city hall constantly look for ways to improve things, while local restaurateurs are letting their imaginations run amok. So forget Ukraine's capital of humour, Odesa, you'll find infinitely more smiles here in forward-looking Lviv.

History

Lviv (luh-*veev*) has had as many names as it has had rulers. It took its first name from Lev, the son of King Danylo Halytsky who founded a hilltop fort here on present-day Castle Hill in the 13th century. When the Poles took over 100 years later, the place became known as Lwo'w, as it still is in Poland. Austrians called it Lemberg between the 18th and 20th centuries, and still do. The Russians, who later christened it Lvov, continue to use this historical name. Most of its names – apart from Lemberg, which has many competing origins – can be traced back to 'lion', and the city has always taken the big cat as its symbol.

Lviv had another set of unwelcome occupiers who also called the place Lemberg – the Nazis. They invaded in 1941 and weren't driven back by the Soviets until 1944. During these three years, 136,000 people are reported to have died in Lviv's Jewish ghetto and nearly 350,000 in nearby concentration camps. For more about this era, read Robert Marshall's *In the Sewers of Lvov: A Heroic Story of Survival from the Holocaust*.

The Galician capital played a major role in the movement that led to Ukrainian independence in 1991. Ukrainian nationalism and the Greek Catholic Church re-emerged here in the late 1980s, and in the early 1990s its people unanimously elected nationalist politicians and staged mass demonstrations. Today, it still has its eyes focused firmly on Europe and has been a stronghold for Western-oriented politicians.

◉ Sights

Ploshcha Rynok SQUARE

Thanks to its splendid array of buildings Lviv was declared a Unesco World Heritage Site in 1998, and this old market square (Map p92) lies at its heart. The square was progressively rebuilt after a major fire in the early 16th century destroyed the original. The 19th-century **ratusha** (Ратуша; town hall) stands in the middle of the plaza, with fountains featuring Greek gods at each of its corners (you'll see these garbed in traditional Ukrainian embroidered shirts around 24 August, Ukrainian Independence Day). Vista junkies can climb the 65m-high neo-Renaissance **tower** (admission 5uah; ◔9am-6pm), though it's a hard slog to the top. Multilingual signs point the way to the ticket booth on the 4th floor.

Around 40 buildings in various states of repair line the square's perimeter. Most of these three- and four-storey buildings have uniform dimensions, with three windows per storey overlooking the square. This was the maximum number of windows allowed tax-free, and those buildings with four or more belonged to the extremely wealthy.

House No 4, the **Black Mansion** (Map p92), has one of the most striking façades. Built for an Italian merchant in 1588–89, it features a relief of St Martin on a horse. The **Kornyakt House** (Map p92) at No 6 is named after its original owner, a Greek merchant. An interesting row of sculptured knights along the rooftop cornice makes it a local favourite. Together, Nos 2 and 6 house the largest portion of the Lviv History Museum.

Lychakivske Cemetery CEMETERY

(Личаківське кладовище; Map p90; admission 10uah; ◔9am-6pm) Don't even think of leaving town until you've seen this amazing cemetery only a short tram ride from the centre. This is the Père Lachaise of Eastern Europe, with the same sort of overgrown grounds and Gothic aura as the famous Parisian necropolis (but containing less-well-known people). Laid out in the late 18th century, when Austrian Emperor Jo-

sef II decreed that no more burials could take place in churchyards, it's still the place Lviv's great and good are laid to rest.

Eagle eyes can try to spot the graves of revered nationalist poet Ivan Franko, Soviet gymnastics legend Viktor Chukarin, early 20th-century opera star Solomiya Krushelnytska, and some 2000 Poles who died fighting Ukrainians and Bolsheviks from 1918 to 1920. There's also a memorial to the Ukrainian insurgent army (UPA), who fought for independence against both the Nazis and Soviets. But ultimately you needn't recognise a single soul to be moved by the mournful photos of loved ones, ornate tombstones and floral tributes.

A good strategy is to combine a trip to the cemetery and the Museum of Folk Architecture and Life. The cemetery is one stop past the stop for the open-air museum on tram 7.

Prospekt Svobody BOULEVARD

Just in case it should ever slip your mind that Lviv is Ukraine's most patriotic large city, an enormous **statue of Taras Shevchenko** (Пам'ятник Тарасу Шевченку; Map p92) rises up in the middle of Prospekt Svobody (Freedom Avenue). A gift from the Ukrainian diaspora in Argentina, the statue of the revered national poet stands beside a wave-shaped relief of religious folk art. In summer, the broad pavement in the middle of the *prospekt* is the town's main hangout and the hub of Lviv life, where lovers pose for photos at Shevchenko's feet. People promenade along the strip of park, kids scoot around in rented electric cars, impromptu choirs form on park benches and wedding parties mill around shouting photo instructions. At the northern end of the boulevard is the 1897–1900 **Solomiya Krushelnytska Lviv Theatre of Opera and Ballet** (Map p92). At the southern end a **statue of Adam Michiewicz** (Статуя Адаму Міцкевичу; Map p92), the Polish poet, stands in pl Mitskevycha. Pr Svobody is closed to traffic at weekends.

Latin Cathedral CATHEDRAL

(Романо-Католицький собор; Map p92; pl Katedralna; admission 2uah) With various bits dating from between 1370 and 1480, this working cathedral is one of Lviv's most impressive churches. The church's exterior is most definitely Gothic while the heavily gilded interior, one of the city's most ornate, has a more baroque feel. The cannonball hanging by a chain off the cathedral's

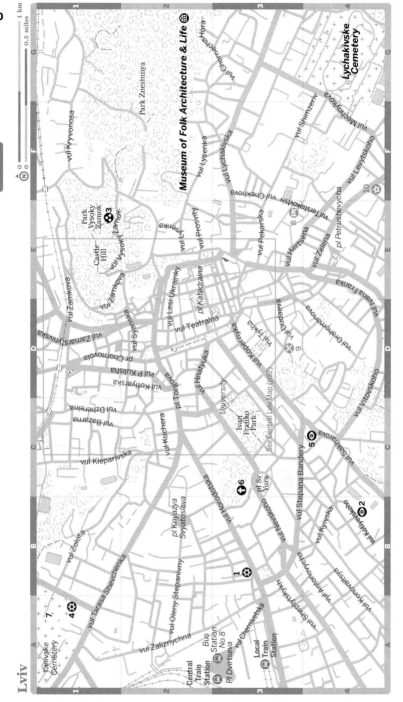

Lviv

N

0 _____ 1 km
0 _____ 0.5 miles

Museum of Folk Architecture & Life 🏛

Lychakivske Cemetery

Park Znesinnya

Park Vysoky Zamok

Castle Hill

vul Kryvonosa

vul Zamkova

vul Zamkova

vul Vysoky Zamok

vul Klymentia Hora

vul Lysenka

vul Lychakivska

vul Prosvity

vul Lysenka

vul Tershakivtsiv vul Chekhova

vul Mechnykova

vul Shimzeriv

vul Levytskoho

pl Petrushevycha

vul Petrushevycha

vul Zelena

vul Herstena

vul Pekarska

vul Nana Franka

vul Drahomanova

pl Katedralna

vul Lesi Ukrainky

vul Teatralna

pl Teatralna

vul Syanska

pr Chornovola

vul P Kulisha

vul Kotlyarska

vul Dzherelna

vul Bazarna

vul Kleparivska

vul Kuchera

vul Zamkova

vul Zamarstynivska

vul Dudaeva

vul Doroshenka

vul Kopernyka

vul TyKlia

University

Ivan Franko Park

See Central Lviv Map (p92)

vul Stepana Bandery

vul Horodotska

vul Nekrasova

pl Sv Yura

pl Knyazya Svyatoslava

vul Oleny Stepanivny

vul Tarasa Shevchenka

vul Zolota

Yanivske Cemetery

vul Zaliznychna

Bus Station No 8

Central Train Station

Pl Dvirtseva

Local Train Station

vul Chernivetska

vul Stryjsky

vul Antonovycha

vul Konovaltsia

vul Kyivska

vul Kolbereshko

vul Sakharova

vul Vitovskoho

1 🏟

2 ◎

3 😋

4 🏟

5 ◎

6 ✝

7 ✝

8 😋

10 ⚽

Lviv

corner miraculously failed to penetrate its walls during a historic battle. If you walk around the cathedral, you'll see a relief of Pope John Paul II on the other side, erected to commemorate his visit to Lviv in 2001.

Dominican Cathedral — CATHEDRAL
(Костьол домініканців; Map p92; pl Museyna) Dominating a small square to the east of pl Rynok is one of Lviv's signature sights, the large rococo dome of the Dominican Cathedral. Attached to the cathedral and to the left of the entrance is the **Museum of Religious History** (Музей історії релігії; admission 5uah; ⊙11am-6pm Tue-Sun), which was an atheist museum in Soviet times. The exhibition looks at all religions currently active in Ukraine and includes an 11th-century silver Byzantine reliquary holding the bodies of two saints.

East of the cathedral is a square where you'll see a **statue** of a monk holding a book. This is Federov, who brought printing to Ukraine in the 16th century. Fittingly, there's a second-hand book market here on weekends.

Armenian Cathedral — CATHEDRAL
(Вірменський собор; Map p92; vul Virmenska 7) By some accounts, Lviv has more than 100 churches and it's all too easy to overdose on ornate interiors and golden iconos-tases, but one church you should not miss is the elegant 1363 Armenian Cathedral. The placid cathedral courtyard is a maze of arched passageways and squat buildings festooned with intricate Caucasian detail. Stepping into the courtyard feels like entering another era. Outside, quaint, cobbled vul Virmenska was once the heart of the old Armenian ('Virmenska' in Ukrainian) quarter.

Lviv History Museum — MUSEUM
(Історичний музей; Map p92; per branch 5uah; ⊙all branches 10am-5.30pm Thu-Tue) Lviv's main museum is split into three collections dotted around pl Rynok. The best branch is at **No 6**. Here you can enjoy the Italian-Renaissance inner courtyard and slide around the exquisitely decorated interior in cloth slippers on the woodcut parquetry floor made from 14 kinds of hardwood. It was also here on 22 December 1686 that Poland and Russia signed the treaty that partitioned Ukraine. **No 2** covers 19th- and 20th-century history, including two floors dedicated to the Ukrainian nationalist movement. **No 24** expounds on the city's earlier history. The highlight is an enormous painting depicting the old walled city of Lviv in the 18th century. Pr Svobody was a moat. None of the branches of this museum have English translations.

Museum of Folk Architecture and Life — OPEN-AIR MUSEUM
(Музей народної архітектури і побуту; Muzey Narodnoyi Arkhitektury i Pobutu; Map p90; www.skansen.lviv.ua; vul Chernecha Hora 1; admission 10uah; ⊙9am-dusk Tue-Sun) This open-air museum displays different regional styles of farmsteads, windmills, churches and schools, which dot a huge park to the east of the city centre. Everything is pretty spread out here and a visit involves a lot of footwork. As an exhibition, it doesn't hold a candle to Kyiv's Pyrohovo Museum, but it's worth checking out if you're not heading to the capital. To get to the museum, take tram 7 from vul Pidvalna up vul Lychakivska and get off at the corner of vul Mechnykova. From the stop, walk 10 minutes north on vul Krupyarska, following the signs.

Boyim Chapel — CHAPEL
(Воїм Каплиця; Map p92; pl Katedralna; admission 5uah; ⊙11am-5pm Tue-Sun) Just off pl Rynok's southwest corner, the blackened façade of the burial chapel (1617) belonging to Hungarian merchant Georgi Boyim

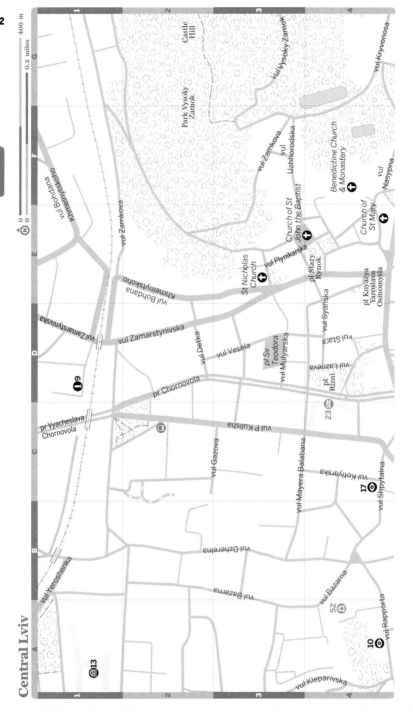

Central Lviv

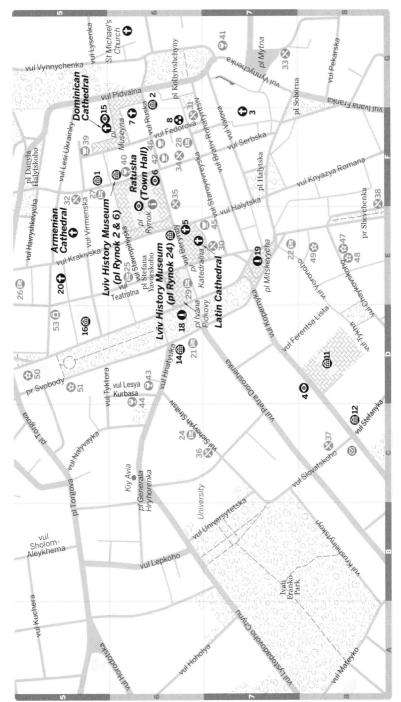

LVIV & WESTERN UKRAINE LVIV

Central Lviv

and his family is covered in magnificent if somewhat morbid carvings. Atop the cupola is an unusual sculpture of Christ sitting with his head in one hand, pondering his sorrows. The interior is dizzying, featuring biblical reliefs with cameo appearances by members of the Boyim family. There are more images of the family patriarchs on the exterior above the door and on the wall flanking vul Halytska.

High Castle   RUINED FORT
(Високий замок; Vysoky Zamok; Map p90) Visiting the High Castle on Castle Hill (Zamkova Hora) is a quintessential Lviv experience. The 14th-century ruined stone fort at the summit was Lviv's birthplace

and offers the best vantage point of the modern city. Good times to visit are at sunset and in winter, when there are no leaves obstructing the view. Newlyweds like to pop the cork on a bottle of champagne here, while enterprising locals rent binoculars and sell souvenirs.

There are several ways to reach Vysoky Zamok. The easiest is to make your way to the corner of vul Vynnychenka and vul Kryvonosa and just head up the hill towards the TV tower. The castle is east of the tower; follow the steel stairs behind the restaurant at the first crest of the hill. If you're feeling lazy, you can take a taxi most of the way up, approaching from the east via vul Vysoky Zamok.

Dormition Church   CHURCH
(Успенська церква; Map p92; Uspenska Tservka; vul Pidvalna 9) This Ukrainian Orthodox church is easily distinguished by the 65m-high, triple-tiered **Kornyakt bell tower** rising beside it. The tower was named after its Greek benefactor, a merchant who was also the original owner of Kornyakt House on pl Rynok. It's well worth going inside to see the beautiful interior of the church, accessible through the gate to the right of the tower. Attached to the church is the diminutive **Three Saints Chapel** (Каплиця трьох святителів).

Transfiguration Church   CHURCH
(Храм Преображення Господнього; Map p92; cnr vul Krakivska & vul Lesi Ukrainky; ⊘7am-7pm) The tall copper-domed church just west of the Armenian Cathedral is the late-17th-century Transfiguration Cathedral, the first church in the city to revert to Greek Catholicism after Ukrainian independence in 1991. This place is particularly impressive during a service (6.45am to 10am and 5pm).

Lviv Art Gallery   GALLERY
(Львівська художня галерея; Map p92; vul Kopernyka 15 & vul Stefanyka 3; per branch 10uah; ⊘11am-6pm Tue-Sat, noon-5pm Sun) Lviv's main art repository has two wings – one in the lavish **Pototsky Palace** (Палац Потоцького), the other around the corner on vul Stefanyka. The former houses an impressive collection of European art from the 14th to 18th centuries, including works by Rubens, Bruegel, Goya and Caravaggio. The wing on vul Stefanyka contains 19th- and early-20th-century art, most of it Polish and Russian.

(Національний музей-меморіал жертв окупаційних режимів; Map p90; vul Bryullova; admission free; ⊘10am-5pm) This infamous building in vul Bryullova was used as a prison by the Poles, Nazis and Communists in turn, but the small and very moving ground-floor exhibition focuses on Stalinist atrocities in the early years of WWII. Left exactly as it was when the KGB bailed out in 1991, the brutally bare cells, horrific statistics posted throughout and Nazi newsreel from summer 1941 will leave few untouched. Some English explanations.

Lvivske Museum of Beer and Brewing   MUSEUM
(Львівський музей пивоварення; Map p92; www.lvivske.com; vul Kleparivska 18; admission 15uah; ⊘10.30am-6pm Wed-Sun) The oldest still-functioning brewery in Ukraine turns 300 in 2015, and a tasting tour, which runs roughly every 1½ hours, through the mainly underground facilities is well worth the trek out of the centre. One old storage vault has been turned into an atmospheric beer hall where you can sample even more frothy Lvivske, one of the most popular brands in the country. To reach the museum, take tram 6 to the Dobrobut stop then walk north along vul Kleparivska for around 10 minutes.

St George's Cathedral   CATHEDRAL
(Собор Святого Юра; Map p90; pl Sv Yura 5) On a hilltop beyond Ivan Franko Park stands the historic and sacred centre of the Greek Catholic Church in Ukraine, which was handed back after 44 years of compulsory Orthodox control. Constructed in 1774–90, this yellow building is pleasant enough, especially since a refurbishment for the Pope's 2001 visit. However, it's perhaps not as striking as some of Lviv's less important churches. For many, the most memorable element will be the 3-D icon of Christ near the far right corner, if looking from the door. It presents Christ's face from one angle, and the image from the shroud of Turin from another.

Museum of Ethnography, Arts and Crafts   MUSEUM
(Музей етнографії та художнього промислу; Map p92; pr Svobody 15; admission 5uah; ⊘11am-5pm Wed-Sun) Exhibits of furniture, clothing, woodcarvings, ceramics and farming implements give a basic introduction to Carpathian life. However, the

Museum of Hutsul Folk Art in Kolomyya is superior.

National Museum   MUSEUM
(Національний Музей; Map p92; pr Svobody 20; admission 9uah; ⊙10am-6pm Tue-Sun) Dedicated to Ukrainian art of the 12th to 20th centuries, this extensive museum is probably only for diehard enthusiasts of Ukrai-

nian culture. The old religious icons and medieval books are extraordinary, but the temporary exhibitions by local artists are of a more variable quality. Taras Shevchenko's moustachioed death mask is also here.

Apteka Museum   MUSEUM
(Аптека-музей; Pharmacy Museum; Map p92; vul Drukarska 2; admission 3uah; ⊙9am-6pm

JEWISH LVIV

Jewish sites in Lviv may be more about what's been destroyed than what remains, but a tour through the city's rich Jewish past can still elicit a range of emotions. There were more than 100,000 Jews in Lviv before WWII, not including the several thousand Jewish refugees who arrived from Germany and western Poland before the war. The Nazis murdered nearly all of them at Lviv's Janowska concentration and forced labour camp, and at Belzec, another hideous extermination camp in present-day Poland, where, it is believed, some 600,000 people were killed and only two survived. Today Lviv's Jewish community numbers only about 2000.

Before the tragic events of WWII there were two Jewish districts in Lviv: a wealthy inner district around vuls Staroyevreyska (Old Jewish Street), Fedorova and Ruska in the old town; and a larger outer district covering a vast area north and west of the Theatre of Opera and Ballet.

The late-16th-century **Golden Rose Synagogue** (Map p92; vul Staroyevreyska) stood at the heart of the inner district before the Nazis blew it up in 1941. Today there's not much to see at the fenced-off site, but the local Jewish community plans to rebuild a replica of the synagogue in the coming years. Another synagogue once stood in the decrepit open lot directly across vul Staroyevreyska.

In the outer district, you'll find the **Jewish Hospital** (Єврейська лікарня; Map p92; vul Rappoporta), one of Lviv's architectural highlights. From afar this Moorish, dome-topped building looks like a mosque, but up close Jewish motifs are evident in the striking, eclectic façade. Krakivsky Market, right behind the hospital, was a Jewish cemetery in medieval times. Writer Sholem Aleichem lived not far away, at Kotlyarska 1, in 1906. There's a **plaque** (Map p92) to Aleichem on the side of the building. South of here, on vul Nalyvayka, a few old Yiddish shop signs remain. About 500m north of the Theatre of Opera and Ballet on pr Chornovola is the **Holocaust memorial** (Map p92), a vaguely cubist statue of a tormented figure looking skyward. The Lviv ghetto began here after most of the city's Jews were killed or deported to Belzec in the 'Great Action' of August 1942. Nazi hunter Simon Wiesenthal was the most famous resident of the ghetto, which was liquidated in June 1943.

The **Yanivske Cemetery** (Янівське кладовище; Janowska Cemetery; Map p90; vul Tarasa Shevchenka), northwest of the city centre, has a large Jewish section accessible from vul Yeroshenka (a side street off vul Tarasa Shevchenka). A 15-minute walk west of the cemetery are a plaque and a billboard marking the spot of the **Janowska concentration camp** (vul Vynnytsya, off vul Tarasa Shevchenka), now a prison. About 200m further west on vul Tarasa Shevchenka is **Kleparivska train station**, the last stop before Belzec on the Nazi death train. A plaque commemorates the 500,000 doomed Galician Jews who passed through here.

Artefacts of Lviv's Jewish heritage are scattered around various museums in the old town. There's a small Holocaust exhibit in the Lviv History Museum branch at pl Rynok 6, while the Museum of Religious History attached to the Dominican Cathedral has a collection of Jewish relics and the **Hesed-Arieh Jewish Centre** (Map p90; vul Kotlyevskoho 30; ⊙9.30am-6pm Sun-Fri) has a tiny museum on Jews in Galicia. Lviv's only functioning synagogue is the attractive **Beis Aharon V'Yisrael Synagogue** (Map p90; vul Brativ Mikhnovskykh 4), built in 1924.

For more Jewish sites, see the Lviv Walking Tour.

Mon-Fri, 10am-5pm Sat & Sun) Ukraine's only pharmacy museum is located inside a still-functioning chemist's shop dating from 1735. Entrance into the eerie *pidval* (basement) is by request only. Bottles of medicinal wine with a high iron content can be bought here (temporary tooth discolouration is all part of the fun); just ask for *zalizne vyno.*

Bernardine Church and Monastery
MONASTERY COMPLEX

(Бернардинців костьол і монастир; Map p92; vul Vynnychenka) Lviv's most stunning baroque interior belongs to the 17th-century now Greek Catholic Church of St Andrew. The highlight is the long ceiling covered in recently restored frescoes. Sunday masses spill out into the street, filling the surrounding square with song.

Arsenal Museum
MUSEUM

(Музей старовинної зброї; Map p92; vul Pidvalna 5; admission 5uah; ☉10am-5.30pm Thu-Tue) The town's former arsenal (1554–56) is now a museum where you can check out suits of armour and various cannons and weapons.

☞ Tours

If you want to dig deeper or see the main sights in a short time, we recommend the following tours. Contact the travel agencies listed later for more options.

Chudo Tour
TOURIST TRAIN

(Map p92; www.chudotour.com.ua; pl Rynok; tour 40uah; ☉10am-6pm) Ukraine's first and only tourist train leaves every hour from the right-hand side of the *ratusha* on pl Rynok. The 50-minute tour with recorded commentary takes in most of the major sights in the city centre. The company also run themed walking tours.

Kumpel Tour
THEMED TOURS

(☏067 373 8900; www.kumpel-tour.com) Expert Lviv historian, university lecturer and part-time local radio presenter Ihor Lylo runs the best English-language tours in town for visitors looking to get under the skin of this intriguing city.

MP3Tours
DOWNLOADABLE TOURS

(www.visitlviv.net) Lviv once again leaves other Ukrainian cities (and the vast majority of the ex-USSR's other tourist 'hotspots') open-mouthed in confused wonderment with the country's first English-language MP3 tours, downloadable from the tourist office website to the device of your choice – free! Yes, free.

🛏 Sleeping

In preparation for Euro 2012, Lviv's hotels are busy adding beds, tiling bathrooms, giving staff English lessons and generally banishing all vestiges of the Soviet past. The result will be the best range of accommodation outside Kyiv.

Lviv's hostel situation seems to be in constant flux, with expats setting up then selling up with alarming speed. Check that those listed below are still up and running before turning up without a booking. Most hostels seem to have a no-alcohol policy.

TOP CHOICE Vintage
HOTEL $$$

(Вінтаж; Map p92; ☏032-235 6834; www.vintagehotel.com.ua; vul Staroyevreyska 25/27; s/d/ste 750/950/1550uah; ✳🛜) Lviv's first real boutique hotel is this delightfully intimate 12-room place, tucked away up a quiet street in the historical centre. Rooms ooze period style with hardwood floors, polished antique-style furniture and Victorian-style wallpaper, successfully blended with flat-screen TVs and 21st-century bathrooms. You'll be looking forward all night to the cooked-to-order breakfast served in the hotel's stylish cafe. The genuinely friendly staff are glad to help with anything Lviv-related, plus onward travel arrangements and the like. The hotel is busy expanding into the building next door, but this shouldn't take away any of its cosiness.

Leopolis Hotel
HOTEL $$$

(Готель Леополіс; Map p92; ☏032-295 9500; www.leopolishotel.com; vul Teatralna 16; s/d 1800/2000uah; ✳🛜) Slowly emerging as the city centre's finest place to catch some Zs, the Leopolis comes to you from the same designer who fashioned Tallinn's Telegraaf Hotel. Every understated guestroom in this 18th-century edifice is slightly different, but all have a well-stocked minibar, elegant furniture and Italian marble bathrooms with underfloor heating. There's even a wheelchair-friendly room, a rarity indeed in these parts. This hotel is also expanding sideways, and the new wing, with spa centre and conference facilities, should be ready in good time for Euro 2012.

Kosmonaut Hostel
HOSTEL $

(Map p92; ☏032-260 1602; www.thekosmonaut.com; vul Sichovykh Striltsiv 8; dm/tw 100/250uah; ➠🛜) Not as space-age as the branding implies, this place resembles a slightly ramshackle but cool student household in Australia. That said, there

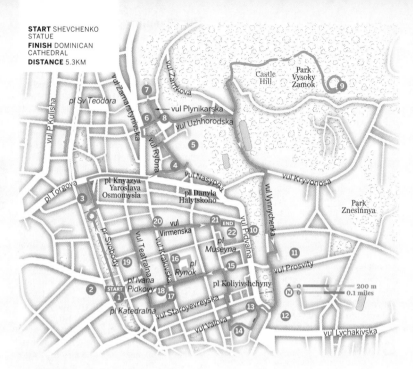

Walking Tour
Lviv's Historical Centre

❭ Lviv's relatively compact centre makes for an easy, pleasant walking tour that will get you to most of the major sites. This tour will take approximately 1¾ hours – 2½ hours if the Castle Hill loop is included. It starts at the spiritual centre of modern-day Lviv, the Taras Shevchenko statue on pr Svobody, and ends at enchanting vul Virmenska in the heart of the old city.

With your back to the **❶ Shevchenko statue**, start walking right, glancing up at the interesting cast of stone-carved characters (one resembling New York's Statue of Liberty) on the parapet of the **❷ Museum of Ethnography, Arts & Crafts**. The small gift shop inside is one of the best places to pick up authentic souvenirs. Continue north on pr Svobody toward the **❸ Solomiya Krushelnytska Lviv Theatre of Opera and Ballet**. Skirt right around the theatre and its recently installed fountain then take a right on vul Horodotska and carry on for about 250m until you reach the **❹ Church of**

St Mary, parts of which date from 1340. Carry on past the church then take a right into **❺ vul Chornomorska**, scene of Cold War tragedy. Vibration from Soviet tanks heading to Hungary in 1956 shook several houses to the ground, hence the gap now occupied by a children's playground. A few steps further bring you to pl Stary Rynok, where the 1845 **❻ Progressive Jews Synagogue**, once stood. Destroyed by the Nazis during WWII, it's marked by a plaque.

Glance up at the old buildings around pl Stary Rynok before performing a quick there-and-back movement up vul Plynikar-ska to see the **❼ Church of St Nicholas**. Local historians claim this is Lviv's oldest church, but only elements of the building date back to the 13th century. Back on pl Stary Rynok head east, passing the diminutive **❽ Church of St John the Baptist**, now a book museum, on your left, then bear right on vul Uzhhorodska. Continue uphill about 200m to the corner of vul Zamkova. From here you can easily spot the TV tower that tops **9 Castle Hill**. If you've got your walking boots on, High Castle (Vysoky Zamok) is about a 45-minute round-trip walk from here, and it worth it for the views across the city. If you're not up for the climb, take a right on vul Zamkova, which leads to the old town.

Proceed about 300m on vul Zamkova to a three-way intersection and bear right down vul Vynnychenka. In the park on your right is the 16th-century **10 Gunpowder Tower**, part of the old system of walls and bastions, which now houses a seasonal restaurant. The twin-spired church looming up the hill on your left is the Greek Catholic **11 St Michael's Church**. It's worth taking a peek inside to see its striking baroque sanctuary. Continue south to vul Valova at the south end of the park.

If you need a breather, **12 Kabinet Cafe** is a fine place to grab a coffee. If not, backtrack about 30 paces and cross the park and tram tracks. You will see No 20 Bapova on your left. Skirt inside the fenced sidewalk and continue along the old brick walls on your right. This is the last standing section of **13 Lviv's medieval fortifications**. Go down the steps and duck right through the arched passageway. You are in the yard of the splendid **14 Bernardine Church and Monastery**.

Head north across the square in front of the church's main entrance, cross vul Valova and continue north on vul Fedorova for about 200m until you come to vul Ruska. **15 The Dormition Church** and its Kornyakt bell tower loom on your right. Go left on vul Ruska, keeping the **16 ratusha** on your right as you cross pl Rynok. You can come back and wander around pl Rynok later. For now, look for the black façade of the **17 Boyim Chapel**, on pl Katedralna, and have a look inside. When you exit, head straight down the path in front of you, keeping the **18 Latin Cathedral** on your right, and take the next right on vul Teatralna.

You're now close to where you started, walking north parallel to pr Svobody. Continue past the **19 Jesuit Church**, stopping to admire its interesting baroque and Renaissance façade. Your home stretch, vul Virmenska, is easy to spot – it's the prettiest little street in Lviv. Hang a right and set your sights on the eastern terminus of the street – your finish line, where the Dzyga awaits. But before you get there, pop your head into the courtyard of the **20 Armenian Cathedral**. At the **21 Dzyga Café**, choose an outdoor table with a view of the **22 Dominican Cathedral** and order yourself a well-deserved Lvivske beer, or best of all, a cup of Lviv's legendary coffee.

are plenty of Gagarins, Lenins and other fun and scary USSR-era memorabilia scattered about the place for guests to play with (have no fear, none of the weaponry is active). Remarks in the guestbook would indicate no one leaves this relaxed and convivial place in an angry huff and the staff come in for specific praise.

Soviet Home Hostel
HOSTEL **$**

(Map p92; ☎032-225 8611; www.homehostels .com.ua; vul Drukarska 3, top fl; dm/s/d 100/280/320uah; ☻🛜) Festooned in Soviet-era junk, this friendly, 20-bed hostel is small-scale enough to not feel overcrowded yet big enough for a party crowd to form. Dorms are generously cut with not too many bunks, there's a small kitchen where the free breakfast is laid out and the double has a less-than-sleep-inducing Lenin portrait above the bed. Fun digs for budget nomads.

Hotel George
HOTEL **$$**

(Готель Жорж; Map p92; ☎032-232 6236; www.georgehotel.com.ua; pl Mitskevycha 1; r from 600uah; 🛜) Seasoned travellers to Lviv will be saddened to learn that the George is renovating and has lost its elusive 'Soviet chic' vibe. A prime candidate for a show-stopping five-star establishment, instead this gorgeous 1901 art nouveau building is receiving a crass, skin-deep makeover – plasticky, faux-antique furniture clashes with the rooms' high-ceilinged period style and cheapo carpets conceal the wonderfully creaky parquet floors. However, communal spaces remain untouched, the English-speaking staff are great and the buffet breakfast is still served in the amazing Oriental-style restaurant.

APARTMENTS

As in most Ukrainian cities, apartments are better bang-for-the-buck than hotels. **Lviv Ecotour** (www. lvivecotour.com) has a couple of apartments. The following have English-speaking proprietors.

» **www.rentinlviv.com** (☎067 670 0951; apt from 250uah) Ask for Yaroslav.

» **www.inlviv.info** (contact@inlviv. info; apt from 250uah).

» **www.rent-lviv.com** (☎032-238 6193; apt from 400uah) Well-appointed pads for a bit more cash.

Wien Hotel
HOTEL **$$**

(Готель Вена; Map p92; ☎032-244 4314; www.wienhotel.lviv.ua; pr Svobody 12; s/d from 450/500uah; ❄) Tucked behind the Wiener Kaffeehaus just off Lviv's main boulevard, cosy little Wien has 20 fresh, if slightly small, rooms. The kind reception, tasteful and elegant décor, and totally agreeable pricing draw a steady stream of people in the know. The free Wiener Kaffeehaus breakfasts for guests are excellent. Book ahead as it's popular.

Grand Hotel
HOTEL **$$$**

(Гранд Готель; Map p92; ☎032-272 4042; www.ghgroup.com.ua; pr Svobody 13; s/d 980/1200uah; ☻❄🛜🏊) Having rested too long on its laurels as the only real luxury show in town, the Grand is no longer top dog in Lviv. The rooms, while still holding on to their olde-worlde flavour, are beginning to fade a bit and the service has been caught flat-footed by other more up-to-speed establishments. Fortunately its prime location on pr Svobody will never fade. Prices come down by around 20% at weekends.

Hotel Lviv
HOTEL **$**

(Готель Львів; Map p92; ☎032-242 3270; pr Chornovola 7; s 100uah, s/d with bathroom 200/250uah) You're looking at the cheap, no-frills singles here, which are a super deal considering the location; stay away from the slightly overpriced 'renovated' doubles. While Soviet in character, the Lviv lacks the deal-breakers that dog many hotels of this ilk. The common bathrooms, for instance, aren't gross, and the beds don't sag too badly. Street noise is one problem; ask for a room at the back.

Art Hostel
HOSTEL **$**

(Map p92; ☎032-297 5195; www.arthostel.lviv.ua; pl Rynok 3/4; dm 85uah; @🛜❄) Bright, messy and ever so slightly institutional, the main drawcard here is the location on pl Rynok. The price is the same whether you stay in the six-bed dorms or the 10-bed, and there's a dinky kitchen. A vague art theme runs throughout, but this hostel just lacks that frayed, lived-in feel that seasoned hostel dwellers know and love.

Nataliya-18
HOTEL **$$**

(Наталія-18; Map p92; ☎032-242 2068; www. natalia18.lviv.ua; pl Knyazya Yaroslava Osmomysla 7; s/d from 400/580uah; ❄) Located on the edge of the former Armenian quarter, this solid midrange choice features big bath-

Local historians regularly lock horns on the issue of where the world's original 'masochist' was born. Some claim he came into the world at vul Kopernyka 22 opposite the Pototsky Palace, others assert he must have first seen light of day in a house where the Grand Hotel now stands. Wherever the exact location may have been, the author of *Venus in Furs* was definitely born in Lviv in 1835, although he spent most of his subsequent 60 years begging to be whipped in Austria, Germany and Italy.

If you'd like to experience a light-hearted version of some of Masoch's practices, the waitresses at the **Masoch Cafe** (Мазох-Кафе; vul Serbska 7; ⊙11am-1am) will handcuff and whip you after a meal selected from the lightly erotic menu (don't worry, there's nothing distasteful about an evening here and it's all just a bit of fun). A bronze of Masoch himself greets 'diners' at the door.

rooms with mirrors worthy of a porn set and the softest, fluffiest towels in Ukraine. The 22 odd-shaped rooms are anchored by queen-sized beds draped in fine linens.

Eurohotel　　　　　　　　　　HOTEL **$$**
(Єврoготель; Map p90; ☏032-275 7214; www.eurohotel.lviv.ua; vul Tershakovtsiv 6A; s/d from 500/600uah; ❀❉🛜) This unexciting place is a good example of just what you can do with a surplus Soviet lumpen-hotel. The 90 bog-standard but comfortable rooms are for those who want to sleep, shower and access the web, but little else.

✖ Eating

Lviv is more famous for cafes than restaurants, but the food scene has seen dramatic developments in recent years with some weird and wonderful theme restaurants popping up across the city centre.

[TOP CHOICE] **Masonic Restaurant**
　　　　　　　　　　　　　MASONIC THEMED **$$$**
(Map p92; pl Rynok 14; mains before discount 300-800uah; ⊙11am-2am) It's hard to know where to start with this place. Finding it is the first obstacle – head to the 2nd floor and open the door of apartment 8 (the number is changed occasionally to throw people off the scent). You'll be accosted by an unshaven bachelor type, into whose Soviet-era kitchen you appear to have inadvertently wandered. Having barred your way for a few minutes, he eventually opens the door to a fancy beamed restaurant full of Masonic symbols and portraits of bygone masons. The next shock is the menu – advertised as Galicia's most expensive restaurant, prices are 10 times higher than normal...so make sure you pick up a 90% discount card at Dim Lehend or Livy Bereh beforehand. The food, by the way, is great and the beer and

kvas come in crystal vases. The loo is a candlelit Masonic throne. Ukraine's weirdest restaurant experience? Probably.

Dim Lehend　　　　　　　LVIV THEMED **$$**
(Дім Легенд; Map p92; vul Staroyevreyska 48; mains 20-75uah) Dedicated entirely to the city of Lviv, there's nothing dim about the 'House of Legends'. The menu pamphlet you receive at the door is more a map used to explore the five floors, which house a library stuffed with Lviv-themed volumes, a room showing live webcam footage of Lviv's underground river, rooms dedicated to lions and cobblestones, and another featuring the city in sounds. A GDR Trabant occupies the roof terrace, the views from which will have you reaching for your camera. Having chosen a room, the menu is a work in progress, but the coffee and desserts are Central European bliss.

Kupol　　　　　　CENTRAL EUROPEAN **$$**
(Купол; Map p90; vul Chaykovskoho 37; mains 40-80uah; ⊙11am-9pm) This place is designed to feel like stepping back in time – to 1938 in particular, 'the year before civilisation ended' (ie before the Soviets rolled in). How well this former mansion and arts salon recreates that specific year is moot, but goodness, is the overall effect winning. The olde-worlde interior is lined with framed letters, ocean-liner ads, antique cutlery, hampers and other memorabilia. The Polish-Austrian-Ukrainian food is delicious and beautifully garnished.

Livy Bereh　　　　　　INTERNATIONAL **$$**
(Левий Берег; Map p92; pr Svobody 28; mains 20-80uah; ⊙10am-2am; 📶) Buried deep beneath the Theatre of Opera and Ballet, this superb restaurant-cum-coffeehouse serves European fare with a few Ukrainian and

Hutsul favourites thrown in. The vibe is easy-going and the service respectful, and you can even ask the waitress for pencil and paper to leave an arty memento of your visit (guests once expressed their thanks with musical instruments, but this quickly got out of hand). The name (meaning 'Left Bank') refers to Lviv's subterranean River Poltva, which flows under the theatre.

Kumpel MICROBREWERY **$$**

(Кумпель; Map p92; vul Vynnychenka 6; mains 20-90uah; ⊘24hr; ⓐ) Centred on two huge copper brewing vats cooking up Krumpel's own beer (1L 29uah), this superb round-the-clock microbrewery restaurant has a low-lit art deco theme. The menu is heavy on international meat and two veg combos, with a few local elements included. Locals love it.

Amadeus INTERNATIONAL **$$**

(Амадеус; Map p92; pl Katedralna 7; mains 40-200uah; ⓐ) The refined interior, peaceful music and perfectly placed patio are reason enough to plop down in one of Amadeus' stylish wicker chairs. But it's the food that puts it on another level. The menu leans toward fancy European fare like fondue and risotto, but there are stuffed baked potatoes, pizza-sized omelettes, *shashlyk* (shish kebab) and *varenyky* (dumplings) on offer for the price-conscious hryvnya hoarders.

Veronika DESSERT RESTAURANT **$$**

(Вероніка; Map p92; pr Shevchenka 21; mains 40-150uah; ⓐ) This classy basement restaurant shares the same owners and the same menu as Amadeus. Need we say more? In addition there's a street-level *Konditorei* (cafe-bakery), with criminally delicious desserts, which will make you think you've died and gone to Vienna.

Puzata Khata CANTEEN **$**

(Пузата Хата; Map p92; vul Sichovykh Striltsiv 12; mains from 10uah; ⊘8am-11pm) Puzata Khata is a small mercy anywhere, but this super-sized version of Ukraine's number-one restaurant chain stands out for its classy, Hutsul-themed interior and pure Ukrainian-rock soundtrack.

Also recommended:

Pyrizhky PIE CANTEEN **$**

(Пиріжки; Map p90; vul Slovatskoho 4; pyrizhky 3-5uah) This blast from the Soviet past has been serving budget *pyrizhky* (pies/turnovers) here for over 50 years.

Kilikiya ARMENIAN **$$**

(Кілікія; Map p92; vul Virmenska 13; mains 20-70uah) Armenian food in the Armenian quarter.

Drinking

Be careful: Lviv has so many lovely cafes luring you in with olde-worlde charm and the scent of arabica that disciples of the bean risk over-caffeination. Lviv also has a fine and growing selection of watering holes and more are likely to spring up for Euro 2012.

Dzyga CAFE

(Дзиґа; Map p92; vul Virmenska 35; ⊘9am-11.30pm; ⓐ) This cafe-cum-art gallery in the shadow of the Dominican Cathedral has a relaxed vibe. It's particularly popular with bohemian, alternative types, but seems to attract pretty much everyone, really. The summertime outdoor seating is gathered around the city's Monument to the Smile. If it's full, there are other attractive options for a nibble or a cuppa joe nearby on postcard-pretty vul Virmenska.

Smachna Plitka CAFE

(Смачна Плітка; Map p92; vul Kurbasa 3; ⊘11am-11pm; ⓐ) Head down the stairs behind an anonymous wooden door in the façade of the Kurbasa Theatre to find a basement cafe that's everything you want a central European coffeehouse to be – small cafe tables tucked furtively into corners, hard-to-beat coffees and beers, and turtle-necked revolutionaries filling the air with schemes. Hard to find, but one of Lviv's longest established cafes.

Pid Synoyu Plyashkoyu CAFE

(Під синьою пляшкою; Under the Blue Bottle; Map p92; vul Ruska 4; ⊘11.30am-10pm) With its nostalgia for the Polish-Austrian past and its dark interior, this tiny cafe at the back of a courtyard has a cosy, secretive atmosphere. It serves sandwiches and fondues, as well as wine and coffee with pepper. It's hard to find; look for the blue bottle.

Svit Kavy CAFE

(Світ Кави; Map p92; pl Katedralna 6; ⊘8am-10pm Mon-Sat, 9am-11pm Sun; ⓐ) Pick of the bunch on pl Katedralna, with no theme, no gimmicks, just a focus on Lviv's best coffee-making traditions. Beans come from almost every continent, and if you like the drink, you can buy the unground raw ingredient in the shop next door.

Robert Doms Beer House BEER HALL
(Map p90; vul Kleparivska 18; ☺noon-midnight)
This fantastic, utterly unique beer hall
is located three storeys underground in a
centuries-old beer-storage vault once used
by the neighbouring Lvivske brewery. It's
named after the brewery's founder and
features fresh Lvivske served in litre steins,
plus German food and nightly live music in
one of the vault's four chambers. Another
chamber has a mammoth TV screen for
sports viewing.

Italyansky Dvorik CAFE
(Італ'янський дворик; Italian Courtyard; Map
p92; pl Rynok 6; ☺10am-8pm) Even if you decide to skip the Lviv History Museum, it's
worth popping in for a coffee in its aptly
named inner courtyard. There's a 1uah fee
to enter the courtyard.

Zoloti Dukat CAFE
(Золотий дукат; Map p92; vul Fedorova 20;
☺10am-10pm) The mirrored ceiling in this
faux bat-cave creates all sorts of optical
illusions – this place would be a real hit
in Amsterdam. No cannabis here, though,
just what may be Lviv's best (and best-
smelling) coffee in a mercifully smoke-free
environment.

Kabinet Cafe CAFE
(Кафе Кабінет; Map p92; vul Vynnychenka 12;
☺10am-11pm) Despite the nationalist symbols plastered on the walls, there's still a
brown-wrapping-paper, Soviet atmosphere.
You can curl up with a book (there's a small
library) in a cosy antique throne, or play a
game of billiards.

Praga Pub PUB
(прага; Map p92; vul Hnatyuka 8; ☺11am-mid-
night) This relatively new Czech-style pub
serves some of the best draught ales from
the land of ice hockey and Skodas. There's
lots of stodgy soak-up material to go with
it too.

☆ Entertainment
Clubs

Kult MUSIC CLUB
(Культ; Map p92; www.kult.lviv.ua; vul Chaykovskoho 7; admission 10-20uah; ☺noon-2am) This
superb basement venue next to the Philharmonia reverberates with live Ukrainian
rock music every night of the week.

Picasso NIGHTCLUB
(Пікассо; Map p90; www.picasso.lviv.ua; vul
Zelena 88; admission 15-30uah; ☺Fri-Wed) Lviv's

most atmospheric club, inside a former theatre, has consistently good DJs and a consistently festive crowd paying proper homage to them.

Rafinad People NIGHTCLUB
(Map p92; www.rafinad-club.com; vul Rudanskoho
1; admission from 50uah) If you can get past
the face control (no sports shoes please),
this is possibly Lviv's classiest mainstream
club with something happening every night
of the week.

Opera, Theatre & Classical Music
Advance tickets for all Lviv's venues are
sold at the **Teatralna Kasa** (Театральна
каса; Theatre Box Office; Map p92; pr Svobody 37;
☺10am-1pm & 3-5pm Mon-Sat).

**Solomiya Krushelnytska Lviv Theatre of
Opera & Ballet** THEATRE
(Театр Опери та балету ім Соломиї
Крушельницької; Map p92; ☏032-272 8672;
www.opera.lviv.ua; pr Svobody 28). For an evening of high culture, and to enjoy the ornate building, take in a performance at
this Lviv institution. For some local colour
catch a performance of *Zaporozhets za Du-
nae*, which runs once or twice a month. The
theatre shuts down for most of July and
August.

Philharmonia ORCHESTRA
(Філармонія; Map p92; ☏032-274 1086; www.
philharmonia.lviv.ua; vul Chaykovskoho 7). If classical music is more your thing, let yourself
be wooed by the sweet strains of Lviv's regional philharmonic orchestra. Things are
very quiet from July through to mid-
September.

🛍 Shopping

Outdoor Arts & Crafts Market MARKET
(Відкритий ринок по продажу виробів
мистецтва та художнього промислу;
Map p92; cnr vuls Lesi Ukrainky & Teatralna;
☺10.30am-6pm) This large market sells
rugs, embroidered blouses, wooden *pysanky* (patterned eggs), woodcrafts and
lots of everyday knick-knacks.

Ravlyk SOUVENIR SHOP
(Равлик; Map p92; pr Svobody 15; ☺10am-6pm)
Located in the pr Svobody branch of the
Museum of Ethnography, Arts and Crafts,
the quality of the souvenirs at Ravlyk is
second to none in Lviv, particularly the
pysanky, which use real eggshells and are
arguably better than those in the museum
itself.

Svitoch
CHOCOLATE SHOP

(Світоч; Map p92; pl Rynok 10) Lviv-produced Svitoch (Світоч) is one of Ukraine's most popular brands of chocolate, and the company has many own-brand shops, including this one on the main square.

Krakivsky Market
MARKET

(Краківський ринок; Map p92; vul Bazarna) Fans of outdoor markets will enjoy this real, bustling Soviet-style *rynok* (market) with all the fresh fruit, raw meat and cheap junk that entails.

ℹ Information

Central telephone office (Укртелеком; vul Petra Doroshenka 37; ☺8.30am-7pm Mon-Fri, 9am-4pm Sat)

Central post office (Поштамт; Map p92; vul Slovatskoho 1)

Chorna Medea (Чорна мідія; vul Petra Doroshenka 50; per hr 6uah; ☺24hr) Lviv's greatest internet cafe, with drinks, Skype and cheap, speedy web connection.

InLviv (☑032-235 7630; www.inlviv.info) InLviv runs a variety of tours and has a website with loads of information on Lviv.

Krylos.com (☑032-225 8215; www.krylos. com) Runs a range of themed tours and arranges transport tickets, hotels and apartment rental.

Lonely Planet (www.lonelyplanet.com/ ukraine/western-ukraine/lviv) Head here for planning advice, author recommendations and travel reviews.

Lviv Ecotour (www.lvivecotour.com) Owner Slav knows the region very well, has plenty of experience in guiding foreigners and speaks fluent English. Highly recommended. Can also arrange accommodation.

Lviv Regional Hospital (Map p90; ☑032-275 5020; www.hospital.lviv.ua; vul Chernihivska 7) Hospital with some English-speaking staff.

Lviv Today (www.lvivtoday.com.ua) Glossy English-language lifestyle and listings magazine available at many hotels.

Tourist Information Centre (Map p92; ☑032-254 6079; www.visitlviv.net; Ratusha, pl Rynok 1; ☺10am-7pm Mon-Fri, to 6pm Sat, to 5pm Sun) Finally Lviv has a proper municipal tourist office! The friendly staff can help with accommodation and produce a daily digest of what's on in the city. When it's closed, there's a touch-screen information portal just outside – yes, you *are* still in Ukraine.

ℹ Getting There & Away

More and more tourists are flying to Poland on budget airlines and proceeding overland to Lviv from there. See p278 for more details.

Air

By the time you read this Lviv will be the proud proprietor of a shiny new **airport** (www.airport. lviv.ua) bolted together about 9km west of the centre in preparation for Euro 2012. To reach the

---

FROM LVIV TO POLAND

With budget airlines flying into neighbouring Polish cities, Lviv is a popular transit point in and out of Ukraine. However, Poland's EU accession and rampant cigarette smuggling have made border delays even longer.

There are several routes between Lviv and the Polish airports in Krakow and Rzeszow, and different travellers have different preferences. Some recommend the train to and from the Polish border town of Przemysl, where you can at least sit during the average two- to three-hour waiting time. Others prefer to jam themselves on the much quicker *marshrutka* 297 between Lviv train station and the road crossing at Shehyni/ Medyka (15uah; 1½ hours, every hour), where they alight, walk across the border, and take another *marshrutka* onwards. This can be the quickest route and handy if you need to leave Lviv for Poland after the last train has departed. Beware though; the *marshrutky* are crowded and you have to stand in often long border queues (EU passport holders are sometimes sent to the front of the line).

Most agree that taking a bus from Lviv's inconveniently located Main Bus Station is the slowest option leaving Ukraine – although not as dire coming in. Hopefully Euro 2012 will ease the situation on the border slightly as new and sorely needed border facilities are built and completely new crossings created.

For further information on the Polish side of the border, head to shop.lonelyplanet. com to purchase a downloadable PDF of the Poland chapter from Lonely Planet's *Eastern Europe* guide.

city centre, take trolleybus 9 to the university or *marshrutka* (fixed-price minibus) 95.

Domestically you can fly from Lviv to Kyiv (four daily), Donetsk (daily) and Simferopol (weekly, summer only). Book through **Kiy Avia** (Кий Авіа; Map p92; ☎032-272 7818; www.kiyavia.com; vul Hnatyuka 20-22; ☺8am-8pm Mon-Sat, to 6pm Sun).

For a Ukrainian city Lviv is relatively well connected to Western Europe and the new airport is likely to attract even more airlines. There are currently daily flights to and from Vienna, Munich, Warsaw, Timişoara, Istanbul and Moscow.

Bus

Lviv has three bus stations of use to travellers. The extremely inconveniently located **Main Bus Station** (Holovny Avtovokzal; vul Stryska) is a whopping 8km south of the centre. To reach the city centre take trolleybus 5.

From the Main Bus Station, buses serve all major southern, eastern and central cities, including Kyiv (50uah to 90uah, nine hours, four daily), Kamyanets-Podilsky (71uah to 78uah, eight hours, twice daily) and Odesa (77uah, 16 hours, once daily). Western Ukraine destinations include Ivano-Frankivsk (35uah, three hours, hourly until 6pm), Chernivtsi (74uah, eight hours, at least twice daily), Kolomyya (54uah, six hours, nine daily), Uzhhorod (64uah, six hours, three daily), Lutsk (43uah, three hours, every hour), Rivne (58uah, three to four hours, 12 daily), Ternopil (36uah, three hours, every 30 minutes) and Kremenets (30uah, four hours, once daily) via Olesko and Pochayiv.

Many southbound buses depart from Bus Station No 8 (Map p90) in front of the Central Train Station. Destinations served include Ivano-Frankivsk (30uah, 3½ hours, seven daily), Uzhhorod (50uah, 6½ hours, two daily), Odesa (daily), Kyiv (twice daily).

Bus station No 2 is 3km north of the centre near the end of tram line 6 but is only good for services to Zhovkva and Olesko.

Train

Lviv's train station is 2km west of the centre, connected to town by trams 1 and 9.

The quickest way to Kyiv is on an express day train (100uah, 6½ hours, daily except Tuesday). There are also at least 10 regular trains per day, many overnight (150uah, nine to 11 hours). Most services to Kyiv pass through Ternopil (68uah, 2½ hours) and Vinnytsya (85uah, 6½ hours). Slow *elektrychky* service Ternopil (11uah, four hours, three daily), Lutsk (15uah, six hours, once daily) and Rivne (15uah, six hours, two daily).

Heading south, there are trains to Ivano-Frankivsk (70uah, three hours, twice daily), Kolomyya (67uah, five hours, twice daily),

Uzhhorod (65uah, seven hours, at least three daily), Chop (100uah, six hours, 11 daily), Rakhiv (60uah, 8½ hours, once daily) and Chernivtsi (70uah, 5½ to 11 hours, at least four daily).

There are daily trains to all major cities in central, southern and eastern Ukraine, including Odesa (132uah, 12 hours, up to five daily), Simferopol (190uah, three daily) and Kharkiv (205uah, 20 hours, three daily). To get to Kamyanets-Podilsky take a train to Khmelnytsky (four hours) and transfer to one of the frequent *marshrutky* (1½ hours).

International trains serve Moscow (270uah, 25 hours, up to six daily), St Petersburg (850uah, daily), Prague (390uah, daily) and Minsk (370uah, twice daily), among other destinations.

The most painless way to acquire a train ticket is to use the centrally located **train ticket office** (Центральні залізничні каси; vul Hnatyuka 20; ☺8am-2pm & 3-8pm Mon-Sat, to 6pm Sun).

❶ Getting Around

From the Central Train Station, take tram 1 or 9 to the southern end of pr Svobody; tram 6 will take you to the northern end. With freshly laid tram lines heading to the football stadium, a few new options and routes may spring up over the next couple of years.

If you must travel by taxi, and Lviv's good public transport network means you can probably avoid it, call **Vashe Taksi** (☎063 854 8995).

Zhovkva ЖОВКВА

☎03252 / POP 13,300

With your own wheels, the most impressive day trip from Lviv is probably Pochayiv Monastery. However, it's too difficult to visit quickly on public transport, leaving the fairly low-key historical town of Zhovkva at the top of the list. Its cluster of pastel-coloured buildings, handful of impressive churches and city-wall remnants will happily occupy you for an hour or two.

Built in the 16th century in an imitation of Italian-Renaissance style, Zhovkva was the birthplace of legendary Cossack Bohdan Khmelnytsky, who reportedly led his men through the 17th-century **Zvirynetska Gate** when liberating the town from the Poles in 1648. Ironically, however, the town's heyday was actually under the Poles, when it became the preferred residence of 17th-century king Jan III Sobiesky. Today roughly a dozen buildings – a monastery, lesser churches, a synagogue and a 'castle' that's not really a castle – cluster around the market square.

There are several ways to make the 32km journey north from Lviv, but the easiest route is via *marshrutka* 151 (3uah, 30 minutes), which leaves approximately every 15 minutes from the stop on vul P (Panteleymona) Kulisha (see Map p92), a 10-minute walk northwest of the Opera Theatre. Other frequent services leave from Lviv's Bus Station No 2.

Olesko ОЛЕСЬКО

☎ 03264 / POP 1800

Some 70km east of Lviv, Olesko boasts a French chateau-style hilltop castle visible for miles around. The current castle dates back to the 18th century but it was built on the site of a medieval fortress, destroyed by Tatar attacks in the 15th century. To get to Olesko, take a bus (1½ hours, eight daily) from Bus Station No 2 in Lviv. Alternatively, travel agencies in Lviv organise day trips.

Drohobych ДРОГОБИЧ

☎ 0324 / POP 77,000

Once home to Jewish-Polish writer and artist Bruno Schulz, Drohobych is of most interest to his fans, who might hope (possibly in vain) to recognise the town from his magic-realist novella *The Street of Crocodiles* (1934). Otherwise this quiet provincial town is mildly diverting if not gripping. There are plenty of historical monuments and some faded Polish and Austro-Hungarian homes. The leafy **Bandera Park** above the town square is lovely today, but it was around here that a vengeful German SS officer shot Schulz in 1942.

Indeed, while up to 40% of Drohobych's 35,000 inhabitants were once Jewish, only a handful remain. The truly enormous **New Synagogue** (1865) was a Soviet furniture store and has long lain derelict, although stop-start renovations began in 2005. You pass the building on the left when making the 10- to 15-minute walk from the bus station into town.

Frescoes that Schulz painted for his Nazi 'protector' in WWII were, controversially, taken to Jerusalem's Yad Veshem Holocaust Museum in 2001. But the town schedules a Schulz festival every second November (including in 2012), has plans for a museum and displays a memorial plaque on vul Y Drohobycha. If you speak Ukrainian, Polish or German, a tour organised by a local uni-

versity faculty (☎ 442 4322; frgf@drohobych. net) might be the thing for you.

The town lies some 80km southwest of Lviv. *Marshrutky* 722 and 122 (25uah, two hours) leave approximately every hour for Drohobych from Lviv's Bus Station No 8 (in front of Lviv's central train station). In Drohobych; other frequent *marshrutky* take you the 10km to Truskavets.

TERNOPIL REGION

This triangular-shaped region at the heart of Western Ukraine may have some stunning countryside, but it's fairly difficult for independent travellers to reach. Not many foreigners even make it to the larger population centres, although a couple of the smaller towns like Pochayiv and Kremenets are worth the effort.

Ternopil ТЕРНОПІЛЬ

☎ 0352 / POP 217,600

Arrive in Ternopil on the right day, and this city, which lends its name to the wider region, has a laid-back, leafy almost European feel, rather like an anonymous piece of Poland or the Czech Republic. Its signature feature is a huge artificial lake that's pleasant enough to stroll around of an evening, and the tiny old-town centre is quite appealing, but that's about it. For those with time, the town could be a low-key, off-the-radar stop-off between Chernivtsi or Kamyanets-Podilsky and Lviv. Most snore through it on a sleeper train in the early hours.

The town centre sits between the artificial lake (to the west) and the train station (to the east). To reach the centre from the station, exit into the square in front of the train station, and crossing vul Bohdana Khmelnystkoho, continue straight ahead down vul Zaliznychna for two blocks until you arrive at bul Taras Shevchenko, with the central maydan Tealtralni at its northern end.

◉ Sights

Dominican Church CHURCH
(vul Hetmana Sahaydachnoho) At the western end of vul Hetmana Sahaydachnoho, where it opens up into maydan Voli, the cream and pea-green Dominican Church and monastery complex hoists the city's finest silhouette. Built in the mid-18th century, its twin towers rise from a baroque façade.

TRUSKAVETS ТРУСКАВЕЦЬ

Truskavets is an old-fashioned spa town that in another country and another time might have given the Czech Republic's celebrated spa town Karlovy Vary a run for its money. Unfortunately, that sort of rivalry is a long way off, but the town still makes a fun day trip from Lviv. Its heart is the mineral water *buvet* or spring (Бювет Мінеральних Вод) in the central park, where locals supposedly once came to drink from the fountain of good health.

Two 'cures' are on tap. Sodova water is reputedly good for the digestive tract; Naftusya for kidney, urinary tract and liver ailments. The springs only run at certain hours and you're supposed to drink the water at a certain temperature, but you can find extensive instructions posted in several languages, including English. Oddly shaped spa cups are used here, with a long spout for sucking. They are so designed because the mineral-rich water is allegedly good for other bodily parts, but not the teeth. You can buy yourself a cup in one of the park kiosks.

Away from its park, Truskavets is mostly a grid of unappetising concrete sanatoria with names like Dnipro, Mir and Moldova, but one hillside hotel stands out if you fancy an overnight stay. The foreign-owned **Rixos-Prikarpatye** (☑032-477 1111; www.rixos.com.ua; vul Horodyshche 8; d/tw from 1440uah; ☺❄@☂) is an oasis of luxury with a professional medical centre, trendy modern spa treatments, German patients and Ukrainian oligarchs. It even has its own supply of Sodova and Naftusya – drunk elegantly through straws up here.

Alternatively, for both a pleasant and well-priced stay, try the **Oriana** (☑032-476 9435; www.oriana-hotel.com; prov Tikhy 8; s/d from 150/240uah; ❄), right by Truskavets' joint train and bus station. Its staff generally speak no English.

From Lviv take any of the eight trains a day (10uah to 20uah, 2½ to three hours) that pass through or terminate in Truskavets. Buses (15uah, two hours, every half hour) also leave regularly from Lviv's Bus Station No 8 in front of the train station. They're just marked 'Truskavets'.

Rizdva Khrystovoho Church   CHURCH
(vul Ruska) Ternopil's most attractive ecclesiastical interior belongs to the 17th-century Church of the Nativity. Inside this oasis of calm, the nave explodes in gilded colour, musty murals and polished-brass incense burners.

Bul Taras Shevchenko   BOULEVARD
(bul Taras Shevchenko) The town's leafy showpiece, with landscaping and fountains, is a popular hangout and a nice spot for a stroll. Heading north you stumble upon maydan Teatralni, which at the time of writing was being re-slabbed in rather inappropriate multicoloured crazy paving. It's dominated by the neoclassical **Shevchenko Theatre**. Around 100m along the boulevard, another impressive architectural opus in the neoclassical style is the old **cinema**, also receiving a much-needed post-Soviet facelift.

Ternopil Lake   LAKE
(access behind Hotel Ternopil) Don your best fake D&G, grab a bottled beer and head to the lake, the place to see and be seen

on summer evenings. There are boat trips on the good ship *Geroy Tantsorov,* aquazorbing, a beer-tent strip and a generally jolly atmosphere.

🛏 Sleeping & Eating

The two major hotels have eateries of sorts. You can also try the old town, particularly around vul Hetmana Sahaydachnoho.

Hotel Ternopil   HOTEL **$$**
(☑524 263; www.hotelternopil.com; vul Zamkova 14; s/d from 325/450uah; ☎) Conveniently located between the lake and the Dominican Church, the Ternopil is a renovated former Intourist wedge that now leaves its sister hotel across the water to specialise in shabbiness. The hotel's unusual slogan is 'Time just never stops here' – you may be glad this is true after a night in one of its garish bedrooms.

Hotel Halychyna   HOTEL **$**
(☑533 595; www.hotelhalychyna.com; vul Chumatska 1; standard s/d: 298/360uah) Across the lake, this semi-renovated, Soviet-style

monolith offers the classic miserable Ukrainian hotel experience. The day we visited the receptionist wasn't old enough to remember the USSR, but was well versed in tutting, eye-rolling and general bad manners. The cafe waitress was asleep in the lobby. If you must stay here, go for the standard en-suite room, as everything else is either overpriced or too grotty. Breakfast is served in the adjoining supermarket.

Hotel Globus   HOTEL **$**
(☑550 044; www.globus-hotel.com.ua; vul Stepana Budnoho 18; s from 100uah, d 220-290uah; ✆) This modern, privately run hotel arguably offers a better correlation between price and general amenities than the city's two monoliths. However, it's less conveniently located and even the staff recommend catching a taxi to get here.

❶ Getting There & Away

There are four regional *elektrychky* a day to Lviv (11uah, three to four hours), although the two cities are also linked by numerous other mainline services (40uah, usually 2½ hours) to onward destinations. Frequent trains run to Kyiv (110uah, eight hours), several a day to Odesa (122uah, 10 to 12 hours) and Simferopol (190uah, 22 to 23 hours), as well as one or two a day to Kharkiv (175uah, 19 hours).

Ternopil's frantic bus station lives up to its role as a regional hub. At least 14 direct services a day go to Pochayiv (17uah, 1½ hours), which can also be reached via Kremenets (18uah, 1¼ hours, at least 25 daily). Additionally, buses to Rivne (42uah, four hours, nine daily) and Lutsk (44uah, four hours, at least eight daily) all stop in Kremenets and Dubno (30uah, 2½ hours).

Heading west, several buses an hour go to Lviv (36uah, three hours). Southern destinations include Ivano-Frankivsk (36uah, roughly 30 a day) and Kamyanets-Podilsky (47uah, up to 10 daily).

❶ Getting Around

The train station is on the eastern perimeter of the old city centre and within walking distance of the lake and Hotel Ternopil. The bus station is about 1km south of the centre; trolleybus 9 will get you from the bus station to the train station and the centre.

Pochayiv ПОЧАЇВ

 03546 / POP 8000

Its ornate golden domes rising up from the surrounding plain, **Pochayiv Monastery** (Pochayivska Lavra; admission free; ⊘grounds 24hr, excursion bureau 11am-4pm) is a beacon of Ukrainian Orthodoxy (Moscow Patriarchate) on the edge of a largely Ukrainian Catholic region. Indeed, it's the country's second largest Orthodox complex after Kyiv's Kyevo-Pecherska Lavra and was founded by monks fleeing that mothership when the Mongols sacked Kyiv in 1240.

Visitors will find the monastery's ornate golden dome and church interiors beautiful and its mystical aura intriguing. The atmosphere is much more devout than at the *lavra* in Kyiv.

Pochayiv is frequently packed, but tourists are still outnumbered by pilgrims visiting the Mother of God icon (1597) or the 'footprint of the Virgin Mary'. The busiest religious festivals are the Feast of the Assumption on 28 August and the Feast of

---

WORTH A TRIP

PIDKAMIN ПІДКАМІНЬ

Known today primarily for its striking natural hilltop standing stone, the village of Pidkamin was once most celebrated for its huge fortified monastery. This was founded at the same time as Pochayiv by monks hightailing it from Kyiv before the Mongols hit town in 1240, and was later beefed up to protect the icon of the Blessed Virgin. The icon was spirited away to Wroclaw at the end of WWII when most of the region's Polish population was sent packing. The crumbling remains of the monastery rise just a short amble from the 17m-high rock from which Pidkamin, meaning 'under the rock', takes its name. This was a significant place of pagan ceremony, but the graves circling its base probably belong to 17th-century Cossacks.

Pidkamin comes alive once a year during the large **Pidkamin Ethnofestival** (http://pidkamin.ridne.net) in late July, which attracts acts and audiences from across the Ukrainian-speaking provinces.

As the village is in a different region to Pochayiv, there are virtually no 'cross-border' buses between the two. Regular services run from Brody 22km away, which has good connections to Lviv.

The figure of Queen Bona Sforza looms large over the Kremenets ruins. Polish King Sigismund I presented the castle as a gift to his Italian wife in 1536, and she began levying such onerous taxes on Kremenets that its townsfolk began spinning stories about this greedy 'evil witch'.

In her quest for eternal youth, Bona was rumoured to have bathed in the blood of virgins, some 300 of whom were supposedly spiked on one of the castle's towers. She was said to have been a serial adulterer and a murderous mother-in-law. According to another legend, her ghost still lurks in a well below the castle, emerging each Easter with the key to her gold-filled treasury in her mouth for safekeeping. At the end of the day, however, the only thing certain is that Bona gave her name to the hill on which the castle ruins now stand.

St Iov, a 17th-century Pochayiv abbot and the *lavra's* most important monk, on 10 September.

Both of the monastery's famous religious relics are found in the baroque **Uspensky Cathedral** (1771–83), whose entrance is straight ahead and to your left, on the crest of the hill after you enter the main gate. The famed footprint of Mary, reportedly left after the Virgin appeared to a local monk and a shepherd, has a holy spring with purportedly healing waters. The Mother of God icon is imbued with the power to work any miracle. Both are to the right of the central aisle.

The 65m-tall baroque **bell tower** (1861–71) is worth climbing for the view, if you can sneak in with a tour group or monk. Its central knocker weighs over 315kg.

On the far side of the Uspensky Cathedral is a building with a door leading down to the **Cave Church**. Pilgrims come here to pay their respects to the relics (ie remains) of St Iov.

Because this is an Orthodox place of worship, men aren't allowed to wear hats or shorts, and women must cover their head, knees and hands (no trousers, shorts or skirts above the knee, but six-inch heels seem to be fine). This applies to the churches *and* the grounds. Trouser-clad women can borrow a wraparound skirt from the excursion bureau. The souvenir stalls on the way up to the monastery do a roaring trade in headscarves. No photography is allowed anywhere once through the gates, but a snap of the views from the monastery ramparts is possibly worth a ticking-off from a monk.

Tourists almost always visit Pochayiv as a day trip, either from Ternopil, Kremenets, Dubno or even, if they have a car, from Lviv. Little white *marshrutky* shuttle back and forth almost constantly to and from Kremenets (5uah, 30 minutes), from where you can pick up services on the main Lutsk–Ternopil or Rivne–Ternopil routes (see Getting There & Away sections for each city). They drop off and then wait to fill up at the bottom of the hill below the monastery.

Kremenets КРЕМЕНЕЦЬ

☎ 03546 / POP 22,000

The remains of a hill-top **fortress** (admission 3uah) overlook picturesque Kremenets' cluster of pastel-coloured, freshly renovated churches. The Mongols never managed to capture this castle during their sweep through Kyivan Rus in 1240–41 (despite reaching Kremenets' outskirts), but today it's easily breeched by individual hikers and day-trippers. Dating from at least the 12th century, and possibly earlier, the *zamok* (castle) on Bona Hill now lies in ruins, with only a ring of walls and a gate tower remaining. However, it's a surprisingly pleasant spot for longer-term travellers in Ukraine to while away a few hours and the views from the hill are magnificent.

Unlike the Mongols, Ukrainian Cossacks did manage to conquer Kremenets 400 years later. During the Khmelnytsky uprising against Poland in 1648, the town was liberated by a band of Cossacks, who principally starved out the Poles. Some 100 or so of the Cossacks who died in the accompanying skirmishes are buried in the remarkable **Pyatnystke Kladovyshche** (Pyatnystke Cemetery), where weathered stone crosses bear faint Slavonic inscriptions. The cemetery is completely untended with many of the stubby stones lost in the long grass, but this only adds to its magical atmosphere.

When the Poles regained control of Kremenets, they sealed their victory by building another of the town's main sights, the **Jesuit Collegium** (1731–43) on the main drag through town. In turn the Soviets sealed their triumph in WWII by plonking a bombastic **war monument** right in front of the church.

Yet another of Kremenets' claims to fame is as the birthplace of renowned Jewish violinist Isaac Stern in 1920. Jewish communities lived here, on and off, from the 15th century until 1942, when the Nazis massacred 15,000 people herded into the ghetto here.

The old town centre and fortress both lie 2.5km south of the bus station along the main artery, vul Shevchenko. Turn right when exiting the bus station or bus station office, and walk 30 to 40 minutes to the town, which is strung out along the road. To climb the hill, keep going to just past the edge of the town until you reach a turn off marked with a yellow sign bearing the words замкова гора. The entire walk from the bus station to the summit takes roughly 1¼ hours. Alternatively, take one of the many buses or *marshrutky* from the bus station to the centre to halve your journey on foot.

To reach the Cossack cemetery, look for the town market, with the word рунок across an arch. Heading from here back north to the bus station, take the next right. Bear left where the road forks and walk about 10 minutes uphill.

The most convenient place to stay is **Hotel Vika** (☑238 83; vul Dubenska 57; r 140-190uah), a big yellow building between the bus station and the centre with unexciting, but clean, new rooms and friendly staff. If full, the owners have another hotel with a restaurant.

From Kremenets, there are some 40 daily buses and *marshrutky* to and from Ternopil (18uah, two hours), and a regular service to and from Pochayiv (5uah, 30 minutes). In addition, hourly buses go to and from Rivne and Lutsk (both 15uah, 2½ hours) and two buses daily to Lviv (35uah, 3¼ hours).

Ternopil Caves ПЕЧЕРИ ТЕРНОПІЛЬЩИНИ

The Ternopil region is home to dozens of karst caves, including the 212km-long **Optimistic Cave**, one of Europe's largest. These are all 100km south of Ternopil, near Bor-

shchiv. It's not really safe to visit without a tour, but unfortunately, as with so many Ukrainian sightseeing gems, tours are sometimes tricky to arrange. Your best bet is to try to organise something well in advance with Lviv's **Fund of Support for Scientific and Creative Initiatives** (☑0322-404 624; www.cave-ua.narod.ru).

VOLYN & RIVNE REGIONS

Lutsk ЛУЦЬК

POP 211,200

Infinitely more charming than Ternopil to the south and Rivne to the east, Volyn's chief city of Lutsk has a split personality. The modern town is a relatively successful example of Soviet architecture, with broad boulevards and monumental squares creating a feeling of freedom and space. But the real jewel in Lutsk's crown is its historic quarter. A small, refurbished enclave of cobbled streets is lined with architecture from centuries past, harking back to Lutsk's Lithuanian, Polish and Russian history. It hardly gives, say, Krakow much competition, but in Ukraine it's a rarity.

Starting from modern Lutsk's central hub of maydan Teatralny, traffic-free vul Lesi Ukrainky heads southwest towards the picturesque old town, which nestles across busy vul Kovelska in a bend of the Styr River. The leafy vul Lesi Ukrainky is only rivalled by pr Voli, leading east off maydan Teatralny, as the city's most popular pedestrian strip.

◉ Sights

Lutsk Castle   CASTLE
(vul Kafedralna 1; admission 10uah; ⊙10am-7pm Tue-Sun) Lutsk's 14th-century castle stands surrounded by ornate 17th-century churches and homes and is in fairly decent shape for a Ukrainian fortress. Known as Lubart's Castle after the Lithuanian prince who ordered it built, it has sturdy 13m-high ramparts topped with three tall towers, one containing a collection of bells. There are also the archaeological remains of a 12th-century church and 14th-century palace, a small dungeon, a museum of books and small art collection (extra 3uah). In late August the castle is the main venue for the **Artjazz Festival** (www.artjazz.info) held simultaneously in Lutsk and Rivne.

Saint Peter's and Paul's Cathedral
CATHEDRAL

(vul Kafedralna) The Jesuit complex on vul Kafedralna was designed in the early to mid-17th century by Italian architect Giacomo Briano. The stately white-and-blue façade of the cathedral dates from 1640, the renovated interior – painted in pink and yellow tones – resembling a massive Easter egg. Closed following WWII, the building served as a museum of atheism in the 1970s. To the right you'll find the entrance to the town's huge network of **underground tunnels** (admission 5uah; ☉10am-5pm Sat & Sun). Created in the 16th century, these were used by locals to move about freely without being seen by the authorities, whether Polish, Nazi or Soviet. Tours are guided but some may be put off by the passageways' derelict state. In summer this is the coolest place in Lutsk.

Trochenbrod shtetl
JEWISH SITE

The former Jewish *shtetl* (village) of Trochenbrod – fictionalised as Trachimbrod in Jonathan Safran Foer's cult novel *Everything is Illuminated* (2002) – used to lie some 30km northeast of Lutsk. There are four Jewish memorials within the former town's footprint, but this area is exceedingly tricky to find. If you're really set on visiting, we recommend contacting an agency like Lviv Ecotour well in advance.

Trinity Church
CHURCH

(maydan Teatralny) The main Orthodox church in Lutsk dates from 1752 and is a much more atmospheric affair than the Catholic cathedral, not having been stripped of its gilding and icons by the Soviets. The interior is perfumed with beeswax candles and infused with 260 years of worship.

🛏 Sleeping

Hotel Zaleski
HOTEL $$

(☎0332-772 701; www.zaleski-hotel.com; vul Krivy Val 39, s/d from 500/700uah; ✳🛜) Finally Lutsk has an alternative to (un)renovated Soviet-era digs in the shape of this purpose-built hotel just off vul Lesi Ukrainky. Immaculate rooms brim with reproduction antique style, the up-to-the-minute bathrooms are sparkling clean and the English-speaking staff will bend over backwards to assist. The economy singles are a bit poky, but imagine badly varnished parquet floors and transparent curtains and you'll cheer-

fully squeeze yourself into these velveted quarters.

Hotel Ukraina
HOTEL $

(☎0332-788 100/118; www.hotel-lutsk.com; vul Slovatskoho 2; s/d from 250/380uah) A central location overlooking maydan Teatralny, 128 modern rooms offering good standards, and decent prices make this the hotel of choice in Lutsk. Sure, the place has foibles, like a penchant for gold satin bedspreads and hideous 'theme' wallpaper, but with a decent restaurant, pleasant staff and even a spa, the net result is positive. Rates even include a buffet breakfast.

🍴 Eating & Drinking

Korona Vitovta
MEDIEVAL UKRAINIAN $$

(pl Zamkova; mains 25-130uah; ☉noon-midnight; ✳🛜) The idea behind Lutsk's grandest restaurant, which guards the entrance to the castle, came from a recipe book – unearthed during an archaeological dig – that belonged to the cook of King Vitovta of Lithuania. The current chef remains as faithful as possible to those 15th-century recipes (though a few tomatoes and potatoes have crept in somewhere) and the menu is as meat heavy as feasting medieval royals would have demanded. The wall in the entrance hall is hung with photos of the rich and good who have dined here, including Viktor Yushchenko (before he was president).

Celentano
PIZZERIA $

(vul Lesi Ukrainky 57; pizzas 20uah; ☉8am-11pm) This cheery, upbeat and well-kept branch of Ukraine's favourite home-grown pizza chain isn't huge, but sharing a table is a good way to meet the locals.

Rose Cafe
CAFE $

(pr Voli 11; snacks 12-50uah; ☉9am-10pm; ✳🛜) This violet-and-rose postmodern cafe is not only a chic place to be seen, it serves pretty good coffee, sandwiches, milkshakes, cocktails and spirits, too.

Brave Schwejk
BEER RESTAURANT $$

(vul Lesi Ukrainky 56; mains 25-100uah; ☉9am-11pm) Named for the famous fictional Czech soldier Švejk (or Schweik in German) in *Good Soldier Schweik* by Jaroslav Hašek, this place harks back to the novel's Austro-Hungarian era with its mix of sausages, goulash, pigs' knuckles, milk veal and similar specialities. The atmosphere is that of a small beer hall, where you'll find the likes of Paulaner and Warsteiner beer from Germany alongside Staropramen and Krušovice from the Czech Republic. The 48uah business lunch is a filling deal.

ⓘ Getting There & Around

The bus station is 2km northeast of the centre, right next to a market (зал рунок); trolleybuses 5, 8 and 9, plus numerous *marshrutky*, link it to central maydan Teatralny (look for signs like центр or цум).

There are buses to and from Lviv (from 44uah, three hours, twice hourly), including two more comfortable **Autolux** (www.autolux.ua) services heading to and from Kyiv each day. Autolux has a counter at the bus station. *Marshrutky* and buses to Rivne (20uah, 1¼ hours) leave half-hourly and services also run to Ternopil (50uah, 4½ hours), passing through Dubno (16, 1½ hours) and Kremenets (26uah, 2½ hours).

The train station is just a little south of the bus station, and also northeast of the centre. Trolleybuses 4 and 7, plus numerous *marshrutky*, shuttle between here and maydan Teatralny. There are three trains to and from Kyiv (76uah, seven to 9½ hours); the best service from Lutsk is the overnighter leaving at 11.40pm.

Shatsky National Nature Park ШАТСЬКИЙ ЗАПОВІДНИК

The Shatsky National Nature Park lies 160km northwest of Lutsk in the corner between Belarus and Poland, and has some 200 lakes, rivers and streams. However, while fascinating to scientists, Ukraine's wild 'Lake District' and its deep Lake Svityaz is a long way from appealing to all but the most adventurous of (camping and rafting) tourists.

If you are interested in heading to this park, catch one of the frequent buses to Kovel and change for the village of Shatsk. Twelve buses a day also go direct to Shatsk from Lutsk. Don't even consider heading this way without lashings of mosquito repellent.

Dubno ДУБНО

☏ 03656 / POP 37,700

Some 50km south of Lutsk, Dubno is one of several towns in the region with a **castle** (vul Zamkova 7A; admission 5uah; ☺8am-5pm Apr-Oct, to 7pm Nov-Mar), making it a relatively interesting stopover. This is where Andry, the son of Cossack Taras Bulba, falls in love with a Polish princess in Gogol's famous story, *Taras Bulba,* and crosses over to join the princess and her fellow Poles, while his Cossack brothers are busy trying to starve these enemies into submission. There's not that much to see inside, but the views of the sluggish River Ikva from the ramparts are pretty enough. Dubno's only other attraction is the crumbling 1630 **Church of St Nicholas** (vul D Halytskoho), whose telltale plain interior suggests it was used for secu-

THE WORLD OF NIKOLAI GOGOL

Although Taras Shevchenko is the greatest literary figure within Ukraine, one of the best-known Ukrainian writers outside the country's borders must be Nikolai Gogol. He was born in 1809 to impoverished parents in the Cossack village of Sorochyntsi near Poltava. It was here, in deepest rural Ukraine, that Gogol spent his formative years before leaving for St Petersburg in 1828.

Often claimed as a great Russian writer, Gogol was Ukrainian through and through. Many of his stories set in Ukraine are inspired by the supernatural world and the rural superstitions and folk tales of his youth in the Poltavshchina. His tales are set in a land of sun-drenched fields and blue skies, where faded nobles nap in the afternoon heat, Cossacks gulp down bowls of *borshch,* kitchen gardens overflow with tobacco and sunflowers, and shy Ukrainian beauties fall in love under star-dusted skies. Gogol's short novel *Taras Bulba* is a rollicking Cossack tale flush with romantic nationalism, adventure and derring-do.

During his years in St Petersburg, where he was employed in the civil service, his mood changed and his later stories such as *The Nose, Nevsky Prospekt* and *The Inspector General* are darker, gloomier, and riddled with ill health, crime and vice. In fact, the capital had such a bad effect on Gogol that he died in 1852 after burning the second half of his last novel, *Dead Souls,* in a fit of madness.

Gogol is an inspirational companion to pack into your rucksack on long train journeys across the snowbound steppe or midsummer bus trips through Ukraine's endless landscapes.

lar purposes during the decades of Soviet communism.

Every July, Dubno hosts the increasingly popular **Taras Bulba Festival** (www.tarasbul ba-fest.kiev.ua) featuring rock music.

Dubno is conveniently located only 41km from Kremenets and 66km from Pochayiv, making it a good base from which to explore. The unimaginatively renovated **Hotel Dubno** (☑410 86, 418 02; vul D Halytskoho 9; s/d from 200/300uah; ☻✳) with its spotless, reasonably priced accommodation is a good spot to stay while visiting these, though the restaurant seems almost permanently reserved for Dubno's unremitting stream of weddings. If you'd rather not fall asleep to the back catalogue of *Modern Talking*, the five-room, hunting-themed **Antique House** (☑050 579 5905; vul Zamkova 17; s/d from 300/430uah; ☻✳) is an astonishingly well-appointed guesthouse for rural Ukraine and the location at the gates of the castle is superb.

Marshrutky and buses travelling Rivne– Ternopil, Lutsk–Ternopil, Lutsk–Brody and more routes mean there are plentiful connections to/from Dubno. Prices are 16uah from Lutsk and Rivne, 9uah from Kremenets and 27uah from Ternopil.

Rivne PИВНE

☑0362 / POP 249,000

Standing in Rivne's central maydan Nezalezhnosti, you couldn't be anywhere else but Ukraine; the **statue** of poet Taras Shevchenko and the golden-domed **Resurrection Cathedral** (1895) are both emblematic national features. Unfortunately, though, the modestly sized, shiny cathedral is just about the city's only attractive building, for as the Nazis' administrative capital in Ukraine, Rivne took a battering during WWII. It's since been rebuilt in a way only the Soviets knew how.

Frequently bustling with people, this regional hub has more energy than charm, and it's hard to imagine anyone specifically coming to see the sights here. However, if you're in town, there's a large park to wander in. In summer, the **market** is worth checking out for the region's semitranslucent cherries, while locals flock to **Gilcha Lake**, about 20km south of Rivne on the road to **Ostroh**, where there's an attractive 'castle hill' (namely, castle ruins).

Rivne is easy to negotiate. The central district stretches about 3.5km west to east along a long boulevard that starts off as vul Soborna and becomes vul Kyivska. At the western end is the market, with the train station a couple of blocks north of this. In the east lies the bus station along vul Kyivska. The town centre and maydan Nezalezhnosti lie approximately halfway in between, and most *marshrutky* and buses heading east from the market or west from the train station pass through it.

Overnighters on a budget can try the **Hotel Tourist** (☑267 413; www.rivnetourist. com.ua; vul Kyivska 36; s/d from 180/220uah), a freshly painted concrete hulk looming over the bus station with hideously done-up rooms. Much further up the hotel evolutionary scale, the **Hotel Marlen** (☑690 600; www.marlen.com.ua; cnr vuls Hrushevskoho 13 & Pushova; r from 370uah; ☎✳) is the city's poshest lodgings but has only nine rooms. Despite its slightly snooty attitude and trappings of 'luxury' (like a small casino), the décor is generally tasteful, especially in the light-filled upper atrium.

There are frequent bus services between Rivne and most outlying towns and larger cities, including half-hourly buses to Lutsk (20uah, one to 1½ hours) and hourly services to Ternopil (35uah, four hours via Kremenets). There are four trains a day to and from Kyiv (54uah, six to seven hours), plus daily services to Minsk (10 hours) and Warsaw (17 hours).

The Carpathians
Карпати

POP 3.5 MILLION

Best Places to Eat

» Reflection (p133)

» Olenka (p130)

» Beer Club 10 (p118)

Best Places to Stay

» On the Corner (p125)

» Smerekova Hata (p130)

» Good Morning B&B (p125)

» Old Continent (p136)

» Atrium (p117)

Why Go?

Clipping the country's southwest corner, the Carpathian arc has endowed Ukraine with a crinkled region of forested hills and fast-flowing rivers, a million miles from the flatness of the steppe. This is the land of the Hutsuls, whose colourful folk culture is laced through thin villages stretching languidly along wide valley floors. The Carpathians are rural Ukraine at its best, where tiered wooden churches dot hillsides, horse-drawn carts clip-clop along potholed roads, *babushkas* shoo geese, and *marshrutka* (fixed-price minibus) passengers cross themselves as they whizz past roadside chapels.

The 'Hutsulshchyna' may be Ukraine's epicentre of rural folk culture, but this is also a leading holiday spot. The local peaks have been a long-term hit with Ukrainian hikers and skiers; the Carpathian National Nature Park, the country's biggest, lies in this region, and within the park's boundaries rises Mt Hoverla – Ukraine's highest peak at 2061m. It's also home to Bukovel, Ukraine's glitziest ski resort.

When to Go?
Ivano-Frankivsk

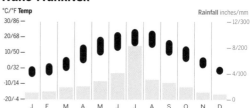

July Picnic on flower-filled *polonyna* (summer pastures) as you listen to the tinkle of cow bells.

September Say 'cheese' at the Hutsul cheese-making festival in Rakhiv.

December Enjoy some hearty Hutsul après-ski during the Carpathian ski season.

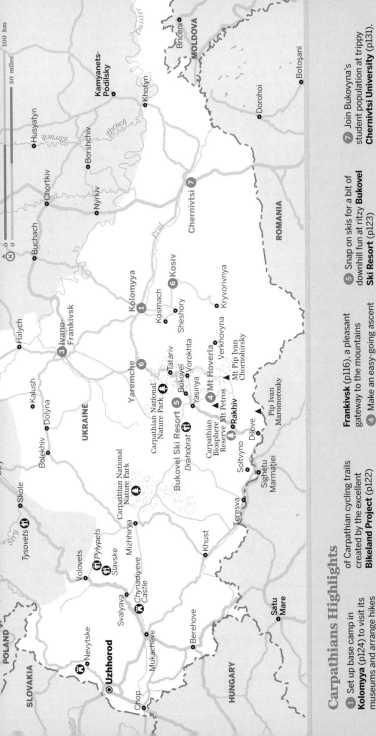

Carpathians Highlights

1 Set up base camp in **Kolomyya** (p124) to visit its museums and arrange hikes into the hills

2 Hire a two-wheeler to enjoy the ups and downs of Carpathian cycling trails created by the excellent **Bikeland Project** (p122)

3 Wander the pastel-coloured heart of **Ivano-Frankivsk** (p116), a pleasant gateway to the mountains

4 Make an easy-going ascent of Ukraine's highest peak, **Mt Hoverla** (p120)

5 Snap on skis for a bit of downhill fun at ritzy **Bukovel Ski Resort** (p123)

6 Bargain hard for Hutsul souvenirs at markets in **Kosiv** (p127) and **Yaremche** (p121)

7 Join Bukovyna's student population at trippy **Chernivtsi University** (p131), one of Eastern Europe's most mind-boggling places of learning

History

Formed some 50 million years ago, during the same geological upheavals that produced the Alps, the crescent-shaped Carpathians were the cradle of Hutsul civilisation, and they're still home to this hardy mountain tribe.

A natural barrier between the Slavic countries and Romanised Dacia (Romania), the Carpathians have always provided a refuge from conquest and authority. When the Mongols sacked Kyiv in 1240, many of the city's citizens fled here, and when Poland and Lithuania invaded in the 14th century it's questionable how much control they exercised in the region's higher altitudes. The Poles' lengthy struggle to capture the 'Ukrainian Robin Hood' Oleska Dovbush (see p123) suggest it was very little.

Signs of 19th-century Austro-Hungarian culture haven't penetrated deeper than Ivano-Frankivsk and Chernivtsi. And when the Soviets rolled up after WWII, locals didn't exactly get out the salt and bread. The Ukrainian Insurgent Army (UPA) survived as guerrillas in the Carpathians well into the 1950s, using the mountains as a stronghold from which to launch attacks on the authorities (the UPA is a controversial entity because of its probable, but unquantified, role in the extermination of Ukrainian Jews during WWII). However, even ordinary Carpathian villagers resisted Russian rule.

The Soviets weren't initially keen on the Hutsuls' folklore and pagan traditions, but came to see their culture as a tourist attraction and largely let them be. However, the Hutsuls have long been integrated into mainstream western Ukrainian culture. Their arts, crafts, cuisine and farming lifestyle all survive, but they reserve their traditional dress, music and dancing for celebrations, ceremonies and other special occasions.

Ivano-Frankivsk
ІВАНО-ФРАНКІВСЬК

📲 0342 / POP 240,000

With pastel-coloured neoclassical buildings, neatly landscaped gardens and orderly, tree-lined cobblestoned pavements, the spruced-up city of Ivano-Frankivsk is increasingly becoming one of Ukraine's most pleasant.

'Ivano' was a closed city until 1991 but you'd never guess it today. The city's pedestrianised thoroughfares, street cafes and a well-established tourist office now make this one of the west's more visitor-friendly cities. Add to that a couple of decent places to eat and sleep and an overnight stay here becomes even more attractive.

For many Ivano-Frankivsk is merely a gateway to the Carpathians and a popular jumping-off point for the northern peaks, but the city is very much worth a day of exploration in its own right.

⊙ Sights

'Ivano' is somewhere nice to wander through, rather than a place offering loads of individual things to see. The main pedestrian drag and Ivano's single most attractive street is **vul Nezalezhnosti** with rows of refurbished neoclassical buildings in differing pastel colours, housing restaurants, cafes and boutiques.

Former Armenian Church
CHURCH

(Колишня Вірменська церква; Українська католицька церква; vul Virmenska 6) A few steps off Rynok Square stands this eye-pleasingly symmetrical baroque church built by the Armenian community in 1762. Beyond the golden doors the interior is a typically fragrant affair busy with head-scarved *babushkas* lighting beeswax candles and praying before gilt icons.

Cathedral of the Holy Resurrection
CATHEDRAL

(Кафедральний собор Страсного Воскресіння; maydan Sheptytskoho 22) The city's freshly renovated Greek Catholic cathedral is another example of baroque symmetry crafted in the mid-18th century. The beautiful and aromatic interior is dark, musty and best experienced during one of the many services held here daily.

Regional Museum
MUSEUM

(Краєзнавчий музей; pl Rynok 4A; admission 5uah; ⊙8.30am-5.30pm Tue-Sun) Ivano's heart is Rynok Square (Площа Ринок), which is ringed with numerous colourful buildings. The star-shaped town hall at its centre houses the vaguely distracting Regional Museum, which displays the results of various archaeological digs in the region, some pieces of folk art and exhibits relating to the history of Ivano-Frankivsk. The town hall building is also home to the city's superb tourist office.

Ivano-Frankivsk is the most prominent example of the many places in Ukraine named after a poet, politician, translator, writer, journalist and academic whom locals revere. Ivan Franko (1856–1916) was a typical 19th-century polymath and, alongside Taras Shevchenko, became a leading figure in the revival of Ukrainian language and culture under the Austro-Hungarian regime.

Born the son of a village blacksmith near Lviv, Ivan Frank (he added the 'o' later to make his name sound Ukrainian) studied Ukrainian literature at the Lviv university that now bears his name. Over his short lifetime, he wrote countless poems and articles, edited numerous (often banned) newspapers and led several left-wing workers' groups. His nationalist and Marxist leanings saw him serve three terms in imperial jails for political agitation. Ironically, some of his most eloquent works date from his time in prison.

Franko died in 1916 in a house purchased for him in 1902 by Lviv University students who were ashamed to see such an inspirational figure living alone in poverty. Today, hundreds of streets, squares and buildings across the country bear his name. Indeed, in 1962 the Soviets offered up his moniker as an olive branch to Ukrainian nationalist guerrillas in the Carpathians, who'd been taking pot shots at them since WWII. That's when the one-time Polish town known as Stanyslaviv became Ivano-Frankivsk.

Art Museum   ART MUSEUM
(Художній музей; maydan Sheptytskoho 8; admission 5uah; ⊙10am-5pm Tue-Sun) Ensconced in the 17th-century Church of the Blessed Virgin Mary, the city's oldest building, this museum is packed with a jumble of religious sculptures and paintings from around Central Europe.

Egg Fountain   FOUNTAIN
(Фонтан-яйце; maydan Vichevy) The dominating feature on maydan Vichevy is the Egg Fountain, a popular meeting spot. If you descend the steps below the fountain's main 'bowl', you can stand beneath the cascading water without getting wet – a little factoid of which locals are inordinately proud, especially those posing for wedding photos.

Taras Shevchenko Park   PARK
(vul Shevchenka) Around 20 minutes' walk south from maydan Vichevy, the city's main stretch of green is a great place to shake out the picnic blanket, hire a rowboat on the lake or chill with an ice cream to do a spot of people-watching of a balmy eve. The approaches to the park are lined with refurbished Austro-Hungarian mansions and the grounds have been beautifully landscaped thanks to EU money.

Regional Administration Building
                    OFFICIAL BUILDING
(Обласна державна адміністрація; vul Hrushevskoho) This Soviet-realist hulk is worth seeing for its sheer size and bombast. The two traditional Ukrainian musician statues that guard the entrance are particularly impressive.

🛏 Sleeping

Atrium   MINI-HOTEL **$$**
(Атріум; ☑557 879; www.atrium.if.ua; vul Halytska 31; s 300uah, tw & d from 400uah; ❄🛜) Ivano's most central beds can be found in this new and soothingly well-heeled mini-hotel looking out across Rynok Square. Rooms are studies in leathery luxury, bathrooms dazzle and staff are keen to show off their well-tuned English. Guests receive a 10% discount in the hotel's first-rate restaurant and cafe. One slight downside is that smoking is permitted in five of the 11 rooms, but you can hardly tell.

Hotel Auscoprut   HOTEL **$**
(Готель Аускопрут; ☑234 01; www.auscoprut.if.ua; vul Hryunvaldska 7/9; s 200-260uah, d 330-400uah; ❄) This slightly faded Austro-Hungarian *grande dame* has much more character than its slicker rivals. Past the duck-egg blue, baroque exterior, you'll find creaky parquet flooring, stained-glass windows and wrought-iron lacework, all of which is offset by some amusingly dated furniture. Modern bathrooms, efficient service and a decent restaurant make this hotel near the train station well worth considering.

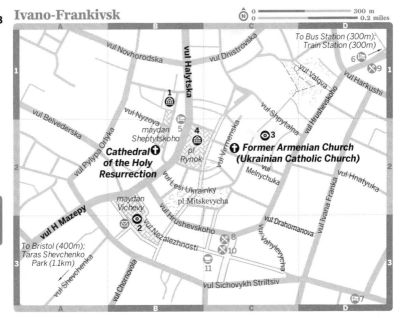

N 0 ——— 300 m
0 ——— 0.2 miles

To Bus Station (300m);
Train Station (300m)

vul Novhorodska

vul Halytska

vul Dnistrovska

vul Harkushi

vul Valova

vul Nyzova

vul Shpytalna

vul Hrushevskoho

maydan
Sheptytskoho

pl
Rynok

vul Shpytalna

vul Belvederska

Cathedral
of the Holy
Resurrection

vul Pylypa Orlyka

vul Virmenska

Former Armenian Church
(Ukrainian Catholic Church)

vul
Melnychuka

vul Hnatyuka

vul Lesi Ukrainky

pl Mitskevycha

vul Ivana Franka

maydan
Vichevy

vul Drahomanova

vul H Mazepy

vul Hrushevskoho

vul Nezalezhnosti

vul Vahylevycha

To Bristol (400m);
Taras Shevchenko
Park (1.1km)

vul Shevchenka

vul Chornovola

vul Sichovykh Striltsiv

Hotel Nadiya   RENOVATED SOVIET **$$**

(Готель Надія; ☎727 077; www.nadia.if.ua; vul Nezalezhnosti 40; s/d from 330/500uah; ➋@🛜) If you're looking for generic, Western-style comfort, the central, brightly painted Nadiya is the one for you. The floral rooms are well equipped with 21st-century bathrooms, and there's a sound buffet breakfast served in the restaurant adjoining the sparkling, tiled lobby. However, for this price you'd expect free wi-fi.

Stanislavsky Dvir   SMALL HOTEL **$**

(☎550 808; www.s-dvir.if.ua; vul Depovska 97; r 250uah; ❄🛜) This newly built, family-run place has 13 immaculate rooms with typically busy décor and a celebrated Ukrainian theme restaurant. The location on the wrong side of the tracks behind the train station is not ideal, but we were assured train noise is not an issue at night.

🍴 Eating & Drinking

TOP
CHOICE
Beer Club 10

MICROBREWERY RESTAURANT **$**

(Півний Клуб Десятка; vul Shashkevycha 4; mains 7-25uah; ⏰noon-10pm) Good for a light lunch or a night on the house-brewed Klubne beer, this warren of brick cellars decorated with an assortment of international beer paraphernalia has a decidedly

Central European vibe. Insert yourself at one of the hefty wooden tables, wait for your golden ale to arrive (with free peanuts) then choose from the thirst-inducing menu. Service is unusually brisk, and the crowd gets more good-natured as the night progresses.

Slovan   INTERNATIONAL **$**

(Слован; vul Shashkevycha 4; pizzas & other mains 15-50uah; ⏰8am-11pm) Slovan's white walls, dark wooden panelling and brown floor tiles make it one of Ivano's most stylish restaurants and its wooden-decked terrace is a popular spot to be seen in summer. Breakfasts (French, Italian or Hutsul) are complemented by homemade pastas, gourmet fillets of beef and humble fare such as jacket potatoes and pizza.

Sadko   CHINESE **$$**

(vul Hetmana Mazepy 138; mains 33-150uah; 🅿) With a balcony offering primo views across the lake, Sadko produces a fine interpretation of Chinese cuisine. There's sushi in the clubby room downstairs too. Duck and seafood feature heavily, at least eight veggie options satisfy non-carnivores and you can wash it all down with one of the 35 cocktails (23uah to 60uah) or a delicately brewed cup of tea.

Ivano-Frankivsk

Marrakesh   NORTH AFRICAN $
(Маракеш; vul Hryunvaldska 4A; mains 9-28uah)
This friendly North African restaurant
might have been more memorable if it always served the tagine, couscous and *plov*
dishes on the menu. Usually you have to
improvise with salad, baba ganoush–style
pickled eggplants, spicy sauce or other alternatives. Still, the oriental-style concrete
basement is cool when the heat's up, and
the summer terrace is a winner.

Bristol   INTERNATIONAL $$
(vul Shevchenka 68; mains 12-75uah) Treat your-
self at this elegant Ukrainian-European-
French establishment where the menu
includes such delights as Caesar salad,
spaghetti, veal, frogs' legs and even pâté de
foie gras.

Cafe Kimbo   CAFE $
(Кафе Кімбо; vul Nezalezhnosti 10A) This sum-
mer street cafe and indoor winter retreat is
generally regarded as serving the best cof-
fee in town. The desserts aren't bad either.

🛈 Information

Central post office (Поштамт; maydan Vi-
chevy; ⊙8am-7pm Mon-Fri, 9am-5pm Sat)

Karpaty Tour (Карпати тур; ☑050 434 0958;
www.karpaty-tour.com; vul Nezalezhnosti
40) Located in Hotel Nadiya, this agency runs
Carpathian tours.

Tourist Information Centre (Центр
туристичної інформації; ☑502 474; www.rtic.
if.ua; pl Rynok 4A; ⊙10am-4pm Mon-Fri) This
excellent, NGO-run centre hands out city maps
and English-language pamphlets. There's no
booking service.

Ukrtelekom (maydan Vichevy; internet per hr
3.60uah; ⊙internet centre 8am-10pm, tele-
phone centre 8am-10pm Mon-Fri, 9am-7pm Sat
& Sun) Go to the left for long-distance phone
calls and right for internet access.

🛈 Getting There & Away

BUS The brand new bus station (Автовокзал)
building is next to the train station on pl
Pryvokzalna. There are numerous services into
the Carpathians including to Yaremche (16uah,
70 minutes, half-hourly), Kolomyya (14uah, one
hour, every 15 to 30 minutes), Chernivtsi (32uah,
four hours, at least three daily) and Rakhiv
(25uah, four hours, three daily).

Heading north from Ivano-Frankivsk, at least
12 buses daily go to Lviv (30uah, three hours),
leaving every hour until early evening. Longer-
distance buses also go to Kyiv (90uah, 12 hours,
twice daily).

TRAIN There are three daily trains to Kyiv
(152uah, 12 hours) and Lviv (from 78uah, 3½ to
seven hours), plus services to Uzhhorod (75uah,
seven to eight hours, daily), among others.

Local trains serve Kolomyya (20uah, four to
five daily) and Rakhiv (11uah, 5½ hours, twice
daily). Three to four trains daily pass through to
Chernivtsi (56uah, 3½ hours), but only one at a
sensible time.

CARPATHIAN NATIONAL NATURE PARK & AROUND КАРПАТСЬКИЙ НАЦІОНАЛЬНИЙ ПРИРОДНИЙ ПАРК

This is Ukraine's largest national park and
the heart of the Carpathians. However, it's
a very different sort of national park – in-
dustrial logging occurs here, for example.
Only about a quarter of the area is com-
pletely protected, but that hasn't detracted
too much from the natural beauty of the
place...yet.

Founded in 1980, the Carpathian Na-
tional Nature Park (CNNP) covers 503 sq
km of wooded mountains and hills. Parts

KIPPING IN THE CARPATHIANS

Several websites advertise homestays and other accommodation in the Carpathians, including www.adventurecarpathians.com, www.greentour.com.ua, and www. bikeland.com.ua. However, none is as well maintained, organised and user-friendly as the outstanding www.karpaty.info, which features more listings than any guidebook could ever feasibly include. Hotels, guesthouses and B&Bs are visited by the website's administrators, who post photos, prices, the languages that the hosts speak as well as basic transport information. Most of the website's content is now in English, too.

If you're looking for something a little cheaper still, wild camping is allowed within most of the Carpathian National Nature Park, apart from the eastern side of Mt Hoverla. You'll have to pay the CNNP entrance fee, but this is just a few hryvnya.

There are no mountain huts or properly equipped camp sites. You will find some well-used fireplaces, even though fires are officially prohibited throughout the park. This rule is now enforced quite strictly in summer due to the heightened risk of forest fires.

of it shelter small numbers of animals and the alpine meadows are carpeted with species of flora. Realistically, however, hiking and skiing are the main reasons to head this way.

The Carpathian National Nature Park straddles the Ivano-Frankivska and Zakarpatska oblasti. From the city of Ivano-Frankivsk, the A265 cuts southwards into the heart of the park. Yaremche, 60km south of Ivano-Frankivsk, sits across the park's northern boundary. Yasinya, 37km further south along the A265, marks the park's westernmost point. Rakhiv, 62km south of Yaremche on the A265, is just outside the southwestern boundary.

Because it stands a little apart from the main CNNP, the adjoining Carpathian Biosphere Reserve is discussed under its main entry point, Rakhiv.

Train services are less frequent and extensive in the mountains than in other Ukrainian regions, so be prepared to ride the crowded buses and *marshrutky,* and budget for the occasional taxi. Otherwise, agencies and hotels in Lviv, Ivano-Frankivsk and Kolomyya can organise guided tours and transportation.

Maps featuring varying degrees of detail are becoming easier to source and are available from most tourist information centres throughout the Carpathians. Maps 165 and 184 in the old *Topograficheskaya Karta* map series cover the park and surrounding area (1:100,000 scale), but feature few hiking trails. The superb new Bikeland maps (1:70,000 scale) will soon be downloadable from www.bikeland.com.ua and cover large areas of the park.

 Activities

First, a word of warning: hiking 'trails' crisscross the Carpathians, but until recently no serious attempt had been made to systematically signpost them. Most Ukrainians rely on a combination of personal family memory, logging roads and topographical maps to find their way. However, the trail to Ukraine's highest peak, **Mt Hoverla** (2061m), is well marked, as is the continuing journey along the Chornohora ridge.

These trails aside, hiking in the Carpathians is usually best done in the company of locals and there is no shortage of guides and tours, official and unofficial, in the area.

For information about skiing destinations, see Bukovel, plus the boxed text, Off Piste (p124).

Hiking Hoverla

It's hardly the most remote trail in the Carpathians, nor the most litter-free, but the popular ascent to Ukraine's highest peak is relatively easy to achieve. On a clear day, the expansive views from Mt Hoverla are also breathtaking. Initially, the trail follows the Yaremche–Vorokhta–Zaroslyak road, so how much of the way you want to hike and how much you want to cover by *marshrutka* (which go as far as Vorokhta) or taxi is up to you.

About 7km south of Vorokhta (guides know the place as 'sedmoy kilometr'), you will need to take the right fork in the road, heading west to Zaroslyak, where there's a **hotel** (☎034 344 1592; r from 80uah). En route, you will cross the CNNP boundary and pay the entrance fee (adult/child 15/5uah). From

Zaroslyak (20km from Vorokhta) it's about 3.5km to the summit of Mt Hoverla, which is marked with a big iron cross and a huge Ukrainian national flag (and occasionally a provocative EU flag, too).

Along the Chornohora Ridge

The southern Chornohora peak of **Mt Pip Ivan Chornohirsky** (2028m; not to be confused with Mt Pip Ivan Maramorosky) is well known for the abandoned **astronomical observatory** atop it. The Poles completed this observatory just before WWII, and anything of value has been looted, but the place stills retains atmosphere.

One of the easiest routes to Pip Ivan is along the crest of the Chornohora ridge from Mt Hoverla via Lake Nesamovyte. It's hard to get lost this way, as your views are unimpeded, and the route follows the former interwar border between Poland and Czechoslovakia, passing the old boundary markers. At more than 40km return, the hike will take at least three days.

Chornohora Mountains

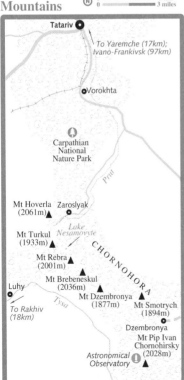

Other routes to Pip Ivan include coming from the village of Verkhovyna via Dzembronya and over Mt Smotrych (requiring at least one night's camping out). Alternatively, you can approach the mountain from Rakhiv.

ℹ️ Information

Visitors tend to pay the CNNP entrance fee (adult/child 15/5uah) as they pass one of the rangers' huts that are on virtually every trail into the park. In the unlikely event you'll need it, the **CNNP Headquarters** (📞03434 211 55; www.cnnp.yaremcha.com.ua; vul Stusa 6, Yaremche; ⊙9am-5pm Mon-Fri), a white concrete building with a distinctive stained-glass window, can be reached by heading uphill from the railway line in central Yaremche. This is also where you will find the excellent, EU-funded **Ecotourism Information Centre** (📞03434 222 59; ⊙10am-5pm), which includes an exhibition on the culture and natural history of the Carpathians.

Yaremche Яремче

📞03434 / POP 7600

Stretching for around 10km along the valley of the Prut River, your average Ukrainian shuns Yaremche (also sometimes known as Yaremcha) as too touristy and overcrowded. True, the blitz of Hutsul souvenir markets and naff theme restaurants can be a turn-off, but Yaremche is, in the end, all about heading out into the wilds and not about the town itself. Plus it has more guesthouses and eateries than any other Carpathian valley community and is also a good place to look for a guide.

The town is an easily reachable staging point for an ascent of Mt Hoverla. By catching a *marshrutka* or taxi to Vorokhta or beyond you can get to Ukraine's highest peak and back in a day or two, depending on your preferred pace. As the epicentre of the Bikeland project, Yaremche is one of the best places in the Ukrainian Carpathians to strike out on two knobbly wheels. With more cycle-hire places than Kyiv, there are plenty of people around here willing to help you do it.

⊙ Sights & Activities

Dovbush Cliffs

The most popular activity in Yaremche (second only to souvenir shopping) is a hike to the nearby Dovbush Cliffs. To get there, pass the Hutsulshchyna restaurant

BIKELAND

In recent years no other single initiative has caused such a kerfuffle in the Carpathians as **Bikeland** (Велокраїна in Ukrainian, 098 1025 500; www.bikeland.com.ua). The brainchild of Yaremche-based cycling fanatic Viktor Zagreba, this project to construct a network of cycling routes throughout the Carpathian region attracted EU funding as well as an army of eager mountain-biking volunteers who pedalled off into the wilds to create the 1300km of marked trails. Hotels and guesthouses affiliated to the Bikeland project guarantee bike-friendly facilities, such as storage and a place to wash two-wheelers, and the initiative has also spawned a number of cycle hire centres (mountain bikes 90-100uah per day), most notably in Yaremche, meaning there's no need to haul your velocipede through customs at Boryspil Airport.

For more details the Bikeland website is a mine of information not just on cycling, but on the Carpathians in general, and the maps the project produces are superb, even if you're not heading up into the hills to cycle. The Bikeland magazine is published yearly and can be downloaded from the web, as can maps and GPS coordinates for all 52 routes. According to Viktor Zagreba, other Ukrainian regions are ripe for the Bikeland treatment, with Lviv and Crimea currently top of the list.

to where a trail rises left off the road. This is the beginning of the not-too-taxing trek. The caves are actually a series of boulders, which were pushed off a cliff to form shelters that outlaws once used as hideouts. With several looped trails around here, you could spend anything from half an hour to three hours walking.

🛏 Sleeping & Eating

U Lesi
B&B $

(213 04, 067 907 6432; mama86yaremche@ meta.ua; vul Kovpaka 24; d 80uah; P) What this youthful family home lacks in space it makes up for in friendliness and laughter. This is a top choice for language students or budget travellers with some Ukrainian language skills. Should the bonhomie ever get too overwhelming, there's also a nice gazebo for chilling.

Mriya
B&B $

(221 68, 067 902 1718; vul Hnata Hotkevych 8A; d from 250uah) Having built a brand new wooden cottage, Mriya's owners have then bizarrely filled it with old-fashioned furnishings in green-grey tones. However, the bathrooms, price and riverside location are all pretty decent, while the sauna and 'smoking room' with open fire lend a touch of elegance. To get here, find the Favorit store (фаворіт) on the main road, head south, take the next left, first right and next left and then keep going to the end of the street.

Krasna Sadyba
HOTEL $

(212 75, 222 53; vul Ivasyuka 6; s/d from 150/200) In a secluded corner yet just min-utes from the centre, this red-brick hotel on the river looks like something from 'Hansel and Gretel'. Most of the 15 rooms are spacious and fashionable, and the few more basic rooms are good bargains. The river here is unusually free of litter, making a dip quite appealing.

Hotel Edelweiss
HOTEL $$

(reception 225 78, reservations 0342-559 546; www.bukovel.com; vul Petrasha 60; s/d from 210/370; ❄ ❋) All Yaremche's top-end hotels – Edelweiss, Vodospad, Karpaty, Stanyslav – lie in this enclave south of the town centre, and if you're going to spend this sort of money, the Edelweiss is the best pick. Its panoramic glass lift takes you up to the admittedly compact but elegant rooms, decorated in classic French style. Getting to Edelweiss might be tricky without your own car, but the hotel belongs to the Bukovel resort, so you should be able to arrange transfers to the snowfields from here.

Kolyba Krasna Sadyba
HUTSUL $

(vul Ivasyuka 6; mains 12-34uah; ⏰11am-midnight; 🍴) Krasna Sadyba's *kolyba* (wooden hut) is rightfully considered the best eating spot in Yaremche. That's despite slightly pushy waiters and a smoky grill room that overheats in summer, because you can't beat eating sumptuous spit-roasted pork, beef *shashlyk* (shish kebab), chicken wings or salmon on a terrace overlooking a leafy, quiet stretch of river. *Borshch,* forest mushroom soup, carp, trout, *kulesha* or *banosh* (polenta) are other options.

(vul Svobody; mains 20-90uah) Quite understandably the backdrop to many souvenir photos, this ornate log cabin, with its central spire and faint sprinkling of Hutsul colour, serves pretty decent food. The menu includes river fish, forest mushrooms, polenta, pancakes and all sorts of other regional fare.

Getting There & Around

There are regular buses and *marshrutky* to Yaremche from Ivano-Frankivsk (13uah, 1¼ hours) and Kolomyya (10uah, 70 minutes). Yaremche also lies on most routes in and out of Rakhiv (18uah, three hours), one of which heads to Chernivtsi (32uah, 3¼ hours) daily. Nearby destinations include Bukovel and Vorokhta.

All the following services stop at Yaremche train station Kolomyya–Rakhiv (one each way daily), Lviv–Rakhiv (one each way daily), Ivano-Frankivsk–Rakhiv (two each way daily).

Tatariv Татарів

Tatariv is little more than a cluster of buildings clinging to an intersection. However, its proximity to leading ski resort Bukovel makes it a popular winter destination. In summer, it's also a useful base for hikes into the Eastern Horhany Mountains, particularly Mts Khomyak and Synyak. Six-room **Prutets Sadyba** (☏03434 352 95; lileja@gmail.com; vul Nezalezhnosti; s/d 120/150uah; ❄) is a surprisingly chic place for such a rural setting. With sheepskin rugs and a vaguely Scandina-

vian fireplace in the open living room, it seems a bit like a ski pad straight from a vodka advert. A short distance along the road is the slightly more homely **Anastasiya** (☏03434 352 54; vul Nezalezhnosti; s/d 80/120uah), where you can choose between rooms with or without a Hutsul theme. The owners also run a small tourist information office out front.

Regular Yaremche–Vorokhta *marshrutka* and bus services go through Tatariv.

Bukovel Буковель

☏03434

Hard-core regional skiers were sceptical when this ritzy resort opened in 2003–04 and immediately began attracting oligarchs from Kyiv and other 'new Ukrainian' guests. However, as the country's first fully planned ski area, **Bukovel** (☏0342-559 546, toll-free 0800 5050 880; www.bukovel.com) soon won doubters over with its sensible network of lifts and trails, printed trail maps, orderly queues, snowmaking machines and 'night-time' slopes (5pm to 8pm).

Here are the numbers: over 50km of runs range from 900m to 1370m in altitude. Following recent expansion there are 16 lifts making this one of Eastern Europe's largest ski resorts. Plans to bid for the 2018 Winter Olympics were scrapped in 2008 when the Ukrainian National Olympic Committee admitted the region lacked the required infrastructure to host such a major event. However, reports of a potential bid for 2022 have recently appeared in the Ukrainian media.

THE CARPATHIANS TATARIV

UKRAINE'S ROBIN HOOD

All around the Carpathians you'll discover cliffs, rocks, trees and caves bearing the name 'Dovbush'. Legend has it that these are spots where the 'Robin Hood of the Carpathians', Oleska Dovbush, and his band of merry Hutsuls slept while on the run.

Like his Sherwood Forest–dwelling counterpart, Dovbush robbed from wealthy merchants, travellers and nobles and distributed the loot to the poor – in his case Ruthenian peasants and poor Hutsul villagers. Born in 1700 near Kolomyya, he joined and later led a band of *opryshki* (outlaws). Many other bandits operated in the region, but Dovbush's particular generosity to the highlanders led to his legendary status.

Despite the best efforts of a hapless Polish army, which sent thousands of troops into the mountains after him, he was never captured. In the end it was his mistress who betrayed him in 1741 to her husband, a Polish official. Arrested in the village of Kosmach (see boxed text, p126) he was executed without trial and his body parts displayed in villages around the Carpathians as a warning to other outlaws.

Western Ukraine continued to have a reputation for banditry until the 20th century. This dubious 'tradition' was even revived for several years in the early 1990s when whole convoys of trucks would mysteriously vanish from the region's highways.

The Carpathians are one of Eastern Europe's premier skiing regions, and if you're already coming this way, these slopes provide an unusual alternative to those in the continent's west. Outside pricey Bukovel, ski passes in this area are about 50uah to 100uah a day, and equipment rental costs around the same. Hotel rooms can go up to 500uah a double in high season, but homestays can be as cheap as 100uah. **Piligrim** (☎032-297 1899; www.piligrim.lviv.ua) and **SkiUkraine** (www.skiukraine.info) both have useful information and bookings. The latter's 'Peculiarities of Skiing in the Carpathians' (www.skiukraine.info/info/skiing.shtml) makes entertaining reading.

In addition to the following resorts, a new $60 million resort is planned near Bystrets village, some 6km from Verkhovyna. This would be the first resort built on the higher Chornohora peaks.

Drahobrat (www.ski.lviv.ua/Drahobrat, in Ukrainian) Want to go skiing in April? At snowy Drahobrat, 1300m above sea level, you often can. Ukraine's only truly 'Alpine' skiing spot is remote and its conditions are suitable only for the experienced. It's also popular with snowboarders. The resort is 18km from Yasinya.

Slavske (www.slavsko.com.ua, in Ukrainian) This still-popular resort has blue, red and black runs, but slopes tend to get bumpy and icy by the season's end. Slavske is 130km south of Lviv, on the rail line to Uzhhorod.

Podobovets & Pylypets (www.ski.lviv.ua/volovets-podobovets, in Ukrainian) These neighbouring resorts are slowly developing, with fewer crowds and new tow lifts, but less accommodation than other resorts. Volovets on the Kyiv–Uzhhorod line is the nearest train station, 12km away.

Tysovets (www.ski.lviv.ua/tysovets, in Ukrainian) You'll hear this former Soviet Army winter-sports base mentioned, but its facilities are a little lame. Skole train station is 32km away.

As Bukovel is by far the most expensive ski resort in the country, the major gripe here among Ukrainians (and some foreigners) is the cost of ski passes. But at 75uah on weekdays (slightly more at weekends), they're still cheaper than in major western European resorts.

There are regular and seasonal bus services from Yaremche (via Tatariv) and Kolomyya. There have been fast Lviv–Chernivtsi trains specially put on for Bukovel's high season, but they are sometimes removed, so it's best to enquire at the time you're travelling.

Vorokhta Ворохта

A typical Carpathian sprawl, the village nearest to Mt Hoverla is quite difficult to get a handle on. If you wish to stay here, the best-known accommodation is **Kermanych** (☎034 344 1082; vul Danyla Halytskoho 153; s/d/tr from 200/200/300uah, in winter to 500uah), where log cabins have been built around a restaurant, a Russian *banya* (bathhouse) and a Finnish sauna. However, some guests do complain about noise and frequent par-

ties. Much cheaper, and a good choice for German speakers, is **Raitshtocky** (☎0343 441 501, 067 794 3010; vul Bohdan Khmelnytskoho 38; d/f 160/220uah; ☻). This family-run B&B has a nice feel, but is difficult to find, so read the directions on www.karpaty.info carefully beforehand or ask to be picked up.

Regular *marshrutka* and bus services run from Yaremche (one hour) and Verkhovyna (30 minutes). There's also a daily local train to and from Kolomyya (2½ to three hours).

Kolomyya Коломия
☎03433 / POP 70,000

Pretty as a picture, Kolomyya is one of the best introductions to the Carpathians for foreigners, despite being more than 50km east of the main part of the Chornohora range. Spruced up in the early noughties, it has the feel of an Austrian spa town, with a few good accommodation options and two interesting museums. In another country, Kolomyya might be too twee and touristy, but in Ukraine it's a breath of fresh air.

Kolomyya

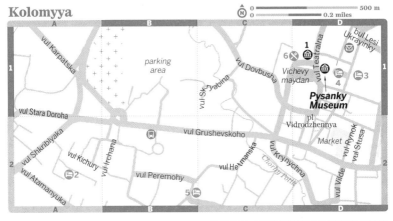

Sights

Pysanky Museum   MUSEUM
(Музей Писанки; vul Chornovola 39; adult/
child 5/2uah; ☺10am-6pm Tue-Sun) Kolomyya's
most eye-catching attraction is a monster
Easter egg, which sits rather self-consciously
on the town's main square. Inside and in an
adjoining building you'll discover a museum
dedicated to the traditional art of egg painting with examples from Ukraine, Romania,
the Czech Republic and as far afield as India,
China and Canada. However, some of the
exhibits, especially those in the main egg
building, could do with a little freshening up
and the outer shell could, ironically, do with
a lick of paint, but nonetheless this remains
Kolomyya's star attraction.

Museum of Hutsul Folk Art   MUSEUM
(Музей народного Мистецтва
Гуцульщини; vul Teatralna 25; admission 12uah;
☺10am-6pm Tue-Sun) Behind the Pysanky
Museum, cut diagonally left towards the
next street to this well-curated exhibition,
probably the best of its kind in Ukraine.
Decorated stove tiles and other ceramics,
musical instruments, carved wooden tools,
boxes, furniture, traditional and embroidered folk dress, woven wall-hangings and
an interesting collection of traditional Hutsul axes fill the museum's grand neoclassical home. Most of the wall texts have been
translated into sound English.

Sleeping & Eating

TOP CHOICE **On the Corner**   GUESTHOUSE $
(☐274 37, 067 980 3326; www.onthe
corner.info; vul Hetmanska 47A; dm 100uah, r per
person 150uah, d with bathroom 330uah; ☻@☎)

Vitaliy, his mum Ira, wife Anna, and the
rest of the extended Pavliuk family, continue to wow guests with their legendary
hospitality, making this not only one of the best
place to stay in Kolomyya, but one of the
best in all Ukraine. Indeed, this six-room
B&B just gets better, with cable TV, wi-fi,
laundry, bike hire, planned disabled access
and myriad other services that other guesthouses wouldn't even consider. With outstanding cooking and coffee, a multitude
of hikes and tours on offer, and assistance
and advice provided in English, German,
Ukrainian, Russian and Italian, comments
praising 'the best place I stayed in Ukraine'
just keep flooding in. Bikeland-affiliated
and motorcycle-friendly.

Good Morning B&B   GUESTHOUSE $
(Садиба Добрий ранок; ☐547 97, 066 162
9870; mvoyetska@hotmail.com; vul Rankova 4;
s/d 120/200uah; @) You'll know you're on

KOSMACH

We hesitate to call Kosmach off the beaten track, as the only road to it is very beaten indeed. The road's infamous potholes and Kosmach's vigilant villagers even managed to keep the Soviets at bay after WWII. Today the place is famous among Ukrainians for the private **Oleska Dovbush Museum**, run by Mykhailo Deidyshyn. It's a very *Pan's Labyrinth* experience.

Deidyshyn claims the hut housing his small museum is the one in which the 'the Ukrainian Robin Hood' was killed and he even shows you Dovbush's very own hat. However, the museum is mostly taken up with the strange figures Deidyshyn has carved from tree roots. Outside, he shows you a meteor, and a little forested plot that really is like the 'Garden of Eden'. Here you'll find the 'holy tree', whose fruit is supposed to have similar powers to a Latin American worry doll – whisper your problems to the fruit and your troubles will disappear.

Even for atheists it's an intriguing place, as you learn about pre-Christian Carpathian mysticism. The fact that you'll see oil – yes, real black gold – bubbling up beside the road to Kosmach just makes a weird day weirder. Public buses do run to the village, but to find the museum, you will need the services of a local guide; ask at one of the hotels in nearby Kolomyya.

the right track to this superb B&B, as the street is signposted in English from around 200m away. Charming hosts, Maria and Yuriy, speak English, after having lived in the US for years and can help with tours, travel and anything else you can think of. The Hutsul-themed room is the most striking of the four immaculate guest bedrooms, the breakfast menu includes real porridge and they'll pick you up for free from the stations.

Hotel Kolomyya
HOTEL $

(Готель Коломия; ☏257 33; www.kolomiya. com.ua; vul Chornovola 26; s/d from 170/250uah) Each of the town's two large hotels has its little idiosyncrasies. Hotel Kolomyya's is that you have to walk through a shopping mall to go from reception to your room. The accommodation is comfortable and generously sized, especially the huge bathrooms. Depending on availability, Hotel Kolomyya may sell beds in its quad rooms individually as dorm accommodation (100uah each). Staff can arrange lots of tours, and the hotel is part of the Bikeland project.

Hotel Pysanka
HOTEL $

(Готель Писанки; ☏203 56; reception@ pysanka-hotel.com; vul Chornovola 41; s/d 105/210uah; ❖) Once the only show in town, Hotel Pysanka's quirk is to have rested on that reputation for too long. It does face the Pysanky Museum and breakfast is included, but its 23 rooms are bland and unexciting, despite the 21st-century bathrooms. Dull but super-central sums things up here.

Trembita
HUTSUL $

(Park Trylovskoho; mains 8-30uah) Buried deep within a rambling leafy park just east of the centre, the Trembita is a relaxing place to chase *vareniki* (filled pasta) around a plate or cool down with a foamy one. The menu is ambitious, so ask what they have first. The thing that slightly spoils this place is the particularly disinterested service.

Kafe Elina
BEER GARDEN $

(Кафе Еліна; vul Taras Shevchenka; mains 10-45uah) This cafe behind the Museum of Hutsul Folk Art is a typical Hutsul *kolyba* arrangement with tables and knick-knacks in a wooden hut serving salad, *shashlyk* and *vareniki*. In summer the set up is reminiscent of a Bavarian beer garden with tables and little fairy-lit pavilions nestling under mature trees.

ⓘ Getting There & Away

BUS From the bus station (Автовокзал) services leave every 30 minutes to Ivano-Frankivsk (14uah, one hour), about every 30 minutes to Kosiv (9uah, one hour) and every two hours to Yaremche (10uah, 70 minutes) and Bukovel, among others. There are three services a day to Rakhiv (24uah, 3½ to four hours) and many to and from Chernivtsi (20uah, 1½ hours).

TRAIN There are at least three trains a day from Lviv to Kolomyya (49uah, 5½ hours), all stopping in Ivano-Frankivsk. Additionally, local trains go to and from Ivano-Frankivsk (7uah, 1½ to two hours, five daily), Chernivtsi (8uah, 2½ hours, four daily) and Rakhiv (11uah, 4½ hours, once daily).

Kosiv Косів

03478 / POP 9000

Sitting pretty in a river valley, tiny Kosiv is synonymous with serious, high-quality Hutsul crafts. They're sold at its famous craft market (☺8am-11am Thu, 6am-noon Sat) and produced in the surrounding hills as well as at the Kosiv State Institute of Decorative and Applied Arts (vul Mitskevycha 2). The latter also has a small museum (admission free; ☺9am-5pm Mon-Fri Sep-Jun), but for a much wider overview of the Hutsuls' artistic skills head for the Museum of Hutsul Folk Art and Life (vul Nezalezhnosti 55; adult/child 8/4uah; ☺10am-6pm Tue-Sun), which has a well-presented display of beautiful 19th- and 20th-century ceramics, carpets, inlaid boxes and embossed leather.

Kosiv is a minor Hassidic pilgrimage destination, though almost all the town's Jews were murdered by the Nazis on the Miska Hora (Town Mountain), a hill rising above the town. One side of the hill is peppered with the toppled graves of the former Jewish cemetery. Ask locals living around the hill to show you, as they're hard to find.

If you want to be here early for the crafts market – and the best buys do go in the first few hours – you could stay at the perfectly comfortable Hotel Kosiv (☎215 57, 246 73; vul Nezalezhnosti 65A; d from 180uah). If you fancy bedding down in these parts for longer, perhaps to do some hiking, Bayka (☎236 58; vul Nad Hukom 150; s/d with breakfast from 295/330uah, cottages from 600uah; ☒) occupies a hillside location in the forest and has comfy en suite rooms, timber cottages, a swimming pool and a fancy restaurant. It's a 40uah taxi ride from the town centre.

There are regular services to and from Kolomyya (9uah, one hour) and one overnight bus from Kyiv.

Sheshory Шешори

3478 / POP 2000

Sheshory is another Hutsul valley village stretched endlessly along the fast-flowing River Pystynka. In fact, it's the river that's the main attraction here, with many opportunities for wading and plunging in the heat of summer. The most dramatic water features are the waterfalls, a loud and impressive sight after rain.

Sheshory used to hold an annual ethnic music festival, but that has since gone

---

THE HUTSULS

Fiercely independent and individualistic, the Carpathian-dwelling Hutsuls are a mainstay of Ukrainian national identity. They were first identified as a separate ethnic group at the end of the 18th century. According to some accounts, the 'Hutsul' encompass several tribes – including Boiki, Lemi and Pokuttian – so who and what they are is open to some interpretation.

Ethnographers describe Hutsul life as dominated by herding sheep from high mountain pastures (polonyny) to lowland fields, with a little agriculture and forestry thrown in. They point to a dialect incomprehensible to other Ukrainians, a canon of pre-Christian, pagan legends and a diet based on mountain ingredients, including mushrooms, berries, brynza (a crumbly cow- or goat-milk cheese tasting like feta) and corn-based mamalyha (like polenta).

Wooden architecture, particularly churches, and a host of handicrafts, from decorated ceramics and embroidered shirts to woollen rugs and embossed leather, are also totems of Hutsul culture.

But whereas a traditional Hutsul would dress colourfully, carry an ornate toporet (hatchet) and play the trembita (a long alpine horn), most modern Hutsuls don't bother much with any of these. The few occasions on which they are likely to drag out their folk costumes include dances and weddings. For the former, men wear baggy trousers and women floral hair arrangements. For the latter, guests deck trees with paper flowers and ribbons, eat special flatbreads and consume lots of vodka.

Hutsul souvenirs are touted throughout the region, particularly in Yaremche. If you want more, keep an eye out for the wandering Hutsul festivals that take place around the Carpathians each summer. For more on the Hutsuls, see the boxed text, p129.

THE CARPATHIANS KOSIV

walkabout (it was last spotted somewhere in rural Podillya). The only other attraction is the verdant peace and tranquillity of the surrounding hills and mountains. Sheshory is a good base for some easy walks up onto the *polonyny* (summer pastures) where the Hutsuls make their cheese and herd cattle. Ask around in Kolomyya if you a need a guide to help you navigate the trails.

It is possible to stay in Sheshory, as many of the villagers rent out their rooms; check out www.karpaty.info for the latest offerings.

Verkhovyna Верховина

☑ 03432 / POP 5400

Among the villages in the Ukrainian Carpathians, Verkhovyna is probably the most gorgeously located (alongside tiny neighbour Kryvorivnya). It sits on a wide valley floor ringed by mountains; Mt Smotrych is just one peak visible from here. While larger towns outside the mountains, such as Kolomyya, were the first to develop the infrastructure to cope with foreign tourists, Verkhovyna is now opening up to adventurous travellers.

Verkhovyna boasts a private **museum** of Hutsul folk instruments. However, you'll almost certainly have to contact a local guide to get the museum to open for you, especially if you don't speak the lingo. As always, to arrange guides in the immediate area, try asking at the hotels in Kolomyya.

Local hiking guide **Vasyl Kobyliuk** (☑ 219 41, 219 71, 096 372 4400, Ukrainian & Russian only; skala2002@ukr.net; vul Stus 4A/8) is good at showing people the region, and also has a handful of humble rooms on offer in his apartment.

Meanwhile, B&B **Nad Cheremoshem** (☑ 222 70, 067 287 4390; vul Popovycha 15; s/d/tr 150/200/250uah; ☀) is picture-postcard idyllic. Covered in climbing flowers, this rustic red-brick cottage sits on the Cheremosh River, and has a barbecue site, aboveground pool, sauna and private apiary. The bedrooms might be quite old-fashioned and dreary, but who cares when you can sample homemade Carpathian cuisine under the arbour?

Bus and minibus services run regularly to Verkhovyna from neighbouring towns and villages such as Kolomyya, Kosiv and Vorokhta.

Yasinya Ясіня

☑ 03132 / POP 17,000

This sprawling village at the turn-off to Drahobrat ski slopes (around 18km away to the southwest) has definitely seen better days. Things are pretty quiet here in summer, but winter sees many a brightly dressed skier heading for the slopes. The planned ski tram/lift that was to be built from Yasinya to Drahobrat remains on paper only, but if you're a skiing novice, the town has two undemanding slopes of its own.

The popular **Hotel Yasinya** (☑ 420 77; www.yasinya.net; vul Maskovskoho 56; r from 180uah; ✴) offers excellent value for money. The staff and rooms get good reviews, and the hotel can arrange transfers to the ski slopes if that's why you're in town. The painting of Lenin and Stalin in the billiards rooms is perhaps the hotel's most memorable feature. If you prefer more intimate, homely digs, try **Zatyshna Domivka** (☑ 423 02; vul Borkanyuka 66; per person 130-150uah), though there are many other similar options in town.

All bus services travelling between Rakhiv and northern or eastern destinations like Yaremche must pass through Yasinya first. This includes some extra services terminating in Solotvyno. A timetable is posted outside the ticket booth at Yasinya's tiny bus station, which opens and closes depending on whether a bus is expected. Many locals prefer to hail private cars instead.

Rakhiv Рахів

☑ 03132 / POP 17,000

An international band of brightly clad hikers slurping *borshch* with weather-beaten Hutsuls; mountain bikers competing with horse-drawn carts and clapped out Ladas for pothole space; wooded mountainsides hoisting a beautiful backdrop as the fast-flowing River Tysa gurgles beneath precariously hung footbridges – this is Rakhiv, chaotically post-Soviet and crudely rural, but the best base from which to explore the southern Carpathians.

While Rakhiv's derelict state is shocking even by Ukrainian standards, the place has a raw energy that draws foreigners in their thousands. Some have even settled here to farm and carry on the traditional ways of the Hutsuls. Peace Corps volunteers posted here love the place.

'A god-forsaken Carpathian region; a land of Ukrainian Hutsuls.' So declares an opening screen of one of the most celebrated Soviet films, Sergei Paradzhanov's *Shadows of Forgotten Ancestors* (1964). Paradzhanov's judgment of the Carpathians is a bit harsh, but it's no doubt made to set the scene for the tragic tale that follows. Part *Romeo and Juliet,* part *Wuthering Heights,* it's the story of how Hutsul shepherd Ivan is haunted by the untimely death of his childhood sweetheart Marika, the daughter of a rival family.

The simple plot is based on an 1894 novel by Ukrainian writer Mikhailo Kotsyubinsky, which itself emanates from folklore. However, it's not the narrative that makes this a spellbinding movie – it's the flamboyant cinematography. Paradzhanov intersperses saturated colour with a black-and-white interlude and uses Hutsul customs and the primeval howl of *trembity* (long alpine horns) to great effect.

Stylised camerawork makes the movie resemble a medieval fairground one moment, and avant-garde Nouvelle Vague the next. Underpinning it all is a gut-wrenching melancholy as a heartbroken Ivan rejects all around him, resulting in tragedy.

The winner of 16 international film awards, this vintage movie makes great viewing before visiting the Carpathians and is now widely available on DVD. For more on Hutsul culture, see the boxed text, p127.

THE CARPATHIANS RAKHIV

Rakhiv is good for a couple of days to take on supplies, have a chuckle visiting a 'geographical centre of Europe' that's not really and to enjoy a little hiking. A Swiss-Ukrainian project, **Forza** (www.forza.org.ua), is working on regional regeneration, including the marking of trails into the Carpathian National Nature Park.

Rakhiv's proximity to the CNNP means that, although it's officially in Transcarpathia, the town is best covered here.

⊙ Sights & Activities

Rakhiv hosts an annual **Hutsul cheese-making festival** on 12 September, but otherwise its main attractions lie outside town.

Carpathian Biosphere Reserve
NATURE RESERVE
(http://cbr.nature.org.ua; Krasne Pleso 77) Declared a Unesco Biosphere Reserve in 1992, this protected area is made up of six separate locations, four of which can be found around Rakhiv. Some 90% of the reserve is made up of virgin forest, home to rare flora and fauna. About 5km southwest of Rakhiv the main road leads to the **Carpathian Biosphere Reserve headquarters**, which isn't so much of interest for itself as for what's surrounding it.

Museum of Forest Ecology
MUSEUM
(Krasne Pleso 77; admission 10uah; ☺8am-5pm) This old-school museum stands on the hill behind the HQ building. The exhibition is surprisingly informative, rich and colourful as well as slightly kitsch, so in between sniggers at the odd moth-bitten, taxidermied sheep, you'll learn a bit from the handy Carpathian Mountains relief map, and the dioramas of forest landscapes and Hutsul festivals – even without reading the signs.

Transcarpathian Hiking Trail
HIKING TRAIL
(www.transcarpathiatour.com.ua) Leaving the museum, turn left at the path just below it, and continue until you see a hiking sign pointing uphill to a spring. This is the start of the so-called Transcarpathian Hiking Trail, which heads south to the village of Kostylivka and is planned to eventually curve back north up the Chornohora ridge and further north towards Poland for 380km.

Geographical Centre of Europe
MONUMENT
Another 7km south of the Carpathian Biosphere Reserve headquarters lies what Ukraine contends is Europe's geographical centre, just before the village of Dilove. Ukraine is not the only country to declare itself the continent's centre: Germany, Lithuania, Poland and Slovakia have all staked rival claims. Furthermore, Austrian experts, quoted in the *Wall Street Journal Europe* in 2004, say the pillar erected by Austro-Hungarian geographers in 1887, in what is now back-country Ukraine, was never intended to mark Europe's middle;

FROM RAKHIV TO ROMANIA

Since the train service from Teresva was suspended in 2007, the only way to reach Romania from Rakhiv is via a car-pedestrian bridge across the Tysa River between Solotvyno and Sighetu Marmaţiei. The English-speaking folks at **Cobwobs hostel** (hostel@cobwobs. com) in Sighet keep abreast of the latest. They recommend foreigners push to the front of the queue as searches of locals and their vehicles (border officials are looking for cigarette and alcohol smugglers) are thorough.

For more information you can purchase a PDF download of the Romania chapter from Lonely Planet's *Eastern Europe* guide at shop.lonelyplanet.com.

its Latin inscription of simple longitude and latitude was mistranslated.

None of this has dented official Ukrainian aspirations to the honour, although some locals are more sceptical. Today, a Soviet-era spire has joined the Austro-Hungarian pillar at the 'geographical centre of Europe', as has a restaurant complex, souvenir stalls and opportunistic photographers equipped with stuffed bears and deer as props.

Make sure you take your passport, as the marker lies after a Ukrainian control point.

🛏 Sleeping & Eating

TOP CHOICE **Smerekova Hata**   GUESTHOUSE **$**
(☑212 92, 096 964 7603; www.smereko vahata.com.ua; vul Shevchenka 39; r per person from 80uah; 🤶) This recently extended B&B near the market just gets better and better. Rooms in the new building are fragrant with pinewood and combine traditional Hutsul bedspreads with ultra-modern showers. Owners Vasyl and Anna can cook you up breakfast (35uah), organise tours and excursions and even run Hutsul cookery classes (Vasyl is involved in Ukraine's embryonic Slow Food movement). Bikeland-affiliated.

U Erika   GUESTHOUSE **$**
(☑215 63; raho_lovagja@freemail.hu; vul Bohdana Khmelnytskoho 86; r per person 80uah; 🅰) The hotchpotch of rooms are more suburban than charmingly folksy here, but there's a friendly, multilingual atmosphere and the hosts like to prepare Hutsul

meals. Guests are free to use the kitchen. Three internet-enabled computers, a sauna, and a large garden complete the package, but it's a good 20 minutes' walk or 10uah to 15uah taxi ride from the bus station. To walk there, take the first right just before the bridge and keep going to No 86.

Hotel Evropa   HOTEL **$**
(☑212 48; vul Myru 42; s/d 60/120uah) Despite the name, there's nothing particularly European about this unexciting hotel. Although quite recently built, it takes a leaf out of the Soviet-style book. Still, it is nice and central and has a cafe-restaurant serving basic meals.

Olenka   INTERNATIONAL **$**
(vul Myru 48; mains 20-60uah; ⊙lunch & dinner; 🍴) Rakhiv's fanciest dining option is a tranquil island of style and efficient service, and a fine place to grab some post-hike grub (though you'll probably want to lose the muddy hiking boots first). Everything on the long menu, from local Hutsul fare to spaghetti Bolognese, was available when we visited, though our food arrived microwaved to the temperature of molten lava.

ℹ Information

At the time of research Rakhiv was erecting its very own, bona fide tourist office near the bridge over the River Tysa. If that hasn't materialised by the time you reach these parts, the 'Hutsul's Place' tourist information centre belonging to **Rakhiv Tour** (☑213 45; www.rakhiv-tour. info; ground fl, Hotel Europa, vul Myru 42) keeps unpredictable hours but is worth a stab.

ℹ Getting There & Away

BUS Many more buses than trains arrive in Rakhiv, but they're often wildly oversubscribed and crowded in summer. Buses winding over the mountains to and from the north and east connect Rakhiv with Chernivtsi (56uah, five hours, four daily), Ivano-Frankivsk (36uah, four hours, five daily), Kolomyya (28uah, 3½ to four hours, two to three daily). Most of these services go through Yaremche (15uah, three hours).

Heading west, there are around 15 sensibly timed services taking two different routes to and from Uzhhorod (49uah to 55uah, six to eight hours) plus four separate services to Mukacheve (41uah, five hours). Four services a week go to Prague (see www.regabus.cz).

TRAIN Only eight daily trains operate to and from Rakhiv's almost completely derelict terminus: two each way from Ivano-Frankivsk (11uah, five hours), one overnight service to Lviv (60uah, 8½ hours) and one return service from

Kolomyya (11uah, 4½ hours). All of these pass through Yaremche.

 **Getting Around**

Travelling south from Rakhiv to the Museum of Forest Ecology and the 'Geographical Centre of Europe' takes patience, as the buses are usually only hourly, and there seem to be few, if any, *marshrutky* in between. Heading north, there are hourly *marshrutky* to Bohdan, which will bring you towards the start of the hiking trail to Mt Hoverla. Two services a day will drop you in Luhy, even closer to the trail.

BUKOVYNA

Chernivtsi ЧЕРНІВЦІ

♪0372 / POP 252,000

Like many cities in the west of Ukraine, energetic Chernivtsi displays the hallmarks of a more elegant past, most obviously in the shape of its star attraction, the phantasmagorical university building. Shabby, leafy and slightly chaotic, this Ukrainian city sometimes has a somewhat un-Slavic flavour, possibly the residue of centuries of Romanian/Moldovan influence. Renovators have been busy with the stucco and whitewash in the city centre, and some of the old Austro-Hungarian tenements are looking pretty dapper, but in general Chernivtsi remains a ramshackle place with a local student population keeping things lively.

Just over six centuries old, Chernivtsi was once the chief city of Bukovyna (Beech Tree Land) in old Moldavia (now Moldova). It belonged to the Habsburg Empire in the 19th century, when much of the city's ornate architecture was built, and after WWI was temporarily drawn into Romania. Today the city remains the 'capital' of the unofficial Bukovyna region, but its past Jewish, Armenian and German communities are now just ghostly presences.

◉ Sights

With Chernivtsi such a jumble of sights, and perhaps only the university a crucial one, the following section offers a mere taster. Keener visitors should go to the tourist office for a map of architectural monuments.

Chernivtsi University   UNIVERSITY BUILDINGS
(Чернівецький національний університет; www.chnu.cv.ua; vul Kotsyubynskoho) University buildings are often called 'dreaming

spires', but Chernivtsi's is more like a trip on LSD. This fantastic red-brick ensemble, with coloured tiles decorating its pseudo-Byzantine, pseudo-Moorish and pseudo-Hanseatic wings, is the last thing you'd expect to see here. The architect responsible was Czech Josef Hlavka, who was also behind Chernivtsi's **Former Armenian Cathedral** (Колишній Вірменський собор; vul Ukrainska 30), as well as large chunks of Vienna. He completed the university in 1882 for the Metropolitans (Orthodox Church leaders) of Bukovyna as their official residence. The Soviets later moved the university here.

The wings surround a landscaped court. To the left as you pass the gatehouse is the **Seminarska Church** (Семінарська церква), now used for concerts and ceremonies. Straight ahead stands the former main **palace residence of the Metropolitans** (Палац-резиденція метрополитів), housing two remarkable staircases and a fantastic, 1st-floor **Marmurovy Zal** (Мармуровий зал; Marble Hall). As a public facility you can wander the buildings at will but the best rooms are usually locked. Alternatively contact **Diana Costas**

JEWISH CHERNIVTSI

One of Chernivtsi's most famous sons was leading 20th-century poet Paul Celan (1920–70) who was born into a German-speaking Jewish family at **vul Saksahanskoho 5** (formerly Wassilkogasse), when 'Cernăuţi' was part of Romania. His parents died in Nazi concentration camps during WWII and Celan himself survived one to write his most famous 1948 poem 'Todesfuge' (Death Fugue). He later drowned himself in Paris' River Seine. There's also a **Celan monument** (Пам'ятник Паулю Целану) on vul Holovna.

Chernivtsi's **former synagogue** (Колишня синагога; cnr vul Universytetska & vul Zankovetskoyi) was once famous for its exotic African/Middle Eastern style, but was turned into a cinema in 1954. The **former Jewish cemetery** is a melancholic jumble of leaning, overgrown headstones. To get there, follow vul Ruska (or catch trolleybus 4) across a bridge. Take the first left, vul Zelena, and continue 750m.

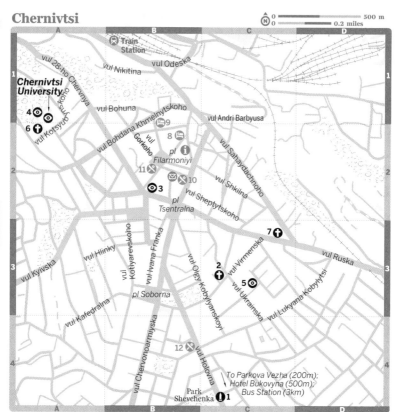

To Parkova Vezha (200m);
Hotel Bukovyna (500m);
Bus Station (3km)

(☎584 821, 050 1764 712; tours in English 40uah), a former student turned guide, who will gladly show you round. Her office is in the Seminarska Church, though you might find her and other guides loitering around the main gate.

The university is about 1.5km northwest of the centre. Trolleybus 2 will get you there.

Kalynivsky Market MARKET
(⊗8am-2pm) With its own police station, first-aid point and dedicated bank branches, this 33-hectare bazaar is like a town unto itself. As a conduit into Ukraine for goods from neighbouring countries, it attracts some 50,000 shoppers a day and is a frenetic, wonderful phenomenon. You might not want to buy anything in particular, although it is good for baseball caps and trainers, but it's great for people-watching. Take any of the numerous *marshrutky* to калинівський рунок; many leave from in front of the train station.

St Nicholas Cathedral CATHEDRAL
(Собор Св Миколи; vul Ruska 35) Chernivtsi's cathedral is nicknamed the 'drunken church', because of the four twisted turrets surrounding its cupola. Painted blue with golden stars, these turrets create an optical illusion, much like an Escher sketch. The cathedral is a 1930s copy of a 14th-century royal church in Curtea de Arges (Romania).

🛏 Sleeping

Hotel Bukovyna RENOVATED SOVIET **$$**
(Готель Буковина; ☎585 625; www.bukovyna -hotel.com; vul Holovna 141; s/d from 190/240uah, ste from 590uah; ❄🞱) Owing to its convenient location, its relative value for money, and its large number of rooms, this jolly yellow giant has an understandably sizable chunk of the local market. Rooms range from 'Economy', where the post-Soviet renovation is skin-deep, to 'Comfort', which comes with air-con and furniture from

Chernivtsi

this century. Guests in 'Economy' class are barred from the unexpectedly good buffet breakfast spread.

Hotel Kaizer　　　　　　　　　　　HOTEL **$$**
(☑585 275; vul Gagarina 51; s & d 250uah, ste from $300; ❄@🐾) Kyiv, Moscow, New York, Berlin, Rome, Warsaw, Istanbul: the world clocks ticking loudly in Kaizer's empty lobby presage Chernivtsi's nicest rooms, which have an appealing mix of new and retro furniture. They, and the lovely grill restaurant out the back (complete with wooden windmill), are wildly underused though – probably because of the slightly out-of-the-way location on the wrong side of the train station.

Hotel Magnat　　　　　　　　SMALL HOTEL **$**
(Готель Магнат; ☑526 420; vul Tolstoho 16A; s 120uah, d from 170uah; ❄) The nine-room Magnat is a midweek hideout for business travellers and you'd be doing well to get a bed here without reserving. It's tucked away in a tiny off-street alley; look for the bed sign. Rooms are superficially pleasant, but they're also a little smoky and their construction is a bit cheap. There's just one single.

Chernivtsi Backpackers　　　　　　HOSTEL **$**
(☑099 261 3645; apt 4, vul Zankovetskoyi 25; dm 120uah; @🐾) The tourist office will tell you it doesn't exist but Chernivtsi's only hostel is just hard to find, and once installed here, the English owner's insider tips, nights out

and summer excursions into the Carpathians make this a great base. Only seven beds, so book ahead.

🍴 Eating

Reflection　　　　　　　INTERNATIONAL **$$**
(Рефлекшн; vul Holovna 66; mains 40-60uah; ◷9am-11pm; 🖬) A completely atypical menu in such an unlikely city makes Reflection worth every kopeck. As if Waldorf and Caesar salads, vegetable fajitas, bruschetta, pesto with penne, teriyaki salad, lentil soup, pork with ripe mangoes etc weren't sufficient reminders of the culinary world you thought you'd left behind when entering regional Ukraine, there are also freshly baked croissants or oatmeal at breakfast. Honestly prepared food at reasonable prices and served by unobtrusive waiters – why can't more Ukrainian restaurants be like this?

Knaus　　　　　　　　　　　BEER HALL **$**
(Кнаус; vul Holovna 26A; mains 15-60uah) Although its menu retains a solid Russian alignment, Knaus does offer Bavarian bratwurst to accompany its range of German beers. The restaurant also rents an apartment on the same courtyard.

Potato House　　　　　　　　FAST FOOD **$**
(картопляна хата; vul Zankovetskoyi 11; mains 20uah; ◷10am-10pm) When all else fails and you just want to fill the hole, Potato House's *borshch*, pancakes, baked potatoes and more exotic stuff such as chilli con carne do the trick. Other cheap eats abound on vul Zankovetskoyi.

Parkova Vezha　　　　　　　　　CAFE **$**
(Park Shevchenka; mains 10-30uah; ◷lunch & dinner) This pretty, half-timbered park cafe next to the open-air theatre serves simple meals in surprisingly stylish surroundings.

ℹ Information

Post office (Поштамп; vul Khudyakova 6)

Tourist Information Centre (Туристично-інформаційний центр; ☑553 684; www. chernivtsy.eu, www.guide.cv.ua; vul Holovna 16; ◷10am-1pm & 2-6pm Mon-Fri) Runs a free city walking tour at noon each day. Staff can be gruff but speak passable English.

ℹ Getting There & Away

AIR Chernivtsi's airport can now call itself 'international' thanks to the Romanian airline **Carpatair** (www.carpatair.com), who fly six times a week to Timişoara. The only other flight is a daily service to Kyiv. Take *marshrutka* 38.

FROM CHERNIVTSI TO ROMANIA

You have to be an early bird to get the scheduled bus to Romania, as there's just one early-morning service a day from Chernivtsi to Suceava leaving at 7.10am. Luckily, many private cars and *marshrutky* also head that way. The best approach is to ask people at Chernivtsi bus station; or just do your best to look lost and they'll ask you.

You can get more info on Romania by buying a PDF download of the Romania chapter from Lonely Planet's *Eastern Europe* guide at shop.lonelyplanet.com.

BUS The bus station (Автовокзал) is 3km southeast of the centre. Services leave for Khotyn (13uah, two hours, half-hourly to hourly), Kamyanets-Podilsky (20uah, 2½ hours, half-hourly), Ivano-Frankivsk (30uah, four hours, at least three daily) and Lviv (45uah, 7½ hours, at least twice daily) among others. Longer-distance services go to Kyiv (90uah to 100uah, nine hours, two daily) and Odesa (100uah, 13 hours, two daily).

Some services to and from Kolomyya (20uah, 1½ hours) do pass through Chernivtsi bus station, but many inconveniently terminate at Kalynivsky Market, where you must change to local *marshrutky*. Heading north, you can catch services from the market to Kolomyya, but the chaos makes choosing the right bus difficult. Much easier is to head for the Drizhdzhi zavod (Дріжджі завод) stop, which is the northern terminus of trolleybus 3, on a huge roundabout. All northward-bound buses or *marshrutky* here go to Kolomyya. Or you can join the local hitchhikers.

TRAIN Mainline services include those to Kyiv (119uah, 15 hours, five daily) and Odesa (170uah, 17 hours, daily). Services to Lviv (70uah, 5½ to 11 hours, five daily) go via Ivano-Frankivsk. Local trains go to Kolomyya (8uah, two to 2½ hours, at least four daily).

❶ Getting Around

Trolleybuses 3 and 5, plus a whole host of *marshrutky*, run between the bus station and the train station. They're normally jam-packed, so be prepared to squeeze in or do a little walking.

Khotyn ХОТИН

You might first pass Khotyn on the way from Chernivtsi, but it's closer to Kamyanets-Podilsky and best visited as a day trip from there.

While Kamyanets-Podilsky is awesome taken as a whole, its castle building is upstaged by **Khotyn Fortress** (admission 10uah; ☉8am-8pm). Eastern European filmmakers love to use this massive fort overlooking the Dnister River as a location; recently refurbished, it served as Warsaw Castle in the highly controversial Russian-language 2009 blockbuster movie *Taras Bulba*. With walls up to 40m high and 6m thick, today's stone fortress was built in the 15th-century, replacing an earlier wooden structure. Its location safeguarded river trade routes making it a sought-after prize. The defining moment in its history came in 1621, with a threatened Turkish invasion. The incumbent Poles enlisted the help of 40,000 Cossacks and managed to rout a 250,000-strong Turkish army. This improbable victory made a hero of Cossack leader Petro Sahaydachny, whose huge statue greets you near the fortress' entrance. However, any notion of the fortress' impregnability was dispelled in 1711 when the Turks finally nabbed it. The Russians took over in the 19th century.

Inside the fortress walls there ain't a whole lot to see, but it's really the large riverfront grounds that make the place. Some of the outer fortification walls remain and you can clamber precariously over these. In one far corner, locals even pose for pictures where it appears they're jumping over the fortress. But whatever you do, don't forget to bring a picnic.

❶ Getting There & Around

BUS There are regular buses and *marshrutky* making the 30km journey between Kamyanets-Podilsky and Khotyn (7uah, 30 to 45 minutes) and every Kamyanets-Podilsky–Chernivtsi bus stops en route. The fortress is about 2.5km north of Khotyn town centre and the best strategy is to get off the bus when locals alight near the market (not at the far-flung bus station). Head along the road through the market and you'll pass a blue church on your right and a Soviet war memorial on your left. Stay on this road for a further 20 minutes until you see an old flaking sign marked Фортеця. Take a right here and you'll soon see the ticket office. A taxi to Kamyanets-Podilsky costs around 70uah.

TRANSCARPATHIA

Most people are only likely to pass this way if entering or leaving Ukraine via neighbouring Hungary or Slovakia. This is a pity, as this corner of the world, where the Soviet Union once faded out and Europe took over, is a melting pot of Hungarian, Slovak, Ukrainian and Roma cultures and has a fascinating social mix. It's also the home of Ukraine's best red wines and most impenetrable dialects (locals claim to speak Transcarpathian). Transcarpathia is so far west that some old timers still set their clocks to Ukrainian time minus one hour, and it's this independent spirit that makes even Lviv seem a long way away, far beyond the high Carpathians.

Uzhhorod УЖГОРОД

📞 0132 / POP 116,400

Uzhhorod (formerly Ungvar) is a typical border town – buzzing, full of energy, and often quite brusque. However, it is quite pretty, particularly the old town centre and tree-lined river embankments.

The main town of the Transcarpathian (Zakarpatska) region, Uzhhorod has large Hungarian and Romanian minorities, giving it a Balkan feel. The long autumn is the best season to visit, with the beech leaves turning and the grape harvest coming in. Troyanda Zakarpatya (a red dessert wine) and Beregivske (a Riesling) are among the best-known Transcarpathian wines.

The old town centre lies on the northern bank of the Uzh River, which wends its way roughly east–west through town. The train and bus stations are 1km directly south. The town has skeletal tourist signposting in English, which generally points in the right direction.

⊙ Sights

Uzhhorod Castle   CASTLE/MUSEUM

(Замок-фортеця; vul Kapitalna; admission 5uah; ⊙9am-6pm Tue-Sun) On the hill overlooking town stands the 15th-century castle with massive walls and beefy bastions built to withstand Turkish assaults. The main palace is now home to the **Transcarpathian Museum of Local Lore** (Закарпатський Краєзнавчий музей), which, while not completely fabulous, does have its moments. The tranquil grounds are also fun to wander and the bastion in the northeast corner provides views across Uzhhorod. If you have an urge to try the local plonk, **wine tastings** (6 wines 45uah; ⊙10am-6pm) take place in the castle's atmospheric brick cellars with friendly sommeliers on hand.

(Музей Закарпатський народної архітектури та побуту; vul Kapitalna; admission 10uah; ⊙10am-6pm Wed-Mon) Next door to the castle, this is one of the tidiest open-air museums in the country, albeit small. Highlights include several Hutsul cottages with their bench-lined walls, a complete timber school and the timber 18th-century

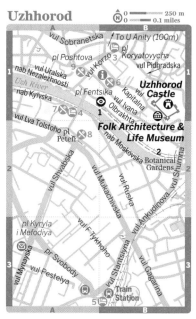

Mykhaylivska Church (St Michael's Church), rescued from the village of Shelestovo near Mukacheve and still a working place of worship.

Philharmonia CONCERT HALL
(Філармонія; pl Teatralna) Built in 1911, it's pretty obvious at first glance that this beautiful concert venue began life as a synagogue. Its intricately carved pink stone façade makes this Uzhhorod's most impressive edifice.

Greek Catholic Church CHURCH
(pl Andreya Bachynskoho) Monumental, recently renovated and built in the neoclassical style, this church is worth a peek inside for its huge iconostasis and striking ceiling frescoes.

Transcarpathian Railway
NARROW-GAUGE RAILWAY
(pl Teatralna) This narrow-gauge railway putts its way from near the Philharmonia building 1km east along the river in summer. However, there wasn't a lot going on here when we visited.

🛏 Sleeping

Old Continent HOTEL **$$**
TOP CHOICE
(Олд Континент; ☎669 366; www.hotel-oldcontinent.com; pl Petefi 4-6; s/d from 590/770uah; ❋🛜) At Uzhhorod's finest digs the choice between 21st-century predict-ability, baroque opulence or swish art deco may be a difficult call, as all the rooms here are immaculate, very well maintained and sumptuously cosy. English-speaking staff are courteous, the location is bull's eye central and there's a decent multitasking restaurant. Our sole complaint – the extra 130uah for breakfast.

Hotel Atlant HOTEL **$**
(Готель Атлант; ☎614 095; www.atlant-hotel.com.ua; pl Koryatovycha 27; s 200uah, d 310-420uah; ❋🛜) These 27 European-style rooms are as sweet as can be and are great value, especially the singles, which are on the top floor (no lift) and have skylights and sloping ceilings. As Uzhhorod's best deal it's popular, so book ahead if you can.

U Anity GUESTHOUSE **$$**
(☎614 019; www.motel-anita.com.ua; vul Bercheni 24; s 260uah, d 250-300uah) This newly built guesthouse to the north of the town centre has eight rooms in two buildings with cheapo furniture and uninspired décor but faultless bathrooms.

Uzhhorod's immaculate, newly built **train station** (r per person 100uah) has better-than-average rooms (at this price, you might have to share with one other person). They're at the eastern end of the main lobby. If the snack bar is on your left, you'll see the stairs to the rooms in the right-hand corner.

FROM UZHHOROD TO HUNGARY & SLOVAKIA

Chop, 22km west of Uzhhorod and 44km northwest of Mukacheve, is the international rail crossing between Ukraine and Hungary or Slovakia. Here, the broader Ukrainian rail gauge meets the narrower standard gauge of the EU, and there's a delay of anything between one and three hours while your train's carriages are lifted in the air and onto different bogies.

Trains affected are long-distance services like the Budapest–Moscow or Kyiv–Bratislava, but half the time these delays occur barely noticed in the wee hours. The other half of the time, you could use the delay as an excuse to break your journey in Uzhhorod or Mukacheve. As Chop is treated as the last stop on the Hungarian rail system, several additional services (eg Budapest–Chop, Bratislava–Chop) originate from and terminate at its station.

On services heading west from Kyiv and Lviv, domestic trains stop at Chop before reaching Uzhhorod; international services don't stop at Uzhhorod at all (think of it as being on a little rail appendix). By comparison, both domestic and international services travelling west stop at Mukacheve before Chop.

The quickest way between Chop and Uzhhorod is to take a *marshrutka;* between Chop and Mukacheve it's usually an *elektrychka* or other train. It's also possible to catch buses from Uzhhorod to Hungary or Slovakia.

For further information head to shop.lonelyplanet.com to purchase a download-able PDF of the Hungary and Slovakia chapters from Lonely Planet's *Eastern Europe* guide.

INDEPENDENCE DAY

The Transcarpathian region must hold the record for the shortest-lived independent state in history. When Czechoslovakia, of which Transcarpathia was a part during the interwar years, fell apart in early 1939, the region declared independence as the Republic of Carpatho-Ukraine on March 15, with Khust as its capital. But that very same day Hungarian troops marched into Transcarpathia and annexed it to Hungary.

✖ Eating & Drinking

Uzhhorod is well endowed with pizzerias and coffeehouses, but traditional local food is hard to track down.

Delfin INTERNATIONAL $
(Дельфін; nab Kyivska 3; mains 10-50uah; 🍴) Locals consider this one of the better restaurants in town. European and Ukrainian dishes are served, but it's known for its grilled meats and rooftop terrace. It's at the end of the pedestrian bridge on the south side of the river. You'll have to go upstairs once you get to the building.

Kaktus Kafe CAFE $
(Кактус Кафе; vul Korzo 7; mains 13-41uah; 🍴) Probably the most popular hang-out in town, this smoky, noisy joint is full of beer- and coffee-drinkers. The theme is decidedly Wild West upstairs; downstairs it seems to be Aztec. The food is pretty good, but the service can be slow.

Cafe Mio CAFE $
(Кафе Mio; vul Kapitalna 5; mains 12-24uah; ◷7am-10pm) Just down the hill from Uzhhorod Castle, funky-arty-bohemian is what this place does. Food is limited to Soviet staples, but it's also a fine spot for a dose of suds.

Jidalnya CANTEEN $
(Їдальня; pl Petifi 15; mains from 10uah; ◷8am-4pm) This no-frills, no-smiles canteen is buried deep in the College of Economics and serves up institutional stodge for subsidised prices. Follow your nose through the building to find it.

ℹ Information

Coffee.net (vul Korzo 5; per hr 3uah; ◷8am-10pm Mon-Fri, 10am-10pm Sat & Sun) Unusu-

ally stylish net cafe where the coffee comes as quick as the web connection. Free wi-fi.

Post and telephone office (Поштамт та Укртелеком; vul Mynayska 4) Opposite Hotel Zakarpattya, this place also has internet terminals. There's another tiny branch at the train station.

Tourist office (☎613 193; www.zakarpattya tourism.info; vul Dukhnovycha 16/1; ◷8am-5pm) Helpful and friendly office selling maps, guides and tours of the Trans-Carpathian region. Little English spoken.

ℹ Getting There & Away

AIR There's at least one daily flight to Kyiv from Uzhhorod's **airport** (☎975 04, 428 71; vul Sobranetska 145), 2km northwest of the centre. Check the website of **Kiy Avia** (www.kiyavia.com) for flight details.

BUS There are long-distance buses to Lviv (57uah, six hours, twice daily) and to Chernivtsi (100uah, 10 to 12 hours, twice daily). Services also run to Rakhiv (49uah, six to eight hours, 11 daily) and Mukacheve (12uah, one hour, every 15 minutes).

Marshrutka 145 goes to Chop (7uah, 45 minutes, every 15 minutes) from the side of the bus station facing the train station. Cross-border buses link Uzhhorod most usefully with Košice (100uah, three hours, three daily) in Slovakia. **Regabus** (www.regabus.cz) operates overnight services to Prague (490uah, 14 hours).

TRAIN Trains to and from Western Europe don't stop in Uzhhorod; you must go to nearby Chop.

Domestic trains go to and from Lviv (83uah, seven to eight hours, four daily) and Kyiv (150uah, 16 to 19 hours, four daily). Other services include one middle-of-the-night train to Solotvyno (60uah, six hours, daily) and slow-but-scenic *elektrychky* to Mukacheve (6uah, 2½ hours, seven daily).

Mukacheve МУКАЧЕВЕ

☎03131 / POP 93,000
Echoes of Austro-Hungary, some fine interwar Czechoslovak architecture, rustic horse-drawn carts competing for cobble space and one of Ukraine's most dramatic castles make Mukacheve a worthwhile stopoff. The town can also serve as an easily reachable, low-key introduction to Ukraine if you're heading into the country by train.

◉ Sights

Palanok Castle CASTLE
(www.zamokpalanok.mk.uz.ua, in Ukrainian; admission 8uah; ◷9am-6pm) Mukacheve's highlight is the hilltop castle that pops up from

the surrounding plain as you approach Mukacheve from Uzhhorod, like something in a fairy-tale fantasy. Famous as the site where Croatian-Hungarian princess Ilona Zrini held off the Austrian Emperor's army for three years before finally capitulating in 1688, the 14th-century castle includes one or two interesting exhibits (folk costumes, archaeological finds) with English explanations, and has some wonderful views. Renovation often gives way to dereliction here and half the fun is getting lost on the various levels of arcading that surround the courtyard. To get here, board bus 3 in front of the church on vul Pushkina or take any *marshrutka* heading to тімірязева.

★ Festivals & Events

With Transcarpathia producing slightly better wine varieties than Crimea, there's an annual **red wine festival** from 12 to 15 January, and a **honey fair** in autumn.

🛏 Sleeping

'Motel'   GUESTHOUSE **$**
(📞050 912 8861, 050 501 2040; vul Yaroslava Mudroho 82-84; s/d 120/150uah) If you're just leaving the train in Mukacheve to stretch your legs for a day or so, staying at this family-run motel makes eminent sense. Beaming a hard-to-miss bright pink just minutes from the station, it's about 15 minutes on foot to the centre. The rooms are cosy, if a little scuffed and tobacco-scented, and the husband speaks some German (hence the flag in the stairwell). No breakfast.

Hotel Star   HOTEL **$$**
(📞320 08, 545 10; www.star-ar.mk.uz.ua; pl Myru 10-12; s/d from 324/480uah; ❄ 🖥) This yellow neoclassical building, in Mukacheve's attractive central pedestrian zone, has rug-lined, flagstaff halls and dark wooden doors leading to spotless rooms with minibar and international satellite TV.

Hotel Palanok   HOTEL
(📞050 351 1008; www.hotelpalanok.com; vul Grafa Shenborna 2A; s/d/tr from 180/220/300uah) Conveniently located under the castle hill, these contemporary lodgings are good for visiting Palanok, but are a long way from anything else.

ℹ Getting There & Away

BUS Bus is the way to go to Uzhhorod (12uah, one hour); services leave every 15 to 20 minutes from the bus station, which is 1.5km east of the centre.

TRAIN The train station is on vul Yaroslava Mudroho, 1.5km southwest of the centre. Heading eastwards from Mukacheve, daily trains go to Lviv (80uah, six hours) and Kyiv (130uah, 15 hours). Heading west, there are at least 15 daily *elektrychka* (6uah) and mainline trains to Uzhhorod via Chop (where you can pick up international services originating in Chop). Alternatively, westbound international services like the Moscow–Budapest or Kyiv–Bratislava train stop in Mukacheve itself.

Odesa & Southern Ukraine Одеса & Південна Україна

POP 4.7 MILLION / AREA: 86,300 SQ KM

Includes »

Best Places to Eat & Drink

» Kompot (p149)
» Shkaf (p150)
» Shuzz (p150)
» Balalaika (p149)

Best Places to Stay

» Hotel Londonskaya (p147)
» Hotel Ayvazovsky (p147)
» Mozart Hotel (p146)
» Pelikan Tour (p158)

Why Go?

Ukrainian nationalists scowl at any mention of Russian empress Catherine the Great, but there's no denying Southern Ukraine wouldn't be what it is today without her. This chunk of no-man's-land between the Cossacks and Crimea formed part of her late-18th-century territorial acquisitions, opening up the balmy Black Sea to a bronchitic St Petersburg. Catherine dispatched lover Grygory Potemkin and a multicultural posse of foreigners to civilise and populate the coast; Potemkin founded Odesa, but died before it was started.

Odesa is still Ukraine's most multicultural city, as well as the self-declared Ukrainian capital of both hedonism and humour. Hedonists flock down from Kyiv for the sandy beaches and wicked nightlife; the humour in this oh-so-Russian city is tougher to find.

It's not all about Odesa's energy and attitude: the south is also home to three major river estuaries, the most spectacular being the Danube Delta, a birdwatcher's paradise.

When to Go?

Odesa

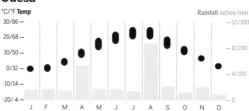

January Feel the warm mist drift onto the Black Sea's deserted beaches.

April Witness Ukraine's funny side at Odesa's Carnival Humorina festival of humour.

October-November Arrive in time for the bird migration in the impressive Danube Delta.

Odesa & Southern Ukraine Highlights

1 Join the tanning and party fest on **Odesa's beaches** (p145)

2 Spot zebra and bison on safari at the **Askaniya Nova Reserve** (p155)

3 Make an ascent of the **Potemkin Steps** (p141) – setting for one of cinema's most famous scenes

4 Launch an assault on the beefy ramparts of **Bilhorod-Dnistrovsky Fortress** (p156)

5 Try to keep your feet dry in **Vylkovo** (p156), epicentre of the Danube Delta Biosphere Reserve

6 Crawl the bars and restaurants in and around Odesa's **vul Derybasivska** (p141)

Odesa ОДЕСА

POP: 1 MILLION

Odesa is a city straight from literature – an energetic, decadent boomtown. Its famous Potemkin Steps sweep down to the Black Sea and Ukraine's biggest commercial port. Behind them, a cosmopolitan cast of characters makes merry among pastel neoclassical buildings lining a geometrical grid of leafy streets.

Immigrants from all over Europe were invited to make their fortune here when Odesa was founded in the late 18th century by Russia's Catherine the Great. These new inhabitants gave Russia's southern window on the world a singular, subversive nature.

As well as becoming a duty-free port, Odesa also attracted ordinary holiday-makers with its sunny climate and sandy beaches. True, the city's appearance grows tattier as you head south past half-empty sanatoriums towards its beachside night-clubs. However, this East–West crossroads makes up for that with sheer panache, and Odesans are known across the old USSR for being stylish, funny, savvy and not easily impressed.

But let's not get carried away here. Barcelona or Brighton it ain't, and the city does have a distinctly seedy feel. Prostitutes, con artists, drug dealers and the mob have all found their niche here, and the city is a magnet for sex tourists, wife hunters and general ne'er-do-wells from around the world. Also, nowhere else in Ukraine do the police hassle foreigners to such an extent, something you might experience firsthand should you head to the beaches in the evening.

History

Catherine the Great imagined Odesa as the St Petersburg of the South. Her lover, General Grygory Potemkin, laid the groundwork for her dream in 1789 by capturing the Turkish fortress of Hadjibey, which previously stood here. However, Potemkin died before work began on the city in 1794 and his senior commanders oversaw its construction instead. The Spanish-Neapolitan general José de Ribas, after whom the main street, vul Derybasivska, is named, built the harbour. The Duc de Richelieu (Armand Emmanuel du Plessis), an aristocrat fleeing the French Revolution, became the first governor, overseeing the city's affairs from 1803 to 1814.

In 1815, when the city became a duty-free port, things really began to boom. Its huge appetite for more labour meant the city became a refuge – 'Odesa Mama' – for runaway serfs, criminals, renegades and dissidents. By the 1880s it was the second-biggest Russian port, with grain the main export, and an important industrial base.

It was the crucible of the early 1905 workers' revolution, with a local uprising and the mutiny on the battleship *Potemkin Tavrichesky*. Then, between 1941 and 1944, Odesa sealed its reputation as one of Stalin's 'hero' cities, when partisans sheltering in the city's catacombs during WWII put up a legendary fight against the occupying Romanian troops (allies of the Nazis).

Odesa was once a very Jewish city, too, from which its famous sense of humour presumably derives. Jews initially came to Odesa to escape persecution, but tragically suffered the same fate here. In the early 20th century, they accounted for one third of the city's population but after horrific pogroms in 1905 and 1941 hundreds of thousands emigrated. Many moved to New York's Brighton Beach, now nicknamed 'Little Odessa'.

◉ Sights & Activities

Odesa may lack the must-see sights of a Kyiv or a Lviv, but it still packs plenty of charm with its splendid architecture, eye-popping panoramas and quirky monuments. The city centre's shaded avenues are tailor-made for strolling, so lace up your best walking shoes. Just avoid staring at them, as most of Odesa's attractions are overhead in the form of intricate turn-of-the-20th-century façade details, onion-domed church spires and towering statues.

Potemkin Steps   STEPS
(Потёмкинские ступеньки; Map p140) You've seen the steppe, now see the steps, the Potemkin Steps, the site of one of cinema's most famous scenes. Designed by Italian architect Franz Boffo, the last of the 192 granite steps was slotted into place in 1841. The lower steps are wider than those at the top creating an optical illusion – the steps seem to be the same width all the way up. The Potemkin steps are certainly best appreciated from the bottom from where you can't see the tatty bits of tarmac, and if you don't fancy the climb back up to the top, take the free **funicular railway** (фунікулер; ⊘8am-11pm) that runs parallel.

Vul Derybasivska   STREET
(Map p140) Odesa's main commercial street, pedestrian vul Derybasivska, is jam-packed with restaurants, bars and, in the summer high season, tourists. At its quieter eastern end you'll discover the **De Ribas statue** (Map p140), a bronze of the general who built Odesa's harbour and after whom the street is named. At the western end of the thoroughfare is the pleasant and beautifully renovated **City Garden** (Городской сад; Gorodskoy Sad; Map p140), surrounded by several restaurants. You'll find various touristy knick-

AS SEEN ON SCREEN

Regularly voted one of the most influential films of all time, Sergei Eisenstein's *Battleship Potemkin* (1925) has guaranteed Odesa cinematic immortality. The black-and-white classic's most renowned sequence is that of a massacre of innocent civilians on the Potemkin Steps, during which a baby in a pram is accidentally pushed off the top and bounces in agonising slow motion down the 192 stairs.

As with much great art, however, the scene is partly fiction. Sailors aboard the battleship *Potemkin Tavrichesky* did mutiny over maggot-ridden food rations while in Odesa harbour, and that mutiny did spark a revolution in 1905. However, locals running to the shore to support the sailors were never shot by tsarist troops on the steps – although they were killed elsewhere in the city.

None of this detracts from the drama of the legendary Russian director's brilliant edit, which still moves audiences today. In 2004 the Pet Shop Boys wrote a new soundtrack to the movie, and a reconstructed version of *Battleship Potemkin,* including scenes cut by Soviet censors, appeared at the 2005 Berlin Film Festival. The scene can also now be viewed on YouTube.

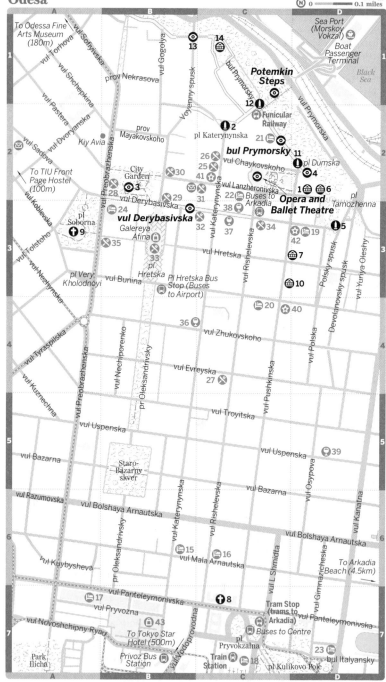

ODESA & SOUTHERN UKRAINE

knacks for sale here and you can have your photo taken with a monkey or a snake, but the main draw is people-watching.

Across the street, the swanky **Passazh** (Map p140) covered shopping arcade is the best-preserved example of the neo-renaissance architectural style that permeated Odesa in the late 19th century. Its interior walls are festooned with gods, goblins, lions and nymphs. Shabbier but equally ornate representations of this style are huddled around pl Soborna at vul Derybasivska's western terminus, including the Passazh Hotel.

Opera and Ballet Theatre   THEATRE
(Map p140; Chaykovskoho 1) The jewel in Odesa's architectural crown was designed

in the 1880s by the architects who also designed the famous Vienna State Opera, namely Ferdinand Fellner and Herman Helmer. After being closed for several years amid botched reconstruction efforts, the theatre reopened to great fanfare in 2007. You can take a tour of the theatre or, better yet, take in a performance.

Bul Prymorsky   BOULEVARD
(Map p140) Sooner or later everyone gravitates to this tree-lined pedestrian zone with replica 19th-century gas lamps, park benches and more photographers armed with a small zoo of animals with which to have your photo taken. At the boulevard's eastern end, you'll spot the pink and white colonnaded **City Hall** (Городской совет;

Take a park bench in Odesa's City Garden on a busy summer afternoon, and before long your eye will be drawn to a bit of commotion surrounding a single bronze chair fixed on vul Derybasivska, just outside the park's perimeter. Girls strike provocative poses for camera-toting friends, Russian males pose he-man style beside it and the odd foreigner copies the fun for the hell of it, oblivious to what all the fuss is about.

The chair in question is 'the 12th chair', the illusive star of a satirical novel called *The Twelve Chairs* by Soviet authors Ilf and Petrov. Set in Odesa, the book, and later film adaptations, beautifully capture the chaos and absurdity of life in the newly minted USSR of the late 1920s, and shed light on the shady Odesan character.

The story is about a down-at-heel aristocrat, Ippolyte, whose dying mother confesses she's concealed the family's jewellery inside one of the dining room chairs. These have, unfortunately, been confiscated by the Bolsheviks. Undeterred, Ippolyte sets out to track down the family's fortune, but the set of chairs has been split up and sold individually. So assisted by Odesa spiv, Ostap Bender, he roots out one chair after another, but none contain the jewellery. Meanwhile a priest, who overheard the mother's confession, is also searching for the chairs, as are a mean band of other treasure hunters. When Ippolyte discovers where the last, 12th chair is located, he bumps off Bender who wants a share of the loot. But the treasure has already been found – this is too much for Ippolyte who goes insane.

Map p140), originally the stock exchange and later the Regional Soviet Headquarters. The cannon here is a war trophy captured from the British during the Crimean War. In the square in front of the City Hall is Odesa's most photographed monument, the **Pushkin statue** (Памятник Пушкину; Map p140). The plaque reads 'To Pushkin – from the Citizens of Odesa'.

Continuing along the boulevard, at the top of the Potemkin Steps you'll reach the **statue of Duc de Richelieu** (Памятник Ришелье; Map p140), Odesa's first governor, looking like a Roman in a toga. The view from here is of the passenger port, the towering Hotel Odessa and the Black Sea.

At the western end of bul Prymorsky stands the semi-derelict **Vorontsov Palace** (Воронцовский дворец; Map p140). This was the residence of the city's third governor, built in 1826 in a classical style with interior Arabic detailing. The Greek-style colonnade behind the palace offers brilliant views over Odesa's bustling port.

Tyoshchyn Most

(Тёщин Мост; Map p140; bul Mystetsv/bul Prymorsky) The drab, Soviet-era footbridge behind the Vorontsov Palace is nicknamed 'Mother-in-Law's Bridge'. It was erected in the 1950s for a communist official who wished to facilitate visits from his wife's mother or – in the story's more popular version – wanted to leave her no excuse to stay overnight. Local superstition requires newlyweds to clamp inscribed locks to its railings and throw away the key – this supposedly ensures decades of marital bliss.

Panteleymonivsky Church

ORTHODOX CHURCH

(Пантелеймоновская церковь; Map p140; vul Panteleymonivska 66) Near the train station you can't help but spy the five silver onion domes of this Russian Orthodox church, built by Greek monks with stone from Constantinople in the late 19th century. According to legend, every time the Soviets painted over the church's elaborate frescoes, they would miraculously reappear. While the Soviets eventually succeeded in covering them up, many of the frescoes are once again visible thanks to vigorous restoration efforts.

Museum of Western and Eastern Art

GALLERY

(Музей западного и Восточного искусства; Map p140; www.oweamuseum.odessa.ua; vul Pushkinska 9; admission 15uah; ☉10.30am-4pm Thu-Tue) Housed in a beautifully renovated (at least on the outside), mid-19th-century palace the museum's star turn used to be one of 12 known versions (most likely not the original) of Caravaggio's brilliant painting *The Taking of Christ*. However, in July 2008 the canvas was cut from its frame in Ukraine's biggest art heist and only recovered by police two years later. The museum's Western Art section is currently closed indefinitely 'while security improvements are made' the ticket lady claimed. Stable doors and bolting horses come to mind. The Eastern Art section has displays of porcelain and other artwork, mostly from Japan, China, Tibet and India.

Pushkin Museum   MUSEUM
(Музей Пушкина; Map p140; vul Pushkinska 13; admission 8uah; ⊙10am-5pm Tue-Sun Jul & Aug, Mon-Fri Sep-Jun) This is where Alexander Pushkin spent his first days in Odesa, after being exiled from Moscow by the tsar in 1823 for radical ideas. Governor Vorontsov subsequently humiliated the writer with petty administrative jobs, but it took only 13 months, an affair with Vorontsov's wife, a simultaneous affair with someone else's wife and more radical ideas for Pushkin to be thrown out of Odesa too. Somehow, he still found time while in town to finish the poem 'The Bakhchysaray Fountain' (see p168), write the first chapter of *Eugene Onegin* and scribble the notes and moaning letters found in this humble museum.

Odessa Fine Arts Museum   MUSEUM
(Художественный музей; off Map p140; http://museum.odessa.net/fineartsmuseum; vul Sofiyivska 5A; admission 20uah; ⊙11am-6pm Wed-Mon) Located in the former palace of one Count Pototsky, this museum has an impressive collection of Russian and Ukrainian art, including a few seascapes by master talent Ayvazovsky and some Soviet realist paintings. Temporary shows can push the price of tickets up slightly.

Preobrazhensky Cathedral   CATHEDRAL
(Преображенский собор; Map p140; pl Soborna) Leafy pl Soborna is the site of the gigantic, newly rebuilt Preobrazhensky (Transfiguration) Cathedral, which was Odesa's most famous and important church until Stalin had it blown up in the 1930s.

Archaeology Museum   MUSEUM
(Археологический музей; Map p140; vul Lanzheronivska 4; admission 20uah; ⊙10am-5pm Tue-Sun) Gold jewellery and coins from early Black Sea civilisations are joined by a few Egyptian mummies at this under-visited museum.

Literature Museum   MUSEUM
(Литературный музей; Map p140; ☎0482-223 370; vul Lanzheronivska 2; admission 25uah; ⊙10am-5pm Tue-Sun) Another old palace housing a collection of interest to Russian literature fanatics. Nothing in English.

Black Sea Coast
Lots of people do swim at Odesa's crowded, dirty beaches in summer, but that's not really what going to the beach here is about. Rather, it's about strolling dishevelled promenades observing beach life, Ukrainian style. Should you choose to

---

MONUMENTAL CONTROVERSY

It may seem incomprehensible to outsiders, but by the time you read this Odesa may have won the dubious honour of erecting Ukraine's first Stalin monument. Backed by a petition of 30,000 signatures, the local branch of the Communist Party is keeping the monument's exact location secret, but on Victory Day 2011 (9 May) local activists were planning to unveil Stalin, accompanied by WWII commanders Zhukov and Malinovsky, somewhere around a Soviet war memorial (Memorial 411-y Batarey) in the city's far south. Understandably Ukrainian nationalists are in uproar and even the Odesa city council isn't keen on the idea.

But the kerfuffle caused by Stalin et al is nothing compared to the furore kicked up in 2007 by the Catherine the Great statue (Памятник Екатерине II; Map p140), raised in place of a monument honouring the soldiers who staged the mutiny aboard the battleship *Potemkin Tavrichesky*. Ukrainian nationalists hold a long-time grudge against the temperamental Russian empress, who dealt a crippling blow to Ukrainian statehood in 1775 when she ordered the dismantling of the Cossack's Zaporizhska Sich (fort; see p228). But she remains a hero to Odesa's majority Russian population for founding the city and bringing much of southern Ukraine under Russian rule. Tatars and Ukrainian nationalists protested the move vigorously, but to no avail, and a stone rendition of Catherine II now stands tall on the square that bears her name (pl Katerynynska). The once popular *Potemkin Tavrichesky* is set to make a comeback somewhere in the city, but has yet to be given a new home.

swim, exercise caution: the Black Sea is still notoriously polluted around Odesa despite local government clean-up efforts. Be aware that drinking is now banned on and around Odesa's beaches, so don't give the ever-present police an excuse to extract money from you by carrying a cool one.

Arkadia Beach BEACH

(Map p146) An evening at Arkadia is a must when in Odesa and this is definitely the city's best place to see and be seen. Here you can play old-school arcade games, dress up like a tsar or tsarina for a photo op, or hang out in a variety of cafes, bars and clubs. If crowds aren't your thing, it might be worth paying 15uah to 30uah to enter the private **Tropicana Club** (Клуб Тропикана; Map p146), where you can order cocktails from your chaise longue and use the pool.

Arkadia is easy to reach: take tram 5 from the tram stop near the train station, in front of the McDonald's on vul Panteleymonivska, to the end of the line via the lovely tree-lined bul Frantsuzsky, where the crème de la crème of Odesa's aristocracy lived in tsarist times. Enjoy the views of the old mansions and sanatoriums along the way. Public transport to Arkadia gets extremely crowded in the summer, so consider taking a taxi (around 40uah).

The crowds begin to thin out and the water gets cleaner as you head south to the area known as **Bolshoy Fontan**; take tram 18 from the tram stop near the train station.

Otrada Beach

(Пляж Отрада) This beach can be reached via a primitive **chairlift** (Канатная дорога к пляжу Отрада; kanatnaya doroga; 1-way 12uah). Like eating *salo* (cured pig fat), riding one of these chairlifts is one of those 'when-in-Ukraine' experiences that probably shouldn't be missed. To the south of Otrada Beach is a **nudist beach**.

Other attractions:

Lanzheron Beach BEACH

Closest to the centre, this beach is reachable on foot via Shevchenko Park, east of the city centre.

Oceanarium OCEANARIUM

(Океанариум; ⊙10am-8pm Mon-Fri, 10am-10pm Sat & Sun) On the coast next to Shevchenko Park, this place puts on entertaining **dolphin shows** (⊙noon, 3pm & 6pm).

★ Festivals & Events

Odesa's annual **Carnival Humorina**, celebrated on 1 April, is no joke. The festival fills the streets with carnival floats, music and drunks, and is the biggest party of the year for most Odesans. No less frivolous is **Odesa City Day**, which is held annually on 2 September.

🛏 Sleeping

Odesa is popular among Russians and Ukrainians, especially in July and August, but rarely are its hotels and hostels full and turning up without a booking is still feasible, even in high season. The city's hostel situation is in constant flux, with expats setting up shop, partying for a couple of seasons then moving on. It may be a good idea to check whether the hostels listed below are still operating before turning up at 4am unannounced.

Mozart Hotel HOTEL **$$$**

(Гостиница Моцарт; Map p140; ☎0482-377 777; www.mozart-hotel.com; vul Lanzheronivska 13; s 1104-2722uah, d 1635-3785uah; ❸❄@ ❧❄) As the name suggests, this top choice epitomises European luxury, with elegant furnishings and a calm, light-filled interior

Arkadia

⊙ 0 ——— 200 m
0 ——— 0.1 miles

Gagarinskoe plato
vul Genuezka
Arkadia Tram Stop
vul Tinysta
prov Khrustalny
Arkadia Beach
Black Sea

Arkadia

If there is one place in Ukraine where you're likely to be singled out by the cops for a bit of special treatment it's the pedestrian alley leading to Arkadia Beach. Officers occupy strategic sites here, cherry-picking foreigners out of the crowd for a little shakedown. In fact we spoke to one traveller who'd been selected four nights out of eight for the grave offence of looking foreign.

If you're heading this way of an eve, make sure you're carrying your passport (you really should have it with you at all times anyway, but some travellers are afraid of losing their documents while under the influence). If the police want a bribe even after they've seen your papers, stand your ground, don't hand over any money and ask to be taken to the station. After a certain time the officers will see they're onto a loser and wander off to bother someone else. US visitors could also try calling their embassy in Kyiv, which scares the clappers out of most Ukrainian patrols.

lurking behind its refurbished neoclassical façade. The 40 rooms are individually decorated and the location across from the Opera and Ballet Theatre is perfect.

Hotel Ayvazovsky HOTEL $$$
(Отель Айвазовский; Map p140; ☑0482-429 022; www.ayvazovsky.com.ua; vul Bunina 19; s/d from 800/1080uah; 🖙❄🛜) From the Chesterfield sofas in the lobby to the spacious, high-ceilinged, European-standard bedrooms to the design-magazine perfect bathrooms, this soothing, 27-room sleepery in the heart of the city centre is worth every kopeck. Continental breakfast is delivered every morning to your room and staff can book tours and countless other services.

Hotel Londonskaya HOTEL $$$
(Гостиница Лондонская; Map p140; ☑048-738 0110; www.londred.com; bul Prymorsky 11; s 1100-2910uah, d 1360-3170uah; 🖙❄🛜🐾) Last refurbished in the early 1990s, the rooms of Odesa's oldest luxury hotel are becoming slightly dated, but with iron-lace balustrades, stained-glass windows, parquet flooring and an inner courtyard, the place still oozes Regency charm and is still the lodgings of choice for the smart set. It boasts a primo position, an excellent restaurant and even a small museum paying tribute to past guests.

Continental HOTEL $$$
(Континенталь; Map p140; ☑048-786 0399; www.continental-hotel.com.ua; vul Derybasivska 5; s/d from 1220/1460uah; 🖙❄🛜) If you're a businessperson arriving in Odesa on expenses, this smart hotel in a pretty much perfect location is probably where you'll be staying. The stylish rooms have high ceilings, exquisite oak desks, and plenty

of unused space. Well-briefed staff, 24-hour room service and a gaggle of cable TV channels are ideal for perking up your down time.

Babushka Grand Hostel HOSTEL $
(Map p140; ☑063 070 5535; vul Mala Arnautska 60; dm from 100uah; 🛜) While Odesa's other hostels are decidedly for the young, day-sleeping crowd, the wonderfully named Grand Babushka, occupying a palatial apartment near the train station, has a more laid-back, traveller vibe. The stuccoed interiors and crystal chandeliers are stunning, the staff fun and at least once a week a real Ukrainian *babushka* comes in to cook up a feast (100uah).

Black Sea Hotel Odessa HOTEL $$
(Гостиница Черное Море Одесса; Map p140; ☑048-230 0911; www.bs-hotel.com.ua; vul Rishelevska 59; s/d from 500/650uah; @🐾) This ugly 1970s concrete tower shelters generic but surprisingly well appointed and spacious rooms, most of which have been smartly renovated (the exception is the shabby and far-from-chic singles). The once-surly staff are now friendly, helpful and speak English. Breakfast is extra.

Black Sea Hotel Privoz HOTEL $$
(Гостиница Черное Море Привоз; Map p140; ☑0482-365 411; www.bs-hotel.com. ua; vul Panteleymonivska 25; s/d/tw from 550/1150/540uah; ❄@) Although in a slightly dodgy area, this hotel stretches your hryvnya a long way at the midrange level. While the décor is hit or miss, the generous size of the rooms, professional service and overall modernity of this 100-room high-rise make up for it. Breakfast costs 70uah extra.

Palladium Hotel HOTEL $$
(Гостиница Палладиум; Map p140; ☎048-728 6651; www.hotel-palladium.com.ua; bul Italyansky 4; r from 785uah; ❄☞☎) With attractive, pastel-hued rooms featuring minimalist décor and fine-textured carpets and a wonderful swimming pool, this definitely qualifies as a good deal for Odesa. Admission to the popular downstairs nightclub (closed during summer) is free for hotel guests, as is admission to the summer club Itaka.

TIU Front Page Hostel HOSTEL $
(off Map p140; ☎093 566 6278; vul Koblevska 42, top fl; dm 50-120uah; @) The current owners inherited the premises from a publishing company that had wallpapered the entire place in magazine front pages, hence the name. Sadly they no longer rent out the private double decorated in Playboy centre-folds. Definitely a party hostel with never a dull moment, so sleep may not come easily here. English proprietor Marcus runs a weekly bus between this and his other hostel in Kyiv (TIU). The bus is free if you book two nights or more in both hostels.

Chillout Hostel HOSTEL $
(Map p140; ☎063 867 7828; vul Derybasivska 5; dm from 120uah; ❄☎) Odesa's best located hostel is this modern, Polish-run affair next door to the Continental Hotel, mere stumbling distance from the city's best bars. The high-ceilinged dorms have loads of space to unpack and there's a free breakfast. As with all apartment hostels in the former USSR, the bathroom facilities are a bit inadequate,

but few seem to mind. Air-con means this place lives up to its name in summer.

Passazh Hotel HOTEL $
(Гостиница Пассаж; Map p140; ☎048-728 5500; www.passage.odessa.ua; vul Preobrazhenska 34; s/d from 180/230uah) The Passazh is the epitome of faded glory, but my, how glorious it must have been. Everything here is *big*. A giraffe could preen itself in the enormous mirrors flanking the grand central stairway, and frankly, you could almost swing a giraffe in the cavernous corridors too. The rooms feature lots of Soviet fixtures, bad wallpaper, saggy beds and shoddy tile-work, but they are large and come with old-world amenities such as full-length claw-footed bathtubs.

Tokyo Star Hotel MINI-HOTEL $
(off Map p140; ☎048-700 2191; vul Vodoprovodna 1A; s/d 100/200uah; ❄☎) This no-frills mini business hotel near the Privoz bus station is for those who use their room to sleep and wash but little else. The singles have no windows and rooms are so small, you'll be constantly climbing over a large pack or suitcase. With the doubles, make sure you know the person you're travelling with well, as there's very little dividing the bed from the toilet and shower.

Hotel Yunost HOTEL $$
(Гостиница Юность; ☎048-738 0412; www.hotel-yunost.com.ua; vul Pionerska 34; s/d/tw from 400/360/740uah; ❄) Occupying a hard-to-miss monolith out towards Arkadia, Yunost's rooms range from unrenovated Soviet with appalling décor and creaky parquet

ODESA'S ARCHITECTURE

Odesa's underrated architecture can look Kyiv and Lviv square in the eye. The city emerged from WWII largely unscathed, and it remains awash with beautiful, if often dilapidated, pre-Soviet structures, many reflecting eclectic neo-renaissance and art nouveau styles.

While building buffs are liable to find unheralded architectural gems along any street in the centre, the mother lode is on vul Gogolya (west of the Potemkin Steps), where the city's best 19th-century architects were apparently in a contest to create the city's most elaborate buildings. With its odd patterns, bright colours and eccentric balconies, No 14 is probably the most eye-catching, followed by No 6, where a row of gods supports the 2nd-floor balcony. The street's namesake, Nikolai Gogol, lived at No 11 for several months in the 1850s – just one of several prominent names to have had an address here.

Other buildings not to be missed include Passazh, the Opera and Ballet Theatre, the main synagogue and the recently renovated building of the Museum of Western and Eastern Art. A large number of Odesa's buildings were made with limestone taken from the city's catacombs and many are now undergoing much needed facelifts.

As in most Ukrainian cities, many hotels tend to be quite poor value, and apartments offer more bang for your buck. The cheapest flats are offered by the 'babushka mafia', as locals call it, whose members hang out around the train station (though not in the numbers they once did) and ask around 50uah for a room, or roughly double to triple that for a one-bedroom apartment. Beware: babushkas often falsely claim their apartments are located v tsentre (in the centre) or u morya (by the sea). Carry a map to check. Otherwise contact the following apartment-rental agencies:

Central Vokzal Apartment Bureau (Квартирное бюро-Центральный вокзал; Map p140; ☎048-727 1381; Odesa train station; beds from 50uah, apt from 250uah; ☺6.30am-8pm) If you don't want to deal with finicky babushkas and haven't booked anything in advance, this is your best walk-in bet. It's across from platform 4 near the station's rear exit.

American Business Center (Map p140; ☎048-777 1400; www.odessa-apt-rentals.com; vul Derybasivska 5) Only suitable for long-term visitors, as there's a seven-day minimum stay requirement.

Odessa Rent-A-Flat (Map p140; ☎048-787 3444; www.odessarentaflat.com; vul Rishelevska 11)

Odessaapts.com (☎067 708 5501; www.odessaapts.com)

floors to comfortable pads with air-con and sea views. The more you pay, the better standard you'll enjoy. Surprisingly the rate includes breakfast. It's a few stops before Arkadia on tram 5.

✖ Eating

Kompot — TOP CHOICE — FRENCH $$
(Компот; Map p140; vul Derybasivska 20; mains 40-90uah; ☺8am-11pm; ⚑) Spilling out onto busy Derybasivska to a jolly Gallic soundtrack, this French-style eatery is good for any meal of the day. Fresh pastries and an early start are a godsend for caffeine-craving Westerners, light lunches can be devoured in the faux Parisian interior over a newspaper and you can dine out on the cobbles till late with a bottle of something nice. Service here can be escargot-paced when busy.

Balalaika RUSSIAN $$
(Балалайка; Map p140; vul Katerynynska 12; mains 40-100uah; ☺11am-midnight; ⚑) If you were looking forward to Odesa for its Russian-ness, this brightly lit, timber-lined restaurant decorated with colourful Russian knick-knackery is the place to indulge. There are Siberian pelmeni (dumplings), imaginatively filled pancakes, heaps of meat and fish, and a mangal (grill) working overtime to supply diners with shashlyk (shish kebab). Real beluga caviar comes in at 925uah for 100g. Sadly this place gets lambasted on Russian restaurant review sites for its brazen service.

Tavriya CANTEEN $
(Таврія; Map p140; Galereya Afina mall, pl Hretska; mains from 15uah; ☺8am-10pm) This squeaky-clean food mecca in the basement of Odesa's flashiest mall has become the city's most popular quick eat. It consists of a Ukrainian-food stolova (cafeteria), a pizza and pasta bar, and a large supermarket. The caf has a larger choice of dishes than the city's other canteens, but can be a much more Ukrainian-style push-and-shove affair and the service stinks.

Zharyu Paryu CANTEEN $
(Жарю Парю; Map p140; vul Hretska 45; mains from 10uah; ☺8am-10pm) When lunchtime strikes, going where the local student and office-worker population find nourishment usually makes sense. This clinical self-service canteen of the factory or school variety is such a place, and with cheap and cheerful Ukrainian favourites on the menu board it's ideal for cash-strapped nomads.

Pulcinella ITALIAN $$
(Map p140; vul Lanzheronivska 17; mains 30-50uah) The bright teal interior gives this place a seaside Mediterranean feel, but it's the scrumptious five-course meals that will really make you feel like you're in southern Italy. The culinary highlights are the lasagne and the brick-oven-fired pizza.

Puzata Khata
CANTEEN $

(Пузата хата; Map p140; vul Derybasivska 21; mains from 10uah; ☺9am-10pm) Take the lift to the 6th floor of the Evropa shopping mall to find the Odesa branch of this national chain. The theme here is vaguely Greco–Black Sea, but the serving staff still look as though they've just stepped off the steppe. The cut-priced fare here is as tasty as at any other branch and a three-course meal with a drink should fit into 40uah.

Fat Mozes
BISTRO $$

(Map p140; vul Katerynynska 8/10; sandwiches 39-55uah, mains 65-105uah) Sounds like a New York deli, doesn't it? However, apart from the roast-beef sandwiches, it isn't quite. The atmosphere is more of a cosy, unpretentious bistro, serving an eclectic mix that includes souvlaki, goulash and Jamaican chicken.

Klarabara
INTERNATIONAL $$

(Кларабара; Map p140; City Garden; mains 35-100uah) Tucked away in a quiet corner of the City Garden, this classy, cosy, ivy-covered cafe and restaurant is awash with antique furniture and fine art. The food is a mixed bag, but every week there's also a theme menu showcasing the cuisine of this or that country.

Kumanets
UKRAINIAN $$

(Куманець; Map p140; vul Havanna 7; mains 35-80uah) A kitsch little island of Ukraine in Russian Odesa, this veritable Ukrainian village produces affordable *holubtsy* (cabbage rolls), *varenyky* (dumplings) and *deruny* (potato pancakes) in addition to pricier mains.

Zara Pizzara
PIZZERIA $$

(Map p140; vul Rishelevska 5; mains 40-60uah; ☺9am-midnight) Odesa's best pizzeria has an enviously located summer terrace, real Italian-style thin-crust pizza loaded with toppings, and hefty calzones.

Khevron
KOSHER $$

(Хеврон; Map p140; vul Rishelevska 30; mains 28-110uah; ☺Sun-Fri; ❄ⓘ) This excellent underground kosher eatery is beneath Odesa's main synagogue.

Drinking

Just about anywhere along vul Derybasivska is a good place for a drink.

TOP CHOICE Shkaf
BAR

(Шкаф; Map p140; vul Derybasivska 14; ☺7pm-late) Often the best watering holes in Ukraine are hidden behind unmarked doors and buried deep below anonymous buildings. That's the case with this heaving basement bar cum club, a sure-fire antidote to Odesa's trendy beach-club scene and pick-up bars. To find it, pass through a pair of varnished wooden doors at Derybasivska 14, flanked by official-looking blue signs, walk to the building's rear then down the stairs.

Shuzz
MUSIC BAR

(Шузз; Map p140; www.shuzz.od.ua; vul Uspenska 22; admission 30uah; ☺5pm-3am) Occupying a former shoe factory, this is the latest addition to Odesa's night scene. The vibe is laid-back, so grab a cloudy Chernihivske Bile and chill to whatever's playing, as this is also the best alternative-music venue in Odesa. There's all sorts on the bill, from Ukrainian indie bands to Spanish guitar acts.

Friends and Beer
RETRO BAR

(Map p140; vul Derybasivska 9) This charming re-created USSR-era living room littered with photos of Russian film stars is proof that 'Retro Soviet' doesn't have to mean political posters and Constructivist art. The huge TV screen is possibly not authentic for the period, but it's great for sports.

Mick O'Neill's Irish Bar
IRISH BAR

(Ирландский бар Мик О'Нилз; Map p140; vul Derybasivska 13; ☺24hr) This longstanding

---

WHAT THEY SAID ABOUT ODESA

'I have not felt so much at home for a long time as I did when I "raised the hill" and stood in Odessa for the first time.'

Mark Twain, Innocents Abroad, 1869

'Odessa has more colour, more spunk, more irreverence than any other Soviet city.'
Maurice Friedberg, How Things Were Done in Odessa, 1972

'Odessans, from the city's raffish gangsters to its lissom girls, are convinced that they are superior in culture and style to anyone in Moscow or London, let alone the hicks from Kiev... And they are absolutely right.'

Simon Sebag-Montefiore, the Independent, 2000

Irish pub is a great place to start an evening and an even better place to finish it, as it's the only outdoor patio on vul Derybasivska that's open round the clock.

Captain Morgan BAR
(Map p140; vul Zhukovskoho 30; ⏱24hr; 🐦) By day Captain Morgan (the name is pirated) is a pretty benign breakfast or lunch spot or early-evening drinks stop. But at night capable DJs spin till the wee hours and there's a funky downstairs lounge. The crowd of expats, local heavies/beauties and sex tourists never fails to generate a 'colourful' atmosphere.

☆ Entertainment
Clubs

Odesa's raucous club scene has two seasons: summer (June–August) and the rest of the year. In summer, the action is at Arkadia Beach, which boasts two huge, Ibiza-style nightclubs that produce heightened levels of madness seven days a week. At other times of the year, the action is closer to the city centre. Unless otherwise noted, the following clubs charge 50uah to 100uah on weekends, and much less on weekdays. Discounted or free admission for women is the norm.

Ibiza NIGHTCLUB
(Ибиза; Map p146; www.ibiza.ua; Arkadia Beach; ⏱summer) This white, free-form, open, cave-like structure is Arkadia's most upmarket and most expensive club. European DJs and big-ticket Russian and Ukrainian pop bands often play here. Ticket prices can be high when a big act is in town.

Itaka NIGHTCLUB
(Итака; Map p146; www.itaka-club.com.ua; Arkadia Beach; ⏱summer) It's slightly more downmarket than Ibiza and consequently often rowdier (in a good way). The Greek columns and statues are a tad much, but you'll hardly care when it's 5am and you are out of your gourd. Like Ibiza, it also draws big regional pop acts.

Palladium NIGHTCLUB
(Палладиум; Map p140; www.palladium.com.ua; bul Italyansky 4; ⏱Sep-May) Itaka's sister club takes up the slack downtown when Itaka shuts down in September. There's a nightly show at around 11pm, followed by general debauchery.

Cosmo NIGHTCLUB
(Космо; Map p146; Gagarinskoe plato 5; ⏱Fri & Sat Sep-May) This spaceship-shaped club out

by Arkadia is Odesa's biggest club in the low season, attracting a relatively young and boisterous crowd.

Shede GAY CLUB
(Шеде; Map p140; www.shedeclub.com.ua; Derybasivska 5) One of Ukraine's best openly gay nightclubs with Friday and Saturday night shows beginning at 1am.

Praetoria Music Club MUSIC CLUB
(Map p140; vul Lanzheronivska 26) This is one of the few city-centre clubs that has a pulse in the summer.

Classical Music & Opera

Theatre, concert and opera tickets can be purchased at the venues or at a **Teatralna Kasa** (Театральная касса; Map p140; Theatre Kiosk; ⏱9am-5pm). There's one on the corner of vul Derybasivska and vul Rishelevska.

Odessa Philharmonic Hall CONCERT HALL
(Одесская филармония; Map p140; www.odessaphilharmonic.org; vul Bunina 15; ⏱closed Jul & Aug) The best regional orchestra within the former Soviet Union is the **Odessa Philharmonic Orchestra** led by charismatic and energetic American conductor Hobart Earle, a former student of Leonard Bernstein. This orchestra accounts for half the symphonies put on here.

Opera and Ballet Theatre THEATRE
(Театр оперы и балета; Map p140; www.opera-ballet.tm.odessa.ua; Chaykovskoho 1) In addition to being architecturally magnificent, Odesa's theatre is also known for its marvellous acoustics. Unfortunately, the local opera company does not do justice to the theatre's impressive physical attributes, but performances are eminently affordable and the Odessa Philharmonic Orchestra performs here from time to time.

🛍 Shopping
Privoz Market MARKET
(Привоз базар; Map p140; vul Pryvozna) Odesa is home to two of Southern Ukraine's largest and most famous markets. The centrally located market is possibly the largest farmers market in the country and a must-visit for *rynok* lovers. On hot days you may want to breathe through your mouth in some of the overheated halls.

7-Kilometres Bazaar MARKET
(www.7km.net) The sprawling bazaar on the city's southwest edge is one of the largest markets of any kind in the former Soviet

MARCUS NIMMO: ODESA CONNOISSEUR

Brit Marcus Nimmo is founder of the TIU (This Is Ukraine) chain of hostels located in every tourist hotspot in Ukraine. But he hasn't spent the last four years just fitting out and opening hostels – partying, especially in Odesa, has also been high on his agenda. Here Marcus gives us his top tips for a great time by the Black Sea.

Best Nightclub

In summer it's got to be Itaka, as it's more relaxed on dress code and face control than its Arkadia competitors. In winter I'd recommend Palladium, as it's quite backpacker friendly.

Best Place to Drink

At TIU we love Shkaf. It has a budget Bohemian atmosphere and there's live music.

Best Place to Eat

Kompot would be my choice in Odesa. They have an English menu, the waiters are friendly and the food is superb, and not too pricey.

Best Experience

It's got to be the catacombs just out of town. Try to set up an English guide for a more in-depth experience.

Best Beach

Everyone has their favourite, but mine's an obvious choice – Arkadia. It's definitely Odesa's cleanest beach and the best for a barbecue.

Top Tips

Many travellers arrive in Odesa intending to continue their journey by boat. Sadly the local ferry operators are an unpredictable bunch and no one should base their travel plans around their timetables. My other tip is simple – always take your passport when you head down to the beach!

Union. Nicknamed the *tolkuchka* or *tolchok* (both meaning 'push' in Russian), its appeal lies in its sheer size, rather than its shopping selection, which mainly entails row after row of the same old cheap knock-offs and junk. The official name comes from its location about 7km outside the city. To get there, take a *marshrutka* (fixed-route minibus) marked '7KM' from Privoz bus station.

ⓘ Information

Angar18 (Ангар-18; vul Velika Arnautska 52; per hr 6uah; ⊙24hr) Internet at any time of day plus Skype and photocopying.

Central post office (Почта; vul Sadova 10)

European Business Center (vul Preobrazhenska 34; per hr 6uah; ⊙9am-midnight) Modern internet place on the ground floor of the Passazh Hotel.

Lonely Planet (www.lonelyplanet.com/ukraine/odesa) You'll find planning advice, author recommendations and travel reviews here.

Tourist Office (☑048-731 4808; www.odessatourism.in.ua; bul Italyansky 11; ⊙9am-1pm & 2-6pm Mon-Fri) Stop the presses, Odesa has a tourist office! This office is one of only a handful of municipally funded information points in the entire country, and it's a decent one too. Staff can book anything, including hotels, all kinds of tickets and city tours. The website is superb as well.

ⓘ Getting There & Away

Air

Odesa airport (www.airport.od.ua) is better linked to Europe than any other Ukrainian airport, with the exception of Kyiv's. Malev, Air Baltic, Czech Airlines, Carpatair and Turkish Airlines all have regular flights to Odesa, and various regional carriers fly to Georgia, Armenia and Russia.

Domestic airline Dniproavia flies between here and Kyiv up to five times a day. **Kiy Avia** (Map p140; www.kiyavia.com; vul Preobrazhenska 15; ⊙8am-8pm) can sort you out with tickets and timetables.

Boat

Ferry services to and from Odesa are notoriously unreliable, with services to Istanbul, Varna in Bulgaria and Poti in Georgia ceasing for months on end without explanation. Boats are in theory operated by **Ukrferry** (www.ukrferry.com), but planning onward travel around these guys is folly indeed. The only reliable passenger service from Odesa (not run by Ukrferry) is the boat to Crimea (850uah, 20 hours, five to seven sailings a month). For tickets and timetables contact London Sky Travel.

Bus

Odesa has two bus stations that are useful for travellers. The conveniently located, but slightly chaotic, **Privoz bus station** (Привоз Автвокзал; Map p140; vul Vodoprovodna), 300m west of the train station, is mainly for shorter trips. *Marshrutky* leave from here to Mykolayiv every 15 minutes throughout the day (46uah, 1½ hours), and to Vylkovo (50uah, three to four hours, about every two hours).

Most international and long-haul domestic buses leave from the **long-distance bus station** (vul Kolontaevska 58), 3km west of the train station. Frequent **Gunsel** (☑048-232 6212) and **Autolux** (☑048-716 4612) buses are the most comfortable and quickest way to travel to Kyiv (125uah to 175uah, six to seven hours). The latter's non-stop VIP service has airline-style seats and a stewardess serving free refreshments; it runs four times a day. Otherwise speedy *marshrutky* leave from just in front of the station building (150uah, six hours). Other destinations include Izmayil (60uah, four hours, hourly), Donetsk (130uah, 13 hours, one daily), Simferopol (100uah, 12 hours, six daily), Yalta (125uah, 14 hours, three daily), Lviv (140uah, 15 hours, two daily) and Chernivtsi (130uah, 13 hours, two daily) via Kamyanets-Podilsky.

There are at least 10 buses per day to Chişinău via Tiraspol, and two via Palanka (65uah, five to seven hours). The latter avoid Transdniestr (see p281).

Train

Odesa is well connected by train to all major Ukrainian, Russian and eastern European cities. Despite the addition of 'summer trains' on the most popular routes (eg Kyiv, Moscow, Simferopol and Lviv), seats to/from Odesa fill up fast from June to August, so book ahead.

There are up to eight trains to Kyiv (110uah, 10 to 12 hours), four of which are overnighters. Other destinations include Kharkiv (190uah, 14 hours), Lviv (180uah, 12 hours), Kamyanets-Podilsky (130uah, 18 hours) and Simferopol (140uah, 12 hours). Longer-distance services go to Moscow, Minsk, Rostov and (during summer only) to St Petersburg. There are still no trains to Chişinău.

ⓘ Getting Around

Odesa airport is about 12km southwest of the city centre, off Ovidiopilska doroha. Bus 129 goes to/from the train station; infrequent bus 117 runs to/from the pl Hretska stop.

To get to the centre from the train station (about a 20-minute walk), go to the stop near the McDonald's and take any bus saying 'Площа Грепка' (pl Hretska), such as bus 148. Trolleybuses 4 and 10 trundle up vul Pushkinska before curving around to vul Prymorska past the passenger port and the foot of the Potemkin Steps.

Tram 5 goes from the train station to the long-distance bus station. From the Privoz bus station to pl Hretska take bus 220.

If you must travel by taxi, **Servis-Taksi** (☑0482-345 077) and **IgAl** (☑0482-348 080) come recommended by the tourist office.

Rental cars are especially useful for exploring Bessarabia or the Kherson area. Try **Europcar** (☑048-777 4011) in the Black Sea Hotel Odesa.

Around Odesa

The limestone on which Odesa stands is riddled with some 2000km of tunnels, which have always played an important part in the city's history. Quarried out for

TRAVEL AGENCIES

Odesa's travel agencies can show you the city, its surroundings and places further afield such as the Danube Delta and Askaniya Nova.

» **Eugenia Travel** (☑048-722 0331; www.eugeniatours.com.ua; vul Rishelevska 23) Runs a variety of tours.

» **London Sky Travel** (☑048-729 3196; www.lstravel.com.ua; Boat Passenger Terminal, vul Prymorska 6) Specialises in ferry tickets but also does the standard city and regional tours.

» **Salix** (☑048-728 9738, 048-799 0796; www.salix.od.ua; vul Torhova 14) A rare, authentically 'green' Ukrainian travel agency, with responsible tours to Vylkovo and the Danube Delta, as well as Crimea and other southern destinations.

building in the 19th century, they were first used to hide smuggled goods. During WWII they sheltered a group of local partisans, who waged a war of attrition against the occupying Romanians and forced the Nazis to keep greater troop numbers in the area.

Most of the catacomb network lies well outside the city centre. The only tunnels that can be visited are in the suburb of Nerubayske, about 15km north of the centre of Odesa. Here a resident speleologist offers 45-minute **catacomb tours** (☑048-725 2874; ⊙9am-4pm Tue-Sun) that wend through what was the headquarters of Odesa's WWII partisan movement. Tours cost 10uah per person (plus a 100uah flat fee for the guide) and are in Russian, so you may wish to bring a translator along, although you don't necessarily need one to enjoy the catacombs. Tours exit into the musty Partisan Museum.

Marshrutka 84 to Nerubayske leaves every 10 minutes from Odesa's Privoz bus station (2uah, 35 minutes). Ask the driver to let you off at the 'Katakomby' stop, easily identifiable by the hulking Soviet realist statue depicting five defiant partisans. Tour agencies in Odesa run tours out here for about 600uah per group, or in summer you can look for one of the Russian-speaking guides touting tours in front of the train station.

Mykolayiv МИКОЛАЇВ

☑0512 / POP 500,000

The juggernaut of the Soviet Union's shipbuilding industry fell upon hard times when Ukraine gained independence, but is beginning to emerge from its malaise on the back of renewed demand for its ships – and its women. Mykolayiv (Nikolayev in Russian) is the centre of Ukraine's marriage industry, and the city's pleasant, pedestrian main drag, **vul Radnyanska** (although just about everybody uses its Russian name, Sovetskaya), is eavesdropping central if you're looking for a little insight into this curious subculture.

Mykolayiv is also home to Ukraine's most famous zoo, although, as with any zoo in the former Soviet Union, you should temper your expectations.

With Odesa's Ship Museum long since reduced to ashes, there is no longer any debate about which city has the best boat museum in Ukraine. Mykolayiv's **Shipbuilding Museum** (vul Admiralska 4; admission 5uah; ⊙10am-5pm Tue-Sun) features loads of exquisitely crafted models, through which you can observe the evolution of Mykolayiv-built warships over the last 300 years: from wooden schooners to Leviathan steel aircraft carriers. There are some stunning antique globes and extensive exhibits on the naval campaigns of the Crimean War, WWI and WWII. There's nothing in English, but it's still interesting for non-Russian speakers.

If you decide to overnight here or get stuck, the best beds in town can be found at the **Hotel Ukraine Palace** (☑582 700; www.palace.nikolaev.ua; pr Lenina 57; r from 600uah), a sparkly new place for well-heeled *byznysmeny*. Slightly lower down the hotel food chain is **Hotel Kontinent** (☑477 520; www.continent.in.ua; vul Admirala Makarova 41; s/d from 300/420uah; ✳), which has its main entrance on vul Radnyanska. It's especially popular with the wife-seeking set, so book ahead.

Speedy private *marshrutky* to Odesa's Privoz bus station (46uah, 1½ hours) leave from behind the bus station. There are also half-hourly *marshrutky* to Kherson from the bus station (15uah, 1¼ hours).

Mykolayiv is a jump-off point of sorts for the Nuclear Missile Museum in Pervomaysk (see p78); *marshrutky* zip up to Pervomaysk from behind the bus station every half hour or so (40uah, 2½ hours).

Kherson ХЕРСОН

☑0552 / POP 347,000

Kherson is pleasantly situated at the mouth of the Dnipro River, but the main reason to come here is, rather, for what lies around it. The city is a popular, if not terribly convenient, jumping-off point for the Askaniya Nova Reserve, and there are also several less-ballyhooed excursions closer at hand.

One such excursion is to the Swedish village of **Zmiyivka**, whose first citizens begged Catherine the Great to move them here to escape serfdom in Russian-governed Sweden in the late 18th century. Zmiyivka remains a quirky enclave of Swedishness in today's Ukraine. To get to Zmiyivka take a *marshrutka* to Nova Kakhovka, which is about a 20-minute taxi ride from Zmiyivka (70uah).

From Kherson it's a pleasant 50-minute ferry ride south to **Hola Prystan** (two per day, April to October), the last town of any significance on the Dnipro. A seldom-travelled road leads west from here along the border of the bird-infested **Black Sea Biosphere Reserve** to **Heroyske**, an old Cossack settlement with a famous salt mine. You can do this beautiful drive on your own in a hired vehicle, but to enter the reserve you'll have to take an organised tour – inquire at the Fregat hotel in Kherson or at the **reserve office** (☑05539 267 75; vul Lermontova 1) in Hola Prystan.

Hotel Fregat (☑491 342; www.hotelfregat. com; vul Ushakova 2; s/d from 352/612uah) clearly has Soviet skeletons in its cupboards but the renovated rooms are comfy enough for a night or two. The in-house travel agency organises tours to various locations in the area, including Zmiyivka, Heroyske and Askaniya Nova. Another decent place to kip is **Meridian** (☑264 156; www.meridian.biz center.com.ua; Richkovy Vokzal - River Station; s/d from 130/180uah; ❄), which has sublime views of the Dnipro delta, so ask for a room with a view (and air-con).

Marshrutky depart every half hour to Mykolayiv (15uah, 1¼ hours) and every hour or so to Odesa (40uah, 2½ hours) until about 7.30pm. Trains and public buses to Odesa are more sporadic and take about twice as long. Buses also serve Simferopol (90uah, five hours). Kherson lies on the main train line between Kyiv (12 hours) and Simferopol (seven hours), and there are also five buses per day to Kyiv (120uah, 12 hours).

Askaniya Nova АСКАНІЯ НОВА

☑05538

Just a few kilometres north of the border between Ukraine proper and Crimea lies a vast plain populated by roaming buffaloes, playing deer and antelopes, as well as sturdy, wild Przewalski horses and other exotic species. The 2300-hectare **Askaniya Nova Reserve** was the brainchild of a 19th-century German settler who acted on his slightly mad idea of importing animals from different continents to this unique natural steppe. In addition to the above-mentioned animals, there are zebras, camels, gnus, rare Central Asian saiga antelopes and all manner of birds, from pink flamingos to rare steppe eagles.

These animals live in incongruous harmony on what is Europe's largest remaining natural steppe. This is what the Ukraine of the Cossacks looked like – a parched, isolated, sprawling, yellow expanse. It evokes the central plains of Africa and, as in Africa, the best way to see the animals is on a safari.

Alas, that's easier said than done. The reserve does organise safaris in horse-drawn carts at 400uah for groups of four or less. Reserve-organised minivan safaris are also possible for larger groups. However, the reserve limits the number of visitors, and safaris are shut down entirely when there's an elevated risk of fire, which seems to be more often than not, especially during the dry summer months. Booking three days in advance is mandatory for safari tours, and you should call to confirm the day before you arrive. Book through the **reserve office** (☑612 86, 612 32; askania-zap@mail.ru; vul Lenina 16; ❤8am-5pm mid-Apr–mid-Nov) in front of the zoo in Askaniya Nova.

If you can't get on a safari tour, Askaniya Nova is still of interest for its zoo, its botanic garden and its austerely beautiful landscape. However, these features alone are probably not worth the hassle of getting out here. A few specimens of each species found in the reserve occupy well-kept open-air pens in the **zoo** (admission 10uah; ❤8am-5pm mid-Apr–mid-Nov).

Lastly, a word of warning: most travel agencies running package tours to Askaniya Nova out of Crimea and Kherson have no intention of taking you on safari. If you are coming on a package tour, confirm that your tour includes a safari rather than the standard three-hour zoo and botanic-garden tour.

🛏 Sleeping

Spending a night in Askaniya Nova is highly recommended to get a proper feel for the place.

Fortuna　　　　　　　　　　HOTEL **$**
(☑615 86; d & tr with shared bathroom per person 60uah) This backpacker's delight, located right next to the bus station, has basic rooms with perfectly cosy beds and big, clean common bathrooms.

Kanna　　　　　　　　　　HOTEL **$**
(☑613 37; www.askania-nova-kanna.com.ua; vul Krasnoarmeyska 22; d from 300uah; ❄) The rooms here are squeaky clean and cavernous, but most definitely overpriced considering the rural location.

ⓘ Getting There & Away

Getting to Askaniya Nova by public transport is tricky; your best bet is to go to Nova Kakhovka and shell out 175uah for the scenic one-hour taxi ride. There are two early-morning and two early-afternoon *marshrutky* to Nova Kakhovka (16uah, 1½ hours), but these are often sold out. One of those originates in Kherson (30uah, at least three hours).

Nova Kakhovka is connected by bus to Kyiv (130uah, 13 hours) and Kherson (15uah, 1½ hours).

SOUTHERN BESSARABIA
ПІВДЕННА БЕСАРАБІЯ

Not too many Westerners venture into the fertile wedge of Ukraine that lies between the Danube and Dnister rivers. That's too bad because, in addition to being beautiful in spots, it's also one of Ukraine's most culturally peculiar regions.

Its history is equally peculiar. From the late 15th century until Russia's victory in the Russo-Turkish War of 1806–12, this region was part of the Ottoman Empire. The Turks named it 'Bessarabia' after the Wallachian family – the Basarabs – who controlled the area during the late medieval period. When the Russians took over, they expanded Bessarabia to include most of present-day Moldova (plus a small slice of Carpathian Ukraine). The section of Bessarabia lying east of the Moldovan border in present-day Ukraine was dubbed Southern Bessarabia, or Budzhak. Between the world wars it was part of Romania before the Soviets annexed it in 1940 and made it part of Ukraine.

Bilhorod-Dnistrovsky
БІЛГОРОД-
ДНІСТРОВСЬКИЙ

🕿 04849 / POP 58,400

A simple day-trip from Odesa, the 'White City on the Dnister' is an ordinary industrial port, but with an impressive **fortress** (vul Pushkina 19; admission 5uah; ◷9am-6pm) built by Moldavians, Genoese and Turks in the 13th to 15th centuries. Today the castle is among Ukraine's largest and best preserved. You can walk along most of the walls, which stretch nearly 2km in total.

Marshrutky departing every 10 minutes or so from Odesa's Privoz bus station cover the 55km to Bilhorod-Dnistrovsky in about

1½ hours (15uah), terminating at the train station. Each day, there are also five *elektrychky* (electric trains; 7uah, 2¼ hours). To reach the fortress from the train station, walk along vul Vokzalna, and after the park, turn right onto vul Dzerzhinskoho. From here, the fortress is a 1.5km walk.

Vylkovo ВИЛКОВО

🕿 04843 / POP 8000

A network of navigable canals has earned Vylkovo the nickname 'the Venice of Ukraine'. Frankly, the comparison is preposterous. This sleepy little fishing village feels light years removed from Venice – or any other form of civilisation. And while the canals – along which many villagers live – are interesting, you won't spend much time on them unless you take a special tour. But Vylkovo does have one thing going for it that Venice lacks: the heavenly Danube Delta Biosphere Reserve.

The lion's share of the marshy, bird-laden **Danube Delta Biosphere Reserve**, Europe's largest wetland, lies in Romania. Few tourists enter from the Ukrainian side, but those who do are rewarded with extremely affordable half- to full-day boat tours through the delta's unique waterways. You can visit the Danube's terminus (dubbed the '0km mark') or take a bird-watching tour. Guides can drop you off on small islands populated by thousands of terns and their just-hatched chicks. On other islands flocks of cormorants and white pelicans roost (the reserve is home to 70% of the world's white pelicans).

In the centre of Vylkovo you'll find the **Biosphere Reserve office** (🕿446 19; reserve@it.odessa.ua; vul Povstanniya 132A; ◷9am-6pm), with an on-site museum and informational videos (in German and Russian). The staff speak some English and can set you up with a local tour operator to take you into the reserve by boat.

Vylkovo's **canals**, built by the town's original Lipovan settlers, are the other main attraction. The villagers who live along the canals still use traditional, narrow fishing boats known as *chaika* (seagull) to fish and get around. Locals say there are 3000 such boats in Vylkovo, compared with only 600 cars. While touring the canals, drop by a local's house and purchase a bottle of the local wine, known as *novak*.

Booking tours in advance is a good idea, particularly on weekends. The largest and

Bessarabia has spent the better part of the past half-millennium getting tossed around like a hot potato by various regional powers. As a result of shifting borders, Moldovans, Romanians, Russians, Turks, Germans and Ukrainians have all called this region home, as have several more obscure groups.

Lipovans

One such group is the Lipovans, Russian 'Old Believers', who were exiled from Russia in the 18th century for refusing to comply with Russian Orthodox Church reforms instituted by Peter the Great. Most of them settled near the Danube Delta, where they still continue to live and practice Old Believer traditions such as crossing themselves with two fingers, and not shaving. Lipovan churches – one example is the St Nicholas Church in Vylkovo – are built in the shape of a boat instead of a cross, and have two spires and separate entrances for men and women. The interior walls are completely devoid of frescoes.

Gagauz

Next up are the Gagauz, an Orthodox-Christianised Turkish group, originally from Bulgaria, who ended up in Bessarabia when the Russians annexed the area from the Turks after the Russo-Turkish War of 1806–12. Today most Gagauz live in Moldova (where they have their own autonomous republic, Gagauzia), but you'll find Gagauz communities throughout Southern Bessarabia, including an active one in Vylkovo. The Gagauz language, Gagauzi, is a Turkish dialect influenced by Russian via the Russian Orthodox Church.

Zaporizhsky Cossacks

From a Ukrainian perspective, the most significant group to settle in this area was the Zaporizhsky Cossacks, who founded the Danube Sich just south of the Danube (in present-day Romania) after being driven out of Zaporizhzhya by Catherine the Great in 1775. Its loyalties split by the Russo-Turkish Wars, the *sich* collapsed in 1828, and most of its inhabitants migrated back east. A few thousand Cossacks, however, remained in the area, ensuring that a dash of hearty Cossack blood would forever be ingrained in the populations of Southern Bessarabia and northern Romania (where a strong Ukrainian community persists to this day).

most organised tour operator is **Pelikan Tour** (Пеликан Тур; www.pelican-danube-tour.com.ua in Russian) Vylkovo (☑067 483 5207; Primorskoye beach); Odesa (Map p140; ☑777 1205; vul Gogolya 8). Boat hire costs 150/300uah for a half/full day for up to six people. English-speaking guides cost around 100uah per hour (much more per hour for a professional ornithologist who speaks English). A half day should be enough time to visit both the reserve and the canals. A one-hour canal tour costs about 50uah.

Odesa travel agencies offer Vylkovo as a day trip, but they can charge anything up to 1200uah for transport, a boat trip and lunch. Joining a group can bring the cost down to around 300uah, but it is far more rewarding to spend a night in Vylkovo and use the extra time to absorb some local flavour. In Odesa, we recommend Salix travel agency.

🛏 Sleeping

In addition to the following options, ask Salix tours about its secluded riverside cabin available for around 100uah per person per night, exclusive of boat hire (300uah). Bring your own food.

Venetsiya HOTEL $
(☑313 74; vul Lenina 19A; r per person from 100uah; ☀) The 'Venice' represents exceptional value for money, with big, bright, comfy rooms and fluffy rugs. Most rooms share pristine bathrooms and there's also a restaurant.

Since the Black Sea was formed six millennia ago, the Danube Delta has grown into Europe's second largest river delta (after Russia's Volga Delta). Here are some facts and figures about this remarkable area:

» **Area:** 4178 sq km

» **Rate of growth:** 80 sq m per year

» **Number of resident bird species:** 240

» **Area included in Unesco Biosphere Reserve:** 14,851 hectares

» **Percentage of Danube Delta on Ukrainian side of border:** 18%

» **Number of languages spoken in the delta:** seven

Pelikan Tour　　　　GUESTHOUSE/COTTAGES **$**
(☎067 483 5207; guesthouse d with shared bathroom per person 150uah, cottages 500uah) Pelikan Tour runs a homey, 14-bed guesthouse on the banks of the Danube, a short walk from the centre. You'll have to resist the urge to take up duck hunting when awakened by the loudly frolicking, nocturnal waterfowl in the small marina. The company has also built four comfortable timber cottages in a tranquil spot on the riverbank. They have large glazed verandas for bird spotting and to let the river views flood in.

✖ Eating & Drinking

Yakar　　　　　　　　　　　　　CAFE **$**
(Belhorodsky canal; dishes from 10uah) This friendly little cafe is the only place in town for a canal-side beer and snack. The food is basic Russian fare and the Obolon draught beer is cheap.

Venezia　　　　　　　　　　　　CAFE **$**
(vul Lenina 22; mains 10-20uah) Located on the main street in the centre of town, Venezia features diversions like billiards and a weekend disco in addition to run-of-the-mill Russian and Ukrainian food.

ℹ Getting There & Away

Fast *marshrutky* to Vylkovo leave every two hours or so until late afternoon from Odesa's Privoz bus station (50uah, three to four hours). The occasional buses that depart from Odesa's long-distance bus station are slower, taking up to twice as long to do the run.

Izmayil ІЗМАЇЛ

☎04841 / POP 84,800
It's probably not worth a special trip, but Izmayil's interesting history and edgy border-town feel make for a fine stopover if you're heading to/from Romania or Moldova. If you prefer to avoid other tourists, you won't have to worry about bumping into any here.

Izmayil was named after a Turkish khan who sacked the city – then called Smil – in the 15th century. In subsequent centuries the fortress of Izmayil attained legendary status as the Turks gradually made it one of the world's most impregnable bastions. Measuring 7km around, it overlooked the Danube and boasted supposedly impenetrable walls, which were 4m thick and 24m tall. The successful sacking of the fort by General Alexander Suvorov and his men on 22 December 1790 (during the Russo-Turkish War of 1787–92) is regarded as one of the most impressive military feats in Russian history – and one of the most disastrous blows ever dealt to the Ottoman Empire.

This battle is recreated in a brilliant diorama at the **Suvorov Museum** (vul Krepostnaya; admission 5uah; ⊙9am-5pm). Dioramas of famous battles are a dime a dozen in Ukrainian museums, but this one truly stands out in terms of the quality of both the visual presentation (complete with light show) and the 20-minute audio presentation (in English!). The 16th-century former mosque housing the museum is all that remains of the once-mighty fortress.

If you need a place to crash, the **Hotel Grin Kholl** (☎583 83; pr Suvorova 374; s/d from 150/190uah) doesn't look much from the outside, but the inside conceals clean and comfy bedrooms and rates include breakfast. Shevchenko Park runs along pr Suvorova and has several pleasant outdoor eating and drinking options.

There are two slow *marshrutky* a day to/from Vylkovo (20uah, 2¼ hours). Buses (four hours) and *marshrutky* (three hours) depart every 15 minutes or so to Odesa (about 40uah).

Crimea Крим

POP: 2 MILLION / AREA: 26,200 SQ KM

Best Places to Eat

» Kezlev Kyavesi (p166)

» Aliye (p171)

» Barkas (p184)

» Izbushka Rybaka (p186)

» Kubdari (p202)

Best Places to Stay

» Sevastopol (p183)

» Kichkine (p193)

» Knyaz Golitsyn (p198)

» Dolina Privideny Lodge (p196)

» Dacha Koktebelica (p200)

Why Go?

Diamond-shaped Crimea is a gem that has adorned many different crowns. From ancient Scythians to Russian tsars, everyone wanted to possess this little subtropical paradise with its bluff limestone plateaus, lush coastal forests and turquoise bays. If you were an army roaming in the vicinity, we bet you'd soon be invading it, too!

The latest horde to swarm the peninsula is that of ex-Soviet holiday-makers, who fill every patch of Crimea's narrow pebbly beaches in summer. Yet few foreigners are here on a beach holiday. Instead many of them are lured by infinite opportunities for outdoor adventure as well as the peninsula's fascinating ethnic mishmash.

Still, the main pull of Crimea for foreign visitors is its history. You'll encounter ruins of an ancient Greek colony and Genovese fortresses, medieval cave cities and Crimean War battlefields, residences of Tatar khans and Russian tsars – even a short holiday in Crimea turns into a dizzying journey through time.

When to Go?
Simferopol

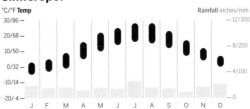

May-June Feel the flower power as orchards bloom and mountains are covered in wild tulips.

July-August Beaches are packed but the sea is warm and the Kazantip rave is under way.

September-October Crowds wash away. Time for jazz in Koktebel and mountain hikes.

Crimea Highlights

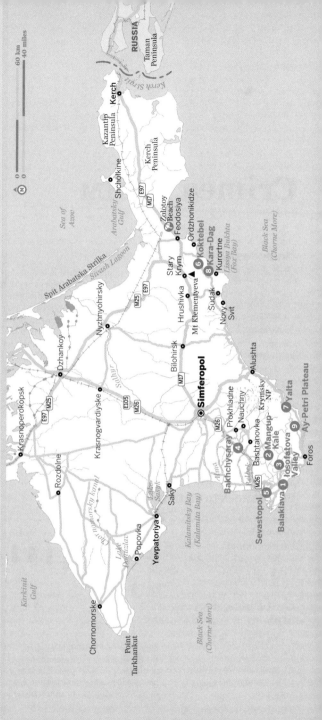

1. Enter a top-secret Soviet nuclear facility and sample Black Sea fish in the beautiful bay of **Balaklava** (p185)

2. Conquer the cave-city of **Mangup-Kale** (p171)

3. Get spooked by thousands of gravestones covered in ancient Hebrew script at **Iosofatova Valley** (p169)

4. Stay with Crimean Tatars, learn their heartbreaking story and sample their food in **Bakhchysaray** (p167)

5. Explore Crimean War battlefields and party in a **Sevastopol** (p172) gay bar

6. Soar above Crimea in the paragliding paradise of **Koktebel** (p199)

7. Get decadent touring the paradise lost of royal estates near **Yalta** (p187)

8. Trek through the striking volcanic formations of **Kara-Dag** (p199) nature reserve

9. Take a breathtaking cable-car ride to the top of **Ay-Petri plateau** (p193)

History

The stage is littered with cameo appearances, from ancient Greeks who built Chersoneses (now Khersones) to the 15th-century Genoese merchants behind the impressive Sudak fortress, as well as Cimmerians, Scythians, Sarmatians and Jews. However, the central theme of Crimean history revolves around the struggle between the Turkic and Slavic peoples for control of the peninsula.

This began in 1240, when Mongols conquered Crimea. Two centuries later, control passed to their descendants, the Tatars, who held it for centuries. The Crimean Khanate became an independent political entity under Haci Giray in 1428, and after the 1475 invasion, was a vassal state of the Ottoman Empire. Although advanced in culture and arts, its main economic activity was trading in slaves, captured during raids into Russian, Ukrainian or Polish territory.

While a Turkish vassal state, Crimea enjoyed much autonomy. The same was not true when the Russians arrived in 1783 and began a campaign of assimilation. Three quarters of Crimean Tatars fled to Turkey, while Russians, Ukrainians, Greeks, Bulgarians, Germans and even some French were invited to resettle Crimea.

Such Russian expansionism soon began to worry the great powers, Britain and France. As Russia tried to encroach into the lands of the decaying Ottoman Empire, the Crimean War erupted in 1854 (see p181).

With close ties to the monarchy, Crimea was one of the last White bastions during the Russian revolution, holding out till November 1920. It was occupied by German troops for three years during WWII and lost nearly half its population. In the war's aftermath, Stalin deported all remaining Crimean Tatars and most other ethnic minorities.

In 1954 Soviet leader Nikita Khrushchev, a self-styled Ukrainian, created the Autonomous Crimean Soviet Socialist Republic and transferred legislative control to the Ukrainian SSR from the Russian Federation.

When the USSR disintegrated, Russia and Ukraine wrestled over the region. They came to a temporary compromise over Russia's Black Sea Fleet, allowing it to stay in Crimea until 2017. Soon after being elected in 2010, President Viktor Yanukovych extended this lease until 2035.

Over 60% of the Crimean population are ethnic Russians and most of the others are Russian speakers. Russian is an official language in Crimea, along with Ukrainian and Crimean Tatar. Locals weren't particularly chuffed by Ukrainian independence, even less so by the Orange Revolution.

Crimean Tatars started returning from Central Asian exile in the late 1980s. Restitution of the property lost in 1944 was out of the question. Penniless and unwelcome by the Russian majority, they resorted to grabbing unused land. Pro-Russian 'Cossack' vigilantes launched a series of violent attacks on Tatar squatters, but by the time of writing-tensions have largely subsided.

CENTRAL & WESTERN CRIMEA

Simferopol
СІМФЕРОПОЛЬ

☑ 0652 / POP 345,000

With its odd mixture of Levantine and Soviet, the Crimean capital is not an unpleasant city, but there is no point lingering here, as everything else on the peninsula is much more exciting – and it's only a short bus ride away! If you have a night to spend in Simferopol, use this opportunity to chill out in one of its quality restaurants and cafes – a bit of a rarity on the coast.

◉ Sights

Taurida Central Museum HISTORY MUSEUM
(Центральный музей Тавриды; vul Gogolya 14; admission 15uah; ◷9am-5pm Wed-Mon) Crimea's largest museum has a vast collection of archaeological finds and books representing different cultures that flourished on the peninsula. Sections dedicated to the Hellenised Goths of the Feodoro Princedom and Genovese colonists are of particular interest to those who plan to visit Mangup-Kale and Sudak.

Neopolis SCYTHIAN CITY
(btwn vuls Vorovskogo & Krasnoarmeyskaya) There's little sense of history about the hilltop site, where archaeologists have unearthed remnants of Crimea's Scythian capital (300 BC–AD 300), but it offers a good view of Simferopol in all its Soviet-constructivist glory.

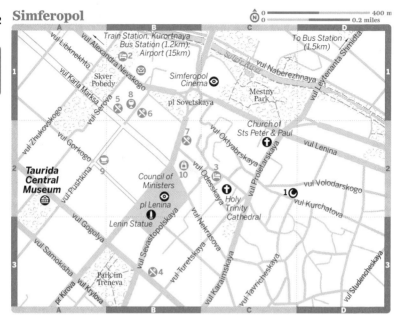

Kebi-Djami Mosque   MOSQUE
(Мечеть Кеби-Джами; vul Kurchatova 4) The
restored 16th-century mosque dates back
to the Tatar town of Ak-Mechet (White
Mosque), a predecessor of Simferopol.

🛏 Sleeping

Hotel Valencia   NEW HOTEL **$$**
(Гостиница Валенсия; ☑510 606; www.va
lencia.crimea.ua; vul Odesskaya 8; d from 400uah;
❄🛜) Fusing Crimea and Spain, this cen-
trally located, friendly and well-run hotel is
justifiably popular, so book ahead. The sole
windowless 'economy' single goes for just
150uah, but without air-con it's uncomfort-
able in summer. Breakfast not included.

Hotel Ukraina   NEW LUXURY **$$**
(Гостиница Украина; ☑510 165; www.
ukraina-hotel.biz; vul Rozy Lyuxemburg 7; s/d
from 470/640uah; ❄🛜) Admittedly, the baroque public areas of this central, forward-
thinking hotel are a bit OTT, but rooms are
restrained and well finished – the standard
class in sandy ochre and red-earth tones.
Staff speak English, plus it has a sauna and
hammam (Turkish bath).

Hotel Moskva   RENOVATED SOVIET **$$**
(☑620 615, 620 600; www.moskva-hotel.com;
vul Kievskaya 2; s/d from 390/580uah; remod-
elled 480/650uah) Under the same manage-

Simferopol

ment as Ukraina, this Soviet-period high-
rise by the central bus station is a popular
escape for those who can't find a decent
room in the centre. From Silpo take any
marshrutka (fixed-price minibus) heading
to автовокзал (main bus station).

Turbaza Tavriya RENOVATED SOVIET **$$**
(☏638 914; vul Bespalova 21; www.tavriya.krym
tur.com; s without/with air-con 360/450uah, d
510/630uah) This tranquil, hillside place is
popular, despite being a bit far from the
centre. It is, however, convenient for Neopo-
lis. *Marshrutky* 15 and 17 go here from pl
Sovetskaya. Breakfast is included.

Soma Youth Hostel HOSTEL **$**
(☏063 225 2896; vul Sevastopolskaya 41/6, apt
28; dm 135uah, r without bathroom 400uah; 🛈)
About 15 minute by *marshrutka* from the
centre, this typical semi-clandestine West-
ern-run hostel was operating here in sum-
mer 2010. Cheap guided tours of Crimea's
southern coast were on offer.

✕ Eating

Café Motivi MIDDLE EASTERN **$**
(Кафе Мотивы; basement, vul Karla Marksa
9; mains 30-60uah) This opulently decorated
and moodily lit Persian restaurant is one of
Simferopol's hip hangouts. The food, which
consists mainly of stews and stir-fries, is
delicious but usually takes ages to arrive.
From Thursdays to Saturdays, locals come
for the DJs and the bar (cocktails 30uah to
45uah) rather than the food.

Grand Café Chekhov RUSSIAN **$$**
(Гранд-кафе Чехов; vul Chekhova 4; mains 30-
80uah) In this beautifully designed oasis of
whiteness and coolness, you can just imagine that Anton Pavlovich himself is treating
you to classic Russian specialities, such as
ukha fish soup and *bliny* (pancakes), at his
Crimean *dacha* (holiday house). We loved
pork stir-fried with apples, cooked and
served in an iron pan.

Piroga CALZONES **$**
(Пирога; vul Pushkina 4/6; mains from 16uah)
Brightly coloured murals give this casual
eatery the atmosphere of a world food cafe.
The eponymous *pirogi* are in fact like large
flat calzones, and you choose individual
toppings for them as for pizza. Salads and
desserts also served.

Veranda Chirakhova & Piramida
EUROPEAN **$$**
(Веранда Чирахова и Пирамида; vul
Odesskaya 22/2; mains 30-70uah) This cluster
of restaurants (all under the same owner-
ship) is dominated by the open-air Chi-
rakhova terrace with its pastel-coloured
wooden furniture and comfy couches. Eu-
ropean and Russian/Ukrainian standards
are on the menu. The glassy Piramida is for

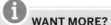
For in-depth information, reviews and
recommendations, head to the www.
lonelyplanet.com/ukraine/crimea.

patrons to escape the winter chill. The once
popular Falstaff Pub, located on the same
premises, was closed for reconstruction
when we visited.

Taj Café INDIAN **$**
(Тадж Кафе; Dormitory 5, vul Rechnaya 2A;
mains 20-30uah; ⊙10am-9pm) Enjoy a change
at this medical-school canteen catering to
the numerous Indian, Malaysian and Arab
students. The chicken tikka masala, Pattaya
noodles, egg sambals and lassis are cafete-
ria food, but you won't find it anywhere else
in Crimea. Enter through the guardhouse
opposite the Arab-run cafe Prinzesa, recog-
nizable by its red chairs. If asked, say you
are you going to the 'cafe'.

♉ Drinking

Kofein COFFEE
(Кофеин; vul Pushkina 8; espresso 15uah, mains
35-70uah; ⊙24hr; 🛈) The 'exoticism' at this
trendy African-themed cafe overdoes its ap-
preciation of the female form. But if you can
position yourself where your eye's not being
poked out by a photographed nipple, you'll
find it takes its coffee seriously and turns
out a good brew.

Cotton Club PUB
(vul Pushkina 3; beer 6uah; ⊙10am-9pm Sep-May)
The name is hilariously misleading, but if
moody tattooed patrons and a statue of Lu-
cifer don't put you off, this pub has some of
the cheapest drinks in the whole of Crimea
and Russian underground music for its
soundtrack. Enter through an arch.

🛍 Shopping

Silpo SUPERMARKET
(Сільпо; inside Univermag, pr Kirovaya 19; ⊙gro-
cery 24hr, mini-mall 10am-6.30pm) Self-caterers
should make a beeline to this conveniently
located, Western-style supermarket. The
grocery section is on the ground floor; the
mini-mall is on the 1st.

ℹ Information

Central post office (Почтамт; vul Aleksandra
Nevskogo 1; internet per hr 4.5uah) Contains a
telephone centre and a 24-hour internet cafe.

Pro-Internet Center (☑549 805; vul Karla Marksa 1; per hr 4uah; ☉24hr) Although full of noisy teenage boys, this has 112 high-speed computers, where you can plug in USBs and other media.

❶ Getting There & Away

Air

Simferopol airport (☑295 516, 295 545; www. airport.crimea.ua) is 15km northwest of the town centre and is accessible by trolleybus 9 (1.5uah, 30 minutes) as well as myriad *marshrutky,* including numbers 49, 50, 98, 113 and 115.

Aerosvit (VV), Air Baltic (BT), Turkish Airlines (TK), El Al (LY) and Ukraine Airlines (PS) all fly in from abroad, as do several Russian carriers. Most notably, the budget carrier Wizzair connects Simferopol with London Luton via Kyiv. If lucky, you can get a ticket to Kyiv for less than 300uah.

Kiyavia (☑272 167; www.kiyavia.crimea.ua; bul Lenina 1/7; ☉9am-6pm Mon-Fri, to 5pm Sat) sells both international and domestic air tickets.

Bus

There are three main roads originating in Simferopol. One leads to Sevastopol via Bakhchysaray. Another one crosses the main ridge near Alushta before turning west towards Yalta. The third road heads east to Feodosiya and Kerch, branching off for Sudak.

Buses to pretty much anywhere in Crimea leave from the chaotic **Kurortnaya bus station**, located on the train station square. There are frequent services to Yevpatoriya (17uah, 1½ hours, every 20 minutes), Sevastopol (22uah, two hours, every 20 minutes), Yalta (20uah, 1½ hours every 10 minutes), Sudak (25uah, 2½ hours, hourly) and Feodosiya (27uah, three hours, every 20 minutes).

Buses for Kerch (50uah, 4½ hours, every 30 minutes) that go via Feodosiya and long-distance buses to continental Ukraine depart from the **main bus station** (☑275 211; vul Kievskaya 4) on the other side of town. There are daily services to Dnipropetrovsk (60uah, nine hours), Donetsk

A LA TARTAR

When in Crimea, you may often find yourself staring at a menu with a 'what the hell is it?' expression on your face. Most problematic are Crimean Tatar and Black Sea fish restaurants where people find nothing but endemic Crimean dishes they've never heard of.

Crimean Tatar cuisine is similar to Turkish, but half a century in Central Asian exile left a significant imprint. Here is the list of the most ubiquitous eats.

» *Cheburek* (Чебурек) – a fried turnover filled with minced meat and onions

» *Plov* (Плов) – a variation of the Asian pilaf rice dish, usually with pieces of mutton, carrots and raisins

» *Qashiq ash* (Кашик Аш) – small, ravioli-style, meat-filled dumplings, usually served in broth

» *Manty* (Манты) – large Central Asian dumplings filled with minced mutton

» *Sarma* (Сарма) – grapevine leaves stuffed with minced meat

» *Dolma* (Долма) – green paprika stuffed with a mixture of minced meat and rice

Studying the menu at a Crimean fish restaurant, you'll be confronted by two questions: which fish to choose and how it should be cooked. For the latter, you can have your fish grilled, fried or cooked in the Greek-Jewish *shkara* style, where fish and vegetables are boiled in a frying pan until most of the liquid evaporates. For the former, here are the most common types of fish.

» *Barabulka* or *sultanka* (Барабулька, Султанка) – surmullet, small fish that locals often swallow whole, although the fillet is easy to separate from the bones

» *Sargan* (Сарган) – garfish, small needle-shaped fish rolling itself into neat-looking rings when fried

» *Lufar* (Луфарь) – bluefish, medium-sized fish

» *Kefal* (Кефаль) – mullet, the best known Black Sea fish, mentioned in classical Odesa songs

» *Katran* (Катран) – a small (and totally harmless!) Black Sea shark

» *Kambala* (Камбала) – sole

(130uah, nine hours) and Krasnodar in southern Russia (221uah, 13½ hours).

Locals usually catch *marshrutky* to Bakhchysaray (6uah, one hour) from the west bus station; they leave every 20 minutes. For newcomers, it's easier to use the main bus station, where direct or through services leave at least hourly.

Train

Simferopol is Crimea's main railway junction, with five trains daily to/from Kyiv (147uah to 196uah, 15 hours), including two through services to/from Sevastopol, plus services to/from Dnipropetrovsk (110uah, seven hours, six daily), Lviv (322uah, 21 hours, daily), Kharkiv (190uah, 16 to 17 hours, five daily) and Odesa (125uah, 12 hours, daily). There are also services to Moscow, St Petersburg, Rostov-on-Don and Minsk.

Local *elektrychka* run regularly along the Crimean peninsula to/from Yevpatoriya (two hours, seven a day in each direction) and Sevastopol (two hours, seven daily in each direction). The latter service stops en route in Bakhchysaray (40 minutes). Prices are all 8uah or less. Be warned that if you're trying to leave Crimea in August you might have to upgrade to 1st-class to get a ticket, and that can cost three times as much.

Getting Around

Marshrutka 49 plies the route between the airport, the train station, the centre and the central bus station. Trolleybus 9 goes from the airport to the train station. To get to the centre from here, you need to take trolleybus 5 or 2 eastwards, or a *marshrutka* or bus from near McDonald's with 'Сільпо' (Silpo) on its side.

Yevpatoriya ЄВПАТОРІЯ

☏ 06569 / POP 103,000

Touted by local tour operators as a mini-Jerusalem, Yevpatoriya lures visitors with its Muslim, Christian and – most intriguingly – Karaite (see p166) places of worship. Although in the Soviet era the town became a major health resort for children, and its western waterfront is still a dense grid of such sanatoria, since celebrating its 2500th birthday in 2003 it's been reclaiming its historic multiculturalism. For history buffs, it is worth knowing that the Allied forces landed here at the start of the Crimean War before moving on to besiege Sevastopol.

Sights

All major sites are located near or inside the Old Town Medina, which dates back to the Ottoman period.

A fun, if very slow method of getting to Yalta from Simferopol is by trolleybus. Powered by electricity, those ancient dinosaurs used to be the pride of Soviet Crimea, since they began plying the world's longest trolleybus route long before clean transport became an issue in the West. They have no other virtues we can think of. Seats are cramped and trolleybuses get jam-packed as drivers collect passengers, stopping every 50 metres in central Simferopol. Yet looking at the long queues at the Kurortnaya bus station, you might be really tempted to get a ticket from a booth across the road and board the trolleybus with no hassle. Trolleybus 52 serves Yalta (12uah, 2½ hours, every 20 minutes between 5.30am and 8pm). Trolleybus 51 only goes to/from Alushta (7uah, 1½ hours, every 20 minutes). Large bags need a separate ticket.

Dervish Tekiye   MUSLIM MONASTERY

(Текие дервишей; vul Karayeva 18; admission with guided tour in Russian or Turkish 10uah; ◷10am-5pm) Early 20th-century travel guides to Crimea still touted dervishes whirling in a breathtaking shamanic dance as one of the peninsula's main attractions, but today unfortunately this site is about the only legacy left by the once influential Sufi mystics. The 15th-century monastery served as a retreat for the wandering monks of the Mevlevi order who slept and meditated inside the arched niches of the main building. Sadly today there are no dervishes here – only tourists and nostalgic Crimean Tatars. Women are required to wear a scarf.

Gezlev Firewood Gate   MEDIEVAL STRUCTURE

(Дровяные ворота Гезлева; vul Karayeva 13A; guided tour 10uah; ◷9am-9pm) Apart from an excellent cafe (see p166), the restored gates of the medieval Gezlev (Yevpatoriya's Turkish name) house a small museum with a new, skilfully created 3-D model of the walled medieval city.

Karaite Kenassas   TEMPLE

(Караитские кенассы; vul Karaimskaya 68; admission 5uah, tours 10uah; ◷10am-8pm May-Sep, to 6pm Oct-Nov, service Sat 10am) The beautiful whitewashed colonnaded complex became the main place of worship for Karaites in the aftermath of the Russian takeover of Crimea, when they were allowed to abandon cave cities and live where they pleased. Tsar Alexander I inaugurated the main *kenassa* (temple) in 1807. Staunch monarchists, the Karaites later erected his statue on the premises. During the Crimean War, the allies converted the *kenassas* into stables, which were targeted by Russian artillery – look out for a cannon ball left in the *kenassa* wall.

Dzhuma-Dzhami Mosque TEMPLE

(Мечеть Джума-джами) Built in 1552, the landmark mosque is attributed to Mimar Sinan, the architect of Istanbul's famous Blue Mosque. Although not in Backhysaray, it was considered the main mosque of Ottoman-ruled Crimea. It served as a venue for enthroning Crimean khans, who disembarked in Yevpatoriya after an obligatory inauguration visit to Istanbul. From the port, they proceeded straight to the mosque, where they presented the sultan's *firman* (license to rule) to the citizens.

Other notable religious buildings in Yevpatoriya include the synagogue **Yegiya-Kopay** (vul Prosmushkinykh 34), the Armenian church **St Nikogayos** (Internatsionalnaya, 44) and the Russian Orthodox cathedral of **St Nicholas** (vul Tuchina 3).

🛏️🍴 Sleeping & Eating

Krym HISTORIC HOTEL $

(Крым; ☎60364, 23412; vul Revolyutsii 46; r without breakfast 200uah) This no-frills Tatar-run hotel is good value for the price, considering its location in the historic part of Yevpatoriya, close to Dzhuma-Dzhami mosque.

Ukraine Palace NEW LUXURY $$

(☎94 111, 94 110; cnr pr Lenina & ul Frunze; s/d from 500/650uah; P❄️🛜🏊) With its large open-air pool, modern and tastefully decorated rooms, Ukraina is about the best place to stay in Yevpatoriya, but you need to book two or three weeks in advance in high season.

Kezlev Kyavesi CRIMEAN TATAR $

(Кезлев Кьявеси; vul Karayeva 29; sweets plate 25uah, coffee 25uah) The gorgeous looking and tasting Tatar sweets and Turkish coffee served in this cafe, inside Gezlev park, alone justify a visit to the town. The adventurous may try *kypchak* tea made with milk, pepper, salt and sugar. For more substantial Crimean Tatar meals, head to the excellent Dzheval restaurant across the road, run by the same people.

Karaman KARAITE $

(Караман; Karaimskaya 68; mains 20-30uah; ⏱noon-6pm) The former charity canteen in the *kenassa* now houses this excellent cafe

---

DEATH DEBATE

At the height of WWII, the Nazis summoned three Jewish professors who were imprisoned in the Warsaw and Vilnius ghettoes and told them to voice their opinion on the subject they had studied all their lives. The question was – are Crimean Karaites Jewish or not? In a series of debates with leading scholars all of them independently gave a negative answer, which largely contradicted everything they said before in their long scholarly careers. Their names were Meyer Balaban, Yitzhak Schiper and Zelig Kalmanovich. None of them survived the Holocaust. But the Karaites did – following the debate, the Nazis classified them as 'impure' but not warranting extermination. They even reopened the *kenassa* in Yevpatoriya, which had been closed by the Bolsheviks, allowing services in Hebrew! All Crimean Jews captured by the Nazis were killed.

Today, the Karaites number about 2000, with 650 living in Crimea, mostly in Yevpatoriya and Feodosiya. Although their leaders deny it – perhaps a legacy of their survival tactics – the name of the people probably derives from the ancient Hebrew word for 'reader'. Initially, it was an early medieval Jewish sect in Baghdad, which rejected the Talmud, believing the Old Testament to be the only source of holy wisdom. No one is sure how this teaching spread to Crimea, but by the Medieval Ages it became the second most important religion for the Turkic population of Crimea after Islam. It mixed with shamanism and the pagan beliefs of the ancient Turks. To this day, the Karaites worship sacred oak groves (p169) and call their god Tengri, as did their pre-Judaist ancestors. Speaking a pure version of ancient Turkic, the Karaites even donated 330 words to the modern Turkish language when Kemal Ataturk was getting rid of Arabisms in the 1920s.

Most people west of Berlin have yet to hear of it, but long-term attendees complain that the annual rave **Kazantip** (www.kazantip.com) in July/August has become too commercial. Launched in the early 1990s as an après-surf party near a half-finished nuclear reactor on the northeastern Kazantip peninsula, the five-week-long festival moved, because of local pressure, to Popovka, north of Yevpatoriya. Today 'the republic of Kazantip' is a huge Ibiza-style operation with enormous stage sets, international DJs such as Timo Maas, more than 100,000 punters, many of them half-naked (or naked), dodgy food, deliberately humorous rules and lots of serious security.

Too commercial? Probably, but the only way you'll make up your own mind is to visit. Once you book, the organisers can arrange to pick you up, but for the duration of the festival *marshrutky* meet major services arriving in Simferopol and also leave from outside Yevpatoriya's bus station, on vul Internatsionalnaya.

which gives you a chance to sample Karaite cuisine. Similar to Crimean Tatar, it's arguably more Levantine than Central Asian. Try meat or cheese and paprika *chir-chir* – the Karaite version of *cheburek* – and *yazma* (similar to the Greek *tsatsiki*). Wash it down with *buza* – a minimally alcoholic drink made of wheat.

ⓘ Information

Elken (☑433 33, 095 850 3738; www.elken. com.ua; vul Karayeva 13a; tours 20uah; ☉tours 10am, 4.30pm May-Sep) Located inside the Timber Gate, Elken offers a Russian-language tour of Yevpatoriya that may save you time since it takes in most major sights in the medina and its environs.

ⓘ Getting There & Around

BUS In summer there are buses approximately every 20 minutes from the bus station adjoining the Simferopol train station (20uah, 1½ hours).

TRAIN In summer, there are seasonal trains to Kyiv and Moscow.

TRAM & MARSHRUTKY In Yevpatoriya, the bus and train stations are next to one another on vul Internatsionalnaya, northwest of the old town, and you can buy a map at the stalls in front of the train station. Then take tram 3 south down vul Frunze to the Hotel Ukraine Palace and pr Lenina. Trams and *marshrutky* heading east (left away from the hotel) will take you to the old town and waterfront.

Bakhchysaray
БАХЧИСАРАЙ

☑06554 / POP 27,500

More a village than a town, the former capital of Crimean Tatar khans is cradled in a narrow valley squeezed between two limestone escarpments. Its name means 'garden-palace', and it's a garden that needs a lot of tilling after 50 years of neglect, when its owners lived in exile. Now the Crimean Tatars are back, and although lacking resources, they have already orchestrated a minor renaissance, which benefits travellers more than anyone else.

Forget the nouveau-riche tackiness of seaside resorts! This is the place to stay with local families, drinking Turkish coffee on their verandas and gorging on home-made Tatar sweets. But that's not all – the place is full of remnants of past civilizations and is a great base for outdoor adventure in the Crimean mountains.

⊙ Sights

Bakhchysaray's sights are strung on the town's main axis, vul Lenina, like pieces of mutton on the *shashlyk* skewers served in local restaurants. The road begins in the new part of town, 500m from the train station. Khans' Palace is in its middle section. Uspensky Monastery and Chufut-Kale are another 2km up the same road, which becomes vul Basenko. Near a cluster of Tatar restaurants, a paved path heads up the hill on the right to Uspensky Monastery (a five- to 10-minute walk) and Chufut-Kale beyond.

Khans' Palace   PALACE
(Ханский дворец; Khansky Dvorets; www.han saray.iatp.org.ua; vul Leninaya 129; adult/child & student 20/10uah; ☉9am-5.30pm) When she was busy ordering the mass destruction of Bakhchysaray's mosques in the 18th and early 19th centuries, Catherine the Great spared the Khans' Palace. Her decision was reportedly based on the building being 'romantic',

and it is sweet. While it lacks the imposing grandeur of Islamic structures in, say, Istanbul, this is a major landmark of Crimean culture and history. Erected in the 16th century under the direction of Persian, Ottoman and Italian architects, it was rebuilt a few times, but the structure still resembles the original.

Passing through the back of the finely carved, Venetian Renaissance **Demir Qapi Portal** (also called Portal Alevizo after its Italian designer, who also authored parts of Moscow's Kremlin), you enter the west wing and the dimly lit **Divan Hall**. This was the seat of government, where the khan and his nobles discussed laws and wars.

Through the hall lies the inner courtyard, containing two fountains. With its white marble ornately inscribed with gold leaf, the **Golden Fountain** (1733) is probably the more beautiful. However, the neighbouring **Fountain of Tears** (1764) is more famous, thanks to Alexander Pushkin (see the boxed text, p168). It's tradition that two roses – one red for love and one yellow for chagrin – are placed atop the fountain; Pushkin was the first to do this.

Behind the palace is the only surviving **harem** of the four that were traditionally attached to the palace and belonged to the khans' wives. Across the yard you can see the **Falcon Tower**.

The **Khans' Cemetery** is beside the mosque, and way back in the grounds' southeast corner is the **mausoleum of Dilara Bikez**, who may or may not be the Polish beauty who bewitched the khan.

Usta Workshop   CRAFTS REVIVAL

(www.usta.rcf.crimea.ua; vul Rechnaya 125; ☉10am-5pm) Ten years ago Crimean Tatar handicrafts were on the verge of extinction, but Ayshe Osmanova resolved to rescue her people's culture from the precipice. Retrieving old manuals from the Khans' Palace, she taught herself the ancient art of Crimean embroidery and was soon teaching the craft to other Tatar women returning from exile. A veteran silversmith (p169) and other craftsmen joined in.

These efforts culminated in a small workshop, where you can watch artists at work and buy embroidered shawls and tablecloths, woven rugs and hangings, pottery and filigree jewellery. The shop is minutes from the Khans' Palace and well signposted from vul Lenina. The turn-off to vul Rechnaya is just before the palace when coming from the station.

Uspensky Monastery   CAVE CHURCH

Stop for a moment and say 'aah!' at possibly the cutest little church in a country absolutely jam-packed with them. Part of the small Uspensky Monastery, the **gold-domed church** has been built into the limestone rock of the surrounding hill, probably by Byzantine monks in the 8th or 9th century. Whitewashed monks' cells, a 'healing' fountain and tiled mosaics cling to the hillside too. Of course, the Soviets closed the place down, but it's been operating again since 1993.

Chufut-Kale   CAVE CITY

(Чуфут-Кале; adult/student 30/15uah; ☉10am-5pm) Rising 200m, this long and bluff plateau houses a honeycomb of caves and structures where people took refuge for centuries. It's wonderful to explore, especially (gingerly) the burial chambers and casemates with large open 'windows' in the vertiginous northern cliff. These are truly breathtaking, as is the view into the valley below.

First appearing in historical records as Kyrk-Or (Forty Fortifications), the city was settled sometime between the 6th and 12th centuries by Christianised descendants of

---

THE BAKHCHYSARAY FOUNTAIN

The Fountain of Tears in the Khans' Palace is a case of life imitating art imitating life.

The fountain was commissioned for the last Crimean khan, Giri, whose hard heart was revealed to have a chink when he fell in unrequited love with a Polish beauty enslaved in his harem. But she resisted his advances and wasted away, unable to endure harem life. After this the khan began weeping uncontrollably day and night. Worried that important state matters were being neglected, the court ordered the Persian master craftsman Omer to build the fountain to give an outlet to the khan's grief.

On visiting the fountain, Russian writer Alexander Pushkin was so moved by the tragedy he wrote the poem 'The Bakhchysaray Fountain' (1823).

The artful verse became so famous in Russia it ensured the survival of the palace itself.

When you disembark from an *elektrychka* in Bakhchysaray, you might notice a plaque on the left side of the station building. It commemorates Crimean Tatars who were herded here on 18 May 1944, forced into cattle cars and sent on an arduous journey to Central Asia. Stalin had decided to punish a whole people for collaboration with German occupiers, ignoring the fact that 9000 Crimean Tatars fought in the Soviet army and thousands more joined Soviet partisans.

Ayder Asanov, 82, is one of the few who lived to return from the exile in the 1990s. Sitting in the Usta Workshop, he is only 50m away from the place he was born. 'It was a jeweller's district,' he explains. 'My father, my grandfather and my grand-grandfather all were filigree silversmiths.' Aged 16 when he was deported to the desert known as Famine Steppe, Asanov had already mastered the craft, but there was little chance to develop his skills in exile. He faced punishment for making jewellery and there were no materials anyway. Still, from time to time he worked secretly, procuring little pieces of wire at the machinery plant, where he was forced to work.

By the time he returned, Asanov was the only person who knew the secrets of Crimean Tatar filigree. But this last link to the past proved very durable. 'I am amazed how my hands remembered it after all these years. Tatar filigree is much finer than, say, Russian, but I could still do it,' says the old man. Nowadays he has about a dozen students, guaranteeing that the craft will not be facing extinction again anytime soon.

A total of 180,000 Crimean Tatar were deported from Crimea, followed by 37,000 members of smaller minorities – Greeks from Balaklava, Italians from Kerch, Bulgarians from Koktebel, Armenians from Feodosiya and all ethnic Germans. They were usually given only a few minutes to take vital belongings and very few of them lived to see their homes again.

Sarmatian tribes. The last powerful ruler of the Golden Horde, Tokhtamysh, sheltered here after defeat in the 1390s, and the first Crimean khanate was established at Chufut-Kale in the 15th century, before moving to nearby Bakhchysaray. After the Tatars left, Turkic-Jewish Karaites occupied the city until the mid-19th century, which won the mountain its current name of 'Jewish Fortress'.

Following the track from Uspensky, the best idea is to keep bearing right. The main entrance is not under the flat tin roof to the left of the Chufut-Kale sign, but further up the hill to the right. At this, the 14th-century main **South Gate**, you'll usually be hit for a 12uah entrance fee.

Soon after the gate, you enter a Swiss-cheese composition of carved-out rooms and steps. Behind this a stone path heads along the top of the plateau, past two locked **kenassas** (Karaite prayer houses) in a walled courtyard to the right. There is a **Karaite cultural centre and cafe** (mains 30uah) in the adjacent former house of the city's last resident, Karaite leader Avraam Firkovich.

To the left of the first intersection stands the red-tile roofed **Muslim mausoleum** (1437) of Dzhanike-Khanym, daughter of Tokhtamysh; to the right is an archway. Head left behind the mausoleum towards the cliff edge and enjoy the view into the valley below. To the right (east), a grassy track leads to two **burial chambers** in the northern side of the cliff.

From here it's hard to get lost; there are more caves until you reach the locked **East Gate**, where the road loops back on itself towards the main gate.

Iosofatova Valley   KARAITE CEMETERY
(Иософатова Долина; adult/student 30/15uah; ☺10am-5pm) The forested Iosofatova Valley beneath the Chufut-Kale plateau hides a breathtaking and spooky sight. Thousands of moss-covered gravestones covered in Hebrew script stand, lie upturned at precarious angles in the shade of ancient oak trees. For over a millennium the Karaites brought their dead to the sacred grove, which they called Balta Tuymez, meaning axe-don't-touch in ancient Turkic. The scene is straight out of Michael Jackson's 'Thriller' and at sunset it's hard to escape the chilly sensation of being watched by thousands of empty eye sockets.

TEPE-KERMEN

If the view of Iosofatova Valley left you unshaken, you may follow the path to its other side where it abuts the road leading to this minor cave-city. After a few hundred metres you'll find a small clearing on your left with the word ТЕПЕ-КЕРМЕН (Tepe-Kermen) and an arrow laid in pebbles on the ground. It marks the start of a path that descends into a valley, where it hits another road. Follow it and you will soon come in full view of Tepe-Kermen mountain on your right. At the fork where the road starts descending to the plain, turn right and follow the Tepe-Kermen signs. An early Byzantine basilica is the main attraction here. Otherwise people mostly come here for a workout and for the view. The trek takes about an hour one way. If lost, descend to any village below and catch a bus to Bakhchysaray.

Zyndzhyrly Medrese   MEDIEVAL SCHOOL
(Зынджырлы Медресе; Chain Medrese; vul Basenko 57; admission 20uah; ◷10am-6pm) Carefully restored and reopened as a museum in 2010, the *medrese* (Muslim religious school) and the adjoining 15th-century mausoleum where 18 members of the Crimean khan's dynasty are buried is set to become one of Bakhchysaray's must-sees once the planned exhibition of medieval books and teaching appliances is up and running. The eponymous chain is hanging at the school's entrance, ensuring that even the khan humbly bows his head when entering the house of god. It's a short detour on the way to Uspensky Monastery. To get here, bear left shortly before the monastery.

🛏 Sleeping

Thanks to Crimean Tatars' entrepreneurial skills, Bakhchysaray is now a great base for budget travellers, but guesthouses are rarely signposted and hard to find, so it's better to call ahead and arrange a pickup.

Dilara Hanum   GUESTHOUSE $
(☏050 930 4163, 063 227 3120, 065 544 7111; www.bahchisaray.net; vul Ostrovskogo 43; r without breakfast 320uah) Almost under the escarpment at the end of vul Ostrovskogo, which branches off vul Lenina, this little guesthouse is 'managed by two grannies and a grandson', as their ad goes. However, Dilara is only a part-time granny and hotel manager – she is also the leader of the Crimean Tatar teachers' union and a mine of knowledge on all Tatar-related issues. Rooms are modern and come with attached bathrooms. There is large dining area on the first floor with a kitchen, a library and a ping-pong table. Dilara's daughter speaks English.

Efsane   GUESTHOUSE $
(☏478 61; 066 570 7845; vul Basenko 32 & 32A; r without/with bathroom 200/250uah) Like other hosts in Bakhchysaray, Shevkiye is a bit of a cultural ambassador for the Crimean Tatar people, but unlike most she speaks impeccable English having taught the language to generations of local children. Cultural immersion starts at breakfast – each day it is a presentation of a new Tatar dish. Tours, mountain treks and free cooking classes are on offer. Call ahead for free pickup from the station.

Villa Bakhitgul   GUESTHOUSE $$
(☏050 174 3167; www.bahitgul.com.ua; vul Basenko 32; B&B 400uah, half board 500uah) The closest you get to a boutique hotel in Bakhchysaray, this place has two large and stylishly decorated rooms – one with dark wooden, art nouveau furniture, another looking more oriental. It can organise trips to various parts of Crimea. Free pickup from the train or bus station.

Enver & Lenmara   GUESTHOUSE $
(☏44 114, 095 156 2733; vul Kom Podpolshchikov 12/3; r without/with bathroom per person 40/70uah) An amiable former military man, Enver built his guesthouse around a small garden. Rooms are spartan, but clean and excellent value for the price. From the Khans' Palace walk in the direction of Chufut-Kale, turn right after cafe Eski-Kermen (there is a 'Turbaza Prival' turn sign), then bear left at the fork. After you pass a post office on your left, look out for a trilingual 'Rooms' sign near an abandoned mosque on your right.

Meraba   GUESTHOUSE $
(☏067 731 5235, 050 930 4164; www.meraba. crimea.ua; vul Rechnaya 125b; d/tr without breakfast 300/360uah) A Polish-owned guesthouse associated with the Usta Workshop

and located right behind it, Meraba is a long-time favourite. However, you might get a more rewarding experience if you stay in family-run guesthouses, such as Efsane.

Turbaza Prival   HOTEL **$$**
(Турбаза Привал; ☑478 46, 522 70, 472 35; www.prival.crimea.com; vul Shmidta 43; dm/d 80/300uah, 2-3 person cottages 420uah; ✶✶) The only proper hotel in town, this renovated *turbaza* (simple resort) is not a bad choice, but all the other options reviewed here are really better. Popular with school groups.

✗ Eating

Musafir   CRIMEAN TATAR **$**
(Мусафир; vul Gorkogo 21, enter from vul Lenina; mains 15-25uah; 🖻) A specially invited Uzbek *plov* master is conjuring a magic stew in the *kazan* (traditional wrought-iron bowl), while patrons marvel at the view of the nearby Khans' Palace while squatting on Turkish-styled rugs. Apart from the usual Tatar dishes, they make excellent *yantyk* pastry and Bakhchysaray's best Turkish coffee. The latter is served with lumps of sugar that you are expected to put straight in your mouth, rather than in your cup.

Aliye   CRIMEAN TATAR **$**
(Алие; vul Lesi Ukrainki; mains 18uah) Popular with locals and tour groups, this superfriendly cafe on the main drag has Turkishstyled rugs on the upper terrace surrounded by a garden and European tables on the lower terrace, which features an artificial waterfall. The *shashlyks* are superb and we also loved the small *yerash* dumplings with walnut paste.

Visiting the Khan   CRIMEAN TATAR **$**
(В гостях у хана; vul Lenina; mains 6-15uah) Not all Crimean Tatars are teetotal, despite being Muslim, and the sociable owner of this pleasant, casual restaurant can often be seen sharing shots of vodka with her guests as she works the room. Nab a bench seat on the terrace, order *plov* (lamb, carrot and rice stew) or *chebureky* (meat or cheese turnovers/pastries) and gaze over the netting at the valley beyond.

Karavan Sarai Salachik   CRIMEAN TATAR **$**
(Караван-сарай Салачик; vul Basenko 43A; mains 28uah) Hookah pipes replace alcohol at this restaurant, in which individual gazebos with low Turkish-style seating (or *topchans*) are dotted across a landscaped lawn. There are all the usual Crimean Tatar dishes, in-

cluding *sheker keyeks* (a little bit like traditional Turkish baklava) for dessert.

❶ Getting There & Away

BUS Bakhchysaray's bus station is just off the road linking Simferopol and Sevastopol, where you can a catch a bus in either direction. Frequent direct *marshrutky* go to the inconveniently located western bus station in Simferopol (7uah, 30 minutes). Buses originating in Sevastopol terminate at Simferopol's train station (9uah, 50 minutes).

ELEKTRYCHKA Local trains shuffle back and forth between Sevastopol (5.60uah, 1½ hours) and Simferopol (5uah, 50 minutes) seven times a day in each direction.

❶ Getting Around

Marshrutka 2 shuttles constantly between the bus station, train station, Khans' Palace and Uspensky monastery. A taxi ride inside the city costs 20uah.

Mangup-Kale
МАНГУП-КАЛЕ

If you liked Chufut-Kale and want more, head to **Mangup-Kale** (admission 15uah), the peninsula's most spectacular cave city. Located 22km south of Bakhchysaray, this remote plateau is in the shape of a hand with four fingers. Allocate at least three hours for the return hike from the base of the plateau.

Formerly the ancient capital of Feodoro, the principality of the 6th-century 'Crimean Greeks' (actually Greeks, Goths and Sarmatian descendants), this was an excellent fortress due to its sheer cliffs. It was finally abandoned in the 15th century.

The village at the base of the trail is called Khadzhi-Sala, reached from Bakhchysaray by *marshrutka* bound for Rodnoye (Родное, 6uah, five daily) or by taxi (100uah). There are several guesthouses where you can overnight in case you are stuck. The large village Zalisne (Zalesnoye in Russian), 2km before Khadzhi-Sala (coming from Bakhchysaray), has more transport options.

In Khadzhi-Sala, there is a booth selling tickets (15uah) and useful Russian-language maps of the cave city. A trail leading up the plateau between two fingers begins about 100m to your right. At the top of the ridge follow the trail to the furthest finger of land until you see a large stone gateway and a long wall. Beyond are carved-out chambers and caves. The most impressive is the final cave room, carved out of the very tip of the cliff with stairs leading down the west side to a burial chamber.

Sevastopol
СЕВАСТОПОЛЬ

📞 0692 / POP 330,000

It is easy to understand why the Russians are lamenting the loss of Sevastopol more than any other chunk of their vast empire. Orderly and clean as the deck of a ship, with whitewashed neoclassical buildings surrounding a cerulean bay, it has everything most Russian cities badly lack.

Not that the loss is complete – an agreement hastily signed by President Yanukovych stipulates that Sevastopol will remain the base of the Russian Black Sea fleet for another 25 years. Most locals are linked to the navy in one way or another and maintain a strong allegiance to Russia. This results in a peculiar cultural microclimate, similar to Gibraltar.

A favourite playground for military history fans, Sevastopol is also attractive to those with no interest in weapons and uniforms. Simply put, it is the most pleasant Crimean city – civilised, easy-going, but largely bypassed by the recreational mayhem of Crimea's southern and eastern coasts.

History

Sevastopol has much to say about the irony of fate. Purpose-built as an impregnable sea fortress to shelter the imperial fleet, it fell three times after being attacked from land. Anglo-Franco-Turkish allies were the first to lay siege and capture it during the Crimean War. In 1920, the city became the last stronghold of the retreating White Russian army. It saw steamships carrying away the cream of Russian society into a lifelong exile before surrendering to the Bolsheviks.

History repeated itself in 1942, when the Germans captured Sevastopol after a devastating 250-day siege. There was hardly a building left standing when they entered. But very soon Sevastopol was rebuilt by the Soviets with an atypical regard for its historic outlook.

◉ Sights & Activities

Primorsky Boulevard   PROMENADE
The city's bay-facing showcase greets seafarers with an array of whitewashed colonnaded buildings. Fresh from a Russian-funded spruce-up, the boulevard is also a pleasant place to walk or hide from the scorching sun in the shade of trees. It begins at **Grafskaya Pristan** (Графская пристань; Count's Jetty) – the city's official gateway marked by a colonnaded arch. Here you can hop on a **bay cruise** (50uah, 1½ hours). The square behind is dominated by the **Admiral Nakhimov monument** (Памятник адмиралу Нахимову; 1959), dedicated to the man who led the city's defence during Crimean War. Walking further along the seafront, you will soon spot the **Eagle Column** (Памятник затопленным кораблям; 1904). Set atop a rock in the sea, it commemorates Russian ships deliberately scuppered at the mouth of the harbour in 1854 to make it impossible for enemy ships to pass. The boulevard ends at **Artbukhta** (Artillery Quay) – the city's main nightlife area.

Panorama of Sevastopol's Defence   WAR MEMORIAL
(http://sev-museum-panorama.com; bul Istorichesky; adult/student 40/20uah; ⊙9am-5pm, last entry 4.30pm Tue-Sun Jun-Sep, Wed-Sun Sep-May) The focus of Sevastopol's wartime memories, this is a circular building, its inner wall covered in a mammoth-sized painting. Supplemented with 3-D props, it brings to life the 349-day siege of Sevastopol. Entry is only as part of a group tour, leaving at allotted times. English- or German-language tours cost 500uah per group.

Black Sea Fleet Museum   NAVAL MUSEUM
(Музей Черноморского флота; ul Lenina 11; admission 20uah; ⊙10am-5pm Wed-Sun) Full of ship models and Crimean War snippets, this small museum is visually impressive, even though all inscriptions are in Russian. The upper-floor exhibition is less interesting and reflects the Soviet view of the Russian Civil War and WWII.

Khersones   ANCIENT RUINS
(Херсонес; www.chersonesos.org; ul Drevnyaya 1; admission 20uah, student 15uah; ⊙grounds 9am-9pm, museum 9am-9pm May-Oct, to 5pm Nov-Mar) The ruins of the ancient Greek city founded in 422 BC are of great significance to local visitors. This is the place where Volodymyr the Great was famously baptised into Christianity in AD 988, launching

(Continued on page 181)

Ukrainian Gems

Cultural Tapestry »
Great Outdoors »
Religious Artistry »
Soviet Relics »

Swallow's Nest (p193), Crimea

Cultural Tapestry

Invasion, occupation and settlement from outside have bequeathed Ukraine a patchwork of cultures, from the woolly Hutsul traditions of the Carpathians to the exotic Middle Eastern world of the Crimean Tatars and the colourful Orthodox customs of the Slavic majority.

Pysanky

1 With their flashes of colour, intricate designs and pleasing shape, Ukraine's decorated eggs are an iconic symbol of traditional Slavic folk crafts. Kolomyya's Pysanky Museum (p125), itself housed in a monster egg, is the place to go to admire the egg-decorator's skill.

Slavic Knees-Up

2 Whether it's the on-the-spot jitter of a Hutsul hop, a boot-slapping Russian shindig, the swirling veils and curling hands of Crimean Tatars or the drama of Cossack acrobatics, dance is at the heart of all Ukraine's cultures.

Bandura Players

3 Hey, Mr Bandura Man. *Kobzary* minstrels (p260) were the keepers of Ukrainian folklore, travelling from village to village reciting epic poems across the steppe while strumming the 65-string *bandura*. Stalin had them all shot, but the tradition is making a slow comeback.

Taras Shevchenko Statues

4 Chiselled in classic stone, set in 19th-century bronze and moulded in art deco concrete, old and young, moustachioed and clean-shaven, statues of the national poet Taras Shevchenko (p261) can be found in almost every city across Ukraine.

Jewish Ukraine

5 Jewish communities were virtually wiped out in the Holocaust and depleted further by post-independence emigration, but remnants of Ukraine's Jewish past can be seen in Berdychiv, Uman, Bratslav, Lviv and Medzhybizh.

Clockwise from top
1. Basket of *pysanky* 2. Traditional folk dancing
3. Musician strumming a *bandura*

Great Outdoors

The Ukrainian steppe, traversed by mighty rivers, rolls on to far-flung horizons. The Carpathians, in the country's west, and the Crimean peninsula, jutting into the Black Sea in the south, provide striking landscapes and show-stopping vistas.

Kara-Dag Nature Reserve

1 Eerie volcanic rock formations on Crimea's east coast create an otherworldly landscape (p199) that can be explored on foot or aboard pleasure boats, which approach from the adjacent Black Sea and sail right through the formations.

Black Sea Coast

2 A balmy Black Sea slaps its tepid waves against almost 2800km of coastline, much of which is hemmed with golden sand or shingle. Odesa (p145) and Crimea (p187) are where most bucket-and-spade fun is to be had.

Snow Fun

3 Popular with Ukraine's steppe dwellers, and enjoying a relatively long winter season, the Carpathian ski resorts are slowly getting their act together. The most developed winter sports centre at Bukovel (p123) is even considering a bid for the 2018 Winter Olympics.

Summer in the Carpathians

4 With soothingly forested peaks and broad valleys, western Ukraine's Carpathian Mountains (p119) is the best place to head for some warm-weather hiking and mountain biking. Trails are faint or unmarked, but locals are working on them.

Mt Hoverla

5 At a mere 2061m, Ukraine's highest peak (p120) hardly has the Himalayas quaking with fear, but it makes up for its modest altitude with some soothing Carpathian vistas. The trails to the top are easy, but get busy in summer.

Clockwise from top left
1. Crimea's east coast 2. Gurzuf, Black Sea coast, Crimea 3. Winter hiking in the Carpathians 4. Summer landscape, the Carpathians

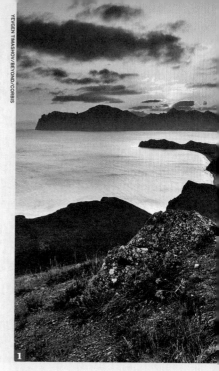

Religious Artistry

A highlight of Ukraine is its churches; from the golden domes of Orthodox monasteries to the Gothic arches of western Ukraine and the timber spires of the Carpathians, there's certainly nothing austere about its places of worship.

Inside an Orthodox Church

1 With their elaborately carved iconostases, riotously frescoed walls and neck-stiffeningly high domes, the colour, atmosphere and scent of many Ukrainian churches will have you looking on in awe.

Carpathian Timber Churches

2 If there's one commodity the Carpathians have in ample supply, it's wood! Locals have been cobbling together timber churches since at least the 16th century, and although fire and woodworm have destroyed many, a surprising number still dot the landscape.

Call to Prayer

3 Catherine the Great had many Tatar religious buildings pulled down and Stalin did his best to wipe Islam off the Crimean map, but the Tatar call to prayer has returned in the last two decades, and more mosques and schools are planned.

Onion-Domed Beauty

4 The sight of the gilt onion domes of an Orthodox cathedral or monastery catching the fiery rays of a Ukrainian sunset is one of the strongest images travellers take home from these parts.

Temple Fatigue in Lviv

5 Lviv (p88) is said to have over 100 churches, not bad for a city of just over 700,000. The most interesting examples hoist their spires above the city centre, where it's easy to overdose on beautiful church interiors.

Clockwise from top
1. Bernardine Church and Monastery (p97) 2. Carpathian timber church 3. Mosque minaret, Bakhchysaray

Soviet Relics

Ukraine may have shaken off its Soviet shackles, but its towns, cities and villages are still peppered with hammers and sickles, great-coated Lenin statues and stern war memorials. These often well-tended sites look like they're here to stay.

Defence of the Motherland

1 There are taxi-hailing Lenins, plinthed tanks and brutish Red Army conscripts seemingly emerging from the bedrock, but the queen of Soviet relics must be Kyiv's sword-wielding Defence of the Motherland Monument (Rodina Mat; p47).

Kyiv's Ornate Metro

2 Blasted deep into the rock below the city, Kyiv's metro system (p67) is a time-warped subterranean realm of ornate Stalinist-era stations, brave-new-world frescoes and socialist-realist reliefs.

Stalin's Back

3 Somewhat incredibly, new Stalin statues are planned in several Russian-speaking cities in the south and east of the country. Look out for Joseph Dzhugashvili (Stalin's real name) making an unlikely return in Odesa (p145) and Zaporizhzhya, moustache and all.

Nuclear Missile Museum

4 The Cold War is long over and much of Ukraine's military infrastructure has been left to crumble into the steppe. But the fascinating Nuclear Missile Museum (p78) near Pervomaysk is a real missile base preserved in the middle of the Ukrainian countryside.

Kharkiv's Derzhprom Building

5 Proof that big can be quite clever, Kharkiv's mammoth Derzhprom (House of State Industry; p213) used pioneering construction techniques when it was built in the 1920s. Now in a bit of a state, its granite and concrete hulk still dominates the world's second-largest city square.

Right
1. Defence of the Motherland Monument 2. Metro station, Kyiv

what would become the Russian Orthodox Church. Earlier that year, he sacked the city, helping the Byzantine emperor to put down a local rebellion. Nowadays, the best-preserved structure is the **ancient theatre** (p184). There's also the restored **Vladimir-sky Cathedral** and an interesting **museum** displaying items excavated on the site. History apart, Khersones provides a nice photo opportunity, particularly with the **stone arch**, whose bell comes from a Crimean War cannon. In May, the place is ablaze with blooming poppy flowers.

Local bus/*marshrutka* 22 goes directly to Khersones. Or catch trolleybus 2 or 6 westwards to the Rossiya (россия) stop, turn back to the first street (vul Yeroshenko or Ерошенко) and walk for 15 minutes.

Mikhaylovskaya Battery   WAR MUSEUM
(Михайловская Батарея; ul Gromova 35; admission with tour 20uah; ⊘10am-6pm) A massive piece of fortification seen across the bay from central Sevastopol, the battery served as a hospital when the Russians withdrew to the northern side of the bay during the Crimean War. It has recently been transformed into a museum dedicated to Sevastopol's military history with the emphasis on the Crimean War. Original uniforms, weapons, photos and tonnes of other memorabilia are on display, but if that's not enough, you can listen to old military marches and speeches by historic figures. English-language tours are available – ask for Danil. To get there, take a ferry bound for Radiogorka from Artbukhta (2.5uah every 40 minutes).

Cape Fiolent   SCENIC BEACH
(Фиолент) The southernmost tip of Sevastopol municipality is a spot of a rare, *Le Grand Bleu* type of beauty. But this aesthetic pleasure comes at a cost – an 800-step descent from the cliff-top Georgievsky monastery to the city's most scenic beach – Yashmovy. Reaching Fiolent is not easy, either. You have to transfer to the often crowded *marshrutka* 3 at 5km terminal (see Getting Around, p185). In summer, there are boats to Balaklava (one hour, 50uah).

RESULTS OF THE CRIMEAN WAR

An example of particularly pointless bloodshed, the Crimean War started over France and Russia struggling to be proclaimed the sole 'protector of Christians' in Turkish lands. Essentially it was about carving up the Ottoman Empire, which Russian Tsar Nicholas I famously described as 'the sick man of Europe'. A chain of events led to the destruction of the Turkish fleet by Russians at Sinop and the subsequent siege of Sevastopol by a coalition force consisting of French, British, Turkish and Sardinian troops.

As one of the first wars to be properly reported by the free press, the Crimean War came to be remembered not so much for valour and chivalry as for gross mismanagement, fraud and outright stupidity on both sides of the conflict. The siege ended a year later when the French stormed Malakhov Mound, forcing the Russians to withdraw from Sevastopol's centre to the northern side. The subsequent Paris Treaty stipulated full demilitarisation of the Black Sea, but left Sevastopol under Russian control. Just 15 years later, the fall of French emperor Napoleon III allowed the tsar to discard the treaty, rebuild the fleet and muscle the Turks out of the Balkans.

But although the actual results of the war seemed inconsequential, there were side effects of tectonic proportions, such as the abolition of serfdom in Russia in 1861 and the sale of Alaska to the US in 1867. Cash-strapped Russia was only too keen to get rid of the seemingly useless American possessions bordering on hostile British Canada.

A cruise of Sydney harbour in Australia reveals another effect of that war. Fort Denison was built by the British, who feared a Russian geographical expedition could attack Sydney. But instead it kept hoisting the Russian flag on small atolls in present-day Kiribati.

Finally, blamed for supplying poor ammunition and rotten food to the Russian army, one St Petersburg German had to flee Russia fearing criminal charges. Named Heinrich Schliemann, he turned to archaeology and discovered the ancient city of Troy with all its immense treasures. When he later requested permission to repatriate, Alexander II – incidentally the most liberal tsar in history – allegedly replied, 'Hang him upon crossing the border'.

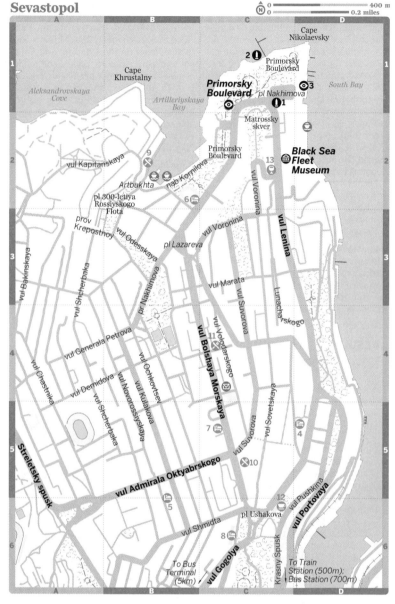

N 0 ————— 400 m
0 ————— 0.2 miles

Sleeping

The shortage of decently priced accommodation in Sevastopol is acute, so renting an apartment deserves extra special consideration. English-run **Travel 2 Sevastopol** (☎050 757 5952; www.travel2sevastopol.com)

responds promptly and is knowledgeable and remarkably helpful.

Funny Dolphin HOSTEL **$**
(☎050 146 4194, 095 501 3343; www.funnydol phin.hostel.com; vul Vasiliya Kuchera 5, apt 2; dm/d 140/300uah;❄@) A fan of military

Sevastopol

history and vintage Soviet cars, Yury converted a small flat in a quiet part of central Sevastopol into a modern-looking hostel with bunk-beds in two brightly coloured rooms. On a cobbled road veering uphill from vul Lenina, the place is unsigned and the ancient lady next door is not terribly good as a receptionist, so call ahead to be met by the owners. Two rooms with double beds, shared bathroom and kitchen are in a separate flat a short walk away.

Ukraina   RENOVATED SOVIET $$
(Отель Украина; 📞542 127; www.ukraine-hotel
.com.ua; vul Gogolya 2; economy s & d with breakfast 360-470uah, standard 550/650uah; 📶) This friendly hotel with the blackwood interior so favoured by former Intourist establishments is excellent value for the price. Without an expensive renovation, it somehow succeeds in making even the cheapest rooms look homely. Most of what are called economy rooms are in fact discounted standard rooms minus breakfast.

Gostevoy Dom K&T   GUESTHOUSE $
(Гостевой дом K&T; 📞553 228; www.ghkandt.com; vul Chertsova 27; s/d from 236/383uah; 🌀) The drive leading towards this pretty little hotel is jokingly called an 'ecopath'. In fact, it is a dirt track cutting through a *dacha* sprawl in a ravine close to Khersones. De-

spite the slightly unfortunate location, the place is favoured by Russian rock and cinema stars whose photos adorn the lobby. There is a neat-looking garden with a small pool. Take a taxi – the place is hard to find on your own.

Sevastopol   INTERNATIONAL CHAIN $$$
(Отель Севастополь; 📞539 060; www.sev astopol-hotel.com.ua; pr Nakhimova 8; s/d from 540/607uah; ❄@📶) Designers at Best Western must have been overexcited when the chain took over this landmark building overlooking the bay from Primorsky Blvd. Thick carpets mute sounds in the high-ceilinged corridors and the neoclassical lobby, which seems suitable for an opera performance. But nothing can protect bay-facing rooms from pop-music blasted by seafront bars.

TIU Bolshaya   HOSTEL $
(📞096 834 4074; vul Bolshaya Morskaya 38, apt 16; dm 120uah, d without bathroom 300uah; @📶) In a converted flat, this hostel run by a friendly Brit opens in summer only. It may or may not be in the same location as we found it in 2010. Check hostelworld.com for updated info.

Delfin   NEW HOTEL $$
(Дельфин; 📞479 252; vul Yeroshenko 20; d from 510uah, apt 750uah; ❄@) The imposing whitewashed colonnaded edifice on the quiet street leading to Khersones has 19 large and modern, but fairly standard, rooms.

Olymp   NEW HOTEL $$$
(Отель Олимп; 📞455 789, 095 479 7889; www.olymp-hotel.com; vul Kulakova 86; r from 750uah; ❄❄) Very helpful staff, a location on a quiet street and comfy pistachio

FLAG DAY

Tourists flock to Sevastopol and hotels greedily raise prices during the last weekend of July, when the city celebrates Russian Navy Day with an impressive show of battleships manoeuvring in the bay, planes flying overhead and marines landing on Grafskaya Pristan. This show of force is largely symbolic. With half of the Black Sea and the straits controlled by NATO member-countries, the Russian fleet has no strategic role to play, apart from guarding the coast of Georgia's breakaway Abkhazia.

coloured rooms are Olymp's main virtues. But the lobby could do without those faux-Greek motifs.

✕ Eating & Drinking

Hungry, thirsty or in desperate need of a Segway ride? Head straight to Artbukhta, Sevastopol's Soho, where many restaurants and fast-food outlets are located. Some of the sleaziest nightclubs and bars are also to be found here.

Injir Cafe   PIZZA $$
(vul Bolshaya Morskaya 35; mains 40-60uah; 🛜📖) A local hipster fave, this pizzeria cum bar exudes positive vibes, musically and gastronomically speaking. Totally unpretentious, it is equally good for eating and social drinking. Pizzas are properly thin and served on wooden plates by friendly waiters clad in uniform jeans shorts, while the DJ spins summery tunes.

Barkas   SEAFOOD $$
(Баркас; Pinnace; Artbukhta, vul Kapitanskaya 2A; mains 40-80uah; 📖) The motto – 'we store our fish in the sea' – suggests that only the fresh catch is served in this naval-themed restaurant with a blue-coloured interior and waiters dressed as sailors. Check our mini-guide to Black Sea fish (p164) to make an informed decision about your order. This is also the place to sample all kinds of Crimean wine.

Madame Shoco   EUROPEAN $
(vul Bolshaya Morskaya 13A; mains 30-50uah; ⏲24hr; 🛜) Not quite sure about her true identity, this Madame has a bit of every-thing – slightly bizarre but edible break-fast meals and main courses, coffee drinks, shishas and live jazz during weekends. The psychedelically designed, open-air terrace attracts a girly crowd, with many *Sex and the City* types chatting nights away while emptying one glass after another.

Kofein   COFFEE & BREAKFAST $$
(Кофеин; vul Lenina 55; salads & mains 20-60uah; ⏲24hr; 📖) No other Kofein outlet in Ukraine can boast such a scenic location – with a terrace perched above Yuzhnaya (Southern) bay, where Russian navy ships are moored. The smartly designed picture menu makes it easier to choose from the extensive list of coffee drinks, salads, main courses and cocktails. But the unnecessary 'exotic' in-gredients in iced teas and milkshakes are slightly annoying.

Qbar   COCKTAILS $$
(vul Lenina 8; mains & cocktails 40-60uah) So if an old Soviet seadog, his chest adorned with medals and his memories revolving around LA and Florida as seen from the periscope of a nuclear submarine, is look-ing for his grandchildren on a Friday night, where does he find them? In a gay bar, why not? For this Rhodes-styled courtyard is the place to hang out with Sevastopol's gilded youth, gay and straight alike. It's supposed to be a pre-party place, but it is heaving till early morning.

☆ Entertainment

Khersones Theatre   OPEN-AIR THEATRE
(📞544330; vul Drevnaya 1; tickets 40uah) Sev-astopol's Russian theatre stages costumed historical dramas amid the ruins of an-cient Khersones. For schedules and tickets, drop in at **Lunacharsky theatre** (pr Nakhi-mova 6).

❶ Information

Battlefield Tours (📞44 121 430 5348; www.battlefieldtours.co.uk; tours £1950) A branch of the UK War Research Society runs Crimean War tours twice a year.

Central post office (Почтамт; vul Bol-shaya Morskaya 21; internet per hr 4.5uah; ⏲counters 9am-7pm Mon-Fri, to 2pm Sat, internet centre 8am-6pm Mon-Fri, to 5pm Sat & Sun) Internet available too.

Telephone office (Укртелеком; ⏲9am-10pm) In the side street next to the post office.

❶ Getting There & Away

AIR Sevastopol's Belbek airport, once used by Soviet leaders travelling to their Crimean *dachas*, is now catering to ordinary folks, with several Dniproavia flights to Kyiv and Moscow, in summer only.

BUS There are buses every 20 to 30 minutes to/from Bakhchysaray (13uah, one hour), Yalta (22uah, two hours) and Simferopol (20-38uah, two hours).

FERRY Two boats a week leave the **port of Sevastopol** (Севастопольский порт) for Istanbul (from 1300uah including meals, 26 hours). Schedules are available at www.stam-bul.com.ua and www.omegaship.com.ua (in Russian).

TRAIN There are two trains a day from Kyiv direct to Sevastopol (180uah, 17 hours), as well as *elektrychka* trains to/from Simferopol (8uah, two hours, seven daily in each direction). The latter service stops en route in Bakhchysaray (5.60uah, 1½ hours).

ℹ Getting Around

TO/FROM THE TRAIN STATION The train station is south of the town centre and main seafront. To get into town, cross the metal pedestrian bridge over the tracks and hop on any bus or *marshrutka* – all of them trudge uphill to the centre. Main central streets (vul Lenina, pr Nakhimova and vul Bolshaya Morskaya) form a circle with one-way anti-clockwise traffic movement.

BALAKLAVA & FIOLENT The chaotic 5km terminus comes into the equation here. To reach it, hop on any *marshrutka* marked 5KM in the centre. Once there, look for a large square where trolleybus routes terminate. Walk to its far edge – you'll have apartment blocks on your right and market stalls across the street on your left. You'll find Fiolent *marshrutka* 3 on the same side of the street as the trolleybuses. *Marshrutka* 9 for Balaklava stops across the street and around the corner.

TAXI This is the most sensible option for Balaklava and Fiolent. The reliable **Taxi Metro** (☏ 050 424 1556, 050 424 1558) charges around 40uah in both directions.

Balaklava Балаклава

☏ 0692

From the bloodthirsty pirates featuring in Homer's *Odyssey* to the Soviet nuclear submarine fleet – everyone used this beautiful curving fjord, invisible from the sea, as a secret hideout.

The British army wintered here during the Crimean War when a storm destroyed many supply ships moored outside the bay. Reading about it in the *Times*, concerned women back home began knitting full-cover woolly caps for the freezing sailors. These garments became known as balaclava helmets, or simply balaclavas.

Nowadays, the bay's turquoise waters surrounded by arid, scrub-covered hills shelter an armada of yachts, while pretty much the entire Ukrainian navy is tucked in the far corner.

History

The 2500-year-old settlement became a Genovese trading post in the medieval period. In 1475, it fell to the conquering Turks who gave Balaklava its current name, which means Fish's Nest. After the Russian takeover of Crimea, the area was settled by Greek refugees escaping Ottoman rule.

During the war Florence Nightingale ran a field hospital on one of the plateaus above

the village, and the infamous charge of the ill-fated Light Brigade took place in a valley north of the city.

Stalin deported Balaklava Greeks to Central Asia in 1944. Few of them returned to their hometown, which was turned into a top-secret Soviet submarine base.

⊙ Sights & Activities

Genovese Fortress of Cembalo
MEDIEVAL RUINS

(Генуэзская крепость Чембало; admission 10am-5pm 20uah, after hrs free) All that remains of the 15th-century Genovese fortress are three semi-ruined towers on top of a strategic hill, guarding the mouth of the harbour. But the view of the bay and the sea coast, stretching to Cape Aya, is breathtaking. The fortress was the site of the last stand of Balaklava's garrison, which was composed of local Greek fishermen who defended their town from the Allied troops during the Crimean War.

Cold War Museum
NUCLEAR BUNKER

(Музей Холодной Войны; Tavricheskaya nab 24; adult/student 20/15uah; ⊙10am-6pm, ticket desk to 4.45pm) The town's quirkiest sight lurks across the bay from the main promenade. The concrete opening in the harbour wall is the mouth of a natural underwater cave the Soviets turned into a secret nuclear submarine factory officially known as Facility-825. Today, you can breach the huge nuclear-blast-proof doors and wander through parts of the facility, which features repair docks, mess rooms and, thankfully, an arsenal that is now empty. It is possible on a one-hour Russian-language walking tour or on a ½-hour boat tour, leaving on the hour and at 4.45pm. But perhaps the best method is to get a ticket to the **Crimean War Exhibition** (admission 20uah) from a stall near the main ticket booth. The Sheremetyev brothers' excellent collection of Crimean War memorabilia, including a replica of a British officer's winter flat, occupies a large hall at the far end of the facility, where an underground canal opens into the sea. This allows you to wander around the bunker on your own. The exhibition will be based here at least until May 2011, but probably much longer. Take a jumper; it gets chilly inside.

Balaklava beaches
BEACHES

In summer, there are frequent boats to beaches with names like Golden and Silver. Tour agency stands also tout sea tours to Cape Aya and Cape Fiolent (100uah).

INTO THE VALLEY OF DEATH

Unquestioning loyalty, bravery and inexplicable blunders leading to tragedy – these ingredients turned an engagement lasting just minutes into one of the most renowned battles in military history. The action in question is the ill-fated charge of the Light Brigade, which occurred during a Russian attempt to cut British supply lines from Balaklava to Sevastopol during the Crimean War.

The battle began northeast of Balaklava early on 25 October 1854. Russian forces based on the east–west Fedioukine Hills wrested control of Allied (Turkish-held) gun positions lining the parallel southern ridge of Causeway Heights. Then they moved towards Balaklava itself.

Initially the Russians were blocked by the 'thin red line' of the British 93rd Highlanders, and repulsed by Lord Lucan's Heavy Cavalry Brigade. But four hours later, they appeared to be regrouping at the eastern end of the valley between the Fedioukine Hills and Causeway Heights. British army commander Lord Raglan sent an order for the cavalry 'to try and prevent the enemy carrying away the guns'.

The order was vague – which guns exactly? – and misinterpreted. The Earl of Cardigan headed off down the wrong valley, leading his Light Cavalry Brigade into a cul-de-sac controlled on three sides by the enemy. The numbers are disputed, but nearly 200 of 673 were killed.

'*C'est magnifique, mais ce n'est pas la guerre*,' exclaimed a watching French general. ('It's magnificent, but it's not war.') Later, romantic poet Lord Alfred Tennyson would lionise the 'noble six hundred' who rode into 'the valley of death'. His poem 'The Charge of the Light Brigade' did more than anything to mythologise the event for posterity. On its 150th anniversary, the charge was even recreated in front of British dignitaries, including Prince Phillip.

The 'Valley of Death' is now a vineyard, just north of the M18 road from Sevastopol to Yalta. You can look down on it from the hill of Sapun Gora (Сапун-гора), where there's a WWII **diorama** (⊙9.30am-6pm Tue-Sun Apr-Oct, to 4pm Nov-Mar) and Memorial. *Marshrutka* 107 (1.50uah) will get you there from downtown Sevastopol.

Akvarmarin   DIVING
(☑637 348; www.voliga.ru; vul Nazukina 1) This PADI-approved outfit offers dives through the watery channels of the factory, or in the bay or sea.

🛏 Sleeping

Kefalo Vrisi   PENSION $$
(Кефало Вриси; ☑050 398 7147; www.kefalo-vrisi.com; vul Istoricheskaya 15; d from 450uah; P✳) Flower and fruit trees cover every patch around this excellent pension set in a secluded valley, about 15 minutes' walk along a footpath from the embankment. All rooms face Cembalo fortress. Book well in advance in summer and call to arrange a pickup – not all taxis will agree to take you there and carrying luggage uphill to this place is quite an exercise. It's about a 30-minute walk to the first of Balaklava's beaches.

Listrigon Motel   HOTEL $
(Мотель Листригон; ☑463 191, 455 150, 455 870, 467 283; www.listrigon.com; vul 7th Noyabrya 5D; economy s/d/tr 80/150/180uah, standard d/tr 500/555uah; P✳) This Lego-like motel curving around a hillside offers great views, reasonable accommodation and decent prices. The cheapest, economy rooms (April to October only) are dormitory-style with shared bathrooms and breakfast not included; however, there's a cafe where you can pay for it. More expensive accommodation includes a private bathroom and is open year-round.

🍴 Eating

Izbushka Rybaka   SEAFOOD $$
(Избушка Рыбака; Fisherman's Hut; ☑455 049, 050 153 3922; www.isbushka.net.ua; nab Nazukina 33; mains 40-70uah; ⓘ) We heard people dubbing this the best fish restaurant in Crimea. Located on a floating platform at the far end of the main promenade, it specialises in *shkara* – a style of cooking favoured by local Greeks.

Piratskaya Kharchevnya   SEAFOOD $$
(Пиратская Харчевня; Pirate's Inn; ☑050 278 4116; ul Mramornaya 17; mains 50-100uah) Near

the entrance to the Naval Museum, this is another excellent fish restaurant with waiters dressed as *Peter Pan* pirates. All kinds of Black Sea fish are on offer, which is no wonder, since the Fish's Nest is just around the corner.

❶ Getting There & Around

Marshrutka 9 for Balaklava (2uah, every 20 minutes) departs from Sevastopol's chaotic 5km terminus. See Getting Around Sevastopol, p185, for details. In Balaklava, boatmen will take you across the harbour to the Cold War Museum for 20uah. Otherwise it's a 30-minute walk around the bay.

SOUTHERN COAST

Sevastopol to Yalta

The drive between Sevastopol and Yalta is one of the most scenic in Crimea. The road twists and turns along a coastal escarpment, with the Black Sea far below and the sheer cliffs of the Crimean Mountains rising behind. Vineyards and cypress trees line the route.

Thirty kilometres from Sevastopol is the small village of **Foros**, notable for three

things. First, this is where Gorbachev was held under house arrest during the 1991 coup attempt in Moscow. Locals will happily point out his *dacha*, which has a terracotta roof.

Second, there's the small, gold-domed Resurrection Church, also known as the **Church on the Rock** for its dramatic perch on a precipitous crag overlooking the sea. The 19th-century tea tycoon Alexander Kuznetsov built the church in thanks for the survival of his daughter, whose runaway horse stopped at the edge of the cliff.

Third, Foros is popular with rock climbers because of the left-hand face of Mt Mshat-Kaya, the **Forosskiy Kant**, which rises above the village. The face lies above today's Sevastopol–Yalta road, near the Baydarsky Vorota pass. For details contact guide **Sergey Sorokin** (www.mt.crimea.com).

Yalta ЯЛТА

☎ 0654 / POP 80,500

Yalta's air – an invigorating blend of sea and pine forest sprinkled with mountain chill – has always been its main asset. Back in the 19th century, doctors in St Petersburg had one remedy for poor-lunged aristocrats: Yalta. That is how the Russian royal family and other dignitaries, such as playwright

Southern Crimea

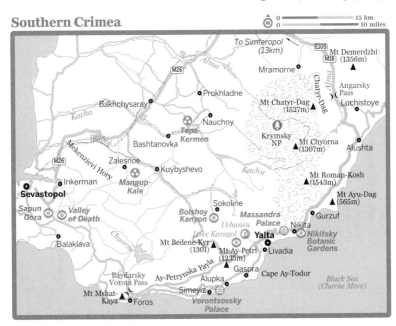

Yalta

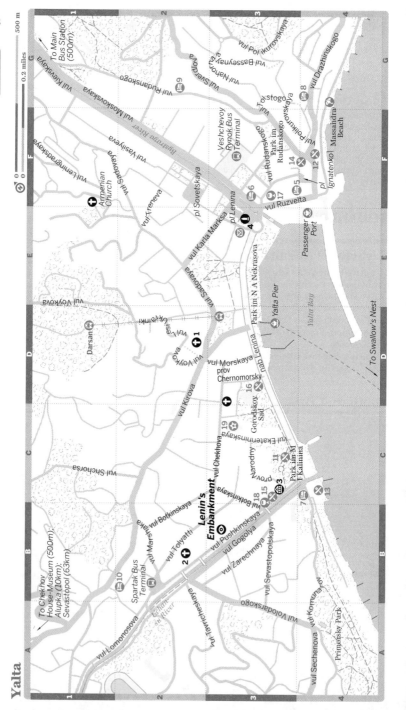

Anton Chekhov, ended up here. Old parts of Yalta are still full of modest and not-so-modest former *dachas* of the tsarist-era intelligentsia, while the coast around the city is dotted with the luxurious palaces of the aristocracy. But back in 1913, a Russian travel guide remarked that Yalta was a long way from the Riviera in terms of comforts and civilization. And it hasn't got any closer, despite the extremely beautiful setting in the shade of the chalk-faced Mt Ay-Petri.

A workers' paradise in the Soviet times, Yalta was badly hit by the wild commercialisation of the 1990s, but it is undergoing a visible gentrification. The view from the spruced-up seaside promenade, lined with swaying palm-trees, is no longer obscured by the rusting carcasses of sunken boats in the harbour. And a very happy-looking granite Lenin seems particularly pleased when *babushkas* gather at sunset to dance the waltz and polka on the plaza that still bears his name.

⊙ Sights & Activities

Chekhov House-Museum   MUSEUM
(www.chekhov.com.ua; vul Kirova 112; adult/student 30/15uah; ⊙10am-5pm, last entry 4.30pm Tue-Sun Jun-Sep, Wed-Sun Sep-May) With many of Yalta's attractions a short distance away, the Chekhov House-Museum is the only must-see in town. It's sort of *The Cherry Orchard* incarnate. Not only did Anton Chekhov (1860–1904) pen that classic play here, the lush garden would appeal to the most horticulturally challenged audience.

A long-term tuberculosis sufferer, the great Russian dramatist spent much of his last five years in Yalta. He designed the white *dacha* and garden himself and when he wasn't producing plays like *Three Sisters* and *The Cherry Orchard,* he was a legendary host and bon vivant, welcoming the Russian singer Feodor Chaliapin, composer Rachmaninov and writers Maxim Gorky and Leo Tolstoy.

After the exhibition at the entrance, you head down the path to the *dacha,* where all nine rooms are pretty much as Chekhov left them upon his departure from Yalta for Germany in May 1904. Explanation sheets are available in several languages.

Take *marshrutka* 6 from Veshchevoy Rynok terminal or *marshrutka* 8 from the Spartak cinema to the Dom-Muzey Chekhova stop. It takes 15 to 20 minutes to walk from the Spartak Cinema.

Lenin's Embankment   PROMENADE
Everyone's favourite pastime in Yalta is walking up and down the seafront nab Lenina and the pedestrian zone along the Uchan-su River, where you'll find a small **History Museum** (Pushkinskaya 5A; admission 15uah; ⊙10am-5pm Wed-Sun) and a **Catholic church** (vul Pushkinskaya 25). A popular attraction here is a flimsy plastic-bucket-style **chairlift** (vul Kirova, behind nab Lenina 17; return trip 30uah; ⊙11am-5pm Apr-Sep, to 11pm Jul & Aug) that swings above the rooftops to the Darsan hill. To see **old dachas,** venture into the quiet neighbourhood along vul Botkinskaya and vul Chekhova.

Massandra Winery   WINE CELLARS
(vul Vinodela Yegorova 9; tour 70uah; wine-tasting 40uah) Memoirists claim that Tsar

Yalta

Nicholas II would always keep a flask of Massandra port hidden in his high boot during his daily **Sunny path** walks, while his wife sipped the very same drink listening to Rasputin's prophesies. The imperial court's winery is now open to visitors. On a mandatory Russian-language tour (leaving every two hours from 11am to 7pm, you get to see the tsar's wine cellars, which contain over a million dust-covered bottles, including a 1775 Spanish Jerez de la Frontera claimed to be the oldest preserved wine in the world. The tour itself might seem a little boring, if you don't understand Russian. Subsequent wine-tasting sessions are more fun, but you must have a sweet tooth to appreciate local wines. There is a shop selling bottles for collection at modest prices. To reach the winery, take *marshrutka* 40 from Veshchevoy Rynok terminal. Ask the driver to stop at Vinzavod Massandra.

Alexander Nevsky Cathedral   CATHEDRAL
(vul Sadovaya 2) A beautiful piece of neo-Byzantine architecture with fantastic detailing.

🛏 Sleeping
Apartments
The entire city seems to be for rent in summer. Apartments come in all shapes from four walls and a bed for 250uah to fully furnished multi-bedroom cottages that may cost up to $500 a night. Prices drop drastically off-season – you can get a nice flat in the centre for as little as 60uah in winter. The biggest concentration of holiday houses and apartment dealers carrying signs like Жилье, Квартиры or Сдается can be found at the beginning of ul Drazhinskogo above Massandra beach.

Yalta Apartment   APARTMENT AGENCY
(☎050 970 9446; www.yaltaapartment.com; flats from 260uah) English-speaking Lyudmila operates several nicely furnished flats in the heart of Yalta, at the beginning of pr Karla Marksa.

Travel 2 Sevastopol   APARTMENT AGENCY
(☎050 757 5952; www.travel2sevastopol.com) Apartments are available from this Crimean-based, English-run outfit.

Black Sea Crimea   APARTMENT AGENCY
(☎44 780 816 0621; www.blacksea-crimea.com) This UK-based operator has slightly more expensive offerings.

Hotels
Bristol   HISTORIC HOTEL **$$$**
(Бристоль; ☎271 606, 271 603; www.hotel-bristol.com.ua; vul Ruzvelta 10; standard s/d 875/980uah, business class 1130/1240uah; ☀) Few of us ever really need more comfort than this central, three-star establishment provides. The town's oldest hotel is in a heritage-listed, 19th-century building, but its rooms were thoughtfully renovated in 2003, many in yellow and blue hues. Throw in a good breakfast buffet and reasonable service, and your stay will usually be straightforward and uncomplicated.

Vremena Goda   SPA HOTEL **$$**
(Времена года; ☎230 852, 234 111; www.hotel-seasons.com.ua; vul Rudanskogo 23; s/d from 570/980uah; ☀ ☀) For something a little special, visit this spa hotel and medical centre for its chocolate massages and mud treatments. With clean, modern lines complemented by a few art nouveau stained-glass windows, the 'Four Seasons' is within fairly easy reach (a 10- to 15- minute walk) of the high-season action.

Oreanda   HOTEL **$$$**
(Ореанда; ☎274 274, 274 250; www.hotel-oreanda.com; nab Lenina 35/2; s/d 1175/1785uah; ☀ ☀ @ ☀) The crème de la Krim is favoured by oligarchs, expense-account bunnies and others who wish their wealth to be seen. Rooms are elegant and tasteful – which is more than can be said for the hotel's casino and club. However, they're also small and only superior accommodation enjoys sea views. So this place for special occasions is wildly overpriced on any everyday analysis.

Otdykh   PENSION **$**
(Отдых; ☎353 069; www.krim-yalta.com.ua; vul Drazhinskogo 14; economy d 250uah, standard 475uah; ☀) Hotel 'Relaxation' was a 19th-century brothel; now it's a decent enough budget pension. Some of the bathrooms are a bit whiffy and there's some street noise, but staff speak OK English and the location is convenient.

White Eagle   BOUTIQUE HOTEL **$$**
(Белый Орел; ☎327 702, 050 324 2161; prov Krutoy 13; s/d $90/100; ☀summer; ☀) Judge for yourself the ethics of the face-control policy that bars most Ukrainians and Russians, while welcoming all foreigners. Otherwise, this is a chic, relaxed residence with six air-conditioned rooms that are comfort-

ably and tastefully furnished. Contact Igor Brudny of Travel2crimea.com (p192) if you can't contact the hotel.

Yalta-Intourist SOVIET HIGHRISE **$$**

(Ялта-Интурист; ☑270 260, 270 270; www. hotel-yalta.com.ua; vul Drazhinskogo 50; s/d from 670/770uah; ❇@✉) No one chooses the famous Yalta for comfort or convenience. They stay for the novelty of checking in to a 2230-bed ex-Soviet behemoth. Rooms are ordinary and the hotel is as poorly located as the neighbouring Massandra. However, given 10 bars, seven restaurants, numerous shops, a dolphinarium, a sauna, a lift to a private beach and myriad sporting activities, some guests probably never set foot off the premises.

Krym SOVIET-STYLED **$**

(Крым; ☑271 701; baza@hotelkrim.yalta.crimea. ua; vul Moskovskaya 1/6; s/d 90/150uah, d with bathroom from 280uah) Despite its best efforts to be dour and utterly unwelcoming, this ex-Soviet number remains mega-popular for its low prices and central location (expect noise). To save on water bills, the management opens shower cabins in shared bathrooms only for a few hours during the day. Breakfast is not included.

✖ Eating & Drinking

The waterfront and adjacent street are lined with restaurants offering standard 'European' (that is – post-Soviet) menus. A myriad of Столовая signs mark *stolovaya* cafeterias, where you can choose from displayed dishes.

Khutorok La Mer CREATIVE UKRAINIAN **$$**

(Хуторок ля Мэр; ☑271 815; vul Sverdlova 9; mains 60-170uah; ☉10am-2am) If this is a *khutorok* (a traditional Ukrainian farm), then designers must have salvaged it from the bottom of the sea. The menu is also a wild fusion of rural Ukrainian and marine themes. Nothing prevents you from ordering fried *barabulka* (see the box, p164) and cabbage *varenyki* at the same time. Cooking and service are both excellent in this restaurant overlooking Massandra beach.

Nobu JAPANESE **$$$**

(Нобу; ☑274 246; nab Lenina 35/2; mains 90-400uah) Unlike the Greek *galera* (galley) nearby, *Espagnola* used to be a real seafaring *caravella* that sailed as far as Georgia on the whims of Soviet cinema directors who used it as a prop. Now it stands on stilts in front of Hotel Oreanda and hous-

es – no, not a tapas bar, but an upmarket Japanese restaurant. What else can you expect in a sushi-crazy country! It also has a separate Black Sea fish menu. We especially liked *sultanka* in ginger sauce.

Apelsin EUROPEAN, JAPANESE **$$**

(Апельсин; nab imeni Lenina 35A; mains 30-150uah; ☉9am-midnight) A glassy structure set in a park, Apelsin is one of the few places in Yalta where you can have a decent breakfast. At other times, you can choose from an extensive menu that has a bit of everything – from standard international meat and poultry dishes to Black Sea fish and sushi.

Teatralnoye Café CRIMEAN TATAR, EUROPEAN **$$$**

(Театральное Кафе; ☑320-352; prov Chernomorsky 2; mains 50-200uah) A stylish upmarket place set in a garden, off the seafront promenade, Teatralnoye Café serves refined versions of Crimean Tatar dishes, such *plov* and *dolma,* as well as mouth-watering Black Sea fish *shashlyks.*

Smak CRIMEAN TATAR **$$**

(Смак; vul Pushkinskaya 7A; mains 50-150uah) This simple open-air eatery and takeaway makes more than 10 different kinds of mouth-watering *chebureki* (10uah), an impressive array of Crimean Tatar dishes, great *shashlyks* (25uah to 30uah for 100g) and Black Sea fish – the latter about half the price of upmarket restaurants albeit the same quality.

Pelmennaya DUMPLINGS **$**

(Пельменная; vul Sverdlova 8; mains 5-15uah) This is the best workers' caf in town because it makes your order fresh, rather than doing the usual of placing dishes in a glass display cabinet for hours. *Varenyky, blyny, borshch* and good, crisp salads all join the namesake dish of *pelmeni* (Russian dumplings).

Pinta BEER **$$**

(Пинта; vul Pushkinskaya 7; vul Ignatenko 7; ☉9am-2am) Beer-drinkers, you are not forgotten in this sweet-wine kingdom! Two Pinta pubs are strategically located on both sides of the promenade. International beers brands, such as Belgian Leffe and Czech Staropramen, are on tap. Meat dishes dominate the extensive menu.

☆ Entertainment

Nightclubs tend to gear towards main hotels such as Yalta-Intourist and Oreanda, but in a way all of Yalta turns into a sleazy nightclub after dark.

Chekhov Theatre of Russian Drama

THEATRE

(vul Ekaterininskaya 13) For a slightly more re-fined entertainment, head to this recently refurbished theatre. Despite its name, musicals and jazz gigs, not *Uncle Vanya,* dominate its schedule.

Information

Dozens of tourist booths line the waterfront and around, selling reasonably priced Russian-language day trips and, occasionally, maps. Remember, some attractions don't need much commentary. Many hotels can also help with information.

Central post office (pl Lenina 1; ⊙8am-9pm Mon-Fri, to 6pm Sat, to 4pm Sun summer, reduced hr in winter)

Intourist (☑327 604, 270 260/70; Hotel Yalta, vul Drazhinskogo 50; ⊙8am-8pm summer, 9am-5pm rest of year) If you're happy to tag along on one of Intourist's many crowded day tours, great. If you want something different, tough. Customisation isn't a speciality here.

Kiyavia (☑231 210, ul Ruzvelta 10) Book your air tickets here.

Travel2crimea.com (☑272 546, 050 324 2350; www.travel2crimea.com; Hotel Massandra, vul Drazhinskogo 35; ⊙9am-5pm Mon-Fri year-round, Mon-Sat May-Sep) With years of experience, excellent English and a helpful manner, owner Igor Brudny runs a superior travel service. The website is in conjunction with guide Sergey Sorokin.

Ukrtelekom (vul Moskovskaya 9; per hr 6uah) Telephone and internet centre.

ⓘ Getting There & Away

BOAT Some international cruise ships now stop here but Yalta's **passenger port** (morskoy vokzal; ☑320 094; vul Ruzvelta 5) is largely underused. In the summer of 2010, there were two boats a week to Novorossiysk in Russia (832uah, five hours). There were plans to resume catamaran service to Sinop in Turkey in 2010, but this failed to materialise.

BUS & TROLLEYBUS Buses depart from Yalta's **main bus station** (☑325 777, 342 092; vul Moskovskaya 8) to Sevastopol (21uah, two hours, every 20 minutes) and Simferopol (20uah, two hours, every 20 minutes). Buses to Feodosiya (49uah, five hours, two daily) go via Sudak.

ⓘ Getting Around

There are several bus/*marshrutka* stations in town. You'll arrive at the main bus station, which is about 1.5km from the waterfront. From here, trolleybuses 1, 2 and 3 go down the hill along vul Kievskaya to the centre.

Behind the main bus station, on the lower level, you'll find the buses and *marshrutky* going to the sights around Yalta. But perhaps more useful are Veshchevoy Rynok and Spartak cinema bus stations. See the West of Yalta and East of Yalta sections for more details.

There are several metered taxi firms and they're definitely cheaper for journeys within the city. **Akva-Trans Taxis** (☑231 085, 067 563 0444) is good, but you can generally find some sort of metered cab at the intersection of vul Ruzvelta and nab Lenina.

West of Yalta

☑0654

Yalta's most popular attractions are lined up like ducks in a row several kilometres west of the city. Many *marshrutka* routes (most notably the 32 and the 27) pass them all. From piers 7 and 8 in Yalta in summer there are eight boats a day to Alupka via Miskhor (for Ay-Petri Cable Car) and Swallow's Nest. Additional boats go to Swallow's Nest only.

◉ Sights & Activities

Livadia Palace   HISTORIC RESIDENCE

(Дворец Ливадия; Dvorets Livadia; adult/student 40/20uah ⊙10am-5.45pm Tue-Thu) It's not the most sumptuously fur-nished Crimean interior, but Livadia Palace reverberates with history. It's the site of the 1945 Yalta Conference, where dying US president Franklin Roosevelt and heat-allergic British prime minister Winston Churchill turned up to be bullied by Soviet leader Josef Stalin. While here, Churchill declared steamy Crimea 'the Riviera of Hades'. No wonder, given the high temperatures and the company he was keeping. Stalin's insistent demands to keep Poland and other swathes of Eastern Europe shaped the face of postwar Europe. Even as huge tour groups nearly trample you in a race to the overflowing souvenir shops in the furthest rooms, it's hard not to be awed wandering these corridors of power.

In the enormous **White Hall**, the 'Big Three' and their staff met to tacitly agree that the USSR would wield the biggest influence in Eastern Europe, in exchange for keeping out of the Mediterranean. The crucial documents, dividing Germany and ceding parts of Poland to the USSR, were signed on 11 February in the English billiard room. The most famous Yalta photograph of Churchill, Roosevelt and Stalin is hung on a wall, along with the awkward outtakes, which bring history to life.

It's upstairs, however, that Livadia's other ghosts genuinely move you (yes, even complete antimonarchists). This Italian Renaissance-style building was designed as a summer residence for Russian Tsar Nicholas II in 1911. But he and his family spent just four seasons here before their arrest by Bolshevik troops in 1917 and execution in Yekaterinburg the following year. Photos and some poignant mementos of the doomed Romanovs are still in their private apartments.

From the row of souvenir stands at the entrance, a signposted path leads to the palace's former power station (800m away), which has been transformed into an **organ hall**. In summer, concerts take place daily at 4pm and three times a day during weekends.

Marshrutka 47a from Veshchevoy Rynok terminal and *Marshrutka* 5 (3uah; summer only) from the Spartak bus terminal drop you right in the palace grounds. A taxi to Livadia will cost around 20uah.

Sunny Path
SCENIC TRAIL
(Солнечная тропа) Starting in Livadia's lush coastal gardens, this trail was built on the recommendation of Tsar Nicholas II's doctor, who believed that regular outdoor exercise would improve the royal family's tuberculosis. The tsar typically walked the route with a rifle and in full soldier's gear, his adjutants following him at a respectful distance. The trail stretches for nearly 7km to Roza Lyuksemburg Sanatorium in Miskhor. From there, you can catch bus 26 either further to Alupka or back to Yalta. Shortly before the end of the trail, there is a turn to **Gaspra/Miskhor** and Ay-Petri Cable Car station. Although the trail is generally well-signposted, some stretches are disturbed by new development. If you lose it, keep walking in the same direction and you'll find the trail again.

Swallow's Nest
CASTLE
(Ласточкино Гнездо; Lastochkino Gnezdo; admission 5uah; 8am-6pm Tue-Sun) Like many movie stars, Swallow's Nest is shorter in

real life than it appears in pictures. This toy-town castle is a favourite subject for Crimean postcards, but it's only big enough to house an expensive and exceedingly disappointing Italian restaurant.

Instead, it's the castle's precarious perch on the sheer cliff of Cape Ay-Todor, 10km west of Yalta, that elicits a minor thrill. On the surrounding walkway, you realise that the castle actually overhangs the cliff. Although the castle looks medieval in style, it was built in 1912 for German oil magnate Baron Steingel, as a present to his mistress.

The most spectacular approach to the castle is over the water, via the ferry (adult 20uah, child 10uah; up to 20 daily in high season, four in October), which heads from Yalta pier to the beach and jetty just below the Swallow's Nest.

Buses 32, 26 and 27 also pass this way, stopping directly in front of a row of souvenir stalls above the castle. Stairs, leading to the castle, are on the left side of the row.

Ay-Petri Cable Car
CABLE CAR
(Канатная дорога; Kanatnaya doroga; one way 50uah; ticket office 10am-4pm, services to 5pm) On the coastal road in Miskhor, behind a little cluster of market stalls, is the cable car up the cliff of Mt Ay-Petri. It's a truly dizzying ride across the foothills and up the mountain's sheer face, during which you

overlook the coast and the sea. Views from the top are stunning, while Mt Ay-Petri's dry plateau itself feels otherworldly, or at least Central Asian. There are also several nice Tatar eateries. Buses 27 and 32 shuttling between Yalta and Alupka stop here; cable cars depart every 20 minutes.

Vorontsovsky Palace FAIRYTALE PALACE
(Воронцовский дворец; Vorontsovsky dvorets; adult/student 40/20uah; ⊙9am-6pm Tue-Sun Jun; 8am-7.30pm Tue-Sun Jul & Aug; 9am-5pm Tue-Sun Apr, May, Sep & Oct; 9am-4pm Tue-Sun Nov-Mar) Crimea's most exotic palace-park complex is wedged between the coast and Mt Ay-Petri, in a stunning setting 16km west of Yalta at Alupka. The palace was designed by English architects for the English-educated Count Mikhail Vorontsov, the immensely rich regional governor, and it's a bizarre combination of Scottish castle on its landward side and Arabic-Asian fantasy on its seaward side. Its towers are said to repeat the contours of the Ay-Petri plateau looming above it. Vorontsov brought serfs from his estates all over Russia to build the palace and park in 1828–46. A century later Winston Churchill stayed here during the 1945 Yalta Conference.

Tours take you firstly into the palace's luxurious interior, which includes an imitation Wedgwood 'blue room', an English-style dining hall and an indoor conservatory. However, the best views are from the lush gardens behind the palace, where six marble lions flank the staircase framed against the backdrop of Mt Ay-Petri. British PM Churchill joked that one of the lions looked like him – minus the trademark cigar.

Bus 32 from Veshchevoy Rynok and Bus 27 from Avtovokzal shuttle back and forth to Alupka (7uah).

Uchansu Waterfall to Grand Canyon
MOUNTAIN ROUTE
Heading northwest from Yalta, bus 30 from the main bus station takes you within walking distance of two beauty spots in the mountains off the Bakhchysaray road. From the Vodopad (Waterfall) stop about 11km out, you can walk to a platform (5uah) beside the 100m-high Uchansu Waterfall. From the Karagol stop, 3km further up the road, a track leads to forest-ringed Lake Karagol. Both spots have a restaurant.

Continuing past the Karagol stop by car, the road winds spectacularly up to the top of the range 13km on; the summit of Mt

Ay-Petri (1233m) sits to the left. This route, and several others up Mt Ay-Petri, are ideal for **mountain biking** (for more details, see www.mountainbiking.velocrimea.com).

On the inland side of the range is Crimea's so-called Grand Canyon (Bolshoy Kanyon) – not very big, really, but a pleasant enough walk. There are several tourist lodges in nearby Sokoline, which can only be reached by taxi from either Yalta or Bakhchysaray – buses are not allowed on this derelict road.

East of Yalta
☑0654

Massandra Palace PALACE
(Дворец Массандра; Dvorets Massandra; adult/student 40/20uah; ⊙9am-5pm Wed-Mon May-Oct, to 4pm Wed-Mon Nov-Apr) A cutesy hunting lodge built to resemble a French chateau, the turreted palace was completed by Tsar Alexander III in 1889. It's better known, however, for what it became: Stalin's summer *dacha*.

The restored palace contains paintings and antique furniture, although the surrounding parkland is probably more beautiful. Outside there are sphinxes with female heads guarding a pretty pond with water lilies and an art nouveau power-station building.

The palace is best visited by taxi (20uah). Otherwise, take trolleybus 2 or 3, heading uphill opposite the Yalta main bus station and ask the driver to drop you at the turn to the palace. Cross the road (carefully!) and walk uphill for about 20 minutes.

Nikitsky Botanic Gardens PARK
(Никитский Ботанический Сад; admission 15uah; ⊙8am-6pm) These gardens let you sample a wide range of the world's flora, just wandering around the 3 sq km of their hillside (and seaside) grounds. Founded under the order of the tsar in 1812, they were designed by British gardener Christian Stephen to collect and then disseminate the planet's species throughout Russia. Today 'Nikita', as they're nicknamed, house up to 28,000 species, including olive trees and roses, cacti, ancient yews and pistachios. An on-site cafe only improves the experience.

From Yalta's Veshchevoy Rynok terminal, take bus 34 or bus 2 from Veshchevoy Rynok bus station to the Upper Gate bus stop. For a pleasant tour, boats (20uah) also sail from the Yalta waterfront to the gardens. Walk to the right of the entrance taking in the bamboo grove and the rosarium then follow the steps to the lower and older part of the park. There are several refreshment stalls on the premises.

Gurzuf ГУРЗУФ

Gurzuf's steep, winding streets and old wooden houses, backed by Mt Roman-Kosh (1543m), were traditionally a magnet for artists and writers. Today they're a site for more inquisitive travellers. The village, 18km northeast of Yalta, is built around a picturesque bay with the rocky Genoese Cliff (Skala Dzhenevez) at its eastern end. Mt Ayu-Dag (Bear Mountain or Gora Medvid, 565m) looms along the coast to the east, protruding into the sea.

Overhanging wooden balconies, a few cafes and the odd shop adorn the curving, picturesque main street.

Gurzuf Park   ARISTOCRATIC ESTATE
The local recreational dinosaur, **Gurzufsky Sanatorium** occupies what used to be the *dacha* of the Duc de Richelieu, governor of Odesa (1803–14). The word *dacha* is a serious understatement, especially if you compare it with Chekhov's modest dwelling in Gurzuf. It really is a large coastal estate with palatial buildings and a vast subtropical park, where you'll find the **Pushkin in Crimea Museum** (⊙10am-5pm Wed-Sun, closed winter). The Russian poet was hosted here by governor Rayevsky and had a great time courting his host's daughters. You can visit the estate on official tours that start at 11am and 4pm from the guard's booth on the beach promenade, or you might try sneaking past the guard to see the park on your own.

Chekhov's Dacha   MUSEUM
(Дача Чехова; vul Chekhova 22; admission 15uah; ⊙9am-6pm) Tired of being a local celebrity in Yalta, Chekhov sought refuge in this little Tatar farmhouse tucked in a solitary cove under the Genovese Cliff. The melancholy of this place inspired him to create one of his best plays – *The Three Sisters*. There is nothing much to see apart from the original furniture and photos of actors playing *Seagull* and *Uncle Vanya,* so sit or lie back on the rocky beach and Chekhov's muse might decide to pay you a visit.

🛏 Sleeping and Eating

Hotel Marina   HOTEL $$$
(Марина; ☎067 620 4419, 067 654 3291; www.hotel-marina.crimea.ua; vul Leningradskaya 68A; r from 750uah; P✱) A reasonable distance from Gurzuf beach, on the way to the Artek children's camp, Marina has large and airy *lyuks* (luxury) rooms that come with balconies and a sea view. The slightly cramped *polulyuks* (standards) have none of that and are only 100uah cheaper.

Motel Bogema   PENSION $$
(Богема; ☎363 802, 095 526 0788; www.bogema.crimea.com; vul Leningradskaya 9; d Jul & Aug 600uah, May, Jun & Sep 400uah; P) The Motel Bogema features large but rather tastelessly furnished rooms with ugly linoleum on the floor and an odd choice of furniture. Prices are officially subject to bargaining.

Meraba   TATAR, ITALIAN $$
(Мераба; nab Pushkina; mains 45-120uah; ⊙11am-11pm; 🍴) A combination of Crimean Tatar and Italian on the menu at this excellent restaurant is an apt representation of Gurzuf, a place where these two peoples rubbed shoulders for centuries. Black Sea fish is also available. To wash it down, try the *makhsma* tonic drink made from wheat.

⊙ Getting There & Away

Bus 31 (every 30 to 45 minutes) links Gurzuf with Yalta's main bus station. There are also buses for Alushta (every 30 minutes). In summer there are boats from Yalta and Alushta.

Alushta АЛУШТА
☎06560
Dusty and crowded, Alushta is the second-largest resort on the southern coast, but lacks a hint of Yalta's elegance. In fact, it epitomises all the worst things about post-Soviet recreation. Beaches are dumpy and hotels are laughably overpriced.

If you absolutely need to stay here, consider splurging on **Radisson Blu** (☎262 26; vul Lenina 2; r from €129; P✱🛜🏊), which has its own beach. Alushta lies on the Simferopol–Yalta trolleybus route, but buses are more convenient. There are services to Simferopol (20uah, every 20 minutes), Sevastopol (21uah, every 20 minutes) and Feodosiya (49uah, two daily).

Around Alushta

Although the following natural attractions are closest to Alushta, they can also be visited from Yalta (on organised tours) or Simferopol (if hiking from the Simferopol–Alushta road).

Mt Demerdzhi   MOUNTAIN

(Гора Демерджі) The **Valley of the Ghosts** under Mt Demerdzhi contains some stunning rock formations created by wind erosion of sandstone. The freaky pillars have vaguely human features and are certainly memorable. The nearby village of **Luchistoye** (Лучистое) has a couple of lodges boasting spectacular views of the coast below. The friendly young people who own **Dolina Privideny Lodge** (☑067 945 5058, 095 895 9891, 067 115 8614; vul Severnaya 11, Luchistoyeper; person half-board 130uah) offer inexpensive mountain treks varying in length, including a two-day trek to their other base on Karabi-Yayla plateau in eastern Crimea.

Luchistoye, from where you can hike to the Valley of the Ghosts, can be accessed from Alushta bus station by *marshrutka* (2uah, every 40 minutes). A taxi from Alushta should cost around 60uah. You can also walk from the Luchistoye bus station on the Simferopol–Yalta road. Travelling from Simferopol it is after Angarsky Pass – get off when the sea comes into view.

Two other options include taking an organised **mountain-bike tour** (www.mt.crimea.com) or booking an organised tour from a stall in Yalta (75uah), although the latter usually only leave on certain days.

Mt Chatyr-Dag   MOUNTAIN

(Чатир-Даг) Mt Chatyr-Dag (1527m) lies west of the Alushta–Simferopol road and is renowned for the numerous caves that lie beneath it. The most famous are the **Mramornaya Cave** (Marble Cave; 1hr tour 50uah) and the **Eminé-Ba'ir-Khosar** (Well of Maiden Eminé; 1hr tour 50uah). They're not world-beating, but maybe are worth seeing if you're staying longer in Crimea.

Mramornaya Cave is a long, shallow cave (68m deep and nearly 2km long) full of strangely shaped stalactites and stalagmites, nicknamed after various animals, objects, fairytale characters and international buildings, such as the Leaning Tower of Pisa.

Eminé-Ba'ir-Khosar spirals down to 120m, with jade-like stalagmites, crystal flowers and a lake. According to legend, Eminé threw herself to the bottom of the cave after her lover was killed by her father's family.

Unless you're hiking in the region, the simplest way to reach the caves is via a day trip from one of the tour stalls in Yalta (95uah). 'Extreme' tours of the lower level of the Mramornaya Cave (three hours) are organised by **Onyx Tour** (☑065 224 5822 Russian only).

EASTERN CRIMEA

Sudak СУДАК

☑06566 / POP 14,500

As an important stop on the Silk Route from China, Sudak was a major and well-defended trading centre run by the Genovese. Its central claim to fame is the fortress that survives from that era, but that's not quite all in this overcrowded resort. Just a few kilometres away lie the popular beaches of Novy Svit.

◉ Sights & Activities

Genovese Fortress   MEDIEVAL CASTLE

(Sudakska Krepost; adult/child 30/20uah; ☺9am-10pm Jun-Sep, 9am-5pm Oct-May) Its vertiginous location is one of the major appeals of Sudak's Fortress. This once-impregnable complex is perched on a massive seaside cliff and in true Ukrainian fashion you're allowed to clamber all over it, at times perhaps unsafely.

Built during the 14th and 15th centuries, the fortress still cuts a magnificent silhouette. The remains of its crenulated walls (6m high and 2m thick) extend for 2km, encircling more than 30 hectares of dry sloping terrain.

Ten original towers remain, most of them bearing the grand-sounding names of Genovese nobles who ruled the city: Francesco di Camilla or Cigallo Corrado, for instance. Open for visitors are the seafacing **Consul's Tower** and **13th-century temple**. Originally a mosque, it was at different times used by Italian Catholics, German Lutherans and Russian Orthodox Christians.

Every summer the fortress plays host to the medieval festival **Genovese Hel-**

met (adult/child 40/20uah), held on set days between mid-July and the end of August, where you can watch actors dressed as knights fight with swords or 'storm' the fortress on horseback. Stalls offer blacksmithing, crafts from the Middle Ages and, erm, AK-47 shooting.

🛏 Sleeping & Eating

Pretty much every room and house in the city is for rent in summer. You find yourself a bed for 40uah, but expect to pay 300uah to 400uah for a hotel-quality room with hot water during high season. There is a cluster of pensions on vul Morskaya and nearby streets that skirt the fortress hill. Cheaper accommodation is found along vul Ayvazovskogo and elsewhere around town.

Hotel Bastion HOTEL **$$**
(Бастион; ☎223 88, 945 24, 050 200 2710; www.hotel-bastion.info; vul Ushakova 3 & Morskaya 3B; d from 510uah; ✳ ❄) Spread across five buildings below the fortress, with excellent amenities and prices targeted at differing budgets, this is the hotel to book. Relatively tasteful modern rooms join an alfresco restaurant, outdoor heated pool and jet skis to rent. The cheapest cottage rooms in building No 2 close for winter; building No 3 usually also shuts.

TOK Sudak RENOVATED SOVIET **$**
(ТОК Судак; ☎21 033, 21 965; www.toksudak.crimea.com; vul Lenina 89; s/d from 290/335uah) Set amid a lush garden that occupies a large part of Sudak's coastal area, TOK Sudak is the flagship of the town's tourist industry and good value for money if it's not fully booked by a conference of ophthalmologists, librarians or dill growers. There are rooms to fit all budgets.

Hotel Forum HOTEL **$$**
(Форум; ☎338 76; www.hotel-forum.crimea.com; vul Lenina 89; d without air-con 650uah, standard s/d from 475/685uah; ✳ @) If you really must have generously sized, well-appointed bedrooms and a downtown location, book in here. It's the big concrete building opposite the city court and the route to the embankment; the nameplate is not so visible from street level. The gym is 35uah for nonguests.

Pansionat Edem PENSION **$**
(Пансионат Эдем; ☎320 52, 050 055 6564; http://edem.eurasium.com; vul Ayvazovskogo 17; s/d $20/26, with bathroom $40/46; 🐾) One of many similar affairs, Edem is popular with

foreigners because it advertises itself as a hostel on English-language booking sites. The large house with a patio has about 20 spacious, but dull brownish lino-clad rooms. There are gazebos to cool down after a day by the sea. The owner is super-nice, but speaks only basic English. It's about 15 minutes' walk along the street that begins opposite Sudak's main square. At the fork turn left. No signs on the door.

Tok Gorizont SOVIET-STYLED **$$**
(ТОК Горизонт; ☎221 79, 222 83; www.tokgorizont.com.ua; vul Turistov 8; s/d from 366/542uah; P ✳ ❄) A large Soviet *pansionat* (resort) in transition to normality, but still not quite there. Rooms look a little Soviet, but the furniture and bathroom equipment are new. Breakfasts are heavy on greasy mains courses, so don't expect any muesli. But sea-facing rooms come with an excellent view of the fortress. The pool is 25uah for nonguests.

Arzy TATAR, INTERNATIONAL **$**
(Арзы; vul Morskaya 5; mains 20-50uah; ⏰24hr) This Tatar-run place with wicker chairs on a beachside terrace is popular for its relaxed, almost Goan ambience and stunning views of the illuminated fortress in the evening. Italian and Japanese food on the menu are hilariously unauthentic, but all the Crimean Tatar dishes are competently cooked and delicious.

ℹ Getting There & Away

There are frequent bus services to both Simferopol (26uah, 1¾ hours, every 15 minutes) and Feodosiya (15uah, 1½ to 1¾ hours, every 15 minutes) via Koktebel (10uah, one hour). There are also four daily buses going along the coastal road to Yalta (27uah, three hours).

ℹ Getting Around

The town centre is 1.2km south of the bus station. It's another few hundred metres ahead to the beachfront *naberezhnaya* (promenade) and a further 2km right (west) to the fortress. From the bus station, *marshrutky* bound for Novy Svit (Новый свет) and Uyutne (Уютное) all stop at the fortress, passing the town centre on the way. Novy Svit is 7km away from Sudak

---

Novy Svit НОВЫЙ СВІТ
☎06566

Its name meaning New World, the beautiful bay of Novy Svit used to be the realm of Prince Lev Golitsyn – an idealistic aristocrat

CRIMEAN GUIDES

Crimea has some fantastic hiking and bicycling opportunities but a scarcity of really good topographical maps with marked routes. In addition, a total lack of English signs means that Westerners will find the going more challenging than usual.

If you're still determined to strike out by yourself, read the tips on camping restrictions, registration and mountain rescue at www.tryukraine. com/crimea/hiking.shtml beforehand. If you'd prefer to go with a guide, the following are highly recommended:

Sergey Sorokin (☑067 793 9100; www.mt.crimea.com) Excellent hiking and bicycle tours.

Outdoor Ukraine (☑097 327 8698, 067 915 1257; www.outdoorukraine.com) A highly recommended Kyiv-based operator.

Marat Pavlenko (☑067 306 7318, 095 528 7232; www.bashtanovka.crimea.ua) Marat's well-established operation runs bicycle tours from his base in the village of Bashtanovka.

turned winemaker. Obsessed with changing Russian drinking culture, he spent all his fortune selling wine and champagne at cheaper prices than vodka. This was a noble, but a rather hopeless cause – innovative drinkers soon realised they could achieve stunning results by mixing champagne with vodka. The resulting killer-cocktail became known as Northern Lights.

Financially broke, Golitsyn was rescued by Tsar Nicholas II, who appointed him the royal winemaker and commissioned him to build the Massandra winery (p189).

These days, buses and *marshrutky* wind regularly across the slightly hairy but breathtakingly gorgeous mountain road connecting Sudak with this popular satellite. Each bus is jam-packed with day-trippers coming to do Golitsyn's favourite walk and sample some bubbly from his winery.

◉ Sights & Activities

Golitsyn's Path   COASTAL TRAIL
(Тропа Голицына; Tropa Golitsyna; adult/child 20/10uah) Starting at the far (western)

end of the beach, this trail takes you on a picturesque, if rather slippery, seaside walk through Novy Svit Botanic Reserve. Winding around the base of Mt Orel, the path leads to a seaside grotto where local Prince Golitsyn used to hold high-society parties. You can plunge into the crystal-clear water of the Blue Bay before ascending the headland for the view of Tsar's Beach, once favoured by Nicholas II. It is, however, off limits to visitors (what else can you expect from such a VIP beach!) and there is a surly policeman to enforce this arrangement.

Novy Svit Champaign Plant   WINERY
(www.nsvet.com.ua; ul Golitsyna 21; tour & tasting 70uah; ⊙tour 8pm) As in Massandra, the tour through the winery's museum may seem boring if you don't understand Russian (and even if you do), but champagne sampling sessions in the chilly wine cellar, accompanied by live classical music and a hilariously sombre presentation, are fun. Since five small glasses of the bubbly that you get during the sampling session seem extremely insufficient to some visitors, they get bottles in the local shop and open them right in front of the winery. Here is your chance to get drunk with total strangers.

🛏 Sleeping

As everywhere else in this part of Crimea, if you speak basic Russian you can shop around and find a much better deal than any hotel can offer. Pensions and rooms for rent are all over the place.

Turbaza Novy Svet   HOLIDAY CAMP **$**
(Турбаза Новый Свет; ☑33 456, 33 511; vul Golitsyna 11A; per person without/with bathroom from 200/217uah; ☀) Novy Svit's flagship *turbaza* (small resort) has a few dozen dilapidated cottages (like those you find on Thai beaches) scattered around a lush garden. Cottages equipped with both air-con and water heater cost over 300uah per person.

Knyaz Golitsyn   NEW LUXURY **$$$**
(Князь Голицын; Prince Golitsyn; ☑33359, 050 583 5949; www.hotel-golitsyn.com; vul Lva Golitsyna 5; d without/with sea view from 1150/1200; ☀🐾) A chalet-styled building under a red-tiled roof set on the Sudak road away from the sea, this brand new luxury hotel has large tastefully decorated rooms, cool marble-clad corridors and a wonderful garden with gazebos.

Kurortne КУРОРТНЕ

✔06562

Kurortne is one of those rare places in Crimea where you can still relax on a relatively uncrowded beach. Besides, it is the gateway to the striking volcanic formations of Kara-Dag Nature Reserve.

Another local attraction is the nearby **Lisya Bukhta** (Fox Bay). For the full libertarian experience, you can pitch a tent at this long sandy beach about a 2.5km walk west from Kurortne. Clothing is optional here and the place is isolated. There are several Tatar beach restaurants with a Jamaican twist.

The easiest way to reach Kurortne is on а биостанция (bio-station) *marshrutka*. These travel from the downtown Feodosiya bus station via Koktebel to central Kurortne (6uah), before continuing to the Kara-Dag Nature Reserve. Travelling from Sudak, get off at Shchebetovka on the Sudak–Feodosiya road, then change for the bio-station *marshrutka*.

🛏 Sleeping & Eating

Kolybel Koktebelya NEW LUXURY $$
(Колыбель Коктебеля; Koktebel's Cradle; ✔067 541 3838; www.kolibel-koktebelya.com; vul Morskaya 2; r from $70, ste from $105; P❄☻) Opened in 2009, this is as modern as it gets in Crimea. Large rooms with eye-catching, red-and-black furniture are in two-floor cottages with glassy front walls that you can open to catch the breeze at night, if you prefer it to the air-con.

Seit-Nebi Baza Turist HOLIDAY CAMP $
(Турбаза Сеит-Неби; ✔26 235, 050 827 7064; www.nebi-hotel.com; vul Pionerskaya 14; d without breakfast from 260uah; P❄) Slightly incongruous low-rise buildings surround the grass-covered courtyard of this Tatar-run establishment. Rooms are clean, though unremarkable. There is a large cheap cafeteria on the premises.

Café Rushanna TATAR, UZBEK $$
(Кафе Рушана; vul Morskaya 1; mains 30-80uah) An upmarket beachside restaurant with wall carpets, tablecloths and armchairs covered in oriental floral ornaments straight out of 1001 nights. A creative take on traditional Central Asian food.

The local Soviet-era flagship *pansionat* **Krimskoye Prymorye** doesn't welcome walk-in travellers, preferring to deal with tour operators. However, its swimming pool is open for guests (20uah). Another place to ask for rooms is at the **bio-station**. Employees rent them for $15 to $20.

Kara-Dag Nature Reserve ЗАПОВІДНИК КАРА-ДАГ

✔06562

The Kara-Dag Nature Reserve is a true Jurassic Park. Its dramatic landscape is the work of an extinct volcano (Kara-Dag, or 'Black Mountain' in Tatar) that spewed lava and debris over land and sea during the Jurassic period. Over millennia, the elements have moulded the volcanic rocks into striking shapes, with names like 'The Devil's Finger', 'The King and the Earth', and the most striking, 'Golden Gate' (Zolote Vorota), a freestanding arch in the sea. These all circle the 575m craggy Mt Kara-Dag; the friends of Koktebel-based poet Maximilian Voloshin used to tell him he looked like it!

The Kara-Dag Nature Reserve **bio-station** (⊙9am-8pm Wed-Mon May-Sep) is on the outskirts of Kurortne. Anyone is free to visit the aquarium, dolphinarium and botanic gardens, but for environmental reasons you're not allowed in the main part of Kara-Dag territory without a guide.

The park administration offers several **group hikes** a day (except Tuesdays), which cover 7km and last four hours (50/30uah per adult/child). It's sometimes easiest to buy these hikes via the many 'excursion' stalls in Koktebel, Feodosiya or Sudak.

An alternative is a **boat trip** around the Kara-Dag coast from Koktebel or Feodosiya. The three- to four-hour journey on the deck of a tug-sized ship doesn't get as up close and personal to the reserve as a hike. However, it's less strenuous and your boat does sail through the arch of the lava-formed Golden Gate. Bring your swimming costume for one of the most pleasant dips in Crimea, when the boat stops for 20 to 30 minutes in a deep, clean stretch of the Black Sea.

In very hot or rainy weather the Kara-Dag administration may cancel all hikes and then a boat trip is the only option.

Koktebel КОКТЕБЕЛЬ

✔06562 / POP 2500

A merry band of Russian bohemians led by the gregarious bearded artist Maximilian Voloshin descended in the 1900s on what was then a small and remote village of Bulgarian refugees, transforming it into a favourite playground for the intelligentsia. This boho atmosphere lingered for a century, but the tide of wild capitalism has largely washed it away. Still with two major jazz festivals, a couple of good musical venues and a naturist beach on the eastern side of the bay, Koktebel is not your average mainstream Crimean resort town, even though the majority of Ukrainian and Russian youngsters who flood it in summer are so very mainstream and provincial.

⊙ Sights & Activities

Voloshin's House   MUSEUM
(Дом Волошина; admission 25uah; ⊙10am-6pm Tue-Sun) Poet Maximilian Voloshin came to live on this bay beneath the anthropomorphic shapes of the Kara-Dag mountains (which his friends claimed looked like him), and his home turned into a meeting place for intellectuals of all professions and political convictions. He stayed here even while the Civil War was raging in Crimea, 'waiting for the Reds to shoot me for being White, or for the Whites to hang me for being Red', as he noted in a letter.

Aquapark   WATER PARK
(Аквапарк; admission 250uah; ⊙10am-8pm) Max Voloshin's big jaw would drop at seeing this symbol of Koktebel's commercialisation, but heck – this is a ruddy great aquapark with multicoloured slides like liquorice and many pools.

⚑ Festivals & Events
Every September, when students leave and the village reverts to being the relaxing idyll it once was, it hosts the **Koktebel International Jazz Festival** (http://jazz.koktebel.info/), which is attended by major musicians from Eastern Europe and beyond. Koktebel is also a regular stop on the route of the travelling **Mamakabo Art-festival** (www.mamakabo.ru).

⌂ Sleeping
Most people stay in rooms for rent and nameless private pensions that come in all shapes and sizes. Look for Есть свободные номера (Rooms available) signs. None of these places have receptions as such, so you normally need to dial a mobile number posted at the entrance. That's obviously bad news for those who don't speak Russian.

Dacha Koktebelica   GUESTHOUSE $
(Дача Коктебелика; ☎050 535 7173, 050 988 3135; www.koktebelika.com; dm/d $7/40; ⓟ❋❄) This one is a particularly cute black sheep in Crimea's dull accommodation family. Accommodation is in tube-shaped mobile houses, once used by oilers in Siberia, which a young polyglot couple from Simferopol installed in their garden in the foothills of Karadag. Solar batteries provide at least part of the energy and there are more breakthroughs planned on the sustainability front. The place is away from the centre, but with free bicycles provided, you can ride as far as Kurortne and Feodosiya. The operators also organise mountain treks from their refuge on the remote Karabi-Yayla plateau. English and Spanish are spoken.

There are several overpriced hotels, but one good-value establishment is **Talisman Hotel** (☎244 76, 244 80; vul Lenina 97; high season s/d from $56, superior d $70, winter s/d $12/24, superior d $36; ⓟ), across the road from the bus station. Passionately recommended by some travellers is **Villa Altaris** (☎056 788 7007, 097 699 0345; http://pdcllc.com.ua/en; vul Solnechnaya 26; d & tr per person with shared bathroom €25).

✗ Eating & Entertainment
You will not get hungry in Koktebel. *Shashlyks*, Tatar pastry, fruit and *churchkhelis* (nut-based sweets) are jumping into your mouth from the myriad food stands that line the beachfront. There are dozens of modern *stolovaya*-styled cafeterias and cheap restaurants, but you will be hard-pressed to find anything more sophisticated.

Bogema   JAZZ
(Богема; vul Lenina 110; concert 50uah) A small and unpretentious place hidden on the premises of Pansionat Goluboy Zaliv, Bogema is perhaps the best-known jazz venue in the whole of Crimea. At least it is the only place on the peninsula that Enver Izmaylov, a Crimean Tatar virtuoso guitarist of international fame, finds worthy of his performances. Besides, it is one of Koktebel's better restaurants (mains 60uah to 100uah), with a good selection of Black Sea fish and Russian/European food.

❶ Getting There & Around
Koktebel's bus station is at the far end of vul Desantnikov – the main drag leading to the beach. From here you can catch a bus to Sim-

The Soviet aviation and aerospace industries were born in the hills outside Koktebel, and paragliders still come here to enjoy the thermal uplifts where sea breezes meet the sun-drenched, long mountain ridges and steppes beyond. In the 1920s and '30s, aircraft designers Sergey Korolyov (father of the Soviet space programme), Sergey Ilyushin and Oleg Antonov tested gliders on the 180m tall, 6km long ridge of Mt Klementyeva (Uzun-Syrt in Tatar). Koktebel was initially called Planerskoye because of this (*planer* meaning 'glider' in Russian).

Today there are still paragliding, hang-gliding and speed-flying schools up here, complete with a landing strip, museum, accommodation and competitions. If you speak Russian, stalls in Feodosiya and Koktebel sell paragliding (about 250uah), gliding (350uah to 800uah) and microlight (400uah) flights, or you can contact the paragliding school **Breeze** (☑065 622 4526/3071, 050 598 1311; zhukarin@feo.net.ua; www.breeze.crimea.ua, in Ukranian; ⊘Apr-Nov). The mountain ridge is off the Feodosiya–Koktebel road, signposted полеты.

For flights elsewhere in Crimea with an English-speaking guide, visit www.paragliding-crimea.com.

feropol (27uah, two hours, every 30 minutes), Sudak (11uah, one hour, every 30 minutes), Feodosiya (5uah, 40 minutes, every 30 minutes), or a *marshrutka* to Kurortne (6uah, every 20 minutes).

Feodosiya ФЕОДОСІЯ

☑06562 / POP 72,000

Neighbourhood names like Chumka (Plague) and Quarantine are not exactly romantic, but they hark back to the city's illustrious past. Founded by the Greeks in 6th century BC under its current name, it was rebranded Kaffa by the Genovese who took over the city in 13th century AD, turning it into meeting point for caravans from the Orient and European merchants. Mutual interest in silk and slaves brought together people of all nationalities, notably Armenians, who left a significant imprint on the city.

Kaffa's fortress, still partly intact, protected it from plundering nomad armies, but not the biological weapon used by the Mongols during one of the sieges. They started catapulting bodies of people who died from bubonic plaque, which was devastating their camp. It is believed that the fleeing Genovese subsequently brought the disease to Europe, which led to the worst epidemics in the continent's history.

Imperial Russians built opulent seafacing palazzos that they modestly called *dachas*. Some of them survived the Soviet period and still soar above the myriad of tacky souvenir stands and fast-food joints,

which look like flotsam washed ashore by a recent storm, and seem destined to be swept away by the next one.

⊙ Sights

The centre's tiny axis, vul Galereynaya, abuts the sea, with the promenade beginning on your left. For Sub-Sarkis church and the Genovese Fortress, walk right past the fenced-off port.

Ayvazovsky Gallery   ART MUSEUM
(Галерея Айвазовского; vul Galereynaya 2; adult/student 20/10uah; ⊘9.30am-8pm Thu-Mon, to 1pm Tue) Born in 1817, the most celebrated son of Feodosiya and of its Armenian community, Ivan Ayvazovsky became the official painter of the Russian navy, assigned with recording all of its victories and defeats on canvas. Mesmerised by the sea, he seemed obsessed with cataloguing all its conditions. During his long and happy life Ayvazovsky produced thousands of paintings, which is why you can hardly find an ex-Soviet museum that doesn't own at least a couple of them.

Prospekt Ayvazovskogo   PROMENADE
(Проспект Айвазовского) With the cacophony of tourist agents touting their services through loudspeakers, terrible music, junk-food smells and a train line right on the beach to complete the picture, Feodosiya's seaside promenade is not exactly relaxing. Once it was lined with opulent palazzos. Standing next to each other are **Villa Victoria** (pr Ayavazovskogo 31) and **Villa Milos** (pr Ayavazovskogo 31). But those are

easily outshone by the Ottoman-style **Dacha Stamboli** (pr Ayavazovskogo 47) – an Arabesque fantasy straight out of *1001 Nights* built by a Karaite tobacco merchant.

Sub-Sarkis Church   ARMENIAN CHURCH

(Церковь Суб-Саркис; vul Armyanskaya 1) Small and almost literally down-to-earth, the town's main Armenian church was built in 1363. Its walls are adorned with numerous *khachkar* – stone plaques with crosses marking historic events. Ivan Ayvazovsky got christened and married in this church. His large **tomb** is also here in the garden, almost overshadowing the ancient temple. To get there, walk west along vul Gorkogo past the ornate **Ayavazovsky fountain**, which the painter built for his fellow citizens. The church is hiding behind a small park that will appear on your right.

Genovese Citadel   FORTRESS

(Генуэзская крепость; admission free) Not nearly as spectacular as its Sudak counterpart, and neglected by the authorities, this is still a beautifully melancholic place where you can get away from the crowds and check out several medieval Armenian churches scattered around the premises. The fortress is in the western part of the city known as Quarantine. To reach it, walk to the end of vul Gorkogo and turn left to vul Portovaya.

🛌 Sleeping

Roza Vetrov   GUESTHOUSE $

(Роза ветров; 315 30; fiord06@mail.ru; vul Kuibisheva 28A; r from 250uah; ⊜✳) Cute as a button, this private hotel's most eye-catching feature is its tiny atrium, with slit windows, oleanders, tea roses, a marble floor and a curved staircase. The seven cosy bedrooms and equally snug bathrooms are well cared for and comfortable. But low pipe pressure sometimes makes you abandon the idea of taking a shower.

Hotel Alye Parusa   NEW LUXURY $$$

(Алые Паруса; Scarlet Sails; 295 29; www.a-parusa.com; pr Ayvazovskogo 47B; high season s/d 710/1280uah, winter 380/580uah; ⊜✳≋) Far from the habitual post-Soviet tackiness, this is a nicely designed and professionally run, top-notch hotel with friendly and very attentive staff. The sea view is complemented by that of Dacha Stamboli. There is an excellent bar-restaurant on the rooftop terrace.

U Sestry   MINI-HOTEL $$

(У сестры; 302 35; www.ysestri.narod.ru; vul Russkaya 2; r from 300uah; ✳) Aqua walls and brownish furniture somehow conspire to give this humble, central hotel, which used to be the house of Ayvazovsky' sister, a vaguely art deco feel. Decent bathrooms too.

Hotel Lidiya   HOTEL $$

(Лидия; 309 01, 211 11, 211 12; www.lidiya-hotel.com; vul Zemskaya 13; s/d from 380/610uah; ⊜✳≋) Rub shoulders with visiting Russian celebrities in this upmarket hotel that's still quite affordable for Western tourists. Built in 2001, its rooms are a tiny bit disappointing for the price. But the swimming pool on the 3rd floor (yes, really) is fantastic and the location can't be beaten. The breakfast buffet (17uah for nonguests) is a major plus.

Sunflower   GUESTHOUSE $$

(Подсолнух; 432 881, 050 769 3421; www.lidiya-hotel.com; vul Fedko 59; r from 410uah; ⊜✳) Hotel Lidiya's cheap little sister is lovely in a Spartan sort of Ikea fashion, and there's a kitchen. Only its location is a wee bit inconvenient.

As elsewhere in Ukraine, it makes a lot of sense to rent a flat in Feodosiya, rather than get ripped off by hotels. The incredibly helpful people at **Rentmyflatinfeodosia.com** (097 375 1552, 067 652 4418; www.rentmyflatinfeodosia.com; vul Revolutsionnaya 16/7; r from 400uah; Ⓟ✳) operate three tastefully decorated flats with internet connections and lots of books.

🍴 Eating

Kubdari   GEORGIAN $

(Кубдари; vul Generala Gorbachyova 7; mains 30uah; ☺summer) Two Georgian men in a spotlessly clean kitchen make a spectacular show of baking simply the best *khachapuri* (Georgian cheese pastry), *khinkali* (large meat-filled dumplings) and *kubdari* (similar to calzone) this side of the Black Sea. It's hard to miss their green-coloured kiosk opposite Mechta bar on the busy restaurant row.

Mercury   CRIMEAN TATAR $

(Меркурий; pr Ayvazoskogo 1; mains 20-40uah, pizzas 10-33uah) Behind the Krym Kino Teatr, this popular Tatar restaurant is just as famous for owner Sakine's ability to read your future in the grounds of your Turkish coffee as it is for its excellent cuisine. The *basturma* (pork steak) comes highly recommended and the 1kg 'Kazan kebab' (100uah) will feed four or five people.

SJ-Café
COFFEE $

(vul Galereynaya 12; ⊘8am-midnight) Religious about coffee, this place is a welcome addition to Feodosiya's rather unsophisticated cafe scene.

❶ Information

Kiyavia (☑30 132; www.kiyavia.crimea.ua; ul Voykova 5) Buy your air tickets out of Crimea through this nationwide agency.

Rentmyflatinfeodosia.com (www.rentmy flatinfeodosia.com) This private apartment rental agency also has an informative English website, with detailed museum, restaurant and bar listings.

❶ Getting There & Away

BUS Feodosiya has two bus stations. The main bus station, serving long-distance destinations, is 4km north of the centre. Buses go to/from Simferopol (30uah, 2½ hours, every 30 minutes), Sudak (15uah, 1¾ hours, hourly) and Kerch (24uah, two hours, hourly). A taxi to the bus station should cost around 25uah.

There's a bus station downtown where *marshrutky* and smaller buses leave for nearby resorts such as Koktebel (5uah), the Kara-Dag bio-station (6uah), Ordzhonikidze (4uah) and Zolotoy (2.50uah).

Local bus 2, or indeed any *marshrutka* leaving from just outside the main outlying bus station (same side of the road), will take you into the centre.

TRAIN Rail services are less useful, although in summer there are services to Moscow and Kyiv.

Kerch КЕРЧЬ

☑06561 / POP 151,000

Many people feel grateful when the holiday tsunami, which engulfs the rest of Crimea in summer, throws them on this quiet shore. A decidedly untouristy town of ramshackle low-rise buildings, Kerch is the place to chill out and dream of new fron-

tiers. Looming across a narrow strait, the Russian coast invites for a Eurasian adventure. Unfortunately, only visa-holders can embark on it straight away.

Stuck out on a 100km limb from Feodosiya, Kerch is one of Ukraine's oldest cities. As the ancient Greek colony of Panticapaeum, it was the capital of the Bosporan Kingdom from the 5th to 2nd centuries BC. Nowadays, Kerch is a mecca for archaeologists, who arrive in droves each year, hoping to unearth Greek and Scythian treasures.

◉ Sights

Mithridates Hill
HISTORIC SITE

The first thing to do in Kerch is to take the 432 stairs up the central Mithridates Hill. The view from the summit is brilliant, and on the leeside the ruins of the ancient city of **Panticapaeum** have been revealed in an ongoing archaeological dig.

Back on the central pl Lenina, check out the candy-striped **Church of St John the Baptist**. Dating back to 717, this Byzantine building is officially Ukraine's oldest surviving church.

Adzhimushkay Defence Museum CATACOMB

(tour 40uah; ⊘9am-5pm Tue-Sun) Catacombs in the Kerch suburb of Adzhimushkay (Аджимушкай) have been a source of construction material for the city from time immemorial. Early Christians held their clandestine services here in the 2nd century AD. When the Germans sacked Kerch in May 1942, 10,000 Soviet troops and civilians (many of them Jewish) descended into the catacombs and held them for 170 days until all of them were gassed or captured. You can relive their experience on a tour of this museum, which takes you through the unlit caverns turned by the defenders into barracks, hospitals, classrooms and cemeteries. The tour is in Russian, but the scenery speaks for itself. To get here, catch the hourly bus 4 for the 'Muzey' stop from the bus station.

FROM KERCH TO RUSSIA

Regular ferries (35 minutes) travel from Kerch's **Port Krym** (☑695 88; adult/child 32/16uah, car 176uah) to the Kafkaz Port in Russia's southern Krasnodar region. There are eight services a day in summer, six in winter (see p281 for more details). *Marshrutka* No 1 gets you from Kerch's bus station to the port in about 45 minutes.

For further information on the Russian side of the border, head to shop.lonelyplanet .com to purchase a downloadable PDF of the Russian Caucasus chapter from Lonely Planet's *Russia* guide.

Tsarsky Kurgan BURIAL MOUND
(admission 10uah; ☺9.30am-6pm Tue-Sun) Eight hundred metres from the Adzhimushkay Defence Museum, there is a monument from a completely different epoch. This empty, 4th-century-BC burial mound is thought to be the grave of a Bosporan king. Its exterior is Scythian, but its symmetrical interior was built by the Greeks. The grass-covered mound surrounded by electric pylons is visible from the bus stop. Just walk straight in that direction along the tarmac road until you find a fairly anatomical slit in the hill – when you see it, you'll know what we mean! Once inside, look out for small crosses and the name *Kosmae* left on the walls by the 2nd-century AD Christians.

Melek-Chesmensky Kurgan BURIAL MOUND
(Мелек-Чесмеский Курган; bus station; admission 5uah; ☺10.30am-6pm Tue-Sat) Hardly any bus station in the world can boast a Scythian burial mound on the premises, but there is one in Kerch. Much smaller than Tsarsky Kurgan, it was the grave of a small boy, thought to be a Bosporan prince.

🛏 Sleeping & Eating

Hotel Meridian RENOVATED SOVIET $
(Меридиан; ☎615 07; avers@kerch.com.ua; vul Marata 9, cnr Sverdlova; d from 240uah) Although far from perfect, this is easily the best choice for most Westerners. It's a hard-to-miss high-rise not too far from the centre with plenty of modern, clean and well-priced rooms. There's also a good supermarket in the same building. Take *marshrutka* 3, 5, 6, 19 or 20 to the Bosforsky stop.

Seasons PIZZA $
(☎920 89; vul Lenina 43; pizzas 30-55uah; ☺10am-11pm) Acquaint yourself with one of Kerch's main eating avenues in this stylish pizzeria and cocktail bar. If an absinthe mojito is not your cup of booze, they make great iced tea and milkshakes.

Penguin Brewery BEER RESTAURANT $$
(Пивоварня Пингвин; vul Lenina 32; mains 40-70uah; ☺10am-2am) Serious beer lovers will have to travel all the way to Kerch to find this rare breed – a Crimean micro-brewery. Three kinds of local brew – lager, red and brown ale – are complemented with excellent food, from gourmet burgers and Central European dishes, such as goose fillet with apples, to the grilled *barabulya* and boiled crayfish – a quintessential Russian beer snack.

Chainy Dom TEA SHOP $
(Чайный дом; vul Teatralnaya 42; tea 15-25uah; ☺10am-10pm Tue-Sun) This charming tearoom in another nice stretch of restaurants is good for beverages, hookah pipes and snacks such as fruit salads and *bliny*.

ℹ Getting There & Around

BUS The most useful bus connections are to Feodosiya (25uah, two hours, hourly), Sudak (40uah, 3½ hours, two daily), Yalta (70uah, six hours, five daily) and Simferopol (52uah, 4¾ hours, hourly). Five buses a day pass on the way to Krasnodar (95uah, 8½ hours), across the strait in Russia.

LOCAL TRANSPORT *Marshrutka* 5 is the most frequent of many services between the bus station and the centre, leaving whenever full. *Marshrutka* 16 is just one of several routes between the bus and train stations.

TRAIN Kerch's small train station is a lot quieter than its bus station, with services including a snail-like overnight train to Simferopol (67uah, eight hours) and trains to Dzhankoy (61uah, six hours, four daily), from where you can change for Simferopol. Trains also head to Moscow (980uah, 28 hours, every second day) and Kyiv (138uah, 23 hours, daily).

Eastern Ukraine
Східна Україна

POP 19.6 MILLION

Why Go?

East of the Dnipro, Ukraine starts blending into Russia. It is the land of Surzhyk – a hybrid dialect, finetuned by its speakers to make it sound more Russian or more Ukrainian, depending on the situation. This part of Ukraine is often dismissed as 'not Ukrainian enough' compared to the folkloric West, but from the economic and demographic point of view it is the country's core. Most political heavyweights, including both leaders of the Orange Revolution, hail from here. So do major oligarchs. East Ukraine might be full of fuming industrial giants, but it also contains places that are key to understanding Ukraine, such as Zaporizhzhya Sich, a few underrated beauty spots and some unspoiled, quintessentially Ukrainian countryside. Done all that? How about playing football in a salt mine, 300m below surface? If only to warm up for Euro 2012, hosted by Donetsk and Kharkiv.

Best Places to Eat

» Stargorod (p216)
» Marrakesh (p221)
» Yuzovskaya Pivovarnya (p221)
» Reporter (p226)
» Sto Dorih (p211)

Best Places to Stay

» Sokolyny Khutir (p209)
» Liverpool Art Hotel (p220)
» Palazzo Hotel (p210)
» Hotel Caspian (p226)
» Hotel Cosmopolit (p215)

When to Go?
Kharkiv

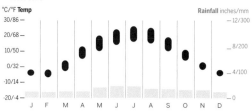

May All the country is aflame with blooming lilacs and fruit trees.

July Weather is mild in the northeastern countryside. Pumpkins ripen and sunflowers bloom.

September Catch modern Ukrainian theatre and dance at Zaporizhzhya's Golden Khortitsa festival.

Eastern Ukraine Highlights

1 Play football in the **Soledar salt mine** (p224), 300m underground

2 Visit a pretty cave monastery burrowed into dazzling chalk cliff in **Sviatohirsk** (p223)

3 Watch Shakhtar's domestic games and the Euro 2012 semi-final at the sparkling new **Donbass arena** (p219)

4 Learn all you need to know about Cossacks on **Khortytsya Island** (p228) in Zaporizhzhya

5 Set off to explore aristocratic estates from your Cossack hut in **Trostyanets** or **Kachanivka** (p209)

6 Check Ukraine's latest musical trends in **Kharkiv's clubs** (p218)

7 Sleep, eat and dance at the Beatles-themed alternative universe of **Liverpool** (p222) in Donetsk

8 Play Polovets Dances on your iPod while exploring Prince Igor's fiefdom in **Novhorod-Siversky** (p208)

9 Procure a pair of jeans and a bowl of Vietnamese noodles at **Barabashova Market** (p215) in Kharkiv

Chernihiv ЧЕРНІГІВ

☏ 0462 / POP 305,000

A Kyivan Rus heavyweight, Chernihiv has never been as prominent since, which is why it retains many early medieval monuments and exudes lots of provincial charm. Apart from observing a tight cluster of churches on a green bluff in the city's historical core, there is the sleepy Desna River to swim or kayak in and a couple of nice places to eat or have a glass of locally brewed beer. Chernihiv makes a relaxing, rather than exciting, retreat from Kyiv's madness and provides a good base for exploring the beautiful countryside and historical sights of northeast Polissya.

◎ Sights

Ploshcha Krasna   SQUARE

Life in Chernihiv revolves around pl Krasna (Red Square). As with its Moscow namesake, there is nothing remotely left wing in the word, which simply meant 'beautiful' in old Slavonic. In the park extending southeast of the square along vul Shevchenko is the **St Paraskevy Pyatnytsi Church**, named after the patroness of the large outdoor market that once occupied pl Krasna. Despite its sturdy, fortress-like appearance, only about one-third of the church survived WWII. With its imposing brick walls and single cupola, it reflects the style popular when it was built in the 12th century – a style epitomised by the Nereditsa Church in Novgorod.

Dytynets   MEDIEVAL FORTRESS

From pl Chervona it's a three-minute walk southeast along pr Myru to the historic core, known as Dytynets ('citadel' in old Russian) or simply 'Val' (ramparts). Today it's a leafy park dotted with domed churches overlooking the Desna River. The 12th-century **Boryso-Hlibsky Cathedral** (admission 6uah, ⊗9am-6pm) is in the same short, squat style as the Pareskevy Pyatnytsi Church. It's worth visiting for the stunning silver **Royal Doors**, commissioned by the famous Cossack leader Ivan Mazepa. Those are very well-travelled doors – they appeared to be on holiday in New York's Ukrainian museum when we turned up!

The gorgeous building next to it is the 18th-century **collegium** (admission 9uah, ⊗9am-6pm), built in a style known as Ukrainian baroque. It houses an interesting exhibition of primitivist village icons.

Nearby is the **Spaso-Preobrazhensky Cathedral** (Transfiguration of the Saviour; 1017), with its two distinctive missile-like corner bell towers. Within its dark interior are the tombs of several members of the Kyivan Rus royalty, including the younger brother of Yaroslav the Wise. Lining the southwestern edge of the Val is a row of 18th-century **cannons**, from where you get a prime view of the five sparkling golden domes of **St Catherine's Church** in the immediate foreground. This is the church you see from several kilometres away if you drive into town from Kyiv.

Antoniy Caves, Illynsky Church & Trinity Monastery   CAVE MONASTERY

About 2km southwest of St Catherine's Church you'll spot the 58m bell tower of the **Troyitsko-Illynsky Monastery** (Trinity Monastery). The **Antoniy Caves**, Chernihiv's answer to Kyiv's Kyevo-Pecherska Lavra, lurk beneath the ground a short walk north of this monastery, under the early 11th-century **Illinsky Church** (admission church & caves 6uah; ⊗9am-5pm Sat-Thu, 9am-4pm Fri). The caves consist of 315m of passageways, galleries and chapels constructed from the 11th to 13th centuries. These are very different from those in Kyiv in that they lack both dead mummies and, for the most part, live tourists. The conditions here were too cold and humid to support mummification. Instead, the bones of monks killed during the Mongol invasion are preserved in a windowed sarcophagus; touching the sarcophagus is considered good luck. The cave's benefactor and namesake, St Antoniy of Pechersk, also helped burrow the Lavra caves.

While you're out here, it's worth checking out the monastery and climbing the **bell tower** (admission 2uah; ⊗10am-7.30pm), which looks right down on the 17th-century **Trinity Church**, an important pilgrimage site that is often mobbed with worshippers.

It's about a 3km walk to the monastery from the Dytynets, or you can jump on trolleybus 8. To get to Illynsky Church get off at the stop before the bell tower and follow the dirt path downhill through the park across the street from the bus stop.

☞ Tours

Dima of the **Centre for Green Tourism** (☎097 284 8068, 063 262 4894; www.explore chernigov.narod.ru; 2/3-day canoe trip per group of four 400/550uah) runs canoe trips on the Desna with overnight homestays or camping in rural villages. A good route is the three-day trip from Novhorod-Siversky to Chernihiv.

Prydesnyasky Hotel has an efficient **travel agency** (☎954 828, 093 794 8976; www.chernigivhotel.com.ua; city tour per person 180uah) running English-language tours of the city and the region.

⛏ Sleeping

Most people do Chernihiv as a day trip from Kyiv, but there are plenty of places to lay your head should you wish.

Sloviansky RENOVATED SOVIET **$$**
(☑698 344; pr Myra 33; s/d 290/490uah; ✸)
Having preserved some of the provincial
Soviet grandeur in the carpeted corridors,
Sloviansky, commonly known under its old
name 'Ukraina', offers modern well-priced
rooms with bedcovers that look like Persian
rugs.

Prydesnyasky RENOVATED SOVIET **$**
(☑954 802; www.chernigivhotel.com.ua; vul
Shevchenko 99a; standard s/d 180/300uah, su-
perior 240/360uah) This quiet option is locat-
ed slightly northeast of the centre. Rooms
are moderately renovated Soviet, but not
too bad. A three-minute walk from here
is a cluster of restaurants and some primi-
tive beach facilities on the Desna River. To
get here take any bus heading down vul
Shevchenko from the corner of pr Myru.

For some rural flavour call Sergei and
Tanya, a hospitable couple who run a log
cabin-style **B&B** (☑933 914, 050 352 2968,
050 352 2968; andrlakes.org.ua; full board cabins
per day from 250uah) on a lake in the ancient
village of Andriyivka, about 25km south-
west of Chernihiv.

✖ Eating & Drinking

Sharlotka Шарлотка COFFEEHOUSE **$**
(pr Myru 21; ◷8am-10pm) Named after an
apple cake that it serves, Sharlotka attracts
cultured types and local foreigners. There is
a small book exchange, albeit without Eng-
lish titles. In 2010, they were also selling a
CD titled *Hear Che* with a nice selection of
songs by local bands. Good for breakfasts
and lunches.

Falvarek CENTRAL EUROPEAN **$**
(Фальварек; pr Myru 20; mains 30-50uah; ☎) A
vaguely Central European cellar pub with
chatty waiters who like to show their pro-
ficiency in foreign languages (mostly Ger-
man). Meat in all shapes dominates the
menu.

Senator GRILL & BEER **$**
(Сенатор; vul Magistratska; dishes 30-50uah)
Shashlyks and steaks are great in this Wild
West–themed restaurant on pl Krasna, but
they take a long time to arrive.

❶ Getting There & Around

BUS The best way here from Kyiv is on a
marshrutka (fixed-price minibus) from Lisova
metro station (30uah, 13 hours, every 15 min-
utes until mid-evening), which will drop you off
anywhere in Chernihiv centre. The departure
point to return to Kyiv is around the corner from

the Hotel Slovyansky on pr Pobedy. Buses for
Novhorod-Siversky leave hourly from the central
bus station (18uah, 3½ hours), located near
the train station. One bus daily goes to Poltava
(85uah, nine hours).

LOCAL TRANSPORT The train and bus sta-
tions are right next to each other 2km west of
pl Krasna, on pl Vokzalna. Take trolleybus 3 or
11, or just about any *marshrutka* to the 'Hotel
Ukraina' stop in the centre.

TRAIN The train station comes in handy if you
are heading to Belarus, with five daily trains to
Gomel (from 47uah, three hours) and two trains
daily to Minsk (370uah, eight hours).

Novhorod-Siversky
Новгород-Сіверський
☑0462 / POP 305,000
Life in this sleepy town, which hides in the
deep forest in Ukraine's extreme north,
may seem uneventful, but back in the Kyi-
van Rus times it was a happening place. It
is from here that Prince Igor set out on his
ill-fated expedition against the Polovtsy,
which became immortalised in *The Tale
of Igor's Campaign,* the 12th-century epic
later made into an opera by Alexander
Borodin.

Dating back to Igor's era (but rebuilt sev-
eral times since then) is the idyllic **Spaso-
Preobrazhensky Monastery** (Transfigura-
tion of the Saviour; admission free; ◷sunrise-
sunset), a complex of wood-shingled build-
ings and golden-domed churches perched
over the leafy banks of the Desna River.

Strolling around the quiet grounds pick-
ing fruit off the monastery trees, you'll
definitely feel like you're in another era. A
wooden walkway atop the monastery fence
provides prime views of the forested Desna
valley, and it's an easy walk down to the
river bank should you care for a swim or a
picnic. On the monastery grounds there's a
museum (admission 3uah; ◷9am-6pm) dedi-
cated to Igor.

The town's history can be safely fast-
forwarded from Kyivan Rus times to 2004,
when president Kuchma, who hails from a
local village, hosted Putin and Lukashenko
at a trilateral summit. This resulted in sev-
eral significant improvements. One came
in the shape of the top-end **Hotel Slovy-
ansky** (☑046 583 1801; vul Lunacharskoho 2;
r from 400uah; ℗✸), which is a remarkable
deal considering what you get – four-star
comfort, albeit without the four-star ser-
vice. Budget travellers can still stay in the

COSSACK RETREAT

East of Chernihiv, lies the land of sunflowers, haystacks and particularly fat pumpkins. Before the Russian takeover, local Cossacks led double lives, keeping their households here, while dashing off to the all-male republic of Sich (p228) every now and then. In the imperial period, aristocrats divided the land into vast estates, complete with grand mansion houses and landscaped parks. Some of these have survived the Russian revolution, and an embryonic rural tourism industry is now popping up around them. Travelling in these parts might be tough without basic Ukrainian/Russian.

The flagship operation here is **Sokolyny Khutir** (☑0463 324 134, 067 956 6751; www.hutir.net; vul Naberezhnaya 68, Petrushivka; bed per person from 85uah; ☻Thu-Sun), set on a grassy bluff above a placid lake, walking distance from **Kachanivka Palace** (admission 3uah), which belonged to the prominent Tarnovsky family. Dressed in full Cossack gear and sporting a traditional *chub* – a long ponytail growing from the front part of the otherwise shaven head – ex-paratrooper Mykola Cherep (his surname translates as 'skull') runs the show, and what a show it is! There is an equestrian Cossack theatre, a Cossack sailboat on the lake and a shooting range for bows, arbalest, and muskets. Cherep is also dead serious about *martial hopak* (a much-ridiculed Ukrainian version of Brazilian capoeira), which he and his son are happy to demonstrate and teach. Guests are treated to excellent Ukrainian food (150uah per day) and put up in traditional hay-thatched *khaty*. Horse-carriage and bicycle tours of nearby sights are on offer.

Another ex-paratrooper Rostyslav Malyarenko runs **Myslyvska Palanka** (☑097 384 5205; www.palanka.com.ua; vul Asaulyuka 6, Trostyanets; r with full board per person from 120uah), a modest one-*khata* operation in the village of Trostyanets, near the beautifully landscaped **Trostyanets Dendropark**. This once surrounded the palace, which belonged to the family of Ivan Skoropadsky, Ukraine's last *hetman*. Malyarenko only accepts groups of four and more people booking for at least two nights. Individual travellers are outsourced to fellow villagers, who are not so choosy and give them an even warmer welcome in their homes. Opt for Yury, the moustachioed beekeeper, who looks like his colleague Panko from Nikolai Gogol's *Evenings on a Farm Near Dikanka*.

There is one daily bus to Trostyanets from Kyiv's Darnitsa bus station and two buses daily from Chernihiv. For Sokolyny Khutir get off at Parafiivka and take a taxi (20uah, 15 minutes) or arrange a pickup. Chernihiv buses stop by the train station at Nizhin, on the busy Kyiv–Shostka railway line. This allows you to build a circuit itinerary including Novhorod-Siversky.

good old **Pasvyrda Hotel** (☑046 582 1225; vul Karla Marksa 3; r from 100uah) located in the city centre.

The other improvement was a railway line with new trains that look space-age by Ukrainian *elektrychka* standards, though it is a *Star Trek* kind of space age. Three such trains link Novhorod-Siversky to Shostka (6uah, one hour) on the main line, from where there are numerous trains for Kyiv.

Buses for Chernihiv (18uah, 3½ hours) depart hourly from the nearby bus station. Most convenient is the Kyiv–Yatsevo luxury bus that leaves Kyiv at 7am and passes both Chernihiv and Novhorod-Siversky before heading towards Bryansk in Russia. It stops in Novhorod-Siversky at 15.25 on the way back.

Poltava ПОЛТАВА

POP 318,000

Quaint and leafy Poltava is all about one particular turning point in history. Had Russian Tsar Peter I lost the decisive battle on the town's outskirts in 1709, he wouldn't have become Peter the Great and Ukraine could have celebrated the 300th anniversary of its independence in 2009. But the Russians defeated a joint Swedish and Cossack force, marking this event a century later by rebuilding the city's centre so that it looked like a mini St Petersburg. This is a fairly odd sight, considering that Poltava is surrounded by quintessentially Ukrainian countryside, which nurtured the talent of writer Nikolai Gogol and served as the scene for many of his stories. Besides, Poltava became the centre of Ukrainian cultural renaissance in the 19th century, as if avenging the lost battle.

☉ Sights

Korpusny Park   PARK
The focal point is the circular Korpusny Park, laid out in the early 19th century in an attempt to emulate the grand planning ideals of St Petersburg. Eight streets radiate off the plaza, and in its centre is the **Iron Column of Glory**, topped by a golden eagle. Southeast of Korpusny Park, the city's main pedestrian drag – vul Zhovtneva (better known under its Russian name, Oktyabrskaya) – leads down to leafy Zhovtnevy Park.

Poltava Regional Museum   MUSEUM
(admission 2uah; ⊙9am-5pm Thu-Mon) Located on the southeast edge of Zhovtnevy Park, the museum exhibits random archaeological and cultural artefacts, its collection almost overshadowed by its gorgeous art nouveau building (1903), adorned with the ceramic crests of each district capital in the Poltava oblast.

Maydan Soborny   SQUARE
Further down, vul Zhovtneva terminates on a bluff at Cathedral Sq, the prettiest little spot in Poltava, with sweeping views of Khrestovozdvyzhensky Monastery across the valley to the northeast. The square is dominated by the newly rebuilt **Uspenska Church**. A footpath leading to the **Friendship Rotunda** on the edge of the bluff is flanked by two quirky statues, namely a *halushky* monument on the left (*halushky* are the beloved local dumplings) and a monument to Igor Svyatoslavych on the right.

Kotlyarevsky Museum   MUSEUM
(admission 5uah; ⊙10am-6pm Tue-Sun) Near madan Soborny, surrounded by a lovely flower garden, this is the lovingly restored former home of Ivan Kotlyarevsky (1739–1838), one of the fathers of Ukrainian literature. The museum provides a glimpse into traditional Ukrainian life in the early 19th century.

Spaska Church   CHURCH
A block northwest of maydan Soborny up vul Parizskoyi Komuny is the quaint wooden Spaska Church (1705), with its newly rebuilt bell tower. It's faced by an odd monument to Tsar Peter I (Peter the Great) across the street on vul Parizskoyi Komuny.

Khrestovozdvyzhensky Monastery   MONASTERY
About 3km east of Korpusny Park is the early 18th-century Khrestovozdvyzhensky Monastery (Elevation of the Cross). The main cathedral is one of only two in the country with seven cupolas, rather than five (the other is St Michael's Monastery in Kyiv). The monastery is a long (30-minute), straight walk east on vul Radyanska (Sovetskaya) from Korpusny Park.

Poltava Battlefield   BATTLEFIELD
The famous battle was fought over a large area around what's now vul Zinkivska, about 7km north of the centre. The best starting point is the **Poltava Battle Museum** (Shvedska mohyla 32; admission 6uah; English-language excursion 30uah; ⊙10am-5pm, box office to 4.20pm) by the Peter I statue. Inside are displays relating to the battle, including maps, paintings and Peter I's original uniform. English signs that appeared during president Yushchenko's term curiously refrain from mentioning Russia, instead using the term 'Moscow Realm'. Aside from the museum, the battlefield contains numerous monuments and various redoubts of the old fortress, many of which have been restored.

Buses 5 and 37 head here from vul Zinkivska near Avtovokzal 3. The museum stands next to Shvedska Mohyla station, one stop away from Poltava's Kyivska Station. A taxi should cost 30uah one way from the centre.

🛏 Sleeping
Breakfast costs extra in the following establishments unless otherwise noted.

Palazzo Hotel   NEW LUXURY **$$**
(☎0532-611 205; www.palazzo.com.ua; vul Gogolya 33; s/d from 450/570uah; P🚗❄🖥🛜) This is the place for people travelling on a medium-range budget to enjoy four-star luxury (well, almost). The attractive king-sized beds have firm mattresses that will have your back feeling like butter after a lengthy snooze. That and the suave, tawny toned design almost make up for the small size of the allegedly smoke-free rooms. Don't go for the bed-and-breakfast option – you essentially commit yourself to spending 70uah for breakfast, which you will still have to order from the menu.

Kyiv Hotel
RENOVATED SOVIET $

(☎0532-224 286; vul Sinna 2/49; budget r 140-220uah; standard s/d 310/460uah) This former ugly duckling has received a complete facelift and now touts its stylishly 'remonted' rooms with blinding blonde-wood floors and polished bathroom fixtures. You could swaddle a newborn in the luxurious towels. Unrenovated rooms with shared bathrooms are Soviet, but not too bad either.

Hotel Turyst
SOVIET-STYLED $

(☎0532-220 921; vul Myru 2; www.tourist. velton.ua; budget s/d 90/160uah, renovated 180/300uah) Some 500m west of the Pivdenniy Vokzal, across the bridge and to the left, this incredible Soviet hulk is unappetising and terribly located, but relatively friendly on the wallet.

✗ Eating & Drinking

Be sure to sample the local delicacy, *halushky* – unfilled dumplings with various rich toppings. The Hotel Palazzo's restaurant does a good rendition.

Sto Dorih
BEER RESTAURANT $

(Hundred Roads; vul Parizkoy Komuny 18; beer from 6uah; mains 10-20uah; ☺10am-10pm) An upmarket version of Poltavske Pivo, this new place has been an instant success, so it is already not so easy to get a table on the summer terrace. Out of 10 kinds of local brew on offer Rizke Firmove is our favourite. It goes really with what passes for Georgian *suluguni* cheese on the menu, but is, in fact, Armenian *chechil* cheese. The place doubles as a musical venue, with rock bands playing during weekends.

Zefir
UKRAINIAN/RUSSIAN $$

(vul Zhovtneva 24; mains 40-80uah;☎) With limited success, Zefir is trying to evoke the ambience of imperial-period Poltava. It is nonetheless a good place to taste Poltava *halushky* and *varenyky*. The service is very attentive.

Poltavske Pivo
OUTDOOR PUB

(vul Zhovtneva; ☺8am-10pm) Beer and nothing but beer. This place is really just a kiosk with outdoor seats and a kindly old man pumping four kinds of the fresh local brew, some of the best in Ukraine.

Also recommended:

Celentano
PIZZA $

(vul Lenina 16) An outlet of the nationwide pizza chain is right in the centre.

Kofein
COFFEEHOUSE $

(vul Kotlyarevskoho 1/27) The Poltava branch of the African-themed coffee chain is also in the centre.

Shopping

Ukrainian Souvenirs
SOUVENIRS

(vul Komsomolska 19; www.vushuvanka.pl.ua/ en_main.php) Beautifully embroidered traditional shirts, blouses and tablecloths are on display in this excellent souvenir shop. Items on sale are handmade by villagers from the Poltava region.

❶ Information

Mikhail Ishchenko (☎067 401 2069, 097 695 0452; m.ishchenko@mail.ru; walking/car tours per hr €20/25) A popular private English-speaking guide doing tours of Poltava and the Gogol circuit.

Rentcars.poltava.ua (☎0532-690 888, 067 418 6818; www.rentcars.poltava.ua; vul Polovka 105) Try them if you need a car for the Gogol circuit.

Ukrtelecom (vul Kuybysheva 5; per hr 5.6uah; ☺8am-11pm) Internet access right off Korpusny Park.

Vilmat (☎0532-596 950/960, 096 235 4499; www.travel.poltava.ua; vul Rozy Lyuksemburg 63; tours per hr €10-17) Tours of Poltava battlefield and the Gogol circuit. It can also organise your stay in village houses in Dikanka (60uah to 100uah per night) and elsewhere in the region.

❶ Getting There & Around

BUS Buses go pretty much everywhere from distant **Avtovokzal 1** (Bus station 1, vul Velikotyrnivska), about 7km east of the centre reached by trolleybus 6, 7 and 8. The most useful are to Myrhorod (7uah, 1½ hours, hourly), Kharkiv (50uah, 2½ to three hours, eight daily) and Dnipropetrovsk (15uah, three to four hours, eight daily).

For the Gogol circuit, however, more convenient is **Avtovokzal 3** (Bus station No 3, vul Zhinkinvska 6b), just outside Kyivsky shopping mall and close to Kyivsky train station. Dikanka buses leave hourly (6uah). For Hoholeve take the Shishaki bus (every two to three hours, 19uah).

TRAIN Most services stop at Pivdenniy Vokzal, including the slow night trains to Kyiv (110uah, five hours, two nightly), Kharkiv (63uah, two to three hours, at least 11 daily) and Odesa (137uah, 13 hours, daily). To get to the centre from Pivdenniy Vokzal, take trolleybus 1, 2, 4, 6 or 11.

Crucially, however, the two daily Kyiv–Kharkiv express trains (Kyiv 58uah, three hours; Kharkiv 62uah, two hours) stop only at **Kyivska station**

THE GOGOL CIRCUIT

North of Poltava lies Gogol-land: textbook Ukrainian countryside in which lived writer Nikolai Gogol (1809–52) – who authored *Dead Souls* and *The Nose* – and which he populated with his characters. Witty, humorous, imaginative and very laidback, locals still have very much in common with Gogol's contemporaries.

Travelling with them in overcrowded buses is part of the fun if you are doing the circuit of Gogol-related sites. However, this method is exhausting and time-consuming – you'll need at least two days to see everything. One day is probably enough if you rent a car. All crucial turns are marked with English-language signs with the writer's trademark long-nosed profile. For Gogol Circuit tours and accommodation in local villages see p211.

To fully appreciate the trip, you may procure Gogol's *Evenings on a Farm near Dikanka* – a collection of funny and surreal stories inspired by the customs and superstitions of local villagers.

Dikanka

In *Evenings on a Farm near Dikanka*, the red-haired beekeeper Panko starts narrating his macabre tales to a group of eager listeners whiling away a summer evening at a farm near this large village, 30km north of Poltava. Once in the centre, look out for signs pointing to **Troitska church**. If we are to believe Gogol, its frescos were authored by the local smith Vakula, who underwent a hair-raising trial while guarding a coffin of a beautiful witch inside this church. Troitska church is tucked in a small lane diagonally across the square from the **Regional Museum** (vul Lenina 68; admission 4uah).

Opishne

Not directly related to Gogol, this potters' village another 20km north of Dikanka has an excellent interactive **Museum-Preserve of Ukrainian Pottery** (vul Partizanska 102; www.opishne-museum.narod.ru; admission 17uah). A pottery class is included in the price and you can buy some great souvenirs here. From Opishne, road P42 goes west towards Velyki Sorochyntsi and Myrhorod.

Hoholeve

Away from the main roads and reachable from Poltava via Dikanka or from Myrhorod/Velyki Sorochyntsi via Shishaki, Gogol's family estate is surrounded by a tranquil park with a pond, and houses a lovingly curated, old-fashioned **museum** (admission 10uah; 8.30am-4.30pm Tue-Sun).

Velyki Sorochyntsi

This sleepy village comes to life in August during the annual **Sorochynska farmers' fair** masterfully described by Gogol in *Evenings on a Farm near Dikanka*. The writer himself was born here in 1809. Outside the fair period, the main sight is the **Spaso-Preobrazhenska Church**, with its unique seven-tier wooden iconostasis. Frozen in time, the local **regional museum** (vul Hoholya 28, admission 2uah) could easily be rebranded as a Soviet-era village museum.

Myrhorod

When Gogol decided to publish a sequel to *Evenings on a Farm near Dikanka*, he simply called the new story collection after this historic town. Belatedly reacting to the writer's satirical ode to the giant Myrhorod puddle that used to occupy most of the central square, the local authorities transformed it into a lovely pond surrounded by bronze figures of Gogol's characters. Today the town is centred on the Soviet-era **Myrhorod Spa Resort**. It is a nice park area in which to walk or swim in the Khorol River. Myrhorod is a major station on the Kyiv–Poltava railway, with frequent services in both directions.

(Stepana Kondratenka 12). Almost all the transport from this train station heads into town. Just check by asking '*do tsentra?*' Trolleybus 1 goes through the centre on the route between Kyivsky and Pivdenniy train stations.

Kharkiv ХАРКІВ

♪ 057 / POP 1.45 MILLION

Kharkiv (or Kharkov in Russian) is one of those ex-Soviet cities that have much to say about themselves, but fairly little to show. Wars and Soviet development reduced its historical centre, boasting some pretty fin de siècle buildings, to a narrow triangle between vul Sumska and Pushkinska. The rest is Soviet monumentalism in all its glory – a delight for architecture buffs, but hardly exciting for the uninitiated.

In the 1920s, Kharkiv was the seat of the Ukrainian Soviet government, which orchestrated a short-lived renaissance of Ukrainian culture and language. But Stalin accused its members of nationalism and launched purges that eventually led to Holodomor (Ukrainian famine).

Nowadays, it is the city of Russian-speaking intelligentsia – scientists and engineers who turned Kharkiv into the brain centre of the Soviet defence industry in the 1960s. Their children, however, were more into rock and alternative music, setting up one of the liveliest scenes in the ex-USSR.

◉ Sights

Ploshcha Svobody   SQUARE
(Ⓜ Derzhprom) Locals claim that this huge square is the second-largest in the world after Beijing's Tiananmen Square. Whatever, at 750m long it's indisputably huge and is certainly Kharkiv's most unique sight.

Planned as an ensemble of Ukrainian government buildings when Kharkiv was the republican capital, it was built between 1925 and 1935. The late-1920s **Derzhprom** (Держпром; House of State Industry) at its western end was the first Soviet skyscraper, a geometric series of concrete and glass blocks and bridges. On the southern side of the square is the **university** (early 1930s), formerly the House of Planning, which displays classic Soviet aesthetics. **Lenin** still proudly stands in the midst of it all, his hand outstretched across the vast open space.

Ploshcha Konstytutsiyi   NEIGHBOURHOOD
(Ⓜ Istorychny Muzey) If you are looking for a meeting point in Kharkiv, nothing beats the spot under the **giant thermometer** that adorns Istorychny metro exit to pl Konstytutsiyi. Just west of the square, the gleaming domes of the **Pokrovsky Monastery** (Intercession of the Virgin) are visible from miles away. The predictably peaceful grounds (enter from pl Konstytutsiyi) have two attractive churches. The smaller and more important of the two is the blue, three-domed **Pokrovska Church** (Покровська церква; 1689). As in all Orthodox churches, the altar is under the east-pointing dome, and there's another altar hidden in the basement, which the attendant may show you if you ask. The church is almost always open for services. The yellow church next to it is the **Ozeyansky Church** (Озеяньська церква).

Back on the square, you can't miss the large granite **sculptural ensemble** commemorating Kharkiv's designation as the first capital of Soviet Ukraine on 24 December 1917. Tongue-in-cheek Kharkivites nicknamed it 'five men carrying a fridge' – the resemblance is far from passing. Nearby are several anti-aircraft guns and tanks, including a **British WWI tank** left from the Russian Civil War. These are associated with the **Kharkiv History Museum** (Харківський історичний музей; pl Konstytutsiyi; admission 8uah; ⊙10am-5pm Tue-Sun; Ⓜ Istorychny Muzey), which occupies the big red-brick building that dominates the square. This has an OK guns exhibit for WWII buffs, but can otherwise be skipped.

Shevchenko Park   PARK
(Ⓜ Universytet) Central Shevchenko Park, just south of pl Svobody, is a great place to observe Kharkivites in their element – or win a stuffed animal in one of the myriad arcade games. From the Lenin statue it's a pleasant walk through the park to the **statue of Taras Shevchenko** (Пам'ятник Шевченку; vul Sumska; Ⓜ Universytet), surrounded by 16 peasants, Cossacks and other Ukrainians representing the national history.

Kharkiv Art Museum   MUSEUM
(Харківський Художній музей; permanent collection vul Radnarkomivska 11, exhibit hall vul Radnarkomivska 9; admission per bldg 2uah; ⊙10am-6pm Wed-Sun, to 4.30pm Mon; Ⓜ Arkhitektora Beketova) Kharkiv's most famous museum owns one of many versions of Ilya Repin's *Zaporizhsky Cossacks Writing a Letter to the Turkish Sultan,* which is found in a room full of Repin paintings in

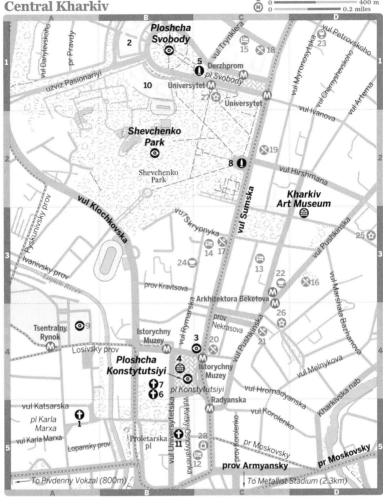

the museum's permanent collection. The entire collection of romantic paintings here is of a high standard for Ukraine, but the neighbouring exhibit hall is hit-or-miss. The museum also curates the little-known Parkhomivka History & Arts Museum (see p217).

Uspensky Cathedral　　　　CATHEDRAL
(Успенський собор; Assumption Cathedral; vul Universytetskaya; MRadyanska) South of the square is this cathedral with its landmark 19th-century bell tower (89.5m tall). This church is now used only as a concert hall; ask your hotel about tickets.

Blahoveshchensky Cathedral　　CATHEDRAL
(Благовещенський собор; pl Karla Marksa; MTsentralny Rynok) The park across the street from Uspensky Cathedral offers the best vantage point of the striking red-and-cream striped cathedral down in the valley, built 1881–1901. Based on Istanbul's Hagia Sophia, it has a beautifully proportioned bell tower resembling a stick of candy.

Metallist　　　　STADIUM
(tickets 10-100uah; MSportyvna) Ready to host the Euro Cup in 2012, the shiny new Metallist arena is home to the namesake team – one of the best in Ukraine. Tickets are sold

in the red neoclassical building with a statue of an athlete on the top. Inside the stadium, there is a shop stocked with T-shirts, scarfs and caps in Metallist's green and yellow colours. The stadium looms all over the place as you come out of the metro.

Tsentralny Rynok　　　　　MARKET
(Центральний ринок; Central Market, also called Blahoveshchensky Rynok; vul Engelsa 33; ⓂTsentralny Rynok) This is well worth a browse for its eclectic collection of everything from fur *shapky* (hats) to vegetables and used car parts.

Barabashova Market　　　　MARKET
(www.barabashka.com; ⓂAkademika Barabashova) For the ultimate post-Soviet bazaar experience, cheap jeans and Vietnamese food, head to this market, which rivals the 7km market in Odesa for the 'biggest in Europe' title. It's really a mind-bogglingly huge affair, run by Africans and Vietnamese who sell clothes and all sorts of junk.

🛏 Sleeping

Preparing for Euro 2012, several large hotels were being renovated when we visited. Look out for the new-old arrivals on Kharkiv's hotel scene, particularly the once popular Hotel Kyivsky.

Hotel Cosmopolit　　NEW LUXURY **$$$**
(☏754 4777; www.cosmopolit-hotel.com; vul Akademika Proskury 1; r from 880uah; ❄❋@) This sets the standard for contemporary design in Kharkiv, with flat-screen TVs and loads of extras like plush robes and 24-hour room service. The theme is Italian, and breakfast in swanky Da Vinci restaurant is divine. The huge 'king' rooms are worth the splurge ($300). If you're here on business, this is your top choice even if it is a short taxi ride from the centre.

Chichikov Hotel　　NEW LUXURY **$$$**
(Готель Чічіков; ☏752 2300; www.chichikov-hotel.com.ua; vul Gogolya 6/8; s/d from 885/1140uah;❋@; ⓂArkhitektora Beketova) We'd like to see more space in the singles in this relatively new (2006) property, but it is elegantly furnished and the location is better than that of its only competitor in this class, the Cosmopolit.

Hotel Kharkiv　　RENOVATED SOVIET **$**
(Готель Харків; ☏758 0008; www.hotel.kharkov.com; ⓂDerzhprom, Universytet; s/d from 350/400uah) Kharkiv's textbook Soviet behemoth looms over pl Svobody, providing adequately equipped, though unremarkable rooms in the heart of the city. Its former 'poor man's wing' was being

reconstructed when we visited. Sad, since the choice of budget accommodation in the city is not great.

Hotel Gloria
SOVIET HIGH-RISE **$**

(✆732 1905; www.hotelgloria.com.ua; Plekhanovskaya 57; old s/d 160/270uah, new 300/520uah; Ⓜ Sportyvna) Old unrenovated rooms are worlds apart from renovated rooms on the upper floors of this former dormitory, 100m from Metallist stadium's main entrance. The former are straight from the Soviet 1960s, with worn-out wooden furniture and parquet floors, but clean and not bad considering the price. The latter are spacious with modern furniture, bathrooms and card locks. Breakfast is not included.

Hotel National
SOVIET-STYLED **$**

(✆702 1628, 702 1624; pr Lenina 21; s & d from 250uah; Ⓜ Naukova) Muted lights, dark wood panelling and stained glass – Soviet designers must have been reminiscing about their holiday in socialist Czechoslovakia. But signs of decay, such as broken tiles in the bathroom and furniture graffiti left by generations of vandalizing guests, are ubiquitous. In summer, you may find hot water switched off for month-long maintenance. It's 1.7km north of the centre.

Old Kharkov Hostel
HOSTEL **$**

(✆050 323 3502; Poltavsky Shlyuakh 41, apt 7a; d/tr per person from 150/130uah; 🛜; Ⓜ Pivdenny Vokzal; @) A welcome addition to the local accommodation scene and convenient for the train station, this typical converted-flat hostel has had mixed reviews. But we hope

APARTMENTS

As is the case elsewhere in Ukraine, a fully equipped apartment is often cheaper than a musty Soviet-era hotel room.

Apartments-in-Kharkov (✆719 0879, 067 577 3758; http://apartments.inkharkov.com; pl Konstytutsiyi 1, Dvorets Truda, entrance No 7, office 72-12; Ⓜ Istorychny, Muzey) Proprietor Dima offers outstanding service and lets clients use the office internet.

Kharkov Apartment (✆093 405 6600, 067 572 7867; www.kharkov apartment.com; vul Bakulina 11, office 2-3) Managers Svetlana and Anna speak English.

we'll find it in the same place when we visit next.

Gostinny Dvor
BOUTIQUE HOTEL **$$$**

(Гостинний двір; ✆705 6086/7; www.hotel-gd.com.ua; vul Rymarska 28; s/d from $120/160; ✳@; Ⓜ Arkhitektora Beketova) A pretty little boutique hotel set in a courtyard behind the posh Chateau restaurant.

🍴 Eating

IT Café
EUROPEAN **$**

(✆760 3060; pr Pravdy 10a; mains 30-50uah; ⊗24hr; Ⓜ Universytet; 🛜📶) A project by the legendary Russian web designer Artemy Lebedev, this is the place to open your laptop and catch up with all that email and Facebook news, while sipping great milkshakes, smoothies and lemonade. But if you need none of that, this is still an excellent breakfast or lunch option. They also sell bizarre-looking souvenirs designed by Lebedev's studio.

Stargorod
BEER RESTAURANT **$$**

(Старгород; ✆700 9030; vul Lermontovska 7; mains 50-110uah; beer 14-32uah; ⊗24hr; Ⓜ Pushkinska) Rivers of beer cut through mountains of meat to the sound of um-pah-pah music in this Kharkivite version of a German biergarten. There is a microbrewery on the premises pumping out fresh lager and ale, which contributes to the overall happy party atmosphere and triggers wild, table-crushing dances slightly more often than you need it. A full-sized sheep or pig is grilled on an open fire each Saturday and Sunday.

Metropol
EUROPEAN **$$$**

(Метрополь; ✆719 4040; vul Sumska 50; Ⓜ Universytet) Under reconstruction when we visited, the expensive and exclusive Metropol dedicates itself to quality European cuisine. Its popular outdoor terrace brings you eye-to-eye with the Taras Shevchenko monument across the street. The terrace used to have a slightly scaled-down, affordable menu.

Huong Viet
VIETNAMESE **$**

(Barabashova Market; mains 25uah; Ⓜ Akademika Barabashova) This huge Vietnamese cafeteria is the nerve centre of Barabashova market, where traders talk business while munching on spring rolls and noodles. The place is near the intersection of the market's five main lanes – look for the red sign. If lost, ask African jeans traders, many of whom speak English or French.

WAITING FOR VAN GOGH *GREG BLOOM*

Possibly Ukraine's best collection of Western art isn't in Kyiv, Kharkiv or Odesa. Rather, it lies deep in rural Kharkivska oblast near the obscure town of Krasnokutsk. We say 'possibly' because it has not been verified that all of the works at the **Parkhomivka History & Arts Museum** (☑057 569 5369, 097 825 5877; vul Kontorska 1; ☺9am-5pm Wed-Sun) belong to the names they are ascribed to – names like Van Gogh, Gauguin, Manet, Rembrandt, Picasso and Renoir.

But before you conclude that we've fallen for a classic Ukrainian scam, think again. Many of the works by big-name artists *have* been verified, and if you can avoid being star-struck, there's also a fabulous collection of Chinese and Japanese etchings, not to mention a stunning Ukrainian collection. Pieces that are still in the process of being authenticated are clearly marked with a '?'. In total, the museum has more than 6000 works; however, only a fraction of them can be shown at once because of space constraints.

How did such a rich collection land here? The man responsible is one Afanasy Lunyov, a teacher and master networker who ran an art school here in the heart of the Khrushchev and Brezhnev years. He used to take his students on field trips to art museums across the Soviet Union, in the process becoming close with artists, collectors and curators. Many of the works by Western artists here were surplus pieces that museums like the Hermitage donated to Lunyov's school, which he eventually turned into a museum. Many Ukrainian and Russian pieces were donated by the artists themselves.

If Lunyov, who ran the museum until his death in 2004, had marketing skills as good as his schmoozing skills, the Parkhomivka museum might be Ukraine's best-known art museum. One obstacle he faced is that the museum, a branch of the Kharkiv Art Museum, is state-owned – and thus poorly funded.

Parkhomivka is about 10km west of Krasnokutsk, about halfway between Poltava and Kharkiv (but well off the main road between the two). *Marshrutky* leave every hour or so from Kharkiv's Tsentralny Rynok (three hours). Connections are less frequent from Poltava.

Bukhara   UZBEK **$$**
(Бухара; ☑716 2045; vul Pushkinska 32; mains 40-80uah; Ⓜ Arkhitektora Beketova) The chef here fries up a mean *plov* (pilaf) and other Uzbek treats, and of course there are hookah pipes to help settle all that lamb. There's also a prime summer terrace.

Kharkiv's 'restaurant row' of sorts is vul Petrovskoho (Ⓜ Pushkinska), where you'll find all brands of cuisine, including Italian at marvellously affordable **Adriano** (☑750 7360; vul Pushkinska 79/1; mains & pizzas 35uah; Ⓜ Pushkinska) and French at funky **Parizh** (☑714 3963; vul Petrovskoho 30/32; mains 30-50uah; Ⓜ Pushkinska).

Useful outlets of nationwide chains include **Puzata Khata** (Пузата хата; cnr of Sumska & pl Konstitjutsii; ☺8am-11pm; ☏; Ⓜ Muzey) and **Celentano** (Челентано; Sumska 23; ☺10am-11pm; Ⓜ Arkhitektora Beketova). Kharkiv's own answer to the above is the excellent aviation-themed cafeteria-cum-bar **Syty Lyotchik** (Сытый Летчик; Well-fed

Pilot; vul Pushkinska 22; mains 9-16uah; Ⓜ Arkhitektora Beketova).

Drinking

Irish Pub   BEER & SPORT
(Ирландский Паб; vul Myronosytska 46; beer 18-43uah; Ⓜ Derzhprom, Universytet) Offers exactly what you'd expect: plenty of beer (fine imports and inexpensive domestic lagers), sports on TV, a few strange Irish dishes and the chance to hobnob with Kharkiv expats.

Pivobar   BEER & FOOD
(vul Frunze 3; Ⓜ Pushkinska) This place actually has a better beer selection than Irish Pub, including beloved English ales like Owd Rodger and Riggwelter, as well as an encyclopaedic food menu.

Major east Ukrainian coffee chains are present, with a few centrally located outlets including **Coffee Life** (vul Pushkinska 43; ☺24hr; ☏; Ⓜ Arkhitektora Beketova) and **Kofein** (Кофеïн; vul Rymarska 15; Ⓜ Arkhitektora Beketova).

☆ Entertainment

Kharkiv is one of the cradles of Russian-language rock and indie music, with major bands, such as Piatnizza, hailing from here. These days look out for the folksy *Selo i Lyudi*. Check Russian-language http://kharkov.nezabarom.com.ua for entertainment listings.

Churchill's Music Pub   LIVE MUSIC
(vul Darvina 9; admission 10-100uah; Ⓜ Pushkinska) A smoke-filled dive pub with excellent live music and an eager, bohemian crowd.

Jazzter   LIVE MUSIC
(www.jazzter.com.ua; prov Teatralny 11/13; admission 30-100uah; Ⓜ Istorychny Muzey) A more upmarket bar with same excellent music and crowd as Churchill's.

For downmarket dancing action in the summer try the **outdoor clubs** (admission 5uah) in Shevchenko Park near the pl Svobody entrance.

🛍 Shopping

Ye   BOOKSHOP
(Є; vul Sumska 3; ⊙9am-9pm) This modern bookstore on a seemingly hopeless crusade to Ukrainianise a Russian-speaking city serves as a club for Kharkiv's Ukrainian speakers and cosmopolitans. English speakers are welcome to participate in regular meetings with students of the language – this is a great way to find local friends.

ℹ Information

Post office (Поштамп; pl Pryvokzalna; ⊙8am-7pm Mon-Sat, to 4pm Sun) Also has a 24-hour telephone centre and internet (5.6uah per hour).

ℹ Getting There & Away
Air

The new terminal of Kharkiv's **Osnova airport** (☏775 5343), built in anticipation of the Euro Cup, was almost ready when we visited, but **Austrian** (www.austrian.com) was still the only European airline present. **Aerosvit** (VV; www.aerosvit.com) flies to Kyiv. **Kiy Avia** (☏732 8441; vul Sumska 77/79) can sort you out with schedules and tickets.

Bus

Buses go to numerous destinations from the **central bus station** (tsentralny avtovokzal; ☏732 6502; pr Gagarina 22; Ⓜ pr Gagarina). The most useful are to Poltava (30uah, 2½ hours, at least eight a day), Dnipropetrovsk (51uah, 4½ hours, 10 per day) and Donets (60uah, 4½ hours, six per day).

Autolux (☏732 5471; www.autolux.com.ua) and **Gunsel** (☏719 9719; www.gunsel.com.ua) have overnight trips to Kyiv.

Kharkiv Metro

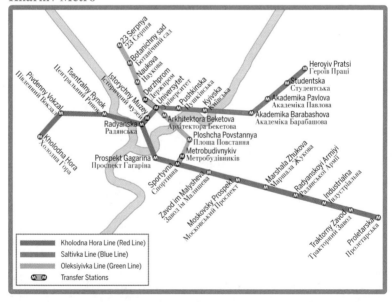

Train

The main station is **Pivdenny Vokzal** (South Station; ☎724 4183; ⓜPivdenny Vokzal).

The fast *Stolichny Express* to Kyiv (102uah, six hours) departs at 7.06am and 4.27pm and goes via Poltava (62uah, two hours). There is also a direct overnight train service (124uah, 8½ to 10 hours), including a few more transit trains.

There are six regular passenger trains, including one fast *elektrychka* to Donetsk (72uah, six to eight hours) and three trains to Sviatohirsk (44uah, 2½hr).

Other popular destinations are Moscow (830uah, 13½ hours, 13 daily), Odesa (153uah, 14 hours, daily) and Simferopol (127uah, 9½ hours, at least two daily).

An office marked as Міжнародні Каси (open 7.30am-8.30pm) – on the right as you walk from the main hall to the ticket booths – has English-speaking staff and sells tickets without queues or surcharge, unlike in the nearby service centre.

🛈 Getting Around

The airport is 8km south of the centre, off pr Gagarina. Trolleybus 5 and *marshrutka* 115 from the pr Gagarina metro stop terminate at the airport. Bus 119T runs between pr Lenina and the airport.

The train station has its own metro stop, 'Pivdenny Vokzal'. Metro tokens cost 1.5uah. There are no cashiers selling tokens – only machines that don't accept notes with denominations higher than 10uah.

Donetsk ДОНЕЦЬК

POP 1.03 MILLION

The Ukrainian coal troll is working hard to become Europe's prince charming as it prepares to host the European football cup in 2012. Its streets flooded with neon and fancy cars, Donetsk is the hometown of the country's richest man Rinat Ahmetov and the president, Viktor Yanukovych. Coal money, coupled with the understandable escapism of the younger generation, results in peculiar clubbing and restaurant cultures. Having been founded by Welshman John Hughes' and originally named 'Yuzovka' after him, the city is obsessed with all things British. In true *Full Monty* style, it is twinned with Sheffield in the UK. Even its grid street plan is attributed to the Brits.

◉ Sights & Activities

Donbass Arena   STADIUM
(vul Chelyuskintsev 189E) A post-Soviet oligarch without a football team is like a boy scout without badges, so Rinat Ahkmetov invested all his energy and resources into making Shakhtar Donetsk a top-end club deserving to play at the best stadium in Ukraine. You can book a tour of the arena (250uah), which is slated to host one of the Euro 2012 semi-finals, in the **cash office** (pr Mira). At these counters you can also buy tickets for Shakhtar's domestic games (from 100uah). Right inside the arena, there is a great shop selling sportswear in Shakhtar's anarchist red-and-black colours.

Nearby is the old **Olympic Stadium** (vul Artyoma 88), fronted by a tall **statue** of pole-vault great and hometown hero Sergei Bubka. Now it is mostly used for track-and-field competitions, as well as shows.

Lenin Komsomol Park   PARK
Believe it or not, for many years the sci-fi sounding *terrikony* – slag heaps – were the city's main attraction. 'They change their colour depending on season and time of the day', locals still reflect dreamily. The best place to observe those changes is in Lenin Komsomol Park, where chiselled socialist realist sculptures dot the sprawling **Liberators of Donbass memorial**. But turn around and you will see what completely outshines *terrikony* these days – the brand new Donbass Arena.

Donetsk Art Museum   ART GALLERY
(Донецкий музей искусств; bul Pushkina 35; admission 10uah; ☺9am-5pm Wed-Sun) It's surprising that Donetsk lacks a world-class art museum given that it counts several billionaires among its patrons. However, this gallery does have a large collection spanning the last three centuries, including a notable Soviet-realist collection.

In the centre, you'll also find a full-sized copy of the Kremlin's Tsar Cannon standing in front of the city's **town hall**. Behind it, there is a garden dotted with a peculiar **forged-iron sculpture** – a tribute to the local metallurgical industry. If tired, you may relax on a bench under two street lamps tied in a passionate embrace.

⌸ Sleeping

Expect to pay more in Donetsk than you would elsewhere, but it's generally worth it, as Donetsk's hotels are second to none in Ukraine. Unfortunately, pickings at the budget end of the spectrum are slim. The higher-end properties include breakfast in their rates.

0   400 m
0   0.2 miles

To Town
Hall (500m);
Putilovsky
Bus Station (7km);
Train station (7km)

To Donbass-Arena (800m);
Lenin Komsomol
Park (800m)

pr Bohdana Khmelnytskoho
To Intours-Donetsk
(100m)

pr Oreshkova

pl
Oktyabrskaya

bul Shevchenko

**Donetsk Art
Museum**

pr Teatralny

pr Teatralny
pr Teatralny

vul Shchorsa

vul Universytetska

bul Pushkina

vul Artyoma

vul Postysheva

vul Chelyuskintsev

vul 50-letnya SSSR

pr Gurova

pr Grinkevicha

pr Komsomolsky

pr Illicha

pr Komsomolsky

vul Rozy Lyuksemburg

To Pivdenny
Avtovokzal (700m)

To Hotel
Velikobritaniya (800m)

Liverpool Art Hotel BOUTIQUE HOTEL **$$**
(062-312 5474/5; vul Artyoma 131A; www.liver
pool.com.ua; s/d from 495/540uah; P❄🌐)
Gilded figures of John, Paul, George and
Ringo greeting you in the archway may not
be a good sign, but there is much more to
Liverpool than belated provincial Beatle-
mania. In fact this is one of the city's funki-
est alternative universes, which, apart from
the hotel, includes a great cafeteria and
one of the best musical venues in eastern
Ukraine. Pink-coloured attic rooms are
full of character, but are cramped and only
50uah cheaper than more spacious stan-
dard rooms.

TOP CHOICE **Azania Boutique Hotel**
MODERN LUXURY **$$**
(062-349 3314; www.azaniahotel.com; pr Teat-
ralny 3; s/d ste 650/720uah; ❄@) When you
enter your suite in this extraordinary boutique hotel, you might feel you are dreaming already, your body swallowed by one of

the California king beds. It only gets better: *two* flat-screen TVs in each cavernous
suite, DVD collection, kitchen, furniture
worthy of a *Home & Design* cover, Jacuzzi
etc. Pinch yourself when you look at the
price – it's real.

Hotel Velikobritaniya HISTORIC HOTEL **$**
(062-305 1951; vul Postysheva 20; s/d
150/250uah, with bathroom 220/360uah) This
pillar of the city's budget accommodation
has heaps of olde-worlde charm. However,
the location is crummy and it gets stiflingly
hot in the summer.

Hotel Ukraina SOVIET-STYLED **$**
(Гостиница Украина; 062-304 4535; vul
Artyoma 88; s/d 228/330uah, with bathroom
420/540uah) Don't be turned off by the common showers, which are huge and sparkling
clean. The rooms, while nothing fancy, also
fit that description. Those that lack toilets/
showers at least contain sinks. It occupies

two floors of a large building right in the centre.

Hotel Econom   TIDY MINIMALISM **$**
(Отель Эконом; ☑062-381 7686, 050 331 7686; vul 50-letiya SSSR 144/4; www.hotel -econom.com.ua; s/d/tr with shared bathroom 160/220/280uah; ☎) Occupying the 3rd floor of a decrepit 1930s house, Econom has 38 clean rooms equipped with a small TV and fridge, but lacking bathrooms or even sinks. There are only four shared bathrooms, which creates a bit of a rush hour in the morning, while thin walls engage you in eavesdropping, whether you want to or not.

Hotel Center Victoria   NEW UKRAINIAN **$$$**
(☑062-381 4700; www.victoria.ua; pr Mira 24a; s/d from 910/1320uah; ☒❋@☒) If this lags behind Donbass Palace in any respect, we failed to notice. Frankly the rooms best the Palace's and are equally capacious. The not-so-central location by Donbass Arena means there's plenty of spare real estate for the four tennis courts, bowling alley and luxury gym (with TVs attached to every treadmill!). Rooms go for half the price on weekends.

Donbass Palace   NEW UKRAINIAN **$$$**
(Дворец Донбасс; ☑062-343 4333; www. donbasspalace.com; vul Artyoma 80; s/d from 2470/3460uah; ☒❋@☒) The country's first five-star property when it opened in the mid-1990s, the Donbass Palace has a lot more competition of late, but it remains the number-one choice among well-heeled *biznesmeny*. It boasts four superb restaurants if you're entertaining, and a casino if you're feeling lucky (well are you, punk?).

Hotel Central   MODERN HOTEL **$$**
(Гостиница Центральная; ☑062-332 3875; www.hotel-central.com.ua; vul Artyoma 87; r from 650uah; ❋@) Midrange corporate-orientated establishment with a prime location.

✗ Eating & Drinking

Elaborate theme restaurants – some of them extremely well done – are the norm in Donetsk. For fine dining hit the Donbass Palace.

Yuzovskaya Pivovarnya   FOOD **$$**
(Юзовская пивоварня; Johh Hughes Brewery; ☑062-208 9800; vul Artyoma 129b; mains 40-60uah; ☺11am-1.30pm; ☎) A tribute to the city founder John Hughes, this place is full of shiny brass – that of the mini-brewery pumping fresh brew into the pipes that take it straight to your table. All you need is to open the tap. A large, airy hall is divided into compartments with red leather couches seating about six people. Meaty Central European dishes dominate the menu.

Liverpool Foodmarket   CAFETERIA **$**
(vul Artyoma 131A; mains 10-20uah; ☺7am-11pm) With walls draped in Union Jacks and the Beatles for the soundtrack, this food factory churns out tonnes of European and Asian meals immediately devoured by a horde of hungry students. Payment is with a deposit card, which you get at the cash office near the entrance. You can cash the unspent money on the way out.

Marrakesh   FRENCH, MOROCCAN **$$**
(Маракеш; ☑062-381 7474; vul Artyoma 127; mains 80-120uah; ☺11am-1.30am) With its harem-styled décor, this place flies you on

a magic carpet to the Sahara. Once inside, you feel so removed from all things Donbass, you can almost hear camels stepping on desert dunes behind the dark-red curtains. However, food here is mostly French, with just a hint of Moroccan. It's very tasty nonetheless.

3 Tolstyaka RUSSIAN $
(Три Толстяка; 3 Fat Guys; pr Gurova; mains 35-60uah; ⏰10am-11pm) The 3 Tolstyaka is enormously popular for a reason: authentic Russian food at awesome prices. Its popularity is also proof that average Donetsk denizens can't afford the gaudy prices at all those top-end restaurants.

Golden Lion IRISH PUB
(vul Artyoma 76A; beer 9-40uah; ⏰11am-1.30pm; 🛜) Far from your run-of-the-mill Irish pub, and not just because it's spacious enough to hold a rugby game and stays open after midnight. Here you'll also encounter 5uah Sarmat beer to go along with the standard selection of imported brew. Mains are available for 60uah to 100uah.

Kayut-Kompaniya COFFEEHOUSE $
(Кают-компания; vul Grinkevicha 9; espresso 14uah, cocktails 30-40uah; ⏰9am-11pm) Descend to the bottom of the sea and travel to faraway lands in this little cellar coffeehouse cum cocktail bar designed to look like Captain Nemo's submarine. Another striking example of local escapism.

Also recommended:

Khinkali GEORGIAN $$
(Хинкали; bul Pushkina 20A; mains 50-80uah; ⏰11am-2pm; 🛜) Good place to try meaty Georgian food, although *khinkali* (meat dumplings) filled with cherries are a sacrilege!

Bassano del Grappa ITALIAN $$$
(☎062-381 0858; pr Grinkevicha 8; mains 120-300uah; ⏰noon-11pm) This bright Italian restaurant has a great wine list and an inviting street-side patio for sipping that wine.

☆ Entertainment

Listings in Russian can be found at http://donetsk.afisha.ua.

Chicago Biker's Bar UNDERGROUND LABYRINTH
(vul Artyoma 113; ⏰10am-2am) Soviet chic to the core, this place features a pellet-gun gallery, private rooms like KGB prison cells, and beer taps on the tables. There's live music nightly and Shakhtar Donetsk games are shown on televisions embedded in oil barrels. It's part of the multifunctional Chicago nightclub and entertainment complex.

Liverpool Live Music Bar LIVE MUSIC
(vul Artyoma 131A; cocktails 50uah) This imaginatively designed place claims to have the longest bar in Eastern Europe. The catwalk stage is placed so that musicians find themselves in the middle of the crowd. Some major Ukrainian bands play here.

Other options:

Opera & Ballet Theatre OPERA & BALLET
(Театр Оперы и балета; ☎922 348; vul Artyoma 82) Culture vultures can catch *Swan Lake* here.

Philharmonic Concert Hall CLASSICAL
(Концертный зал филармонии; ☎304 5031; bul Postysheva) Soak up some classical sounds.

ℹ Information

Intours-Donetsk (☎062-304 7192; www.intours.donetsk.ua; vul Universytetskaya 55) With advance notice (a week is often needed to set things up), this office can organise excursions to Sviatohirsk, Soledar salt mine and the salt mine of the Artyomivsk champagne factory, which is used as a wine cellar.

Post & Telephone Centre (Почтамт; vul Artyoma 72; internet per hr 4uah; ⏰24hr).

Salt Symphony (Соляная симфония; ☎062-208 9148; vul Shchorsa 29; www.saltsymphony.com.ua) City office of Soledar salt-mine sanatorium.

ℹ Getting There & Away

AIR **Donbassaero** (www.donbass.aero) flies to **Donetsk airport** (☎062-344 7322; http://airport.dn.ua) from Kyiv, Moscow, Athens and a host of other international destinations. Turkish Airlines, Lufthansa, Austrian Airlines and Aerosvit also serve Donetsk (for contact details see p278).

TRAIN Trains from the **train station** (☎062-319 0005; pl Pryvokzalna) include six a day to Kyiv (127uah, 12 hours) and one to Odesa (137uah, 16½ hours) via Zaporizhzhya (81uah). There are two fast *elektrychka* daily to Dnipropetrovsk (30uah, 3½ hours). To Kharkiv there's one overnight 'fast *elektrychka*' (61uah, 6½ hours) and about six slower trains.

BUS Catch buses to Sviatohirsk (38uah, hourly), Artyomivsk (23uah, hourly) and Soledar (28uah, twice daily) at the **Putilovsky bus station** (☎062-312 0509; vul Vzletnaya 1) north of the centre.

To head toward Crimea, Odesa and the Azov Sea use the more centrally located **Pivdenniy Avtovokzal** (☑0622-665 119; South bus station; pl Kommunarov).

Handle all your ticketing needs at the **central booking office** (vul Universytetskaya 35; ☉7am-7pm), where there's an advance train-ticket window and Donbassaero and Kiy Avia plane-ticket booths.

ℹ Getting Around

The airport is about 8km north of the centre, about 1km beyond Putilovsky bus station. Both are accessible by trolleybus 9 or 10 heading up vul Universytetskaya.

A little further south is the train station, a straight shunt down the city's main axis, vul Artyoma on bus and trolleybus 2. Tram 1 plies the parallel vul Chelyuskintsev.

Sviatohirsk Святогірск

☑06262

Built into a dazzlingly white chalk cliff above the dreamy Siversky Donets River, the Sviatohirsk (Svyatogorsk in Russian) cave monastery is a heavenly sight, complemented rather than spoilt by the gigantic statue of the Bolshevik hero Artyom, which tops an adjacent hill. All that contrasts sharply with the hellish sprawl of *pansionaty* (Soviet-style workers' resorts) and tacky outdoor cafes on the other bank of the river. The reason is that apart from being the holiest Orthodox site in Eastern Ukraine, Sviatohirsk is also the main recreational zone for the Donbass region. Vacationing miners find time for the spiritual and for the mundane, putting candles in the monastery by day and washing down their shashlyk with gallons of beer and vodka by night.

◉ Sights & Activities

Sviatohirsk Lavra　　　　MONASTERY
(Svyatogorskaya Uspenskaya Lavra in Russian; ☑admission 20uah 10am-5pm, after hours free) One of only three *lavras* (super-monasteries) in Ukraine, Sviatohirsk monastery obtained this status in 2004. It is probably not nearly as ancient as Kyevo-Pecherska – monks moved in here in 1620, burrowing into the chalk cliff, which they transformed into a five-storey dwelling, complete with several chapels and monk cells. These **caves** now form the monastery's upper part. In the following years it grew to become a prominent religious centre, but in 1790 Catherine II decided to close it, handing the surround-ing lands to her lover Grygory Potemkin. The monastery reopened in 1844 when its lower, riverside part was built. In 1920, the Bolsheviks shot the monks and set up a car-dio-centre on the premises. But the clergy was back in 1992 taking over the entire monastery by 2004. You can check out the riverside part of the *lavra* on your own. To visit the caves in the upper part of the mon-astery, join a group of pilgrims organised by the **monastery's excursion bureau** (tours 3uah, ☉9am-noon & 1-4pm), located at the far end of the monastery's riverside part.

Artyom Monument　　　VANGUARD SCULPTURE
After the monastery visit, consider taking a taxi (30uah) or hiking to the top of the adjacent hill dominated by 27m monu-ment of local Bolshevik leader Artyom. It was designed in an unusual cubist style by Ivan Kavaleridze, who authored some of the worst monuments in Kyiv. Fortu-nately, this early (1927) work is nothing to be ashamed of. Also dazzlingly white, it looks like (and in many way is) an idol of a rival religion, but it and the Orthodox monastery create a wonderful ensemble. If you came by taxi, you may choose to return on foot. The descent begins near a wood-en hermitage, 300m away in the *lavra* direction.

🛏 Sleeping

Zeleny Gai　　　　RENOVATED SOVIET $
(☑55 888, 55 844; www.zeleny-gay.dn.ua; vul 60 let Oktyabrya; s/d from 270/295uah; ☑☎✉) There are dozens of Soviet-era *pansionaty* making a painful journey into the modern hospitality world with a little help from Donbass oligarchs. Zeleny Gai (gai stands for grove, in case you are wondering) is one of the better examples. Grey Soviet *korpusy* may look uninviting, but rooms are modern and good value for money. From the bus sta-tion, walk away from the centre for about 700m until you find the entrance marked by the Russian-language sign Зеленая Роща.

CONE ART

The local specialty at Sviatohirsk is jam made of baby pine cones. One-litre jars are sold for 30uah at the market behind the parking lot near the monastery bridge. It is also served with pancakes at the Roche Royal's hotel restaurant.

So typical of Ukraine. You chat to someone and in 20 minutes you know their whole life story. That's what happened when we met 72-year-old Roman Mankevich while waiting for a *marshrutka* outside the Soledar mine.

His parents moved here when he was two. Soon the war broke out, and as the Germans rolled across Ukraine, Mankevich's father said publicly that they were no joke and that the enemy should be taken seriously. He was instantly arrested as a defeatist and sent to a Gulag camp where he died four years later. 'We became enemies of the people. My mother couldn't get a job. But soon the Germans came, as my father predicted,' he said. Ironically, life became better. 'We had no Gestapo, only mining engineers – cultured people. One of them stayed with us and we liked him.'

After the war, Mankevich went to work in the Soledar mine, where he spent 10 years digging out salt. It might sound like serving a sentence, but he doesn't regret one minute he spent there: 'Our mine is a hundred times better than coal mines. No methane explosions and your lungs only get better thanks to being there'. Mankevich firmly told us that being in the vicinity and not visiting his mine is a crime. 'Look, it is the bottom of a prehistoric ocean. Have you been to the bottom of the ocean? See, me neither. It's a unique deposit, no such thing exists elsewhere in the world. It's like going into space, or to the North Pole, or to Africa...'

Roche Royal MODERN LUXURY **$$$**
(☑533 05, 050 701 7272; www.rocheroyal.com.
ua; vul 60-letiya Oktyabrya 21; r from 850uah;
P❄) Right by the bus station, Roche Royal sets new standards for Sviatohirsk's hospitality scene with huge stylish rooms, a spa and all the amenities a coal mogul might dream of. It also boasts the best restaurant for miles around.

❶ Getting There & Around

TRAIN Sviatohirsk train station, 5km away from the town and reached by a fairly frequent bus, is convenient for Kharkiv, with at least two fast *elektrychka* a day (45uah, 2½ hours). Krasny Liman, a few stops away by *elektrychka*, is a major junction with frequent services to Donetsk, Artyomivsk and Sil (for Soledar). For Sil, look for trains bound for Debaltsevo and Mykytivka (Nikitovka).

BUS From the bus station, buses leave for Donetsk at least hourly (2½ hours, 38uah). Still, you may sometimes find them fully booked, in which case change at Slovyansk.

Soledar Соледар
☑06274

The medieval *chumaki*, Ukrainian salt traders, risked their lives trudging hundreds of miles across the hostile steppe to the salt deposits in Crimea without realizing that Europe's largest deposit of salt lay almost under their doorstep. If you are concerned about the planet's shrinking natural

resources, relax about salt. In the Artyomivsk deposit alone, there is enough of it to supply the whole of humanity for tens of thousands of years.

The reason why you are reading about it here is that you can penetrate this giant salt crystal on a tour of the Soledar salt mine (☑42 573, 050 802 0707; excursion 100uah; ◷11am, 1pm & 3pm Tue-Sun), 75km from Donetsk. Three hundred metres below the surface, there is salt everywhere – you're actually encouraged to lick the walls, as guides are adamant no bacteria survive at this depth. Licking the mine's protector gnome brings you luck, they will surely add. There are a few more salt statues in the wide, high-ceilinged galleries. You are unlikely to feel claustrophobic at the end of the tour when they bring you into a giant hall decorated by a Christmas tree – so that guests can have a New Year party here at any time of the year. There is also a football pitch where you can practice your strikes while listening to Bach and Chopin records. Approximately once every two years a whole orchestra descends into the mine to play a full concert. The acoustics are stunning. While here, some visitors choose to walk (or play football) barefooted – it is a strange and rather pleasant sensation and they say it is good for your health, too.

Unlike coal mines, salt mines are very safe and even have a curative effect. In fact, the mine houses the Salt Symphony Speleosanatorium (☑209 91 48; www.salt

symphony.com.ua; per day from 155uah) for people suffering from asthma and other lung diseases. You can book your stay there with **Salt Symphony** (Соляная симфония; ☑208 9148; vul Shchorsa 29; www.saltsymphony.com.ua) in Donetsk. The mine can be reached by a *marshrutka* (1.5uah) that goes between Artyomivsk, 13km away, from where there are frequent connections to Donetsk (see p222) and Soledar's train station, Sil, which comes into the equation if you go to Sviatohirsk.

Dnipropetrovsk
ДНІПРОПЕТРОВСЬК

POP 1.08 MILLION

With its portly 19th-century houses, trams trundling along leafy boulevards and beautiful river vistas, Dnipropetrovsk has the potential to become an attractive city. But unfortunately its fathers (and godfathers) are too preoccupied with opening new boutiques and shopping emporiums, while heritage buildings are crumbling away and whole blocs are bulldozed, giving way to yet another glassy rectangle. A major centre of space and aviation industry, Dnipropetrovsk became a springboard for such political heavyweights as ex-president Leonid Kuchma and Orange Revolution leader Yulia Tymoshenko. Local oligarchs rival those of Donetsk in wealth and power.

Sights & Activities

Window shopping is one pleasant Dnipropetrovsk experience. Another favourite activity is wandering the two riverfront promenades – along nab Lenina and nab Pobedy.

Monastyrsky Island   ISLAND

At the eastern end of nab Lenina is Monastyrsky Island, the site of the area's first human settlement. Crossing the bridge to the island, you immediately come face to face with a **Taras Shevchenko statue**, the immense size of which would put most Lenin statues to shame. Turning left (west) you'll come to the beautiful, fortress-style **St Nicholas Church** (Свято-Николаевская церковь). Nearby, a cross depicting the site of the island's original monastery sits in a fragrant, lovingly cared-for garden. The southeast portion of the island is dominated by sandy **beaches**, popular among locals in the warm months.

Back on the mainland, walking up the hill from the bridge's southern terminus

brings you to **Shevchenko Park**, where you can watch old men playing chess.

History Museum   MUSEUM

(Исторический музей; pr Karla Marksa 16; admission 8uah; ⊙10am-5pm Tue-Sun) South of Shevchenko Park is pl Zhovtneva (pl Oktyabrskaya), site of the excellent History Museum, which has large visually attractive rooms dedicated to the Cossacks, the Russian empire, the Civil War and Holodomor. Adjoining the museum is a **diorama** (Диорама; admission 4uah), an 840-sq-metre painted canvas depicting the WWII Battle of the Dnipro, which was fought near here.

Preobrazhensky Cathedral   CATHEDRAL

Outside the museum, anti-aircraft batteries are aimed towards the glistening gold spire and dome of Preobrazhensky Cathedral (Спасо-Преображенский кафедральный собор; Transfiguration), a classical structure dating from 1830 to 1835. This is Dnipropetrovsk's holiest church, so don't barge in wearing beach clothes.

🛏 Sleeping

As elsewhere in Ukraine, it is totally reasonable to rent an apartment. **Mystay.org** (☑067 563 5906; www.mystay.org; pr Karla Marksa 60/16; flats from 350uah) not only secured a prime internet domain, but provides a good choice of inexpensive apartments in the city centre to primarily foreign clientele.

Dnipropetrovsk   SOVIET HIGH-RISE **$$**

(☑056-744 1158; www.hotel.dp.ua; nab Lenina 33; standard/superior 330/470uah; ✴) Located on the river about a 15-minute walk from the centre, this renovated 11-storey concrete block is the best value in town. Look past its Soviet husk and the loud furniture and you'll find surprises like toothbrushes, colourful soaps, minibars and comfy foam mattresses, even in the economy rooms. Air-con is by request.

Grand Hotel Ukraine   MODERN LUXURY **$$$**

(Гостиница Украина; ☑056-790 1441, 056-740 1010; vul Korolenko 2; www.grand-hotel-ukraine.dp.ua; s/d from $130/180, ste from $300; ⊖✴@≋) It's known as *the* business hotel in town, and has the fitness centre, business centre, conference facilities and free wi-fi to back it up. However, the standard rooms are surprisingly small and lame; upgrade to a suite if you want more space. Breakfast costs (a lot) extra.

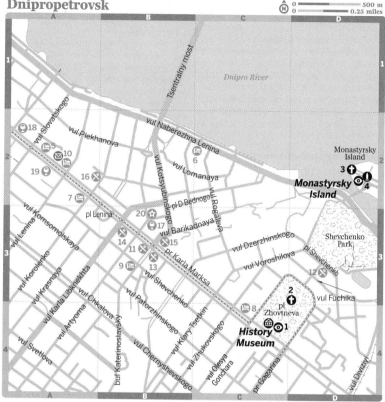

0 — 500 m
0 — 0.25 miles

Hotel Caspian

MODERN LUXURY **$$$**

(Отель Каспий; ☎056-371 0002; www.kaspiy.com.ua; vul Shevchenko 53A; r from 1240uah; ☺✿) Beautiful Turkish carpets, expensive Italian furniture and sumptuous king-sized beds are among the many highlights of this lavish boutique. Service is friendly, rooms are huge and the location is ideal. Arguably tops among Dnipropetrovsk's many luxury hotels.

Hotel Academy

ANTIQUARIAN SOVIET **$$$**

(Гостиница Академия; ☎056-370 0505; www.academya.dp.ua; pr Karla Marksa 20; s/d from 1000/1700uah; ✿) Fans of Soviet-realist art need look no further than this museum-like hotel. The walls in the lobby and corridors are covered in brilliant paintings epitomising the best of the genre. While the service is outstanding, the rooms (which, curiously, bear Cézanne prints) are simply average. Breakfast in Deja Vu restaurant downstairs is a highlight.

Astoria

HISTORIC HOTEL **$$**

(Отель Астория; ☎056-376 0300; www.astoria.com.ua; pr Karla Marksa 66; r from 850uah; ☺✿) Olde-worlde charm mixes with post-Soviet lack of taste in this historic hotel, which housed the headquarters of anarchist warlord Nestor Makhno. He led a ragtag Ukrainian peasant army in the Russian civil war.

✗ Eating

For a pleasant dining experience, there are a number of restaurants and outdoor food stands on the riverside promenade across from the Hotel Dnipropetrovsk. For economy eats and beer try the *shashlyk* stands on either side of the bridge to Monastyrsky Island.

Reporter

EUROPEAN **$$**

(Репортёр; cnr pr Karla Marksa & vul Barikadnaya; mains 60-120uah; ☺24hr) Reporter has three wings: a ground-floor coffeehouse serving breakfasts and possibly the plumpest, tastiest homemade *varenyky* (dumplings) in the land; a chichi restaurant upstairs; and a superb basement 'warm-up bar' with a great in-house DJ getting the city's hipsters fired up for a night on the town. You'll find at least one of the three open at any time of the day and night.

Yaffo   JEWISH $$
(Яффо; bul Yevropeysky; meals 40-115uah; ◷11am-11pm) With its large and influential Jewish community, it's only natural for Dnipropetrovsk to have a restaurant that serves competently cooked Levantine food. An assortment of *meze* (light snacks) watered down with homemade lemonade make an ideal lunch on a hot summer day.

Beer House   STEAKS $$
(Пивной дом; bul Katerinoslavsky 2; mains 45-60uah; ◷11am-midnight) Beer House must have a versatile chef – there are separate European, Russian and, of course, sushi menus in the downstairs restaurant. Be warned: those juicy-looking steak prices are 'per 100g'. Personal 3L kegs are the speciality of the beer room upstairs and there are 14 kinds of Ukrainian and international beer to choose from.

Da Vinci   SUSHI $$
(Кофейня Да Винчи; vul Yavornitskoho 6) An exquisitely designed terrace cafe strategically placed at the entrance to Shevchenko Park. Inevitably, sushi is on the menu – rolls 36uah to 80uah, cocktails 50uah. Design inspired by Da Vinci's frescoes.

Nobu   JAPANESE $$$
(pr Karla Marksa 49; meals 100-200uah) The best sushi in a sushi-mad city.

Puzata Khata   FAST FOOD $
(Пузата Хата; pl Petrovskogo 5; vul Karla Libknekhta 1) There are outlets near the train station and in the centre.

▼ Drinking

Café Cuba   BAR $
(vul Kharkovskaya 2; cuba libre 25uah) It might look like a tiny bar doubling as souvenir shop, but the black Cuban owner, Miguel Angel, sees it as his island's cultural embassy. Spanish and salsa lessons are on offer.

Tsepi   BAR $
(Цепи, Chains; pr Karla Marksa 77; beer 9-14uah) The décor in this slightly grim, though very cheap, pub involves many chains hanging from the ceiling, a few motorcycles and their spare parts. Soundtrack is Nick Cave-ish. Mains are 40uah to 60uah.

L'Orangerie   COCKTAIL BAR $$$
(vul Polovitskaya 2; cocktails 50uah; ◷11am-11pm) People come here to sit outside in wicker chairs, sip cosmopolitans and look cool.

☆ Entertainment

Labyrinth   NIGHTCLUB
(Лабиринт; cnr vul Kharkovskaya & vul Hopner; admission Sun-Thu free, Fri & Sat 50-100uah) True to its name, this is an underground maze of corridors and halls, each with its own bar and soundtrack. Don't buy the full ticket for 100uah unless you are desperate to see a striptease show in the upstairs 'VIP' lounges.

ⓘ Information

Handle both your snail mail and email needs at the **post office** (Почтамт; pr Karla Marksa 62; internet per hr 6uah; ⌚8am-8pm Mon-Fri, to 7pm Sat). Check out http://gorod.dp.ua for the latest hotel, restaurant and club news.

ⓘ Getting There & Away

AIR International carriers Austrian Airlines, Turkish Airlines and Aeroflot (see p278 for airline contact information) all have flights to **Dnipropetrovsk International Airport** (☑395 209), which is about 15km southeast of the city towards Zaporizhzhya (the airport is also convenient for that city). Local carrier **Dniproavia** (www.dniproavia.com) flies to Kyiv, Odesa, Simferopol (summer only) and a few international destinations. Aerosvit also flies to/from Kyiv.

BUS Dnipropetrovsk has the country's largest **bus station** (☑008, 778 4090; www.dopas.dp.ua; vul Kurchatova 10), located west of the centre about a 10-minute walk from the train station. To save time take *marshrutky*, not buses, to Zaporizhzhya (24uah, 1½ hours, every 15 minutes). 'Luxury' bus operators **Autolux** (☑371 0353) and **Gunsel** (☑778 3935) have overnight trips to Kyiv (80uah, seven to eight hours), and you'll find plenty of buses to Poltava, Kharkiv, Odesa and Simferopol.

TRAIN From the **central train station** (☑005 395 209; pr Karla Marksa 108) the fast *Stolichny Express* (108uah, six hours) to Kyiv runs early in the morning and late evening, plus there are other services to Kyiv (112uah, eight hours). Trains also rumble to Odesa (120uah, 11½ hours, at least daily), Simferopol (90uah, seven hours, five daily), and all other major cities.

There are daily fast *elektrychky* to Kharkiv (70uah, 4½ hours) and Donetsk (31uah, 4½ hours) plus a few slower passenger trains to both destinations. Some slow trains pass through nearby Zaporizhzhya, but it's much easier and quicker by *marshrutka*.

ⓘ Getting Around

From the airport, take bus 60 or 109 to the train station and tram 1 into the centre from there. A taxi should cost about 50uah to 60uah.

Tram 1 runs the length of pr Karla Marksa, originating at the train station. The metro is useless to the average visitor, as it does not go near the centre.

Zaporizhzhya
ЗАПОРІЖЖЯ

☑0612 / POP 815,000

So, so Soviet! For a visitor, Zaporizhzhya is essentially one avenue lined with sometimes imposing Stalinesque architecture.

Named after its Moscow equivalent, pr Lenina runs from Avtozaz, the birthplace of the Zaporizhets – USSR's most ridiculed car model – to the Soviet industrial icon, Dniproges power station. Neither of which are the reason people come here on holiday. The reason is Khortytsya - a rocky forested island where Cossacks set up their all-male free-rule republic, which prospered from raids on neighbouring empires and duties levied on anyone who used the river trade route. Today, it is the place to learn about Cossack culture and history, admire beautiful river vistas and spend a day hiking or bicycling.

◉ Sights

Khortytsya Island   COSSACK STRONGHOLD

The Zaporizhska Sich on Khortytsya Island was the most important cradle of Ukrainian Cossackdom, where *hetman* (leader) Dmytro Baida united disparate groups of Cossacks in the construction of a *sich* (fort) in 1553–54. The island was perfect: strategically located below the Dnipro rapids and beyond the control of Polish or Russian authority. Any man could come to join the Cossack brotherhood, irrespective of social background, and like Galicia under self-rule in the 14th century, the *sich* is revered as a leading forerunner of an independent Ukraine.

At the height of its power the community numbered some 20,000 fighters, under the authority of one *hetman*. On the battlefield they were formidable opponents; off it, formidable vodka drinkers. However, there was a code of discipline, and no women were allowed on Khortytsya. Even Russian empress Catherine the Great was prohibited from setting foot on the island and was reduced to spying on it from a nearby rock. Some laughingly suggest that this, as well as the threat the Cossacks posed to Russian imperial ambitions, was why she had the *sich* destroyed in 1775.

Since 1965 the 2690-hectare island has been a reserve, although it's tough to imagine the Cossack revelry of the past with a massive bridge to the mainland and the Dniproges Dam in plain view, and nary a rapid in sight. Nevertheless, you can visit the informative **Historical Museum of Zaporizhsky Cossacks** (admission 6uah, English tours per group 120uah; ⌚10am-7pm Tue-Sun), which includes painted dioramas and various Cossack weaponry and bric-abrac excavated from the island and nearby Baida Island. Also interesting are the photographs of the island surrounded by rapids before the dam was built.

Nearby, a prime spot on the cliff edge is now occupied by the **Sich Reconstruction** (admission 6uah; English tours per group 120uah; ☺10am-7pm Tue-Sun), a wooden fortress, complete with churches and about a dozen thatched-roof *khaty* (dwellings), built for the epic movie *Taras Bulba* in 2007.

The museum grounds sprawl across the island's rocky northern end, offering prime views of the Dniproges Dam. Scrambling around this area, you will come across various Scythian ruins and burial mounds thought to be more than 3000 years old.

Cossack haunts on the island include the **Cossacks' jetty** and the **Hadyucha Peshchera** (Snake Cave). Also here is the **Chyorna Skala** (Black Cliff), where the Kyivan Rus King Svyatoslav was reportedly killed by the Pechenegs in AD 972 (there's a diorama of this battle inside the museum).

There's an **amphitheatre** on the southern portion of the island where highly entertaining horse shows and mock fights are put on periodically by Cossack descendants; check with the travel agency at the Hotel Intourist for details.

With its network of forest paths and tarmac roads, Khortytsya Island is a haven for hikers and bicyclists. You can usually find a **bicycle-renting stand** (20uah per hour, 100uah per day) at the museum's parking lot.

Public transport can get you to the island but not to the museum (see p230).

Dniproges Dam

HYDROPOWER STATION

Here's a quick quiz. What's missing from the following list? The Eiffel Tower, the Golden Gate Bridge, the Empire State Building, the Panama Canal, the Suez Canal and the Alaska Highway? Perhaps the Sydney Opera House? Nope. Try again. Apparently, until 2007, when the list was refreshed, the seventh declared wonder of the modern world was Zaporizhzhya's Dniproges Dam.

At 760m – two and a half times longer than the famous Hoover Dam – the wall of the USSR's first dam certainly represented a monumental engineering feat when constructed under US supervision in 1927–32. In some ways, it's still impressive, but it's not especially tall and you have to reflect that its concrete walls, stained by years of local pollution, are really rather less appealing than the Sydney Opera House. Little known in the West, it was not considered for inclusion on the 'New Seven Wonders' list unveiled in 2007.

🛏 Sleeping

Hotel Intourist-Zaporizhzhya

RENOVATED SOVIET **$$$**

(☎330 554, 332 5564; www.intourist.com.ua; pr Lenina 135; s/d from 810/930uah; ✴@) This frog-turned-prince might very well have replaced the Dniproges Dam as one of the world's seven wonders. Smiling young receptionists mete out four-star service, beds have firm double mattresses and there is a great breakfast buffet. Throw in some quality restaurants plus a nightclub and you'll find few reasons to leave the place, apart from the Khortytsya excursion.

Ukraina

SOVIET-STYLED **$$**

(☎289 0404; www.ukraine.zp.ua; pr Lenina 162A; s/d from 330/390uah, q per person 190uah) Reception staff are super-friendly and maids do exceptional handiwork, but saggy beds, thin walls and sometimes rowdy clientele make the short distance that divides Ukraina from Intourist seem like a million light years.

🍴 Eating & Drinking

The main restaurant row is on bul Shevchenka, but you'll find a few good places along pr Lenina.

Politbureau

RETRO-SOVIET **$$**

(pr Lenina 208; mains 45-70uah) Looking perfectly appropriate in such a Soviet city, this place has waiters dressed like young pioneers and rooms designed to resemble the flats of Soviet citizens from different walks of life – workers, peasants, party officials and intelligentsia. There is an extensive, though not too inventive, menu of European and Russian/Ukrainian food. Go for pancakes.

Mustang

THEME RESTAURANT **$$$**

(pr Lenina 143; mains 50-170uah; ☺9am-11pm; 🛜) It's a theme restaurant dedicated to the legendary WWII fighter plane, not the car. A massive model of the plane hangs above the bar, while a wax pilot cheers you with a shot of whiskey at the entrance. There are hundreds of black-and-white photos, model airplanes, various guns and a huge menu of overpriced food. Fondue and steaks are the house specialities.

Bosfor   TURKISH **$$**
(vul Yakova Novitskogo 3; mains 40-70uah; 🛜)
Turkish expats run this pleasant eatery not
far from Intourist. The convenient picture
menu features lots of kebabs and appetising
Turkish snacks. Patrons smoke shisha on an
open-air terrace.

Trattoria Bambola   ITALIAN **$**
(bul Shevchenko 8; mains 40-60uah; ⊘10am-
11pm) In the city's main restaurant row,
this is a nice unpretentious place that
knows how to make pizzas. Cool Japanese
soundtrack.

Coffee Life   COFFEEHOUSE **$**
(pr Lenina 145; 🛜) For a cup of competently
brewed coffee, a range of smoothies and
fast wi-fi, head to this useful outlet near
Intourist.

☆ Entertainment

Crow Bar   NIGHTCLUB
(pr Lenina 135; admission 120uah) This club
may be in the same building as the Hotel
Intourist, but it's head and shoulders above
your ordinary hotel nightclub. We prom-
ise. It has plenty of local flavour and draws
top DJs.

❶ Information

Just about every service you need is found
around pl Festyvalna – many inside Hotel
Intourist-Zaporizhzhya (p229), which has a travel
agency among myriad other services.

Post office (pr Lenina 133; internet per hr
1.50uah; ⊘post office 8am-7pm Mon-Sat, 9am-
5pm Sun, internet 8am-9pm, telephone centre
24hr) Besides postal services, an internet and
telephone centre, there is also an ATM.

❶ Getting There & Away

TRAIN **Zaporizhzhya-1 train station** (☑224
4060; pr Leninaya 2) is at the southeastern

end of pr Lenina. Trains trundle to Simferopol
(97uah, five hours), Kyiv (130uah, 10 hours),
Kharkiv (87uah, 4½ hours), Lviv (166uah, 20
hours) and Odesa (98uah, 16 hours). Many trains
going north stop in Dnipropetrovsk (50uah, 2½
hours), but you're much better off on a bus. You
can buy train tickets at booths in the lobby of the
Hotel Intourist.

BUS *Marshrutky* for Dnipropetrovsk (15uah,
1½ hours, every 15 minutes) leave from the bus
station or from pl Lenina near the dam. The **bus
station** (☑642 657; pr Leninaya 20) is near
Zaporizhzhya-1 train station. **Autolux** (☑642
558) has four buses per day to Kyiv (90uah, 9½
hours). The Kyiv–Simferopol bus stops through
here (40uah to Simferopol).

❶ Getting Around

The main street, pr Lenina, stretches for
10km from Zaporizhzhya-1 train station at its
southeastern end to pl Lenina overlooking the
Dniproges Dam. Halfway down there's a centre
of activity around pl Festyvalna, where you'll
find both listed hotels. Three to four bus stops
further northwest is bul Shevchenka. Most trol-
leybuses and *marshrutky* run the length of pr
Lenina between Zaporizhzhya-1 train station and
pl Lenina, but you can bank on trolleybus 3.

Khortytsya Island lies in the Dnipro, 2km
southwest of the Dniproges Dam wall. To get
there, take the infrequent *marshrutka* 46 from
anywhere on pr Lenina. It goes across the dam
and then south along the riverside bul Vintera.
Get off as soon it turns right, away from the river,
and walk. Return to bul Vintera and walk for
another 700m before the road turns left to Khor-
tytsya's northern bridge. Once you have crossed
it, find a footpath leading to the museum on
your left.

Alternatively, take a *marshrutka* marked
Хортица (eg 87 or 58), leaving from the corner
of pr Lenina and pr Metallurgov, and get off
after it crosses Khortytsya's southern bridge.
From there, it is a 30-minute walk north to the
museum.

Understand Ukraine

>

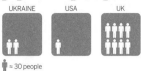

population per sq km

UKRAINE   USA   UK

♟ ≈ 30 people

Ukraine Today

RIP Orange Revolution

The Orange Revolution of 2004, a popular pro-Western uprising which forced a rerun of disputed elections, seems a very distant memory in today's Ukraine. The man behind the alleged electoral fraud was pro-Russia candidate Viktor Yanukovych, who was finally elected the country's president in 2010. The post-mortem of failed post-revolution politics continues, but as those orange days and nights on Kyiv's Independence Square fade into folk memory, Ukrainians enter a new and uncertain chapter in their history as the focus of power shifts once again.

Divided Nation

Even the most optimistic Ukrainians would admit that theirs is a divided nation. The Orange Revolution was driven by Ukrainian-speaking politicians with their support base in the west of the country, but President Yanukovych represents the interests of the Russian-speaking east and south. East of the River Dnipro the Orthodox Church rules supreme; west Ukrainians observe a mishmash of faiths. The east bathes in cosy nostalgia for the Soviet Union, while west Ukrainian nationalists rename streets after Stepan Bandera (controversial WWII leader of the Ukrainian Nationalist Organisation), and hanker to be enveloped in the EU's Russia-proof bubble. Odesa and Zaporizhzhya erect new Stalin monuments as west Ukrainians drag Moscow through international courts to gain compensation for relatives exiled to Kazakhstan and Siberia. 'How do these people live together?' you might ask yourself – but they do. To the outsider the differences are small, seemingly insignificant – people eat the same food, look the same, dress in the same cheap clothes, drive the same bad cars on the same bad roads, and vodka unites Ukraine's east and west. But a turbulent history still makes

Faux Pas

» Leaving your shoes on when entering someone's house, even if implored to do so.

» Giving an even number of flowers; that's for funerals.

» Tucking straight into food before your hosts have said *smachnoho* (bon apetit).

» Not bringing a gift when invited to someone's house.

» Gulping vodka without waiting for a toast.

» Shaking hands across a threshold – it brings bad luck.

» Leaving an empty bottle on the table – again, bad luck.

Top Films

Shadows of Forgotten Ancestors (1964) Shaggy Hutsul customs and symbolism.

Za Dvumya Zaytsami (Chasing Two Hares; 1961) Diverting romp through early-20th-century Kyiv.

Orange Revolution (2007) Steven York's doco on the events of 2004.

belief systems
(% of population)

50
Ukrainian Orthodox
(Kyiv Patriarchate)

26
Ukrainian Orthodox
(Moscow Patriarchate)

8
Greek
Catholic

7
Ukrainian
Autocephalous
Orthodox

9
Others

if Ukraine were 100 people

77 would be Ukrainian
17 would be Russian
6 would be Others

waves here, and Yanukovych's victory in the elections of 2010 was just the latest to crash onto Ukraine's troubled shores.

Ukraine Hit Hard

Ukraine's economy was hit harder than most in the world economic woes of 2008, and ordinary people are still feeling the pinch. The hryvnya, took a pummelling and has yet to recover. Reminders of the bad old days of the 1990s have appeared as locals retreat to the dollar and the euro for security, hoarding wedges of cash under the bed, safely out of the banking system. Though things have started to move again recently, for a couple of years all building work ceased in the capital as funds dried up; new bridges ended mid-arch, cranes loitered idly on the skyline and new high-rises froze mid-storey. At one point even the future of the biggest sporting event in the country's history looked in doubt.

Euro 2012

The one thing that unites Ukrainians is the fact that whatever their differences, whatever the economic and political weather, the country must be ready to host the world's third-largest sporting event, the UEFA European Football (Soccer) Championships in 2012, which it will co-host in an unlikely partnership with neighbouring Poland. For just over three weeks in June of 2012 the eyes of the world will be on Ukraine, and although many cynical locals anticipate international humiliation, talking to the officials in charge of hosting the tournament it's obvious the country will be ready. A successful hosting of Euro 2012 is certain to spark new interest in a bid for the Winter Olympics, another potential opportunity for Ukrainians to unite, at least for a moment, beneath their flag of navy and gold.

» Population: 45.7 million

» Official unemployment: 8.8%

» Population below poverty line: 35%

» Internet users: 10.3 million (2008)

» National anthem: 'Ukraine Has Not Yet Died'

Top Books

Evenings on a Farm near Dikanka Nikolai Gogol's stories, mostly set in his native Poltava region.
Borderland Anna Reid's journey through Ukrainian history.
Death and the Penguin Andrey Kurkov's Kafkaesque tale set in the troubled early 1990s.

Top Websites

www.tatar.net The lowdown on the Tatars, their history, culture and contemporary issues.
www.risu.org.ua A detailed portrait of all Ukraine's major and minor religions.
www.artukraine.com All you want to know about Ukrainian art.

www.cossacks.kiev.ua Ukrainian Cossacks in action.
www.ukrainianclassickitchen .ca Huge online Ukrainian recipe book.
www.umka.com.ua Online Ukrainian music store offering international shipping.

History

Although their northern neighbours disparagingly refer to Ukrainians as 'little Russians', it was Ukraine that was home to the first eastern Slavic state. So historically Ukraine is the birthplace of Russia rather than vice versa. Another irony is that this initial state, Kyivan Rus, was founded in the 9th century by neither Russians nor Ukrainians, but by Vikings – an indication of just how much foreigners have meddled in the region's convoluted history.

Invaded by Mongols from the east, encroached upon by Poland and Lithuania from the west and requisitioned by Russia from the north, Ukraine's national culture was principally forged in the wild, Cossack-held steppes in the middle. The baton of nationalism was taken up again in the 19th century by western Ukrainians under Austro-Hungarian rule, but it took the 1991 collapse of the Soviet Union for a centuries-old dream of an independent state to be realised.

Cimmerians to Khazars

Before Kyivan Rus, Ukraine's prehistory is tribal. First came the Cimmerians in the 12th century BC. Then, fierce warrior Scythians from Central Asia settled the steppe in the 7th century BC, while Greeks from western Asia Minor established city-states around the Black Sea. The two groups formed a symbiotic relationship. The famous gold work found in Scythian tombs is believed to have been commissioned from Greek artisans; a fine collection is found in Kyiv's Kyevo-Pecherska Lavra.

Successive waves of nomadic invaders (Sarmatians from the east, Germanic Ostrogoths from northern Poland and Huns from Mongolia) continued to sweep into Ukraine. However, the Slavs, thought to originate from near the borders of present-day Poland, Belarus and northwestern Ukraine, remained untouched by these invasions. Turkic-Iranian Khazars from the Caucasus were probably the first to bring the Slavs under subjugation, in the 8th century AD.

Orest Subtelny's 700-page *Ukraine, A History* is widely considered the definitive work on the subject, narrowly edging out Paul Magosci's equally long *History of Ukraine*. Both have been updated to cover the Orange Revolution. However, the most readable account of Ukraine's history is Anna Reid's *Borderland*, which neatly divides events into digestible chunks.

TIMELINE	482	879	989
	One of Eastern Europe's oldest settlements, Kyiv's origins aren't crystal-clear. Legend has it that Slavic brothers Ky, Shchek and Khoriv and their sister Lybid founded it.	Nordic King Oleh travels to Kyiv. Liking its strategic position on the Dnipro between Scandinavia and Constantinople, he wrests it from his own emissaries Askold and Dir – by killing them.	With Kyivan Rus now established as the first eastern Slavic state, Volodymyr the Great adopts Orthodox Christianity. A mass baptism in the Dnipro River seals this early pro-European decision.

Kyivan Rus

Meanwhile, Scandinavians – known as Varangians or Rus to the Slavs – had been exploring, trading and setting up small states east of the Baltic since the 6th century AD. Travelling south from the Rus power centre of Novgorod (near modern-day St Petersburg) in 879, King Oleh stopped just long enough to declare himself ruler of Kyiv. The city handily lay between Novgorod and Constantinople on the River Dnipro, and under Oleh's urging it became capital of a huge, unified Rus state. At its largest, under the rule of Volodymyr the Great (978–1015), this empire stretched from the Volga to the Danube and to the Baltic, its prosperity based on trade along the Dnipro. Despite Nordic rule, the territory's underlying culture remained essentially Slavic.

As well as consolidating Rus territory, Volodymyr firmly established Orthodox Christianity as the pre-eminent religion. By accepting baptism in 989 and marrying the Byzantine emperor's daughter (at Khersones outside Sevastopol), he opened the door to Byzantine artistic influences and cast Kyivan Rus as a European, rather than Islamic Asian, state. St Sofia's Cathedral in Kyiv is still testament to Kyivan Rus' greatness and the importance of Orthodox Christianity within the state.

For an easy-to-absorb, chronological listing of Ukrainian events from the 9th to the 20th centuries, set alongside those in the rest of the world, head to www.brama.com/ukraine/history.

After the death of Kyivan Rus's last great ruler, Yaroslav the Wise, in 1054, the empire began disintegrating into separate princedoms. When Mongol warriors sacked Kyiv in 1240, it largely ceased to exist. According to Russian and Western historians, who believe present-day Russia, Ukraine and Belarus all stem from Kyivan Rus, the centres of power then simply shifted north and west, with Russia evolving from the northern princedoms of Novgorod and Vladimir-Suzdal. Some Ukrainian historians, however, prefer to treat Russia as a distinct civilisation – emanating from and returning to Novgorod after 1240.

Mongols, Tatars & Turks

The Mongol invasion that sounded the death knell for Kyivan Rus in 1240 was led by Genghis Khan's grandson Batu. As a result of his handiwork, a large swathe of the Rus empire was subsumed into the so-called Golden Horde ('horde' meaning region) of the Mongol empire. This encompassed much of eastern and southern Ukraine, along with parts of European Russia and Siberia, with the city of Sarai, on the Volga, as its capital.

Over time, Mongol leaders were gradually replaced by their Tatar colleagues and descendants, and when the horde began to disintegrate in the 15th century, it divided into several smaller khanates.

One of these – the Crimean Khanate – eventually became a client state of the Constantinople-based Ottoman Turk Empire in 1475. The Crimean Tatars, as the people of the khanate were known, made

1199	1240	1349	1475
West of Kyiv, Prince Roman Mstyslavych merges the provinces of Galicia and Volynia into one Grand Duchy. Although landowners continue to rebel against his rule, a thriving agricultural society emerges.	A pivotal moment in Kyivan Rus history is reached, as Mongols sack the capital. The already fragmented empire's eastern regions are absorbed into the Mongolian Golden Horde. Many Kyivans flee west.	Ukraine comes under attack from the opposite direction, as Poland overruns Galicia and its capital Lviv. Nearly 40 years later, Poland teams up with Lithuania as they both inch eastwards.	The Crimean Khanate, which succeeded the Mongolian Golden Horde in 1428, becomes a client state of the Ottoman Empire, remaining so until 1772. Crimean Tatars frequently take slaves from mainland Ukraine.

frequent slave raids into Ukrainian, Russian and Polish territory until the 18th century. When Russia overran Crimea in 1783, it retaliated. The Tatars suffered dreadfully and often have ever since. Reminders of their once-powerful civilisation can be seen in Bakhchysaray, which is finally becoming resurgent in the 21st century.

Galicia-Volynia

Meanwhile, from 1199 under the rule of Prince Roman Mstyslavych, the region of Galicia-Volynia (most of present-day western, central and northern Ukraine, plus parts of northeastern Poland and southern Belarus) became one of the most powerful within Kyivan Rus. This enclave's geography differentiated it from the rest of the empire. It was far enough west to avoid conquest by eastern invaders like the Mongols and more likely to fall prey to its Catholic neighbours Hungary and Poland – or, later, Lithuania. More densely populated than any other part of Kyivan Rus, it developed a rich agricultural society.

Until 1340 Galicia-Volynia (also called Halych-Volhynia) enjoyed independent rule under Roman, his son Danylo, grandson Lev and descendants, who kept the Mongols at bay and helped Lviv and other cities to flourish. Political control was wrested from this local dynasty by the Poles and Lithuanians in the 1340s, who split the kingdom between them and used it as a base to expand eastwards into other areas of Ukraine, including Kyiv. However, its brief period of early self-determination seems to have left Galicia-Volynia with a particularly strong taste for Ukrainian nationalism, which is still evident today.

Roxelana, the powerful wife of Ottoman emperor Suleyman the Magnificent, was originally a Ukrainian slave from near Lviv, who was sold at Kaffa (today's Feodosiya) and taken to 16th-century Turkey.

Cossacks

Later lionised – perhaps overoptimistically – by nationalist writers such as Taras Shevchenko and Ivan Franko, the Cossacks are central to the country's identity. They arose out of the steppe in the country's sparsely populated mid-south. In the mid-15th century, this area was a kind of no-man's-land separating the Polish-Lithuanian settlements in the northwest from the Tatars in Crimea.

However, the steppe offered abundant natural wealth, and poorer individuals in Polish-Lithuanian society began making longer forays south to hunt or forage for food. The area also attracted runaway serfs, criminals, bandits and Orthodox refugees. Along with a few semi-independent Tatar bands, the hard-drinking inhabitants formed self-governing militaristic communities and became known as *kozaky* (Cossacks in English), from a Turkic word meaning 'outlaw, adventurer or free person'. The people elected the ruling chieftain (hetman). The most famous group of Cossacks was based below the rapids *(za porozhy)* on the lower Dnipro, in a fortified island community called the Zaporizhska Sich (see p228).

1554	1569	1648
Some 60 years after Cossacks first appear in the historical record, the fiercest and most famous band of warriors – the Zaporizhzhya Sich – sets up on an island in the Dnipro River.	The Union of Lublin builds on existing links to establish the Polish-Lithuanian Commonwealth. This monarchical democracy includes parts of Belarusia, Estonia, Latvia, Russia and Ukraine.	Central Ukrainian Cossacks become weary of foreign rule and, under the leadership of Bohdan Khmelnytsky, rebel against the Poles.

» *Bohdan Khmelnytsky*

PARADISE LOST

To avoid offending Ukrainians, one should never say out loud that one of their country's greatest heroes ultimately led it to defeat. Unfortunately, it is at least partly true.

The hero in question is the Cossack Hetman Bohdan Khmelnytsky, who led a huge rebellion against the Poles in 1648. Aided by Tatar cavalry, the Cossacks destroyed the Polish army at the Battle of Pyliavtsi (near present-day Khmelnytsky). Storming past Lviv, Khmelnytsky was poised for an invasion of Poland, but decided to accept an armistice and returned triumphantly to Kyiv.

The following year, at another battle against Polish King Casimir, near Zboriv, Khmelnytsky was betrayed by his Tatar allies and forced to sign an armistice. A further forced armistice in 1651 made Khmelnytsky finally realise that foreign support was necessary for a decisive victory over the Poles. He signed a military alliance with Russia in 1654, which eventually also betrayed him.

Instead of supporting the Cossacks, Russia went into battle against Poland in 1660 for control of Ukraine. In 1667 and 1668 the two powers signed treaties carving up the country between them. Russia got control over Kyiv and northern Ukraine east of the Dnipro. The Poles kept territory to the west of the river.

Later, Hetman Ivan Mazepa, aiming to unite Polish- and Russian-dominated Ukraine, allied with Sweden against Russia's Peter the Great but was beaten at Poltava (1709). After victories against the Ottomans, Catherine the Great destroyed the Cossack Sich at Zaporizhzhya in 1775.

Bohdan Khmelnytsky, though, is still revered for his initial storming victory against the Poles. He's remembered not as a man who hesitated, but as one who was fatally betrayed.

HISTORY COSSACKS

Although they were officially under Polish-Lithuanian rule from 1569, and sometimes joined the commonwealth army as mercenaries, the Cossacks were, for the most part, left to their own devices. They waged a number of successful campaigns against the Turks and Tatars, twice assaulting Istanbul (in 1615 and 1620) and sacking the Black Sea cities of Varna (in today's Bulgaria) and Kaffa (modern-day Feodosiya). While millions of peasants in the Polish-Lithuanian state joined the Uniate Church, the Cossacks remained Orthodox.

As Poland tried to tighten its control in the 17th century, there were Cossack-led uprisings to try to win greater autonomy. In 1654 the Cossacks formed their own so-called Hetmanate to assert the concept of Ukrainian self-determination. While initially successful, ultimately the Cossacks' military uprisings only led to a change of overlord – from Polish to Russian.

1654	1709	1772	1775
Cossacks enter into a military alliance with Russia against Poland. The Cossacks form their own fledgling state – whose initial success is shortlived – called a Hetmanate.	Cossacks seize another chance to throw off the colonial yoke, by joining Sweden in its 'Northern War' with Russia. But the Battle of Poltava doesn't go their way and victorious Tsarist forces execute them.	Under the three Partitions of Poland, Russia, Prussia and Habsburg Austria divvy up the weakened Polish-Lithuanian Commonwealth.	As her army moves south, and her lover Grygory Potemkin follows, blithely building film-set villages, Catherine the Great orders the destruction of the Cossack settlement at Zaporizhzhya.

Russian Control

Without Ukraine and its abundant natural wealth, Russia would never have become such a powerful nation. Ukraine also offered access to the Black Sea, so after a series of wars with the Turks in the 18th century, Russia was keen to expand into southern Ukraine. Catherine the Great led the charge to colonise and 'Russify'. In 1775, the same year she destroyed the Zaporizhska Sich, she annexed the region to the imperial province of 'New Russia' and charged governor Grygory Potemkin with attracting settlers and founding new cities. Potemkin helped establish today's Dnipropetrovsk, Sevastopol and Simferopol, but died before Odesa was completed.

In 1772 powerful Prussia, Austria and Russia decided to carve up Poland. Under the resulting Partitions of Poland (1772–95), most of western Ukraine was handed to Russia, but the far west around Lviv went to the Austrian Habsburg empire. The Ukrainian nationalist movement was born in Kyiv in the 1840s, but when the tsarist authorities there banned the Ukrainian language from official use in 1876, the movement's focus shifted to Austrian-controlled Lviv.

Neal Ascherson's *Black Sea* is a fascinating tale of the civilisations – and barbarians – that jostled for supremacy around this coast, from prehistory's Scythians to multicultural Odesa's 19th-century founders.

Civil War

Following WWI and the collapse of the tsarist monarchy, Ukraine had a shot at independence, but the international community was unsupportive and none of the bewildering array of factions could win decisive backing. In Kyiv, the first autonomous Ukrainian National Republic (UNR) was proclaimed in 1918 under president Mykhailo Hrushevsky. Meanwhile, Russian Bolsheviks set up a rival Congress of Soviets in Kharkiv. Civil war broke out, with five different armies – Red (Bolshevik), White, Polish, Ukrainian and Allied – vying for power, while various anarchist bands of Cossacks (the most famous led by Nestor Makhno) roamed the land. Author Mikhail Bulgakov estimated that Kyiv changed hands 14 times in 18 months.

Just as any UNR victories in Kyiv proved short-lived, so too did the West Ukrainian National Republic (ZUNR) in Lviv. Proclaimed in October 1918, it was overrun by Polish troops the following summer. Under the 1919 Treaty of Versailles negotiated after WWI and the following Treaty of Riga in 1921, Poland, Romania and Czechoslovakia took portions of western Ukraine, while Soviet forces were given control of the rest. Nationalist leader Semyon Petlyura set up a government in exile, but was assassinated in Paris in 1926.

Terry Brighton's *Hell Riders: The True Story of the Charge of the Light Brigade* interweaves participants' accounts and factual reports to unravel the Crimean War's greatest blunder.

Soviet Power

Thus handed to the Soviets, Ukraine was at the founding of the USSR in 1922. Behind Russia, it was the second largest and second most power-

1783	1825	1854	1861
Russia establishes its sovereignty over Crimea by demolishing mosques. Many Crimean Tatars flee. The Khans' Palace at Bakhchysaray survives because Empress Catherine finds it 'romantic'.	Many of the Decembrists behind a doomed St Petersburg coup hail from Ukraine. The most famous of the Decembrist wives, Maria Volkonskaya, also has close links to the country.	France and England have watched Russia's moves south with unease and decide to put a stop to it. The Crimea War sees Sevastopol come under 349 days' siege.	Tsar Aleksander II abolishes serfdom across the Russian Empire. That same year the first railway on Ukrainian soil is opened between Lviv and Przemysl (in today's Poland).

ful republic in the union, but despite – or perhaps because of – that 'little brother' status, it came in for some particularly harsh bullying from the top. When Stalin took power in 1927, he looked upon Ukraine as a laboratory for testing Soviet restructuring while stamping out 'harmful' nationalism. In 1932–33 he oversaw a famine (see the boxed text, p240). Executions and deportations of intellectuals and political 'dissidents' followed, along with the destruction of numerous Ukrainian palaces, churches and cemeteries. During the great purges of 1937–39, an estimated one million people in the USSR were executed and a further three to 12 million (the numbers are difficult to quantify) sent to labour camps, a high proportion of them from Ukraine.

New York Times journalist Walter Durranty is a controversial Pulitzer Prize winner because he covered up the Ukrainian famine when reporting from the 1930s USSR.

WWII

Even by the standards of Ukrainian history, WWII was a particularly bloody and fratricidal period. Caught between Soviet Russia, Nazi Germany and an ongoing struggle for independence, some six to eight million Ukrainians, at least 1.6 million of them Jews, were killed. Entire cities were ruined. The Red Army rolled into Polish Ukraine in September 1939, the Germans attacked in 1941, and the Nazis and their Romanian allies occupied most of the country for more than two years. Two million Ukrainians were conscripted into the Soviet army and fought on the Russian side. However, some nationalists hoped the Nazis would back Ukrainian independence and collaborated with Germany. This was a source of much post-war recrimination, but many partisans in the Ukrainian Insurgent Army (UPA) fought both German and Russian troops in a bid for an independent state. The catacombs just outside Odesa sheltered a celebrated group of partisans.

Mikhail Bulgakov's novel The White Guard enlivens the confusion reigning in Kyiv during the 1918 Civil War – and better explains the competing factions than most history books do.

In the end the Soviet army prevailed. In 1943 it retook Kharkiv and Kyiv before launching a massive offensive in early 1944 that pushed back German forces. In the process any hopes for an independent Ukraine were obliterated. Soviet leader Stalin also saw fit to deport millions of Ukrainians or send them to Siberia for supposed 'disloyalty or collaboration'. This included the entire population of Crimean Tatars in May 1944.

Towards the war's end, in February 1945, Stalin met with British and US leaders Churchill and Roosevelt at Yalta's Livadia Palace to discuss the administration of post-war Europe, among other things. The fact that the Red Army occupied so much of Eastern Europe at the end of WWII helped the USSR hold onto it in the post-war period.

Postwar Period

For most, WWII ended in 1945. The Ukrainian Insurgent Army (UPA) continued a guerrilla existence well into the 1950s, taking pot shots at

1876	1918	1917–1934	1928
With a new Ukrainian nationalist movement bubbling up since the 1840s, Tsar Aleksander II issues a decree banning the use of the Ukrainian language in public.	In the chaotic aftermath of WWI, Ukrainians try to form an independent republic but are hamstrung by internecine fighting. Fourteen different factions control Kyiv in 18 months.	The capital of the Ukrainian SSR is moved to Kharkiv by the Soviets. The city is still often referred to as Ukraine's 'first capital'.	Stalin's first Five Year Plan sees rapid and brutal industrialisation and massive immigration from the countryside into cities across Ukraine. Industrial output subsequently increases fourfold.

Between 1932 and 1933, some three to five million citizens of Ukraine – 'Europe's breadbasket' – died of starvation while surrounded by fields of wheat and locked government storehouses full of food. How did this happen? Stalin collectivised Soviet farms and ordered the production of unrealistic quotas of grain, which was then confiscated.

Many historians believe this famine was part of the Soviet leadership's wider plan to solve the 'nationality problem' within several troublesome republics, especially Ukraine. Undoubtedly the agricultural collectivisation of the time was ideologically driven. However, as the USSR's leading farmlands, Ukraine was particularly hard-hit, and documents released in 2006 suggest that Ukrainians were deliberately targeted in the 'Great Hunger'. For example, Ukraine's borders were reportedly shut to prevent people leaving.

A total of seven to 10 million people died throughout the USSR. (It's difficult to quantify, partly because those who took the next census were, in Stalin's inimitable style, immediately ordered shot.) Yet the true scale of the disaster has rarely been appreciated in the West.

As Soviet collectivisation began in the 1930s, combining individual farms into huge state-run communes (*kolkhozes*, or *kolhospy* in Ukrainian), wealthier peasants (*kulaks*, or *kurkuli* in Ukrainian) who resisted were deported or starved into submission. By 1932, Communist Party activists were seizing grain and produce from collectives and houses. Watchtowers were erected above fields. Anyone caught stealing was executed or deported. As entire villages starved, people committed suicide and even resorted to cannibalism.

At the time Soviet authorities denied the famine's existence, but damning facts have emerged since Ukrainian independence. In 2003 Kyiv designated the Holodomor, or Ukrainian famine, as genocide, and a handful of other governments followed suit. In 2005 president Viktor Yushchenko declared 26 November as official Holodomor Remembrance Day, and called on the international community to recognise the famine as genocide. Critics, however, continue to argue that the famine was aimed at certain social, rather than ethnic, groups. The Council of Europe adopted this stance in 2010, Russia remains firmly opposed to any 'genocide' description and new president Yanukovych has declared the events of the early 1930s a tragedy, but not genocide.

the Soviet authorities, especially in the Carpathian region. A government in exile was led by former partisan Stepan Bandera, until he was assassinated in Munich in 1959.

Elsewhere, Ukraine rapidly developed into an important cog in the Soviet machine. Eastern regions became highly industrialised, with

1932–33	1941	1943	1944
Millions of Ukrainians die in a famine caused by Stalin's farm collectivisation. Some historians believe that other grain-grabbing, border-closing measures deliberately targeted its people.	During WWII, Ukraine becomes a bloody battleground for opposing Nazi, Soviet and nationalist forces and some six million locals perish. The death toll includes almost all of Ukraine's Jews.	The Red Army liberates Kyiv from the Nazis on 6 November. Earlier, retreating Soviets had dynamited buildings along the main street of Khreshchatyk; these were replaced post-war with Stalinist structures.	Stalin deports the entire 250,000-strong Crimean Tatar population in just a few days, beginning 18 May. He accuses them of 'Nazi collaboration'. Thousands die during this genocidal journey of 'Sürgün'.

coal and iron-ore mining around Donetsk, arms and missile industries in Dnipropetrovsk, and Dniproges, a huge hydroelectric dam near Zaporizhzhya.

Ukraine acquired strategic technological and military importance during this era, and at least one Ukrainian rose to become Soviet leader. Leonid Brezhnev graduated from metallurgy engineer to Communist Party General Secretary from 1964 to 1982. Brezhnev's predecessor, Nikita Khrushchev (Soviet leader from 1953 to 1964) was born just outside Ukraine but lived there from adolescence and styled himself as a Ukrainian. Khrushchev's post-Stalin reformist agenda led him to create the Autonomous Crimean Soviet Socialist Republic in 1954, and transfer legislative control over Crimea to the Ukrainian Soviet Socialist Republic.

Nationalism Reappears

The rotten underbelly of Soviet high tech was cruelly exposed by the nuclear disaster at the power plant Chornobyl on 26 April 1986. Ukrainians weren't just killed and injured by the radioactive material that spewed over their countryside, but also appalled by the way the authorities attempted to cover up the accident. The first Kremlin announcement wasn't made until two days after the event – and only then at the prompting of Swedish authorities, who detected abnormal radiation levels over their own country. However, by then Kyiv was awash with rumour that something was afoot and many promptly decamped to the Carpathians and Crimea as fast as they could.

As more information came to light, discontent over Moscow's handling of the Chornobyl disaster revived nationalist feeling. Ukrainian independence had become a minority interest, mainly confined to the country's west, but slowly, the hard-core in the west started to take the rest of Ukraine with them. In 1988 marches rocked Lviv, and the Uniate Church, banned by Stalin in 1946, emerged from the underground as a pro-independence lobby. In 1989 the opposition movement Rukh (Ukrainian People's Movement for Restructuring) was established. By 1990 protest marches and hunger strikes had spread to Kyiv.

Independent Ukraine

With the nationalist movement snowballing and the USSR disintegrating, many politicians within the Communist Party of Ukraine (CPU) saw the writing on the wall. After the Soviet counter-coup in Moscow in August 1991 failed, they decided that if they didn't take their country to independence, the opposition would. So, on 24 August 1991, the Verkhovna Rada (Supreme Council) met, with speaker Stanyslav Hurenko's wonderfully pithy announcement recorded by the *Economist* for posterity: 'Today we will vote for Ukrainian independence, because if we don't

Leading 20th-century artist Joseph Beuys was rescued by Crimean Tatars when he crash-landed on the peninsula during WWII, and his oeuvre of sleds, felt and honey recalls their healing methods.

1945
Winston Churchill and an ailing Franklin Roosevelt travel to 'the Riviera of Hades' so Stalin can bully them. At the Yalta Conference, the Soviet leader demands chunks of Eastern Europe.

1959
Stepan Bandera, the exiled Ukrainian Insurgent Army (UPA) leader, is killed in Munich by the KGB. Ukrainian partisans had continued ambushing Soviet police until the mid-1950s.

» *Livadia Palace (p192), site of the Yalta Conference*

we're in the shit.' In December some 84% of the population voted in a referendum to back that pragmatic decision, and former CPU chairman Leonid Kravchuk was elected president.

As the new republic found its feet, there were more than the usual separation traumas from Russia. Disagreements and tensions arose, particularly over ownership of the Black Sea Fleet harboured in the Crimean port of Sevastopol. These were only resolved in 1999 by offering Russia a lease until 2017, controversially extended by the new government in 2010 to 2042.

Economic crisis forced Kravchuk's government to resign in September 1992. Leonid Kuchma, a pro-Russian reformer, came to power in July 1994 and stayed for 10 years.

During Kuchma's tenure, the economy did improve. The hryvnia was introduced and inflation was lowered from a spiralling 10,000%

CHORNOBYL: 'A MONSTER WHICH IS ALWAYS NEAR'

In perhaps the blackest of ironies in history, the world's worst nuclear disaster was the result of an unnecessary safety test. On the night of 25 April 1986, reactor No 4 at the Chornobyl power plant was due to be shut down for regular maintenance. Workers decided to use the opportunity to see if, in the event of a shutdown, enough electricity remained in the grid to power the reactor core cooling systems, and turned off the emergency cooling system. For various reasons, including a design flaw, operational errors and flouted safety procedures, the result was a power surge, a steam explosion and a full-blown nuclear explosion. At 1.26am on the morning of 26 April 1986, the reactor blew its 500-tonne top and spewed nearly 9 tonnes of radioactive material into the sky in a fireball. Radioactive material was blown north and west during the next few weeks, fallout dropping mainly over Belarus, and Ukraine. Some material also wafted over Sweden, whose scientists were the first to alert the world.

The Soviets initially remained silent while the emergency unfolded. Two people died in the explosion and another 29 firemen – sent in to clean up without proper radiation protection – died in the following weeks. Some 135,000 people were evacuated from the satellite town of Prypyat and a 30km radius around the plant, but were told it was only 'temporary'. Six days after the disaster, May Day parades in Kyiv went ahead.

Today the long-term effects of the disaster are still being felt and assessed. The most obvious impact has been an upsurge of thyroid cancer in children, with nearly 2000 cases reported. Studies suggest that of the 600,000 'liquidators' brought in to clean up, more than 4000 have died from exposure and 170,000 suffer from terminal diseases. In addition, some 35,000 sq km of forest remain contaminated, and the meat, milk, vegetables and fruit produced there have radioactivity levels higher than normal. It's estimated that by 2015 the disaster will have cost the economy $200 billion, although, of course, all the figures are disputed.

1986	1991	1991	1994
Reactor No 4 at the Chornobyl nuclear power plant explodes, after a failed safety test. More than 90 Hiroshimas are spewed out over the Ukrainian and Belarusian countryside.	President Gorbachev is held prisoner at his country retreat in Crimea while a coup led by hardliners takes place in Moscow.	As the Soviet Union falters, Ukraine's parliament votes for independence. Some 90% of the population figures that's about right and backs the decision in a referendum.	Former rocket scientist Leonid Kuchma becomes president. With inflation running at 10,000%, he moves to reform the economy, but his popularity wanes when he's implicated in a series of corruption scandals.

in 1993 to 5.2% in 2004, by which time GDP was growing at a rate of 9%. Kuchma's reign is also remembered for its extreme cronyism. Foreign investors complained that companies being privatised were often sold to Ukrainian ventures with presidential connections, sometimes for well under market value, and international watchdog Transparency International named Ukraine the world's third most corrupt country.

One major scandal surrounded the mysterious beheading of campaigning opposition journalist Georgiy Gongadze in 2000. Kuchma was widely rumoured to have ordered the killing. Although this was never proved, Gongadze became a posthumous cause célèbre.

The last working reactor at Chornobyl, No 3, was finally shut down in 2000.

The Orange Revolution

Former central banker Viktor Yushchenko had proved too reformist and pro-European for his masters when he was Leonid Kuchma's prime minister from 1998 to 2001. However, in 2004 as Kuchma prepared to stand down, Yushchenko re-emerged as a strong presidential contender.

Kuchma's anointed successor, the Kremlin-friendly Viktor Yanukovych, had expected an easy victory and the popularity of Yushchenko's Nasha Ukraina (Our Ukraine) party looked threatening. During an increasingly bitter campaign, and seven weeks before the scheduled 31 October election, Yushchenko underwent a remarkable physical transformation – disfiguration that Austrian doctors later confirmed was the result of dioxin poisoning.

After an inconclusive first round, a second vote was held on 21 November. A day later, contrary to the exit polls and amid widespread claims of vote-rigging by overseas electoral observers, Yanukovych was declared the winner.

Over the next few days and weeks Yushchenko supporters staged a show of people power unlike any Ukraine had ever seen. Despite freezing temperatures they took to the streets, brandishing banners and clothes in the opposition's trademark orange. They assembled to listen to Yushchenko and his powerful political ally Yulia Tymoshenko at mass rallies in Kyiv's maydan Nezalezhnosti (Independence Square). They surrounded parliament and established a demonstrators' tent city along Kyiv's main Khreshchatyk boulevard to keep up pressure on the authorities.

The Yanukovych camp refused to respond to a parliamentary vote of no-confidence in the election result and his eastern Ukrainian supporters threatened to secede if Yushchenko was declared president. Despite this, on 3 December the Supreme Court annulled the first election result, and the way was paved for a second poll on 26 December which

The 'Ukrainian Katyn' (mass grave) was revealed globally in 2007, when authorities reburied 2000 victims of the Soviet Secret Police (NKVD). The deaths at Bykovyna, near Kyiv, occurred in the 1930s and '40s.

Yushchenko, Yanukovych, Tymoshenko, Kuchma and the Supreme Court – want to understand the key players and sequence of events of 2004? *Ukraine's Orange Revolution* by Andrew Wilson helps you do it.

2000	**2004**	**2006**	**2007**
After opposition journalist Georgiy Gongadze is murdered, a recording emerges of President Kuchma asking his staff to 'deal with' the journalist. Kuchma later claims the tape has been selectively edited.	Thousands take to the freezing streets to protest that vote-rigging has robbed Viktor Yushchenko, of the presidency. The 'Orange Revolution' leads to a fairer second election, which Yushchenko wins.	Russia cuts off gas supplies on 1 January. Kyiv suspects punishment for becoming more pro-European. Moscow says it just wants a fair price – nearly five times the existing level.	Some 100 people die in the worst mining accident in Ukraine's history. The disaster at Zasyadko, eastern Donetsk, highlights safety concerns about all of the country's ageing coalmines.

Yushchenko won. The tent city was dismantled just in time for Yushchenko's swearing-in on 3 January 2005.

The Orange Glow Fades

A highly individual, entertaining and ultimately moving short photo-essay, www.theorange revolution.com looks back on Ukraine's momentous winter of 2004.

Alas, the course of true reform never did run smoothly in Ukraine (to paraphrase a *Time* magazine observation on Russia) and anyone hoping for a fairy-tale ending would be swiftly disappointed. Less than a year after they had stood shoulder to shoulder on the maydan in Kyiv, the Orange Revolution's heroes had fallen out with each other.

If you've been able to follow the ins and outs of Ukrainian's political scene since the Orange Revolution, you probably should get out more. In the late naughties the blond-braided Yulia Tymoshenko, a weak president Yushchenko and a resurgent Viktor Yanukovych engaged in an absurd political soap opera featuring snap elections, drawn out coalition deals, fisticuffs in parliament and musical chairs in the prime minister's office. Russia turned off the gas at opportune moments and the West got bored and moved on. The upshot was complete disillusionment with the Orange Revolution among the population and Viktor Yanukovych's victory in the April 2010 presidential elections.

2007	**2009**	**2010**	**2010**
The Ukraine-Poland bid to host the 2012 European Football (Soccer) Championships is successful. Immediately, doubts about Ukraine's ability to hold the event are voiced.	Russia once again turns off the gas on 1 January as Moscow claims Kyiv has failed to pay its bills. This time the EU steps in to resolve the dispute.	Despite allegations of a fraudulent election in 2004, Viktor Yanukovych becomes president in a closely fought February poll. Many Ukrainians fear press freedom and democracy will suffer under his rule.	In the Ukrainian parliament, fights break out and eggs and flour bombs are thrown by the opposition as a treaty allowing Russia's Black Sea fleet to remain in Sevastopol until 2042 is ratified.

The People

The National Psyche

Having endured centuries of many different foreign rulers, Ukrainians are a long-suffering people. They're nothing if not survivors; historically they've had to be, but after suffering a kind of identity theft during centuries of Russian rule in particular, this ancient nation that 'suddenly' emerged some 20 years ago is starting to forge a new personality.

Traditionally, many patriots would unite behind a vague sense of free-spirited Cossack culture and the national poet Taras Shevchenko. This is a religious society, a superstitious society and one in which traditional gender roles, strong family and community ties still bind. It's a culture where people are friendly and sometimes more generous than they can really afford to be. Paradoxically, it's also one in which remnants of the Soviet mentality – of unofficial unhelpfulness and suspicion of saying too much – remain. As in Russia, many people lead a kind of double life – snarling, elbowing *homo sovieticus* outside the house, but generous, kind and hospitable Europeans around their kitchen tables.

However, as contemporary commentators love to point out, Ukraine is also a patchwork nation. City dwellers and farmers, east and west, young and old, Russian-speaking and Ukrainian-speaking, Hutsul and Tatar have very different attitudes. Broadly speaking, Russian-speaking easterners look right towards the former Soviet Union, while Ukrainian-speaking westerners look hopefully left towards a future in Europe. But for every rule, there's an exception too.

In *The Ukrainians: Unexpected Nation* academic Andrew Wilson examines Ukraine's founding myths, how its history and culture have shaped its national identity and what it all means for this ancient but young nation.

Lifestyle

Just as there is no one 'typical' Ukrainian, so there is no single average lifestyle. This is still a relatively poor, second-world country. However, it's fair to say that daily life has become marginally easier for most households in the last decade. Until 2008 the average national wage had been increasing quite rapidly, though it has stagnated at around 1500uah ($190, €150) per month in recent years. However, since the economic downturn of 2008 prices, particularly of food, have shot up, meaning a decrease in many people's standard of living.

Middle-class Ukrainians have always had ways of getting by, holding down several jobs, pursuing a number of money-making schemes and looking out for each other. Outside big cities, it's also been common for people to grow food in their back garden and for extended families to divvy up domestic duties. *Baba* (grandma) is frequently a respected household member, very often in charge of the kids while parents go off to work.

Old appliances or unreliable hot water and power supplies mean domestic life can be more arduous and time-consuming for both urban apartment-dwellers and rural inhabitants. Old Soviet apartments are

IDENTITY

quite compact and old-fashioned, but people always remove their shoes carefully at the door. Some Ukrainians still do laundry in the bathtub and eating out is an event.

Yet, amid the old housing stock and creaking public transport infrastructure, young Ukrainians are avid users of new technology and media. Everyone has at least one mobile phone (usually more), internet cafes are usually packed and social networking sites are as popular as they are in the West. Even 3-G technology is catching on and wi-fi buzzes through all but the cheapest of hotels, cafes and restaurants.

Mind the Gap

Even after two decades of 'reforms', there's still a mammoth and ever-widening gap between average Ukrainians and the super-rich elite. It's the country's oligarchs and 'new Ukrainian' businesspeople you see driving the black Mercedes SUVs and shopping in Kyiv's designer boutiques. Had the aspirations of the Orange Revolution been fulfilled, this gap may have narrowed, but under Yanukovych most expect more of the same.

A CARPATHO-RUSYN WEDDING *LISA DUNFORD*

Hospodi pomiluj, Hospodi pomiluj... Long forgotten Old Church Slavonic chants from my childhood came back to me as I stood, about to be married, in the Greek Catholic Cathedral in Uzhhorod – a hundred years to the month after my great-grandfather was married, and subsequently ordained, there. Growing up I'd thought we were Hungarian, until I tried to translate a novella he wrote and it turned out to be in a Slavic dialect.

The confusion is understandable given the history of the Carpathian region. The origins of the first Slavic settlers are a bit fuzzy – a mixture of White Croats, Slavs who came with the Huns, and Slavs from Galicia (Poland). How they got their Orthodox religion is also unclear, as the region was never part of Kyivan Rus; from the 11th century until WWI it was under Hungarian and Austrian rule. So perhaps they brought it west with them or maybe it was spread by wandering Kyivan Rus missionaries. What's better known is that in 1646, at the Union of Uzhhorod, a group of Orthodox churches in Transcarpathia accepted the authority of Rome, creating the unique hybrid that is the Greek Catholic (or Uniate) religion. The traditions of Orthodoxy remain – plain-chant liturgies, onion-dome architecture, icon veneration, married priests – but the leader of the church is the Pope, and the theology Catholic.

Faith was the defining factor in the identity of the Carpatho-Rusyns like my great-grandfather who lived in the region before the war. As a priest, he spoke Slavonic, Rusyn, Hungarian, Slovak and probably a Polish dialect. Under the Soviet Union, Greek Catholicism was outlawed, priests were sent to hard labour in Siberia and churches were seized. The Rusyn and Hungarian languages were taken out of schools – only Russian and Ukrainian were allowed. Post-communism, the Greek Catholics recovered some of their churches, including the cathedral. And in 1996 the Rusyn language was codified. That's the language Grandpa's book was written in; the story tells of a village wedding party where a gypsy played.

Standing before the two-storey gold icon screen shimmering in the soft light as crowns of flowers were placed on our heads, I realised the ancient words being chanted were the same words sung a hundred years before. Sixteen relatives, descendents of my great-grandfather's brother who we'd lost touch with for decades after WWII, stood behind me at the dais. My great-grandparents had a town wedding, so probably no three-day feast and gypsy violinist for them. We had a cousin serenade us with a Mozart piano recital. At the dinner party the relatives spoke in a mishmash of languages: me in English, Hungarian and Slovak; them in Hungarian, Ukrainian and English. In Transcarpathia, a Greek Catholic wedding and a mix of languages seemed entirely appropriate.

At the lower end of the scale are the elderly and other pensioners. Although the basic pension has increased to around 700uah per month (2010), over 30% of Ukrainians remain below the poverty line. Due to losses in WWII, industrial accidents, deadly roads, vodka and general bad health among males, many of the elderly are women. They can often be seen selling their home-grown produce on the street to make ends meet.

Population

As a crossroads between Europe and Asia, Ukraine has been settled by numerous ethnic groups throughout history and has a fascinating underlying mix. However, most people still describe themselves as Ukrainians and, hence, of Slavic origin. According to the last census (2001), 77% of the country's population are ethnically Ukrainian. The other large ethnic group is Russian, who account for 17% of the population, and are mainly concentrated in the south and east. However, these figures are not reflected in the language people speak; many claiming to be Ukrainian use Russian as their first language.

Minorities

Ukraine's ethnic minority groups include, in order of size, Belarusians, Moldovans, Tatars, Bulgarians, Hungarians, Romanians, Poles and Jews. Almost all of the country's 260,000 Tatars live in Crimea. No one measures the size of western Ukrainian Hutsul communities, which in any case are seamlessly integrated into the wider community. In 2007 the 800,000 Rusyns (an ethnic group of the Carpathians spread across Ukraine, Poland and Slovakia) were recognised by Transcarpathian authorities as distinct from mainstream Ukrainians.

Dying Nation

Since independence, Ukraine's population has fallen more dramatically than that of any other country not affected by war, famine or plague. The number of citizens plummeted from 52 million in 1993 to around 45.8 million in 2010, as birth rates and life expectancy dropped concomitantly. This demographic trend has slowed in the last few years, and there's even been a mini baby boom, but the overall situation has only improved slightly with population growth figures for 2010 estimated at -0.6%. Also, due to the bureaucratic system of registering citizens at a certain address, population figures include a huge chunk of the nation that has emigrated in search of a better life, but still officially resides in Ukraine for legal reasons. This means the actual population figure may be as low as 39 million.

A large Ukrainian diaspora of some 2.5 million people exists. Many live in North America, particularly Canada.

Multiculturalism

The 'ethnic' schism between western and eastern Ukraine has been under the spotlight since the Orange Revolution, when there were brief but serious fears the country might split. With Russian immigration into Ukrainian territory from the late 17th century, some Russian Ukrainians still feel their allegiance lies more with Moscow than with Kyiv. This immigration is the single reason Ukrainian nationalists refuse to see an east–west split as a solution to the country's ethnic strife. Though the cause of countless problems, the divisions are neither as clear-cut nor as intractable as some politicians like to suggest.

Patriotic western Ukrainians often liken the difference between themselves and Russians to that between Canadians and Americans (other slightly better comparisons include the Spanish and the Portuguese or,

THE PEOPLE POPULATION

Buying produce such as milk, honey and vegetables from old ladies on the street means you are contributing directly to the local economy, and not funding an oligarch supermarket owner's lifestyle in the Bahamas.

Former Israeli prime minister Golda Meir and film star Milla Jovovich were both born in Kyiv, Bolshevik Leon Trotsky hailed from outside Odesa, and both Dustin Hoffman and Sylvester Stallone have Ukrainian roots.

According to local superstition, women should never sit down on steps, walls or anything concrete, lest their ovaries freeze and they can't bear children. Remember this when tired from sightseeing!

THE PEOPLE RELIGION

It involves fire, water, dancing, fortune-telling, and strong overtones of sex. So is it any wonder the Soviets tried to quash the festival of Ivan Kupala, a pagan midsummer celebration? Indeed, leaders since the Middle Ages – including Cossack *hetmans* (leaders) – have tried to outlaw it, but all without success. The festival is still marked across Ukraine and beyond.

To ancient pre-Christians, Kupala was the god of love and fertility, and young people would choose a marriage partner on this eve. Today's rituals vary, but typically begin with folk singing and a maypole-style dance performed by young women wearing white gowns and flower wreaths in their hair. After this, the women float their wreaths (symbolising virginity) down the requisite nearby river or other body of water. A wreath that sinks indicates bad fortune in love for its owner.

Later a bonfire is lit, around which young couples dance. Couples will also jump over small fires, holding hands, to test whether – if they maintain their grip – their love will last. In ancient times, the young men would go off into the woods to seek a special 'magical' fern before dawn.

After Kyivan Rus adopted Christianity, the festival became mixed up with the birthday of John the Baptist. This not only means the festival has largely been shifted from the summer solstice on 22 June to 7 July, it sometimes means people walk in the fire or jump in the river as a 'cleansing' act. A good spot to join Kupala celebrations is Pyrohovo (p48) in Kyiv, or head to the countryside for more traditional rituals.

perhaps most accurate historically, the British and Irish). However, not all Ukrainians feel quite so strongly about their most powerful neighbour and in public the divisions are principally played out in religion and language.

Crimea

Only 11 countries in the world have a lower birth rate than Ukraine, with 2010 estimates putting the average number of children born per woman at just 1.24. The world average is 2.56.

Different tensions exist in Crimea, where some 260,000 Tatars have resettled since the 1990s. After early clashes, 14 Tatar seats were granted in the Crimean parliament and the situation quietened down. Disturbingly, there have been attacks by skinhead 'Cossack paramilitary' groups on Tatars and their property. In August 2006 there was a particularly ugly confrontation between Tatars who wanted a market removed from one of their burial grounds, and other small-scale skirmishes have continued. Whether or not they're in the news, the Crimean Tatars undoubtedly face racism, of both a casual and deep-seated nature, on a daily basis. Tatar leaders have also expressed concerns over Ukraine's shift towards a more Russia-friendly policy in Crimea since the Yanukovych administration took over in 2010.

Religion

As the sheer number of churches in Ukraine attests, religion in this country is pivotal. It has provided comfort during many hard times and even shaped Ukrainian identity, as by accepting Orthodox Christianity in 989, Volodymyr the Great cast Kyivan Rus as a European, rather than Islamic Asian, state.

For the lowdown from Tatars themselves on their history, culture and contemporary issues, visit www.tatar.net.

Ukraine's Many Churches

Today the country's sizable Christian population is confusingly splintered into three Orthodox churches and one major form of Catholicism.

In the 17th century, when Ukraine came under Russian rule, so did its Orthodox Church. Even now, nearly two decades after independence, the largest Orthodox congregation in the country belongs to the Ukrainian Orthodox Church (UOC-MP), the former Ukrainian section of the Russian Orthodox Church that still pays allegiance to the Moscow Patriarch. There are also two smaller, breakaway Orthodox churches, which are both more 'Ukrainian' in nature. A Ukrainian Orthodox Church (UOC-KP) was formed in 1992 after independence to pay allegiance to a local Kyiv Patriarch. Meanwhile, the Ukrainian Autocephalous Orthodox Church (UAOC), formed during the 19th century in western Ukraine and suppressed by the Soviets, has bounced back since independence.

To complicate matters, another five to six million Ukrainians follow another brand of Christianity entirely. In 1596 the Union of Brest established the Uniate Church (often called the Ukrainian Catholic or Greek Catholic Church). Mixing Orthodox Christian practices with allegiance to the Pope, this essentially Catholic church was, and is, popular in the western part of the country once controlled by Poland. In 2005 it shifted its headquarters to Kyiv to position itself as more of a pan-Ukrainian faith.

'Well the Ukraine girls really knock me out, they leave the West behind' – even the Beatles sang the praises of Ukrainian females in their song, 'Back in the USSR'.

Religious Rivalry

The two main Orthodox churches – Moscow Patriarchate and Kyiv Patriarchate – have had territorial disputes in the past. The Ukrainian government's 1995 refusal to allow Kyiv Patriarch Volodymyr Romanyuk to be buried inside Kyiv's St Sophia's Cathedral, for fear of reprisals from Moscow, is a good example. They have since confined themselves to more low-level bickering, about how many adherents each has, for example. The Moscow Patriarchate has the greater number of parishes at 10,875, but in some polls up to 50% of Orthodox believers claim to follow the Kyiv Patriarchate, so the picture is completely muddled.

Tensions between these two churches have been rising recently, especially as the Moscow Patriarch Kirill I, has made a couple of controversial visits to Ukraine since the more pro-Russia government took over in 2010. The UOC-MP favours close ties with Russia and backed Viktor Yanukovych during the Orange Revolution. The UOC-KP, the UAOC and the Uniate Church all welcome greater Western ties.

For a detailed portrait of all Ukraine's major and minor religions, head to the excellent www.risu.org.ua, which also offers relevant news and statistics.

Other Faiths

Minority faiths include Roman Catholicism, Judaism and, among Crimean Tatars, Sunni Islam. Ukraine's religious freedom means Evangelical, Buddhist, Jehovah's Witness and neo-pagan communities have also emerged since independence from the atheist USSR.

Sport

Every Ukrainian will tell you his or her country is sports mad, but as with most ex-USSR countries, you'll hardly ever see anyone actually engaging in sporting activities, especially outside of the big cities.

TEMPLE DOS & DON'TS

Religious Ukrainians are a pretty tolerant lot, but women should cover their heads when entering Orthodox churches. There's an even stricter dress code (no above-knee skirts for women and no hats for men) when visiting particularly holy sites such as the Kyevo-Pecherska Lavra and Pochayiv Monastery. Taking photos during a service, touching the icons and affectionate hand-holding may incur the wrath of the church's elderly custodians.

Crimean Tatars are Muslim, but only a few are really devout and many others even drink alcohol. Nevertheless, women should dress modestly when entering mosques. A scarf to cover the head and shoulders is definitely needed when visiting Yevpatoriya's Whirling Dervish Monastery, possibly the strictest Muslim site in Ukraine.

THE ROAD TO EURO 2012

With football the leading spectator sport in Ukraine, the country was delighted, and not a little surprised, to be chosen with Poland as joint hosts of the European Football Championships in 2012. Ukraine team captain Andriy Shevchenko, boxer Vitaly Klytschko and former president Viktor Yushchenko were all cheerleaders for the Euro 2012 bid, the first time Ukraine will be involved in hosting such a major soccer event.

Games are to be played in four far-flung Ukrainian cities – Kyiv, Donetsk, Kharkiv and Lviv. (the Polish cities of Warsaw, Poznan, Gdansk and Wroclaw are the other four venues). Fears of a late kick-off have been allayed recently with the required investment going into infrastructure and stadium reconstruction. The main legacy for the country will be a high-speed rail link between Kyiv and Boryspil airport, a new airport in Lviv and a complete rebuild of the Kyiv–Chop highway, the country's main road transport artery. It even looks as though the country's hotels will get their act together, though in 2010 there were still worries about Donetsk and the standard of team training bases. One problem that probably won't be solved in time are the new border crossing points between Poland and Ukraine, and border queues may prove the biggest obstacle to holding a trouble-free tournament.

The final will be held in Kyiv, but the most impressive stadium is Donetsk's Donbass Arena. Eastern Europe's most technically advanced soccer stadium was funded by football-crazy oligarch Rinat Akhmetov, Ukraine's richest man and owner of the Shakhtar Donetsk football team. None other than American R&B singer Beyoncé performed at the opening.

Football

Dynamo Kyiv's official website at www.fcdynamo.kiev.ua now has an English section. You can also follow the domestic Ukrainian league at www.ukrainiansoccer.net.

As football continues its inexorable domination of sports TV schedules, Dynamo Kyiv is no longer the only well-known Ukrainian team. Play-offs between foreign clubs and Shakhtar Donetsk, Metallist Kharkiv or Karpaty Lviv have also guaranteed those teams prominence. Former Chelsea striker and national team captain, Andriy Shevchenko, threatened to overshadow his namesake Taras Shevchenko (the Ukrainian national poet) on the world stage at one point, but his failure to make a mark at Roman Abramovich's London club and Ukraine's poor showing on the international scene has seen his fame wane slightly. He returned to Dynamo Kyiv in August 2009.

Of course 2012 will see Ukraine take footballing centre stage when it co-hosts the UEFA European Football Championships with neighbouring Poland. Lviv, Donetsk, Kharkiv and Kyiv will host matches, with the final played at the newly rebuilt Olympic stadium in the capital.

Other Sports

Vitaly Klytschko is still punching his weight in the political ring and in 2010 even founded a new political party called the Ukrainian Democratic Alliance for Reform.

Ukraine also enjoys ice hockey (though the national team brings little joy) and has an international presence in boxing with the brothers Vitaly and Volodymyr Klytschko. Vitaly in particular gained prominence as the world heavyweight champion. Injury forced him to retire in November 2005, when he was still the titleholder, and this staunch backer of Viktor Yushchenko announced a desire to become involved in politics. After running unsuccessfully for mayor of Kyiv, Klytschko announced a boxing comeback and now holds the WBC heavyweight title.

Tennis has also gained popularity since independence, and Ukraine now has three men in the top 100 (but only one woman). A decade and a half ago there were virtually no bicycles on Ukraine's roads, but all kinds of cycling has since gained in popularity, especially mountain biking in the Carpathians and Crimea.

Women in Ukraine

Cynically speaking, women have been one of independent Ukraine's biggest tourist attractions. Combine their legendary beauty, devotion to personal grooming and sometimes outrageous, sexualised fashion sense with a relatively impoverished society, especially in the early 1990s, and you were always going to have fertile ground for online 'dating agencies', 'marriage agencies' and straight-out sex tourism. Sex trafficking of Ukrainian women and girls is now a serious problem, too.

These myriad dating agencies, introducing sometimes not-so-attractive overseas men to beautiful Ukrainian women, are the reason you'll notice an awful lot of oddly matched couples in Ukraine. Victor Malarek, author of *The Natashas: The New Global Sex Trade,* even contends: 'These agencies...are usually nothing more than online brothels'.

There are over 3½ million more women in Ukraine than there are men. This despite slightly more boys being born on average than girls.

Gender Roles & Discrimination

Traditional gender roles are quite entrenched in Ukraine's paternalistic society. Even the country's many young career women unashamedly place much greater emphasis on their looks than their Western counterparts would. The press coverage devoted to high-flying politician and billionaire businesswoman Yulia Tymoshenko is a case in point, with its continual habit of commenting on her beauty, even once questioning whether her typically Ukrainian blonde braid was real.

In 2003, Human Rights Watch was concerned that Ukrainian women faced job discrimination, with age, appearance and family circumstances often excluding them from roles they were professionally qualified for, and because they were most likely to be given the lowest-paying roles. The group opined: 'The job market in Ukraine reflects some highly archaic stereotypes about women's capabilities'. Little has changed since.

GENDER

THE PEOPLE WOMEN IN UKRAINE

Food & Drink

'*Borshch* and bread – that's our food.' With this national saying, Ukrainians admit theirs is a cuisine of comfort – full of hearty, mild dishes designed for fierce winters – rather than one of gastronomic zing. And yet, while it's suffered from negative stereotypes of Soviet-style cabbage slop and pernicious pickles, Ukrainian cooking isn't bad these days. In recent years, chefs have rediscovered the wholesome appeal of the national cuisine. Plenty of Ukrainian-themed restaurants offer the chance to sample *varenyky* (stuffed, ravioli-like dumplings), *kruchenyky* (beef roulades with prunes, bacon and spinach), elaborately stuffed fish dishes or red-caviar pancakes, washed down with chilled vodka or freshly pressed cranberry juice.

Obviously, the country's weather has influenced its cuisine. As London restaurant reviewer Tom Parker-Bowles put it, this is 'the sort of food you eat before venturing out into the snow to wrestle a bear'. However, successive invaders and immigrants have left their mark on a menu heavily reliant on local produce. So while Ukrainians love the carp, pikeperch and salmon found in their rivers, the pork and game roaming their lands, and the wheat and barley from their fields, they're also familiar with Siberian *pelmeny* (filled pasta like ravioli) and Jewish-style dishes.

If Ukraine has a culinary capital, it's probably Kyiv, but there are interesting regional sidelines, too. The Hutsul people of the Carpathians favour berries and mushrooms, plus their own speciality cheese *brynza* (a cross between cottage cheese and feta) and polenta-style *banush* or *mamalyha*. Central Asian–style Tatar cuisine spices up the menus in Crimea, with specialities like *shashlyk* (shish kebab). For more on Crimean food, see the boxed text, p164. Another unmistakable feature across the country is the recent success of restaurant chains (see p255), which can be a godsend for travellers on a budget or those who just want to grab a quick bite to eat.

Staples & Specialities

Many of the country's specialities stem from down-to-earth peasant dishes, based on grains and staple vegetables like potatoes, cabbage, beets or mushrooms, then seasoned with garlic and dill.

Borshch Locals would have you know that *borshch* (борщ) is Ukrainian – not Russian, not Polish, but Ukrainian – and there's nothing better than a steaming

---

Ukrainians love *salo* (raw pig fat) so much they even smuggle it. In 2007, one group was caught at the Russian border near Donetsk trying to illicitly bring three tonnes of the stuff into Ukraine.

You can learn how to cook everything from different types of *borshch* to delicious *medovyky* (honey cakes) with Hippocrene's *Best of Ukrainian Cuisine* (1998) by Bohdan Zahny.

RESTAURANT PRICES

Price categories used in this guide per main course:

» **$** budget less than 50uah for meals
» **$$** midrange 50uah to 150uah
» **$$$** top end more than 150uah

Ukrainian food could sometimes be described as bland, but there's nothing shy and retiring about the following delicacies.

Salo Eating this raw pig fat is a centuries-old tradition that runs deep and thick, quite literally, in the Ukrainian blood. Songs and poems are even dedicated to this product, which long provided a cheaper and more preservable alternative to meat. Some Ukrainian doctors even recommend 30g each morning for a long and healthy life! You'll find *salo* (сало) flavoured with garlic, and salt and occasionally smoked, on most menus and occasionally you'll even alight on the 'Ukrainian Snickers bar' – *salo* in chocolate. Never suggest to a Ukrainian that eating *salo* could be unhealthy.

Churchkheli Originally from Georgia, these nut-based sweets could easily be mistaken for a thin sausage or candle. What's slightly alarming about the Ukrainian versions, seen predominantly in Crimea, is just how brightly coloured they are – are there E-numbers in there? In the final analysis, though, *churchkheli* (чурчхелі) turn out to be delicious. They're an innocuous combination of hazelnuts (walnuts are more traditionally used in Georgia) dipped in a gel of wine, or in apple or pomegranate juice.

Sheep and bull's testicles Sold charcoal-grilled at some Tatar roadside stalls and restaurants in Crimea, this he-man dish reportedly tastes like kidneys crossed with that old staple – chicken.

bowlful in winter. A typical version of the national soup is made with beetroot, pork fat and herbs, but there's also an aromatic 'green' variety, based on sorrel. Regional *borshch* recipes can include sausages, red kidney beans, marrows or marinated apples. If you don't like *smetana* (сметана, soured cream), you'd better pipe up early, as this is normally added automatically.

Bread Visiting Ukraine in the 1840s, French writer Honoré de Balzac counted '77 ways of preparing bread'. Dark and white varieties of *khlib* (хліб) are available every day, including the white *pampushky* (soft rolls rubbed with garlic and oil and then fried) served with *borshch*. Bread is often used in religious ceremonies and on special occasions. Visitors are traditionally greeted with bread and salt.

Cabbage Rolls *Holubtsy* (голубці) are cabbage rolls stuffed with seasoned rice and meat and stewed in a tomato and soured cream sauce.

Kasha Pretty much any grain is called *kasha* (каша) in Ukrainian, and while the word might be used to describe what Westerners would call porridge, more commonly it turns out to be buckwheat. The latter appears as a side dish, as stuffing or as an unusual but filling breakfast gruel. More strongly flavoured than you'd expect, it's an acquired taste.

Pancakes Three types of pancake might land on your plate. *Deruny* (деруни) are potato pancakes, and are served with soured cream and vegetables or meat. *Nalysnyky* (налисники) are thin crepes; *mlyntsy* (млинці) are thicker and smaller, like Russian *blyny*.

Varenyky Similar to Polish *pierogi*, *varenyky* (вареники) are to Ukraine what dim sum is to China and filled pasta to Italy. These small half-moon-shaped dumplings have more than 50 different traditional vegetarian and meat fillings. They're usually served with soured cream.

Drinks

On street corners in summer, you'll see small drinks tankers selling *kvas* (квас), a gingery, beer-like soft drink, which is made from sugar and old black bread and is mildly alcoholic; look for the big vats with hosepipe attachments. *Kvas* is proffered in plastic beakers but the communal mug on a chain that everyone shares seems to have made something of a comeback. If the tankers have scuttled away for the winter, you can buy *kvas* in plastic bottles at the supermarket, but it's over-carbonated and lacks that zingy 'live' taste.

A series of updated and adapted traditional recipes from American-Ukrainian homes is brought together in *Ukrainian Recipes* (1996), edited by Joanne Asala. Daily staples and festive fare are both included.

A phrase you often hear in Ukrainian restaurants, particularly in smaller towns, is 'ne-ma-ye', meaning 'there isn't any'. It turns out many menu items aren't always available. This is because eating out is still quite a treat for many Ukrainians, who mostly only come for slap-up feasts and celebrations booked in advance. Many restaurants, in turn, have written their menus for these banqueting groups. While they might be happy to pre-order ingredients for a party, shark fin and kangaroo steak won't normally be in their pantry, even if these dishes stay on the menu. Since only nouveau riche Ukrainians eat out regularly, restaurants outside Kyiv are often quite empty.

It may come as a surprise to hear that Ukraine, a country where every occasion or meeting is steeped in vodka, produces some very quaffable beers. In fact, the beer market is booming, with many young people, especially in the cities, turning their backs on vodka for it.

Breweries produce various light, dark, unfiltered and flavoured lagers; there are at least 40 different domestic varieties, including the following leading brands:

Chernihivske (Чернігівське; www.chernigivske.com.ua/en) This brewery originally hails from Chernihiv, but now has some beers from Mykolayiv on its roster of light, premium, strong and dark labels. The fashionable stand-out of late has been its Bile (біле), a cloudy, German-style wheat beer.

Lvivske (львівське; www.lvivske.com) In the Galician capital from which it originates, you can learn more about delicious Lvivske on a brewery tour (p95).

Obolon (Оболонь; www.obolon.com) Named after a Kyiv suburb, Obolon is the third-largest brewery in Europe, and Ukraine's largest manufacturer and number-one export beer.

Slavutych (Славутич; www.slavutich.ua) Hailing from Zaporizhzhya, Slavutych comes in four varieties including a flavoursome non-alcoholic version.

Nearly 20 *borshch* recipes can be found at www.borshchrecipe.info – just a tiny sample of more than 300 different varieties that exist.

The situation with Ukrainian wine is not so rosé, with production having fallen by almost three quarters since Gorbachev's 'dry law' saw many vines pulled up in the late 1980s. Crimea still produces wines, but most of them are sugary dessert wines akin to Madeira or sherry. Some Koktebel-label whites and Inkerman reds are probably the best you will drink in Ukraine. Wines are also grown in the Transcarpathian region, and some top restaurants in Kyiv now source their wines from this area. Sadly, the best wines available in Ukraine still come from neighbouring Moldova.

The biggest name in Ukrainian vodka is undoubtedly **Nemiroff** (www.nemiroff.ua). However, although they seem to imbibe an awful lot of the stuff, surveys show Ukrainians don't drink anything like as much as Russians – which is probably a good thing.

Celebrations

Ukrainian food truly comes into its own during Christmas, Easter and wedding celebrations. Marta Pisetska Farley's *Festive Ukrainian Cooking* (1990) will give you chapter, verse and recipes.

At Easter, certain foods are taken to church in a covered basket to be blessed. These usually include hard-boiled eggs, baked cheese and Easter breads like round *paska* (паска; decorated with crosses) or tall, cylindrical *babka* (бабка; a sweet egg bread). Think hot-cross bun meets panettone.

On their wedding day, bride and groom break a spectacular round bread called a *korovay* (Коровай) – whoever gets the bigger half will be the dominant partner in the marriage.

Where To Eat & Drink

Restaurant (ресторан) and cafe (кафе) sound similar in English and Ukrainian. Some Ukrainian restaurants specialise in a particular dish, such as a *varenychna* (варенична), which serves only *varenyky*. A *stolova* (столова) is a Russian-style self-service canteen. Visiting Ukraine, you should probably swallow any dislike you may have of theme restaurants – they're as trendy here as in Russia.

Most restaurants are open from 11am or noon to 11pm or midnight, serving food constantly throughout. Cafes and canteens often open at the earlier time of 8am, but frequently stay open late too.

When eating in restaurants, be aware that prices for many meat and fish dishes are listed on the menu by weight. For example, the *shashlyk* that looks good value at 10uah, might actually be 10uah per 100g, so read the menu carefully, and if in doubt, ask. Bread and condiments are never complimentary, but they cost very little.

Tipping is virtually unheard of except in big-city places where waiters have become used to foreigners adding something to the bill. Out in the sticks, a tip may even be returned – the staff believing you've overpaid by accident.

Quick Eats

Food kiosks selling drinks and snacks sprout up on every spare inch of pavement in Ukraine, especially around train and bus stations. Mostly they deal in cigarettes, sweets and the ever-present chewing gum. The bottles on the shelves range from water and soft drinks to beer, which is also considered a soft drink by most Ukrainians but is now illegal to drink in most public places (though you'd hardly guess this was so).

Other stalls sell pastries or warm snacks, including newcomers such as hamburgers and hot dogs, as well as Soviet favourites such as *shashlyky* (шашлик) and *perepichky* (перепічки, fairground-style frankfurters deep-fried in dough) and *chebureky* (чебуреки, fried meat turnovers). It's not as if you need triple-strength health insurance to eat at these, but if you have a delicate stomach, give them a wide berth.

If you're self-catering, head to the local market *(rynok)*, which always provides a colourful experience. Old-style food stores *(gastronomy)* tend to be reminiscent of the USSR, but these are becoming less common as modern supermarkets take over.

For details of more than 450 great restaurants, with reviews and ratings, log on to www.chicken.kiev.ua/eng. Rival website www.lasoon.com.ua/eng even includes some menus.

Vegetarians & Vegans

While most Ukrainians are carnivores by nature, vegetarians won't find eating out too trying, especially in the larger cities where pizza joints and international restaurants abound. Even Ukrainian cuisine can be meat-free if you stick to a fairly bland diet of *deruny* or potato-and-mushroom *varenyky*. However, it's always a good idea to specify that you want a meat-free salad and *borshch* is, sadly, best avoided if

THE UKRAINIAN FOOD CHAIN

It if ain't broke, don't fix it...just open another one. That seems to be the mantra among Ukrainian restaurateurs. For it seems that when they find a formula that works they certainly stick to it. This has recently led to the emergence of several dominant fast-food chains. The mega-successful **Pizza Celentano** (www.pizza-celentano.com) has joined the widespread **Kartoplyanoye Khata** (www.potatohouse.biz) and **Dva Gusya** (www.dvagusya.ua) on many city streets, but none of these compare to the king of Ukrainian fast-food outlets, **Puzata Khata** (www.puzatahata.com), which has huge self-service restaurants in most big cities and some shopping centres.

you're strict about your diet. Even 'vegetarian' versions are often made using beef stock.

Vegans are much worse off. In a land that adores *smetana* (soured cream) and slathers its salads in mayonnaise, dining out will prove a trial. The best thing to do is stay in apartments and visit the local markets for cooking ingredients. While most Ukrainians have heard of vegetarianism, veganism is an unknown concept and will seem to most like abstinence from rice would to the Chinese.

According to some enthusiasts, *Borshch* is imbued with all kinds of magical powers, including the ability to melt the hardest heart.

Habits & Customs

Ukrainians will tell you the midday meal is the main feed of the day, but changing lifestyles mean many workers now eat lunch on the run. Breakfast (sni-*da*-nok in Ukrainian) is usually very similar to lunch (o-*bid*) or dinner (ve-*che*-rya); you'll rarely see cereal, muesli or toast.

The best Ukrainian food is home-cooked, and if you get invited to someone's house for a meal, you're in for a treat. Ukrainian hospitality is legendary and having guests around turns the meal into a drawn-out, celebratory banquet, with plenty of courses and toasts.

Art & Architecture

Painting & Sculpture

Most don't associate Ukraine with the arts and architecture, but as anyone who's been to the country will tell you, the country's museums and galleries showcase exquisite local art and traditional crafts, much of it with a folksy rural theme, and Ukrainian architecture is not all about USSR-era concrete blocks and Stalinist pomp.

Icons

Icons are small holy images painted on a lime-wood panel with a mix of tempera, egg yolk and hot wax. Brought to Ukraine from Constantinople by Volodymyr the Great in the 10th century and remaining the key religious art until the 17th century, icons were attributed with healing and spiritual powers. Icon painters – mostly monks – rarely signed works, and depicted only Christ, the Virgin, angels and saints. Church murals, mosaics and frescoes, as well as manuscript illuminations, developed at the same time. Some of the oldest frescoes are found in Kyiv's St Sophia's Cathedral.

Pysanky

Painted Easter eggs *(pysanky)* are an ancient Slavonic art found across Eastern Europe. Designs are drawn in wax on the eggshell (these days hollowed out beforehand), the egg is dyed one colour and the process continually repeated until a complex pattern is built up. Different symbols represent varying natural forces – a circle with a dot in the middle is the sun, and so on – but each Ukrainian region has its own traditions. The country's largest collection of *pysanky* is found at Kolomyya's Pysanky Museum.

Ukraine's most celebrated sculptor is Oleksandr Arkhipenko (1887–1964), who was born in Kyiv but spent most of his life abroad. His works are scattered across many galleries, mostly in the US.

SCULPTOR

BUYING SOUVENIRS

If you're looking for arty souvenirs, there are numerous souvenir markets in the major cities. Among other things, these markets sell embroidery *(vyshyvka)* in various forms, including long, narrow towels *(rushnyky)*, men's shirts *(sorochky)* and women's blouses *(bluza)*. Ceramics *(keramiky)* and woollen blankets *(lyzhnyky)* are other souvenirs on offer. Most Ukrainian patterned eggs *(pysanky)* for sale are wooden imitations. You can buy the real thing in Lviv at the Museum of Ethnography, Arts & Crafts.

Tatar handicrafts are available in Crimea at the Usta Workshop and Store. Several antique shops in Kyiv sell old, hand-painted wooden icons – most of which are officially illegal to take out of the country.

Romanticism

The first break from religious art occurred during the Cossack Hetmanate. A secular, romantic trend of folk painting slowly developed, common themes being the *Kozak Mamay* (a Cossack playing a *bandura* or *kobza*), country life and folk traditions. Most of these paintings remained unknown, but Ukrainian-born Ilya Repin gained international fame. His famous *Zaporizhsky Cossacks Writing a Letter to the Turkish Sultan* and other Romantic paintings are found in the Art Museum in Kharkiv. The art museums in Kyiv and Odesa also display typical Romantic art.

Ivan Ayvazovsky is regarded as one of the world's best painters of seascapes. Ethnically Armenian, he was born and lived in Feodosiya, Crimea, where hundreds of his works are found in the Ayvazosky Museum.

Soviet Era & Beyond

Socialist realism propagated Soviet ideals – the industrialised peasant, the muscular worker and the heroic soldier. Take, as an example, the sculptural reliefs near Kyiv's Museum of the Great Patriotic War. Ukrainian nationalism asserted itself through the age-old tradition of folk art, leading the Soviet authorities to ban folk embroidery.

In the aftermath of independence, Ukrainian art enjoyed a reawakening, with art schools in Kyiv producing new stars, like painter Maxim Mamsikov (b 1968), sculptor Zhana Khadyrova (b 1981) and multimedia artist Kyril Protsenko (b 1967). One of the most important artists to emerge at this time was the Ukrainian photographer Boris Mikhailov. Born in Kharkiv in 1938, he now divides his time between there and Germany (see the boxed text, p259).

Since 2006, art lovers in Kyiv have been making a beeline to the PinchukArtCentre. This gallery not only has major international exhibitions and pieces by the likes of Damien Hirst, Anthony Gormley and Andreas Gursky, it's also a good place to see works by leading local artists.

There have been three new books of Boris Mikhailov's photography in recent years. *Yesterday's Sandwich* (2007) is a collector's edition of 52 artfully double-exposed prints. *Crimean Snobbism* (2006) and *Suzi Et Cetera* (2007) go back to the 1980s, the latter in Kharkiv.

Architecture

Church design has wrought a vast influence on Ukrainian architecture. Byzantine layout has at various times been merged with traditional wooden Hutsul churches (colonnaded porches and freestanding belfries) and 17th-century baroque to produce unique styles. 'Ukrainian baroque', with its trademark green, helmet-shaped dome, is typified by St Andrew's Church in Kyiv.

UKRAINIAN SYMBOLS

The colours of the Ukrainian flag, yellow and blue, are unusual for a Slavic nation; most opt for red, white and blue. Several theories exist as to why this might be. Some claim the combination, officially adopted in 1918, dates from pagan times when it represented fire and water. Others say it reflects Ukraine's 18th-century alliance with Sweden, whose flag is a yellow cross on blue. But the most common, and yet still not definitive, theory is that the band of blue over a strip of yellow represents swaying fields of wheat under an azure sky. Another informal Ukrainian symbol is also yellow. It's the sunflower, fields of which cover the steppes in summer.

On a more official note, the *tryzub* (trident) adorns government buildings, police officers' epaulettes, banknotes and stamps. This insignia, officially the country's coat of arms adopted in 1917, dates back to 11th-century Kyivan Rus, where it was embossed on seals, coins, pottery and bricks. It symbolises the three elements – air, water and earth – as well as a universe divided into heaven, earth and the beyond.

He paid one homeless Kharkiv woman to pose for his camera in the snow, with her knickers pushed to her knees and her blouse above her breasts and scarred stomach. In another picture, a naked woman with a large cancerous growth jutting from her stomach tends a flower bush. Yet Ukrainian photographer Boris Mikhailov wasn't censured or censored for such shocking images. He was awarded the prestigious Citibank Photography Award. That same year, 2000, he also won the Hasselblad Photography Award for a career in which he has continually challenged viewers.

Like all his work, Mikhailov's award-winning *Case History* – 450 photos of Kharkiv's *bomzhy* (homeless) – is about the 'dissolution of beauty'. And it's an aesthetic that has kept him in the public eye.

Still the most important Eastern European photographer today, he first entered professional photography in the 1970s, after the KGB found some nude amateur shots of his wife and had him fired from his engineering job. Originally satirising Soviet realism, he later shifted to documenting society in independent Ukraine, including its poverty. Rebutting claims of voyeurism, he says homelessness didn't exist in the Soviet Union, and it's better to bear witness to the suffering of these people than to wish it away.

Whatever his politics, Mikhailov's work is always compelling and ironically often beautiful. He continues to exhibit at big-hitting galleries around the world, bringing the harsh and mundane realism of post-Soviet Ukraine to an international audience.

Otherwise various styles have come in and out of vogue. After St Petersburg proved such a success in Russia, its planned layout and neoclassical architecture was copied in Odesa and Korpusny Park in Poltava. In the 19th century there were revivals of Byzantine design (as seen in St Volodymyr's Cathedral in Kyiv) and Renaissance style merged with baroque – for example in the opera houses in Kyiv, Odesa and Lviv. A modern Ukrainian style based on art nouveau featured in the Regional Museum in Poltava and the eclectic Metropolitan Palace, or university, in Chernivtsi.

The Soviets had a penchant for pompous 'monumental classicism', with enormous temple-like state edifices. Extensively rebuilt after WWII, Kyiv is full of such buildings. The Soviets were also responsible for the most widespread architectural style seen in Ukraine's big cities, the apartment block. Even these can be divided into periods, starting with the so-called Khrushchyovka, a normally five-storey brick or concrete tenement built in the 1960s during Khrushchev's tenure at the Kremlin. However, most of Kyiv and Kharkiv's housing stock was erected in the 1970s and '80s. The acres of shabby blocks that ring the capital are made of prefabricated concrete panels that could be locked together in a matter of weeks. Despite their dilapidated outward appearance, most Ukrainian apartments are very comfortable inside and warm in winter, but not terribly cool in summer.

Some of Kyiv's most impressive Soviet architecture can be found underground in the shape of its ornate metro stations.

Music & Literature

Music

Folk Music: Blind Kobzary & Huge Banduras

Ukrainian folk music developed as a form of storytelling. The guardians of Ukrainian folklore, *kobzary* were highly respected wandering minstrels who travelled from town to town spreading news through an extensive repertoire of songs. These included *bylyny*, epic narrative poems relating the courageous deeds of the heroes of Kyivan Rus, and *dumy*, lyrical ballads glorifying the exploits of the Cossacks.

Traditionally, *kobzary* were required to be blind and they used the lute-like *kobza* to accompany their historical narratives. In the 18th century the *kobza* was replaced by the *bandura*, a larger instrument with up to 65 strings. Popular *bandura* choirs accompanied Ukrainian national songs and folk dances, and this unparalleled instrument soon became a national symbol.

The Ukrainian Bandura Chorus (www.bandura.org) was founded in Kyiv in 1918 and still performs worldwide today (mainly in the US). To find a *bandura* concert in Ukraine, check listings magazines. The National Philharmonic in Kyiv is a reasonable bet.

Traditional *kobzary* themselves suffered the all-too-familiar and miserable fate of many who lived under Stalin. During the Soviet era, they kept Ukrainians apprised of collectivisation, famine and repression. When Stalin heard about them, he immediately ordered a national *kobzary* conference, feigning great interest – and then killed all attendees.

Bandura 'buskers' can often be seen strumming in Kyiv and Lviv for the tourists. In Lviv, look outside the Grand Hotel.

Classical Music & Opera

The most notable local composer remains Mykola Lysenko (1842–1912). The 'father of Ukrainian national music' applied the logic of Ukrainian folk songs to piano-based classical music. Ukrainian operettas combine more acting and dancing than typical operas.

Rock Music

Ukraine's active rock scene provides a welcome antidote to the Russian pop streaming in over the border. Broadly, the scene can be split into four categories: the legends, the nationalists, mainstream alt rock and hip-hop.

The legends are Vopli Vidopliasova (VV) and Okean Elzy. Both have been going since the 1990s and have charismatic front men – Oleh Skrypka and Svyatoslav Vakarchuk respectively – who seek to promote the Ukrainian identity through music. Both tend toward the progressive; VV is more up-tempo, Okean Elzy more melancholic.

The most famous Ukrainian songstress of the last 40 years, bar none, is Sofia Rotaru (1947–), an ethnic Moldovan born near Chernivtsi. Dubbed the 'Nightingale of Bukovyna' her voice is as familiar to Ukrainians as it is to music followers in Riga, Irkutsk or Vladivostok. Indeed, across the ex-USSR, only the immovable Alla Pugacheva comes anywhere near her profile. Rotaru began her career in the early 1970s, gaining many 'People's Artist of...' and 'Hero of...' titles before making a successful transition to the new order of the 1990s. Singing in three languages (Russian, Ukrainian and Romanian), she still has huge appeal among the over-40s.

The nationalists, from Lviv and the west, are defenders of Ukrainian heritage. This category, including Plach Yeremiyi, Mertvy Piven and Mandry, might also fit into the category of folksy alt-rock, alongside the edgier but higher profile Druha Rika.

Next up are popular hip-hop acts, like TNMK, Tartak, Boombox and Vova z Lvova. Acoustic reggae duo 5'nizza and ska band Haydamaky boast large followings thanks to their often exceptional arrangements.

Pop

Ukrainian chick pop follows the tried-and-tested formula of scantily clad singers belting out studio-driven pop. Ukraine's Eurovision entries – including Tina Karol (2006) and even 2004 winner Ruslana – tend to hail from this group, as do high-profile video stars Ani Lorak and all-girl band Via Gra (geddit?). The vast majority of what you see on Ukrainian MTV and other music channel start-ups, usually porno-pop highlighting the physical attributes of female singers, hails from across the border in Russia.

www.umka.com.ua is an online music shop with an international shipping service, offering anything from Transcarpathian folk to the latest Donetsk hip-hop.

Others

Ukraine's 2007 Eurovision entry and the overall runner-up – cross-dressing comedian/singer Verka Serduchka – occupies a category all his/her own. The same is true of NYC gypsy punk outfit Gogol Bordello, whose eccentric singer, Eugene Hutz, is originally from Kyiv. Another unusual hit are the hard-rock Death Valley Screamers, fronted by a Yorkshireman, Sean Carr, now married to politician Yulia Tymoshenko's daughter, Evgeniya.

Literature

Taras Shevchenko is *the* figure towering over all Ukrainian literature. Literally: statues of Shevchenko now stand on pedestals vacated by Lenin across the entire west of the country. Shevchenko (1814–61) embodied and stirred the national consciousness, while achieving literary respectability for a Ukrainian language then suppressed under tsarist Russian rule. Born a serf and orphaned as a teenager, Shevchenko studied painting at the Academy of Arts in St Petersburg, where in 1840 he published his first work, *Kobzar* (The Bard), a book of eight romantic poems. It was a great success and his epic poem *Haidamaky* (1841) and ballad *Hamaliia* (1844) followed soon afterwards. Later works, such as *Son* (The Dream), *Kavkas* (Caucasus) and *Velyky i Lokh* (The Great Dungeon), were not immediately published but are now held in great affection.

Alexander Pushkin spent some of his scandal-filled 20s in Ukraine, most notably in Odesa and Crimea. He was also friends with Gogol and some of the Ukraine-based Decembrists.

Through Shevchenko's prolific work, Ukrainian was elevated from a peasant tongue to a vehicle of eloquent and poetic expression. Combining vernacular expressions and colloquial dialects with Church Slavonic, he formed a unique voice. He passionately preached social justice, in universal terms as well as to the downtrodden peasant and to the Ukrainian nation, referring to 'this land of ours that is not our own'. A staunch anti-tsarist, the poet was banished to Siberia for 10 years, which led to his premature death in 1861. In 1876 Tsar Alexander II banned all Ukrainian books and publishing, but Shevchenko's message remained. He was a Ukrainian hero.

Some of Shevchenko's works – namely *Kobzar* – have been translated widely, but English editions are usually out of print or expensive collectors' books. However, among other extensive details, 24 Shevchenko poems can be found in English at www.infoukes.com/shevchenko museum.

In addition to Shevchenko there are three other Ukrainian writers who rate a mention. Ivan Franko (1856–1916) is another hero who promoted the Ukrainian language. His better-known writings include *The Turnip Farmer, The Converted Sinner* and *During Work,* while some of his poems can be found at www.franko.lviv.ua/ifranko/franko_eng.html.

Equally distinguished was Larysa Kosach (1871–1913), known by her pen name, Lesia Ukrainka. Her frail health inspired her to compose deeply moving poetry expressing inner strength and inspiration – symbolic beatitudes for the Ukrainian people. Her *Forest Song* inspired a ballet, an opera and a film.

Greatly influenced by Taras Shevchenko, Mikhailo Kotsyubinsky (1864–1913) was probably the finest Ukrainian literary talent around the turn of the century. His novels are a snapshot of Ukrainian life in the late 19th and early 20th centuries and some, including the famous *Shadows of Forgotten Ancestors*, were made into films during the Soviet era.

There are several other proudly Ukrainian authors, but none are translated into English. On the other hand, two internationally renowned authors usually claimed by Russia are Ukrainian-born. Mikhail Bulgakov's (1891–1940) first novel, *The White Guard,* is set in his native Kyiv. Nikolai Gogol's (1809–52) novels *Evenings on a Farm near Dikanka* and *Dead Souls* and short story 'Taras Bulba' (about a Cossack hero and included in the collection *Mirgorod,* in Ukrainian *Myrhorod*) all have links to his country of birth. Odesa-born Isaac Babel (1894–1939) was the most famous chronicler of that city.

The star of the Ukrainian contemporary literature scene, Andrey Kurkov has had his works translated from Russian into no less than 25 languages – including Ukrainian.

Contemporary Writers

As far as contemporary writers go, Kyiv-based author Andrey Kurkov (b 1961) has been called Bulgakov's heir. That might be taking things a bit far, but Kurkov is widely known abroad and his *Death and the Penguin, Penguin Lost* and *The President's Last Love* do indulge in the

---

TOP 10 READS

» *The White Guard* (1925) by Mikhail Bulgakov

» *Street of Crocodiles* (1934) by Bruno Schulz

» *Taras Bulba* (1835) by Nikolai Gogol

» *Dead Souls* (1842) by Nikolai Gogol

» *Death and the Penguin* (1996) by Andrey Kurkov

» *Borderland* (1998) by Anna Reid

» *Recreations* (1998) by Yuri Andrukhovych

» *Everything Is Illuminated* (2002) by Jonathan Safran Foer

» *Complete Works* (reissued 2005) by Isaac Babel

» *A Short History of Tractors in Ukrainian* (2005) by Marina Lewycka

Only a handful of authors – of either fiction or nonfiction – have made their way across Ukraine. So take your diary: there's a gap in the market here. Anna Reid's excellent *Borderland*, her observations of the country during her time here as an *Economist* correspondent in the 1990s, functions as much as a travelogue as a history book.

Everything Is Illuminated, by Jonathan Safran Foer, follows a Jewish American searching for the Ukrainian woman who saved his grandfather during WWII. Letters between him and his language-mangling translator and guide build up a wacky, almost stream-of-consciousness novel. (Liev Schreiber's 2005 film of the book had the benefit of starring Elijah Wood and Gogol Bordello singer Eugene Hutz, but suffered from giving the story a happy ending.)

In *Long Way Round*, actor Ewan McGregor and friend Charley Boorman cross Europe, including Ukraine, on their motorbikes. However, they're not travel writers and devote at least as much space to their practical tribulations as to the countries.

More recently *Australian Geographic* Adventurer of the Year 2006, Tim Cope, spent 14 months crossing Ukraine on horseback as part of a longer, three-year epic to follow in the footsteps of Genghis Khan from Mongolia to Hungary. He completed the trip in late 2007 and has since chronicled his wanderings in *On the Trail of Genghis Khan*, due for publication in 2011. Until that time, you can read about his many adventurous journeys at www.timcopejourneys.com, or purchase the DVD of the television documentary at http://shop.abc.net.au.

same flights of fancy as Bulgakov's classic *The Master and Margarita*. In *Death and the Penguin*, for example, would-be novelist Viktor is eking out a miserable existence with his pet penguin Misha, when suddenly he gets a great gig writing stock obituaries for still-living prominent people. Then suddenly, one by one, the subjects of his profiles all start dying.

More for the Ukrainian cognoscenti are the works of Yuri Andrukhovych (b 1960), a western Ukrainian and cofounder of the Bu-Ba-Bu (loosely 'burlesque, side-show, buffoonery') poetry group. Andrukhovych's *Recreations* is a burlesque retelling of four poets' time at a pagan festival cum orgy-of-excess, while *Perverzion* presents a twist on *Death in Venice*.

Oksana Zabuzhko (b 1960) is another major contemporary name, best known for her 1990s Ukrainian-language novel *Field Research on Ukrainian Sex*.

Survival Guide

Directory A-Z

Accommodation

Accommodation will be your single biggest expense in Ukraine, but with the recent fall in value of the hryvnya, rooms are slightly more affordable than they once were. Kyiv, Crimea and eastern Ukrainian cities are the most expensive places to stay; smaller towns and the Carpathians are better value. Room prices in rural towns can be as low as 100 to 200uah a night, with prices plummeting to 50uah in a few places.

Note we list room rates in hryvnya, as do most hotels, guesthouses and hostels. But you may still come across places where prices are listed in US dollars or euros.

Water problems – hot and cold – still plague Crimea, Lviv and Odesa. The situation is exacerbated in busy periods and is sometimes worse in budget hotels. More expensive accommodation often has private water tanks to guarantee 24-hour supply.

B&Bs

Just a handful of Ukrainian establishments truly fit this description, but they're often the most wonderful places to stay in the country. Kolomyya, Rakhiv and Bakhchysaray have particularly good options.

Camping

If you intend to camp in Ukraine you might need to know the following:

» Wild camping is permitted in the Carpathian National Natural Park apart from the eastern side of Hoverla.

» In Crimea camping is officially permitted in *turstoyanki* (campsites with basic facilities).

» Wild camping is tolerated in most areas of the country but is not recommended.

» Lighting fires in national parks is officially forbidden.

» In summer never light a fire in woodland, as Ukraine is prone to forest fires.

» Most so-called campsites are really former Soviet holiday camps, and slightly more formalised than most Western campers like. Facilities are usually poor.

Homestays

Crashing with a local is not only cheap, but also a great way to get to know individual cities. There are several ways you can do this.

HOSPITALITY CLUBS

Couch Surfing (www.couchsurfing.com) Somewhat surprisingly this stay-for-free club has over 4000 hosts.

Global Freeloaders (www.globalfreeloaders.com) Mostly Kyiv-based hosts.

Hospitality Club (www.hospitalityclub.org) Hook up with almost 6000 Ukraine-based hosts.

ONLINE PROJECTS

Several 'green' tourism organisations have offered homestay programmes in the past, but their websites are mostly outdated. The best current option is **Karpaty Info** (www.karpaty.info), which offers details on B&Bs, homestays and hotels in the Carpathians.

PRIVATE RENTALS

In parts of Ukraine, you will still find people standing outside train or bus stations offering rooms in their houses or private apartment rentals. Look for signs reading кімнати (*kimnaty,* Ukrainian) or комнати (*komnaty,* Russian), садиба (*sadyba,* Ukrainian, seen mainly in the Carpathians) or жильо (*zhilyo,* Russian, seen mainly in Crimea). This is still common in summer holiday spots like Crimea and Odesa. Although the numbers of *babushky* (grannies) doing so are dwindling, it's also just

---

BOOK YOUR STAY ONLINE

For more reviews by Lonely Planet authors, check out hotels.lonelyplanet.com/. You'll find independent reviews, as well as recommendations on the best places to stay. Best of all, you can book online.

TYPE	BREAKFAST	HOT WATER	ENGLISH
Soviet unrenovated	Almost never	Sporadic	No English
Soviet renovated	Rare	Semi-reliable	No English
New rural	Unpredictable	Usually reliable	No English
New city centre	Buffet	Reliable	Some English
Boutique	Cooked or buffet	Reliable	Usually good
Upmarket	Buffet	Reliable	Good

still possible in Kyiv. Prices are usually quite reasonable at around 250uah per night for a one-room apartment (more in Kyiv).

Hostels

Hostelling is now a well-established sector in Ukraine's accommodation market, especially in tourist hotspots such as Kyiv, Lviv and Odesa. However, many hostels are run by expats who open up, party for a couple of seasons then move. See individual town listings or check out the following websites.

Hostelling Ukraine International (www.hihostels.com.ua) Gathers together all of Ukraine's hostels in one place. Online booking available.

Hostelworld (www.hostelworld.com) Still the best international website for booking a hostel in Ukraine.

Youth Tourism & Hostels of Ukraine (www.hostels.org.ua) Hostels listed here tend to be in rather odd locations.

Hotels

As in most countries of the former USSR, Ukraine has a bewildering array of hotel and room types. At the bottom are Soviet-era budget crash pads for as little as 50uah, at the top 'six-star' overpriced luxury in OTT surroundings. Everything in between can be very hit-and-miss and there are no national standards to follow, so forget any star ratings you might see.

Things to know when choosing a hotel in Ukraine:

» Older Soviet hotels often offer the full range of rooms, from semi-luxurious to downright grotty.

» At reception you'll often be presented with a baffling list of room prices and types. Pick your price, then view the room to see if it's acceptable.

» Single rooms in miserable unrenovated or partially renovated Soviet-era hotels cost around the same as a hostel dorm bed.

» Communal heating systems, to which Soviet-era hotels are linked, aren't switched on until early autumn, long after things have got nippy.

» Sometimes a 'luxury' room is renovated and modern; other times it's as bad as cheaper rooms, just larger.

» It's only worth booking ahead in Odesa and Crimea in summer, in big cities in late December and early January and in the Carpathians from November to March.

Renting an Apartment

Even if you never normally think of renting an apartment when abroad, you should consider it in Ukraine. With insufficient midrange hotels available, these help fill the gap. Single-night stays are perfectly acceptable and for longer sojourns, you not only have the benefit of a washing machine and a kitchen, you can save up to half the cost of a hotel. Any agent dealing with apartments should speak English, and you should make sure you deal with one that does, as if things go wrong, language difficulties will compound the problem. See individual chapters for contact details of apartment rental agencies.

Things to check before you commit to renting:

» Does the apartment have its own hot-water supply (the only guarantee of 24-hour, year-round availability)?

» Does it have its own central heating? Communal heating systems come on in October and go off in April/May)

» Does the building have a concierge?

» Is the entrance well lit at night?

ACCOMMODATION PRICE SCALE

Accommodation price scales used in this guide:

» **$** budget up to 400uah

» **$$** midrange 400uah to 800uah

» **$$$** top end from 800uah

» How near to a metro station/the centre/the beach is the apartment?

» Who should you call at 3am when the fuse box blows/key snaps in the lock/neighbours flood you out?

Other Options

Adventurous alternatives to the above:

Railway stations Many Ukrainian train stations have a small 'hotel' or *kimnaty vidpochynku* (Кімнати відпочинку; resting rooms) designed for late-night arrivals or those departing early.

Turbazy These are simple holiday resorts, most common in the Carpathians; the vast majority of them haven't changed from the Soviet era.

Sanatoria These often rundown health resorts can be found on the Black Sea coastline. Minimum stay conditions apply.

Activities

The following outfits will get you active in Ukraine:

Aero-Kiev (www.aero-kiev.com) Paragliding outfit based in Kyiv, but they do most of their flying in Crimea.

Bikeland (www.bikeland.com.ua) The largest cycling initiative in Ukraine, with 1300km of marked trails, approved accommodation and hire centres.

Onyx tour (www.onixtour.com.ua) The only tour company specialising in caving in Crimea.

Outdoor Ukraine (www.outdoorukraine.com) Arranges hiking tours in Ukraine's outdoor hotspots.

Paragliding Crimea (www.paragliding-crimea.com) Dima will soon have you gliding high above Koktebel in Crimea.

Sergey Sorokin (www.mt.crimea.com) Crimea-based guide Sergey can arrange any kind of outdoor activity you care to think of.

Velocrimea (www.velocrimea.com, in Russian) Crimea is perfect for mountain biking, and these guys will help you hit the right trail.

Velokosiv (www.velokosiv.if.ua) Bike trips into the Carpathian Mountains.

Business Hours

Business hours can be hard to pin down in Ukraine. A rule of thumb is that unless an establishment has anything to do with the state, it's normally open when most people are around. Lunch breaks (1pm to 2pm or 2pm to 3pm) are an all-too-common throwback to Soviet days. Sunday closing is rare.

Reviews in this book do not list opening hours unless they differ from those in the table following.

Banks & offices	9am–5pm or 10am–6pm
Shops	9am–6pm, big city shops to 8pm or 9pm
Restaurants	noon–11pm
Sights	9am–5pm or 6pm, closed at least one day a week

Children

Ukraine is not the world's most child-friendly destination, so if you're travelling with young children, it's advisable that you have previous experience of the country, or limit yourself to a short break in a major city like Kyiv.

Minuses:

» Levels of hygiene are still low even in big cities.

» Playgrounds are common but very often slides, swings and other equipment are downright lethal.

» Ukrainian museums have yet to come up with activities for children.

» Long and hot *marshrutka* (fixed-price minibus) rides with kids are no fun.

PRACTICALITIES

» Ukraine weights and measures are metric.

» DVDs sold in Ukraine tend to be Region 2 or Region 5.

» TV channels include **Inter TV** (www.inter.ua), **1+1** (www.1plus1.ua), **5 Kanal** (www.5.ua), state-run UT-1 (www.1tv.com.ua), and pop-music channels **M1** (http://m1.tv/ua/) and **MTV** (www.mtv.com.ua). For English information see www.ukrainatv.com.

» Hundreds of FM radio stations broadcast in Ukrainian and Russian; BBC World Service (594MW) and **Radio Liberty** (www.rferl.org) broadcast in English.

» Newspapers include *Fakti i Kommentarii* (www.facts.kiev.ua), *Segodnya* (www.segodnya.ua), *Ukrayina Moloda* (www.umoloda.kiev.ua) and *Holos Ukrayiny* (www.golos.com.ua). News weeklies include *Korrespondent* (http://korrespondent.net) and English-language *Kyiv Post* (www.kyivpost.com).

» Entertainment tips can be found in *What's On Kiev* (www.whatson-kiev.com). News agencies **Unian** (www.unian.net) and **Interfax Ukraine** (www.interfax.com.ua) also have English pages.

» Attitudes to children's health are outdated and finicky.

» Ukraine's roads are still extremely dangerous, even for adults.

» Car booster seats are rare and very few people use them.

Pluses:

» Ukrainians adore kids and often show it.

» With a child in tow even the old will give up seats for you on public transport.

» Bureaucratic obstacles may suddenly melt away with the appearance of a cute tot.

» A toddler will bring a smile to the lips of even the scariest ticket seller/shop assistant/receptionist.

» Kiddies will love Ukraine's easily accessible animal population.

» You're far less likely to be hassled by the police if accompanied by a child.

For further information on family travel in general, see Lonely Planet's *Travel with Children*.

Customs Regulations

You are allowed to carry up to US$1000 when entering Ukraine without having to sign any documentation. You are also permitted to bring in the following items duty-free:

» 1L of spirits

» 2L of wine

» 5L of beer

» 200 cigarettes or 250g of tobacco

» €50 worth of food (not exceeding 2kg)

If you exceed these limits, you'll have to sign a *deklaratsiya* (customs declaration). Be careful not to lose this completed form – you will need to present it when departing the country. More than US$10,000 in cash

cannot be imported at all without special written permission beforehand.

The duty-free limits for export are the same as for import. You may now also take out local currency up to 1000uah.

It's prohibited to export antiques (including icons), works of art or cultural/historical treasures without special written permission from the **Ministry of Culture** (☏044 226 2645, 226 2902; vul Ivana Franka 19, Kyiv).

Electricity

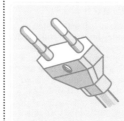

220v/50hz

Embassies & Consulates

The following are in Kyiv (☏044) unless otherwise noted. Call your embassy if you need emergency help. Consulates issue visas and can help their own citizens if there is no embassy.

Australia Honorary Consulate (☏235 7586; Apt 11, vul Kominterna 18; Ⓜ Vokzalna)

Belarus Embassy (☏537 5200; vul Mykhayla Kotsyubynskoho 3; Ⓜ Universytet)

Canada Embassy (☏590 3100; www.canadainternational.gc.ca/ukraine; vul Yaroslaviv Val 31; Ⓜ Zoloti Vorota)

France Embassy (☏590 3600; www.ambafrance-ua.org; vul Reytarska 39; Ⓜ Zoloti Vorota)

Georgia Embassy (☏451 4353, 451 4356; vul Melnikova 83D, Section 4, Kyiv; Ⓜ Lukyanivska); Odesa Consulate (☏0482 726 4727; vul Tolstoho 21, Odesa)

Germany Embassy (☏247 6800; vul Bohdana Khmelnytskoho 25; Ⓜ Zoloti Vorota)

Hungary Embassy (☏230 8001; vul Reytarska 33, Kyiv; Ⓜ Zoloti Vorota) Uzhhorod Consulate (☏615 788; vul Pravoslavna 12, Uzhhorod)

Ireland Consulate (☏285 5902; vul Shchorsa 44; Ⓜ Pecherska)

Moldova Embassy (☏521 2279; www.ucraina.mfa.md; vul Sichnevoho Povstannya 6; Ⓜ Arsenalna)

Netherlands Embassy (☏490 8200; www.netherlands-embassy.com.ua; pl Kontraktova 7; Ⓜ Kontraktova ploshcha)

New Zealand Honorary Consulate (☏537 7444; vul Baggovutivska 17/21; Ⓜ Lukyanivska)

Poland Embassy (☏230 0700; www.polska.com.ua; vul Yaroslaviv Val 12; Ⓜ Zoloti Vorota)

Romania Embassy (☏234 5261; http://kiev.mae.ro; vul Mykhayla Kotsyubynskoho 8, Kyiv; Ⓜ Universytet); Odesa consulate (☏048 725 0399; http://odessa.mae.ro; vul Bazarna 31, Odesa); Chernivtsi Consulate (☏037 545 434; vul Skilna 16, Chernivtsi)

Russia Embassy (☏244 0961; www.embrus.org.ua; pr Vozdukhoflotsky 27, Kyiv; Ⓜ Vokzalna); Consulate (☏284 6816; vul Kutuzova 8, Kyiv; Ⓜ Pecherska); Odesa consulate (☏048 240 164; Gagarinskoe Plato 14, Odesa)

Turkey Embassy (☏284 9964; www.turkembkiev.com; vul Arsenalna 18, Kyiv; Ⓜ Pecherska);

Odesa consulate (☎048 722 7911; bul Lidersovsky 3, Odesa)
UK Embassy (☎24hr 490 3660; http://ukinukraine.fco.gov.uk/en/; vul Desyatynna 9, Kyiv; Ⓜ Maydan Nezalezhnosti); Consulate (☎494 3418; Artyom Centre, vul Hlybochytska 4, Kyiv; Ⓜ Lukyanivska)
USA Embassy (☎24hr emergencies & switchboard 490 0000; http://kyiv.usembassy.gov; vul Yuriya Kotsyubynskoho 10, Kyiv; Ⓜ Lukyanivska); Consulate (☎207 7071; vul Mykoly Pymonenka 6, Kyiv; Ⓜ Lukyanivska)

Gay & Lesbian Travellers

Ukraine is generally more tolerant of homosexuality than is Russia, but that's not saying much. Out-and-proud gay views mix badly with those of the Orthodox Church, hence most people's outwardly conservative attitudes.

» Homosexuality is legal in Ukraine.

» Few people are very out here and attitudes vary across the country.

» Ukraine's gay scene is largely underground.

» Young people and city dwellers are much more tolerant of homosexuality.

» Displays of affection between two men (and perhaps two women) in public could create hostility.

» The biggest scene is in Kyiv, but Kharkiv and Odesa have one or two clubs.

» Simeyz in Crimea is also reportedly a gay mecca in August and early September.

Health

Ukraine's health system is under-resourced and decidedly primitive by Western European standards, so it's important to come prepared. Ukraine has reciprocal agreements with most countries (including the UK and most of the EU), which in theory guarantee foreign citizens free emergency care.

USEFUL GAY WEBSITES

» www.gayua.com
» www.gay.org.ua
» www.gaylvov.at.ua

However, heading to Ukraine without medical insurance would be foolhardy indeed.

RECOMMENDED VACCINATIONS
No jabs are mandatory to enter Ukraine, but the following are recommended:
» diphtheria
» hepatitis A
» measles
» polio
» rabies
» tetanus
» tick-borne encephalitis (if hiking in summer)
» typhoid

MEDICAL FACILITIES
State hospitals and clinics are very basic affairs with

MEDICAL CHECKLIST

Pharmacists in Ukraine are the first port of call for many people suffering minor complaints, and they will usually perform a diagnosis if you can explain or point to the problem. It's always a good idea to bring extra supplies of any medication you are taking and familiarise yourself with the Latin name if it's not on the label. In Ukraine this is often written in the Roman alphabet alongside any medicine's local name. Most common medicines are available, but it might be handy to bring the following:
» adhesive tape
» antibacterial ointment (for cuts and abrasions)
» antidiarrhoeal drugs (eg loperamide)
» antihistamine (for hay fever and allergic reactions)
» anti-inflammatory drugs (eg Ibuprofen)
» aspirin or paracetamol
» bandages, gauze rolls
» DEET-based insect repellent for the skin
» eye drops
» insect spray containing pyrethrin, for clothing, tents and bed nets
» oral rehydration salts
» scissors, safety pins, tweezers
» sun block
» thermometer

HIV & AIDS

Ukraine is the site of Europe's worst HIV epidemic. The country is thought to have more than 10 times the number of HIV cases of equivalent Western European nations, and the virus continues to spread faster here than elsewhere on the continent. New reported HIV diagnoses reached record levels in 2007, and UNAIDS now estimates that 440,000 people – or around 1.6% of the adult population – is HIV positive. That number could be as high as 540,000. Most cases go unreported, which explains the uncertainty and why official figures released by Ukraine's Ministry of Health are much lower.

While the epidemic was originally drug-driven, heterosexually transmitted infection is on the increase. The worst-hit areas are Crimea, Dnipropetrovsk, Donetsk, Odesa and Mykolayiv.

The message is clear: always practise safe sex.

limited supplies and facilities. Patients are expected to supply everything from food to syringes, and doctors expect (unofficial) payment for every stage of treatment. Avoid admittance to this type of hospital if you can by contacting the following Kyiv clinics where Western standards of care are maintained:

American Medical Centre (☑044 490 7600; www.am centers.com; Vul Berdychivska 1, Kyiv; ☺24hr)

Dobrobut (☑044 495 2888; www.med.dobrobut.com; vul Pymonenka 10, Kyiv; ☺24hr)

TAP WATER
Drinking tap water is not recommended anywhere in Ukraine. Bottled water is incredibly cheap and comes both still and fizzy.

Insurance

Make sure you are fully insured before heading to Ukraine. Worldwide travel insurance is available at www.lonelyplanet.com/ travel_services. You can buy, extend and claim online anytime – even if you're already on the road.

If you're staying longer than 90 days in the country

(and therefore will need a visa), you might also be asked to show you have appropriate health insurance, as decided by the Department of Citizenship, Passport & Immigration. If your insurance doesn't make the grade, the major approved Ukrainian insurer is **Pro100 Strakhuvannya** (www. pro100.com.ua/eng).

Internet Access

Internet service in Ukraine can be very intermittent, with networks and servers going down frequently. If an email or web address in this book doesn't work the first time, it's worth trying again the next day (or the next!).

» Many upmarket and midrange hotels now offer free wi-fi internet access.

» Restaurants and cafes are rapidly installing wi-fi technology.

» Upmarket hotels often have a business centre with a couple of terminals hooked up to the internet.

» Internet cafes are not as common as they once were but there's usually at least one in every town.

» Ukrtelekom offers web access at its city centre offices.

» Prices for internet access range from about 4uah in smaller cities to up to 12uah in Kyiv.

Legal Matters

Useful legal advice:

» Carry your passport with you at all times; if stopped by the police, you are obliged to show it.

» If you are stopped by the police, ask to see their ID immediately.

» The police must return your documents at once.

» Do not get involved with drugs; penalties can be severe and the process leading up to them labyrinthine.

» The US embassy in Kyiv maintains a list of Englishspeaking lawyers (http://ukraine.usembassy.gov).

Maps

Accurate city maps (plan mista) are widely available for all reasonably sized cities. They're available from bookshops and news kiosks.

Bikeland (www.bikeland. com) The Bikeland project produces excellent maps of the Carpathians showing cycling trails. These can also be used as hiking maps.

Freytag & Berndt (www. freytagberndt.at) This Austrian company produces comprehensive Ukraine-Moldova (1:1,000,000) maps that can be ordered online.

GPS Server (www.navigation .com.ua) Download very detailed maps of Crimea, the Carpathians and other parts of Ukraine to your Garmin GPS device.

Stanfords (☑0044-20-7836 1321; www.stanfords.co.uk) In the UK, this travel bookshop sells a wide range of road atlases and city maps, including Kyiv and Lviv. Everything can be ordered online.

Topograficheskaya Karta Keep an eye out for this excellent series, based on former Soviet army mapping, which covers the entire country in 286 maps (1:100,000). These are the most detailed maps available and are useful to hikers (even though trails as such are not marked). The maps are printed in Russian only and are quite inexpensive.

Ukrainian Map Server (www.ukrmap.net) Download very detailed, printable regional maps from this website. Many sheets are slightly out of date.

Money

» The Ukrainian hryvnia is divided into 100 kopecks.

» Coins come in denominations of one, five, 10, 25 and 50 kopecks, plus the rare one hryvnia.

» Notes come in one, two, five, 10, 20, 50, 100, 200 and 500 hryvnia.

» Kopecks have become virtually worthless and prices are often rounded up or down.

» There is a chronic shortage of change throughout the country – try to give the correct money whenever you can.

» In Russian-speaking regions people may still quote prices in roubles instead of hryvnia from force of habit.

» It's virtually impossible to buy any hryvnia before you get to Ukraine.

ATMs
» Cash machines/automated teller machines (ATMs) are now almost as common as in some Western countries.

» The best way to manage your money here is to take it out of your account in hryvnia.

» Cirrus, Plus, Visa, MasterCard/EuroCard and other global networks are all recognised.

» *Bankomats*, as ATMs are known locally, are found in major airport terminals, hotel lobbies, central post offices and supermarkets as well as on the street.

» There are several ATMs in the arrivals hall at Boryspil airport.

» Your own bank will charge you a small fee for taking out foreign currency.

» Some ATMs also distribute US dollars.

Cash
Exchanging currency is still very much a part of everyday life for many locals. Hoarding hard currency is still common.

» US dollars, the euro and Russian roubles are the easiest currencies to exchange.

» The British pound is hard to exchange, except in Kyiv.

» In western Ukraine, Polish zloty and Hungarian forints are widely accepted.

» Banks and currency exchange offices will not accept old, tatty notes with rips or tears.

» US dollar bills issued before 1990 cannot be exchanged.

Credit Cards & International Transfers
Ukraine remains primarily a cash economy. Credit cards are increasingly accepted by upmarket hotels, restaurants and shops inside and outside

Kyiv. But be alert to possible credit-card fraud.

Raiffeisen Bank Aval (www.aval.ua), **UKRExim Bank** (www.eximb.com) and **Western Union** (www.ufg.com.ua) all make cash advances (in dollars or hryvnia) on major credit cards, with around 3% commission. The procedure can be bureaucratic and confusing, however.

Western Union will receive money wired from anywhere in the world.

Travellers Cheques
» Travellers cheques should be avoided, or brought only as a backup.

» It's relatively hard to find banks that will accept travellers cheques and the process is lengthy, involving lots of paperwork.

» If you must use them, take Thomas Cook, American Express or Visa cheques in US dollars.

» Cheque-friendly establishments include branches of the nationwide chains Raiffeisen Bank Aval or UKRExim Bank.

» Expect to pay a commission of 2%.

Tipping
Tipping is not common in Ukraine.

Post

The national postal service is run by **Ukrposhta** (www.ukrposhta.com).

» Sending a postcard or a letter of up to 20g costs

5.50uah to anywhere outside Ukraine.

» Major post offices (*poshta* or *poshtamt*) are open from around 8am to 9pm weekdays, and 9am to 7pm on Saturday.

» Smaller post offices close earlier and are not open on Saturday.

» Outward mail is fairly reliable, but you should always send things *avia* (airmail).

» Mail takes about a week or less to Europe, and two to three weeks to America or Australia.

» Take packages to the post office unwrapped, so their contents can be verified.

» Express mail is faster, more reliable and more expensive, depending on weight.

» The state-run International Express Mail (EMS) is available at most main post offices

» Incoming post is still lamentably unreliable.

» DHL and FedEx have offices throughout Ukraine; rates are astronomical.

Public Holidays

Public holidays seem to change every year in Ukraine, depending on which way the political wind is blowing. When a public holiday falls on a Thursday or a Tuesday, employees may work the previous Saturday, earning them a free day, with which to plug the gap between the holiday and the weekend. Currently the main public holidays in Ukraine are the following:

New Year's Day 1 January

Orthodox Christmas 7 January

International Women's Day 8 March

Orthodox Easter (Paskha) April

Labour Day 1-2 May

Victory Day (1945) 9 May

Constitution Day 28 June

Independence Day (1991) 24 August

ADDRESSING MAIL

Traditionally, addresses were written in reverse order (eg Ukraina, Kyiv 252091, vul Franko 26/8, kv 12, Yuri Orestovich Vesolovsky), but the continental European fashion (Yuri Orestovich Vesolovsky, vul Franko 26/8, kv 12, Kyiv 252091, Ukraina) is now common. The return address is written in smaller print in the top left-hand corner on the front of the envelope (not on the back).

When addressing outgoing mail, repeat the country destination in Cyrillic if you can. Incoming mail addressed in Cyrillic, rather than Roman, characters will reach its destination sooner.

Safe Travel

Despite what you may have heard, Ukraine is not a dangerous, crime-ridden place. The infamous mafia are not interested in tourists – in fact, you are infinitely more likely to be knocked down by a *marshrutka* than to be gunned down by the mob.

Crime

Don't be overly worried about crime in Ukraine, which is normally as safe as most Western European countries. However, petty theft is a serious problem, and no matter how hard you try to blend in, you will stand out as a 'rich' Westerner.

Avoiding becoming a victim of theft is a matter of common sense:

» Don't flash your money around.

» Watch your wallet and belongings, particularly on public transport and in crowded situations.

» Stay low-key in appearance and have more than one place on your body where you stash your cash.

» Avoid being alone at night in parks or secluded places.

» In hostels stash your gear away in lockers – traveller-on-traveller crime is all too common.

» Lock your compartment door on overnight trains.

CREDIT-CARD FRAUD

Although Ukraine remains largely a cash economy, credit cards are increasingly accepted by upmarket hotels, restaurants and shops both inside and outside Kyiv. Unfortunately, some embassies have warned of a rise in credit-card fraud. They suggest you use your card only as a last resort, and only in reputable locations. Take all the usual precautions to make sure no one sees or copies down your PIN.

THE DROPPED-WALLET SCAM

This well-known rort starts with you suddenly noticing a wallet or a large wad of cash on the ground near you. If you pick it up, you'll be approached by someone saying it's theirs. They'll thank you... and then say that they had *two* wallets or wads of cash and accuse you of stealing the other. Alternatively, they'll directly accuse you of stealing the first wallet. Accomplices might be brought in as witnesses or 'police'. Don't get involved and walk away quickly.

Racist Attacks

Ukraine has tended to be more welcoming to people of African, Asian and Caribbean appearance than neighbouring Russia, though that's not saying a lot. In the past couple of years, there's been

UKRAINE'S HAZARDOUS HIGHWAYS

You don't need to travel very long in Ukraine to realise that this country has some of the most perilous driving conditions in Europe. The country's mix of poorly lit, potholed roads, an idiotically aggressive driving style and the poor state of many (seatbelt-less) vehicles is a lethal cocktail indeed. Accidents are the norm, and in 2008 almost 8000 people died on the country's roads (compare that to just over 2000 in the UK).

In a bid to stop the carnage and stimulate at least a basic instinct for self-preservation in local drivers, Ukrainian TV channels broadcast daily and weekly programmes detailing horrific RTAs, most of which are caused by mindboggling stupidity and/or drunkenness.

Driving Ukraine's rutted highways will also bring you into contact with the bane of motorists' lives and a widely loathed national institution, the traffic police (Derzhavna Avtoinspektsiya; DAI). Foreign cars come in for special attention.

a worrying increase in seemingly racially motivated attacks – with the UN and the International Organization for Migration (IOM) speaking out about the problem in 2007 and again in 2008, after an asylum seeker from Congo was stabbed 15 times and died outside a Kyiv metro station.

The situation is nowhere near as bad as it is in, say, St Petersburg, but if you're black, Asian or Middle Eastern, stay alert and exercise extreme caution if going out alone at night.

Telephone

Ukraine recently simplified the way numbers are dialled, banishing the confusing system of Soviet-era prefixes and dialling tones for good. All numbers now start with ☎0. If you see a number starting with ☎8, this is the old intercity and mobile prefix and should be left off.

The Ukrainian telephone company Ukrtelecom has been slated for privatisation in the near future, meaning some of the information below may change slightly.

Phone Codes

Ukraine's country code is ☎0038. To call Kyiv from London, dial ☎00 38 044 and the subscriber number.

As the Ukrainian telephone system slowly migrates from analogue to digital, many cities and towns now have two area codes. The longer one (eg ☎0482 for Odesa) is used with the shorter, old numbers. The shorter area code (eg ☎048) just drops the last digit and will be used with longer, new numbers. There's no need to dial the city code if dialling within that city, unless you're calling from a mobile.

To call internationally, dial ☎0, wait for a second tone, then dial 0 again, followed by the country code, city code and number.

Operators

» If you can't dial directly, book a call through the international operator (☎079), who will make the connection for you.

» Kyiv has some multilingual international operators (English ☎0191, French ☎0192, German ☎0193, Spanish ☎0195).

Telephone Offices

Every city has a Ukrtelekom telephone office (many open 24 hours), where you can make international (*mizhnarodny*), intercity (*mizhhorodny, mizhmisky*) or local calls. You pay the switchboard operator first, go to your assigned booth (*kabina*) and dial the number you require. If there is a black button labelled 'ответ' (answer) on the booth phone, press it when the person you are calling responds. After your call, pay the operator, who will give you change for any unused time. In some older telephone offices, the switchboard operator will dial the number for you and direct you to your assigned booth once the connection has been made.

WHEN IT'S NOON IN TRANSCARPATHIA...

Many elderly people in rural areas of the Transcarpathian region still set their watches to Kyiv time, minus one hour. This is a throwback to the days when the westernmost province of today's Ukraine was part of Czechoslovakia, as well as a small-scale protest at rule from faraway Kyiv. It's also quite practical as sunrise and sunset happen much later here than in the capital.

There's a Ukrainian saying: 'Where's the toilet? The toilet is everywhere!' When you see some of the public toilets, you'll understand why. To be fair, vile, stinky, clogged holes with foot markers on either side are far less common than they once were, but when you encounter one, you realise why people so often prefer to go behind a bush. During research for this guide, we even encountered a communal squat toilet (Uman bus station if you're curious).

Where it's not possible to consult nature, pay toilets are the most bearable. An attendant will demand 50 kopecks to 1.50uah and proffer an absurdly small amount of toilet paper in exchange. Public facilities in Crimea are generally much better than elsewhere in the country. The toilets at newly renovated railway stations are quite acceptable, too, if a bit pongy. Avoid free blue Portaloos, which often stand unemptied for days and can be categorically vile.

The bathrooms on the trains are another mucky subject. By the end of a journey, they are usually awash in liquid – but be consoled that it's usually nothing but water that's been splashed around from the tap.

Toilet paper in Ukraine is no longer so bad or so rare that you need to carry a major stash. That said, it's a good idea to always keep a little on hand.

Mobile Phones

European GSM phones usually work in Ukraine; double-check with your provider before leaving. However, if you're going to be making a few calls, it's more economical to get a prepaid SIM card locally. Two operators now give these away for free on the street and others can cost as little as 10uah. Top up credit using vouchers available from mobile-phone shops and news kiosks, or use the special touch screen terminals found in busy places such as bus stations, markets and shopping centres.

The main pay-as-you-go mobile providers:

Djuice (www.djuice.com.ua) Network operator of Kyivstar's prepaid division.

Life:) (www.life.com.ua)

MTC (www.mts.com.ua) Formerly called UMC.

Public Phones

» Public phones on the street can be used for local calls only.

» Most require a phonecard, sold at post and telephone offices.

» Phones in each city require a different brand of card.

» Using a Utel card phone is another way to make international and national calls.

» Cards can be purchased at post offices.

» The cards have printed instructions in English.

» Only Utel phones can be used to make calls with these cards.

Time

Ukraine is located in one time zone – GMT plus two hours. During daylight-saving time, from the first Sunday in April until the last Sunday in October, it's GMT plus three hours.

When it's noon in Kyiv, it's 10am in London, 5am in New York, 11am in Paris, 1pm in Moscow and 8pm in Sydney.

Ukraine generally uses the 24-hour clock (for instance 8pm is 20:00).

Toilets

A women's toilet (*tualet*) is marked with an upwards-facing triangle or ж (for *zhinochy*); men's are marked with a downwards facing triangle, ч or м (for *cholovichy* or *muzhcheny*).

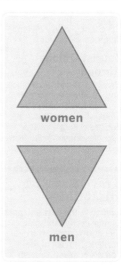

women

men

Tourist Information

Reliable tourist information is not as hard to come by as it once was. That said, cities with tourist offices are still the welcome exceptions to the rule.

Local Tourist Information

You can obtain tourist information in several ways:

Hostels Hostel staff and owners are sometimes very up to speed on what's going on locally, and they speak English.

Hotel receptions Due to the lack of tourist offices, reception staff have become used to fielding travellers' queries.

Internet There's a lot of information on the net if you know where to look. Sadly much of it is out of date.

Ministry of Culture and Tourism Even if you read Cyrillic, the websites http://mincult.kmu.gov.ua and www.tourism.gov.ua are as useless as this meaningless ministry.

Tourist information offices These are more common in the west of the country. See individual chapters for details.

Tourist Offices Abroad

Ukraine has no tourist offices abroad, and the information stocked by its consulates and embassies is very general and basic. Foreign travel agencies specialising in travel to Ukraine are more helpful.

Travellers with Disabilities

Even Kyiv, the best-equipped Ukrainian city, isn't that friendly to people with disabilities. The rest of the country is worse. Uneven pavements, steep drops off curbs, holes in the road, lack of disabled access to public transport and very few wheelchair-accessible hotel rooms mean the only way to have an enjoyable time would be to come on a tour catering specifically for disabled travellers – and these don't exist.

The following companies and organisations can give advice on travel for those with disabilities, though their knowledge of facilities in Ukraine will be very limited.

Access Travel (☑01942 888 8446; www.access-travel.co.uk)

Holiday Care Services (☑0845 124 9971; www.holidaycare.org.uk)

SATH (Society for the Advancement of Travelers with Handicaps; ☑212 447 728 4347; www.sath.org)

Visas

At the time of research there were rumours that a group of MPs in Ukraine's parliament was working on a new law that would see visas reintroduced for citizens of many countries, who at present enjoy visa-free travel. It's not clear whether this law will be passed (Ukraine has slightly more pressing problems to deal with) but in view of this, it may be worth checking the visa situation with your nearest Ukrainian embassy before making any travel arrangements.

Citizens of the EU, Canada, the USA, Iceland, Japan, Norway, Switzerland, Andorra, Liechtenstein, Monaco, San Marino, South Korea and the Vatican can stay without visas for up to 90 days. However, citizens of most other countries, and anyone intending to work, study, take up permanent residency or stay for more than 90 days, will require a visa.

For other matters related to visas:

Embassies The Ministry of Foreign Affairs of Ukraine (www.mfa.gov.ua) has a complete list of embassies.

Letters of invitation These are technically needed for all visas, although this is more of a formality these days.

Limitations You can't stay visa-free in Ukraine for more than 90 days in any 180-day period. It's not possible to leave the country after 90 days and immediately come back across the border by renewing your entry stamp.

Validity Single- and double-entry visas can be bought for one to six months. Multiple-entry visas are valid for three to 12 months.

Visa types Business, tourist and private, with single, double and multiple entries available.

Visa Extensions

Department of Citizenship, Passport & Immigration (☑044 224 9051; bul Tarasa Shevchenka 34, Kyiv; ☉9am-5pm Mon-Fri) If you're staying for longer than three months on a tourist visa or six months on a business visa, or if you want to extend your visa, you'll need to visit this office. The process is a bureaucratic ordeal that's best avoided if at all possible. Take a friend or helper along if you don't speak Russian or Ukrainian.

Volunteering

Volunteers for the US Peace Corps and Soros Foundation have a long history with

GOING SOLO

More independent travellers are making their way to Ukraine, and though the rest of the country still doesn't exactly cater to their needs, the growing network of hostels does. Apart from a few well-trodden international train routes (eg Przemysl, Poland to Lviv), these are the only places you can really bank on meeting other travellers.

However, if you're moving around, rather than staying in one city, you'll never feel alone in Ukraine. Whether pressed against local people on a crowded, long-distance bus seat or sharing a train compartment with them, they will often want to chat – regardless of your respective language skills. It's a good incentive to learn at least a little Ukrainian or Russian.

Similarly, you won't feel particularly like 'Billy No-Mates' in restaurants. With eating out considered such a treat here, almost no locals would do so alone; everyone will immediately realise you're foreign and chalk your solitude up to that.

the country, as do religious missionaries.

Bikeland (www.bikeland. com) As it expands across the country, the Bikeland project will be on the look-out for experienced cyclists to mark out trails. Contact the organisers through the website.

Life2Orphans (www.life2 orphans.org) Volunteers are sorely needed in Ukraine's desperately underfunded orphanages. Life2Orphans is an excellent place to start if you're looking for volunteer opportunities in this sector.

Svit Ukraine (www.svit -ukraine.org) This NGO in east Ukraine organises various volunteer camps and placements for young people with the aim of promoting issues such as sustainable development, human rights and democracy.

Women Travellers

Old-fashioned attitudes (so much for Soviet feminism!) still reign in Ukraine. Here, women are a *devushka* ('miss' or 'young lady') pretty well up until they become a *babushka* and retire, and that quaint quirk says it all. The upside is that security guards and police who might stop male foreigners consider women harmless and usually let them pass. Hotel staff and train conductors, who are often women themselves, frequently take pity on women travelling alone, and will make an unusual effort to be nice.

The likelihood of being harassed is pretty slim. Unless they are extremely drunk, local men tend to be either wary of, or protective towards, foreign women. Young Ukrainian women dress to kill and deflect most sexual attention away from travellers anyway. If you're very cautious, always travel 2nd-class on trains. Sharing the compartment with three other passengers, rather than just one, offers safety in numbers.

Pregnant women get reduced fares on some public transport, but you'll probably need more than just a big bump to prove you are with child. If you do arrive expecting, expect lots of help and smiles wherever you go.

Work

In the past few years, English teachers and a few adventurous entrepreneurs have been attracted to Ukraine to work and do business. Kafkaesque bureaucracy puts many off registering legally. To get a work permit you have to show that a Ukrainian could not do the job you're being hired for.

Online jobs are advertised on the following websites:

www.cicerone.com.ua Kyiv language school.

www.go2kiev.com/view/ jobs.html Jobs and work permit info in English.

http://job.ukr.net Type 'English' next to Ищу работу (Job Search).

www.rabota-ukraine. com.ua Type 'English' or 'Teacher' below Словарный поиск (Search by Key Word).

www.tryukraine.com Advice and help finding English teaching positions.

www.rabota.ua Lists a limited number of jobs for English speakers.

Transport

GETTING THERE & AWAY

The majority of visitors fly to Ukraine – generally to Kyiv. However, low-cost flights to neighbouring countries mean a growing number of travellers are entering the country overland. Flights, tours and rail tickets can be booked online at www.lonely planet.com/bookings.

Entering the Country

» Your passport must be valid for at least one month beyond your intended departure from Ukraine. It must be stamped with a visa if you need one.

» Entry is usually trouble free and border officials ask few questions these days.

» Immigration cards were scrapped in September 2010, so anyone claiming you still need one is up to no good or hasn't heard about the change yet.

Air

Low-cost airlines have struggled to find their way into Ukraine, but this is likely to change once Lviv's new terminal is built. This is sure to attract a budget operator with direct flights from major cities in Western Europe.

Airports & Airlines

Borispil International Airport (KBP; www.airport -borispol.kiev.ua) Most international flights use Kyiv's main airport, 30km southeast of the city centre.

Lviv International Airport (LWO; www.airport.lviv.ua)

Odessa International Airport (ODS; www.airport. odessa.ua)

Ukraine's international airline carriers:

Ukraine International Airlines (PS; www.flyuia.com) Always check this airline's rates against your country's national carrier as UIA's ticket prices can often be lower.

Aerosvit (VV; www.aerosvit. com) Also operates domestic flights.

The following airlines also fly to/from Ukraine:

Aeroflot (SU; www.aeroflot.ru)
Air Baltic (BT; www.airbaltic. com)
Air France (AF; www.air france.com)
Austrian Airlines (OS; www. aua.com)
British Airways (BA; www. ba.com)
Carpatair (V3; www. carpatair.com)
Czech Airlines (OK; www. czechairlines.com)
Delta (DL; www.delta.com)
Dniproavia (Z6; www. dniproavia.com)
El Al (LY; www.elal.co.il)
Estonian Air (OV; www. estonian-air.ee)
Finnair (AY; www.finnair.com)
Germanwings (4U; www. germanwings.com)
KLM (KL; www.klm.com)
LOT (LO; www.lot.com)
Lufthansa (LH; www. lufthansa.com)
Male'v (MA; www.malev.hu)
Transaero (UN; www. transaero.ru)
Turkish Airlines (TK; www. turkishairlines.com)
Wizzair (W6; www.wizzair. com)

Budget Flights to Neighbouring Countries

A cheap way of getting to Ukraine is to take a budget flight to a neighbouring country, then cross the border by land. Poland has the most flights from Western Europe, but Hungary, Romania and Slovakia also provide a handful of options.

Ryanair (www.ryanair.com) This Irish budget airline connects five cities in the UK with the Polish city of Rzeszow, a mere 90km from the border with Ukraine. There are also daily flights to Budapest and Bratislava (Slovakia), from where you can continue by train

easyJet (www.easyjet.com) This no-frills airline links the UK, France and Germany with Budapest and Krakow.

Wizzair (www.wizzair.com) Wizzair has popular direct flights to Kyiv from London Luton, but also connects

FLYING FROM THE USA & CANADA

The only direct flights between North America and Ukraine are with Aerosvit from Kyiv to Toronto (twice a week) and New York's JFK airport (six times a week). Otherwise the best routings are through the European hubs London, Paris and Vienna.

the UK with Katowice and Warsaw in Poland and Cluj-Napoca in northern Romania.

Jet2 (www.jet2.com) Links cities in northern England and Scotland with Krakow and Budapest.

Check the websites www.flycheapo.com and www.skyscanner.net for the latest flight information.

Land

» Crossing the border into Ukraine is a fairly straightforward, if slightly drawn-out, affair.

» Expect customs personnel to scrutinise your papers and search your vehicle.

» Heading out of Ukraine into the EU and Schengen zone, be prepared for delays.

» The Poland–Ukraine and Romania–Ukraine borders are popular cigarette-smuggling routes, hence the thorough customs checks.

» Extra border posts between Ukraine and Poland are being constructed for Euro 2012.

» When heading for Belarus or Russia ensure you have the right visa.

» You might need special medical insurance for

Belarus, purchasable at the border.

» In the unlikely event you are hitchhiking into Ukraine, it may be a good idea to take a local bus or train across the border, as drivers are generally reluctant to take hitchhikers over the line.

» When leaving Ukraine, a train is preferable to bus or car.

» You are permitted to walk across the country's borders.

Belarus

Be aware that to even pass through Belarus, you will need a transit visa.

BUS

In most cases, you're better off going between Ukraine and Belarus by train.

CAR & MOTORCYCLE

Only two crossings are official:

M01 The road north from Chernihiv to Homel crosses just north of the Ukrainian village of Novy Yarylovichy.

M19 The road between Brest and Kovel crosses just southeast of the Belarusian village of Makrany.

TRAIN

The main services are Kyiv–Minsk (463uah, 10½ to 12 hours, one to two daily), the Lviv–St Petersburg train that passes through Minsk, and the summertime Varna–Minsk service, which passes through Lviv. Lviv to Minsk

takes 13 to 14 hours. Change at Minsk for Brest.

Hungary

BUS

Between one and two daily buses go from Uzhhorod to Nyíregyháza (60uah, three hours).

CAR & MOTORCYCLE

The road crossing between Zahony and Chop is open all year. Follow the E573 (M06) from Debrecen and Nyíregyháza. Other crossings are Beregsurány–Luzhanka and Tiszabecs–Vylok.

TRAIN

Chop, 22km southwest of Uzhhorod, is the international junction for trains between Ukraine and Hungary. Because the two countries use different rail gauges, services have a long stop while the carriage bogies are changed to a different gauge. Note that if coming from Budapest, you'll generally save money by buying a domestic ticket as far as Zahony, then a short international ticket to Chop, and purchasing a domestic train ticket onwards. The following are direct trains between Hungary and Ukraine: Kyiv to Budapest (24 hours, one daily), Chop to Budapest (six hours, one daily) and Lviv to Budapest (14 hours, one daily).

Moldova

The unofficial republic of Transdniestr bordering Ukraine for some 500km

CLIMATE CHANGE & TRAVEL

Every form of transport that relies on carbon-based fuel generates CO_2, the main cause of human-induced climate change. Modern travel is dependent on aeroplanes, which might use less fuel per kilometre per person than most cars but travel much greater distances. The altitude at which aircraft emit gases (including CO_2) and particles also contributes to their climate change impact. Many websites offer 'carbon calculators' that allow people to estimate the carbon emissions generated by their journey and, for those who wish to do so, to offset the impact of the greenhouse gases emitted with contributions to portfolios of climate-friendly initiatives throughout the world. Lonely Planet offsets the carbon footprint of all staff and author travel.

causes only minor irritation to travellers these days. The 24 hours you have to cross into Moldova proper are more than enough time. It's another matter if you want to hang around in the 'capital' Tiraspol, which has become an odd kind of I've-been-there tourist attraction in recent years.

EU and US citizens, Canadians, Swiss and Japanese no longer need visas for Moldova. However, Australians, New Zealanders, South Africans and others do.

BUS
There are at least 10 daily buses from Odesa to Chişinău via Tiraspol, and two via Palanka (65uah, five to seven hours). The latter avoid Transdniestr.

CAR & MOTORCYCLE
Most of the dozen border crossings between Ukraine and Moldova enter Transdniestr. To get into Moldova without going through the breakaway republic, you'll need to come up from the south. The most obvious route is the M15/E87 to the crossing at Palanka – a 280km-long diversion.

Train
There are three trains a day from Kyiv to Chişinău (14 to 17 hours), all of which originate in Moscow. There are no services between Odesa and Chişinău because of Ukraine's blockade of troublesome Transdniestr. That situation is unlikely to change soon.

Poland
Most overland travellers enter Ukraine from Poland heading to Lviv. See the boxed text on p278 for details on how to get to Ukraine cheaply by combining budget flights with overland travel to Ukraine's western border.

BUS
While international services do go from Lviv's main bus station, it's best to give this station a miss for cross-border travel. From Lviv there are terrible delays leaving the country (we've heard reports of generally at least four and sometimes even nine hours at the border).

Between Przemysl and Lviv it's quickest to take the *marshrutky* (minibuses) from outside each city's train station to the border, walk across and hop onto an onward *marshrutka*. Leaving Lviv, *marshrutka* 297 runs between Lviv train station and the road crossing at Shehyni/Medyka ($2 to $3, 1½ hours). While they are quick, nimble and handy if you need to leave Lviv for Poland after the last daily train has departed, the *marshrutky* are crowded. If you're unlucky you might get caught in a long pedestrian queue at the border, although Western passport holders are often sent to the front of the line (as they are thought less likely to be professional smugglers of massive amounts of cheap cigarettes).

CAR & MOTORCYCLE
There are several crossings, of which the easiest in terms of both distance and formalities is Shehyni on the M11 between Lviv and Przemysl. Travelling Kyiv–Warsaw via Lutsk, you cross over the border at the Buh River before stopping in the Polish town of Okopy Nowe.

TRAIN
Poland has an online **train timetable** (www.rozklad.pkp.pl) in several languages, including English. The following text lists direct connections, but there are plenty of other services if you are prepared to change. The following are direct trains between Poland and Ukraine: Kyiv to Warsaw Wschodnia (17 hours, one daily), Kyiv to Wroclaw (24 hours, one daily), Lviv to Przemysl (2½ hours, two daily), Lviv to Krakow (six hours, two daily) and Lviv to Warsaw Central (16 hours, one daily).

Romania
BUS
There's only one bus a day from Chernivtsi to Suceava (four to five hours), leaving at 7.10am. The short journey is drawn out by a lengthy border stop, as it's a popular cigarette-smuggling route. Private *marshrutky* will also take you. Look for them at Chernivtsi bus station.

CAR & MOTORCYCLE
There are three Ukraine–Romania road crossings, only two of them important. The main crossing is 40km

south of Chernivtsi, where the E85 (A269) crosses between Porubne in Ukraine and Siret in Romania. The other is the bridge between Solotvyno in Ukraine and Sighetu Marmatiei on the Romanian side.

Note that if you try to cross between southern Ukraine (say, from Odesa) and Romania via Reni, north of Izmayil, you will have to traverse a tantalisingly short stretch of Moldavian soil. If you need a visa, you almost certainly won't get across.

TRAIN
Be aware that all trains listed below run via Moldova. If travelling from Chernivtsi you can change in Ocniţa for services to Bucharest. Direct trains to and from Romania and Ukraine run between Chernivtsi and Ocniţa (six hours, one daily), and Kyiv and Bucharest Nord (25 hours, one daily).

Russia
CAR & MOTORCYCLE
The main route between Kyiv and Moscow starts as the M01 (E95) north of Kyiv, bypasses the town of Chernihiv and becomes the M8 after the border.

TRAIN
Most major Ukrainian cities have daily services to Moscow, all passing through either Kyiv or Kharkiv. Many of the daily international trains between Ukraine and Western Europe either originate or terminate in Moscow. There are many extra services laid on in summer for Russians heading to Crimea, though these tend to sell out quickly. The following are the main direct train routes between Russia and the Ukraine: Kyiv to Moscow (14 to 16 hours, up to 17 daily), Kyiv to St Petersburg (24 hours, one daily), Lviv to Moscow (24 hours, up to five daily), Lviv to St Petersburg (30 hours; odd dates, daily summer) and Kharkiv to

Moscow (17 hours, up to five daily).

Slovakia
BUS
Three buses a day go from Uzhhorod to Košice (100uah, three hours), from where you can catch regular trains and buses to Prague, Bratislava and daily coaches to London.

CAR & MOTORCYCLE
The E50 from Košice crosses at Vyšné Nemecké on the Slovak side to Uzhhorod in Ukraine, becoming the M08 afterwards. Expect long queues, particularly at weekends.

TRAIN
As with services to Hungary, Chop is the gateway to/from Slovakia. Again, because of differing rail gauges, trains have to stop for a couple of hours while the carriages' bogies are changed. The main train routes between Slovakia & Ukraine are Kyiv to Bratislava (29 hours, one to two daily), Chop to Bratislava (11 hours, one to two daily) and Lviv to Bratislava (19 hours, one to two daily)

Sea
Cruise and cargo ships are the main users of Ukrainian ports but some useful scheduled ferry services do exist. However, please note that, as across the ex-USSR, boat services are erratic to say the least, and if the cost of docking and fuel rises, sailings are cancelled without notice. Basing your travel plans around sea or

river travel is probably not advisable.

TO/FROM ILYICHEVSK
Ukrferry (www.ukrferry.com) The main operators from Ilyichevsk, outside Odesa. Be aware that services are regularly cancelled for months on end without explanation. Check the website for the latest sailing times and days (if there are any).

TO/FROM KERCH
Old ferries shuttle regularly between Kerch's Port Krym and Port Kafkaz in Russia's Novorossiysk region. In summer, eight ferries cross every day; in winter there are six ferries.

Beware that timetables change and that travel onwards from Port Kafkaz might not be that easy unless you're on a bus or have your own wheels. Ukrainian authorities are promising a bridge here, but have been for years.

TO/FROM ODESA
London Sky Travel (☑729 3196; www.lstravel.com.ua) Sells tickets for summer ferries and cruise ships to Yalta and Sevastopol. In theory there are five to seven sailings a month.

TO/FROM SEVASTOPOL
There are twice weekly ferries between the port of Sevastopol and Istanbul. For details see www.stambul.com.ua and www.omegaship.com.ua.

TO/FROM YALTA
Services to Sinop in Turkey failed to appear in 2010 and have probably gone for good.

SEA CONNECTIONS FROM ILYICHEVSK

Destination	Duration	Frequency
Varna, Bulgaria	20hr	1 weekly
Poti, Georgia	42-58hr	1 weekly

THE TROUBLE WITH TRANSDNIESTR

The breakaway republic of Transdniestr can be a minor headache for travellers passing between Ukraine and Moldova proper, though not the full-blown migraine it once was. Recent reports from travellers who've crossed the Ukraine-Transdniestr border indicate that the 'entry permit' fee has been dropped and that Transdniestr customs officials seem to have got their act together. However, it may be worth checking the situation before setting off, as Transdniestr is not exactly Europe's steadiest state. Seasoned border-hoppers have told us they have a different experience almost every time they try to cross this border.

The only other services from Yalta are the twice weekly boats to Novorossiysk on Russia's stretch of the Black Sea coast.

Tours

The following agencies provide package tours to Ukraine. Remember that train tickets are much cheaper at Ukrainian railway stations than via booking agents.

Australia

Gateway Travel (☑02-9745 3333; www.russian-gateway. com.au) Offers escorted group tours.

Canada & USA

Black Sea Crimea (www. blacksea-crimea.com) Small but helpful operator, with an informative and up-to-date website.

Meest Travel (www.meest. net) This delivery and travel service has more than 400 representatives throughout Canada, the USA and Ukraine.

Scope Travel (www.scope travel.com) Offers tours from the major cities to the Carpathian countryside and the southern regions.

Ukrainetour (www.ukraine tour.com) Run by Ukrainians now based in Canada.

UK

Panorama Tours (www. panorama-tours.com.ua) City breaks to Kyiv, Lviv and Odesa with this Ukrainian International Airlines partner.

Regent Holidays (www. regent-holidays.co.uk) Knowledgeable company with varied itineraries.

Ukraine Travel (www. ukraine.co.uk) The UK's leading Ukraine specialist, also known as Bob Sopel's. The website lists Ukrainian football fixtures.

Ukraine Adventures (www. ukraineadventures.com) Small, Hampshire-based company capable of organising pretty much anything, including skiing trips.

GETTING AROUND

Air

Ukraine does not have the world's safest airline industry; on the other hand, it's probably not the least safe in the world either. In 2005 the US Federal Aviation Authority downgraded the country's safety rating to Category 2, although both of Ukraine's international airlines meet FAA standards and air fatalities since independence are actually low. (Essentially, the planes are old, while operating procedures do not meet minimum international safety standards.)

The national network mainly uses Kyiv as a hub. To fly from Lviv to Donetsk or from Simferopol to Kharkiv, for example, you almost always need to go through the capital.

Airlines in Ukraine

Aerosvit (www.aerosvit.ua) Based at Boryspil International Airport in Kyiv. Serves Kyiv, Donetsk, Kharkiv, Lviv, Odesa, Simferopol and Uzhhorod.

Dniproavia (www.dniproavia. com) Major domestic airline based at Dnipropetrovsk Airport. Serves Dnipropetrovsk, Kyiv, Ivano-Frankivsk, Donetsk, Kharkiv, Sevastopol, Lviv, Luhansk, Odesa, Simferopol, Chernivtsi and Uzhhorod, with many direct routes between cities (not via Dnipropetrovsk) such as Odesa–Kyiv and Ivano-Frankivsk–Donetsk.

Donbassaero (www.donbass. aero) Based at Donetsk Airport. Serves Donetsk, Kyiv, Odesa and Kharkiv.

Motor Sich (www.m9.com. ua) Based at Zaporizhzhya. Serves Zaporizhzhya and Kyiv.

Ukrainian-Mediterranean Airlines (www.umairlines. com) Based at Boryspil International Airport in Kyiv. Domestically serves Kyiv, Chernivtsi, Kharkiv, Odesa and Simferopol. This airline was banned from the EU for several years due to safety concerns.

Ukraine International Airlines (www.flyuia.com) Based at Boryspil International Airport in Kyiv. Domestically links Kyiv, Lviv and Donetsk, but is essentially an international airline.

Wizzair (www.wizzair.com) While not a Ukrainian airline, Wizzair does operate one handy domestic flight between Kyiv and Simferopol.

Tickets

Kiyavia Travel (www.kiyavia.com) This company has branches across the country and can book most flights with them. The website lists timetables, prices and aircraft used – all in English. You can print out e-tickets, collect paper tickets from offices or have them couriered to you anywhere in Ukraine.

Bicycle

Although you have to keep an eye out for crazy drivers and keep to the road's shoulder, cycling is a great way to see the real Ukraine. The Carpathians and Crimea – in that order – are particularly pleasant cycling country.

» Markets everywhere sell lots of spare parts.

» Rental is rare except in Crimea and the Carpathians.

» To transport your bike on a mainline train, you must remove the wheels, wrap the bike in plastic, and place it in the luggage niche above the top bunks.

» On local *electrychky* trains buy an outsized luggage ticket (3uah to 4uah) from the conductor (if he or she requests you to do so).

Boat

Chervona Ruta (www.ruta-cruise.com) Dnipro River cruises, from Kyiv to the Black Sea, can be booked through many travel agencies, but Chervona Ruta is the principal operator. Check its very comprehensive website for details.

Ukrferry (www.ukrferry.com) This unreliable operator sometimes has Black Sea cruises. Depending on availability, you might be able to nab a berth for just one leg, from Sevastopol to Yalta, for example. For these short hops, contact **London Sky Travel** (www.lstravel.com.ua).

Bus

Buses serve every city and small town, but are best for short trips (three hours or less), as vehicles are generally small, old and overcrowded. If you're travelling around Ukraine for a longer period of time, bus will be your most common mode of transport. There's a very ad-hoc feel to the experience, with buses, minibuses and decrepit coaches continually coming and going, seemingly without rhyme or reason.

Bus Companies

There are literally hundreds of tiny transport companies operating thousands of services across Ukraine. However, on the main intercity routes large operators use Western-standard 'luxury' coaches.

Autolux (www.autolux.ua) Ukraine's top coach operator. Runs services between Kyiv and most regional centres. The company's non-stop 'VIP' coaches between Kyiv and Odesa have airline-style seats, acres of legroom and free refreshments.

Gunsel (www.gunsel.com.ua) Older buses than Autolux but still comfortable. Operate mainly between Kyiv and the south and east of the country.

SURVIVING UKRAINE'S BUSES

Unless you are travelling long distances overnight, bus is likely to be your main mode of transport. For the uninitiated, Ukrainian bus travel can be a bemusing and uncomfortable ordeal. Here are our survival tips.

» Bus can mean anything from an ageing 60-seater Hungarian coach to a 12-seater Russian minivan.

» Your ticket has a seat number printed on it, but on small buses passengers generally just sit where they like (but not always!).

» Don't sit in a seat which has something on it. This means someone else has 'reserved' it while they go shopping/visit the toilet/call on relatives across town.

» Yes, the bleary-eyed guy stumbling towards the bus – one dose of *salo* away from a coronary – is your driver. His job is to drive, not answer questions.

» Luggage should be stored in the luggage space (*bagazhnyk*) under the bus. It's normally free to do so.

» Even if the mercury is pushing 35°C (95°F), all windows will be slammed shut as soon as the bus moves off. However, the roof hatch is left open, so try to sit in the faint airflow it provides.

» Buses often stop at stations for between five minutes and half an hour. Make sure you know how long the break is, as drivers rarely check if everyone is back on board.

ONWARD BUSES

Bus operator **Regabus** (www.regabus.cz) has services from several (mostly Western) Ukrainian towns to Prague and other locations in the Czech Republic. **Ecolines** (www. eco-tickets.net) travels between a handful of Ukrainian cities and the Baltics.

Ukrbus (www.ukrbus.com) Relatively new company operating services out of Kyiv, Odesa, Donetsk and Yalta.

Bus Stations

Bus stations are called *av-tovokzal* or *avtostantsiya*. Some of Ukraine's larger cities have several stations – a main one for long-distance routes and smaller stations that serve local destinations.

Information

Timetables Reliable timetables are displayed near the ticket windows and on boards; don't rely on the Soviet-era route maps.

Information There might be an information window (*dovidkove byuro*; довідкове бюро), but you can usually ask at any window.

Platforms Platforms are numbered and destinations are usually signposted.

Online Timetables etc are listed at www.bus.com. ua, but it's patchy, virtually impossible to navigate and not very reliable.

Tickets

Tickets are sold at the bus station right up to departure and resemble shop-till receipts. Your destination and time of travel is clearly marked, as well as your seat number (*meest*; місп). Tickets from the bus station are valid only for one service. Having bought a ticket, you can't suddenly decide to take a later bus without paying again.

Unless the bus is full, you can always simply pay the driver. Indeed, if the bus is passing through town without a long stop, the fare can only be paid this way. No tickets are issued.

Car & Motorcycle

Unless you're used to developing-world driving conditions, getting behind the wheel in Ukraine is not recommended. The roads are mostly terrible and there's a tacit, unofficial highway code that local drivers understand, but which you probably never will. Traffic accidents are also on the high side, with an average 8000 people killed annually on Ukraine's roads.

Bringing Your Own Vehicle

To bring your own vehicle into the country, you'll need:

» Your original registration papers (photocopies not accepted)

» A 'Green Card' International Motor Insurance Certificate

Your registration number will be noted, and you'll have to explain if leaving the country without your vehicle. For stays over two months, you'll have to register your car with the local authorities.

Driving Licence

Most official sources say an IDP (International Driving Permit) is necessary, and given the Ukrainian traffic police's habit of pulling people over for minor transgressions, it would be silly not to have one.

Fuel & Spare Parts

Petrol stations are very common and frequent on main roads. Innovative, shoestring repairs are widespread; proper spare parts are not quite so unless you have an ageing German vehicle, a Daewoo or a Lada.

Hire

Despite Ukraine's hazardous roads, an ever-increasing number of travellers are hiring cars, especially in the west of the country. Between them, the major companies listed here have locations in Kyiv (airport and downtown), Dnipropetrovsk, Donetsk, Kharkiv, Lviv, Odesa, Simferopol and Yalta. Drivers must be over 21 years of age. Check insurance and hire conditions very carefully.

Avis (www.avis.com)

Europcar (www.europcar. com)

Hertz (www.hertz.com)

Insurance

Third-party insurance is compulsory, which will normally be covered by a 'Green Card' International Motor Insurance Certificate. Hire companies provide their own vehicle insurance.

Road Conditions

While roads are generally poor, the main E/M highways traversing the country are better than most. The reconstructed E93 (M05) between Kyiv and Odesa is OK, though it has its moments. The east–west E40 (M06) between Lviv and Kyiv is being completely rebuilt to Western European standards in preparation for Euro 2012, and the E105 (M18) from Kharkiv to Simferopol is also decent. Generally, roads are better in the east than the west.

Road Rules

» Traffic drives on the right.

» Unless otherwise indicated, speed limits are 60km/h in towns, 90km/h on major roads and 110km/h on highways.

» There's a zero-tolerance policy on drink-driving.

» Believe it or not, it's actually a criminal offence not to wear a seat belt (although everybody completely ignores this rule).

» Legally, you must always carry a fire extinguisher, first-aid kit and warning triangle.

Hitching

You simply can't hitchhike around Ukraine for free. Hitching a ride is common, but it's necessary to pay drivers for the privilege. Also, hitching is never entirely safe anywhere. However, given the prevalence of unofficial taxis in Ukraine, it's reasonably safe to do so during the day, within big cities. Obviously, exercise common sense, particularly if you're a woman travelling solo.

You will need to speak the lingo to discuss your destination and price and it's easiest to get a ride where locals are flagging down cars. Put your hand up in the air, palm down.

Local Transport

Ukrainian cities are navigable by trolleybus, tram, bus and (in Kyiv, Kharkiv and Dnipropetrovsk) metro. Urban public-transport systems are usually overworked and overcrowded. There's no room for being shy or

squeamish – learn to assert yourself quickly.

» A ticket (kvytok or bilyet) for one ride by bus/tram/trolley-bus costs 1uah to 1.50uah.

» There are no return, transfer, timed or day tickets available anywhere.

» It's always simplest to pay the driver or conductor.

» Tickets have to be punched on board (or ripped by the conductor).

» Unclipped or untorn tickets warrant an on-the-spot fine should you be caught.

» For the metros you need a plastic token (zheton), sold at the counters inside the stations for 1.50uah to 2uah.

» Metros run from around 5.30am to midnight.

» A metro station can have several names – one for each different line that passes through it.

Taxis

Travelling by taxi anywhere in the ex-USSR can be a decidedly unenjoyable experience for foreigners, so if there's a bus or tram going to your destination, take it. However, occasionally in Ukraine you may have no choice but to grab a cab (when travelling to remote places, or if you're in a hurry).

» If possible, have your hostel or hotel call a cab for you – they generally use trustworthy companies with set fares.

» Always try to call for a taxi. Some companies now send a text message to confirm the booking, exact fare and make and colour of the car.

» Avoid taxis that tout for business outside airports and stations as these operators are very likely to rip off foreigners (and Ukrainians).

» Calculate the approximate fare between two towns by multiplying the distance in kilometres by two or two and a half.

» Make sure the fare quoted by taxi drivers is the fare to the final destination and not per kilometre (a common scam).

» Never travel in a cab that already has passengers in it.

Train

For long journeys, overnight train is the preferred method of travel in Ukraine. Carriages are old and the network in need of updating, but services are incredibly punctual. You can also move around or get some sleep.

Carriage Classes

All classes have assigned places. Your carriage (vahon)

DAI – OR GIMME

Among the biggest road hazards in Ukraine are the traffic cops. The underpaid DAI (Derzhavna Avtomobilna Inspeksiya) officers are infamous for waving drivers down and demanding a 'fine' for some minor violation (eg not carrying a warning triangle), or even an imaginary breach of the road rules.

In 2005 President Yushchenko sacked the entire force in disgust, after being continually pulled over himself while driving an unmarked car from Kyiv to Poland. The DAI was later reinstated by Prime Minister (now President) Yanukovych.

If you're pulled over when not speeding, they're probably just looking for a little cash (say around 50uah). However, they don't speak English and so some expats suggest that yabbering on until they lose patience is a good way to escape (officers have to collect a certain amount in bribes per shift to hand over to superiors). It's worth trying at least. Amusingly, 'dai', being short for 'dayte', translates as 'gimme' in Russian and Ukrainian.

Main Train Routes

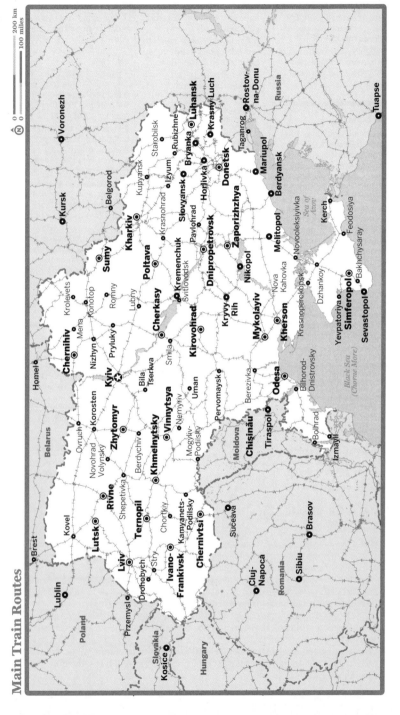

and bunk (*mesto*) numbers are printed on your ticket.

SV *Spalny vahon* (SV) is a 1st-class couchette (sleeper) compartment for two people. This is perfect for couples, but if travelling alone, sharing with a stranger can be a little awkward. Your bed will already be made for you and SV toilets are much cleaner. Not all trains offer SV, which costs two to three times more than *kupe*.

Kupe *Kupe* or *kupeyny* is a 2nd-class sleeper compartment for four people. This is the most popular class – which books up fast on some routes – and also the safest and most fun. Sharing the compartment with two or three others is less awkward and there's safety in numbers. *Kupe* is about twice as costly as *platskart*. Unless otherwise noted, train prices quoted in this guidebook are for *kupe*.

Platskart *Platskart* is a 3rd-class sleeper. The entire carriage is open (no separate compartments), with groups of four bunks in each alcove, along with two others in the aisle.

Zahalny vahon (*obshchy* in Russian) Fourth-class travel means an upright, hard bench seat for the entire journey. This class of carriage is now rare on intercity trains, but most *elektrychky* have this kind of seating.

Train Types

There are basically three types of train:

Pasazhyrsky poyizd (also known as *poyizd, skory poyizd* or *shvydky poyizd*) These are mainline services travelling long distances between cities, often overnight.

elektrychka (*prymisky poyizd*, or *prigorodny poyezd* in Russian) These are slow electric trains running between cities and rural areas. They're often used by locals to reach summer cottages and gardens, and overflow in summer with humanity, tools, vegetables and small farm animals. *Elektrychky* usually leave from a different part of the train station set aside for local trains.

Express trains The Kyiv–Kharkiv express has airplane-style seats, rather than the usual benches, travels much faster than the previous classes of train and makes fewer stops. More of these services are planned.

Tickets

» Tickets are still very cheap.

» Ticket clerks probably don't speak English, so get a local to write down what you need.

GIVE ME A SIGN

There are so many varying classifications of desk across Ukraine's non-English-speaking train stations it would be impossible to list them all. However, a few major signs to watch out for, or words to know of, follow:

» **Довідкове бюро** – Information desk

» **інформація** – Information

» **Добова каса/каса квиткова Добова** – Tickets for today (for departures within the next 24 hours)

» **Продаж квитків** – Ticket booking/advance tickets

» **інвалідів та учасників війни** – Try to avoid windows with this on the glass, unless you're an invalid or war veteran

» **сервіс центр** – Service centre, where you might or might not be sent if you hold a foreign passport. They won't speak English, but the queues are generally less brutal

» **міжнародні квитки** – International tickets

» **приміський вокзал** – Station for local or suburban trains (usually part of, or adjoining, the main train station)

» **приміська каса** – Local or suburban ticket desk

» **камера схову/камера зберігання/камера хранення** – Left-luggage room and/or lockers (sadly the easily pronounceable first option – *skhovu* – is rarely the term used or understood)

» **Кімнати відпочинку** – 'Resting' rooms, or rooms for overnight stays, ie train-station hotel

» **розклад** – Timetable

» **прибуття** – Arrivals

» **відправлення** – Departures

LEFT LUGGAGE

Every train station (zaliznychny vokzal or just vokzal) has a left-luggage counter – which usually goes by the Russian name kamera khranyeninya (камера хранения) or kamera zberihannaya (камера зберігання) in Ukrainian. Many are open 24 hours except for signposted short breaks. You usually pay when you deposit your luggage and retrieve it with the receipt or metal tag you are given.

» When buying tickets you need to know your destination, number of tickets required, class of carriage, the date and perhaps the train number.

» You no longer have to show your passport when buying tickets (but take it anyway, just in case).

» Several cities, such as Kyiv, Lviv and Simferopol, have advance ticket offices in the centre.

» So-called 'service centres' are comfortable, Western-style ticket offices found at big-city stations. Tickets cost slightly more here, but there's no queue.

» Never buy tickets from touts.

Information
ONLINE

Ukrainian Railways (www.uz.gov.ua, in Ukrainian) The official Ukrainian Railway website is extremely difficult and frustrating to navigate, even if you speak Ukrainian, but does include prices and ticket availability from Kyiv.

Poezda.net (www.poezda.net) This online timetable for the entire ex-USSR is available in English, but it's not 100% up-to-date. The search facility uses some downright perverse spellings for town names (eg Ujgorod for Uzhhorod, Harkov for Kharkiv), but is still pretty good.

Seat 61 (www.seat61.com/Ukraine.htm) Worth checking out, especially for trans-border train travel info.

AT THE STATION

» Strictly Russian- or Ukrainian-speaking attendants in information booths (dovidkove byuro; довідкове бюро) are frequently surly and uncooperative.

» There's a charge for any information that staff write down (around 3.50uah).

» Schedules are posted on the wall – once you have mastered some basic words, they're simple to decipher.

» You may find railway timetables in business catalogues, posted in hotels and occasionally at bus stations.

On the Journey

» Each carriage has an attendant called a provodnik (male) or provodnitsa (female), who collects your ticket, distributes sheets, makes morning wake-up calls, and serves cups of tea.

» It's de rigueur to change into sleeping wear in your carriage, so bring tracksuit bottoms, a comfortable top and thick-soled slippers or flip-flops (thongs).

» Dining cars rarely sell anything more than sandwiches, snacks and drinks, so bring food to share with fellow passengers.

» Toilets are locked some 30 minutes either side of a station. Bring your own paper.

» Don't drink the water from the tap or even clean your teeth with it.

WANT MORE?

For in-depth language information and handy phrases, check out Lonely Planet's *Ukrainian Phrasebook*. You'll find it at **shop.lonelyplanet. com**, or you can buy Lonely Planet's iPhone phrasebooks at the Apple App Store.

Language

The official language of Ukraine is Ukrainian, which belongs to the Slavic language family and is most closely related to Russian and Belarusian. It has about 50 million speakers worldwide, including significant Ukrainian-speaking communities in Eastern Europe, Central Asia and North America.

Many Ukrainians speak Russian as their first language and many more know it as a second language; it's predominantly spoken in the east and the south (apart from Crimean Tatar in Crimea). In many places, including Kyiv, you'll hear Russian and Ukrainian inter-mingled to create a dialect commonly known as *surzhyk*. However, many locals – particu-larly those in the west who overwhelmingly speak Ukrainian – still see Russian as the language of an oppressor and it's often more politically correct not to use it.

Ukrainian is written in the Cyrillic alphabet (see the next page), and it's well worth the effort familiarising yourself with it so that you can read maps and street signs. Otherwise, just read the coloured pronunciation guides given next to each Ukrainian phrase in this chapter as if they were English, and you'll be understood. Most sounds are the same as those found in English, and the few differ-ences in pronunciation are explained in the alphabet table. The stressed syllables are indicated with italics.

BASICS

Hello.	Добрий день.	*do*·bry den'
Goodbye.	До побачення.	do po·*ba*·chen·nya
How are you?	Як справи?	yak *spra*·vy
Fine, thanks.	Добре, дякую.	*do*·bro *dya*·ku·yu
Please.	Прошу.	*pro*·shu
Thank you.	Дякую.	*dya*·ku·yu
You're welcome.	Добро пожалувати.	*do*·bro po·*zha*·lu·va·ty
Yes./No.	Так./Ні.	tak/ni
Excuse me.	Вибачте.	*vy*·bach·te
I'm sorry.	Перепрошую.	pe·re·*pro*·shu·yu
What's your name?	Як вас звати?	yak vas zva·ty
My name is ...	Мене звати ...	me·*ne* zva·ty ...

Do you speak English?
Ви розмовляєте
англійською мовою?
vy roz·mow·*lya*·ye·te
an·*hliys'*·ko·yu mo·vo·yu

I don't understand (you).
Я (вас) не розумію.
ya (vas) ne ro·zu·*mi*·yu

ACCOMMODATION

Do you have any rooms available?
У вас є вільні
номери?
u vas ye *vil'*·ni
no·me·ry

How much is it per night/person?
Скільки коштує
номер за ніч/особу?
skil'·ky ko·shtu·ye
no·mer za nich/o·so·bu

Is breakfast included?
Чи це включає
вартість сніданку?
chy tse wklyu·*cha*·ye
var·tist' sni·*dan*·ku

campsite	кемпінг	*kem*·pinh
hotel	готель	ho·*tel'*
youth hostel	молодіжний гуртожиток	mo·lo·*dizh*·ny hur·*to*·zhy·tok

bathroom	ванна	van·na
double room	номер на двох	no·mer na dvokh
shared room	місце	mis·tse
single room	номер на одного	no·mer na o·dno·ho
window	вікно	vik·no

DIRECTIONS

Where is ...?
Де ...?   de ...

What's the address?
Яка адреса?   ya·ka a·dre·sa

Could you write it down, please?
Могли б ви   moh·lu b vy
записати,   za·py·sa·ty
будь ласка?   bud´ la·ska

Can you show me (on the map)?
Ви можете показати,   vy mo·zhe·te po·ka·za·ty
мені (на карти)?   me·ni (na kar·ti)

Go straight ahead.
Ідіть прямо.   i·dit´ prya·mo

Turn left.
Поверніть ліворуч.   po·ver·nit´ li·vo·ruch

Turn right.
Поверніть праворуч.   po·ver·nit´ pra·vo·ruch

at the corner	на розі	na ro·zi
at the traffic lights	біля світлофора	bi·lya svi·tlo·fo·ra
behind	ззаду	z·za·du
in front of	спереду	spe·re·du
far	далеко	da·le·ko
near (to)	біля	bi·lya
opposite	протилежний	pro·ty·le·zhny

EATING & DRINKING

Do you have any free tables?
У Вас є вільні столи?   u vas ye vil´·ni sto·ly

Can I see the menu?
Можна подивитися   mo·zhna po·dy·vy·ty·sya
на меню?   na me·nyu

Do you have a menu in English?
У Вас є меню   u vas ye me·nyu
англійською мовою?   an·hliys´·ko·yu mo·vo·yu

I'm a vegetarian.
Я вегетаріанець/   ya ve·he·ta·ri·a·nets´/
вегетаріанка.   ve·he·ta·ri·an·ka (m/f)

What do you recommend?
Що Ви порадите?   shcho vy po·ra·dy·te

I'd like ...
Я візьму ...   ya viz´·mu ...

Bon appetit!
Смачного!   smach·no·ho

CYRILLIC ALPHABET

Cyrillic	Sound	
А, а	a	as in 'father'
Б, б	b	as in 'but'
В, в	v	as in 'van' (before a vowel);
	w	as in 'wood' (before a consonant or at the end of a syllable)
Г, г	h	as in 'hat'
Ґ, ґ	g	as in 'good'
Д, д	d	as in 'dog'
Е, е	e	as in 'end'
Є, є	ye	as in 'yet'
Ж, ж	zh	as the 's' in 'measure'
З, з	z	as in 'zoo'
И, и	y	as the 'ir' in 'birch', but short
І, і	i	as in 'pit'
Ї, ї	yi	as in 'yip'
Й, й	y	as in 'yell'; usually precedes or follows a vowel
К, к	k	as in 'kind'
Л, л	l	as in 'lamp'
М, м	m	as in 'mad'
Н, н	n	as in 'not'
О, о	o	as in 'pot' but with jaws more closed and lips more pursed
П, п	p	as in 'pig'
Р, р	r	as in 'rub' (trilled)
С, с	s	as in 'sing'
Т, т	t	as in 'ten'
У, у	u	as in 'put'
Ф, ф	f	as in 'fan'
Х, х	kh	as the 'ch' in the Scottish *loch*
Ц, ц	ts	as in 'bits'
Ч, ч	ch	as in 'chin'
Ш, ш	sh	as in 'shop'
Щ, щ	shch	as 'sh-ch' in 'fresh chips'
Ю, ю	yu	as the 'u' in 'use'
Я, я	ya	as in 'yard' (when stressed);
	ye	as in 'yearn' (when unstressed)
Ь, ь	´	'soft sign'; softens the preceding consonant (like a faint 'y' sound)

Cheers!
Будьмо!   bud´·mo

I don't drink (alcohol).
Я не п'ю.   ya ne pyu

Can we have the bill?
Можна рахунок?   mo·zhna ra·khu·nok

The meal was delicious!
Було дуже смачно!   bu·lo duz·he smach·no

Signs

Вхід	Entrance
Вихід	Exit
Відчинено	Open
Зачинено	Closed
Інформація	Information
Заборонено	Prohibited
Туалет	Toilets
Чоловічий	Men
Жіночий	Women

Key Words

bar	бар	bar
bottle	пляшка	plyash·ka
breakfast	сніданок	sni·da·nok
cafe	кафе/	ka·fe/
	кав'ярня	ka·vyar·nya
cold	холодний	kho·lod·ny
cup	чашка	chash·ka
dinner	вечеря	ve·che·rya
food	їжа	yi·zha
fork	виделка	vy·del·ka
glass	склянка	sklyan·ka
hot (warm)	гарячий	ha·rya·chy
knife	ніж	nizh
lunch	обід	o·bid
market	ринок	ry·nok
menu	меню	me·nyu
plate	тарілка	ta·ril·ka
restaurant	ресторан	re·sto·ran
salad	салат	sa·lat
soup	суп	sup
sour	кислий	ky·sly
spicy	гострий	ho·stry
spoon	ложка	lozh·ka
sweet	солодкий	so·lod·ky
with/without	з/без	z/bez

Meat & Fish

beef	яловичина	ya·lo·vy·chy·na
carp	короп	ko·rop
caviar	ікра	i·kra
chicken	курка	kur·ka
crabs	краби	kra·by
duck	качка	kach·ka
ham	шинка	shyn·ka
herring	оселедець	o·se·le·dets'
lamb	баранина	ba·ra·ny·na
pork	свинина	svy·ny·na
salami	салямі	sa·lya·mi
salmon	лосось	lo·sos'
sturgeon	осетрина	o·se·try·na
trout	форель	fo·rel
tuna	тунець	tu·nets
turkey	індик	in·dyk
veal	телятина	te·lya·ty·na

Fruit & Vegetables

apple	яблуко	ya·blu·ko
banana	банан	ba·nan
beetroot	буряк	bu·ryak
cabbage	капуста	ka·pu·sta
capsicum	перець	pe·rets
carrot	морква	mor·kva
corn	кукуруза	ku·ku·ru·za
grapes	виноград	vy·no·hrad
kiwi fruit	ківі	ki·vi
mushroom	гриб	hryb
olives	маслини	ma·sly·ny
onion	цибуля	tsy·bu·lya
orange	помаранча	po·ma·ran·cha
pineapple	ананас	a·na·nas
pomegranate	гранат	hra·nat
potato	картопля	kar·to·plya
raspberry	малина	ma·ly·na
tomatoes	помідори	po·mi·dor·i
watermelon	кавун	ka·vun

Other

biscuits	печення	pe·chen·nya
bread	хліб	khlib
butter	масло	ma·slo
cake	торт	tort
cheese	сир	syr
chewing gum	жувачка	zhu·vach·ka
chips	чіпси	cheep·si
chocolate	шоколад	sho·ko·lad
egg	яйце	yay·tse
honey	мед	med
horseradish	хрін	khrin
ice cream	морозиво	mo·ro·zy·vo
jam	варення	va·ryen·nya
mayonnaise	майонез	ma·yo·nez

mustard	гірчиця	hir·*chu*·tsya
oil	олія	o·*li*·ya
pepper	перець	*pe*·rets
salt	сіль	sil'
sour cream	сметана	sme·*ta*·na
sugar	цукор	*tsu*·kor
tatar sauce	соус татарський	*so*·us ta·*tar*·sky
tomato sauce	кетчуп	*ket*·chup
vinegar	оцет	o·*tset*

Drinks

beer	пиво	*py*·vo
coffee	кава	*ka*·va
juice	сік	sik
milk	молоко	mo·lo·*ko*
red/white wine	вино червоне/біле	*vy*·no cher·*vo*·ne/*bi*·le
tea	чай	chai
vodka	горілка	ho·*ril*·ka
(mineral) water	(мінеральна) вода	(mi·ne·*ral'*·na) vo·*da*
yogurt	кефір	ke·*fir*

EMERGENCIES

Help!
Допоможіть! do·po·mo·*zhit'*

Go away!
Іди/Ідіть звідси! i·*dy*/i·*dit'* zvid·sy (pol/inf)

I'm lost.
Я заблукав/ заблукала. ya za·blu·*kaw*/ za·blu·*ka*·la (m/f)

There's been an accident.
Там був нещасний випадок. tam buw ne·*shcha*·sny *vy*·padok

Call a doctor!
Викличте лікаря! *vy*·klych·te *li*·ka·rya

Call the police!
Викличіть міліцію! *vy*·kly·chit' mi·*li*·tsi·yu

I'm ill.
Мені погано. me·*ni* po·*ha*·no

It hurts here.
У мене болить тут. u *me*·ne bo·*lyt'* tut

Question Words		
How?	Як?	yak
What?	Що?	shcho
When?	Коли?	ko·*ly*
Where?	Де?	de
Which?	Котрий?	ko·*try*
Who?	Хто?	khto

I'm allergic to (antibiotics).
У мене алергія на (антибіотики). u *me*·ne a·ler·*hi*·ya na (an·ty·bi·o·ty·ky)

SHOPPING & SERVICES

I'd like to buy ...
Я б хотів/хотіла купити ... ya b kho·*tiw*/kho·*ti*·la ku·*py*·ty ... (m/f)

I'm just looking.
Я лише дивлюся. ya ly·*she* dy·*wlyu*·sya

Please show me ...
Покажіть мені, будь ласка ... po·ka·*zhit'* me·*ni* bud' *la*·ska ...

I don't like it.
Мені не подобається. me·*ni* ne po·*do*·ba·yet'·sya

How much is it?
Скільки це (він/вона) коштує? *skil*'·ky tse (vin/vo·*na*) ko·shtu·ye? (m/f)

That's too expensive.
Це надто дорого. tse *nad*·to do·ro·ho

Can you make me a better price?
А дешевше не буде? a de·*she*·wshe ne *bu*·de

ATM	банкомат	ban·ko·*mat*
credit card	кредитна картка	kre·*dy*·tna *kar*·tka
internet cafe	інтернетове кафе	in·ter·*ne*·to·ve ka·*fe*
post office	пошта	*po*·shta
tourist office	туристичне бюро	tu·ry·*stych*·ne byu·*ro*

TIME & DATES

What time is it?
Котра година? ko·*tra* ho·*dy*·na

It's (eight) o'clock.
(Восьма) година. (*vos*'·ma) ho·*dy*·na

in the morning	вранці	*wran*·tsi
in the afternoon	вдень	w·*den'*
in the evening	у вечері	u·*ve*·che·ri

yesterday	вчора	*wcho*·ra
today	сьогодні	s'o·*ho*·dni
tomorrow	завтра	*zaw*·tra

Monday	понеділок	po·ne·*di*·lok
Tuesday	вівторок	vi·*wto*·rok
Wednesday	середа	se·re·*da*
Thursday	четвер	che·*tver*
Friday	п'ятниця	*pya*·tny·tsya
Saturday	субота	su·*bo*·ta
Sunday	неділя	ne·*di*·lya

Numbers

1	один	o·*dyn*
2	два	dva
3	три	try
4	чотири	cho·*ty*·ry
5	п'ять	pyat'
6	шість	shist'
7	сім	sim
8	вісім	*vi*·sim
9	дев'ять	de·*vyat*'
10	десять	de·*syat*'
20	двадцять	*dva*·tsyat'
30	тридцять	*try*·tsyat'
40	сорок	*so*·rok
50	п'ятдесят	pya·de·*syat*
60	шістдесят	shis·de·*syat*
70	сімдесят	sim·de·*syat*
80	вісімдесят	vi·sim·de·*syat*
90	дев'яносто	de·vya·*no*·sto
100	сто	sto
1000	тисяча	*ty*·sya·cha

January	січень	*si*·chen'
February	лютий	*lyu*·ty
March	березень	be·re·zen'
April	квітень	*kvi*·ten'
May	травень	*tra*·ven'
June	червень	*che*·rven'
July	липень	*ly*·pen'
August	серпень	*ser*·pen'
September	вересень	ve·re·sen'
October	жовтень	*zhow*·ten'
November	листопад	ly·sto·*pad*
December	грудень	*hru*·den'

TRANSPORT

Public Transport

I want to go to ...
Мені треба їхати до ...
me·*ni* tre·ba yi·*kha*·ty do ...

At what time does the ... leave?
Коли відправляється ...?
ko·*ly* vid·pra·*wlya*·yet'·sya ...

At what time does the ... arrive?
Коли ... прибуває?
ko·*ly* ... pry·bu·*va*·ye

Can you tell me when we get to ...?
Ви можете мени казати, коли ми доїдемо до ...?
vy *mo*·zhe·te me·*ni* ska·za·ty ko·*ly* my do·*yi*·de·mo do ...

boat	пароплав	pa·ro·*plaw*
bus	автобус	aw·to·bus
metro	метро	me·*tro*
plane	літак	li·*tak*
taxi	таксі	tak·*si*
train	поїзд	po·*yizd*
tram	трамвай	tram·*vai*
trolleybus	тролейбус	tro·*ley*·bus
one-way ticket	квиток в один бік	kvy·*tok* v o·*dyn* bik
return ticket	зворотний квиток	zvo·ro·tny kvy·*tok*
first	перший	*per*·shy
next	наступний	na·*stup*·ny
last	останній	o·*stan*·niy
platform	платформа	plat·*for*·ma
ticket office	квиткові каси	kvy·*tko*·vi ka·sy
timetable	розклад	*roz*·klad
train station	залізнична станція	za·li·*znych*·na *stant*·si·ya

Driving & Cycling

I'd like to hire a ...
Я хочу взяти на прокат ...
ya *kho*·chu *vzya*·tu na pro·*kat* ...

4WD	чотирьох привідну машину	cho·ty·*ryokh* pry·vid·*nu* ma·*shy*·nu
bicycle	велосипед	ve·lo·sy·*ped*
car	машину	ma·*shy*·nu
motorcycle	мотоцикл	mo·to·*tsykl*

Is this the road to ...?
Це дорога до ...?
tse do·*ro*·ha do ...

I have a flat tyre.
В мене спустила шина.
w me·ne spu·*sty*·la *shy*·na

I've run out of petrol.
У мене закінчився бензин.
u me·ne za·kin·*chy*·wsya ben·*zyn*

My car has broken down.
У мене поламалася машина.
u me·ne po·la·*ma*·la·sya ma·*shy*·na

diesel	дізель	*di*·zel
helmet	шолом	sho·*lom*
petrol/gas	бензин	ben·*zyn*
pump	насос	na·*sos*
service station	заправка	za·*praw*·ka
unleaded	очищений	o·*chy*·shche·ny

behind the scenes

SEND US YOUR FEEDBACK

We love to hear from travellers – your comments keep us on our toes and help make our books better. Our well-travelled team reads every word on what you loved or loathed about this book. Although we cannot reply individually to postal submissions, we always guarantee that your feedback goes straight to the appropriate authors, in time for the next edition. Each person who sends us information is thanked in the next edition – and the most useful submissions are rewarded with a free book.

Visit **lonelyplanet.com/contact** to submit your updates and suggestions or to ask for help. Our award-winning website also features inspirational travel stories, news and discussions.

Note: We may edit, reproduce and incorporate your comments in Lonely Planet products such as guidebooks, websites and digital products, so let us know if you don't want your comments reproduced or your name acknowledged. For a copy of our privacy policy visit lonelyplanet.com/privacy.

OUR READERS

Many thanks to the travellers who used the last edition and wrote to us with helpful hints, useful advice and interesting anecdotes:

Alexey Andrianov, Minoru Arisawa, Rubinho Bahia, Joop Bakker, Paolo Benvenuti, Brandi N Bernard, Chris Coy, Carol Crickshark, Leni Dam, Lotte van Ekert, Jim Eleazer, Joris van Empel, James Falk, Sebastiaan Garvelink, Richard Griffith, Orest Hawryluk, Jenny Heintz, Anna Hermans, Diarne Kreltszheim, Joerg Lehnert, Unni Lervik, Alexis Leveillee, Marcel Michels, P Mitchell, Markiyan M Mykytka, Matthew Nobes, David Pavlita, Alexis Prokopiev, Andrew Sunil Rajkumar, Michael Richardson, Bart Rooijmans, Peter Slabbynck, Eleanor Stadnyk, William Stricklin, Ichiro Sugiyama, Nickolas Switucha, Barbara Trecker, Tania Zulkoskey.

AUTHOR THANKS

Marc Di Duca

When working on a guide to Ukraine, you're never short of people bending over backwards to help you along the way. Firstly, a huge thanks to Ukraine expert Greg Bloom for all his support and fellow author Leonid Ragozin for his professional approach and enthusiasm. A mammoth дякую to my parents-in-law Mykola and Vira for taking care of son Taras while I was on the road. Big thanks also go to Yuri, Maria and family in Uzhhorod; Dmetro and family in Kosiv; Vasyl in Rakhiv; Stefania and Natalia in Ivano-Frankivsk; Vitaly in Kolomyya; Markiyan, Yarema and Ihor in Lviv; Viktor in Yaremche; Marcus in Odesa; and last, but certainly not least, my wife Tanya, for all the days we spend apart.

Leonid Ragozin

Most of all I'd like to thank my wife Masha Makeeva for her patience, which is not her natural character trait. I am very grateful to Jo Potts for taking me on board on this project and Greg Bloom for making it possible. It's been a great pleasure working with Marc Di Duca and Anna Tyler on this book. In Ukraine, first and foremost, I would like to thank my friends Kolya and Masha Malinovsky for explaining and showing Kyiv to me. Also, many thanks to Aricio in Kyiv,

THIS BOOK

This 3rd edition of Lonely Planet's Ukraine guidebook was researched and written by Marc Di Duca and Leonid Ragozin. The previous two editions were researched and written by Sarah Johnstone, who was ably assisted on the 2nd edition by Greg Bloom. Lisa Dunford contributed additional texts. This guidebook was commissioned in Lonely Planet's London office, and produced by the following:

Commissioning Editors Jo Potts, Anna Tyler

Coordinating Editors Monique Perrin, Simon Williamson

Coordinating Cartographer Csanad Csutoros, Valentina Kremenchutskaya

Coordinating Layout Designer Carlos Solarte

Senior Editors Katie Lynch, Anna Metcalfe

Managing Editors Imogen Bannister, Melanie Dankel

Managing Cartographers Amanda Sierp, Herman So

Managing Layout Designers Jane Hart, Celia Wood

Assisting Editor Anne Mulvaney

Assisting Cartographers Diana Duggan

Cover Research Jane Hart

Internal Image Research Aude Vauconsant

Language Content Annelies Mertens, Branislava Vladisavljevic

Thanks to Mark Adams, David Connolly, Stefanie Di Trocchio, Janine Eberle, Joshua Geoghegan, Mark Germanchis, Michelle Glynn, Lauren Hunt, Laura Jane, David Kemp, Yvonne Kirk, Lisa Knights, Nic Lehman, John Mazzocchi, Wayne Murphy, Trent Paton, Adrian Persoglia, Piers Pickard, Lachlan Ross, Michael Ruff, Julie Sheridan, Kerrianne Southway, Laura Stansfeld, John Taufa, Sam Trafford, Juan Winata, Emily Wolman, Nick Wood

BEHIND THE SCENES

Dima in Kharkiv, Irina in Zaporizhzhya, Yury in Sevastopol and Inna in Feodosiya for their kind advice and assistance.

ACKNOWLEDGMENTS

Climate map data adapted from Peel MC, Finlayson BL & McMahon TA (2007) 'Updated World Map of the Köppen-Geiger Climate Classification', *Hydrology and Earth System Sciences*, 11, 163344.

Cover photograph: All Saints Church, Kyevo-Pecherska Lavra, Kyiv, Peter Thornton/Lonely Planet Images. Many of the images in this guide are available for licensing from Lonely Planet Images: www.lonelyplanet images.com.

index

how to use this book

These symbols will help you find the listings you want:

- 👁 Sights
- 🏃 Activities
- 🥤 Courses
- 👉 Tours

- 🎊 Festivals & Events
- 🛏 Sleeping
- 🍴 Eating
- 🍷 Drinking

- ⭐ Entertainment
- 🔒 Shopping
- ℹ Information/Transport

These symbols give you the vital information for each listing:

- 📞 Telephone Numbers
- 🕑 Opening Hours
- Ⓟ Parking
- 🚭 Nonsmoking
- ❄ Air-Conditioning
- @ Internet Access

- 📶 Wi-Fi Access
- 🏊 Swimming Pool
- 🥗 Vegetarian Selection
- 📖 English-Language Menu
- 👪 Family-Friendly
- 🐾 Pet-Friendly

- 🚌 Bus
- ⛴ Ferry
- Ⓜ Metro
- Ⓢ Subway
- ⊖ London Tube
- 🚊 Tram
- 🚆 Train

Reviews are organised by author preference.

Map Legend

Sights
- 🏖 Beach
- ☸ Buddhist
- 🏰 Castle
- ✝ Christian
- 🕉 Hindu
- ☪ Islamic
- ✡ Jewish
- 🏛 Monument
- 🏛 Museum/Gallery
- 🏚 Ruin
- 🍷 Winery/Vineyard
- 🐘 Zoo
- ⚫ Other Sight

Activities, Courses & Tours
- ○ Diving/Snorkelling
- 🛶 Canoeing/Kayaking
- ⛷ Skiing
- 🏄 Surfing
- 🏊 Swimming/Pool
- 🚶 Walking
- 🏄 Windsurfing
- • Other Activity/Course/Tour

Sleeping
- 🛏 Sleeping
- ⛺ Camping

Eating
- 🍽 Eating

Drinking
- ☕ Drinking
- ☕ Cafe

Entertainment
- 🎭 Entertainment

Shopping
- 🛍 Shopping

Information
- 📮 Post Office
- ℹ Tourist Information

Transport
- ✈ Airport
- ⊗ Border Crossing
- 🚍 Bus
- ✛ Cable Car/Funicular
- ⊶ Cycling
- ⊶ Ferry
- Ⓜ Metro
- ✛ Monorail
- Ⓟ Parking
- Ⓢ S-Bahn
- Ⓣ Taxi
- ✛ Train/Railway
- ✛ Tram
- Ⓣ Tube Station
- Ⓤ U-Bahn
- • Other Transport

Routes
- ▨ Tollway
- ▨ Freeway
- ▨ Primary
- ▨ Secondary
- ▨ Tertiary
- ▨ Lane
- ▨ Unsealed Road
- ▨ Plaza/Mall
- ▨ Steps
- ⊞ Tunnel
- ▨ Pedestrian Overpass
- ▨ Walking Tour
- ▨ Walking Tour Detour
- --- Path

Boundaries
- --- International
- --- State/Province
- --- Disputed
- --- Regional/Suburb
- ▨ Marine Park
- ▨ Cliff
- ▨ Wall

Population
- ⊘ Capital (National)
- ⊙ Capital (State/Province)
- ⊙ City/Large Town
- ⊙ Town/Village

Geographic
- 🏠 Hut/Shelter
- 🗼 Lighthouse
- 👁 Lookout
- ▲ Mountain/Volcano
- 🌴 Oasis
- 🏞 Park
-)(Pass
- 🍴 Picnic Area
- 💧 Waterfall

Hydrography
- ~ River/Creek
- ~ Intermittent River
- ~ Swamp/Mangrove
- ◠ Reef
- ~ Canal
- ◯ Water
- ◯ Dry/Salt/Intermittent Lake
- ◯ Glacier

Areas
- ▨ Beach/Desert
- +++ Cemetery (Christian)
- ××× Cemetery (Other)
- ▨ Park/Forest
- ▨ Sportsground
- ▨ Sight (Building)
- ▨ Top Sight (Building)

OUR STORY

A beat-up old car, a few dollars in the pocket and a sense of adventure. In 1972 that's all Tony and Maureen Wheeler needed for the trip of a lifetime – across Europe and Asia overland to Australia. It took several months, and at the end – broke but inspired – they sat at their kitchen table writing and stapling together their first travel guide, *Across Asia on the Cheap*. Within a week they'd sold 1500 copies. Lonely Planet was born.

Today, Lonely Planet has offices in Melbourne, London and Oakland, with more than 600 staff and writers. We share Tony's belief that 'a great guidebook should do three things: inform, educate and amuse'.

OUR WRITERS

Marc Di Duca

Coordinating Author, Central Ukraine, Lviv & Western Ukraine, The Carpathians, Odesa & Southern Ukraine Driven by an urge to discover Eastern Europe's wilder side, Marc first hit Kyiv one dark, snow-flecked night in early 1998. Several prolonged stints, countless near misses with Kyiv's metro doors and many bottles of *horilka* later, he still never misses a chance to fine-tune his Russian while exploring far-flung corners of this immense land. Overheated buses and *salo* aside, he has an enthusiasm for everything Ukrainian, in particular his favourite region, Gogol's native Poltavshchina. An established travel author, Marc has written guides to Moscow and Lake Baikal, and has worked on Lonely Planet's *Trans-Siberian Railway* and *Russia* books.

Read more about Marc at:
lonelyplanet.com/members/madidu

Leonid Ragozin

Kyiv, Crimea, Eastern Ukraine Leonid Ragozin devoted himself to beach dynamics when he studied geology at Moscow State University. But for want of really nice beaches in Russia, he helped Australian gold prospectors in Siberia and sold InterRail tickets and Lonely Planet books to Russian backpackers before embarking on a journalistic career. After eight years with the BBC, he was poached by the Russian *Newsweek* and became their foreign correspondent. In this capacity, he coerced his superiors into sending him as far as Bhutan, Ecuador and dozens of similarly unlikely destinations, and got away with it. While doing this guide, he returned to the BBC, where he is now discovering the wild and dangerous world of television.

Published by Lonely Planet Publications Pty Ltd
ABN 36 005 607 983
3rd edition – May 2011
ISBN 978 1 74179 328 4
© Lonely Planet 2011   Photographs © as indicated 2011
10 9 8 7 6 5 4 3 2 1
Printed in Singapore

Although the authors and Lonely Planet have taken all reasonable care in preparing this book, we make no warranty about the accuracy or completeness of its content and, to the maximum extent permitted, disclaim all liability arising from its use.